THE ACTS OF ANDREW
and
THE ACTS OF ANDREW AND MATTHIAS
IN THE CITY OF THE CANNIBALS

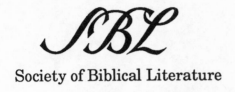

Society of Biblical Literature

TEXTS AND TRANSLATIONS
CHRISTIAN APOCRYPHA SERIES

William R. Schoedel, Guest Editor
Dennis Ronald MacDonald, Editor

Texts and Translations 33
Christian Apocrypha Number 1

THE ACTS OF ANDREW
and
THE ACTS OF ANDREW AND MATTHIAS
IN THE CITY OF THE CANNIBALS
by
Dennis Ronald MacDonald

THE ACTS OF ANDREW
and
THE ACTS OF ANDREW AND MATTHIAS
IN THE CITY OF THE CANNIBALS

Dennis Ronald MacDonald

Scholars Press
Atlanta, Georgia

THE ACTS OF ANDREW
and
THE ACTS OF ANDREW AND MATTHIAS
IN THE CITY OF THE CANNIBALS

Dennis Ronald MacDonald

Library of Congress Cataloging-in-Publication Data

MacDonald, Dennis Ronald, 1946-
    The Acts of Andrew and the Acts of Andrew and Matthias in the city
of the cannibals / Dennis Ronald MacDonald
    p. cm. -- (Texts and translations ; 33)
    Includes bibliographical reference.
    ISBN 1-55540-492-8. -- ISBN 1-55540-493-6 (pbk.)
    1. Acts of Andrew--Criticism, interpretation, etc. 2. Acts of
Andrew and Matthias--Criticism, interpretation, etc. I. Acts of
Andrew. 1990. II. Acts of Andrew and Matthias. 1990. III. Title.
IV. Series: Texts and translations ; no. 33.
BS2880.A372M33 1990
229'.92--dc20   90-39586
                                   CIP

Printed in the United States of America
on acid-free paper

To Peter

TABLE OF CONTENTS

PART III
The Passion of Andrew

PART IV
Related Materials

PREFACE

Photius, a ninth century Byzantine Patriarch, was the last person known to have held a copy of *The Acts of Andrew*. Perhaps no one will do so again. Certainly one must not confuse the ancient Acts with the content of this volume, which is, of necessity, a conjectural reconstruction based on literary debris: quotations, epitomes, fragments, and expansions in Greek, Latin, Coptic, Anglo-Saxon, and Armenian. This volume will have accomplished its goal if it presents the textual survivals accurately, comprehensively, and comprehensibly. At some points the text is secure--as in the case of Andrew's martyrdom--but most materials printed here are textual offspring, more or less resembling their parents but not to be mistaken for them.

In 1911, more than a millennium after Photius, Josef Flamion provided a brilliant assessment of the textual remains, but he did not create an edition of the texts themselves. In the meantime, several other textual witnesses have come to light, most notably, more extensive and reliable versions of the martyrdom of Andrew than had been available to Flamion. During the last decade, Jean-Marc Prieur and I have reassembled from these sundry pieces the jigsaw puzzle known as *The Acts of Andrew*. Our two editions differ significantly, but when possible, I have attempted to harmonize my edition with his in order to minimize confusion. When the editions do disagree, blame my obduracy.

While major sections of the Acts have disappeared nearly without a trace, the textual evidence for other sections is enormous. To provide a comprehensive apparatus in this volume is impractical and unnecessary insofar as the diligent are able to consult Prieur's more exhaustive apparatus. The variants provided here are selective and identify, for the most part at least, only alternative readings potentially original.

I have sought to translate gender-inclusively when doing so would not offend standard English usage or compromise historical reliability. *The Acts of Andrew* issues from the ancient world, and it would be dishonest to disguise its nearly inescapable, if lamentable, patriarchalism. There is, of course, no virtue in making the translation more androcentric than the original, so at times I have changed singulars to plurals or made other subtle adjustments when the author's intentions seem to have been gender-neutral. In order to retain the ambiguity of early Christian employment of ἀδελφοί, I have chosen, somewhat infelicitously, to translate it "brethren," which seems less starkly gendered than "brothers" on the one hand, and less fashionably generic than "brothers and sisters" on the other.

Grants from the National Endowment for the Humanities and the Association of Theological Schools launched this project in 1983, and the Iliff School of Theology brought it safely to port. The staff of Iliff's Ira J. Taylor Library never complained about my exotic interlibrary loan requests, and Dean Jane Smith never looked askance at my requests for a sabbatical, special travel to research collections and experts, or money to obtain a laser printer, special character fonts, and a translator for the Armenian fragments. My students and colleagues at least faked tolerating interests in my carryings on about ant-people, tours of the netherworld,

disarmed soldiers, cancelled weddings, and Homeric conceits. At Harvard Divinity School too, participants in the New Testament Graduate Seminar during the spring of 1986 gave their skeptical encouragement and needed criticism.

Several people merit special thanks. Steven Skiles fortified my flabby Coptic; Rebecca Marshall and Linda Seracuse proofed and beautified the volume. François Bovon, Jean-Marc Prieur, and Jean-Daniel Kaestli, members of l'Association pour l'étude de la littérature apocryphe chrétienne, supplied me with materials otherwise inaccessible and graciously entertained me to discuss topics apocryphal and sublime. Roelof Van den Broek granted permission to reissue his text of *Papyrus Coptic Utrecht 1* which first appeared in Prieur's edition. William R. Schoedel, guest editor for this volume, combed it with care. The Ibycus Corporation of Los Altos, California, by special arrangements made available the character cartridge for the Greek and Coptic fonts. Thomas J. Samuelian capably translated the Armenian fragments of the martyrdom story, while Donald Vance created the Armenian and Syriac fonts. John Strugnell, Gene Tucker, David Suiter, Harold W. Attridge, David Frankfurter, Sandra Smith, Kent H. Richards, Steve Goering, Frank Ames, Kelly DelTredici, Paul Mirecki, and Diane, Katya, and Julian MacDonald deserve thanks for reasons known well to them and perhaps less well to me.

This volume is dedicated to Peter Jonathan MacDonald, lover of languages and libraries, who offered his home in Somerville as a base camp for my serial assaults on Harvard's Widener and Andover-Harvard libraries. Even more, he has, over the years, been my friend, confidant, and intellectual companion. St.

Andrew and I have been similarly blessed, each with a
faithful brother named Peter.

ABBREVIATIONS

AA	*The Acts of Andrew*
AAA	*Acta apostolorum apocrypha*, R. A. Lipsius and M. Bonnet
AAMt	*The Acts of Andrew and Matthias*
AJ	*The Acts of John*
AJPr	*The Acts of John by Prochorus*
AnBoll	*Analecta Bollandiana*
ANRW	*Aufstieg und Niedergang der römischen Welt*
APe	*The Acts of Peter*
APh	*The Acts of Philip*
APl	*The Acts of Paul*
ATh	*The Acts of Thomas*
AV	*Actus Vercellenses*
AXP	*The Acts of Xanthippe and Polyxena*
BHG	*Bibliotheca hagiographica Graeca*, F. Halkin
BHL	*Bibliotheca hagiographica Latina antiquae et mediae aetatis*
BHO	*Bibliotheca hagiographica orientalis*
ByZ	*Byzantinische Zeitschrift*
BZNTW	Beihefte zur Zeitschrift für die neutestamentliche Wissenschaft
CCSA	Corpus Christianorum, Series Apocryphorum
CCSL	Corpus Christianorum, Series Latina
CSEL	Corpus Scriptorum Ecclesiasticorum Latinorum
DOS	Dumbarton Oaks Studies
EETS	Early English Text Society

FAC	*Fragments of Attic Comedy*, J. M. Edmonds
FHG	*Fragmenta historicorum Graecorum*, C. Müller
JAC	*Jahrbuch für Antike und Christentum*
JTS	*Journal for Theological Studies*
Loeb	The Loeb Classical Library
LXX	Septuaginta
MLR	*Modern Language Review*
NovTSup	Novum Testamentum, Supplements
PG	*Patrologia Graeca*, J. P. Migne
PL	*Patrologia Latina*, J. P. Migne
PTSt	Patristische Texte und Studien
PW	Pauly-Wissowa, *Real-Encyclopädie der klassichen Altertumswissenschaft*
RHLR	*Revue d'histoire et de littérature religieuse*
RhMPh	*Rheinisches Museum für Philologie*
StrThSt	Strassburger theologische Studien
TS	Texts and Studies
TU	Texte und Untersuchungen zur Geschichte der altchristlichen Literatur
VC	*Vigiliae Christianae*

Abbreviations relevant to the manuscripts of the Acts appear in the introductions to Parts I, II, and III.

SHORT TITLES

Baker, "Passion of Saint Andrew"

Baker, Alfred T. "The Passion of Saint Andrew." *Modern Language Review* 11 (1916): 420-49.

Blatt, *Bearbeitungen*

Blatt, Franz. *Die lateinischen Bearbeitungen der Acta Andreae et Matthiae apud Anthropophagos.* Beihefte zur Zeitschrift für die neutestamentliche Wissenschaft 12. Giessen: Alfred Töpelmann, 1930.

Bonnet, *Acta Andreae*

Bonnet, Maximilian, ed. *Acta Andreae cum laudatione contexta et Martyrium Andreae Graece: Passio Andreae Latine.* Supplementum codicis apocryphi 2. Paris: C. Klincksieck, 1895. Reprint of *Analecta Bollandiana* 13 [1894]: 309-78.

Bonnet, "Liber de miraculis"

Maximillian Bonnet, "Gregorii episcopi turonensis liber de miraculis beati Andreae apostoli." In *Monumenta Germaniae historica. Scriptores rerum Merovingicarum*, 821-46. Hannover: Impensis bibliopolii Aulici Hahniani, 1883.

Bovon, *Actes apocryphes*

Les Actes apocryphes des apôtres: Christianisme et monde païen, ed. François Bovon, Publication de la Faculté de Théologie de l'Université de Genève 4. Geneva: Labor et Fides, 1981.

Brooks, *Andreas and Fates*

Brooks, Kenneth R. *Andreas and the Fates of the Apostles.* Oxford: Clarendon Press, 1961.

Budge, *Contendings*

> Budge, E. A. Wallis. *The Contendings of the Apostles*. London: Oxford University Press (Humphrey Milford), 1935.

Dvornik, *Apostolicity*

> Dvornik, Francis. *The Idea of Apostolicity in Byzantium and the Legend of the Apostle Andrew*. Dumbarton Oaks Studies 4. Cambridge: Harvard University Press, 1958.

Flamion, *Actes d'André*

> Flamion, Josef. *Les Actes apocryphes de l'apôtre André. Les Actes d'André et de Mathias, de Pierre et d'André et les textes apparentés*. Recueil de travaux d'histoire et de philologie 33. Louvain: Bureaux de Recueil, 1911.

Goodwin, *Anglo-Saxon Legends*

> Goodwin, Charles Wycliffe. *The Anglo-Saxon Legends of St. Andrew and St. Veronica*. Cambridge: Macmillan, 1851.

James, *Apocrypha anecdota*

> James, Montague Rhodes. *Apocrypha anecdota*. Texts and Studies 2,3 and 5,1. Cambridge: Cambridge University Press, 1893 and 1897. Reprint. Nendeln/Liechtenstein: Kraus, 1967.

Junod and Kaestli, *Histoire*

> Junod, Eric, and Jean-Daniel Kaestli. *l'Histoire des Actes apocryphes des apôtres du IIIe au IXe siècle: le cas des Actes de Jean*. Cahiers de la Revue de Théologie et de Philosophie 7. Geneva, Lausanne, Neuchâtel, 1982.

Krapp, *Andreas*

> Krapp, George Philip. *Andreas and the Fates of the Apostles*. Boston: Ginn, 1906.

Leloir, *Écrits apocryphes*

> Leloir, Louis. *Écrits apocryphes sur les apôtres. Traduction de l'édition arménienne de Venise. I. Pierre, Paul, André, Jacques, Jean.* Corpus Christianorum, Series Apocryphorum 3. Turnhout: Brepols, 1986.

Lipsius, *Apostelgeschichten*

> Lipsius, Richard Adelbert. *Die apokryphen Apostelgeschichten und Apostellegenden. Ein Beitrag zur altchristlichen Literaturgeschichte.* 2 vols. in 3. Braunschweig: C. A. Schwetschke, 1883-1890.

Morris, *Blickling Homilies*

> Morris, R. *The Blickling Homilies of the Tenth Century.* Early English Text Society 63. London: N. Trübner, 1880.

Prieur, *Acta Andreae*

> Prieur, Jean-Marc. *Acta Andreae.* Corpus Christianorum, Series Apocryphorum 5 and 6. Turnhout: Brepols, 1989.

Schermann, *Prophetarum vitae fabulosae*

> Schermann, Theodor. *Prophetarum vitae fabulosae indices apostolorum discipulorumque Domini Dorotheo, Epiphanio, Hippolyto aliisque vindicata.* Leipzig: B. G. Teubner, 1907.

Wright, *Apocryphal Acts*

> Wright, William. *Apocryphal Acts of the Apostles. Edited from Syrian Manuscripts in the British Museum and Other Libraries.* London and Edinburgh: Williams and Norgate, 1871. Reprint. Amsterdam: Philo Press, 1968.

Zahn, *Acta Joannis*

> Zahn, Theodor. *Acta Joannis.* Erlangen: Andreas Deichert, 1880. Reprint. Hildesheim: H. A. Gerstenberg, 1975.

INTRODUCTION

Late in the sixth century, Georgius Florentius Gregorius, bishop of Tours, claimed to "have discovered a book of miracles of the holy apostle Andrew, which some dub apocryphal because of its excessive verbosity."[1] This *Liber de virtutibus sancti Andreae apostoli* almost certainly was *The Acts of Andrew*; by the late fourth century ecclesiastical authors were loath to refer to apocryphal Acts as Πράξεις/*Acta*, reserving the title instead for Luke's canonical Acts.[2] Gregory read no Greek, so he must have found the Acts in Latin translation. In order to rescue the book from the smear *apocrifus*, Gregory set out to abstract from his capacious discovery "the miracles only, disregarding whatever would breed disgust."[3] Because no complete text of *The Acts of Andrew* now exists, Gregory's epitome,

----

1. Maximilian Bonnet, "Georgii Florentii Gregorii episcopi turonensis liber de miraculis beati Andreae apostoli," *Monumenta Germaniae historica. Scriptores rerum Merovingicarum* (Hannover: Impensis bibliopolii Aulici Hahniani, 1883), 1:826.

2. See Josef Flamion, *Les Actes apocryphes de l'apôtre André. Les Actes d'André et de Mathias, de Pierre et d'André et les textes apparentés*, Recueil de travaux d'histoire et de philologie 33 (Louvain: Bureaux de Recueil, 1911), 214-15.

3. Bonnet, "Liber de miraculis," 826. Gregory had personal interests in Andrew; he was born on the apostle's "birthday" (*in illius natale*), viz., the day of his martyrdom, 1 December (the official feastday is 30 November).

1

albeit tendentious and frequently garbled, provides our most inclusive overview of its narrative architecture and is the only witness to long stretches of it.

According to Gregory, after the apostles cast lots in Jerusalem to determine where each would preach, Andrew went to Achaea and Matthias to Myrmidonia, whose savage inhabitants immediately seized and incarcerated him. An angel summoned Andrew from Achaea to sail off and rescue Matthias. He did so, converted the city, and continued his adventures through Anatolia, Thrace, Macedonia, and Achaea, until he was executed in Patras. In other words, Gregory's account contains a looping itinerary unique among the early apocryphal Acts which otherwise send the apostles more or less unidirectionally from Jerusalem to the regions of their primary ministries and deaths. Andrew, however, sets out from Achaea and returns there through a series of fabulous ordeals mimetic of Odysseus's Nostos. This erstwhile fisherman, whose name resonates with the Greek word for manliness (ἀνδρεία), appears here as a Christian Odysseus.

Gregory's abstract is by no means all that remains of *The Acts of Andrew*. There also exist eight different recensions of Andrew's Passion, two huge Byzantine Βίοι, two fragments of episodes that circulated independently, several patristic citations, and derivative Andrean apocrypha. This wealth of material, when judiciously compared with Gregory's epitome, allows one to reconstruct much of the original. For several years, Jean-Marc Prieur and I have devoted ourselves to retrieving the ancient Acts, and our two editions, published within a year of each other, for the most part agree.[4] Our most

----

4. *Acta Andreae*, CCSA 5 and 6 (Turnhout: Brepols, 1989).

obvious disagreement concerns how the Acts began. Mine
begins with Andrew going to rescue Matthias from
Myrmidonia, just as in Gregory's epitome. Prieur's
begins instead with chapter 2 of Gregory, with Andrew
healing a blind man in central Anatolia.[5] In this
respect, Prieur follows Josef Flamion in supposing that
the Frankish bishop actually epitomized two books, not
one: *The Acts of Andrew and Matthias in the City of the
Cannibals (AAMt)* and *The Acts of Andrew (AA)*.[6] Gregory's
sloppy weld cannot conceal the original gap between
them. Insofar as the present volume, by including the
AAMt at the beginning of the *AA*, distinguishes itself
not only from the reconstructions of Flamion and Prieur
but also from all other published versions of the Acts,
it is essential here to provide a detailed defense for
doing so.[7]

The Acts of Andrew and Matthias

The *AAMt* begins with the apostles in Jerusalem
casting lots to see where each would preach, a scene

----

5. Ibid., 32-35.

6. *Actes d'André*, 269-324.

7. Several other scholars have claimed that some version
of the *AAMt* might once have begun the *AA*: Richard
Adelbert Lipsius, *Die apokryphen Apostelgeschichten
und Apostellegenden. Ein Beitrag zur altchristlichen
Literaturgeschichte* (Braunschweig: C. A. Schwetschke,
1883), 1:546-53, 601 and 615; Otto Bardenhewer,
Geschichte der altkirchlichen Literatur 2d ed., 3
vols. (Freiburg: Herder, 1912-1914); Adolf von
Harnack, *Geschichte der altchristlichen Literatur bis
Eusebius*, Part 2, *Die Chronologie*, ed. K. Aland and
F. Winkelmann, 2d ed., 2 vols. (Leipzig: J. C.
Hinrichs, 1897-1904), 1:544; Albert Ehrhard, *Die
altchristliche Literatur und ihre Erforschung von
1884-1900*, StrThSt 1 (Freiburg: Herder, 1900), 161;
and Martin Blumenthal, *Formen und Motive in den
apokryphen Apostelgeschichten*, TU 48.1 (Leipzig: J.
C. Hinrichs, 1933).

obviously inspired by Acts 1-2. In both Acts the apostles convene to cast lots, and in both the lot falls on Matthias.[8] The canonical Acts selects him to replace Judas among the Twelve, but the *AAMt* selects him to evangelize the city of the cannibals, which Gregory names Myrmidonia.[9]

When the apostle arrives in the city, the residents gouge out his eyes and imprison him for thirty days of fattening. From this point on, the author borrows freely from the Septuagintal version of Jonah. Jesus appears to Andrew telling him to go to Myrmidonia, just as God appears to Jonah telling him to go to Nineveh.[10] Like Jonah, Andrew objects, but ultimately is compelled to go. He descends to the shore and finds a boat going to Myrmidonia, just as Jonah finds one going to Tarshish,[11] but Andrew's ship is piloted by none other than Jesus himself in disguise. Jonah gives the captain his fare

----

8. Acts 2:1: ἦσαν πάντες . . . ἐπὶ τὸ αὐτό. *AAMt* 1: ἦσαν πάντες . . . ἐπὶ τὸ αὐτό. Acts 1:26: ἔδωκαν κλήρους αὐτοῖς, καὶ ἔπεσεν ὁ κλῆρος ἐπὶ Μαθθίαν. *AAMt* 1: βάλλοντες κλήρους . . . . κατὰ κλῆρον οὖν ἔλαχεν τὸν Ματθείαν.

9. Perhaps it is worth noting that Clement of Alexandria knew a tradition stating that Matthias was a vegetarian (*Paidagogos* 2.1.16). See also *Martyrium Matthaei*.

10. Jonah 1:1 (LXX): καὶ ἐγένετο λόγος κυρίου πρὸς Ιωναν τὸν Αμαθι λέγων, ἀνάστηθι καὶ πορεύθητι εἰς Νινευη τὴν πόλιν τὴν μεγάλην. *AAMt* 4: ἐφάνη ὁ κύριος Ἰησοῦς ἐν *Achaia civitatem* ᾗ ἦν διδάσκων ὁ Ἀνδρέας, καὶ εἶπεν αὐτῷ· ἀνάσθητι καὶ πορεύθητι . . . *in civitatem que dicitur Mermedonia.*

11. Jonah 1:3 (LXX): καὶ ἀνέστη Ιωνας τοῦ φυγεῖν εἰς Θαρσις . . . καὶ κατέβη εἰς Ιοππην καὶ εὗρεν πλοῖον βαδίζον εἰς Θαρσις. *AAMt* 4-6: ἀλλ᾽ ἀναστὰς τῷ πρωὶ κάτελθε . . . καὶ εὑρήσεις πλοῖον . . . καὶ ἀνέληῃς εἰς αὐτὸ . . . . ἀναστὰς δὲ Ἀνδρέας . . . καὶ κατελθὼν . . . εἶδεν πλοιάριον. The boat is headed for Myrmidonia.

(1:3 [LXX]: καὶ ἔδωκεν τὸν ναῦλον αὐτοῦ), but Andrew, because he is a disciple of Jesus, has no fare (AAMt 6: οὐ δίδομέν σοι τὸν ναῦλον ἡμῶν). Captain Jesus lets him board anyway. Like Jonah, Andrew is carried to the city miraculously and again is told to enter it.[12] At the center of the city he finds a large furnace for cooking human prey and a vat for catching blood. Andrew goes to the prison, slays the guards with a prayer, and rescues the prisoners, including Matthias. Andrew sends everyone else away, while he himself sits behind a pillar to see what will happen next, just as Jonah sat under his shelter to see what would happen to the Ninevites.[13]

Discovering their dinners have escaped, fourteen executioners attempt to fillet the dead guards, but Andrew causes their swords to fall from their hands. Then they decide to sacrifice seven of their elderly every day until they capture more victims. One old man convinces the authorities to eat his two children in his place, but again the apostle thwarts them. The residents seize Andrew, drag him through the streets for three days, and leave him for dead. Revived by Jesus himself, Andrew commands a statue to spew forth a flood, thereby drowning many of the residents until the survivors, like Jonah's Ninevites, repent with tears and ashes. Andrew orders the floods to cease, and an abyss swallows the waters along with the executioners and the merciless old

----

12. Jonah 3:2-3 (LXX): ἀνάσθητι καὶ πορεύθητι εἰς Νινευη τὴν πόλιν τὴν μεγάλην καὶ κήρυξον ἐν αὐτῇ . . . . καὶ ἀνέστη Ιωνας καὶ ἐπορεύθη εἰς Νινευη. AAMt 18-19: ἀνάστα, εἴσελθε πρὸς Ματθείαν εἰς τὴν πόλιν καὶ ἐξάγαγε αὐτὸν ἐκ τῆς φυλακῆς . . . . 'Ανδρέας δὲ ἀναστὰς εἰσῆλθεν ἐν τῇ πόλει.

13. Jonah 4:5 (LXX): καὶ ἐκάθητο ὑποκάτω αὐτῆς ἐν σκιᾷ, ἕως οὗ ἀπίδῃ τί ἔσται τῇ πόλει. AAMt 22: καὶ ἐκαθέσθη ὀπίσω τοῦ στύλου ἐκείνου ἕως ἂν ἴδῃ τί ἔσται τὸ γενόμενον.

man. The apostle raises the dead, humans and beasts, and promises to return to rescue those consumed by the abyss, but only after they have observed below the tortures of the wicked and the rewards of the righteous. Andrew then leaves town, in spite of the Myrmidons' begging him to remain. Jesus appears to the apostle as he sails away and rebukes him for his Jonah-like impassibility, for not being moved by their entreaties. Andrew returns and teaches for seven days, but he never retrieves anyone from the abyss.

Like the book of Jonah, the *AAMt* displays a remarkable concern for the salvation of animal life. In Jonah, the king of Nineveh forbids everyone from eating and drinking, not only humans but also "beasts, cattle, and sheep" (4:7 [LXX]: καὶ τὰ κτήνη καὶ οἱ βόες καὶ πρόβατα). Both humans and beasts (κτήνη) wear sackcloth (3:8). The final sentence asks Jonah why he should not have compassion even for κτήνη πολλά. Andrew, however, does have compassion for beasts (κτήνη); he revives them too after the flood.

The Case for Omitting the Cannibal Story from *The Acts of Andrew*

According to Flamion and Prieur, this story never appeared at the beginning of the *AA*: (1) by naming the city of the cannibals Myrmidonia, Gregory demonstrated that he knew only a derivative version of the story, insofar as the city was unnamed in the original; (2) by pasting the story onto the beginning of the Acts, Gregory created a forced and implausible itinerary; and (3) external evidence points to an Acts without Matthias and cannibals. In each case, Flamion and Prieur are wrong.

Myrmidonia

Even though the best Greek texts of the *AAMt* do not contain the word Myrmidonia, it now would appear that the original story, like Gregory's epitome, did. Nineteen years after Flamion's book, Franz Blatt published the first edition of codex *Casanatensis*, a rather faithful Latin translation of the *AAMt*, dating to the sixth or seventh centuries, earlier than the extant Greek witnesses by at least a century.[14] Here one finds several references to Myrmidonia.

In fact, all extant texts in Latin or Anglo-Saxon contain some reference to this city name--even though their copyists were unsure how to spell it. The manuscripts of the epitome by Gregory of Tours variously read Mermidona, Myrmidonia, Mirmidona, Mirmidonia, Myrmidona, and Mirmydona.[15] To make matters even more confusing, other related western documents read Myrmidon, Myrmidonensis, Mermedonia, Marmedonia, Marmadonia,[16] Medea,[17] Margundia,[18] and Mirdone.[19] It would be wrong to conclude, however, that the name was

----

14. *Die lateinischen Bearbeitungen der Acta Andreae et Matthiae apud Anthropophagos*, BZNTW 12 (Giessen: Alfred Töpelmann, 1930).

15. See Bonnet, "Liber de miraculis," 827.

16. See Kenneth R. Brooks, *Andreas and the Fates of the Apostles* (Oxford: Clarendon Press, 1961), xxix; George Philip Krapp, *Andreas and the Fates of the Apostles* (Boston: Ginn, 1906), lxvi; and Blatt, *Bearbeitungen*, 6-7 and 141.

17. An eighth century manuscript of the *Martyrium Matthaei* (AAA 2.1:218).

18. Jacobus de Voragine *Legenda Aurea* (Graesse), 13.

19. The Old French *Vie saint Andrier l'apostle*. See Alfred T. Baker, "The Passion of Saint Andrew," *MLR* 11 (1916): 439.

known only in western Christendom. Greek texts
undoubtedly related to the *AAMt* give the city name as
Μυρμήνη,[20] Μυρμήνις,[21] Μύρνη,[22] Μυρμήκη or Σμυρμήνη,[23]
and Σμύρνα.[24]

Just as baffling as its spelling, and even more
important for determining its function in the *AAMt*, is
the city's location. A monk named Theodosius wrote of
his pilgrimage to Jerusalem which took him also to
Sinope,

> where the lord Andrew freed the evangelist,
> lord Matthew, from prison [at this point in
> the text several lines seem to be missing],
> for at that time Sinope was called Myrmidona
> [a variant reads Mermidona]. Everyone who
> lived there devoured people for their food.
> The misery there was so great that they would
> sit in the street in order to snatch up
> travelers. (*De situ Terrae Sanctae* [Geyer],
> 144; translation mine)

Sinope also was the best guess of the Byzantines.[25]

----

20. An eleventh century manuscript of the *Martyrium
    Matthaei* (*AAA* 2.1:220) and Nicephorus Callistus
    Historia ecclesiastica 2.41.

21. A ninth century manuscript of *Martyrium prius* (*AAA*
    2.1:47).

22. Most manuscripts of the *Martyrium Matthaei* (*AAA*
    2.1:220).

23. *Paris gr. 1313*, unpublished.

24. A tenth century manuscript of the *Martyrium Matthaei*
    (*AAA* 2.1:227 and 262).

25. Epiphanius the monk (*PG* 120:221D--224A), *Narratio*
    5-7, *Laudatio* 7-8, two incipits to the Greek *AAMt*
    (*Paris Gr. 881* and *Escorial Y II, 4*), and two

Others guessed Athens[26] or Titaran.[27] The Syriac text of
the *AAMt* calls it "the City of the Dogs," or ‘Irka. The
location of ‘Irka is unknown, but Theodor Nöldeke
noticed that a slight orthographic alteration of ܡܠܟܒ,
the Syriac word for "dogs," makes it ܡܠܟܒ,
"Colchians," residents of Colchis, a city on the eastern
shore of the Black Sea.[28] A catalogue of the fates of
the apostles falsely attributed to Epiphanius of Cyprus
likewise places Andrew in Sebastopolis Magna, the Roman
name for Colchis.[29]

Modern scholars too have tried to locate the city
of the cannibals. The most convincing identification has
been that of Alfred von Gutschmid, who argued that the
name in Ps.-Abdias (a recasting of Gregory's account)
preserves the most original spelling of the word:
Myrmidona, derived from Myrmiciona "a vulgar form of the
Greek Myrmekion."[30] Myrmekion was a city near Cher-
sonesus Taurica, or the modern Crimean peninsula, in
antiquity frequently related to Scythia. According to

----

unpublished Greek manuscripts (*Ottoban 415* and *Paris
gr. 1313*).

26. A twelfth century Greek manuscript of the *AAMt* (*AAA*
2.1:65).

27. The Ethiopic "Preaching of Saint Andrew and Saint
Philemon Among the Kurds" (E. A. Wallis Budge, *The
Contendings of the Apostles* [London: Oxford
University Press (Humphrey Milford), 1935], 2:137).

28. Lipsius, *Apostelgeschichten*, 1:546-47.

29. Theodor Schermann, *Prophetarum vitae fabulosae,
Indices apostolorum discipulorumque Domini, Doro-
theo, Epiphanio, Hippolyto aliisque vindicata*
(Leipzig: B. G. Teubner, 1907), 108-109.

30. "Die Königsnamen in den apokryphen Apostelgeschichten. Ein Beitrag zur Kenntnis des geschichtlichen Romans," *RhMPh* n.F. 19 (1864): 161-83, and
380-401 (reprinted in his *Kleine Schriften*, ed.
Franz Rühl; [Leipzig: B. G. Teubner, 1890], 332-94).

Eusebius, Origen too (third century) had placed Andrew's ministry in Scythia,[31] and *Recensio Vaticana* (a seventh or eighth century Latin poem about Andrew, Matthias, and cannibals) places "Mirmidonia" (once "Myrmidonensis") in Scythia.[32] A ninth century monk named Epiphanius may have known of this tradition, for he states that when Andrew arrived in Sinope he conversed with the Scythians there.[33] In light of the ancient stereotype of Scythians as cannibals,[34] Gutschmid's identification seems quite plausible and has enjoyed nearly unanimous acceptance.[35] For example, Kenneth R. Brooks claimed the identification of the city "with Strabo's Myrmecium" seemed "practically certain."[36]

This longstanding consensus is wrong. Myrmidonia belongs not on the map of the Roman empire but on the map of the imagination. The significance of Myrmidonia

----

31. Eusebius *Historia ecclesiastica* 3.1.

32. Blatt, *Bearbeitungen*, 141 and 146.

33. *PG* 120:220A. Cf. 221A.

34. For example, Herodotus 4.18 and 26, Aristotle *Politica* 8.3.4, Strabo 11.2.12, Aeschylus *Prometheus* 707-13, Tertullian *Adversus Marcionem* 1.1.

35. So Lipsius, *Apostelgeschichten*, 1:604-10; Bonnet, "Liber de miraculis," 828, n. 2.; Salomon Reinach, "Les apôtres chez les anthropophages," *RHLR* 9 (1904): 316-20; Krapp, *Andreas*, lxvii.; Blatt, *Bearbeitungen*, 6; Francis Dvornik, *The Idea of Apostolicity in Byzantium and the Legend of the Apostle Andrew*, DOS 4 (Cambridge: Harvard University Press, 1958), 205; and Peter Megill Peterson, *Andrew, Brother of Simon Peter, His History and His Legends*, NovTSup 1 (Leiden: E. J. Brill, 1958), 34.

36. *Andreas and Fates*, xxix. A few scholars have preferred instead a setting in Northern Africa or Egypt (François N. Nau, "Actes coptes," s.v., *Dictionnaire d'histoire et de géographie ecclési-astiques*, and Flamion, *Actes d'André*, 313-15).

is not geographical but mythological. In Myrmidonia live
Myrmidons.[37]

Myrmidons appear in Greek literature already in
Homer as allies to Achilles and as

> ravening wolves in whose hearts is fury
> unspeakable--wolves that have slain in the
> hills a great horned stag, and rend him, and
> the jaws of all are red with gore; and in a
> pack they go to lap with their slender tongues
> the surface of the black water from a dusky
> spring, belching forth the while blood and
> gore, the heart in their breasts unflinching,
> and their bellies gorged full; even in such
> wise the leaders and rulers of the Myrmidons
> sped forth round about the valiant squire of
> the swift-footed son of Aeacus. (*Iliad*
> 16.156-66 [Loeb])

According to ancient myth, Myrmidons had a special
relationship to the Aeacus mentioned here.[38] Because
Hera had destroyed all the people on Aegina, Aeacus's
island, he implored Zeus to repopulate it with as many
subjects as the ants marching in file nearby. Zeus
complied by turning the ants (μύρμηκες) into humans. In
Ovid, Aeacus himself tells what happened next.

> I called them Myrmidons, nor did I cheat the
> name of its origin. You have seen their
> bodies; the habits which they had before they
> still keep, a thrifty race, inured to toil,
> keen in pursuit of gain and keeping what they
> get. These men will follow you to the wars
> well matched in years and courage. (*Metamor-
> phoses* 7.614-42 and 649-58 [Loeb])

----

37. So also Vasilij Grigor'evich Vasil'evskij,
    "Choždenic apostola Andreja v strane Mirmidonjan,"
    Žurnal ministerstva narodnago prosveščenija (1877):
    41-82 and 157-85.

38. Excellent discussions of the myth appear in Ludwig
    Preller and Carl Robert, *Griechische Mythologie*, 4th
    ed., 2 vols. in 4 (Berlin: Weidmann, 1964-1967),
    1:75-78; and J. Schmidt, "Myrmidones," s.v. PW.

Undisputed evidences of this etiological, etymo-
logical, entomological myth do not appear in Homer or
elsewhere before Hesiod (fifth or sixth century BCE),[39]
but it likely is much earlier.[40] No matter how deep its
roots, the myth flourished in the Hellenistic and Roman
Imperial periods.

Ovid's depiction of these ant-people, who keep "the
habits which they had before" as ants, emphasizes the

----

39. *Catalogues of Women and the Eoiae* 53.

40. Theagenes (sixth century BCE) already knew the
    tradition that Homer's Myrmidons acquired their name
    from μύρμηκες, but he favored a more rationalistic,
    non-mythological explanation: "some others interpret
    something more persuasive concerning these things.
    They say that when the island had few inhabitants
    they lived in underground caves utterly uncivilized,
    they brought into the caves whatever produce there
    might be, and came up to dig up the earth . . . .
    Wherefore, they are called Myrmidons, because when
    they came out . . . they resembled ants. Aeacus and
    those with him arriving from the Peleponnese lived
    among them, humanized them, gave them laws and
    orderly governance which they observe so completely
    that it seems they are humans made from ants" (*FHG*
    4:511, Theagenes, fr. 17).

    Much later, Strabo (first century CE) gives a
    similar etymological justification: "It is said that
    the Aeginetans were called Myrmidons,--not as the
    myth has it, because, when a great famine occurred,
    the ants became human beings in answer to a prayer
    of Aeacus, but because they excavated the earth
    after the manner of ants and spread the soil over
    the rocks, so as to have ground to till, and because
    they lived in dugouts, refraining from the use of
    soil for bricks" (8.6.16 [Loeb]). Perhaps it is
    worth observing that Aegina is dominated by Mt.
    Oros, which is almost perfectly conical, like an
    anthill. The comic playwright Pherecrates (fifth
    century BCE) wrote a parody on the story in a play
    entitled "The Ant-People" (οἱ Μυρμηκάνθρωποι), the
    few survivals of which depict the ants on Aegina
    deeply resenting their having to become human (see
    FAC 1:251-53). The parody could never have worked
    had the myth of the Myrmidons not been long
    established in popular belief.

positive qualities of ants: industry, thrift, and courage. Apollonius Rhodius domesticated them even further by limiting their formic traits to occasional races in which young Myrmidons would carry heavy jars of water on their shoulders.[41]

As any observant gardener knows, ants also raid, ravage, and plunder, possess Herculean strength, and carry dead insects, including other ants, down into their nests ostensibly to eat. In other words, one might consider them the cannibals of the insect world. These savage implications of the Myrmidon myth did not escape ancient authors. Statius (first century CE) wrote of "the blow of bloodthirsty Myrmidone."[42] The Christian poet Nonnus (fifth century CE) claimed that the ants of Aegina immediately became "an armed host" ready for battle.[43] Lucian (second century CE) says it clearest: the Myrmidons were "the most warlike of races."[44]

Threads of Myrmidonian ancestry are woven so deeply into the fabric of the *AAMt* that even the Greek manuscripts missing the word "Myrmidonia" depict the city as Antville. In order to bake their victims, the cannibals had erected at the center of the city a huge oven (κλίβανος). One built a κλίβανος by digging into the earth a few feet and packing mud and plaster into conical walls with an opening at the top. In other words, a large κλίβανος would have looked very much like an anthill.

----

41. *Argonautica* 4.1765-72.

42. *Thebaid* 5.223-24 (Loeb).

43. *Dionysiaca* 13.205-14.

44. *Icaromenippus* 19 (Loeb).

The social organization of the cannibals also reminds one of ants. They have no king, no proconsul, no magistrate, only "rulers" (ἄρχοντες), "superiors" (μείζονες), "guards" (φύλακες), "executioners" (δήμιοι), and "the young," who sail away in search of prey. Just as some ants bite their victims, poisoning them into submission, the cannibals drug their victims into beast-like domestication. They repeatedly drag Andrew through their streets, like ants hauling quarry. Notice also that in order to punish them, Andrew tries to drown them, a common method for killing ants. When the residents repent, Andrew calls off the flood, walks toward the middle of town, the waters receding before him, until he gets to the vat and the oven, where the earth opens and the abyss swallows the waters along with the most wicked of the cannibals, like ants plunged into their anthole.

Perhaps this reading of the story seems too farfetched, too clever, too modern. Not at all. This interpretation appears in a text earlier than any of our Greek textual witnesses to the AAMt by more than two centuries. The ethnographer Stephen of Byzantium (sixth century) compiled an alphabetical list of place names and attached to them citations from ancient myths, making it a treasury of popular lore. Immediately after his description of Myrmekion, one finds a brief entry on Μυρμιδονία: "Myrmidonia: region of the Myrmidons, for so Aegina is called."[45] Apparently Stephen had seen

----

45. Μυρμιδονία, χώρα τῶν Μυρμιδόνων. οὕτως γὰρ ἡ Αἴγινα
    ἐκλήθη. One early text omits the last three words of
    the preceding entry and the first three words of
    this one. Undoubtedly this omission was caused by a
    haplographic confusion of Μυρμήκιον and Μυρμιδόνων.
    The corruption is apparent not only because earlier,
    more reliable witnesses have the text as translated
    above, but also because the resultant reading is
    incoherent. See August Meineke, *Stephan von Byzanz,*

Μυρμιδονία in a Greek copy of the *AAMt*. His sources were predominantly Greek, and the word Μυρμιδονία itself, in spite of the popularity of the Myrmidon myth, never occurs elsewhere in Greek literature.

It therefore would appear that the textual grandparent behind most extant Greek versions of the *AAMt* tendentiously removed every trace of Μυρμιδονία, presumably because of its fabulous antecedents in Greek myth.[46] Latin and Anglo-Saxon manuscripts, however, retained the name--in thirteen different spellings-- because western readers, for whom ants were *formicae* or *æmette*, were unaware of the disreputable ancestry of Myrmidonia from μύρμηκες. The presence of Myrmidons in the *AA* obviously would encourage the impression that the author wrote with an eye to *The Odyssey*, with its own Myrmidons and cannibals. One thing is certain: Gregory's reference to Myrmidonia does not witness to a Latin, derivative version of the *AAMt*, as Flamion thought, but preserves the city name from the original Greek story.

Gregory's Itinerary

Gregory's clumsy transition from the Myrmidon story to the subsequent episodes has generated other doubts concerning the original unity of the two Acts. Although Richard Adelbert Lipsius thought that the *AAMt* originally commenced the *AA*, he perceived a mistake in Gregory's sending Andrew from Myrmidonia "to his own region" (*Andreas autem recedens ab eo loco, venit in*

Ethnika (Graz: Akademische Druck-und Verlagsanstalt, 1958), 464.

46. Though repressed, the identification of the cannibals as Myrmidons did not escape all later interpreters. Ordericus Vitalis (twelfth century) used Gregory's epitome as a source and in place of Myrmidonia wrote Myrmidons (*PL* 188:139).

regionem suam), that is, to Achaea. The next story in
Gregory takes place not in Achaea but in Amasia, in
north central Anatolia (chapter 2). Lipsius, followed by
Maximilian Bonnet, suggested that Gregory had mistaken
Achaea in Greece for Achaea Sarmata, on the northern
shore of the Black Sea.[47] Flamion, unconvinced by this
clever but forced explanation, argued that the problem
resulted from Gregory's careless conjoining of two
originally independent documents.[48]

This solution creates more problems than it solves.
In the first place, Gregory simply could not have
inherited the alleged Achaean detour from the *AAMt* which
says nothing, absolutely nothing, about Andrew arriving
in Achaea. In fact, if one adopts the ancient
identification of Myrmidonia with Scythia or Sinope, the
AAMt ends with Andrew not far from Amasia.

Second, Gregory claimed to have epitomized one
document, not two. In order to take this claim into
account, Prieur proposes that the combination of the two
Acts already had taken place prior to Gregory in the
Latin translation he epitomized,[49] but this proposal
merely shoves the source of the alleged confusion back a
step; it does not explain it.

Finally, by detaching the Myrmidonian episode from
the *AA* Flamion multiplied one literary mess into two.
Without the Myrmidonian episode at its beginning, the *AA*

----

47. Lipsius, *Apostelgeschichten*, 1:604-10; Bonnet,
    "Liber de miraculis," 828, n. 2. Lipsius and Bonnet
    also could have argued that the confusion might also
    have been visual, between 'Αχαΐα and 'Αμασεία.

48. So also Prieur, *Acta Andreae*, 32-35.

49. "Response," in *The Apocryphal Acts of Apostles*,
    Semeia 38, ed. Dennis R. MacDonald (Decatur, GA:
    Scholars Press, 1986), 28.

begins in landlocked Amasia, without any indication concerning how or why the apostle went there. More glaring is the incompletion of the *AAMt* without additional narrative. The text is quite explicit concerning what should have taken place: Andrew was to leave the city to rejoin his disciples (chapter 32), go with them to "the city of the barbarians" (chapter 33), and return to Myrmidonia to raise the fifteen swallowed by the abyss (chapter 31). Andrew never does any of this. The story stops prematurely, *sans denouement*, with Andrew sailing off to find his disciples.

This unresolved ending bothered ancient readers, as one can see from the attempts to expunge from the text these promises never kept. One Greek manuscript (*Paris suppl. gr. 824*) and an Anglo-Saxon version of the *AAMt* omit any anticipation of Andrew's return to exhume the Myrmidons. The Latin, Syriac, and Ethiopic versions say nothing about Andrew going to the barbarians. By clever omission, a Greek manuscript (*Palat. Vat. 4*) transforms the Myrmidons themselves into the barbarians Andrew was to evangelize, voiding the need for his later return. *Recensio Vaticana*, the Armenian *AAMt*, and *Andreas* (an Anglo-Saxon epic poem based on the *AAMt*) pass over the entire presaging passage of chapter 33 in silence.

Other texts work at the problem from the opposite end by supplying the foreshadowed but wanting episodes. *The Acts of Peter and Andrew* picks up where the *AAMt* broke off by sending Andrew on a cloud to his disciples. Then they go, as anticipated, to the city of the barbarians.[50] In the Syriac and Ethiopic translations of the *AAMt*, Andrew raises the fifteen from the abyss before he leaves the city. According to *Paris gr. 1313*,

----

50. *Acts of Peter and Andrew* 1-3 (*AAA* 2.1:117-18).

the only surviving Greek text of the *AAMt* retaining a variation of the name Μυρμιδονία, Andrew leaves the city for the east, finds his disciples and tells them, "it is time for us to leave for Μυρμήκη (sic), inasmuch as our Lord Jesus Christ commanded that those swallowed up in the abyss be retrieved alive." When they return, Andrew calls forth the fifteen dead from the abyss, revives them, confirms everyone in the faith, and leaves with his disciples for Amasia.[51]

These early readers of the *AAMt* were right: the story obviously is incomplete. To be sure, Gregory's epitome does not narrate the episodes anticipated at the end of the *AAMt*--Excursus A suggests that he and other redactors scotched these episodes because Manichaeans used them to support reincarnation--but Gregory does provide a legitimate beginning to the *AA* and a plausible transition from Myrmidonia to Amasia.

If the Myrmidonian episode originally commenced the *AA*, why did Gregory send the apostle from Myrmidonia back to Achaea before going to Amasia? The answer is embarrassingly simple: Gregory never sent Andrew back to Achaea at all. The phrase *venit in regionem suam* need not mean "he arrived in his own region," it can also quite legitimately mean "he went toward his own region,"[52] which must be what Gregory had in mind, unless one views him as a geographical nincompoop. It would appear that Gregory read in his copy of the *AA* of

----

51. A fuller treatment of this important, unpublished manuscript appears in Excursus A.

52. *Venire in* does indeed usually mean "to come into," but "to go toward" is perfectly acceptable. See for example Gen 12:1 in several manuscripts of the Vulgate where God commands Abraham to leave his home "and to go to a land that I will show you" (*et veni in terram quam monstrabo tibi*).

the apostle's intention to return to Achaea from Myrmidonia, expressed this intention in an admittedly ambiguous clause, and then continued epitomizing the Acts by sending Andrew back toward Achaea through Anatolia, Thrace, and Macedonia.

External Witnesses

Against Gregory's itinerary, Flamion cited, *inter alia*, *The Synaxarion of Constantinople* (ninth century), in which Andrew goes to Bithynia, Pontus, Thrace, Scythia, Sebastopolis, and Patras;[53] there is no explicit reference here to Myrmidons. However, this document surely does not rely on the *AA* directly but on *Ps.-Epiphanius*, *Ps.-Dorotheus*, and *Ps.-Hippolytus*, themselves no older than the eighth century. Furthermore, when one analyzes these sources behind the *Synaxarion*, it becomes reasonable to conjecture that they too knew of Andrew and Matthias among cannibals. *Ps.-Hippolytus* claims Andrew "preached to Scythians, Thracians, and was crucified in Patras,"[54] which conforms with the general geographical movement in Gregory's account, if one sees here the widespread identification of Myrmidons with Scythia. According to *Ps.-Epiphanius*, Andrew:

> preached to the Scythians and Sogdianians and Gorsinians, and in Sebastopolis the Great, where are the encampment of Apsarus and the Bay of Hyssus and the River Phasis, beyond which live the Ethiopians; he is buried in

----

53. Hippolyte Delehaye, *Synaxarium ecclesiae Constan- tinopolitanae. Acta Sanctorum, Propylaea, November* (Brussels: Société des Bollandistes, 1902), cols. 265-66.

54. *PG* 10:952.

> Patras of Achaea after having been put on the
> cross by Aegeus the King of Patras.[55]

Sebastopolis Magna here is home to displaced Africans
not because of firm demographic information, but because
of popular ascriptions of anthropophagy to Ethiopians.[56]
The Syriac version of the *AAMt* likewise identifies "the
city of the cannibals" as Colchis, the Greek name for
Sebastopolis Magna. Elsewhere *Ps.-Epiphanius*, again
followed by the *Synaxarion*, says that Matthias "preached
the gospel of our Lord in interior Ethiopia, and was
martyred there at the Bay of Hyssus by the
Ethiopians."[57] Some manuscripts add: "He [Matthias]
preached the gospel there to *barbarian cannibals*." No
matter which manuscripts preserve the most original
reading of *Ps.-Epiphanius*, the author obviously knew a
tradition of Andrew and Matthias among hostile
barbarians near the eastern shores of the Black Sea as
well as Andrew's mission in Bithynia, Pontus, Thrace,
and Patras. In other words, the *Synaxarion* and its
sources, instead of securing Flamion's position, attest
to an anterior combination of the *AAMt* and the *AA*.

Flamion also appealed to the Syriac *Doctrina
Apostolorum* (fourth century), which locates Andrew in
"Nicea and Nicomedia and all the country of Bithynia and

----

55. Dvornik's translation (*Apostolicity*, 174). Text in
    Schermann, *Prophetarum vitae fabulosae*, 108-109.

56. E.g., Ptolemy *Geographia* 4.8.3 (Αἰθίοπες ἀνθρωπο-
    φάγοι) and Pliny *Naturalis historia* 6.195. Cf.
    Athanasius *Apologia ad Constantium* 29 (*PG* 25:623)
    and Nestorius in Evagrius *Historia ecclesiastica* 1.7
    (*PG* 86 [2]: 2433-43). Dvornik suggests that this
    passage in *Ps.-Epiphanius* might reflect Byzantine
    readings of Herodotus, who mentions Ethiopians
    living in Asia (*Apostolicity*, 174, n. 111).

57. Schermann, *Prophetarum vitae fabulosae*, 113-14.

of Gothia, and of the regions round about it."[58] Flamion emended "Gothia" to read "Thracia" and used this emendation to harmonize this itinerary with Gregory's account, only without cannibals. Francis Dvornik has shown, however, that Flamion's emendation is impossible and that the author of this Syriac text probably had in mind "the Crimea and the Scythian lands around it," once again attesting to Andrew's ministry to Scythia.[59]

Without question, Flamion's most impressive external evidence is a note in Philaster of Brescia (383 or 384).

> For the Manichaeans [have] an apocryphal writing of the blessed apostle Andrew, i.e., an Acts which he performed when traveling from Pontus to Greece, which the disciples who followed the apostle wrote at that time, whence the Manichaeans and such others also have the Acts of the blessed Andrew. (*Diversarum hereseon liber*, 88.5-7.)[60]

----

58. *Actes d'André*, 242. See also William Cureton, *Ancient Syriac Documents Relative to the Earliest Establishment of Christianity in Edessa and the Neighbouring Countries* (London: Williams and Norgate, 1864), 32.

59. *Apostolicity*, 215-16.

60. *Nam Manichei apocryfa beati Andreae apostoli, id est Actus quos fecit ueniens de Ponto in Graeciam, quos conscripserunt tunc discipuli sequentes beatum apostolum, unde et habent Manichei et alii tales Andreae beati . . . Actus* (CCSL 9:255-56). In order to avoid the ellipse indicated in the translation by "[have]" and the redundant second reference to Manichaeans, J.-A. Fabricius emended the text of Philaster. Instead of *Manichaei*, Fabricius read *Matthiae*, rendering the first phrase: "[There is] an apocryphal writing of Matthias and the blessed apostle Andrew" (*PL* 12:1200, n. i). If one prefers this reading--I do not--this passage speaks even more directly in favor of the inclusion of the *AAMt*.

Flamion takes the word "Pontus" here to refer to the province by that name in northern Asia Minor, which would exclude Scythian cannibals. If Philaster indeed had provincial Pontus in mind, he probably was referring to Sinope, the first city of Pontus. Even so, one might argue that he already knew of the tradition locating the Myrmidons in Sinope, a tradition established at least as early as the first half of the sixth century and probably much earlier.[61] Furthermore, Philaster certainly does not perfectly support Flamion's assumption that the Acts began in Amasia, as in Gregory 2; Amasia was in Cappadocia. It is, however, more likely that Philaster intended the more inclusive definition of Pontus, viz., the maritime territories surrounding the Black Sea (*Pontus Euxeinus*). His wording "from Pontus to Greece" suggests that this was the case, insofar as "Greece" too is a regional, not a provincial designation. Obviously, if Pontus here refers to this vast territory, it would include Scythia. In either case, whether provincial or regional, one cannot use this important witness to the ancient Acts decisively to amputate the Myrmidonian episode from it.

The Case for Including the Cannibal Story in *The Acts of Andrew*

Against these few citations advanced by Flamion one might mobilize an army of authors witnessing to the presence of the Myrmidon episode at the beginning of the ancient Acts. Gregory was by no means the only one to have held these stories together.

----

61. Theodosius *De situ Terrae Sanctae* (Geyer), 144.

Andrean Hagiography

Every single witness to the narrative of the Acts prior to the Passion alludes to this story. *Martyrium prius* (late eighth century),[62] whose author, like Gregory, seems to have had access to the entire *AA* (though probably in a derivative recension), likewise begins with the apostolic lottery in Jerusalem. Andrew drew Bithynia, Sparta, and Achaea. In addition, one discovers that Matthew (frequently confused with Matthias) was assigned to τὴν Μυρμηνίδα πόλιν, "the city Myrmenis," undoubtedly a variant of Μυρμιδονία.

Three Byzantine documents narrate Andrew's adventures between Jerusalem and Patras, and each alludes to the Myrmidonian episode: (1) *The Life of Andrew* written by a ninth century monk named Epiphanius, (2) a panegyric conventionally called *Laudatio*, largely dependent on Epiphanius and written by Nicetas the Paphlagonian, and (3) an eighth or ninth century passion of Andrew known as *Narratio*.[63] Gregory, Epiphanius, *Laudatio*, and *Narratio* seldom agree, but they do agree on this: Andrew was sent out from Jerusalem, quickly found himself in the region of the Black Sea, rescued Matthias from savages--his first fully narrated act--and after other exploits traveled to Achaea where he died on a cross.[64] As we have seen, *Martyrium prius* too evidences Matthew's (sic) ministry in Myrmenis (sic) before telling of Andrew's execution in Patras.

----

62. *AAA* 2.1:46-57.

63. These sources are treated more comprehensively in the Introduction to Part II.

64. Gregory 1, Epiphanius 217D-224A, *Laudatio* 7-8, and *Narratio* 5-7.

Around the year 459, Basil of Seleucia claimed that Andrew "filled with grace not only Hellas, but also the lands of the barbarians."[65] A list of apostolic travels attributed to Ephrem claims that Andrew visited *Scythas et Macedones et Archeos* (=*Acheos*).[66] If this reference to Scythia alludes to the cannibals of Myrmidonia, the list corresponds generally with Andrew's itinerary as presented in this edition, with the *AAMt* attached. Nicetas the Paphlagonian (ninth century), the author of *Laudatio*, shows that he knew more of Andrean literature than he presented in that document or than he had read in Epiphanius:

> Hail, for you [Andrew] were considered worthy to see Jesus' own face, you sailed the known and seen sea with him as the pilot, and when you visited those who ate people raw, you were not devoured by them, but having been captured alive by Christ, you were not consumed, and you destroyed the dragon lurking among them. You amazed them with your marvelous works, forced them to believe in the Lord, and you established a church to Christ. (*PG* 105:80)

Neither Nicetas' *Laudatio* nor his source, Epiphanius's *Life of Andrew*, mentions Pilot Jesus as Nicetas does here; the *AAMt* does.

Theophanes Cerameus (twelfth century) assumed that his readers knew both the story of Andrew and the cannibals (*AAMt*) and Andrew's martyrdom in Achaea (*AA*).

> *For all of you have heard* what this great one endured first in Sinope and finally in Patras, and how those wild people sprang upon him like wild beasts and laid hold of their apostolic flesh with their teeth. (Homily 1. *PG* 132: 904D)

----

65. *PG* 28:1108.

66. Prieur, *Acta Andreae*, 70 n.4.

The change in person from the singular to the plural ("*their* flesh") requires one to suppose that the episode known was that of Andrew with Matthias. Nicephorus Callistus Xanthopulus (fourteenth century) gives as Andrew's itinerary Cappadocia, Galatia, Bithynia, Μυρμήνη, in the desert of Scythia, the northern and southern coasts of the Black Sea, Byzantium, Thrace, Macedonia, Thessaly, and Achaea.[67] Μυρμήνη (i.e. Μυρμιδονία) seems to be out of sequence with the order given in the *AA* because Nicephorus arranged the list more or less linearly from east to west.

Testimony to the inclusion of the *AAMt* also comes from the last person known to have had access to all

----

67. *Historia ecclesiastica* 2.41 (*PG* 145:865). See Lipsius, *Apostelgeschichten*, 1:570.

Other witnesses to the combination of Scythian and Achaean traditions are dependent not on the *AA* but on later hagiography. Dvornik cites evidence from Syrian sources that combine the Scythian and Achaean traditions, Michael the Syrian, Salomon of Basrah, and Bar-Hebraeus, but their information almost certainly derives from later traditions and not from reading the *AA* (*Apostolicity*, 262). Even so, these itineraries agree in placing Andrew in Scythia, Nicomedia, Byzantium, and Achaea, which roughly conforms with the itinerary in the ancient Acts with the *AAMt* attached (Prieur, *Acta Andreae*, 75-76). *Ottoban 415*, an unpublished Greek manuscript, contains an abbreviated version of the *AAMt* and continues with a summary of Andrew's travels from Bithynia to Patras, but it seems to be dependent on Symeon Metaphrastes, itself dependent on Epiphanius the monk. Two thirteenth century manuscripts of an Old French poem of Andrew's passion tell of Andrew's exploits in "Mirdone" immediately preceding his death in Patras (Baker, "Passion," 420-49). One Greek manuscript juxtaposes the *AAMt* and *Martyrium prius* (*Cod. Paris gr. 1539*, eleventh century; see Lipsius, *Apostelgeschichten*, 1:545, n. 2). An Arabic *Martyrdom of Andrew* places Andrew in *Askâtya* (Scythia?) and *Argyânos* (Achaea?), but it would seem unlikely that the document displays any knowledge of the ancient Acts (Prieur, *Acta Andreae*, 74).

five of the principal apocryphal Acts, the Byzantine
Patriarch Photius (ninth century). He lists them as "The
Acts of Peter, John, Andrew, Thomas, and Paul" and then
begins discussing them in this same order: *The Acts of
Peter* first, *The Acts of John* second.[68] One should
therefore not be surprised if the comments following *The
Acts of John* obtain to the *AA*.

They do. "He [Leucius Charinus] rejects legitimate
marriages."[69] Andrew breaks up a wedding in Gregory 11
and causes several believers, in particular Maximilla,
to separate from their spouses. "And he says all
procreation is evil and of the evil one." In the
Passion, Andrew tells Maximilla to avoid sexual
intercourse insofar as it is "a foul and filthy way of
life," the result of Eve's eating of the forbidden
sexual fruit (37). "He fantasizes that someone other
[than God] formed the demons." Nowhere in the *AA* do we
find this expressed, even though one does read of
Satan's involvements at the creation of the world.[70]
Eric Junod and Jean-Daniel Kaestli probably are correct
in suggesting that Photius has exaggerated the hostility
in the apocryphal Acts between God and Satan--amply

---

68. *Bibliotheca*, codex 114 (R. Henry, *Photius: Bibliothèque*, 8 vols. [Paris: Collection Byzantine, 1959-1977], 2:84-86). On the arrangement of Photius's comments see Eric Junod and Jean-Daniel Kaestli, *l'Histoire des Actes apocryphes des apôtres du IIIe au IXe siècle: Le cas des Actes de Jean*, Cahiers de la revue de théologie et de philosophie 7 (Geneva, Lausanne, Neuchâtel, 1982), 136-37.

69. This comment, as Junod and Kaestli recognize, does not easily apply to *The Acts of John* which Photius had been discussing (ibid.).

70. Passion 49; cf. *AAMt* 20.

attested in the AA--inflating it into Manichaean dualism.[71]

Photius's next statement is the most important: "He tells fabulous tales about irrational and childish resurrections from the dead of people and cattle and other domestic animals" (Νεκρῶν δὲ ἀνθρώπων καὶ βοῶν καὶ κτηνῶν ἄλλων . . . ἀναστάσεις). Junod and Kaestli claim that nowhere in the remains of the apocryphal Acts do we find a resurrection of animals; Photius must have read a text no longer available to us.[72] NO! Photius here refers to Andrew's reviving those who had drowned in the flood, "men, women, children, and beasts."[73] Photius's Greek copy of the AA began with the Myrmidonian episode, just as Gregory's Latin copy did.

Other Apocryphal Acts

Unfortunately, the external references cited above derive from the fifth to the thirteenth centuries, when hagiographic conflation may have melded together tradi- tions ultimately derived from different sources, or even artificially merged two originally discrete Acts into a single volume. It is possible, however, to push our inquiry back as far as the early third century by analyzing parallels between the AA and other apocryphal Acts to see whether those Acts dependent on the AA also display knowledge of the Myrmidonian episode. From the outset one must keep in mind that synoptic studies of

----

71. *Histoire*, 136.

72. Ibid.

73. *AAMt* 32: ἀνδρῶν τε καὶ γυναικῶν καὶ παιδίων καὶ κτηνῶν; the Latin version: *populus multus erat mortuus, etiam mulieres, et infantes, et iumentas.* Cf. *AAMt* 24 and especially 30: καὶ ἀπέκτεινεν τὸ ὕδωρ τὰ κτήνη αὐτῶν.

this literature are bedeviled by traps, mirrors, and
cul-de-sacs. In some cases, all that remains of these
Acts are late recensions and fragmentary survivals, as
in the case of the *AA* itself. Also, similarities between
these Acts need not indicate direct literary dependence;
they may rather issue from popular literary topoi, or
from independent imitations of other texts--especially
bibilical ones--or even from sources now lost. Even when
literary dependence is apparent, the direction of that
dependence often is not.

Nevertheless, there exists a consensus concerning
the position of the *AA* relative to several other
apocryphal Acts. It knew and imitated *The Acts of Peter*
(*APe*),[74] and in turn influenced *The Acts of Thomas* (*ATh*,
early third century),[75] *The Acts of Philip* (*APh*, fourth
to sixth),[76] *The Acts of John by Prochorus* (*AJPr*, fifth

----

74. Prieur, *Acta Andreae* 400-403. Compare, for example,
    Peter's speech to the cross in *Martyrium Petri* 8
    (=*AV* 37) and Andrew's speech to his cross (Passion
    54).

75. After providing an impressive list of similarities
    between the *AA* and the *ATh*, Prieur concludes: "Les
    ressemblances que nous venons de mettre en évidence
    sont si nombreuses et précises qu'elles nous
    engagent à admettre une dépendance littéraire entre
    les *AA* et les *ATh*" (*Acta Andreae*, 393). The priority
    of the *AA* is apparent from its relative cohesiveness
    and simplicity when compared with the repetition,
    complexity, and occasional confusion of *The Acts of
    Thomas*.

76. François Bovon, "Les Actes de Philippe," in *ANRW*
    II.25.6:4522-23; followed by Junod and Kaestli,
    Histoire, 30. For example, Philip's last words and
    death have been modeled after Andrew's. Andrew:
    ἀναπαυομένων ἐν τῇ σῇ μεγαλειότητι. καὶ εἰπὼν ταῦτα
    παρέδωκεν τὸ πνεῦμα, κλαιόντων οὖν ἡμῶν καὶ
    ἀνιωμένων ἀπάντων (Passion 63). Philip: ἀνάπαυσόν με
    ἐν τῇ μακαριότητί σου. καὶ ταῦτα εἰπών, παρέδωκεν
    τὸν πνεῦμα πάντων τῶν ὄχλων βλεπόντων εἰς αὐτὸν καὶ
    κλαιόντων (*APh* Act 15.38-39).

to seventh),[77] and probably *The Acts of Xanthippe and Polyxena* (*AXP*, fourth to seventh).[78] Obviously, if one could demonstrate that the *AAMt* occupies precisely this same synoptic position, if it too knew the *APe* and in turn influenced these other Acts, the case for the inclusion of some version of the Myrmidonian episode at the beginning of the Acts would be strengthened.

The test case for this dependence will be the parallels between Andrew's voyage to Myrmidonia, Peter's voyage to Rome in *APe* 5, and Thomas's to India in *ATh* 1-3. Parallels with the other, later Acts will follow.

The Acts of Peter. The text for most of the *APe* has disappeared, except for a Latin translation preserved in a single manuscript (*Actus Vercellenses* [*AV*]). It begins

----

77. The dependence of these Acts on the *AA* is beyond dispute (see Eric Junod and Jean-Daniel Kaestli, *Acta Iohannis*, CCSA 1 [Turnhout: Brepols, 1983], 737, and Prieur, *Acta Andreae*, 94). Compare especially chapter 4 of Gregory's epitome (the story of Sostratus' incestuous mother) with pages 135-46 in Zahn's edition (*Acta Joannis* [Erlangen: Andreas Deichert, 1880; Hildesheim: H.A. Gerstenberg, 1975]).

78. As M. R. James and Flamion also recognized (James, *Apocrypha anecdota*, TS 2.3 [Cambridge: Cambridge University Press, 1893], 43-85; Flamion, *Actes d'André*, 263, n. 1). While Polyxena is in Greece, Andrew just happens to pass by (chapter 28). The next two chapters involve Andrew's attempts to help her, and then, just as casually as he appeared, "Andrew went on his way rejoicing and glorifying God" (chapter 31). One senses the scene is Andrew's cameo, celebrity appearance on his way to martyrdom. See Prieur, *Acta Andreae*, 93.

Actually, the *AA* has more affinities with *The Acts of John* than with any of the Acts, but the direction of dependence is not immediately apparent (Prieur, *Acta Andreae*, 394-400). Insofar as there seem to be no parallels here with the Myrmidonian episode, *The Acts of John* contributes nothing to the question at hand.

with Paul's ministry in Rome until Christ tells him to leave for Spain. After Paul's departure, Simon the magician disturbs the Roman church such that Christ visits Peter in Jerusalem and orders him to sail for Rome. The *AAMt* too begins with the ministry of an apostle who soon disappears from the narrative. It is because of Matthias' imprisonment that Christ appears to Andrew and orders him to sail for Myrmidonia. On the following day, both Peter and Andrew go to the shore and find boats headed for their destinations.[79] Peter has no money or food, but Captain Theon—notice the theophoric name!—generously offers passage and supplies; Peter gives thanks. For his part, Andrew finds a boat in which Jesus himself is disguised as the captain. Jesus offers to take the apostle aboard, though he has no fare or food; Andrew gives thanks. Peter converts Theon by narrating the *magnalia Dei* and why "the Lord had selected him as one of the apostles" (*APe* [*AV*] 5: *quomodo dominus elegerit eum inter apostolos*). Andrew tells captain Jesus about the miracles Jesus had performed and the selection of the Twelve (*AAMt* 6: ἐξελέξατο γὰρ ἡμᾶς τοὺς δώδεκα). Both voyages are blessed with remarkable rapidity. Jesus himself is present in both stories, as a youth or as a sailor; the presence of an apostle, Peter or Andrew, guarantees safe travel in both; and in both, passengers fall asleep and receive visions. Because the similarities between these two stories are too close and unusual to be attributed to common nautical topoi, and because, of the two Acts

---

79. Cf. *APe* (*AV*) 5: *crastina die proficiscere, et ibi invenies navem paratum. AAMt* 4: ἀναστὰς τῷ πρωὶ εἰς τὴν θάλασσαν σὺν τοῖς μαθηταῖς σου, καὶ εἰρήσεις πλοῖον . . . . ὁ γὰρ κύριος τῇ ἑαυτοῦ δυνάμει κατεσκεύασεν πλοῖον.

Peter's is undeniably the earlier, one should conclude
that the author of the *AAMt* pirated from the *APe*.[80]

The Acts of Thomas. Not only did the Myrmidonian
episode, like the rest of the *AA*, imitate the *APe*, it
too seems to have influenced the *ATh*, as one can see by
comparing the versions of the famous apostolic land
lottery in the *AAMt* and in the *ATh*. Kaestli shows that
even though the opening episodes of the Acts of Paul, of
Peter, of John, and of Andrew no longer exist, only
those of John, Andrew, and Thomas could have begun with
the disciples casting lots for their fields of
mission.[81] Paul was not one of the Twelve, and Peter
stayed in Jerusalem for twelve years before departing
for Rome. John's case is more complex, but Kaestli
suggests that *The Acts of John* (*AJ*) commenced with the
apostle's three attempts to marry, only to be thwarted
each time by Christ. The *ATh* clearly began with the
apostles casting lots, and Kaestli suggests that the *AA*

----

80. This same story from the *APe* apparently lies behind
    Andrew's voyage from Thrace to Macedonia in an
    undisputed section of the *AA*. Chapter 10 of
    Gregory's epitome, like this section of the *APe*,
    begins with a divine command to board ship and the
    apostle's "discovery" of a boat already destined for
    Macedonia (*APe* [*AV*] 5: *et ibi invenies navem
    paratam, navigantem in Italiam*; Gregory: *et invenit
    ibi navem quae in Machedoniam properaret*). Andrew
    preaches on board, converts "a sailor and all who
    were with him," and, like Peter, is thankful for
    God's presence even at sea (*APe*: *in mari Deus
    providentiam suam voluit eis ostendere qui in navi
    erant*. Gregory: *nec in mari defuit qui audiret
    praedicationem eius aut qui crederet filium Dei
    omnipotentis*).

81. "Les scènes d'attribution des champs de mission et
    de départ de l'apôtre dans les Acts apocryphes," in
    *Les Actes apocryphes des apôtres: Christianisme et
    monde païen*, ed. François Bovon, Publications de la
    Faculté de Théologie de l'Université de Genève 4
    (Geneva: Labor et Fides, 1981), 249-64.

did too. But, alas! bemoans Kaestli, because the
beginning of the AA no longer exists, all that remains
of that earlier scene is an allusion to it in *Martyrium
prius*. Not at all. It appears in its original form in
the *AAMt*. Even *Martyrium prius*, which narrates Andrew's
martyrdom, begins with the apostles casting lots, and
here too Matthew (=Matthias) draws Myrmenis
(=Myrmidonia).

Comparing the opening scenes of the *ATh* and the
AAMt immediately thrusts one into the debate concerning
the compositional language of the *ATh*. Even though Greek
manuscripts generally preserve readings superior to
those in Syriac, many scholars contend the original was
in Syriac. There can indeed be little doubt that its
author lived in the Osröene and was bilingual, but the
following parallels, which are lexical and not merely
thematic, weigh in favor of a Greek original, at least
for these chapters.[82] One might, of course, claim that
the similarities between the Acts are due to the author
of the Myrmidonian episode borrowing from the Greek
translation of the *ATh*; but, as we shall see, the
literary dependence almost certainly moves in the
opposite direction. The first two sentences in both Acts
are nearly identical.

> *AAMt* 1: κατ' ἐκεῖνον τὸν καιρὸν ἦσαν πάντες οἱ
> ἀπόστολοι ἐπὶ τὸ αὐτὸ συναχθέντες, καὶ
> ἐμέριζον ἑαυτοῖς τὰς χώρας, βάλλοντες κλήρους
> ὅπως ἀπέλθῃ ἕκαστος εἰς τὸ λαχὸν αὐτοῦ μέρος.
> κατὰ κλῆρον οὖν ἔλαχεν τὸν Ματθείαν πορευθῆναι
> εἰς τὴν χώραν τῶν ἀνθρωποφάγων (the Latin
> reads: *civitatem que dicitur Mermedonia*).

---

82. Assuming that the *ATh* originally was in Syriac,
    Prieur argues that its parallels with the *AA* are
    best explained by postulating that Andrew's Acts had
    been translated into Syriac at an early date (*Acta
    Andreae*, 393). However, no Syriac fragment of the *AA*
    has yet been found.

(At that time, all the apostles were gathered
together at one place and divided the regions
among themselves by casting lots, so that each
would leave for his allotted share. The lot
fell on Matthias to go to the region of the
cannibals [Latin: the city called Myrmi-
donia]).

ATh 1: κατ' ἐκεῖνον τὸν καιρὸν ἦμεν [some mss.
ἦσαν] πάντες οἱ ἀπόστολοι ἐν Ἱεροσολύμοις
[the next few lines provide the names of the
apostles, taken almost word for word from Matt
10:2-4] καὶ διείλαμεν τὰ κλίματα τῆς οἰκου-
μένης, ὅπως εἷς ἕκαστος ἡμῶν ἐν τῷ κλίματι τῷ
λαχόντι αὐτῷ καὶ εἰς τὸ ἔθνος ἐν ᾧ ὁ κύριος
αὐτὸν ἀπέστειλεν πορευθῇ. κατὰ κλῆρον οὖν
ἔλαχεν ἡ Ἰνδία Ἰούδᾳ Θωμᾷ τῷ καὶ Διδύμῳ.

(At that time, all we apostles were in
Jerusalem . . . and we divided the regions of
the world, so that each of us would go to the
region that fell to his lot and into the
country to which the Lord sent him. The lot
fell for India to be for Judas Thomas, also
called Didymas.)

A comparison with Acts 1-2 shows that both accounts
ultimately derive from Luke's Acts and that the AAMt is
closer to it. Both in Acts and in the Myrmidonian
episode, the apostles are together "at the same
place,"[83] and in both the lot falls on Matthias.[84]
Conversely, the ATh never agrees with Acts against the
AAMt. Furthermore, if the author of the ATh had modeled
the passage directly on the Acts of the Apostles, one
would expect the list of the apostles to have come from
Acts 1:13-14, not from Matthew 10.

----

83. Acts 2:1: ἦσαν πάντες . . . ἐπὶ τὸ αὐτό. AAMt 1:
    ἦσαν πάντες . . . ἐπὶ τὸ αὐτό. ATh 1: ἦμεν πάντες
    . . . ἐν Ἱεροσολύμοις.

84. Acts 1:26: ἔδωκαν κλήρους αὐτοῖς, καὶ ἔπεσεν ὁ
    κλῆρος ἐπὶ Μαθθίαν. AAMt 1: βάλλοντες κλήρους
    . . . . κατὰ κλῆρον οὖν ἔλαχεν τὸν Ματθείαν. ATh 1:
    κατὰ κλῆρον οὖν ἔλαχεν ἡ Ἰνδία.

The *ATh* continues by describing Thomas's fear of going to India in language resonant with Andrew's refusal to go to Myrmidonia.

AAMt 4: οὐ δυνήσομαι φθάσαι τοῦ ἀπελθεῖν ἐκεῖ . . . σὺ γὰρ γινώσκεις κύριε ὅτι κἀγὼ σάρξ εἰμι καὶ οὐ δυνήσομαι τὸ τάχος πορευθῆναι ἐκεῖ.

(I cannot travel there . . . for you know, Lord, that I too am flesh and cannot go there quickly.)

ATh 1: οὐκ ἐβούλετο δὲ ἀπελθεῖν, λέγων μὴ δύνασθαι μήτε χωρεῖν διὰ τὴν ἀσθένειαν τῆς σαρκός, καὶ ὅτι ἄνθρωπος ὢν Ἑβραῖος πῶς δύναμαι πορευθῆναι ἐν τοῖς Ἰνδοῖς;

(He did not want to travel, saying that he could not do so nor leave because of the weakness of the flesh, and "I am a Hebrew man, so how could I go to the Indians?")

Andrew's refusal appears entirely in direct discourse and makes perfect sense. Myrmidonia is so far away that no "flesh," only an angel, could possibly sail there in three days. On the other hand, the expression of Thomas's refusal to sail to India is torturous. The author begins by saying that Thomas "did not want to go," says it again but now in indirect discourse, "saying that he could not go or leave because of the weakness of the flesh," and says it once again, now in direct discourse, "Insofar as I am a Hebrew, how can I go to India?" The author fails to clarify why Thomas's weak flesh forbids travel (seasickness?), or why a Hebrew would have a particularly difficult time in India. Recent studies of the *ATh* demonstrate that the obvious clumsiness and even occasional incoherence of the Acts derive in part from an artless redaction of sources,[85] which seems to be precisely what has happened

----

85. Yves Tissot has shown that the composition of the *ATh* to a large extent is a compilation and

here.

Jesus appears to Thomas, telling him not to fear (μὴ φοβοῦ), for his grace will be with him (ἡ γὰρ χάρις μού ἐστιν μετὰ σοῦ). Similarly, Jesus appears to Matthias, telling him not to be terrified (μὴ πτοηθῇς), and the apostle prays that the Lord's grace be with him (ἡ χάρις σου διαμένῃ μετ᾽ ἐμοῦ).

Similarities likewise exist between the two Acts with respect to the journeys of the apostles to their barbarian lands, although here the parallels are more thematic than lexical. Both apostles arise the next morning, go as ordered to the shore, board the boats they find there, and sit down.[86] Both apostles converse with another passenger about ships: Andrew asks Jesus concerning his remarkable sailing technique (τέχνη); Thomas tells Abban the merchant about his carpentry, including the making of "ships and oars for ships and masts and pulleys." This delights Abban, who is looking for just such a skilled craftsman (τεχνίτης). Only after Abban already has paid for Thomas with three pounds of silver, only after they are already aboard does the merchant bother to ask Thomas about his building abilities. The parallel conversation in the AAMt quite

----

conflation of preexisting materials ("Les Actes apocryphes de Thomas: Exemple de recueil composite," in Actes apocryphes, 223-32. J. Michael LaFargue claims that ATh 1-10 contains a number of incongruities best explained as evidence of a tension between the author's sources and gnosticizing redaction (Language and Gnosis: The Opening Scenes of the Acts of Thomas, Harvard Dissertations in Religion 18 [Philadelphia: Fortress, 1985]), passim but especially 1-11.

86. AAMt 6-7: ἀνῆλθεν ᾽Ανδρέας . . . εἰς τὸ πλοῖον. καὶ εἰσελθὼν ἐκαθέσθη. ATh 3: ἐμβάντων δὲ αὐτῶν καὶ καθεσθέντων.

naturally takes place on board because the topic is
Jesus' piloting.

After remarkably smooth and expeditious voyages,
both apostles put in at seaside cities. The adventures
of Andrew in Myrmidonia and Thomas in Andrapolis share
little apart from two curious traits. First, both cities
are imaginary: Antville and Peoplecity. Second, no one
in either city has a name. In Myrmidonia the reader
encounters "rulers," "guards," "executioners," "an old
man," and "children." In Andrapolis one meets "the
king," "the king's daughter," "one of the cup-bearers,"
and "a flute-player."[87] The characters in the AAMt seem
to have no names either because the story is modeled
after Jonah, which likewise names no Ninevite, or more
likely because the Myrmidons are ant-people. No such
explanation is apparent for the ATh. Once again the
Myrmidonian episode seems more generative and primitive.

In both Acts someone orders a crowd to arrest the
apostle, and in both the crowd cannot find him. In AAMt
24, the devil disguised as an old man says,

> ἀναστάντες ἐπιζητήσατε ὧδέ τινα ἐν τῇ πόλει
> ἐπιδημήσαντα ξένον ὀνόματι 'Ανδρέαν καὶ
> ἀποκτείνατε αὐτὸν . . . . καὶ διαδραμόντες οἱ
> πολῖται ἔκλεισαν τὰς θύρας τῆς πόλεως καὶ
> ἐζήτουν τὸν μακάριον, καὶ οὐκ ἐθεώρουν αὐτόν.

> ("get up and search for a certain stranger
> here residing in the city named Andrew and
> kill him . . . ." The citizens ran about, shut
> the city gates, and searched for the blessed
> one, but did not see him.)

----

87. Flamion noticed the absence of proper names in the
    AAMt, and used it to support the detachment of that
    story from the AA where characters otherwise are
    named (Actes d'André, 274-77). He failed to notice,
    however, that this same phenomenon appears also in
    the ATh.

In *ATh* 16 the king says,

ἐξέλθατε ταχέως καὶ περιέλθατε ὅλην τὴν πόλιν,
καὶ συλλαβόντες φέρετέ μοι ἐκεῖνον τὸν ἄνδρα
τὸν θαρμακὸν τὸν κακῶς παρατυχόντα ἐν τῇ πόλει
ταύτῃ . . . . ἀπελθόντες οὖν περιῆλθον
ζητοῦντες αὐτόν, καὶ οὐχ εὗρον αὐτόν.

("leave quickly and go around the entire city.
Once you have apprehended him, bring that man
to me, the sorcerer who is in this city for
evil . . . ." So they left and went about
searching for him, but they could not find
him.)

Although one might mention several other similarities,[88] from these parallels it would appear that the
author of the *AAMt* modeled the opening sentences after
Acts 1-2 and then combined motifs from Jonah and the
APe. The *AAMt* in turn seems to have inspired the author
of the *ATh*.

It is instructive to observe how complex the
explanation of literary dependence becomes if one
imagines instead that the *AAMt* borrowed from the *ATh*.
According to this scenario, the author of the
Myrmidonian episode becomes a sophisticated weaver who
took woof from Jonah, such as the mention of shipfare,
the double command to enter the city, the concern for

----

88. For example, in both Acts weeping entourages send
the apostles on their ways (*AAMt* 33: προέπεμψαν
αὐτόν; *ATh* 68: προέπεμπον αὐτόν). Both apostles use
miraculous powers to release prisoners (*AAMt* 19-21;
ATh 162). In both Acts people deliberate concerning
how to kill the apostles (*AAMt* 25: καὶ διελογίζοντο
ἐν ἑαυτοῖς λέγοντες· ποίῳ θανάτῳ αὐτὸν ἀποκτένωμεν;
ATh 21: ὁ δὲ βασιλεὺς ἐσκέπτετο ποίῳ θανάτῳ αὐτοὺς
ἀναλώσῃ, but see also John 12:33, 18:32, and 21:19),
and swords miraculously fall from the hands of the
wicked (*AAMt* 22 and 23; *ATh* 63). Notice also that
several people raised back to life in the *ATh*
recount what they observed in the netherworld (esp.
chapters 22-23 and 55-58), which conforms with what
was promised to happen when Andrew returned to raise
the Myrmidons.

animals, and the criticism of missionary obduracy; more woof from the *APe*: one disciple's following another, a captain's generosity, eating on board, sleep and visions; and then skillfully wove them into the warp of the *ATh*, with its dispersal of the apostles by lot, the weakness of the flesh, the discussion of sailing arts, and the imaginary city of no-names. Surely this explanation is unnecessarily Gordian.

The Acts of Philip. François Bovon claims that *APh* 1-7 and 8-15 contain separate blocks of material fused in the fourth century by Encratites in Asia Minor.[89] Both blocks witness to the Myrmidonian episode and undisputed sections of the *AA*. In the first block of material, Act 3 provides the most obvious points of contact. Thanks to Bovon, I was able to see a copy of the text that he and his associates are preparing for Series Apocryphorum, a text based primarily on the unedited Xenophontos manuscript. At the end of this Act, Philip states that the soul is like an eagle. This passage resonates with a speech in the Armenian passion of Andrew (Passion 53). The author of this section of the *APh* undoubtedly had seen this speech in the *AA*.

Earlier in the same Act, however, there exist parallels with the *AAMt*. For instance, the apostle John tells Philip, "that brother Andrew went into Achaea and all of Thrace,"[90] which conforms to the locations in chapters 10 to 21 in Gregory's epitome, "and Thomas into India to violent flesheaters (σαρκοφάγους), and Matthew to ruthless cavemen, for their nature is wild." Thomas's journey to India obviously agrees with his Acts, but one

----

89. "Les Actes de Philippe," 4521-22.

90. See also later in the same Act: τὸν 'Ανδρέαν ἐν τῇ 'Αχαΐα.

reads nothing there about cannibals. It would appear that they and Matthew's (i.e., Matthias's) cavemen derive from the *AAMt*.[91]

Philip then leaves for his field of mission "as Jesus walked with him, in hiding," just as Jesus had hidden his divinity from Andrew on ship. Upset at Jesus' non-disclosure, Philip asks him to reveal himself, just as the disturbed Andrew does in the *AAMt*.[92] Jesus indeed reveals himself, in the form of an eagle, and promises never to abandon him; he will be his pilot at sea.[93] Like Andrew, Philip goes down to the sea and finds a boat going to his destination.[94] He asks to be taken on board,[95] negotiates his fare, and boards.[96] Soon a storm endangers the ship, an episode recalling Andrew's narration of Jesus' stilling of the tempest in *AAMt* 8. Although most of these elements can be found in other apostolic voyages, one dominant motif in both cannot:

----

91. Surely it is no coincidence that the three apostles named here, each with secondary status among the Twelve, are the very three whose fields of mission were determined by lot in the earlier apocryphal Acts.

92. *AAMt* 18: φανέρωσόν μοι σεαυτὸν ἐν τῷ τόπῳ τούτῳ. *APh* Act 3: φανέρωσόν μοι σεαυτὸν ὁ ὢν ἐν κρυπτῷ.

93. Cf. *AAMt* 8: ὁ γὰρ ᾿Ιησοῦς οὐ μὴ ἐγκαταλίπῃ ἡμᾶς, and *APh* Act 3: ἐν θαλάσσῃ δὲ οὐράνιος κυβερνήτης . . . οὐκ ἀποστήσομαί σου οὐδὲ ἐγκαταλείψω σε.

94. *AAMt* 4: κάτελθε εἰς θάλασσαν . . . καὶ εὑρήσεις πλοῖον. *APh* Act 3: ἦλθεν οὖν τότε ὁ Φίλιππος κατὰ θάλασσαν . . . καὶ εὗρεν ἐκεῖ πλοῖον.

95. *AAMt* 5: ducete nos in eadem civitatem. *APh* Act 3: δέξασθε με, ὦ ναυτικοί, καὶ ἀναγάγετε κἀμὲ εἰς Ἄζωτον.

96. *AAMt* 6 and 7: οὐ δίδομέν σοι τὸν ναῦλον . . . καὶ ἀνῆλθεν. *APh* Act 3: δοῦναι αὐτοῖς . . . τὸν ναῦλον . . . καὶ ἀνέβη.

the non-disclosure of Jesus.[97] Therefore, it would
appear that the similarities are due to direct literary
dependence, and the cannibal story almost certainly is
earlier.[98]

Dependence on the *AAMt* is equally likely in the
second block of material in the *APh*, viz., Acts 8-15.
This unit too begins with a division (ἐμέριζεν, cf. *AAMt*
1: ἐμέριζον) of regions (κατὰ πόλιν καὶ χώραν, cf. *AAMt*
1: τὰς χώρας) by lot (κεκληρωμένον, cf. *AAMt* 1:
βάλλοντες κλήρους). According to the unedited Athens
manuscript of *APh* Act 8, the missionary allotments of
several apostles appeared at this point: Andrew went to
Achaea, and Matthew (=Matthias) to "the farthest reaches
of the Black Sea,"[99] which conforms to the traditional
location of the Myrmidons. Philip, however, must go to
"the land of the Greeks." Jesus appears to his apostle
to empower him in a speech that, in the Vaticanus
manuscript at least, may have been assembled largely

----

97. *AAMt* 5: κρύψας τὴν ἑαυτοῦ θεότητα. *APh* Act 3:
ἔκρυψας τὴν δόξαν ταύτην; this phrase appears
fourteen times. *AAMt* 17: οὐκ ἐφανέρωσάς μοι ἑαυτόν,
καὶ διὰ τοῦτο οὐκ ἐγνώρισά σε, and 18: ἐμφάνηθί με
κύριε ᾽Ιησοῦ Χριστέ, ἐγὼ γὰρ γινώσκω . . . . οὐκ
ἐφανέρωσάς μοι σεαυτὸν ἐν τῇ θαλάσσῃ. *APh* Act 3:
ἐμφανίσας σεαυτὸν ὀλίγοις ἐγνώρισας τὴν δόξαν σου.

98. These parallels do not exhaust the points of contact
between *APh* 1-7 and the cannibal story; e.g. *AAMt*
18: τότε ᾽Ανδρέας ἀκούσας ἐχάρη χαρὰν μεγάλην ὅτι
κατηξιώθησαν οἱ μαθηταὶ αὐτοῦ τὰ θαυμάσια ταῦτα
θεάσασθαι, and *APh* Act 3: καὶ ὁ μακάριος Φίλιππος ἐν
αὐτῇ τῇ ὥρᾳ ἐξῆλθεν ἀγαλλιώμενος, ὅτι τῆς τοιαύτης
κατηξιώθη φωνῆς. Notice also that Philip's complaint
in *APh* Act 4 (σὺ γὰρ γινώσκεις τὴν ἀσθένειαν τῆς
ἀνθρωπίνης φύσεως) is nearly identical with Andrew's
in *AAMt* 26 (σὺ γὰρ γινώσκεις κύριε τὴν ἀνθρωπίνην
σάρκα ὅτι ἀσθενής ἐστιν; cf. *AAMt* 4).

99. *APh* Act 8 (Athens): Ματθαίῳ δὲ ἐκληρώθη ἀπελθεῖν εἰς
τὰ ἐσώτερα μέρη τοῦ πόντου.

from the *AAMt*, though they conceivably could have derived also from common topoi.[100]

There are other similarities between Acts 8-15 and the cannibal story that can in no way be explained as independent dipping into the same well of clichés. When Philip arrives in "the land of the Greeks," he encounters snake-people, Ὀφιανοί, who worship a blood-drinking dragon and his viperous brood. Philip is told that the apostles must never return evil for evil (Act 15.25)--a theme common also in the *AAMt* (e.g. chapter 26)--but Philip insists on punishing them by plunging their city into an abyss, just as Andrew had threatened to do to the Myrmidons.[101] Not even their appeals for mercy avert Philip from carrying out his threat.[102] Jesus rebukes him for fighting evil with evil,[103] raises

----

100. Cf. *APh* Act 8: οὐκ ἤκουσας τῆς διδαχῆς μου· ἰδοὺ ἀποστέλλω ὑμᾶς ὡς πρόβατα ἐν μέσῳ λύκων; and *AAMt* 19: οὐκ ἤκουσας τοῦ κυρίου λέγοντος· ἰδοὺ ἐγὼ ἀποστέλλω ὑμᾶς ὡς πρόβατα ἐν μέσῳ λύκων; *APh* Act 8: μὴ οὖν φοβηθῇς αὐτῶν τὴν ἀγριότητα. συνέσομαί σοι ἀεὶ . . . . μεθ᾽ ὑμῶν εἰμι ἐν παντὶ τόπῳ and *AAMt* 3: μὴ πτοηθῇς· οὐ μὴ γάρ σε ἐγκαταλίπω . . . . μετὰ σοῦ γάρ εἰμι πᾶσαν ὥραν καὶ πάντοτε. Cf. *AAMt* 8: μὴ φοβεῖσθε· ὁ γὰρ κύριος Ἰησοῦς οὐ μὴ ἐγκαταλίπῃ ἡμᾶς. *APh* Act 8: ἐν θαλάσσαις ἔσομαι ὑμῶν καλὸς κυβερνήτης and *AAMt* 9, where Andrew comments on how well Jesus piloted: κυβερνῶντα οὕτως ἐν τῇ θαλάσσῃ.

101. Cf. *AAMt* 26 with *APh* Act 15.26, and *AAMt* 31 (καὶ ἀνεῴχθη ἡ γῆ καὶ κατέπιε τὸ ὕδωρ σὺν τῷ γεραίῳ, εἰς τὴν ἄβυσσον κατηνέχθη) with *APh* Act 15.27 (καὶ ἰδοὺ ἐξαίφνης ἠνεῴχθη ἡ ἄβυσσος καὶ κατεπόθη ὅλος ὁ τόπος . . . καὶ ὁ ἀνθύπατος κατεπόθη εἰς τὴν ἄβυσσον).

102. *AAMt* 30: ἐλέησον ἡμᾶς ὁ θεὸς τού ξένου ἄνδρος. *APh* Act 15.27: ἐλέησον ἡμᾶς ὁ τῶν ἐνδόξων σου ἀποστόλων θεός.

103. It should be noted that in the *AAMt* Jesus likewise rebukes Andrew, not for plunging Myrmidons into the abyss but for leaving the city prematurely.

the Ophians from the abyss, but requires Philip to be
martyred for his unfaithfulness.

Before he dies, Philip leaves instructions for his
followers to build a church and to place inside it a
speaking leopard and kid (Act 15.36), which they do (Act
15.41). Andrew too says he will build a church and place
inside it the statue that spewed forth water (30). Just
before he leaves town, Andrew in fact builds a
church.[104]

In addition to these parallels there are several
others, such as calling fire from heaven[105] and the
apostles dragged through city streets.[106] One parallel
is especially curious and telling. As Andrew is dragged
through the streets of Myrmidonia, he complains that his
flesh and hair stick to the earth. A divine voice tells
him to look at what had happened to his flesh and hair.
"Andrew turned and saw large fruit-bearing trees
sprouting" (AAMt 28: μεγάλα δένδρα φυέντα καρποφόρα).
Similarly, Philip tells Bartholomew to "look how my
blood drips to the earth . . . . A plant (φύτον) will
sprout from my blood, and it will become a vine and
produce a bunch of grapes" (APh Act 15.37: ποιήσει
καρπὸν σταφυλῆς). Later (Act 15.42), one reads, "for the
plant (φύτον) which was pre-determined and planted
(φυτευθέν) in this city will yield much fruit

----

104. AAMt 32: καὶ ἐποίησεν οἰκοδομηθῆναι τὴν ἐκκλησίαν
     εἰς τὸν τόπον. APh Act 15.41: καὶ ᾠκοδόμησαν τὴν
     ἐκκλησίαν ἐν τῷ τόπῳ ἐκείνῳ.

105. AAMt 30 and APh Act 15.22.

106. AAMt 25: περιάψαντες σχοινίον περὶ τὸν τράχηλον
     αὐτοῦ διέσυρον αὐτὸν ἐν πάσαις ταῖς πλατείαις. APh
     Act 15.15: ἐκέλευσεν δεθῆναι τοὺς πόδας αὐτῶν καὶ
     σύρεσθαι αὐτοὺς διὰ τῶν πλατείων τῆς πόλεως.

(καρποφορεῖ καλῶς)." Such fertile apostolic deposits appear only in the *AAMt* and in the *APh*.

These elements shared between the two Acts are more integrated, generative, and organic in the Myrmidonian episode than their atomistic, even annoyingly disjunctive, counterparts in the *APh*. Because the Myrmidons retain formic traits, the reader is not surprised to find them dragging Andrew through their streets, or Andrew flooding them, encircling their city with a wall of fire, and plunging the worst into an abyss in the center of town. Andrew's flesh sprouting into fruit trees aptly symbolizes the transformation of the cannibals into vegetarians. No such cohesion or integration appears in the *APh*, suggesting that these motifs are mere survivals, artificial incorporations of the Andrean legend into materials derived from other apocryphal Acts. This is confirmed by references in both major sections of the *APh* to Andrew in Achaea and to Matthew/Matthias among savages.

The Acts of John by Prochorus. This curious document, reasonably dated to the fifth century but perhaps as late as the seventh,[107] freely borrowed from the *AA* for narrating the conversion of incestuous Procliane, mother of Sosipater (135-50 [Zahn], cf. Gregory 4). The section immediately preceeding, however, borrows from the Myrmidonian episode. John and his disciple Prochorus enter an island hamlet named Μυρινοῦσα--no map needed!--through which a river flowed,[108] and where twelve children were in irons awaiting execution at a spot called Πιαστήριον, "Crusher." Every new moon, the

----

107. Junod and Kaestli, *Acta Iohannis*, 744-49.

108. *AAMt* 22: καὶ ἦν κλίβανος οἰκοδομημένοις ἐν μέσῳ τῆς πόλεως. *AJPr* 117: ἦν δὲ ποταμὸς διαρρέων κύκλῳ τῆς πόλεως.

residents sacrificed twelve youths to Lykos, "Wolf," the
local deity. John goes to the temple of Lykos, calls
forth from the river the demon who had passed himself
off as the god, and orders him to leave the island. John
then reveals that he is a disciple of Jesus,[109] the
residents believe, and the apostle orders the children
released.

The resemblances between this story and Andrew
among the Myrmidons are unmistakable. Myrmidonia and
Myrinousa both are dominated by death-dealing struc-
tures, a furnance and vat or the "Crusher," where
executioners would have slaughtered children had the
apostle not defeated the demonic and rescued them. Like
the episodes in Andrew's Myrmidonia and Thomas's
Andrapolis, the residents of Myrinousa have no names.
One reads only of "the first citizens of the city," "the
children," "the man," and "the priests." Other evidences
of the Myrmidonian episode reverberate throughout the
adventures of John and Prochorus, such as an apostolic
lottery (1-7), cannibalism (24 and 100-101), the seaside
city Marmareon (13, 14, and 44), the island Myreon
(53-54), the earth swallowing up a crowd of eight
hundred, and the apostle raising them back to life
(34-35).

The Acts of Xanthippe and Polyxena. The conclusion of
this Acts too seems to have been modeled after the *AAMt*,
although here the evidence is not as conclusive. Compare
the following:

> *AAMt* 33: εἴσελθε εἰς τὴν πόλιν καὶ παράμεινον
> ἐκεῖ ἡμέρας ἑπτά, ἕως οὗ ἐπιστηρίξω τὰς ψυχὰς
> αὐτῶν ἐν τῇ πίστει. . . . ἐχάρησαν χαρὰν
> μεγάλην σφόδρα. καὶ ἐποίησεν ἐκεῖ ἡμέρας ἑπτά

----

109. *AAMt* 6: ἡμεῖς μαθηταί ἐσμεν τοῦ κυρίου ἡμῶν Ἰησοῦ
Χριστοῦ τοῦ ἀγαθοῦ θεοῦ. *AJPr* 119: ἐγώ εἰμι ὁ
μαθητὴς Ἰησοῦ Χριστοῦ τοῦ υἱοῦ τοῦ θεοῦ.

διδάσκων   καὶ   ἐπιστηρίζων   αὐτοὺς   ἐπὶ   τὸν
κύριον.

("Enter the city and stay there seven days,
until I confirm their souls in the faith."
. . . They rejoiced exceedingly and he stayed
there seven days teaching and confirming them
in the Lord. [Then Andrew sails off for "the
city of the barbarians."])

AXP 38: τοῦ διδάξαι τὴν πόλιν· ἐπεμείναμεν οὖν
ἡμέρας ἑπτά, καὶ ἀνέῳξεν ὁ θεὸς τῷ τόπῳ ἐκείνῳ
θύραν πίστεως μεγάλην. καὶ γέγονεν χαρὰ μεγάλη
καὶ ἀγαλλίασις . . . . καὶ ἐπεμείναμεν ἄλλας
ἡμέρας ἑπτά, ἕως οὗ πάντες ἐπίστευσαν καὶ
ἔχαιρον ἐν κυρίῳ.

(teaching the city. So we stayed for seven
days and God opened there a great door for
faith . . . . And there was great joy and
exultation . . . . And we stayed another seven
days, until every one believed and rejoiced in
the Lord. [Then they sail off for an island of
"wild and hardened men" prepared for war.])

This concentration of shared motifs and wording would
seem to indicate that the author not only knew the AA,
as Flamion and others have recognized, but the
Myrmidonian episode as well.

From the evidence cited, it would appear that the
AA probably began with some version of the Myrmidonian
episode, just as it does in Gregory's epitome and in
every other narration of the pre-passion content of the
ancient Acts. Evidence from later hagiographic Andrean
tradition confirms this conclusion: e.g. Basil of
Seleucia, Nicetas the Paphlagonian, Photius, Theophanes
Cerameus, and Nicephorus Callistus Xanthopulus.
Furthermore, as we have just seen, both the AA and the
AAMt occupy precisely the same intertextual location
among the apocryphal Acts insofar as both borrowed from
the APe and both influenced the composition of the ATh,
the APh, the AJPr, and probably the AXP.

Flamion may be correct, however, in his claim that aspects of the *AAMt* suggest a date later than the composition of the *AA*. For example, in *AAMt* 11-15 Andrew explains to captain Jesus why Jews failed to believe in Jesus in spite of miracles and how a stone sphinx summoned Abraham to rebuke Jewish high priests. In this speech, the sphinx seems to anticipate the fifth century transformation of pagan temples into churches.[110] Furthermore, Flamion has demonstrated many affinities between the *AAMt* and other apostolic apocrypha issuing from Egyptian monastic circles of the fourth and fifth centuries, especially *The Acts of Peter and Andrew*, *The Martyrdom of Matthew*, the Old Slavonic *Act of Peter*, and *The Acts of Thomas B*.[111]

It is striking, however, that these chapters and other evidence for a fifth century provenience are entirely unattested by the texts cited here which knew the Myrmidonian episode as part of the *AA*. There is no trace of them in Gregory, Epiphanius, *Laudatio*, *Narratio*, the *ATh*, the *APh*, the *AJPr*, or the *AXP*. These chapters also are missing in the Syriac and Anglo-Saxon versions and in one Greek manuscript (*Ottoban 415*). The

----

110. See especially *AAMt* 14 and 15.

111. *Actes d'André*, 272-300. One must be careful, however, in assessing the significance of these affinities, for they need not imply that all of these documents derive from a common environment. The *AAMt* independently influenced all of the other representatives of Flamion's "Egyptian cycle"; the same mother birthed children who therefore resemble each other. This influence also is apparent in *The Acts of Mark*, *The Acts of Andrew and Bartholomew*, and *The Acts of Andrew and Philemon*. See Dennis R. MacDonald, "*The Acts of Andrew and Matthias* and *The Acts of Andrew*," in *The Apocryphal Acts of Apostles, Semeia 38*, ed. Dennis R. MacDonald (Decatur, GA: Scholars Press, 1986), 20-25.

Ethiopic and Armenian versions abbreviate these chapters without mentioning the articulate sphinx.[112]

In other words, Flamion may have been justified in seeing evidence of the fifth century in *AAMt* 11-15, but manuscriptal and external evidence suggest that this section is a later interpolation. Someone in the fifth century very well may have detached the Myrmidonian episode from the rest of the *AA* and inserted these chapters to justify the controversial Christianization of spaces sacred to the gods. If so, it is entirely possible that this same author altered the text in other ways as well, which may account for the obvious stylistic differences between the *AAMt* and undisputed sections of the Acts, especially the Passion. There is, however, a more plausible explanation for these differences in style: multiple authorship.

Authorship of *The Acts of Andrew*

The three most reliable witnesses to the Passion all conclude with a postscript written in the first person singular. It begins like this:

> Hereabouts I should make an end of the blessed tales (διηγημάτων), acts, and mysteries difficult--or should I say impossible--to express. Let this stroke of the pen end it. I will pray first for myself, that I heard what was actually said (ἀκοῦσαι τῶν εἰρημένων ὡς εἴρηται).

That the passage is not merely a scribal colophon is clear from the author's conscious decision to terminate the nararative here. Its lexical and stylistic

----

112. On the other hand, nothing in chapters 11-15 absolutely requires a later dating. It certainly is conceivable that later copyists deleted these chapters because of their verbosity or offensive hostility for Jews.

agreements with the Acts likewise commend it as the work
of the author.

Unfortunately, this postscript does not square with
two important external witnesses to the authorship of
the Acts, both of which ascribe the book to two or more
people. As we have seen, Philaster of Brescia (prior to
385) attributed the work to "disciples who followed the
apostle," whence it fell into the hands of Manichaeans
(*PL* 12:1200). Perhaps Philaster was mistaken, or naively
perserved Manichaean claims that Andrew's followers
recorded their memoires, but perhaps one should not
reject his testimony so quickly.

Innocent I (early fifth century), in a letter to an
Exuperius of Toulouse, lists books condemned by the
church, including the *AA*. He claims that the *AA* was the
work of "the philosophers Xenocharides and Leonidas"
(*vel sub nomine Andreae, quae a Xenocaride et Leonida
philosophis*).[113] Surely this attribution of the Acts to
two philosophers was made prior to Innocent, who would
have preferred labeling the authors heretics rather than
philosophers. There is no necessary conflict here

----

113. *Epistle* 6.6 (ed. H. Wurm, "Decretales selectae ex
antiquissimis Romanorum Pontificum epistulis
decretalibus," *Apollinaris* 12 [1939]: 77-78).
Notice that the alteration of a single letter in
the text of Innocent transforms Leonidas into
Leonides, the name of the father of Origen, who,
according to Eusebius (*Historia ecclesiastica*
6.1-2), took personal resposibility for his son's
education. This identification, unfortunately, is
little more than speculation, and immediately runs
into serious difficulties; it is risky to ascribe
the radical celibacy of the Acts to a father of
nine.

between Philaster and Innocent; Andrew's faithful all become philosophers (see Passion 59).[114]

If Philaster did not invent Andrew's "disciples," and if Innocent did not invent the names Xenocharides and Leonidas, one must determine when in the compositional or transmissional history of the Acts the names first appeared. Perhaps the names are later, artificial attributions by readers appreciative of the Acts, such as Manichaeans. This explanation would seem unlikely. One might expect that such authenticating pseudonyms would have derived from characters mentioned as Andrew's disciples in the text itself, such as Callistus, Anthimus, Sosius, Antiphanes, or especially Maximilla and Stratocles. Xenocharides and Leonidas, however, appear nowhere, nor can they be securely identified with Manichaeans.

If the names appeared in the ancient Acts, they could have been either pseudonyms or names of the actual authors. If pseudonyms, one again wonders why the author did not select the names of characters mentioned in the Acts. There also is no precedence in early Christian pseudonymity for dual pseudonyms, and no apparent reason for the first person singular postscript apart from taking it as a clever scribal colophon.

Perhaps it is more reasonable to think that Xenocharides and Leonidas actually wrote the Acts. This would match perfectly the statement by Innocent I, conform with Philaster's multiple authorship, and explain the presence of names inexplicable as pseudonyms. There can, in fact, be little doubt that the

----

114. Gregory's epitome mentions several philosophers who disputed with Andrew (17), and Flamion thought they might have been named Xenocharides and Leonidas. See Prieur, *Acta Andreae*, 111-13.

Passion emerged from the pen of a sophisticated
Christian Platonist, from a philosopher. But what about
the single author of the postscript? I suggest that the
two authors wrote the book sequentially; Xenocharides,
say, wrote the first section, the journeys, and Leonidas
perhaps the Passion, including the postscript.[115] The
postscript, therefore, was written in the first person
singular because it indeed was the work of a single
author, even though two authors were responsible for the
whole. This interpretation obviously would explain why
the Myrmidonian episode reads so differently from the
Passion.

Here is what may have happened. Originally, the
Acts began with Xenocharides and Leonidas introducing
themselves, just as "Leucius" apparently did at the
beginning of the *AJ*, or as "the presbyters and deacons
of the churches of Achaea" do at the beginning of a
Latin Andrean passion derived from the *AA*. The *ATh*
likewise begins in the first person plural: "At that
time all of us apostles were in Jerusalem." Prochorus,
the fictitious author of the *AJPr*, identifies himself at
the conclusion of the apostolic lottery.

Presumably Xenocharides and Leonidas identified
themselves as philosophers, co-authors, and transcribers
of Andrean legends they had heard. This would explain
why the author of the postscript does not claim to have
seen what happened but to have "heard what was said,"
what was said by intermediary witnesses. This
corresponds with statements from authors in the second

----

115. Because the narrative between Myrmidonia and Patras
     survives only in Gregory's epitome, in tendentious
     Byzantine recensions, and in a few fragments, it is
     impossible to locate more specifically the seam
     between the two parts.

century that they had heard about the apostles from their followers. Papias:

> whenever anyone came who had followed the ancients (πρεσβυτέροις), I inquired concerning the words of the ancients, what Andrew or Peter or Philip or Thomas or James or John or Matthew, or any other of the Lord disciples had said. (Eusebius *Historia ecclesiastica* 3.39.4)

The word "ancients" in this context seems to refer to people old enough to have heard the apostles. Irenaeus boasts that he heard the preaching of Polycarp who in turn had been "instructed by apostles."[116] If this be the case with the *AA*, the curious and intrusive first person plural immediately after Andrew's death might refer to the witness of these intermediaries: the apostle "handed over his spirit, so that we wept and everyone grieved his departure" (Passion 64).

The names Xenocharides and Leonidas still appeared in the copy of the *AA* known to Innocent I (almost certainly in a Latin translation), and probably in the copy known to Philaster, who mistook them for Andrew's disciples. The names disappeared when Gregory epitomized the Acts and when someone else detached the Myrmidonian episode. The authorial postscript also dropped out of most versions of the Passion. This reconstruction must remain hypothetical; the evidence precludes firm conclusions. Even so, it would seem safest to follow the lead of Philaster and Innocent in referring not to the author of the *AA* but to its authors.

----

116. *Adversus haereses* 3.3.4.

Content and Literary Design

This edition presents the textual survivals of the AA in four Parts. Part I is the *AAMt*, which concludes with an excursus on Andrew's promised return to Myrmidonia. Part II reproduces Gregory's Latin epitome along with parallels from several Byzantine Andrean Βίοι, citations in later literature, and a substantial Coptic fragment. In order to fill in Gregory's gaps or to trim Byzantine expansions, this section also includes six excursus. Although one may be tempted to ignore these excursus as unwelcome interlopers, *caveat lector*: they contain information essential for assessing the content of the original Acts. Part III is an eclectic reconstruction of the Passion based on recensions in Greek, Latin, and Armenian. Part IV reproduces texts related to the Acts, but which may not have been original to it: a quotation from Augustine and a brutalized Coptic fragment. Discussion of the content and relative value of all sources used in creating this edition appear in the Introductions to the various Parts.

When compiled, these materials tell the following story. Andrew leaves Achaea to rescue Matthias from Myrmidons (Part I: *The Acts of Andrew and Matthias*). After doing so and converting the cannibals, he goes to Amasia, where he heals a blind man (Part II: Gregory's *Liber de virtutibus* 2), raises a dead boy (3), and vindicates a lad against his incestuous mother (4). In Sinope he heals a household (5), in Nicea banishes roadside demons (6), and in Nicomedia raises another boy back to life (7). He then sails to Byzantium (8), disarms a gang of robbers in Thrace (9), and converts sailors on his way to Macedonia (10). In Philippi and Thessalonica he disrupts a double wedding (11),

miraculously extinguishes a house fire (12), heals, revives, exorcizes (13-17), convinces a soldier to bolt ranks (18), slays a monstrous serpent (19), and learns in a vision the circumstances of his martyrdom (20). From Macedonia Andrew goes to Patras, Achaea (21), where he converts Lesbius the proconsul (22), rescues a woman from a brothel (23), and raises up forty corpses from the sea (24). Andrew and Lesbius then travel through the Peleponnese while the apostle performs more healings and exorcisms (26-29). By the time he returns to Patras, the rogue Aegeates has become proconsul in Lesbius's place. Andrew heals the infirm, including the wife of Aegeates, Maximilla (30-33).

Part III (the Passion) begins with Andrew healing the slave of Stratocles, Aegeates' brother (1-5). Stratocles converts (6-12). Maximilla, refusing to bed with Aegeates (13-16), bribes her shapely servant Eucleia to sleep with him instead (17-22), but when Aegeates learns the truth, he executes Eucleia and entreats Maximilla to resume sex (23-24). She refuses, so the proconsul imprisons the apostle, but the faithful find ways of sneaking into the prison to listen to him preach (25-50). Aegeates finally decides to crucify this destroyer of his home, and in order to prolong the torture, he ties Andrew to his cross with ropes (51-54). Andrew preaches from the cross for four days (55-58). The crowds successfully pressure Aegeates to release Andrew (59-60), but Andrew chooses rather to die (61-63). Maximilla and Stratocles bury him and devote themselves to holiness. Aegeates leaps to his death. (64).

Several aspects of the AA indicate its authors wanted to write a Christian Odyssey. The Acts begins with Andrew, the former fisherman, sailing with the aid of his god from Achaea to rescue Matthias from

Myrmidons, Achilles' allies in Homer. The worst of the
Myrmidons, like Odysseus, visit the netherworld and see
the wicked punished. After raising the Myrmidons from
the abyss, Andrew begins his journey back to Achaea, a
journey replete with demons, storms, and a monstrous
beast. Patras not only is near Ithaca, Odysseus's island
home, it also allows for a play on the Homeric formula
ἐς πατρίδα γαῖαν, "to the ancestral land." Andrew is
tied to his cross like Odysseus at the mast, symbolizing
the apostle's voyage to his true homeland. His soul
"speeds toward things beyond time, beyond law, beyond
speech, beyond body, beyond bitter pleasures full of
wickedness and every pain." This use of the Siren
episode from The Odyssey correlates with contemporary
allegories of Odysseus as a cipher for the soul seeking
to return to its immaterial home beyond the imperiling
sea of matter.[117] Clement of Alexandria too urged his
pagan readers to sail on to the heavenly harbor past the
sweet but treacherous songs of the Sirens of Greek
culture.[118]

Lesser characters in the AA also play roles mimetic
of characters in The Odyssey. Aegeates, "the one from
Aegae," is "like the raging sea" and functions as a
counter-Poseidon, whose Homeric home is Aegae.[119]
Maximilla, who prefers the attention of a rival to her
own husband, contrasts with Penelope. Whereas Penelope
sequesters herself in her bedroom keeping the suitors in
the hall, Maximilla welcomes "the brethren" into her
bedroom to hear Andrew preach. Stratocles is a counter-
Telemachus. At the beginning of The Odyssey, Telemachus

----

117. See Numenius's allegory in Porphyry's De antro
     nympharum 34.

118. Protrepticus 12.

119. E.g., Iliad 13.17-31 and Odyssey 5.381.

("Fighter-from-afar") is but a babe, but he matures thanks to instruction from the Achaean champions and finally becomes a man when he joins his father in destroying the suitors. Conversely, Stratocles ("Battle-praise") appears in the *AA* first as a soldier on leave to study philosophy. By the end, Stratocles births his own inner fetus, takes on the demeanor of a slave, and forswears violence.

By means of this contrastive characterization, the *AA* replaces the ethically questionable traits of Homeric heroes with Christian virtues. Instead of Odysseus's wealth, sex, and violence, the heroes here represent poverty, chastity, and military disobedience. The authors chose Andrew as the hero not because of a rich anterior tradition about the apostle, but because no apostle could better symbolize the new Odysseus than Peter's brother, Mr. Manliness ('Ανδρέας/ ἀνδρεία), the former fisherman who had brought Greeks to Jesus (John 12:22).[120]

Date and Place of Composition

According to Flamion, the Acts was the product of an anonymous Christian intellectual in Patras, Achaea, who cherished a legend concerning the apostle's visit there.[121] Achaea, however, is the one place in the Greek-speaking oikoumene almost certainly *not* the place of origin. No resident of Achaea would have supplied Patras its own proconsul and praetorium.[122] Moreover,

----

120. For a discussion of the relationship of the *AA* to antecedent traditions about Andrew, see Prieur, *Acta Andreae*, 67-89.

121. *Actes d'André*, 264-68.

122. See Prieur, *Acta Andreae*, 72-80.

apart from the *AA* itself, no evidence exists for a Christian community in Patras until much later. Patras apparently hosts the apostle's martyrdom because it neighbors the traditional location of Ithaca.

Flamion was also mistaken in dating the Acts to the second half of the third century on the basis of its similarities with Neoplatonism. Obviously this date is too late if the Acts indeed influenced the composition of the *ATh*. The Platonic commitments identified by Flamion correlate not only with Neoplatonism but with Middle Platonism as well.[123]

Help in establishing the date and location of composition may come from a controverted passage in Eusebius.

> Thomas, as tradition relates, obtained by lot Parthia, Andrew Scythia, John Asia (and he stayed there and died in Ephesus), but Peter seems to have preached to the Jews of the Dispersion in Pontus and Galatia and Bithynia, Cappadocia, and Asia, and at the end he came to Rome and was crucified head downwards, for so he had demanded to suffer. What need be said of Paul, who fulfilled the gospel of Christ from Jerusalem to Illyria and afterward was martyred in Rome under Nero? This is stated exactly by Origen in the third volume of his commentary on Genesis. (*Historia ecclesiastica* 3.1 [Loeb])

Eric Junod has shown, *contra* Harnack, that Eusebius did indeed receive this information from Origen's commentary, which had been written in Alexandria prior to his flight to Caesarea in 231.[124] Junod also suggests that Origen's listing of the very five apostles featured

----

123. Prieur, *Acta Andreae*, 372-79.

124. "Origène, Eusèbe et la tradition sur la répartition des champs de mission des apôtres (Eusèbe, *HE* III,1,1-3)," in Bovon, *Actes apocryphes*, 233-48.

in the earliest of the apocryphal Acts can hardly be coincidental, especially since Origen mentions John's death in Ephesus, Peter's upside down crucifixion, and Paul's execution by Nero, episodes narrated in the apocryphal Acts of those apostles. Surely Origen's παρά-δοσις somehow relates to the production of apocryphal Acts, but how?

Because the references to Thomas in Parthia and Andrew in Scythia do not correspond precisely with the Acts of those apostles, Junod backed off from claiming that Origen's tradition issued directly from the apocryphal Acts. Albrecht Dihle shows, however, that Origen's statement about Thomas in Parthia need not contradict the *ATh* insofar as Parthian overlords at the time ruled much of northern India.[125] Furthermore, because he was influenced by Flamion and Prieur, the version of the *AA* Junod had in mind had no Myrmidons, whose savagery so frequently identified them with Scythia.[126] Had Origen himself read of cannibals in the *AA*, one can appreciate why he might have substituted historical Scythia for Myrmidonian Never-Land. The conversion of Scythians would demonstrate the universality of the Gospel; the conversion of Myrmidons only its folly. Throughout the centuries, realism and legitimacy have exerted a nearly irresistible pull on the transmission of apostolic memory. Fiction quickly hardens into history, fantasy kowtows before ecclesiastical hierarchy, and fabulosity settles down to foster regional interests. One need only visit the magnificent basilica of Hagios Andreas in modern Patras

----

125. "Neues zur Thomas-Tradition," *JAC* 6 (1965): 54-70.

126. See for example *Recensio Vaticana* (a Latin poem retelling the Myrmidonian episode), the Anglo-Saxon poem *Andreas*, Epiphanius the Monk, Nicephorus Callistus, Ps.-Epiphanius, and Ps.-Hippolytus.

to see how the ancient fantasies of the *AA* have matured
into unquestioned Balkan realities.

Origen's very wording suggests that his tradition
derived from the apocryphal Acts. Thomas, Andrew, and
John are grouped together, each as a subject of the verb
εἴληχεν, "obtained by lot." The verbs change with
respect to Peter and Paul; they are not included in a
lottery. Thomas's Acts undoubtedly began with the
casting of lots; he draws India. Andrew's Acts, if one
includes the Myrmidons, also began with a lottery;
Andrew draws Achaea and Matthias Myrmidonia. The
beginning of the *AJ* is lost, but it too could have begun
with such a scene; and if it did, he would have drawn
Asia, where the apostle ministers in the rest of the
Acts. Surely it is no accident that the three apostles
whose Acts either did or might have begun with a casting
of lots are the same three that Origen makes subject of
the verb εἴληχεν.

There is, however, one serious objection to this
hypothesis. According to the *AAMt*, the lot gives
Myrmidonia to Matthias, not to Andrew; Andrew receives
Achaea. In order to answer this objection one would need
to explain (1) why Origen attributes Scythia to Andrew,
and (2) why he says nothing about the apostle in
Achaea.[127] Concerning the first, in spite of the lot
falling on Matthias to go to the Myrmidons, the *AAMt*
presents Andrew converting them, never Matthias. Second,
Origen's investment in this passage--as well as
Eusebius's in quoting him--lies in the extremities of
the oikoumene evangelized by the apostles: Parthia to

----

127. Eucherius of Lyons likewise located Andrew's
     ministry exclusively in Scythia (*Instructiones ad
     Salonium* 1 [CSEL 31:135]), but he may simply have
     been parroting Origen or Eusebius.

the east, Scythia to the north, and Rome to the west. The placement of Andrew in Achaea obviously would not contribute to this purpose, especially because Achaea already had been spoken for: Paul preached "from Jerusalem to Illyria." Furthermore, one must not insist on precise correspondences when comparing the apocryphal Acts with Origen's παράδοσις. The issue is less direct, literary citation than traditional content.

It would therefore seem reasonable to suggest that Origen's information about Andrew in Scythia and Thomas in Parthia, like his information about John in Ephesus, Peter upside down, or Paul headless, issued from apocryphal Acts. If this be the case, an intellectual of the great church already considered the content of these Acts established tradition by 231. One probably should date the AA no later than 200, inasmuch as it influenced the composition of the ATh. This is also the latest possible date for the AJ, with which the AA shares philosophical commitments, rhetorical patterns, and many literary motifs.[128] Origen's apparent knowledge of the AA, its distinctive version of Middle Platonism, and its similarities with the AJ all point to Alexandria as the most likely place of composition, although other locations also are possible.[129]

----

128. See Prieur, *Acta Andreae*, 413-14.

129. Ibid., 95-96 and especially 414-16.

Part One:

THE ACTS OF ANDREW AND MATTHIAS
IN THE CITY OF THE CANNIBALS

INTRODUCTION TO PART I

No one yet has assembled into a single, comprehensive edition the abundant textual evidence for *The Acts of Andrew and Matthias*. The text presented here takes a step in that direction, but the sheer volume of textual variants, if given due attention, would overflow the apparatus and swamp the reader. Fortunately, the manuscripts organize themselves naturally into two independent, widely attested text-types, distinguished from each other by language and geography. By comparing these two reassembled text-types one achieves a highly reliable reconstruction without accounting for every variant reading. The variants in the notes either have claims to be considered original to the *AAMt* or flag interpretive, grammatical, or transmissional problems.

The first text-type consists of the Greek manuscripts Maximilian Bonnet used to create his eclectic text,[1] as well as translations into Syriac, Ethiopic, Coptic, Armenian, and several Slavonic languages.[2]

----

1. "Acta Andreae et Matthiae" (*AAA* 2.1:65-116), based on nine manuscripts from the tenth to the sixteenth centuries (*BHG* 109-10).

2. These translations and one unpublished Greek manuscript Bonnet did not consult (*Ottoban 415* [*BHG* 110c]) require occasional alterations of his preferred text, but for the most part they represent readings aleady available to him. Syriac (*BHO* 733): William Wright, "The History of Mar Matthew and Mar Andrew," in *Apocryphal Acts Edited from Syrian Manuscripts in the British Museum and Other Libraries*

Readings from this eastern text-type are identified with the letter *Gr* (=Graeci), which generally corresponds with Bonnet's edition. *Gr*m (=Graeci multi) indicates that a reading so designated is attested by many of these manuscripts; *Gr*p (=Graeci pauci) indicates a reading is attested by few.

The second text-type consists of all Latin and Anglo-Saxon translations and is designated with the letter *Lat* (=Latini). These western manuscripts include codex *Casanatensis 1104* (sixth or seventh century),[3]

(London and Edinburgh: Williams and Norgate, 1871. Reprint. Amsterdam: Philo Press, 1968), 93-115; Ethiopic (*BHO* 734, 737, and 739): E. A. Wallis Budge, "The Preaching of Saint Matthias in the City of the Cannibals," and "The Preaching of Saint Matthias," in *The Contendings of the Apostles* (London: Oxford University Press [Humphrey Milford], 1935), 223-40 and 307-34; Coptic (*BHO* 735): Oskar von Lemm, "Koptische apokryphe Apostelakten," *Mélanges asiatiques tirés du Bulletin Impériale des Sciences de Saint Pétersbourg* 10 (1890): 99-171; Armenian (*BHO* 740 and 741 etc.): Louis Leloir, "Actes d'André et Matthias chez les Anthropophages," in *Écrits apocryphes sur les apôtres. Traduction de l'édition arménienne de Venise. I. Pierre, Paul, André, Jacques, Jean*, CCSA 3 (Turnhout: Brepols, 1986), 205-27; Slavonic: Ivan Franko, *Apocrypha and Legends (Codex apocryphus e manuscriptis ukraino-russicis collectus opera doctoris Joannis Franko)*, 5 vols (L'vov, 1896-1910), 3:126-44; K. Istomin, "From the Slavo-Russian Manuscripts About the Apostle Andrew," *Vestnick archeologii i istorii* 16 (1904): 233-80; S. Novaković, "Apocrypha of One Serbian Cyrillic Collection of the Fourteenth Century," *Starine* 8 (1876): 55-69; Julian Andreevich Javorskij, *Novyia rukopisnyia nakhodki v oblasti starinnoi Karpatorusskoi pis'mennosti* (New Manuscript Findings in the Field of Ancient Carpatho-Russian Writings; Prague: Nákl, 1931), 103; and Aurelio de Santos Otero, *Die handschriftliche Überlieferung der altslavischen Apokryphen* 2 vols. PTSt 20 and 23 (Berlin and New York: Walter de Gruyter, 1978 and 1981), 1:69-83.

3. Blatt, *Bearbeitungen*, 32-95.

Codex Vallicellanus (eleventh century),[4] *Bologna 1576* (eleventh century),[5] *Recensio Vaticana* (sixth or seventh century),[6] and the Anglo-Saxon recensions: *Cambridge 198* (late tenth century),[7] *Blickling Homily XIX* (tenth century),[8] and the epic poem *Andreas* (eleventh century).[9]

These two major text-types, *Gr* and *Lat*, also distinguish themselves with respect to the curious name of the cannibals' city. Every single Latin and Anglo-Saxon version of the *AAMt* (i.e., Gregory and the representatives of *Lat*) contain some form of Myrmidonia. On the other hand, every manuscript represented by *Gr* omits the name.

There is, however, a single Greek manuscript of the *AAMt* which contains references to Myrmidonia. *Paris gr. 1313* (=*P* [*BHG* 110b], fifteenth century, unpublished) was known to Bonnet but ignored in his edition. It may, however, represent an independent channel of textual

----

4. *AAA* 2.1:85-88, a Latin fragment of chapters 17-18.

5. Ellen B. Baumler, "Andrew in the City of the Cannibals: A Comparative Study of the Latin, Greek, and Old English Texts." Ph.D. diss., University of Kansas, 1985), 90-112, an abbreviated Latin recension. When this manuscript is cited, the reading corresponds with Baumler's corrected text; the manuscript contains many errors.

6. Blatt, *Bearbeitungen*, 96-148, a poetic Latin recension.

7. Charles Wycliffe Goodwin, *The Anglo-Saxon Legends of St. Andrew and St. Veronica* (Cambridge: Macmillan, 1851), 2-25.

8. R. Morris, *The Blickling Homilies of the Tenth Century*, EETS 63 (London: N. Trübner, 1880), 2:228-49.

9. Krapp, *Andreas*, 1-68.

transmission and supply bridgeheads between the *AAMt* and the rest of the *AA*. *P* once names the cannibals' city Σμυρμήνη and twice Μυρμήκη. Furthermore, unlike *Gr* and *Lat*, *P* narrates Andrew's return to Μυρμήκη to complete his mission there, just as the *AAMt* promised he would. *P* also tells of Andrew's leaving the city with his disciples for Amasia, as in Gregory's epitome. In addition, *P* knows that Andrew received by lot "the region of Pontus (or the Black Sea) and all of Achaea" (χώρα τοῦ Πόντου καὶ ὅλη ἡ 'Αχαΐα) where, at the end of the *AA*, the apostle glorifies his God with martyrdom. The author may indeed have known the ancient *AA* directly, but may merely have known and conflated other Andrean literature and traditions with a version of the *AAMt*. It is particularly disappointing that this manuscript so freely recast its antecedents that it cannot be used with confidence in establishing the text.

The reconstruction of the *AAMt* printed in this volume results from applying the following criteria:

1. A reading is most preferred when *Gr* and any representative of *Lat* agree.

2. When *Gr* and all representatives of *Lat* disagree, the most primitive readings of both text-types are recorded, either in the text or in the footnotes. Unless internal reasons dictate otherwise, the best reading of *Gr* will appear in the text; the best reading of *Lat* in a note.

3. Readings from *P* are recorded only when they help adjudicate between *Gr* and *Lat* or when the content of *P* is independently noteworthy.

The following delimiters indicate the status of particular readings.

(...)	lacuna
<xxx>	emendation
[xxx]	reading only in *Gr*

Because the word Μυρμιδονία probably was in the original, when its presence is attested by *Lat* or otherwise implied, it is restored in its Greek spelling and placed in pointed brackets: viz. <Μυρμιδονία>. In the translation, readings only in *Gr* appear in *italics*; those only in *Lat* in **bold**.

In addition to textual variants, the notes also contain parallel readings from several other documents. The earliest Greek manuscripts of the *AAMt* date to the tenth century; the earliest Latin to the sixth or seventh; the earliest Anglo-Saxon to the tenth. There are, however, several other related documents dating from the third to the ninth centuries whose readings must also be registered and may in fact be preferred: the epitome by Gregory of Tours, *Narratio*, *The Life of Andrew* by Epiphanius the monk, *Laudatio*, *Martyrium prius*, and Photius's *Bibliotheca* 114. Parallels from cognate apocryphal Acts which seem to have known the *AAMt* are cited in the notes to the text: *The Acts of Thomas*, *The Acts of Philip*, *The Acts of Xanthippe and Polyxena*, and *The Acts of John by Prochorus*. Quotations, allusions, and imitations of the Bible and other sources are cited in the notes to the translation.

One must keep in mind that the text printed here is not a comprehensive critical edition of the *AAMt* but an eclectic text based on a comparison of two independent text-types. Furthermore, no attempt is made here to probe behind the fifth-century version of the story in order to reconstruct a more primitive version, such as might originally have appeared in the *AA*.

ABBREVIATIONS TO THE APPARATUS FOR PART I

A   *Andreas.* Krapp, *Andreas,* 1-68.

AJPr   *The Acts of John by Prochorus.* Zahn, *Acta Joannis,* 1-252.

APe   *The Acts of Peter. AAA* 1:45-117.

APh   *The Acts of Philip. AAA* 2.2:1-98.

Arm   Armenian. Leloir, *Écrits apocryphes,* 205-27.

AS   Anglo-Saxon. Goodwin, *Anglo-Saxon Legends,* 2-25, and Morris, *Blickling Homilies,* 2:228-49.

ATh   *The Acts of Thomas. AAA* 2.2:99-291.

AXP   *The Acts of Xanthippe and Polyxena.* James, *Apocrypha anecdota* 2.3:58-85.

B   *Bologna 1576.* Baumler, "Andrew in the City of the Cannibals," 90-112.

C   *Casanatensis 1104.* Blatt, *Bearbeitungen,* 32-95.

E   *The Life of Andrew (BHG* 102), Epiphanius the monk. *PG* 120:216-60.

Eth   Ethiopic *(BHO* 734, 737, and 739). Budge, *Contendings,* 223-40 and 307-34.

Gr   Graeci *(BHG* 109-10). *AAA* 2.1:65-116.

GE   Gregory's epitome *(BHL* 430). Bonnet, "Liber de miraculis," 821-46, reproduced in Prieur, *Acta Andreae,* 555-631.

Grm   Graeci multi

Grp   Graeci pauci

Lat   Latini

L   *Laudatio (BHG* 100). Bonnet, *Acta Andreae,* 3-44.

M   *Martyrium prius (BHG* 96). Prieur, *Acta Andreae,* 675-703.

N   *Narratio (BHG* 99). Bonnet, *Acta Andreae*,
    46-64.

O   *Ottoban 415 (BHG* 110c). Unpublished.

P   *Paris gr. 1313 (BHG* 110b). Unpublished.

Syr   Syriac (*BHO* 733). Wright, *Apocryphal Acts*,
    93-115.

V   *Recensio Vaticana 1274.* Blatt, *Bearbeitungen*,
    96-148.

1. Κατ' ἐκεῖνον τὸν καιρὸν[1] ἦσαν [πάντες] οἱ
ἀπόστολοι ἐπὶ τὸ αὐτὸ συναχθέντες καὶ ἐμέριζον ἑαυτοῖς
τὰς χώρας, βάλλοντες κλήρους ὅπως ἀπέλθῃ ἕκαστος εἰς τὸ
λαχὸν αὐτοῦ μέρος.[2] κατὰ κλῆρον οὖν ἔλαχεν τὸν Ματθείαν
πορευθῆναι εἰς τὴν <πόλιν> que dicitur <Μυρμιδονία>.[3]

Οἱ δὲ ἄνθρωποι τῆς πόλεως ἐκείνης οὔτε ἄρτον ἤσθιον
οὔτε ὕδωρ[4] ἔπινον, ἀλλ' ἦσαν ἐσθίοντες σάρκας ἀνθρώπων
καὶ πίνοντες αὐτῶν τὸ αἷμα.[5] πᾶς οὖν ἄνθρωπος ὃς

----

1. GE: post illum dominicae ascensionis. M 1 (similarly
O, AS, Syr, Arm, E, L and AJPr): μετὰ τὴν ἀνάληψιν
αὐτοῦ.

2. GE: cum beati apostoli praedicare verbum Dei per
diversas   regiones   dispersi   fuissent,   Andreas
apostolus apud Achaiam provinciam adnuntiare Dominum
Iesum Christum exorsus est (cf. M 2: ἔλαχεν καὶ τὸν
Ἀνδρέαν ἡ Βιθυνία καὶ ἡ Λακεδαιμονία καὶ ἡ Ἀχαΐα;
APh Act 3: ὁ ἀδελφὸς Ἀνδρέας ἐπορεύθη εἰς τὴν
Ἀχαΐαν καὶ ὅλην τὴν Θράκην). M 1: ἀναστάντες
βάλλωμεν κλήρους τίς ποῦ ἀπέλθῃ. Cf. ATh 1, APh Act
8, and the beginning of AJPr.

3. Lat: Mermedonia. Gr: τὴν χώραν τῶν ἀνθρωποφάγων. GE:
Matheus   autem   apostolus,   qui   et   euangelista,
Myrmidonae urbi verbum salutis adnuntiavit (cf. C: in
eadem   civitatem   Mermedoniam,   ad   verbum   salutis
predicandum). M 2: καὶ ἐκληρώθη . . . Ματθαῖος τὴν
Παρθίαν καὶ τὴν Μυρμηνίδα πόλιν. Cf. ATh 1 and APh
Act 3.

4. Grm: οἶνον.

5. GE: Sed incolae civitatis dure. N: ἐν ᾗ οἱ ταύτην
οἰκοῦντες αἱμοβόροι τινὲς καὶ ἀνήμεροι καὶ θηρίων
ἀγριωδέστερον τῇ γνώμῃ διέκειντο. E: ἦν δὲ Ἰουδαίων
πλῆθος πολὺ ἐν τῇ πόλει ἐκείνῃ, ἔχοντες καθ' ἑαυτοὺς
αἱρέσεις πολλάς, ἄνδρες τὰ ἤθη βάρβαροι καὶ ἀνήμεροι,
οἱ ἕνεκεν τούτου λέγονται ἀνθρωποφάγοι.

C adds: Habebantque clibanum in medio civitatis
edificatum, insuper et lacus iuxta eodem clibani. In
quo lacu homines interficiebant, ut sanguis illud ibi
colligerent. Alioque lacu iuxta ipsum lacum, in quo
sanguis illud que in ipso priore laco spargentur,

1. At that time,[1] *all* the apostles were gathered together at one place and divided the regions among themselves by casting lots, so that each would leave for his allotted share.[2] The lot fell on Matthias to go to the city **called Myrmidonia.**[3]

The people of that city ate no bread and drank no water,[4] but ate human flesh and drank their blood.[5] They would seize all who came to their city, dig out their

----

1. *GE*: "after the Lord's ascension." *M* 1 (similarly *O*, *AS*, *Syr*, *Arm*, *E*, and *L*): "after his ascension."

2. *GE*: "when the blessed apostles were dispersed throughout various regions to preach the word of God, the apostle Andrew was allotted to proclaim the Lord Jesus Christ in the province of Achaea" (cf. *M* 2: "by lot, Bithynia, Sparta, and Achaea went to Andrew;" *APh* Act 3: "brother Andrew went to Achaea and all of Thrace"). *M* 1: "let us arise and cast lots to determine where someone should go".

3. *Gr*: "the region of the cannibals." *GE*: "But Matthew the apostle and evangelist proclaimed the word of salvation in the city of Myrmidona" (cf. *C*: "into that city Mermidonia to preach the word of salvation"). *M* 2: "And Matthew was allotted Parthia and the city of Myrmenis." Cf. Acts 1:25-26 and 2:1.

4. *Grm*: "wine."

5. *GE*: "but the brutish inhabitants." *N*: "some of the inhabitants of this city were bloodthirsty and savage, with temperaments wilder than beasts." *E*: "There was a large population of Jews in that city, splintered into several parties, men of barbarous and savage habits, who for this reason are called cannibals."

   C adds: "In the middle of the city an earthen oven had been constructed, and, in addition, next to that oven was a trough. They used to slaughter people in the trough in order to collect the blood there. Next to that trough was another into which the blood that was sprinkled into the first trough (...) and flows as though it had been purified (...) for drinking."

ἀπήρχετο ἐν τῇ πόλει αὐτῶν, κατεῖχον αὐτόν, καὶ
ὀρύσσοντες ἐξέβαλλον αὐτοῦ τοὺς ὀφθαλμούς.[6] φάρμακον
αὐτὸν ἐπότιζον ἐκ φαρμακείας καὶ μαγείας σκευασθέν, καὶ
ἐν τῷ αὐτοὺς ποτίζειν τὸ φάρμακον ἠλλοιοῦτο αὐτοῦ ἡ
καρδία καὶ ὁ νοῦς αὐτοῦ μετηλλάσσετο. Menteque iam non
habentes, retrusi in carcere, fenum ut boves vel pecora
conmedebant.[7]

  2. Τοῦ οὖν Ματθεία εἰσελθόντος ἐν τῇ πύλῃ τῆς
πόλεως <Μυρμιδονίας>,[8] ἐκράτησαν αὐτὸν οἱ ἄνθρωποι τῆς
πόλεως ἐκείνης,[9] καὶ ἐξέβαλον αὐτοῦ τοὺς ὀφθαλμούς,[10]
ἐπότισαν αὐτὸν τὸ φάρμακον τῆς μαγικῆς αὐτῶν πλάνης, καὶ
ἀπήγαγον αὐτὸν ἐν τῇ φυλακῇ,[11] καὶ παρέθηκαν αὐτὸν
χόρτον ἐσθίειν.

  Καὶ οὐκ ἤσθιεν, μεταλαβὼν γὰρ ἐκ τοῦ φαρμάκου αὐτῶν
οὐκ ἠλλοιώθη ἡ καρδία αὐτοῦ οὔτε ὁ νοῦς αὐτοῦ μετηλλάγη,
ἀλλ' ἦν εὐχόμενος τῷ θεῷ κλαίων καὶ λέγων· κύριε Ἰησοῦ

  (...) et quasi purgatus discurret, (...) bibendum. A
  similar passage appears in Gr in chapter 22.

6. GE: erutis oculis. N: οὐ μόνον πρὸς ἀλλήλους ἀλλὰ καὶ
   πρὸς πάντας τοὺς ἔξωθεν ἐπεισερχομένους ἐπηλυδάς τε
   καὶ νεήλυδας, τούτοις ἀσπλαγχνία κεχρημένοι καὶ
   ἀνημέρῳ τρόπῳ μετερχόμενοι. Grm add: καὶ μετὰ τὸ
   ἐξενεγκεῖν αὐτοῦ τοὺς ὀφθαλμούς.

7. Similarly Eth and Arm.

8. Lat: Mermedoniam. Gr om.

9. GE: adpraehensum beatum apostolum. E: οἱ Ἰουδαῖοι
   κρατήσαντες αὐτόν.

10. GE: erutis oculis. Grm add: καὶ μετὰ τὸ ἐξενεκεῖν
    αὐτοῦ τοὺς ὀφθαλμούς.

11. GE: circumdatum catenis, in carcere detruserunt. E:
    ἔθεντο εἰς φυλακήν. N: ὡς καὶ τὸν μακάριον ἀπόστολον
    Ματθείαν, καθὰ λόγος κεκράτηκεν, χάριν τοῦ κηρύγματος
    Χριστοῦ τοῦ ἀληθινοῦ θεοῦ ἡμῶν παρ' αὐτοῖς γενόμενον
    κατασχεῖν καὶ ἀνηλεῶς αἰκίσασθαι καὶ κατάκλειστον ἐν
    φρουρᾷ ποιῆσαι ὡς μετὰ ταῦτα τοῦτον σφοδρότερον
    τιμωρησόμενοι.

eyes,[6] make them drink a drug prepared by sorcery and magic. When forced by them to drink the drug, the victims' hearts became muddled and their minds deranged. **Out of their minds and taken to prison, they would eat hay like cattle or sheep.**

2. So when Matthias entered the gate of the city **Myrmidonia**, the people of that city seized him[7] and gouged out his eyes.[8] They made him drink the drug of their magical deceit, led him off to the prison,[9] and gave him grass to eat.

He ate nothing, for his heart was not muddled and his mind not deranged when he took their drug, but he prayed to God weeping, "Lord Jesus Christ, for whom we have forsaken everything to follow you,[10] knowing that

----

6. *GE*: "his eyes were gouged out." *N*: the residents of the city were savage "not only to each other, but also to all those who intruded from the outside, whether strangers or newcomers, inflicting atrocities on them and pursuing them savagely." *Grm* add: "and after removing their eyes."

7. *GE*: "the blessed apostle was seized." *E*: "the Jews seized him."

8. *GE*: "his eyes were gouged out." *Grm* add: "And after gouging out his eyes."

9. *GE*: "they pushed him off to prison bound in chains." *E*: "put him in prison." *N*: "so also with the blessed apostle Matthias. According to the record, when he arrived among them for preaching Christ our true God, they detained him, tortured him mercilessly, and locked him up in a prison, so that they might punish him more severely later."

10. Cf. Matt 19:27.

Χριστέ, δι' ὃν τὰ πάντα κατελείψαμεν καὶ ἠκολουθήσαμέν
σοι, γινώσκοντες ὅτι σὺ εἶ βοηθὸς πάντων τῶν ἐλπιζόντων
ἐπὶ σέ, πρόσσχες οὖν καὶ θέασαι ἃ ἐποίησαν Ματθείᾳ τῷ
δούλῳ σου, πῶς παρεπλησίασάν με τοῖς κτήνεσιν· σὺ γὰρ εἶ
ὁ γινώσκων τὰ πάντα. εἰ οὖν ὥρισάς με ἵνα καταφάγωσίν με
οἱ ἐν τῇ πόλει ταύτῃ ἄνθρωποι ἄνομοι, οὐ μὴ ἐκφεύξομαι
τὴν οἰκονομίαν σου. παράσχου οὖν μοι κύριε τὸ φῶς τῶν
ὀφθαλμῶν μου, ἵνα κἂν θεάσωμαι ἃ ἐπιχειροῦσίν μοι οἱ ἐν
τῇ πόλει ταύτῃ ἄνομοι ἄνδρες· μὴ ἐγκαταλίπῃς με κύριέ
μου 'Ιησοῦ Χριστέ, καὶ μὴ παραδώσῃς με τῷ θανάτῳ τῷ
πικρῷ τούτῳ.

3. Ταῦτα δὲ προσευχομένου τοῦ Ματθεία ἐν τῇ φυλακῇ
ἔλαμψεν φῶς, καὶ ἐξῆλθεν ἐκ τοῦ φωτὸς φωνὴ λέγουσα·
Ματθεία ἀγαπητέ, ἀνάβλεψον. καὶ εὐθέως ἀνέβλεψεν. καὶ
πάλιν ἐξῆλθεν φωνὴ λέγουσα·[12] ἐνισχυρίζου ἡμέτερε
Ματθεία, καὶ μὴ πτοηθῇς· οὐ μὴ γάρ σε ἐγκαταλίπω· ἐγὼ
γάρ σε ῥύσομαι ἀπὸ παντὸς κινδύνου, οὐ μόνον δὲ σὲ ἀλλὰ
καὶ πάντας τοὺς ἀδελφούς σου τοὺς ὄντας μετὰ σοῦ· μετὰ
σοῦ γάρ εἰμι πᾶσαν ὥραν καὶ πάντοτε. ἀλλ' ὑπόμεινον
ἐνταῦθα ἡμέρας κζ' [δι' οἰκονομίαν πολλῶν ψυχῶν],[13] καὶ
μετὰ ταῦτα ἐξαποστελῶ σοι 'Ανδρέαν καὶ ἐξάξει σε ἐκ τῆς
φυλακῆς ταύτης, οὐ μόνον δὲ σὲ ἀλλὰ καὶ πάντας τοὺς μετὰ
σοῦ ὄντας.[14] ταῦτα εἰπὼν ὁ σωτὴρ εἶπεν πάλιν τῷ Ματθείᾳ·
εἰρήνη σοι ἡμέτερε Ματθεία· καὶ ἐπορεύθη πάλιν εἰς τὸν
οὐρανόν.

----

12. *C* om.: Ματθεία . . . λέγουσα. Apparently, these
    words were omitted by haplography caused by the
    repetition of the Greek words φωνὴ λέγουσα, or
    perhaps the Latin words *vox dicens*. *Lat* must have
    included the section absent in *C* inasmuch as it
    appears in *AS*.

13. This phrase is absent also in *Arm* and in an
    important Greek ms.

14. *Grp*: τοὺς ἀκούοντας, a reading perhaps derived from
    a visual confusion between τουϲμεταϲουοντας with
    τουϲακουοντας.

you help all who hope in you, pay attention and see what they have done to your servant Matthias, how they have nearly reduced me to the condition of beasts, for you know all. Therefore, if you have determined in my case that the lawless people of this city should devour me, I will not flee your arrangement. Restore to me, Lord, the light of my eyes, so that I can see what the lawless men of this city are undertaking against me. Do not abandon me, my Lord Jesus Christ, and do not hand me over to this bitter death."

3. As Matthias was praying, a light shone in the prison, and a voice came out of the light saying, "Beloved Matthias, receive your sight." Immediately he received his sight. Again the voice came out saying, "Brace yourself, our Matthias, and do not be terrified, for I will never abandon you. I will rescue you from every danger, not only you but also all your brothers and sisters who are with you, for I am with you every hour and always.[11] But remain here twenty-seven days *for the benefit of many souls,* and then I will send Andrew to you who will lead you out of this prison, not only you but also all who are with you." When the Savior had said these things, he again said to Matthias, "Peace be with you, our Matthias," and he returned to heaven.

----

11. Cf. Matt 28:20.

Τότε ὁ Ματθείας θεασάμενος εἶπεν [πρὸς τὸν
κύριον]·[15] ἡ χάρις σου διαμένῃ μετ' ἐμοῦ κύριέ μου
Ἰησοῦ. τότε οὖν ὁ Ματθείας ἐκαθέσθη ἐν τῇ φυλακῇ καὶ ἦν
ψάλλων.[16]

Καὶ ἐγένετο ἐν τῷ εἰσέρχεσθαι τοὺς δημίους εἰς τὴν
φυλακὴν ἵνα ἐξενέγκωσιν τοὺς ἀνθρώπους εἰς βρῶσιν αὐτῶν,
καὶ ἦν ὁ Ματθείας κλείων αὐτοῦ τοὺς ὀφθαλμούς, ὅπως μὴ
θεωρήσωσιν αὐτὸν βλέποντα.[17] καὶ ἐλθόντες οἱ δήμιοι πρὸς
αὐτὸν ἀνέγνωσαν τὴν ἐν τῇ χειρὶ αὐτοῦ τάβλαν, καὶ εἶπαν
ἐν ἑαυτοῖς· ἔτι τρεῖς ἡμέρας καὶ ἐξάξομεν καὶ τοῦτον ἐκ
τῆς φυλακῆς καὶ σφάξομεν αὐτόν. [ἐπειδὴ πάντα ἄνθρωπον
ὃν κατεῖχον ἐσημειοῦντο τὴν ἡμέραν ἐκείνην ἐν ᾗ κατεῖχον
αὐτόν· καὶ προσέδ<ησ>αν τῇ χειρὶ αὐτοῦ τῇ δεξιᾷ τάβλαν,
ἵνα γνῶσι τὴν πλήρωσιν τῶν τριάκοντα ἡμερῶν.][18]

4. Καὶ ἐγένετο ὅτε ἐπληρώθησαν αἱ κζ' ἡμέραι ἐν τῷ
συλλημφθῆναι τὸν Ματθείαν, ἐφάνη ὁ κύριος Ἰησοῦς ἐν
Achaia civitatem[19] ᾗ ἦν διδάσκων ὁ Ἀνδρέας, καὶ εἶπεν

----

15. *Lat* and *Grp* om.: πρὸς τὸν κύριον.

16. *C* adds: Et tenentes unusquisque tabula in manu sua,
    quas iniquissimi et crudeles carnifices, in eorum
    manibus dederant cum eos retrudebant, erat namque
    per singula tabula scriptum, numerum dierum
    triginta, et cotidie introiebant carnifices illi ad
    eos in eadem carcere, et tabulas illas scripturas
    contemplabantur. Ut quem per ipsam script<ur>am
    invenirent, iam expleti<s> triginta diebus haberet
    reclusum, velud animalia ad saginandum, statim
    eiciebant eum qui triginta dies conpleverant, et
    occidebant, atque judicibus suis preparabant carnes
    eorum ad manducandum, et sanguis eorum ut potum ad
    bibendum.

17. *C* adds: Accepta vero tabula de manu eius, neque
    potuerunt agnoscere oculi eium visum videre.
    Similarly *B*.

18. *GE*: ut, interpositis paucis diebus, interficerent.
    E: τρεῖς ἡμέρας, βουλόμενοι τῇ ἐπαύριον ἀνελεῖν
    αὐτόν.

Seeing this, Matthias said *to the Lord,* "May your grace continue with me, my Lord Jesus!" Then Matthias sat in the prison and sang.[12]

When the executioners came into the prison to carry people away to eat, Matthias would shut his eyes so they would not notice he could see.[13] The executioners came to him, read the ticket on his hand, and said to each other, "In three days we will take this one too from the prison and slaughter him." *They would indicate for everyone they caught the date of their capture, and they tied a ticket to their right hands so that they would know the completion of thirty days.*[14]

4. When twenty-seven days elapsed since Matthias had been captured, the Lord Jesus appeared in **a city of Achaea** where Andrew was teaching and said *to him,*[15]

----

12. Cf. Acts 16:25. *C* adds: "When the wicked and cruel executioners put them in prison they tied on each captive's hand a ticket, and on each ticket was written the number of the thirtieth day. Each day the executioners came to them in the prison and examined those written tickets. Whomever they discovered by means of this writing to have been shut up already for thirty days, like animals for fattening, they would at once remove those whose thirty days had ended, kill them, and prepare the flesh for their judges to eat and the blood as a beverage for drinking."

13. *C* adds: "Indeed, when the ticket was taken from his hand, they could not detect that his eye(s) could see." Similarly *B*.

14. *GE*: "in order to kill him after a few days." *E*: "three days, wanting to kill him on the next."

15. *GE*: "An angel of the Lord came to the apostle Andrew, saying."

[αὐτῷ].[20] ἀνάσθητι καὶ πορεύθητι μετὰ τῶν μαθητῶν σου in
civitatem que dicitur <Μυρμιδονία>,[21] καὶ ἐξάγαγε
Ματθείαν ἐκ τοῦ τόπου ἐκείνου.[22] ἔτι γὰρ τρεῖς ἡμέραι
καὶ ἐξάξουσιν αὐτὸν οἱ τῆς πόλεως καὶ σφάξουσιν αὐτὸν
εἰς τροφὴν αὐτῶν.

Καὶ ἀποκριθεὶς Ἀνδρέας εἶπεν· κύριέ μου,[23] οὐ
δυνήσομαι φθάσαι τοῦ ἀπελθεῖν ἐκεῖ πρὸ [τῆς προθεσμίας]
τῶν τριῶν ἡμερῶν, ἀλλ’ ἀπόστειλον τὸν ἄγγελόν σου τὸ
τάχος ἵνα ἐξάξει αὐτὸν ἐκεῖθεν· σὺ γὰρ γινώσκεις κύριε
ὅτι κἀγὼ σάρξ εἰμι[24] καὶ οὐ δυνήσομαι τὸ τάχος
πορευθῆναι ἐκεῖ· ἀλλ’ οὐδὲ ἐπίσταμαι τὴν ὁδόν.[25]

Καὶ λέγει τῷ Ἀνδρέᾳ.[26] ἐπάκουσον τῷ ποιήσαντί σε,
τῷ καὶ δυναμένῳ λόγῳ εἰπεῖν καὶ μετενεχθήσεται ἡ πόλις
ἐκείνη ἐνταῦθα καὶ οἱ οἰκοῦντες ἐν αὐτῇ πάντες. κελεύω
γὰρ τοῖς κέρασιν τῶν ἀνέμων καὶ ἄγουσιν αὐτὴν ἐνταῦθα.
ἀλλ’ ἀναστὰς τῷ πρωῒ κάτελθε εἰς τὴν θάλασσαν σὺν τοῖς
μαθηταῖς σου, καὶ εὑρήσεις πλοῖον ἐπὶ τὸν αἰγιαλὸν καὶ
ἀνέλθῃς εἰς αὐτὸ μετὰ τῶν μαθητῶν σου.[27] καὶ ταῦτα εἰπὼν

----

19. Similarly *Eth* and *Arm*.

20. *C*: ad beatum Andream. *Grp*: τῷ Ἀνδρέᾳ. *GE*: Venit
    autem angelus Domini ad Andream apostolum dicens.

21. *Lat*: Mermedonia. *Gr*: ἐν τῇ χώρᾳ τῶν ἀνθρωποφάγων.
    GE: Surge et vade ad Myrmidonam civitatem.

22. *GE*: et erue fratrem tuum Matheum de squalore
    carceris quo tenetur.

23. *GE*: Cui ille ait: Domine, ecce.

24. Cf. *ATh* 1 and *APh* Act 4.

25. *GE*: viam nescio, et quo ibo?

26. *Lat* adds: O Andrea.

27. *GE*: Vade . . . ad litus maris, et invenies ibi
    navem, in qua statim ascende.

"Arise, go with your disciples **to the city called Myrmidonia,**[16] and bring Matthias out of that place,[17] for in three days the citizenry will bring him out and slaughter him for their food."

"My Lord," answered Andrew,[18] "I cannot travel there before *the* three day *limit,* so send your angel quickly to get him out of there. For you know, Lord, that I too am flesh and cannot go there quickly. I do not even know the route."[19]

"Obey the one who made you," he told Andrew, "the one who can speak but a word and that city and all its inhabitants would be brought here. For if I were to command the horns of the winds, they would drive it here. But rise up early, go down to the sea with your disciples, and you will find a boat on the shore that you and your disciples should board."[20] Having said

----

16. *Gr*: "to the region of the cannibals." *GE*: "Arise and go to the city Myrmidona." Cf. Jonah 1:1 (LXX).

17. *GE*: "and rescue your brother Matthew from the filth of the prison where he is detained."

18. *GE*: "He said to him,'Lord, behold.'"

19. *GE*: "I do not know the route, and where will I go?"

20. *GE*: "Go . . . to the seashore, and you will find a ship there. Board it at once." Cf. Jonah 1:3 (LXX) and *APe (AV)* 5.

ὁ σωτὴρ πάλιν εἶπεν· εἰρήνη σοι ᾿Ανδρέα ἅμα τοῖς σὺν
σοί· καὶ ἐπορεύθη εἰς τοὺς οὐρανούς.

5. ᾿Αναστὰς δὲ ᾿Ανδρέας τῷ πρωῒ ἐπορεύετο ἐπὶ τὴν
θάλασσαν ἅμα τοῖς μαθηταῖς αὐτοῦ, καὶ κατελθὼν ἐπὶ τὸν
αἰγιαλὸν εἶδεν πλοιάριον μικρὸν[28] καὶ ἐπὶ τὸ πλοιάριον
τρεῖς ἄνδρας καθεζομένους. ὁ γὰρ κύριος τῇ ἑαυτοῦ
δυνάμει κατεσκεύασεν πλοῖον, καὶ αὐτὸς ἦν ὥσπερ ἄνθρωπος
πρῳρεὺς ἐν τῷ πλοίῳ·[29] καὶ εἰσήνεγκεν δύο ἀγγέλους·
μετεμόρφωσεν αὐτοὺς εἰς ἀνθρώπους φανῆναι, [καὶ ἦσαν σὺν
αὐτῷ ἐν τῷ πλοίῳ καθεζόμενοι].

῾Ο οὖν ᾿Ανδρέας θεασάμενος τὸ πλοῖον καὶ τοὺς τρεῖς
ἄνδρας τοὺς ὄντας ἐν αὐτῷ ἐχάρη χαρὰν μεγάλην σφόδρα,
καὶ πορευθεὶς πρὸς αὐτοὺς εἶπεν· ποῦ πορεύεσθε ἀδελφοὶ
μετὰ τοῦ πλοίου τοῦ μικροῦ τούτου;

Καὶ ἀποκριθεὶς ὁ κύριος εἶπεν αὐτῷ· πορευόμεθα ἐν
civitatis <Μυρμιδονίας>.[30]

[῾Ο δὲ ᾿Ανδρέας θεασάμενος τὸν ᾿Ιησοῦν οὐκ ἐπέγνω
αὐτόν· ἦν γὰρ ὁ ᾿Ιησοῦς κρύψας τὴν ἑαυτοῦ θεότητα, καὶ
ἦν φαινόμενος τῷ ᾿Ανδρέᾳ ὡς ἄνθρωπος πρῳρεύς.] Et
respondens Andreas dixit ad eum,[31] κἀγὼ εἰς τὴν <πόλιν>
τῶν <Μυρμιδόνων>[32] πορεύομαι. ergo fratres ducete nos in
eadem civitatem.[33]

----

28. *GE*: Fecit Andreas iuxta verbum Domini et invenit
    litore navem.

29. *GE*: Ego enim ero dux itineris tui. Cf. *APh* Act 8.

30. *Lat*: Mermedonie. *Gr*: ἐν τῇ χώρᾳ τῶν ἀνθρωποφάγων.

31. *Gr*: ἀκούσας τοῦ ᾿Ανδρέου λέγοντος ὅτι.

32. *Gr*: χώραν τῶν ἀνθρωποφάγων.

33. *AS*: Se haliga Andreas him andswarode, and he cwæð,
    Broðer onfoh us mid eow on þæt scip, and gelædað us
    on þa ceastre.

this, the Savior again said, "Peace to you, Andrew, and to those with you," and he went into the heavens.

5. Rising early in the morning, Andrew and his disciples went to the sea, and when he descended to the shore he saw a small boat[21] and seated in the boat three men. The Lord by his own power had prepared the boat. He himself was in the boat like a human captain,[22] and he had brought on board two angels whom he transformed to look like humans, *and they were sitting in the boat with him.*

When Andrew saw the boat and the three men in it he was exuberant. He went to them and said, "Brothers, where are you going with this little boat?"

"We are going **to the city Myrmidonia,**"[23] answered the Lord.

Andrew looked at Jesus but did not recognize him, because Jesus was hiding his divinity and appeared to Andrew as a human captain. "I too am going to the <city> of the <Myrmidons>,"[24] **Andrew answered,**[25] **"so take us to this city, brothers.**"[26]

----

21. *GE*: "Andrew carried out the word of the Lord and found a boat on the shore." Cf. Jonah 1:3 (LXX) and *APe* (*AV*) 5.

22. *GE*: "For I will be the guide for your journey."

23. *Gr*: "to the region of the cannibals."

24. *Gr*: "to the region of the cannibals."

25. *Gr*: "when he heard Andrew say that."

26. *AS*: "'Brother, take us with you into the boat,' said the holy Andrew, 'and take us to that city.'"

Ὁ δὲ Ἰησοῦς λέγει αὐτῷ· πᾶς ἄνθρωπος φεύγει τὴν πόλιν ἐκείνην, καὶ πῶς ὑμεῖς πορεύεσθε ἐκεῖ;

Καὶ ἀποκριθεὶς Ἀνδρέας εἶπεν· πρᾶγμά τι μικρὸν ἔχομεν ἐκεῖ διαπράξασθαι, καὶ δεῖ ἡμᾶς ἐκτελέσαι αὐτό· ἀλλ' εἰ [δύνασαι, ποίησον] μεθ' ἡμῖν τὴν φιλανθρωπίαν ταύτην τοῦ ἀπάξαι ἡμᾶς [ἐν <τῇ πόλει Μυρμιδονία>[34] ἐν ᾖ καὶ ὑμεῖς μέλλετε πορεύεσθαι].

Ἀποκριθεὶς δὲ ὁ Ἰησοῦς εἶπεν αὐτοῖς· si ita vobis est necessarium ἀνέλθατε huc in istam navem, et proficiscite nobiscum.[35]

6. Καὶ εἶπεν Ἀνδρέας· θέλω σοί τι φανερὸν ποιῆσαι νεανίσκε πρὸ τοῦ ἡμᾶς ἀνελθεῖν ἐν τῷ πλοίῳ σου.

Ὁ δὲ Ἰησοῦς εἶπεν· λέγε ὃ βούλει.

Ὁ δὲ Ἀνδρέας εἶπεν αὐτῷ· ἄκουσον ἀδελφέ· ναῦλον οὐκ ἔχομέν σοι παρασχεῖν, ἀλλ' οὔτε ἄρτον ἔχομεν εἰς διατροφήν.

Καὶ ἀποκριθεὶς ὁ Ἰησοῦς εἶπεν αὐτῷ· πῶς οὖν ἀνέρχεσθε μὴ παρέχοντες ἡμῖν τὸν ναῦλον μήτε ἄρτους ἔχοντες εἰς διατροφήν;

Εἶπεν δὲ Ἀνδρέας τῷ Ἰησοῦ· ἄκουσον ἀδελφέ· μὴ νομίσῃς ὅτι κατὰ τυραννίαν οὐ δίδομέν σοι τὸν ναῦλον ἡμῶν, ἀλλ' ἡμεῖς μαθηταί ἐσμεν τοῦ κυρίου ἡμῶν Ἰησοῦ Χριστοῦ [τοῦ ἀγαθοῦ θεοῦ]. ἐξελέξατο γὰρ ἡμᾶς τοὺς δώδεκα,[36] καὶ παρέδωκεν ἡμῖν ἐντολὴν τοιαύτην, λέγων ὅτι πορευόμενοι κηρύσσειν μὴ βαστάζετε ἀργύριον [ἐν τῇ ὁδῷ] μήτε ἄρτον μήτε πήραν μήτε ὑποδήματα μήτε ῥάβδον μήτε δύο χιτῶνας.

----

34. *Gr:* τῇ χώρᾳ τῶν ἀνθρωποφάγων.

35. *AS:* Astigað on þis scip to us, and sellað us eowerne fær-screat.

36. Cf. *M* 1: ἐξελέξατο ἡμᾶς.

"Everyone flees that city," Jesus told him. "How is it you are going there?"

"We have a small task to perform there, and we must finish it," Andrew answered. "But if you *can, do* us the favor of taking us *to <the city Myrmidonia>*[27] *where you too are now going.*"

"If it is so very necessary for you," Jesus answered, "board **this boat and travel with us.**"[28]

6. "Young man," said Andrew, "I want to make something clear to you before we board your boat."

"Say what you want," Jesus said.

"Listen brother: we have no fare to offer you,"[29] Andrew said, "and we have no bread to eat."

"How then can you board if you have no fare for us and no bread to eat?" Jesus asked.

"Listen brother," said Andrew to Jesus, "do not think that we withhold our fare from you as an act of arrogance. We are disciples of our Lord Jesus Christ,[30] *the good God.* He chose us twelve[31] and gave us this command: 'When you go to preach take *on the road* no money, no bread, no packsack, no sandals, no staff, and

----

27. *Gr*: "to the region of the cannibals."

28. *AS*: "Board the ship with us and give us your fare."

29. Cf. Jonah 1:3 (LXX).

30. Cf. Jonah 1:9 (LXX).

31. Cf. *M* 1: "he chose us."

εἰ οὖν ποιεῖς τὴν φιλανθρωπίαν μεθ' ἡμῶν ἀδελφέ, εἰπὲ
ἡμῖν συντόμως· ἢ φανέρωσον ἡμῖν, καὶ πορευθέντες
ζητήσομεν ἑαυτοῖς ἕτερον πλοῖον.

Ἀποκριθεὶς δὲ ὁ Ἰησοῦς εἶπεν τῷ Ἀνδρέᾳ· εἰ αὕτη
ἐστὶν ἡ ἐντολὴ ἣν ἐλάβετε, καὶ τηρεῖτε αὐτήν, ἀνέλθατε
μετὰ πάσης χαρᾶς ἐν τῷ πλοίῳ μου. [ἀληθῶς γὰρ βούλομαι
ὑμᾶς τοὺς μαθητὰς τοῦ λεγομένου Ἰησοῦ ἀνελθεῖν ἐν τῷ
πλοίῳ μου ἢ τοὺς παρέχοντάς μοι χρυσίου καὶ ἀργυρίου·
πάντως γὰρ ἄξιός εἰμι ἵνα ὁ ἀπόστολος τοῦ κυρίου ἀνέλθῃ
ἐν τῷ πλοίῳ μου.]

Ἀποκριθεὶς δὲ ὁ Ἀνδρέας εἶπεν· συγχώρησόν μοι
ἀδελφέ· ὁ κύριος παράσχῃ σοι τὴν δόξαν καὶ τὴν τιμήν.[37]
καὶ ἀνῆλθεν Ἀνδρέας μετὰ τῶν αὐτοῦ μαθητῶν εἰς τὸ
πλοῖον.[38]

7. Καὶ εἰσελθὼν ἐκαθέσθη παρὰ [τὸ ἱστίον τοῦ
πλοίου].[39] καὶ ἀποκριθεὶς ὁ Ἰησοῦς εἶπεν ἑνὶ τῶν
ἀγγέλων· ἀναστὰς κάτελθε εἰς τὴν κοίλην τοῦ πλοίου καὶ
ἀνένεγκε τρεῖς ἄρτους, et appone illos coram omnes
fratres ἵνα φάγωσιν οἱ ἄνδρες, μή ποτε ἄσιτοι ὑπάρχουσιν
ἀπὸ ὁδοῦ μακρᾶς ἐληλυθότες πρὸς ἡμᾶς. [καὶ ἀναστὰς
κατῆλθεν ἐπὶ τὴν κοίλην τοῦ πλοίου καὶ ἀνήνεγκεν τρεῖς
ἄρτους, καθὼς ὁ κύριος αὐτῷ ἐνετείλατο, καὶ παρέθηκεν
αὐτοῖς τοὺς ἄρτους.][40]

Τότε ὁ Ἰησοῦς εἶπεν τῷ Ἀνδρέᾳ· ἀνάστα ἀδελφέ ἅμα
τοῖς ἰδίοις σου· μεταλάβετε ἄρτου τροφῆς, ἵνα ἰσχύσητε
ὑπενεγκεῖν τὸν κλύδωνα τῆς θαλάσσης.

----

37. C adds: et ipse gubernet te semper, tam in mare vel
     ubicumque.

38. GE: ascendensque in eam.

39. Lat: iuxta gubernatorem. P: ἄντικρυς τοῦ κυβερνήτου.

40. Also missing in O.

no change of tunic.'[32] So if you will do us the favor, brother, tell us straightaway. If not, let us know and we will leave to find ourselves another boat."

"If this is the command you received, and if you are carrying it out," Jesus told Andrew, "board my boat joyfully. *Actually, I prefer to bring aboard my boat you disciples of the one called Jesus than those who offer me gold and silver, for I am fully worthy that the apostle of the Lord board my boat.*"

"Brother," responded Andrew, "allow me: May the Lord grant you glory and honor."[33] Andrew and his disciples boarded the boat.[34]

7. After boarding he sat down by *the sail of the boat,*[35] and Jesus said to one of the angels, "Get up and go below to the hold of the boat, bring up three loaves, **and place them before all the brothers**, so that the men may eat in case they are hungry from having come to us after a long trip." *He got up, went below to the hold of the boat,*[36] *and brought up three loaves, just as the Lord had commanded him, and set out the bread for them.*

Then Jesus said to Andrew, "Brother, stand up with those in your party and take bread for nourishment, so that you might be strong enough to endure the turbulence of the sea."

----

32. Cf. Mark 6:8-9, Matt 10:7-10, Luke 9:3, 10:4, and *APe (AV)* 5.

33. *C* adds: "and may he himself pilot you always, on the sea and everywhere."

34. *GE*: "and he boarded it."

35. *Lat*: "by the pilot." *P*: "opposite the pilot."

36. Cf. Jonah 1:5 (LXX).

᾽Αποκριθεὶς <δὲ> ᾽Ανδρέας εἶπεν πρὸς τοὺς μαθητὰς αὐτοῦ· τεκνία μου, μεγάλην φιλανθρωπίαν ηὕραμεν παρὰ τῷ ἀνθρώπῳ τούτῳ. ἀναστάντες οὖν μεταλάβετε ἄρτου τροφῆς, ἵνα ἰσχύσητε ὑπενεγκεῖν τὸν κλύδωνα τῆς θαλάσσης.

Καὶ οὐκ ἠδυνήθησαν οἱ μαθηταὶ αὐτοῦ ἀποκριθῆναι αὐτῷ λόγον· ἐταράχθησαν γὰρ διὰ τὴν θάλασσαν. τότε ὁ ᾽Ιησοῦς ἠνάγκαζεν τὸν ᾽Ανδρέαν ἵνα μεταλάβῃ καὶ αὐτὸς ἄρτου τροφῆς σὺν τοῖς μαθηταῖς αὐτοῦ.

᾽Αποκριθεὶς δὲ ᾽Ανδρέας εἶπεν τῷ ᾽Ιησοῦ, μὴ γινώσκων ὅτι ᾽Ιησοῦς ἐστιν· ἀδελφέ, ὁ κύριος παράσχῃ σοι ἄρτον ἐπουράνιον ἐκ τῆς βασιλείας αὐτοῦ. ἔασον οὖν ἀδελφέ· ὁρᾷς γὰρ τὰ παιδία ὅτι τεταραγμένα εἰσὶν ἔνεκεν τῆς θαλάσσης.

Καὶ ἀποκριθεὶς ὁ ᾽Ιησοῦς εἶπεν τῷ ᾽Ανδρέᾳ· τάχα ἄπειροί εἰσιν οἱ ἀδελφοὶ θαλάσσης· ἀλλ᾽ ἐξέτασον αὐτοὺς εἰ θέλουσιν ἀνελθεῖν ἐπὶ τὴν γῆν καὶ προσμεῖναί σε ἕως ἂν ἐκτελέσῃς τὴν διακονίαν σου καὶ πάλιν ἐπανέλθῃς πρὸς αὐτούς.

Τότε ᾽Ανδρέας εἶπεν τοῖς μαθηταῖς αὐτοῦ. τεκνία μου, εἰ θέλετε ἀνελθεῖν ἐπὶ τὴν γῆν καὶ προσμεῖναί με ἐνταῦθα ἕως ἂν ἐκτελέσω τὴν διακονίαν μου εἰς ἣν ἀπεστάλην;

Καὶ ἀποκριθέντες εἶπον τῷ ᾽Ανδρέᾳ· ἐὰν ἀποστῶμεν ἀπὸ σοῦ, ξένοι γενώμεθα τῶν ἀγαθῶν ὧν παρέσχες ἡμῖν. νῦν οὖν μετὰ σοῦ ἐσμεν ὅπου δἂν πορεύῃ.

8. ᾽Αποκριθεὶς δὲ ὁ ᾽Ιησοῦς εἶπεν τῷ ᾽Ανδρέᾳ· εἰ ἀληθῶς μαθητὴς εἶ τοῦ λεγομένου ᾽Ιησοῦ, λάλησον τοῖς μαθηταῖς σου τὰς δυνάμεις ἃς ἐποίησεν ὁ διδάσκαλός σου, ἵνα χαίρῃ αὐτῶν [ἡ ψυχὴ][41] καὶ ἐπιλάθωνται τὸν φόβον τῆς θαλάσσης· ἰδοὺ γὰρ μέλλομεν ἐ<πα>ναγαγεῖν τὸ πλοῖον ἀπὸ

----

41. *Lat*: corda. *Grm*, including *O*: καρδία.

"My children," Andrew told his disciples, "we have experienced great generosity from this person, so stand up and take bread for nourishment, so that you might be strong enough to endure the turbulence of the sea."

His disciples could not respond to him with as much as a word; they were already seasick. Then Jesus insisted that Andrew and his disciples take bread for nourishment.

"Brother," said Andrew, unaware he was Jesus, "may the Lord grant you heavenly bread from his kingdom. Just leave them alone, brother, for you see that the servants are queasy from the sea."

"Perhaps the brothers have no experience of the sea," Jesus told Andrew. "Ask them if they want to return to land and wait for you until you finish your task and return to them again."

Then Andrew asked his disciples, "My children, do you want to return to land and wait for me there until I finish the task for which I was sent?"

"If we separate from you," they answered Andrew, "we may become strangers to the good things that you provided us. We shall be with you now wherever you go."

8. Jesus said to Andrew, "If you are indeed a disciple of the one called Jesus, tell your disciples the miracles your teacher did so that their *souls*[37] may rejoice and that they may forget the terror of the sea, for we are about to shove the boat off shore." Jesus at

----

37. *Lat* and *Grm*, including *O*: "heart(s)."

τῆς γῆς. [καὶ εὐθὺς εἶπεν ὁ ᾽Ιησοῦς ἑνὶ τῶν ἀγγέλων·
ἀπόλυσον τὸ πλοῖον. καὶ ἀπέλυσεν τὸ πλοῖον ἀπὸ τῆς γῆς.
καὶ ἐλθὼν ὁ ᾽Ιησοῦς ἐκάθισεν παρὰ τὸ πηδάλιον καὶ
διεκυβέρνα τὸ πλοῖον.]⁴²

Τότε ᾽Ανδρέας παρήνει καὶ ἐνίσχυεν τοὺς μαθητὰς
αὐτοῦ λέγων· τεκνία μου οἱ παραδώσαντες τὴν ψυχὴν τῷ
κυρίῳ, μὴ φοβεῖσθε· ὁ γὰρ κύριος οὐ μὴ καταλείψῃ ἡμᾶς
εἰς τοὺς αἰῶνας. ἐν γὰρ τῷ καιρῷ ἐκείνῳ ὅτε ἤμεν σὺν τῷ
κυρίῳ ἡμῶν, ἀνήλθομεν ἐν τῷ πλοίῳ σὺν αὐτῷ, καὶ
ἐκάθευδεν ἐν τῷ πλοίῳ, πειράζων ἡμᾶς· οὐκ ἦν γὰρ
κοιμώμενος. καὶ ἀνέμου μεγάλου γενομένου καὶ τῆς
θαλάσσης κυμαινομένης, ὥστε τὰ κύματα ὑψωθῆναι καὶ
γενέσθαι ὑπὸ τῷ ἱστίῳ τοῦ πλοίου. καὶ ἡμῶν φοβηθέντων
μεγάλως,⁴³ ἀναστὰς ὁ κύριος ἐπετίμησεν τοῖς ἀνέμοις, καὶ
ἐγένετο γαλήνη ἐν τῇ θαλάσσῃ· ἐφοβήθησαν γὰρ αὐτὸν τὰ
πάντα, ὅτι ποιήματα αὐτοῦ εἰσιν. νῦν οὖν τεκνία μου μὴ
φοβεῖσθε· ὁ γὰρ κύριος ᾽Ιησοῦς οὐ μὴ ἐγκαταλίπῃ ἡμᾶς.⁴⁴

Καὶ ταῦτα λέγων ὁ ἅγιος ᾽Ανδρέας ηὔχετο ἐν τῇ
καρδίᾳ αὐτοῦ ὅπως οἱ μαθηταὶ αὐτοῦ ἑλκυσθῶσιν εἰς ὕπνον,
ne amplius expavescerent maris fluctuum.⁴⁵ καὶ εὐχομένου
᾽Ανδρέου εἰς ὕπνον ἐτράπησαν οἱ μαθηταὶ αὐτοῦ.⁴⁶

9. Καὶ ἐπιστραφεὶς ᾽Ανδρέας πρὸς τὸν κύριον, [μὴ
γινώσκων ὅτι ὁ κύριός ἐστιν], εἶπεν αὐτῷ· est aliquid
quod tibi volo dicere.

----

42. This last sentence also is missing in *Arm* and in one
    important Greek ms.

43. *Lat* adds: exclamavimus.

44. *GE*: flantibus ventis congruis, prospere navigavit ad
    urbem.

45. Similarly *Eth*.

46. At this point *AS* has Andrew himself fall asleep and
    does not resume the narrative until chapter 16.

once said to one of the angels, "Cast off the boat," and
he cast the boat off from land. Jesus went and sat at
the rudder and piloted the craft.

Then Andrew encouraged and strengthened his
disciples saying, "My children, you who have handed over
your souls to the Lord, do not be afraid, for the Lord
will never abandon us. At that time when we were with
our Lord, we boarded the boat with him, and he lay
silently on board in order to test us; he was not really
sleeping. A great wind arose, and the sea swelled such
that the waves broke over the sail of the boat. Because
we were terrified,[38] the Lord stood up and rebuked the
winds, and calm returned to the sea.[39] All things fear
him, because they are his creations. So now, my
children, do not be afraid, for the Lord Jesus will
never abandon us."

As the holy Andrew said this, he prayed in his
heart that his disciples would be drawn off to sleep **and
no longer be terrified by the tempest.** As Andrew prayed,
his disciples fell asleep.

9. Andrew turned to the Lord, *still not knowing it
was the Lord,* and said to him, **"There is something I
would like to say to you."**

----

38. *Lat* adds: "we cried out."

39. Cf. Mark 4:35-41, Matt 8:23-27, and Luke 8:22-25.

Et dominus ad eum, dic quod vis.

Λέγε μοι ὦ ἄνθρωπε καὶ ὑπόδειξόν μοι τὴν τέχνην τῆς κυβερνήσεώς σου, quoniam a quo hic intravi, et usque in hanc horam semper te, et tuam gubernationem contemplavi, et miratus sum, ὅτι οὐδένα εἶδον ἄνθρωπόν ποτε κυβερνῶντα οὕτως ἐν τῇ θαλάσσῃ, ὥσπερ νῦν σὲ ὁρῶ. ἑξκαιδέκατον γὰρ ἔπλευσα τὴν θάλασσαν, καὶ ἰδοὺ τοῦτο ἑπτακαιδέκατον, καὶ οὐκ εἶδον τοιαύτην τέχνην· ἀληθῶς γὰρ οὕτως ἐστὶν τὸ πλοῖον ὡς ἐπὶ τῆς γῆς. ὑπόδειξον οὖν μοι νεανίσκε τὴν σὴν τέχνην, quia valde cupio discere eam.

Τότε ἀποκριθεὶς ὁ Ἰησοῦς εἶπεν τῷ Ἀνδρέᾳ· καὶ ἡμεῖς πολλάκις ἐπλεύσαμεν τὴν θάλασσαν καὶ ἐκινδυνεύσαμεν· ἀλλ᾽ ἐπειδὴ σὺ μαθητὴς εἶ τοῦ λεγομένου Ἰησοῦ, ἐπέγνω σε ἡ θάλασσα ὅτι δίκαιος εἶ, καὶ ἡσύχασεν καὶ οὐκ ἐπῆρεν τὰ κύματα αὐτῆς ἐπὶ τὸ πλοῖον.

Τότε Ἀνδρέας ἔκραξεν φωνῇ μεγάλῃ λέγων· εὐλογή<σω> σε κύριέ μου Ἰησοῦ Χριστέ, ὅτι συνήντησα ἀνδρὶ [δοξάζοντι τὸ ὄνομά σου].[47]

10. Καὶ ἀποκριθεὶς ὁ Ἰησοῦς εἶπεν τῷ Ἀνδρέᾳ· εἰπέ μοι μαθητὰ τοῦ λεγομένου Ἰησοῦ, διὰ τί οἱ ἄπιστοι Ἰουδαῖοι οὐκ ἐπίστευσαν αὐτῷ, λέγοντες ὅτι οὐκ ἔστιν θεὸς ἀλλ᾽ ἄνθρωπος; Quomodo potuit homo virtutes dei et magna eius mirabilia facere? φανέρωσόν μοι μαθητὰ τοῦ λεγομένου Ἰησοῦ· ἠκούσαμεν γὰρ ὅτι ἐφανέρωσεν τὴν θεότητα αὐτοῦ τοῖς μαθηταῖς αὐτοῦ.

----

47. At this point P contains a long discourse largely
    drawn from the Gospels but which at places resonates
    the the distinctive theology of the martyrdom of
    Andrew. I include here only one such passage, which
    contains ἐπείγω, frequent and semiotically laden at
    the end of the Acts of Andrew. Jesus tells Andrew:
    ἀληθῶς μακάριος εἶ· σὺ λέγε<ι> τὰ τοῦ Ἰησοῦ· καὶ ἐν
    αὐτῇ τῇ διηγήσει τὸ πλείονα ὄκνος ἐπ<ε>ιχθήσεται
    οὐρανίῳ πνεύματι (118v).

"Say what you wish," the Lord told him.

"Sir, show me your sailing technique, **because from the moment I boarded until now I have constantly observed your piloting and I am astounded.** I have never seen anyone sail the sea as now I see you doing. I sailed the seas sixteen times;[40] this is my seventeenth, and I have never seen such skill. The ship actually responds as though it were on land. So, young man, show me your technique, **for I eagerly desire to learn it**".

"We too have often sailed the sea and been in danger," Jesus told Andrew, "but because you are a disciple of the one called Jesus, the sea knew that you were righteous and so it was still and did not lift its waves against the boat."

Then Andrew cried out in a loud voice, "I bless you, my Lord Jesus Christ, that I have met a man who *glorifies your name.*"

10. "Tell me, disciple of the one called Jesus," Jesus asked Andrew, "why did the faithless Jews not believe in him and say that he was not God but a human? **How could a human do the miracles of God and his great wonders?** Make it clear to me, disciple of the one called Jesus, for we heard that he revealed his divinity to his disciples."

----

40. Or: "sixteen years."

Καὶ ἀποκριθεὶς Ἀνδρέας εἶπεν· ἀληθῶς ἀδελφὲ ἐφανέρωσεν ἡμῖν ὅτι θεός ἐστιν. μὴ οὖν νομίσῃς ὅτι ἄνθρωπός
ἐστιν· αὐτὸς γὰρ ἐποίησεν τὸν ἄνθρωπον.[48]

Καὶ ἀποκριθεὶς ὁ Ἰησοῦς εἶπεν· πῶς οὖν οὐκ
ἐπίστευσαν αὐτῷ οἱ Ἰουδαῖοι; τάχα οὐκ ἐποίησεν σημεῖα
ἐνώπιον αὐτῶν.

Καὶ ἀποκριθεὶς Ἀνδρέας εἶπεν· οὐκ ἤκουσας τὰς
δυνάμεις ἃς ἐποίησεν ἐνώπιον αὐτῶν; τυφλοὺς ἐποίησεν
ἀναβλέψαι, χωλοὺς περιπατῆσαι, κωφοὺς ἀκοῦσαι, λεπροὺς
ἐκαθ<ά>ρισεν, ὕδωρ εἰς οἶνον μετέβαλεν, καὶ λαβὼν πέντε
ἄρτους καὶ δύο ἰχθύας ἐποίησεν ὄχλον ἀνακλιθῆναι ἐν
χόρτῳ, καὶ εὐλογήσας ἔδωκεν αὐτοῖς φαγεῖν· ἦσαν δὲ οἱ
ἐσθίοντες πεντακισχίλιοι ἄνδρες καὶ ἐχορτάσθησαν· καὶ
ἦραν τὰ περισσεύοντα αὐτοῖς δώδεκα κοφίνους κλασμάτων.
καὶ μετὰ ταῦτα <π>άντα οὐκ ἐπίστευσαν αὐτῷ.[49]

Καὶ ἀποκριθεὶς ὁ Ἰησοῦς εἶπεν τῷ Ἀνδρέᾳ· τάχα
ταῦτα τὰ σημεῖα ἐποίησεν ἐνώπιον τοῦ λαοῦ καὶ οὐχὶ
ἐνώπιον τῶν ἀρχιερέων, καὶ διὰ τοῦτο [οὐκ ἐπίστευσαν]
αὐτῷ.[50]

----

48. *Grm*: οὐρανὸν καὶ τὴν γῆν καὶ τὴν θάλασσαν καὶ πάντα
τὰ <ἐν> αὐτοῖς.

49. From here until end of chapter 15 the text is absent
in *AS*, *O*, and *Syr*, and *Eth*, *B*, and *Arm* provide
abbrevated versions, omitting every reference to the
sphinx that spoke. *GE*, *N*, *E*, *L*, and the apocryphal
Acts that seem to have known a more primitive
version of *AAM* likewise do not witness to this
section. Insofar as these chapters tell of a sphinx
forecasting the transformation of temples into
churches, they probably were not composed prior to
the fifth century and thus could not have appeared
in *The Acts of Andrew*.

50. *C*: ideo insurresserunt in eum. *B*: non receperunt
eum.

"Brother," Andrew answered, "he did indeed reveal to us that he is God, so do not suppose he is a human, for he himself created human beings."[41]

"Why then did the Jews not believe?" Jesus asked. "Perhaps he performed no signs before them."

"Have you not heard about the miracles he performed before them?" answered Andrew. "He made the blind see, the lame walk, the deaf hear, he cleansed lepers and changed water into wine.[42] He took five loaves and two fish, made a crowd recline on grass, and after blessing the food gave it to them to eat. Those who ate were five thousand men and they were filled. They took up their excess: twelve baskets of leftovers.[43] And even after all these miracles they did not believe in him."

"Perhaps he did these signs before the people and not before the high priests," Jesus told Andrew, "and for this reason they *did not believe in him*."[44]

----

41. *Grm*: for he himself created "the heaven and the earth and the sea and everything <in> them."

42. Cf. Matt 11:5, Luke 7:22, and John 2:1-12.

43. Cf. Mark 6:32-44, Matt 14:13-21, and Luke 9:10b-17.

44. *C*: "for this reason they rose up against him." *B*: "did not accept him."

11. Καὶ ἀποκριθεὶς 'Ανδρέας εἶπεν· ναὶ ἀδελφέ, ἐποίησεν καὶ ἐνώπιον τῶν ἀρχιερέων, οὐ μόνον ἐν φανερῷ ἀλλὰ καὶ ἐν κρυπτῷ, καὶ οὐκ ἐπίστευσαν αὐτῷ.

'Αποκριθεὶς δὲ ὁ 'Ιησοῦς εἶπεν· ποῖαί εἰσιν αἱ δυνάμεις ἃς ἐποίησεν ἐν τῷ κρυπτῷ; φανέρωσόν μοι αὐτάς.

Καὶ ἀποκριθεὶς 'Ανδρέας εἶπεν· ὦ ἄνθρωπε, ὁ ἔχων τὸ πνεῦμα τῆς ἐπερωτήσεως, τί με ἐκπειράζεις;

Καὶ ἀποκριθεὶς ὁ 'Ιησοῦς εἶπεν· οὐκ ἐκπειράζω σε [ταῦτα λέγων σοι μαθητὰ τοῦ λεγομένου 'Ιησοῦ], ἀλλὰ χαίρει ἡ ψυχή μου καὶ ἀγάλλεται,[51] οὐ μόνον δὲ ἡ ἐμὴ ἀλλὰ καὶ πᾶσα ψυχὴ ἡ ἀκούουσα τὰ θαυμάσια αὐτοῦ.

Καὶ ἀποκριθεὶς 'Ανδρέας εἶπεν· ὦ τέκνον, ὁ κύριος πληρώσει σου [τὴν ψυχὴν][52] πάσης χαρᾶς [καὶ παντὸς ἀγαθοῦ] καθὼς ᾔτησάς μοι νῦν ἀπαγγ<εῖλαί> σοι τὰ σημεῖα ἃ ἐποίησεν ὁ κύριος ἡμῶν ἐν τῷ κρυπτῷ.[53] **(12.)** ἐγένετο πορευομένων ἡμῶν τῶν δώδεκα μαθητῶν [μετὰ τοῦ κυρίου ἡμῶν εἰς ἱερὸν τῶν ἐθνῶν, ἵνα γνωρίσῃ ἡμῖν τὴν ἄγνοιαν τοῦ διαβόλου],[54] καὶ θεασάμενοι ἡμᾶς οἱ ἀρχιερεῖς ἀκολουθοῦντας τῷ 'Ιησοῦ εἶπον ἡμῖν· ὦ ταλαίπωροι, πῶς περιπατεῖτε μετὰ τοῦ λέγοντος ὅτι υἱός εἰμι τοῦ θεοῦ; μὴ ἔχει υἱὸν ὁ θεός; τίς ἐξ ὑμῶν εἶδεν τὸν θεὸν ὁμιλήσαντα γυναικὶ πώποτε; μὴ οὐχ οὗτός ἐστιν ὁ υἱὸς 'Ιωσὴφ τοῦ τέκτονος καὶ ἡ μήτηρ αὐτοῦ Μαριὰμ καὶ οἱ ἀδελφοὶ αὐτοῦ 'Ιάκωβος καὶ Σίμων;

----

51. *Lat* adds: spiritus meus.

52. *Lat*: cor.

53. *Lat* adds: in conspectu eorum.

54. *Lat*: illo, in quo palam fecerunt nobis idolas suas.

11. "Yes, brother," answered Andrew, "he did them also before the high priests, not only publicly but also privately, and they did not believe in him."

"What kind of miracles did he do privately?" Jesus asked. "Disclose them to me."

"O you with an inquisitive spirit," Andrew said, "why do you test me?"

Jesus said, *"By saying these things to you, disciple of the one called Jesus,* I am not testing you, but my soul rejoices and[45] exults--and not only mine, but every soul that hears of his wonders."

"O child," Andrew said, "the Lord will fill your *soul*[46] with all joy *and every good thing,* since you asked me now to tell you the signs which our Lord did privately.[47] **(12.)** When we twelve disciples went with *our Lord into the temple of the gentiles in order for him to make us recognize the devil's ignorance,*[48] because the high priests saw us following Jesus they told us, 'O you wretches, how can you walk with the one who says, "I am the son of God"? God does not have a son, does he? Who of you has ever seen God consorting with a woman? Is he not the son of Joseph the carpenter? Is his mother not Mary, and are not his brothers James and Simon?'[49]

----

45. *Lat* adds: "my spirit."

46. *Lat*: "heart."

47. *Lat* adds: "in their presence."

48. Instead of the words in italics *Lat* reads: "with him, where they made their idols public to us."

49. Cf. Matt 13:55.

Ἡμεῖς δὲ ἀκούσαντες, [μετεστράφησαν αἱ καρδίαι ἡμῶν εἰς ἀσθένειαν. γνοὺς δὲ ὁ Ἰησοῦς ὅτι ἐξέκλιναν αἱ καρδίαι ἡμῶν],[55] παραλαβὼν ἡμᾶς εἰς ἔρημον τόπον ἐποίησεν μεγάλα σημεῖα ἐνώπιον ἡμῶν καὶ ὑπέδειξεν ἡμῖν τὴν θεότητα αὐτοῦ πᾶσαν. [ἡμεῖς δὲ εἴπαμεν τοῖς ἀρχιερεῦσιν λέγοντες ὅτι ἔλθατε καὶ ὑμεῖς καὶ θεάσασθε· ἰδοὺ γὰρ ἡμᾶς ἔπεισεν.][56]

13. Καὶ ἐλθόντες οἱ ἀρχιερεῖς σὺν ἡμῖν καὶ εἰσελθόντες εἰς τὸ ἱερὸν τῶν ἐθνῶν, ὑπέδειξεν ἡμῖν ὁ Ἰησοῦς τὸν τύπον τοῦ οὐρανοῦ, ἵνα γνῶμεν si ἀληθῆ ἐστιν ἢ οὔ. καὶ εἰσῆλθον μεθ' ἡμῶν τριάκοντα ἄνδρες τοῦ λαοῦ καὶ τέσσαρες ἀρχιερεῖς. καὶ θεασάμενος ὁ Ἰησοῦς [ἐκ δεξιῶν καὶ ἐξ εὐωνύμων τοῦ ναοῦ] εἶδεν γλυ<πτ>ὰς σφίγγας marmoreas δύο in similitudinem quasi cherubim, quas colebant et adorabant sacerdotes idolorum, μίαν ἐκ δεξιῶν καὶ μίαν ἐξ εὐωνύμων. καὶ στραφεὶς ὁ Ἰησοῦς πρὸς ἡμᾶς εἶπεν· θεωρήσατε τὸν τύπον τοῦ οὐρανοῦ· ταῦτα γὰρ ὅμοιά εἰσιν τοῦ χερουβὶμ καὶ τοῦ σεραφὶμ τῶν ἐν οὐρανῷ. τότε ὁ Ἰησοῦς ἐμβλέψας τῇ ἐκ δεξιῶν οὔσῃ σφιγγὶ parte ipsius templi εἶπεν αὐτῇ· σοὶ λέγω τῷ ἐκτυπώματι [τ<οῦ>[57] ἐν τῷ οὐρανῷ], ὃ ἔγλυψαν τεχνιτῶν χεῖρες,

---

55. *Lat* shows that some scribe or translator was scandalized that the apostles would weaken:: Nos autem audientes hec verba incredulitatis, nichil eorum respondentibus, sed cor nostrum perseveravit in verbo veritatis eius.

56. *Lat* does not have this invitation to the high priests because the high priests had already followed Jesus and the disciples into the desert to witness Jesus' miracles. The next three chapters display an unusually favorable attitude toward idols. *Lat* repeatedly differs from *Gr* in order to make the section less iconodoulic. Because these variants in *Lat* clearly are secondary, they are not recorded here.

57. *Gr*: τῷ.

"When we heard these words, *our hearts turned weak. But Jesus, knowing that our hearts were giving way,*[50] took us to a desolate place, performed great signs before us, and demonstrated all of his divinity for us. *And we said to the high priests, 'You come too and see, for he has persuaded us.'*

13. "When the high priests went with us and entered into the temple of the gentiles, Jesus showed us the form of heaven, so that we should know **whether** it was real or not. Thirty men of the people and four high priests entered with us. Looking *to the right and left of the sanctuary,* Jesus saw two sculpted **marble** sphinxes **in the likeness of cherubim, which the priests of the idols worship and adore,** one on the right and one on the left. Jesus turned to us and said, 'Behold the replica of heaven, for these are similar to the cherubim and seraphim in heaven.' Then Jesus looked at the sphinx on the right **side of the temple** and said to it, 'I tell you, O model *<of that which> is in heaven,* which the hands of artists sculpted, be loosened from your place, come down,[51] answer, disgrace the high priests, *and prove to them* that I am God and not a human.'

----

50. *Lat*: "When we heard these words of unbelief, we said nothing to them, and our hearts continued in the word of his truth."

51. *Lat* adds: "for the Lord will give you a mouth to speak."

ἀποκολλήθητι ἐκ τοῦ τόπου σου καὶ ἐλθὲ κάτω,[58] καὶ
ἀποκρίθητι καὶ ἔλεγξον τοὺς ἀρχιερεῖς [καὶ ὑπόδειξον
αὐτοῖς] εἰ ἐγὼ θεός εἰμι ἢ ἄνθρωπος.

14. Καὶ εὐθὺς ἀνεπήδησεν de loco suo τῇ ὥρᾳ ἐκείνῃ
ἡ σφὶγξ καὶ ἀναλαβοῦσα [ἀνθρωπίνην][59] φωνὴν εἶπεν· ὦ
μωροὶ υἱοὶ ['Ισραήλ], οἷς οὐκ ἠρκέσθη μόνον ἡ τύφλωσις
τῆς καρδίας αὐτῶν, ἀλλὰ καὶ ἑτέρους θέλουσιν τυφλῶσαι ὡς
[καὶ αὐτοί],[60] λέγοντες τὸν θεὸν εἶναι ἄνθρωπον· [οὗτός
ἐστιν ὁ ἐξ ἀρχῆς τὸν ἄνθρωπον πλάσας καὶ δοὺς τὴν πνοὴν
αὐτοῦ ἐν πᾶσιν, ὁ κινήσας πάντα τὰ ἀκίνητα·][61] οὗτός
ἐστιν ὁ καλέσας τὸν 'Αβραάμ, ὁ ἀγαπήσας τὸν υἱὸν αὐτοῦ
'Ισαάκ, ὁ ἐπιστρέψας [τὸν ἀγαπητὸν αὐτοῦ] 'Ιακὼβ εἰς τὴν
γῆν αὐτοῦ, et apparuit ei in eremo, fecitque ei multa
bona. Hic est qui eduxit et didit eis aqua de petra
fluenti. [οὗτός ἐστιν ὁ κριτὴς ζώντων καὶ νεκρῶν], οὗτός
ἐστιν ὁ ἑτοιμάζων [μεγάλα ἀγαθὰ τοῖς ὑπακούουσιν αὐτῷ
καὶ ἑτοιμάζων κόλασιν τοῖς μὴ πιστεύουσιν αὐτῷ].[62] μὴ
πρόσσχητέ μοι ὅτι ἐγώ εἰμι [ψήφινον εἴδωλον· λέγω γὰρ
ὑμῖν ὅτι καλλίονά εἰσιν τὰ ἱερὰ τῆς συναγωγῆς ὑμῶν].
ἡμεῖς γὰρ ὄντες λίθοι, ὄνομα μόνον ἔδωκαν ἡμῖν οἱ ἱερεῖς
ὅτι θεός, καὶ αὐτοὶ οἱ ἱερεῖς οἱ λειτουργοῦντες τῷ ἱερῷ
καθαρίζουσιν ἑαυτοὺς φοβούμενοι τοὺς δαίμονας· ἐὰν γὰρ
συνέλθωσιν γυναιξίν, καθαρίζουσιν ἑαυτοὺς ἡμέρας ἑπτὰ
διὰ τὸν φόβον τοῦ μὴ εἰσελθεῖν αὐτοὺς εἰς τὸ ἱερὸν δι'
ἡμᾶς, διὰ τὸ ὄνομα ὃ ἔδωκαν ἡμῖν ὅτι θεός. ὑμεῖς δὲ ἐὰν

----

58. *Lat* adds: dabitur enim tibi a domino os ad
    loquendum.

59. *Lat*: magna.

60. *Lat*: et nos sumus.

61. *Lat*: ipse enim deus est qui fecit celum et terram,
    et hominem ad imaginem et similitudinem suam, seu et
    omnia fundamenta terre.

62. *Lat*: ipse est ergo, qui preparavit iudicium et
    ornamenta, et non crediderunt in eum.

14. "And immediately, that very hour, the sphinx leaped up **from its place**, acquired a *human*[52] voice, and said, 'O foolish sons of *Israel*, the blindness of their own hearts is not enough for them, but they want to make others as well blind *like themselves*[53] by saying God is a human. *He it is who from the beginning formed the human and gave his breath to everything, who moves everything immovable.*[54] He it is who called Abraham, who loved his son Isaac, who returned *his beloved* Jacob to his land, **appeared to him in the desert, and made for him many good things. He it is who led them out and gave them water from the gushing rock.** *He is the judge of the living and the dead.* He it is who prepares *marvelous things for those who obey him, and prepares punishment for those who do not believe in him.*[55] Do not suppose that I am merely *a marble idol, for I tell you that the temples are more beautiful than your synagogue.* Although we are stones, the priests gave us alone the name god, and the priests themselves who conduct worship in the temple purify themselves for fear of the demons. If they have sex with women, they purify themselves seven days for fear they cannot enter into the temple because of us, because of the name they gave us: "god." But when you fornicate, you take the law of God, go into God's synagogue, sit, read, and do not reverence the glorious

----

52. *Lat:* "great."

53. *Lat:* "like us," i.e., like us blind idols.

54. *Lat:* "For he is the God who made heaven and earth, the human in his image and likeness, and all the foundations of the earth."

55. *Lat:* "Therefore it is he who has prepared judgment and honors, yet they did not believe in him."

πορνεύσητε αἴρετε τὸν νόμον τοῦ θεοῦ καὶ εἰσέρχεσθε εἰς
τὴν συναγωγὴν τοῦ θεοῦ καὶ καθίζετε καὶ ἀναγινώσκετε καὶ
οὐκ εὐλαβεῖσθε τοὺς λόγους τοὺς ἐνδόξους τοῦ θεοῦ. διὰ
τοῦτο λέγω ὑμῖν ὅτι τὰ ἱερὰ καταργήσουσιν τὰς συναγωγὰς
ὑμῶν, ὡς καὶ γενέσθαι ἐκκλησίας τοῦ μονογενοῦς υἱοῦ
αὐτοῦ. [Ταῦτα εἰπούσης τῆς σφιγγὸς ἐσιώπησεν.

15.[63] καὶ ἡμεῖς εἴπαμεν τοῖς ἀρχιερεῦσιν ὅτι· ἄξιοί
εἰσιν πιστευθῆναι, ὅτι τὴν ἀλήθειαν εἶπαν ὑμῖν καὶ οἱ
λίθοι, καὶ κατῄσχυναν ὑμᾶς.

Καὶ ἀποκριθέντες οἱ ἀρχιερεῖς τῶν Ἰουδαίων εἶπον]·
θεωρήσατε καὶ μάθετε ὅτι ὁ λίθος οὗτος ἐν μαγείᾳ λαλεῖ·
[μὴ νομίσητε ὅτι θεός ἐστιν. εἰ γὰρ ἐδοκιμάσατε ὅ τι
ἐλάλησεν ὑμῖν, ἐγινώσκετε ἄν· ἠκούσατε γὰρ τοῦ λίθου
λέγοντος ὅτι οὗτός ἐστιν ὁ λαλήσας μετὰ τοῦ Ἀβραάμ.
οὗτος ποῦ εὗρεν τὸν Ἀβραὰμ ἢ εἶδεν αὐτόν; ἔ<π>ει[64] γὰρ
Ἀβραὰμ τελευτήσας ἔτη οὐκ ὀλίγα <πρὶν> οὗτος ἐγεννήθη,
καὶ ποῦ οὗτος ἐπίσταται τὸν Ἀβραάμ;

Καὶ ἐπιστρέψας πάλιν ὁ Ἰησοῦς πρὸς τὴν σφίγγα
εἶπεν αὐτῇ· διὰ τί οὗτοι ἀπιστοῦσιν ὅτι ἐλάλησα μετὰ τοῦ
Ἀβραάμ;] ἀλλὰ ἄπελθε καὶ πορεύθητι εἰς τὴν γῆν τῶν
Χαναναίων καὶ ἄπελθε εἰς τὸ σπήλαιον τὸ διπλοῦν εἰς τὸν
ἀγρὸν Μαμβρῆ, ὅπου ἐστὶν τὸ σῶμα τοῦ Ἀβραάμ, καὶ
φώνησον ἔξω τοῦ μνημείου λέγουσα· Ἀβραάμ, Ἀβραάμ, οὗ
τὸ σῶμα ἐν τῷ μνημείῳ, ἡ δὲ ψυχὴ ἐν τῷ παραδείσῳ, τάδε
λέγει ὁ πλάσας τὸν ἄνθρωπον ἀπ' ἀρχῆς, ὁ ποιήσας σε
φίλον ἑαυτοῦ· ἀνάστηθι ἅμα τῷ υἱῷ σου Ἰσαὰκ καὶ Ἰακώβ,

----

63. *C* contains only the last three sentences of this
chapter, presumably because of the fabulosity of the
narrative ommitted. However, *A* contains its own
poetic version of the missing section thereby
proving its presence in some earlier Latin version.
By necessity, the text printed here is based almost
exclusively on *Gr*.

64. Bonnet's text reads: ἔχει.

words of God. Therefore, I tell you that the temples will abolish your synagogues, so that they even become churches of the unique son of God.' *Having said this, the sphinx was silent.*

15. *"'The sphinx's speech is trustworthy,' we told the high priests, 'because even the stones tell you the truth and put you to shame.'*[56]

"The high priests of the Jews answered, 'Observe and learn that this stone speaks through magic. You must not suppose that he is a god. Had you tested what the sphinx said to you, you would have known this, for you heard the stone claim that this is the one who spoke with Abraham. Where did he find Abraham or see him? Since Abraham died not a few years <before> this person was born, how did he know Abraham?'[57]

"Again Jesus turned to the sphinx and said to it, 'Why do these people not believe that I spoke with Abraham? Go and enter the land of the Canaanites, go to the double cave in the field of Mambre where lies the body of Abraham,[58] and outside the tomb call, "Abraham, Abraham, you whose body is in the cave, but whose soul is in paradise, thus says the one who molded human beings at the beginning, the one who made you his own friend: 'Arise with your son Isaac and Jacob, and go into the temples of the Jebusites in order that we might refute the high priests, that they may know that I knew you and you me.'"'

----

56. Cf. Matt 3:9 and Luke 3:8.

57. Cf. John 8:56-58.

58. Cf. Gen 23:9 and 17.

καὶ ἔλθατε εἰς τὰ ἱερὰ τῶν Ἰεβουσαίων, ἵνα ἐλέγξωμεν
τοὺς ἀρχιερεῖς, ὅπως γνῶσιν ὅτι ἐπίσταμαι σὲ καὶ σὺ ἐμέ.

Καὶ ὡς ἤκουσεν τοὺς λόγους τούτους ἡ σφὶγξ εὐθὺς
περιεπάτησεν ἔμπροσθεν πάντων ἡμῶν καὶ ἐπορεύθη εἰς τὴν
γῆν τῶν Χαναναίων εἰς τὸν ἀγρὸν Μαμβρῆ, καὶ ἐφώνησεν ἔξω
τοῦ μνημείου καθὼς ἐνετείλατο αὐτῇ ὁ Ἰησοῦς. καὶ εὐθὺς
ἐξῆλθον οἱ δώδεκα πατριάρχαι ζῶντες ἐκ τοῦ μνημείου, καὶ
ἀποκριθέντες εἶπαν πρὸς αὐτήν· ἐπὶ τίνα ἡμῶν ἀπεστάλης;

Καὶ ἀποκριθεῖσα ἡ σφὶγξ εἶπεν· ἀπεστάλην ἐπὶ τοὺς
τρεῖς πατριάρχας εἰς μαρτύριον· ὑμεῖς δὲ εἰσέλθατε καὶ
ἀναπαύεσθε ἕως τοῦ καιροῦ τῆς ἀναστάσεως.

Καὶ ἀκούσαντες εἰσῆλθον ἐν τῷ μνημείῳ καὶ ἐκοιμή-
θησαν. καὶ ἐπορεύθησαν οἱ τρεῖς πατριάρχαι ἅμα τῇ σφιγγὶ
καὶ ἦλθον πρὸς τὸν Ἰησοῦν καὶ ἤλεγξαν τοὺς ἀρχιερεῖς.
τότε ὁ Ἰησοῦς εἶπεν τοῖς πατριάρχαις· ἀπέλθατε εἰς τοὺς
τόπους ὑμῶν· καὶ εὐθέως ἀπῆλθον.

Καὶ ἐπιστραφεὶς ὁ Ἰησοῦς εἶπεν πρὸς τὴν σφίγγα·
ἄνελθε εἰς τὸν τόπον σου. καὶ εὐθέως ἀνῆλθεν καὶ ἔστη
εἰς τὸν τόπον αὐτῆς. [καὶ ταῦτα θεασάμενοι]65 οἱ
ἀρχιερεῖς οὐκ ἐπίστευσαν αὐτῷ. καὶ ἄλλα πολλὰ [μυστήρια
ὑπέδειξεν ἡμῖν, ἅπερ ἐὰν διηγήσωμαί σοι ἀδελφὲ]66 οὐ
δυνήσῃ αὐτὰ ὑπενεγκεῖν.

Καὶ ἀποκριθεὶς ὁ Ἰησοῦς εἶπεν αὐτῷ· [δύναμαι
ὑπενεγκεῖν]· φρόνιμος γὰρ ἀκούων λόγους [χρηστοὺς
εὐφραίνεται τῇ καρδίᾳ]· διεστραμμένοις δὲ [ὁμιλῶν οὐ μὴ
πείσῃς τὴν ψυχὴν αὐτῶν ἕως θανάτου.67

----

65. Lat: lex omnia que facta fuerant viderunt, et
cognoverunt.

66. Lat: etiam quod et si vultis illa audire nescio.

67. Lat: sicut qui petram in puteum mittit. P contains
more narrative, including a retelling of Peter's
attempt to walk on water and Andrew's visit to Tyre

"When it heard these words, immediately the sphinx walked before us all, went into the land of the Canaanites, to the field of Mambre, and called outside the tomb, just as Jesus had commanded it. At once the twelve patriarchs came out of the tomb alive and said to it, 'To which of us were you sent?'

"'I was sent to the three patriarchs for evidence,' the sphinx answered. 'But as for you, go and rest until the time of resurrection.'

"Hearing this, they went into the tomb and slept. The three patriarchs went with the sphinx, came to Jesus, and refuted the high priests. Then Jesus said to the patriarchs, 'Go to your places.' They left at once.

"Jesus turned to the sphinx and said, 'Go up to your place,' and immediately it arose and stood at its place. Even though the high priests *saw these things,*[59] they did not believe in him. He showed us many other *mysteries, which, should I narrate to you, brother,* you would not be able to endure them."[60]

"*I can endure them,*" Jesus told him, "for when the prudent hear *useful* words, *their hearts rejoice. But when speaking* with the perverted, *you never--not until death--persuade their souls.*"[61]

----

59. *Lat:* "saw and recognized every law that they had made."

60. *Lat:* "even if you wanted to, I do not know if you could hear them."

61. *Lat:* "it is like someone who throws a pebble in a well."

16. Τότε γνοὺς ὁ Ἰησοῦς ὅτι ἔμελλεν τὸ πλοῖον ἐγγίζειν ἐπὶ τὴν γῆν],[68] ὑπέκλινεν τὴν κεφαλὴν αὐτοῦ εἰς ἕνα τῶν ἀγγέλων αὐτοῦ [καὶ ἡσύχασεν καὶ ἐπαύσατο λαλῶν τῷ Ἀνδρέᾳ].[69] καὶ θεασάμενος ὁ Ἀνδρέας ἔκλινεν καὶ αὐτὸς τὴν κεφαλὴν αὐτοῦ εἰς ἕνα τῶν μαθητῶν αὐτοῦ καὶ ἀφύπνωσεν.

Ὁ οὖν Ἰησοῦς γνοὺς ὅτι ἀφύπνωσεν ὁ Ἀνδρέας εἶπεν τοῖς ἀγγέλοις αὐτοῦ· [ὑποστ<ο>ρ<έ>σατε τὰς χεῖρας ὑμῶν καὶ] διαβαστάσατε τὸν Ἀνδρέαν καὶ τοὺς μαθητὰς αὐτοῦ, καὶ [πορευθέντες] θέτε αὐτοὺς ἔξω τῆς πύλης τῆς πόλεως <Μυρμιδονίας>,[70] καὶ θέντες αὐτοὺς ἐπὶ τῆς γῆς ὑποστρέψατε πρός με.

Καὶ ἐποίησαν οἱ ἄγγελοι καθὼς ἐνετείλατο αὐτοῖς ὁ Ἰησοῦς, καὶ διαβαστάσαντες τὸν Ἀνδρέαν [καὶ τοὺς μαθητὰς αὐτοῦ] καθεύδοντας, καὶ ἐπιθέντες αὐτοὺς εἰς ἀέρα ἀπήγαγον αὐτοὺς ἔξω [τῆς πύλης τῆς πόλεως τῶν <Μυρμιδόνων>·[71] καὶ ἀποθέμενοι αὐτοὺς ὑπέστρεψαν οἱ ἄγγελοι πρὸς τὸν Ἰησοῦν· καὶ μετὰ ταῦτα] ἀνῆλθεν ὁ Ἰησοῦς εἰς τοὺς οὐρανοὺς μετὰ τῶν ἀγγέλων αὐτοῦ.

17. Πρωΐας δὲ γενομένης διυπνισθεὶς ὁ Ἀνδρέας καὶ ἀναβλέψας [εὖρεν ἑαυτὸν ἐπὶ τὴν γῆν] καθεζόμενον, [καὶ θεασάμενος] εἶδεν τὴν πύλην τῆς πόλεως <Μυρμιδονίας>·[72] [καὶ περιβλεψάμενος] εἶδεν τοὺς μαθητὰς αὐτοῦ καθεύδοντας ἐπὶ τὴν γῆν, καὶ διύπνισεν αὐτοὺς λέγων·

----

where he raises a corpse that had washed up on shore. Cf. *GE* 24.

68. *Lat*: cum hoc dominus diceret.

69. *Lat*: quasi obdormiente capud suum posuit.

70. *Lat*: Mermedonie. *Gr*: τῶν ἀνθρωποφάγων.

71. *Gr*: ἀνθρωποφάγων.

72. *Lat*: Mermedonia. *Gr*: ἐκείνης.

16. *When Jesus knew that the boat was nearing land,*[62] he laid his head on one of his angels, *was still, and stopped speaking with Andrew.*[63] Seeing this, Andrew too lay his head on one of his disciples and fell asleep.

Jesus knew that Andrew was asleep and said to his angels, *"Spread out your hands,* lift up Andrew and his disciples, *leave,* and place them outside the gate of the city **Myrmidonia.**[64] Once you have set them on the ground, return to me."

The angels did as Jesus commanded them: they lifted Andrew *and his* sleeping *disciples,* raised them aloft, and brought them outside *the gate of the city of the <Myrmidons>.*[65] *After putting them down, the angels returned to Jesus, and then* Jesus and his angels ascended into heaven.

17. Early in the morning Andrew woke, looked up, *and found himself* sitting *on the ground. When he looked,* he saw the gate of the city **Myrmidonia.**[66] *Looking about* he saw his disciples sleeping on the ground, and he woke them by saying, "Get up, my children, and know the *great plan*[67] that has befallen us. Learn that the Lord was

----

62. *Lat:* "When the Lord had said this."

63. *Lat:* "positioned his head as though he were falling asleep."

64. *Gr:* "of the cannibals."

65. *Gr:* "cannibals."

66. *Gr:* "that city."

67. *Lat:* "the mercy of God."

ἀνάστητε τεκνία μου, καὶ γνώσεσθε τὴν [μεγάλην
οἰκονομίαν][73] τὴν γενομένην ἡμῖν, καὶ μάθετε ὅτι ὁ
κύριος ἦν μεθ' ἡμῶν ἐν τῷ πλοίῳ καὶ οὐκ ἔγνωμεν αὐτόν.
[μετεμόρφωσεν γὰρ ἑαυτὸν] ὥσπερ πρῳρεὺς [ἐν τῷ πλοίῳ]
καὶ ἐταπείνωσεν ἑαυτόν, καὶ ἐφάνη ἡμῖν ὡς ἄνθρωπος,
ἐκπειράζων ἡμᾶς. [καὶ ὁ Ἀνδρέας ἐν ἑαυτῷ γενόμενος
εἶπεν· ἐπέγνων σου κύριε τὴν καλὴν λαλιάν, ἀλλ' οὐκ
ἐφανέρωσάς μοι ἑαυτόν], καὶ διὰ τοῦτο οὐκ ἐγνώρισά σε.

Καὶ ἀποκριθέντες οἱ μαθηταὶ αὐτοῦ εἶπον πρὸς αὐτόν·
πάτερ Ἀνδρέα, μὴ νομίσῃς ὅτι ἔγνωμεν ἐν τῷ σε λαλεῖν ἐν
τῷ πλοίῳ μετ' αὐτοῦ· εἱλκύσθημεν ὑπὸ ὕπνου βαρυτάτου,
καὶ κατῆλθον[74] ἀετοὶ καὶ ἦραν τὰς ψυχὰς ἡμῶν καὶ
ἀπήγαγον ἡμᾶς ἐν τῷ παραδείσῳ τῳ ἐν τῷ οὐρανῷ, καὶ
εἴδομεν μεγάλα θαυμάσια. ἐθεασάμεθα γὰρ τὸν κύριον
[ἡμῶν] Ἰησοῦν καθεζόμενον ἐπὶ θρόνου δόξης, καὶ πάντες
οἱ ἄγγελοι κυκλοῦντες [αὐτόν.[75] ἐθεασάμεθα καὶ] Ἀβραὰμ
[καὶ] Ἰσαὰκ καὶ Ἰακὼβ [καὶ πάντας τοὺς ἁγίους],[76] καὶ
Δαυὶδ ᾄδων [ᾠδὴν] ἐν τῇ κιθάρᾳ [αὐτοῦ]. καὶ ἐθεασάμεθα
ἐκεῖ ὑμᾶς τοὺς δώδεκα ἀποστόλους παρεστηκότας ἐνώπιον
τοῦ [κυρίου ἡμῶν Ἰησοῦ Χριστοῦ, καὶ] ἔξωθεν ὑμῶν
ἀγγέλους [δώδεκα κυκλοῦντας ὑμᾶς, καὶ ἕκαστος ἄγγελος
ὄπισθεν ἑκάστου ὑμῶν ἑστηκώς, καὶ ἦσαν ὅμοιοι ὑμῶν τῇ
ἰδέᾳ]. καὶ ἠκούσαμεν τοῦ κυρίου λέγοντος τοῖς ἀγγέλοις
[ὅτι] ἀκούετε τῶν ἀποστόλων κατὰ πάντα ὅσα ἂν ἐρωτῶσιν
ὑμᾶς. ταῦτά εἰσιν ἃ εἴδαμεν πάτερ Ἀνδρέα ἕως οὗ
διύπνισας ἡμᾶς· καὶ ἤνεγκαν τὰς ψυχὰς ἡμῶν ἐν τῷ σώματι
ἡμῶν.

----

73. *Lat:* misericordiam dei.

74. *Grp* add: ἐκ τῶν οὐρανῶν.

75. *C, A,* and *Grp* indicate that at this point the text
    read: καὶ ὑμνοῦντες (= umnumque dicentes).

76. *A:* ond martyra mægen unlytel.

with us in the boat and we did not know him, for *he transformed himself* into a captain *in the boat*. He humbled himself and appeared to us as a mortal in order to test us." *When he had come to himself, Andrew said, "Lord, I recognized your excellent speech,* but I did not recognize you *because you did not reveal yourself to me."*

"Father Andrew," his disciples said, "do not suppose that we were conscious when you spoke with him in the boat, for we were dragged off by a deep sleep. Eagles descended,[68] carried away our souls, brought us to the heavenly paradise, and we saw great marvels. We saw *our* Lord Jesus sitting on a throne of glory and all the angels surrounding *him.*[69] *We saw* Abraham, Isaac, Jacob, *all the saints,*[70] and David singing *a psalm* with *his* harp. We saw you twelve apostles standing there before *our Lord Jesus Christ, and* outside of you *twelve* angels *circling you. One angel stood behind each of you, and they were like you in appearance.* We heard the Lord say to the angels, 'Listen to the apostles with regard to everything they ask of you.' This is what we saw before you woke us, father Andrew, and they brought our souls into our bodies."

----

68. *Grm* add: "from heaven."

69. *C*, *A*, and *Grp* add: "and singing hymns."

70. *A*: "a mighty troop of martyrs."

18. Τότε ᾿Ανδρέας ἀκούσας ἐχάρη χαρὰν [μεγάλην] ὅτι κατηξιώθησαν οἱ μαθηταὶ αὐτοῦ τὰ θαυμάσια ταῦτα θεάσασθαι. καὶ ἀναβλέψας ᾿Ανδρέας εἰς τὸν οὐρανὸν εἶπεν· ἐμφάνηθί μοι κύριε ᾿Ιησοῦ Χριστέ· ἐγὼ γὰρ γινώσκω ὅτι οὐκ εἶ μακρὰν ἀπὸ τῶν σῶν δούλων. συγχώρησόν μοι.[77] [ὡς γὰρ ἄνθρωπόν] σε τεθέαμαι ἐν τῷ πλοίῳ καὶ ὡς ἀνθρώπῳ σοι ὡμίλησα. νῦν οὖν κύριε φανέρωσόν μοι σεαυτὸν ἐν τῷ τόπῳ τούτῳ.

Ταῦτα δὲ εἰπόντος τοῦ ᾿Ανδρέου παρεγένετο ὁ ᾿Ιησοῦς πρὸς αὐτόν, [γενόμενος] ὅμοιος μικρῷ παιδίῳ ὡραιοτάτῳ εὐειδεῖ. καὶ[78] εἶπεν· χαῖρε ᾿Ανδρέα ἡμέτερε.

῾Ο δὲ ᾿Ανδρέας θεασάμενος αὐτὸν πεσὼν ἐπὶ τὴν γῆν προσεκύνησεν αὐτὸν λέγων· συγχώρησόν μοι κύριε ᾿Ιησοῦ Χριστέ· ὡς γὰρ ἄνθρωπόν σε εἶδον ἐν τῇ θαλάσσῃ καὶ[79] ὡμίλησά σοι. τί οὖν [ἐστιν ὅ τι] ἡμάρτηκα κύριέ [μου ᾿Ιησοῦ], ὅτι οὐκ ἐφανέρωσάς μοι σεαυτὸν ἐν τῇ θαλάσσῃ;

Καὶ ἀποκριθεὶς ὁ ᾿Ιησοῦς εἶπεν τῷ ᾿Ανδρέᾳ·[80] οὐχ ἥμαρτες, ἀλλὰ ταῦτά σοι ἐποίησα ὅτι εἶπας· οὐ δυνήσομαι πορευθῆναι εἰς τὴν πόλιν <Μυρμιδονίαν>[81] ἐν τρισὶν ἡμέραις. καὶ ὑπέδειξά σοι ὅτι πάντα ποιῆσαι δυνατός εἰμι καὶ ἑκάστῳ φανῆναι καθὼς βούλομαι. νῦν οὖν ἀνάστα, εἴσελθε πρὸς Ματθείαν εἰς τὴν πόλιν καὶ ἐξάγαγε αὐτὸν ἐκ τῆς φυλακῆς καὶ πάντας τοὺς μετ᾿ αὐτοῦ ὄντας ξένους. [ἰδοὺ γὰρ ὑποδείκνυμί σοι ᾿Ανδρέα ἃ δεῖ σε παθεῖν[82] πρὸ

----

77. *Grp* add: κύριε, ὃ ἐποίησα.

78. *Grm* add: ἀποκριθεὶς ὁ ᾿Ιησοῦς.

79. *Grp* add: ὡς ἀνθρώπῳ.

80. It would appear that the Greek text behind *C* and *AS* read ὦ ᾿Ανδρέα instead of τῷ ᾿Ανδρέᾳ.

81. *Lat*: Mermedonie. *Gr*: τῶν ἀνθρωποφάγων.

82. *Grm* om.: ἃ . . . παθεῖν.

18. When Andrew heard this he was exuberant that his disciples had been considered worthy to see these marvels. Andrew looked up into heaven and said, "Appear to me, Lord Jesus Christ, for I know you are not far from your servants. Forgive me,[71] *for* I beheld you on the boat *as a human* and spoke with you as with a human. Therefore, O Lord, reveal yourself now to me in this place."

After Andrew had said these things, Jesus came to him appearing like a most beautiful small child and[72] said, "Greetings, our Andrew."

When Andrew saw him he fell to the earth, worshiped him, and said, "Forgive me, Lord Jesus Christ, for on the sea I saw you as a human and spoke with you.[73] *My Lord Jesus*, what sin had I committed that caused you not to reveal yourself to me on the sea?"

"You did not sin," Jesus said to Andrew. "I did these things to you because you said, 'I cannot travel to the city **Myrmidonia**[74] in three days.' I showed you that I can do anything and appear to each person in any form I wish. Now stand up, go to Matthias in the city, and bring him and all those strangers who are with him out of the prison.[75] *For behold, I show you, Andrew, before you enter their city what you must suffer.* They will show you many *terrible* insults, contrive tortures,

----

71. *Grp* add: "O Lord, for what I have done."

72. *Grm* add: "Jesus answering."

73. *Grp* add: "as with a human."

74. *Gr*: "of the cannibals."

75. Cf. Jonah 3:1-2 (LXX).

τοῦ εἰσελθεῖν σε ἐν τῇ πόλει [αὐτῶν]. ἐνδείξονταί σοι
ὕβρεις πολλὰς [καὶ δεινὰς] καὶ ἐπάξουσίν σοι βασάνους
καὶ σκορπίσουσίν σου τὰς σάρκας ἐν ταῖς πλατείαις καὶ
ῥύμαις τῆς πόλεως [αὐτῶν]. καὶ τὸ αἷμά σου ῥεύσει ἐπὶ
τὴν γῆν ὥσπερ ὕδωρ· εἰ μὴ μόνον τὸν θάνατον οὐ δύνανταί
σοι παρασχεῖν· πολλὰς δὲ θλίψεις ἐπάξουσιν. ἀλλ᾽
ὑπόμεινον [ἡμέτερε Ἀνδρέα], καὶ μὴ ποιήσῃς κατὰ τὴν
ἀπιστίαν αὐτῶν. μνήσθητι ὧν ὑπέμεινεν [ἡ ψυχή] μου
πολλῶν θλίψεων ὅτε ἔτυπτον καὶ ἐνέπτυον εἰς τὸ πρόσωπόν
μου καὶ ἔλεγεν ὅτι ἐν Βεελζεβοὺλ ἐκβάλλει τὰ δαιμόνια.
[μὴ οὐκ ἤμην δυνατὸς τῷ νεύματι τῶν ὀφθαλμῶν μου
συντρῖψαι τὸν οὐρανὸν καὶ τὴν γῆν ἐπὶ τοὺς ἁμαρτάνοντας
ἐπ᾽ ἐμέ;] ἀλλ᾽ ὑπέμεινα [καὶ συνεχώρησα], ἵνα καὶ ὑμῖν
τύπον ὑποδείξω. νῦν οὖν [ἡμέτερε] Ἀνδρέα, [ἐὰν
παράσχωσίν σοι τὰς ὕβρεις] καὶ τὰς βασάνους ταύτας,
ὑπόμεινον· εἰσὶν γὰρ οἱ μέλλοντες πιστεύειν ἐν τῇ πόλει
ταύτῃ.[83] καὶ ταῦτα εἰπὼν ὁ [σωτὴρ][84] ἐπορεύετο εἰς τοὺς
οὐρανούς.

19. Ἀνδρέας δὲ ἀναστὰς εἰσῆλθεν ἐν τῇ πόλει σὺν
τοῖς μαθηταῖς αὐτοῦ, καὶ οὐδεὶς αὐτὸν ἐθεάσατο, καὶ
ἐπορεύθησαν ἐν τῇ φυλακῇ·[85] [καὶ θεασάμενος] Ἀνδρέας
εἶδεν φύλακας ἑστῶτας ἑπτὰ ἐπὶ τὴν θύραν [τῆς φυλακῆς,
φυλάσσοντ<α>ς τὴν φυλακήν]· καὶ ηὔξατο ἐν ἑαυτῷ, καὶ
πεσόντες οἱ [ἑπτὰ] φύλακες[86] ἀπέπνευσαν· καὶ ἐλθὼν ἐπὶ
τὴν θύραν τῆς φυλακῆς περιεχάραξεν Ἀνδρέας [τὴν θύραν]

----

83. *C* adds: multique hominum de hac urbe capturus es in
sagena tua in me credituri.

84. *L*: dominus.

85. *GE*: ingressusque portam civitatis, venit ad
carcerem. *N*: παραγενόμενος . . . Ἀνδρέας . . . ἐν
τῇ τοιαύτῃ πόλει. *E*: ὁ δὲ Ἀνδρέας κατελθὼν . . .
ἦλθεν εἰς τὴν φυλακήν.

86. *Grp* add: ἐπὶ τὴν γῆν.

scatter your flesh on the public avenues and streets of
their city. Your blood will flow on the ground like
water. They will not be able to kill you, but they will
contrive many afflictions. Stand firm, *our Andrew*, and
do not respond in kind to their unbelief. Remember those
many tortures my *soul* endured when they beat me, spat in
my face, and said, 'He casts out demons through
Beelzebul.'[76] *Am I not able with the blink of my eyes to
crush the heaven and the earth against those who sin
against me?* But I endured *and forgave* in order to
provide a model also for you (pl.!). So now, *our* Andrew,
if they inflict on you these *insults* and tortures,
endure them, for there are those in this city who are
about to believe."[77] After the *Savior*[78] said these
things, he ascended into the heavens.

19. Andrew rose up and went to the city with his
disciples without anyone seeing him.[79] They went to the
prison,[80] and Andrew saw seven guards standing at the
door *of the prison guarding it.* He prayed silently, and
the *seven* guards fell[81] and died. When he came to the

----

76. Cf. Mark 3:22, Matt 9:34, 12:24, 27, Luke 11:15, 19.

77. *C*: "you will capture in your net many people of this
    city who will believe in me."

78. *Lat*: "Lord."

79. Cf. Jonah 3:3 (LXX).

80. *GE*: "and on entering the city gate, he went to the
    prison." *N*: "When Andrew . . . arrived . . . in that
    city." *E*: "After Andrew descended, . . . he went
    into the prison."

81. *Grp* add: "to the ground."

τῷ σημείῳ τοῦ σταυροῦ καὶ αὐτομάτως ἡ θύρα ἠνεῴχθη.[87]
καὶ εἰσελθὼν ἐν τῇ φυλακῇ μετὰ τῶν μαθητῶν αὐτοῦ εἶδεν
Ματθείαν καθεζόμενον καὶ ψάλλοντα καθ' ἑαυτόν.[88] καὶ
ἰδὼν αὐτὸν ἀνέστη, καὶ ἠσπάσαντο ἀλλήλους ἐν φιλήματι
[ἁγίῳ.[89] καὶ ἀποκριθεὶς] ὁ 'Ανδρέας εἶπεν [τῷ Ματθείᾳ]·
ὦ ἀδελφὲ [Ματθεία],[90] πῶς εὑρέθης ἐνταῦθα; ἔτι γὰρ τρεῖς
ἡμέραι, ἐξάξουσίν σε τοῦ θῦσαι, καὶ γενέσθαι βρῶμα τῶν
[ἐν τῇ πόλει ταύτῃ. ποῦ εἰσιν τὰ μεγάλα μυστήρια ἃ
ἐδιδάχθης; ποῦ εἰσιν τὰ θαυμάσια ἃ ἐπιστεύθημεν, ἐξ ὧν
ἐὰν διήγησῃ ὁ οὐρανὸς καὶ ἡ γῆ σείεται;][91]

Καὶ ἀποκριθεὶς ὁ Ματθείας εἶπεν· ὦ ἀδελφὲ 'Ανδρέα,
οὐκ ἤκουσας τοῦ κυρίου λέγοντος· ἰδοὺ ἐγὼ ἀποστέλλω ὑμᾶς
ὡς πρόβατα ἐν μέσῳ λύκων;[92] εὐθὺς γὰρ ὡς εἰσήγαγόν με ἐν
τῇ φυλακῇ καὶ ηὐξάμην πρὸς κύριον καὶ ἐφανέρωσέν μοι
ἑαυτὸν καὶ εἶπέν μοι λέγων· ὑπόμεινον ἐνταῦθα εἰκοσιεπτὰ
ἡμέρας καὶ μετὰ ταῦτα ἐξαποστελῶ σοι 'Ανδρέαν[93] καὶ
ἐξάξει σε ἐκ τῆς φυλακῆς καὶ πάντας τοὺς μετὰ σοῦ. καὶ
νῦν ἰδοὺ καθὼς εἶπέν μοι ὁ κύριος εἶδόν σε· νῦν οὖν τί
ἐστιν ὃ μέλλομεν διαπράξασθαι;

20. Τότε ὁ 'Ανδρέας θεασάμενος [ἐν μέσῳ] τῆς
φυλακῆς εἶδεν τοὺς ἄνδρας τοὺς κατακλείστους γυμνοὺς καὶ
χόρτον ἐσθίοντας ὥσπερ τὰ κτήνη τὰ ἄλογα, καὶ τύψας τὸ

----

87. N: διὰ προσευχῆς ἀπενέκρωσεν τοὺς φύλακας καὶ τὰς
θύρας τῆς φυλακῆς ἀνοίξας. E: ἡ δὲ πύλη τῆς φυλακῆς
αὐτομάτως ἠνοίχθη αὐτῷ.

88. GE: Videns autem Matheum apostolum in squalore
carceris . . . resedentem.

89. V: in osculo sancto.

90. The name is absent also in Grp.

91. Presumably Lat omitted these last two sentences
because of Andrew's rebuking another apostle.

92. Cf. APh Act 8.

93. Lat adds; fratrem tuum.

prison door, Andrew marked *it* with the sign of the cross and it opened automatically.[82] On entering the prison with his disciples, he saw Matthias sitting, singing by himself.[83] When he saw Andrew, Matthias rose, and they greeted each other with a *holy* kiss. "O brother *Matthias*," Andrew said, "how is it that one finds you here? In three days they will take you out for slaughter, and you will become food for *the people of this city. Where are the great mysteries you were taught? Where are the marvels with which we were entrusted, any of which would shake heaven and earth if you were to narrate them?*"

"O brother Andrew," Matthias answered, "did you not hear the Lord say, 'Behold, I send you as sheep in the midst of wolves?'[84] For as soon as they brought me into prison I prayed to the Lord, and he revealed himself to me saying, 'Stand firm here for twenty-seven days, and then I will send you Andrew[85] who will deliver you and everyone with you from the prison.' Now look, I see you just as the Lord said I would. So now what should we do?"

20. Then Andrew looked *into the middle* of the prison and saw the prisoners naked and eating grass like dumb beasts. Andrew beat his breast and said to him-

----

82. *N*: "through prayer he slew the guards and the prison doors opened." *E*: "the prison gate opened to him automatically."

83. *GE*: "On seeing the apostle Matthew sitting in prison filth."

84. Cf. Matt 10:16 and Luke 10:3.

85. *Lat* adds: "your brother."

στῆθος αὐτοῦ ὁ ᾽Ανδρέας εἶπεν ἐν ἑαυτῷ·[94] [ὦ ᾽Ανδρέα,
πρόσσχες καὶ θέασαι τί παρέσχον τοῖς ὁμοίοις σου
ἀνθρώποις, πῶς] παρεπλησίασαν αὐτοὺς τοῖς κτήνεσιν [τοῖς
ἀνοήτοις.[95]

Τότε][96] ἤρξατο ὁ ᾽Ανδρέας διελέγχειν τὸν Σατανᾶν
καὶ λέγειν πρὸς αὐτόν· οὐαί σοι τῷ διαβόλῳ,[97] τῷ ἐχθρῷ
τοῦ θεοῦ καὶ τοῖς ἀγγέλοις αὐτοῦ, ὅτι οὐδέν σοι κακὸν
παρέσχον οἱ ἐνταῦθα miseri et ξένοι, καὶ πῶς ἐπήγαγες
αὐτοῖς τὴν τιμωρίαν ταύτην; O infelix, ἕως πότε πολεμεῖς
μετὰ τοῦ γένους τῶν ἀνθρώπων; σὺ γὰρ ἀπ᾽ ἀρχῆς ἐποίησας
τὸν ᾽Αδὰμ[98] ἐκβληθῆναι ἐκ τοῦ παραδείσου, [καὶ ἔδωκεν
αὐτῷ ὁ θεὸς βρῶσιν χόρτου σπεῖραι ἐν τῇ γῇ.][99] σὺ
ἐποίησας τοὺς ἄρτους αὐτοῦ τοὺς ἐπὶ τῆς τραπέζης λίθους
γενέσθαι· καὶ πάλιν σὺ ἐπεισῆλθες [ἐν τῇ διανοίᾳ τῶν
ἀγγέλων][100] καὶ ἐποίησας αὐτοὺς ἐν γυναιξὶν μιανθῆναι,
καὶ ἐποίησας [ἀδιαθέτους] τοὺς υἱοὺς αὐτῶν τοὺς
γίγαντας, [ὥστε κατεσθίειν τοὺς ἀνθρώπους ἐπὶ τῆς
γῆς],[101] ἕως οὗ ὠργίσθη κύριος [ἐπ᾽ αὐτοὺς καὶ] ἐπήγαγεν
ἐπ᾽ αὐτοὺς τὸν κατακλυσμόν, ἵνα ἐξαλείψῃ πᾶν τὸ

----

94. *GE*: Videns autem Matheum apostolum . . . cum vinctis
aliis resedentem, amarissime flevit, et facta
oratione simul, ait Andreas.

95. *C*: ve mihi peccatori, qualia iniqua et perversa,
iniquissimus ille generis humani fecit in hominibus
istis. Dominus enim tunc quando plasmavit hominem ad
similitudinem suam fecit eum, et nunc diabolus fecit
istos similes iumentis.

96. *Lat*: et conversus.

97. *Lat* adds: quantas inimicitias exercuisti adversus
generis humani inique et perverse.

98. *Lat*, *P*, and one other Greek ms. add: πρωτόπλαστον.

99. This clause is missing also in one Greek ms.

100. *Lat*: in corde filiorum dei.

101. *Lat* and *Grp* om.

self,[86] *"O Andrew, look and see what they have done to people like you, how* they nearly reduced them to the state of *irrational* beasts."[87]

Then[88] Andrew began rebuking Satan saying to him, "Woe to you, Devil,[89] enemy of God and his angels. These **wretches** and strangers did you no harm, so why have you brought this punishment upon them? **O rogue,** how long will you war with the human race? From the beginning you caused Adam[90] to be expelled from paradise.[91] *God caused him to sow a diet of grain on the earth,* but you turned his bread on the table into stones. Later, you sneaked *into the minds of the angels,*[92] made them to be defiled with women, and made their *unruly* sons giants, *so that they devoured the people of the earth,*[93] until the Lord raged *against them and* brought a flood on them in order to obliterate every *structure*[94] *the Lord had made on the*

----

86. *GE*: "On seeing the apostle Matthew . . . sitting with the other prisoners, he cried bitterly, and as he prayed, Andrew said."

87. *C*: "Woe to me a sinner for the cruelties and perversions that enemy of the human race performed against these people. When the Lord formed the human he made him according to his likeness, and now the devil has made these people like beasts."

88. *Lat*: "and turning."

89. *Lat* adds: "who waged such hostilities against the human race, cruel and perverse one."

90. *Lat*, *P*, and one other Greek ms. add: "the first-formed."

91. Cf. Genesis 3.

92. *Lat*: "into the heart(s) of the sons of God."

93. Cf. Gen 6:1-4.

94. *Lat*: "sin."

[ἀνάστημα ὃ ἐποίησεν κύριος ἐπὶ τῆς γῆς]·102 ἀλλ᾽ [οὐκ
ἐξήλειψεν τὸν δίκαιον αὐτοῦ] Νῶε. καὶ πάλιν παρεγένου
καὶ ἐν τῇ πόλει ταύτῃ ἵνα103 και [τοὺς ἐνταῦθα]104
ποιήσῃς καθεσθίειν ἀνθρώπους, eorumque <b>i<b>ere105
sanguinem, ἵνα γένηται καὶ τούτων [τὸ τέλος] εἰς κατάραν
καὶ ἀπώλειαν, νομίζων ἐν σεαυτῷ ὅτι ὁ θεὸς ἐξαλείψει τὸ
πλάσμα αὐτοῦ. Inimice, ἢ οὐκ ἤκουσας ὅτι εἶπεν ὁ
[θεὸς]106 ὅτι οὐ μὴ ἐπάξω ἔτι κατακλυσμὸν ἐπὶ τῆς γῆς;
[ἀλλὰ εἴ τί ἐστιν ἑτοιμαζόμενον κολάσεως ἕνεκεν τῆς σῆς
τιμωρίας γίνεται.]107

21. Τότε ἀναστὰς ᾽Ανδρέας καὶ Ματθείας ηὔξαντο, καὶ
μετὰ τὴν εὐχὴν108 ἐπέθηκεν ᾽Ανδρέας τὰς χεῖρας ἐπὶ [τὰ
πρόσωπα]109 τῶν τυφλῶν [ἀνδρῶν τῶν ὄντων ἐν τῇ φυλακῇ],
καὶ [εὐθέως]110 ἀνέβλεψαν·111 καὶ πάλιν ἐπέθηκεν τὴν

---

102. *Lat*: peccata.

103. *Lat* adds: per iniquas tuas suasiones.

104. *Lat*: homines similes sui.

105. The text reads: vivere.

106. *Lat*: dominum.

107. *Lat*: omnia vero ista que nunc facis inimicitia
generis humani, similia tibi sunt reposita tormenta
in die iudicii.

108. *GE*: ait Andreas, Domine Iesu Christe, quem
fideliter praedicamus et ob cuius nomine tanta
perferimus, qui caecis visum, surdis auditum,
paraliticis gressum, laeprosis munditiam, mortuis
vitam inmensa clementia largire dignatus es, aperi,
quaeso, oculos servi tui, ut eat ad adnuntiandum
verbum tuum. Et statim locus ille contremuit, et
lux magna refulsit in carcere.

109. *Lat*: oculos.

110. *Grp* add: πάντες.

111. *GE*: et oculi beati apostoli restaurati sunt, et
cunctorum catenae confractae sunt, et travis, in
qua pedes eorum coartati erant, scissa est, et

earth. But *he did not obliterate his righteous one,*
Noah. Now you come to this city as well in order to
make[95] its residents[96] eat humans **and to <drink>**[97] **their**
blood so that they too might *end up* accursed and
destroyed. For you assume that God will obliterate what
he has molded. **Enemy!** Have you not heard that *God*[98]
said, 'I will never again bring a flood on the earth?'[99]
If any punishment is prepared, it is for retaliation
against you."[100]

21. Andrew and Matthias then rose up and prayed,
and after the prayer,[101] Andrew put his hands on *the*
faces[102] of the blind *men in the prison,* and *immediately*
they[103] received their sight.[104] He also put his hand

----

95. *Lat* adds: "by your wicked eloquence."

96. *Lat*: "people similar to you."

97. *Lat* literally: "to live."

98. *Lat*: "the Lord."

99. Cf. Gen 9:11.

100. *Lat*: "Whatever hostilities you now perform against
     the human race, similar torments are laid up
     against you for the day of judgment."

101. *GE*: "Andrew said, 'Lord Jesus Christ, whom we
     faithfully preach and for whose name we endure so
     much, who in your boundless mercy deigns to bestow
     sight to the blind, hearing to the deaf, walking to
     paralytics, purity to lepers, life to the dead,
     open, I pray, the eyes of your servant, so that the
     may leave to preach your word.' And immediately the
     place shook, and a great light shone in the
     prison."

102. *Lat*: "the eyes."

103. *Grp* add: "all."

104. *GE*: "and the eyes of the blessed apostle were
     restored, the chains of all were shattered, and the
     stocks in which their feet had been constrained

χεῖρα αὐτοῦ ἐπὶ τὰς καρδίας αὐτῶν, καὶ μετεβλήθη ὁ νοῦς
αὐτῶν [εἰς ἀνθρωπίνην αἴσθησιν]. [112] τότε λέγει αὐτοῖς
'Ανδρέας· ἀναστάντες πορεύεσθε εἰς τὰ κατώτερα μέρη τῆς
πόλεως, καὶ εὑρήσετε ἐν τῇ ὁδῷ συκῆν μεγάλην, καὶ
καθίσατε ὑπὸ [τὴν συκῆν] καὶ ἐσθίετε ἀπὸ τοῦ καρποῦ
αὐτῆς ἕως ἂν ἔλθω πρὸς ὑμᾶς· [113] ἐὰν δὲ βραδύνω τοῦ
ἐλθεῖν [ἐκεῖ], εὑρήσετε τὸ αὔταρκες τῆς τροφῆς [ὑμῶν].
οὐ μὴ γὰρ λείψει ὁ καρπὸς [ἀπὸ τῆς συκῆς], ἀλλ' ὅσον
ὑμεῖς ἐσθίετε, πλείονα καρπὸν ἐνέγκῃ, [καὶ διαθρέψῃ
ὑμᾶς], καθὼς ὁ κύριος διέταξεν.

Καὶ [ἀποκριθέντες] οἱ [ἄνδρες] εἶπαν τῷ 'Ανδρέᾳ·
ἐλθὲ ἅμα ἡμῖν κύριε ἡμῶν, μή ποτε πάλιν [θεασάμενοι
ἡμᾶς] οἱ [τῆς πόλεως ταύτης] ἄνομοι ἄνδρες
κατακλείσουσιν ἡμᾶς καὶ ἐνδείξονται ἡμῖν βασάνους
δεινοτέρας [καὶ πλείους ὧν ἐνεδείξαντο ἡμῖν.]

Καὶ [ἀποκριθεὶς] 'Ανδρέας εἶπεν πρὸς αὐτούς·
πορεύεσθε· [ἐπ' ἀληθείας γὰρ λέγω ὑμῖν ὅτι πορευομένων
ὑμῶν] οὐ μὴ ὑλάξει κύων [ἐν τῇ γλώττῃ αὐτοῦ] ἐφ' ὑμᾶς.

Καὶ ἐπορεύθησαν οἱ ἄνδρες καθὼς εἶπεν ὁ μακάριος
'Ανδρέας. ἦσαν δὲ οἱ [πάντες] ἄνδρες διακόσιοι quadra-

----

omnes magnificabant Deum, dicentes, quia: Magnus
est Deus, quem praedicant servi eius.

112. B: regressus est sensus rationabilis in eis ad
intellegendam naturam humanitatis suae.

113. GE: Tunc educti per beatum Andream de carcere,
abiit unusquisque ad propria sua. N: ἐξήνεγκεν
αὐτόν τε τὸν ἀπόστολον καὶ τοὺς σὺν αὐτῷ
κατεχομένους, ἀπολύσας αὐτοὺς ἔνθα καὶ βούλονται
πορεύεσθαι. E: ἐξαγαγὼν δὲ τὸν Ματθίαν καὶ σὺν αὐτῷ
δεδεμένους πιστεύσαντας, ἔκρυψεν αὐτοὺς ἔξω τῆς
πόλεως ἑπτὰ ἡμέρας, ὡς ἀπὸ μιλίου ἑνός, παρὰ
θάλασσαν. ἦν δὲ συκῶν δάσος ἐκεῖ πολὺ δυσδιόδευτον
ἡμέρων τε καὶ ἀγρίων, καὶ ὁ καιρὸς τῶν συκῶν. ἦν δὲ
καὶ σπήλαιον.

on their hearts, and their minds regained *human consciousness.*[105] Then Andrew said to them, "Stand up, go to the lower parts of the city, and you will find along the road a large fig tree. Sit under *the fig tree* and eat its fruit until I come to you.[106] Should I delay coming *there,* you will find enough food *for yourselves,* for the fruit *of the fig tree* will not fail. No matter how much you eat, it will bear more fruit *and feed you,* just as the Lord commanded."

"Come with us, our lord," the *men* said to Andrew, "lest the lawless men *of this city see us* again, lock us up, and inflict tortures on us more dreadful *and numerous than what they have inflicted on us so far.*"

"Go!" Andrew *answered* them. "*For I tell you truly that when you go* not even a dog will bark at you *with his tongue.*"

The men went off just as the blessed Andrew had told them. *All* the men whom Andrew released *from prison* numbered two hundred **forty-eight**, and the women forty-nine. He made Matthias go with his disciples *out*

----

were broken. Everyone magnified God, saying, 'Great is the God whom his servant preaches!'"

105. *B:* "rationality was returned to them for understanding the nature of their humanity."

106. *GE:* "Then, sent out from the prison by the blessed Andrew, each went off to his or her own home." *N:* "and he brought out the apostle and those detained with him, setting them free to leave for anywhere they desired." *E:* "Having brought Matthias and the believers shackled with him, he hid them for seven days outside of the city, about one mile away, near the sea. There was a thicket of figs there, thick with fruit cultivated and wild; it was fig season. There also was a cave."

ginta octo[114] καὶ γυναῖκες τεσσαράκοντα ἐννέα οὓς
ἀπέλυσεν Ἀνδρέας ἐκ [τῆς φυλακῆς]. Ματθείαν δὲ ἐποίησεν
πορευθῆναι σὺν τοῖς μαθηταῖς αὐτοῦ ἐξ ἀφηλιώτου [τῆς
πόλεως].[115] καὶ ἐπέταξεν Ἀνδρέας νεφέλῃ, καὶ ἦρεν [ἡ
νεφέλη] Ματθείαν καὶ τοὺς μαθητὰς Ἀνδρέου, καὶ ἀπέθετο
αὐτοὺς [ἡ νεφέλη] ἐν τῷ ὄρει ὅπου ἦν ὁ Πέτρος
[διδάσκων], καὶ ἔμειναν πρὸς αὐτόν.

22. Ἀνδρέας δὲ ἐξελθὼν ἀπὸ τῆς φυλακῆς περιεπάτει
ἐπὶ τῆς πόλεως[116] καὶ in quodam vic<o> θεασάμενος στῦλον
καὶ ἀνδριάντα χαλκοῦν[117] ἐπάνω ἑστηκότα καὶ ἐκαθέσθη
ὀπίσω τοῦ στύλου [ἐκείνου] ἕως ἂν ἴδῃ τί ἔσται τὸ
γινόμενον.[118] καὶ ἐγένετο ἐν τῷ πορευθῆναι τοὺς δημίους
εἰς τὴν φυλακὴν ἵνα ἐκβάλ<ω>σιν ἀνθρώπους εἰς βρῶσιν
αὐτῶν [κατὰ τὴν καθημερινὴν[119] συνήθειαν], καὶ ηὗραν τὰς

----

114. The Latin and Anglo-Saxon witnesses consistently
give the number as 248, and three Greek mss. read
249, which may be an accidental variant of 248. For
instance, if the numbers were designated by Greek
letters, the eight, represented by Η, might have
been confused for nine, represented by Θ. Many
Greek mss. read 270, for which there seems to be no
good explanation. It is also possible that the
original number was 217 or 218 (including Matthias)
as in chapter 23. *P* reads 117 once, but after a
long section contradicts itself by reading 9 men
and 9 women.

115. *GE*: Mattheus autem recessit a loco illo. *E*: τὸν δὲ
Ματθίαν λαβὼν ἐξῆλθεν ἐπὶ Ἀνατολήν.

116. *GE*: Denique Andreas apostolus praedicabat incolis
verbum Domini Iesu.

117. *Grp*: στῦλον χαλκοῦν καὶ ἀνδριάντα.

118. *Lat* adds: de eo. Cf. Jonah 4:5 (LXX): καὶ ἐκάθητο
ὑποκάτω αὐτῆς ἐν σκιᾷ, ἕως οὗ ἀπίδῃ τί ἔσται τῇ
πόλει.

119. Following *P* and one other Greek ms. All other Greek
mss. read μακαρίαν. The sentence is absent in the
Latin and Anglo-Saxon versions which therefore are
no help in establishing the text. If μακαρίαν is
original to the ancient Acts, it probably was not

of the city toward the east.[107] Andrew commanded a cloud, and the cloud lifted Matthias and Andrew's disciples[108] and placed them on the mountain where Peter was teaching, and they stayed with him.

22. After Andrew left the prison, he walked about the city,[109] and **by a certain street** he saw a pillar with a copper statue[110] standing on it. He sat behind that pillar in order to see what would happen.[111] When the executioners arrived at the prison to remove people for their food according to their daily[112] custom, they

----

107. *GE*: "Matthew retreated from that place." *E*: "He took Matthias and left toward the east."

108. *Eth* names the disciples: "Rufus and Alexander."

109. *GE*: "Then the apostle proclaimed the word of the Lord Jesus to the inhabitants."

110. *Grp*: "a copper pillar with a statue."

111. *Lat* adds: "concerning him." Cf. Jonah 4:5 (LXX): "and he sat under its shade in order to see what would happen in the city."

112. *Grm*: "blessed."

θύρας τῆς φυλακῆς ἀνεῳγμένας καὶ τοὺς septem φύλακας[120]
νεκροὺς κειμένους [ἐπὶ τὴν γῆν].[121] καὶ εὐθέως
ἐπορεύθησαν [καὶ ἀπήγγειλαν] τοῖς ἄρχουσιν[122] [λέγοντες]
ὅτι τὸ δεσμωτήριον ηὕραμεν ἠνεῳγμένον, καὶ εἰσελθόντες
ἔσω οὐδένα ηὕραμεν. ἀλλὰ τοὺς φύλακας ηὕραμεν νεκροὺς
κειμένους ἐπὶ τὴν γῆν.

Καὶ ἀκούσαντες ταῦτα οἱ ἄρχοντες τῆς πόλεως εἶπαν
ἐν ἑαυτοῖς· τί ἄρα ἐστὶν τὸ γενόμενον; τάχα τινὲς
εἰσῆλθαν εἰς τὴν φυλακὴν τ<ῆς πόλεως> καὶ τοὺς φύλακας
ἀπέκτειναν, ᾖραν δὲ καὶ τοὺς κατακλείστους; τότε
ἐκέλευσαν τοῖς δημίοις [λέγοντες]· ἀπελθόντες εἰς τὴν
φυλακὴν ἐνέγκατε τοὺς ἑπτὰ ἄνδρας,[123] ἵνα κἂν αὐτοὺς
καταφάγωμεν·[124] [καὶ ἀνέλθ<οντες> ἐπὶ τὴν αὔριον,
ἐπισυνάξωμεν πάντας τοὺς γηραιοὺς τῆς πόλεως ὅπως
βάλωσιν κλήρους εἰς ἑαυτοὺς ἕως ἂν ἔλθωσιν οἱ κλῆροι ἐπὶ
ἑπτά, καὶ ἑπτὰ καθ᾽ ἑκάστην ἡμέραν σφαγιάσωμεν· καὶ
ἔσονται ἡμῖν εἰς διατροφὰς ἕως ἂν ἐκλεξώμεθα νεανίσκους
καὶ ὁρίσωμεν αὐτοὺς ἐν πλοίοις ὡς ναυτικούς, καὶ
ἀπελθόντες εἰς τὰς κύκλῳ χώρας καὶ ἐμβαλλόμενοί τινας
ἀγάγωσιν ἐνταῦθα ἵνα ἔσονται ἡμῖν εἰς διατροφάς].[125]

----

used ironically but to suggest the executions were
cultic.

120. *Grp* add: τοὺς φυλάσσοντας.

121. *GE*: Cognoscentes autem homines illi de carceris
vinctis. *N*: ταῦτα ἐνωτισθέντες οἱ τῇ γνώμῃ
ἀποτεθηριωμένοι πρόσοικοι τῆς τοιαύτης πολίχνης.

122. *Grp* add: τῆς πόλεως.

123. *Grp* add: τοὺς τελευτήσαντας.

124. *Grp* add: ἐν τῇ σήμερον ἡμέρᾳ.

125. *Lat*: Quoniam et lacus iste qui nobis sanguis erat
servaturus, inmanens remansit.

found the doors of the prison opened and the **seven** guards[113] lying dead *on the ground.*[114] At once they went *and told* the rulers,[115] "We found the prison opened, and when we went inside we found no one, except for the guards lying dead on the ground."

When the rulers of the city heard these things, they said to each other, "What has happened? Have some people perhaps gone into the <city> prison, killed the guards, and released the prisoners?" Then they commanded the executioners, "Go to the prison and bring the seven[116] men so that we might eat them.[117] *Tomorrow let us go and gather together all the elderly of the city so that they can cast lots among themselves until the lots select seven. Let us slaughter seven each day, and they will be our food until we select some young men and appoint them to boats as sailors. They can invade the neighboring territories and bring captives here for our food.*"[118]

----

113. *Grp* add: "on duty."

114. *GE*: "When those men learned that the prisoners had escaped from the prison." *N*: "When the savagely minded neighbors of this town learned of these things."

115. *Grp* add: "of the city."

116. *Grp* add: "dead."

117. *Grp* add: "today."

118. *C*: "Because that trough which preserves blood for us remains empty."

Καὶ ἀπελθόντες οἱ δήμιοι[126] ἤνεγκαν τοὺς ἑπτὰ [ἄνδρας][127] τοὺς τελευτήσαντας· καὶ ἦν κλίβανος οἰκοδομημένος ἐν μέσῳ τῆς πόλεως, καὶ προσέκειτο ἐν τῷ κλιβάνῳ ληνὸς [μεγάλη] ἔνθα τοὺς ἀνθρώπους ἐσφαγίαζον, καὶ διέτρεχεν αὐτῶν τὸ αἷμα ἐπὶ τὴν ληνόν, καὶ ἤντλουν ἐκ τοῦ αἵματος καὶ ἔπινον.[128] καὶ ἤνεγκαν τοὺς ἀνθρώπους καὶ ἔθηκαν ἐπὶ τὴν ληνόν. καὶ ἐν τῷ ἐπᾶραι [τοὺς δημίους τὰς χεῖρας][129] αὐτῶν ἐπ' αὐτοὺς ἤκουσεν φωνῆς 'Ανδρέας λεγούσης· θέασαι ['Ανδρέα τὸ γινόμενον ἐν τῇ πόλει ταύτῃ.

Καὶ θεασάμενος 'Ανδρέας ηὔξατο][130] πρὸς κύριον λέγων· κύριέ μου 'Ιησοῦ Χριστέ,[131] <ὁ κελεύσα>ς τοῦ εἰσελθεῖν με εἰς τὴν πόλιν ταύτην, μὴ ποιήσῃς τι κακὸν διαπράξασθαι τοὺς ἐν [τῇ πόλει] ταύτῃ, ἀλλ' ἐξελθάτωσαν[132] αἱ μάχαιραι ἐκ τῶν χειρῶν τῶν [ἀνόμων] et fiat manus eorum tanquam lapis.

----

126. Grp add: εἰς τὴν φυλακήν.

127. Lat: custodes.

128. This is where the Gr and P place this reference to the furnace and trough in the middle of Myrmidonia. C places in in chapter 1 and reads: Habebantque clibanum in medio civitatis edificatum, insuper et lacus iuxta eodem clibani. In quo lacu homines interficiebant, ut sanguis illud ibi colligerent. Alioque lacu iuxta ipsum lacum, in quo sanguis illud que in ipso priore laco spargentur, (...) et quasi purgatus discurret, (...) bibendum.

129. Lat: gladios.

130. Lat: numquid non videbis malignitas hec, quid isti faciunt? qui dixit: domine ecce nunc video. unde conversus.

131. Lat adds: qui me creasti in utero matris mea, et fecisti me ad lucem exire, obsecro te per misericordiam tuam.

132. Corrupt for ἐξειληθήτωσαν?

The executioners went[119] and brought out the seven dead *men*.[120] An earthen oven had been erected in the middle of the city, and next to it lay a *large* trough where they used to slay people and their blood would flow into the trough, whence they would draw up the blood and drink it.[121] They brought the men and placed them in the trough. When *the executioners* lifted their *hands*[122] over them, Andrew heard a voice saying, *"Andrew, look what is happening in this city."*

Andrew looked and prayed[123] to the Lord, "My Lord Jesus Christ,[124] <you who commanded> me to enter this city, do not let the residents of the *city* do any harm, but let the swords fall from their *lawless* hands, **and may their hands be like stone."**

----

119. *Grp* add: "to the prison."

120. *Lat*: "guards."

121. *C* places this description of the oven and trough in chapter 1: "In the middle of the city an earthen oven had been constructed, and, in addition, next to that oven was a trough. They used to slaughter people in the trough in order to collect the blood there. Next to that trough was another into which the blood that was sprinkled into the first trough (...) and flows as though it had been purified (...) for drinking."

122. *Lat*: "swords."

123. *Lat*: "'Will you never see this abomination which those people are committing?' He said, 'Lord, now I see.' Then he turned."

124. *Lat* adds: "who created me in my mother's womb, who made me enter into the light, I implore you through your mercy."

Καὶ εὐθὺς ἔπεσαν αἱ μάχαιραι [ἐκ τῶν χειρῶν τῶν δημίων], καὶ ἀπελιθώθησαν αἱ χεῖρες αὐτῶν. καὶ θεασάμενοι οἱ ἄρχοντες τὸ γεγονὸς ἔκλαυσαν λέγοντες· οὐαὶ ἡμῖν, ὅτι [ἐνταῦθα]133 μάγοι εἰσὶν οἱ καὶ ἀπελθόντες ἐν τῇ φυλακῇ καὶ ἐξαγαγόντες τοὺς ἄνδρας· [ἰδοὺ γὰρ καὶ τούτους ἐμάγευσαν.]134 τί οὖν ποιήσωμεν; [ἀπελθόντες νῦν ἐπισυνάξατε τοὺς γεραιοὺς τῆς πόλεως], ἐπειδή ἐσμεν πρόσπεινοι.135

23. Καὶ [ἀπελθόντες] ἐπισυνήξαν omnes seniores civitatis καὶ εὗρον διακοσίους [ιε′],136 καὶ ἤγαγον αὐτοὺς ἐπὶ [τοὺς ἄρχοντας],137 καὶ ἐποίησεν αὐτοὺς βάλλειν κλήρους,138 καὶ ἦλθεν ὁ κλῆρος ἐπὶ ἑπτὰ γεραιούς. καὶ [ἀποκριθεὶς] εἷς τῶν [κληρωθέντων]139 ἔλεγεν [τοῖς ὑπηρέταις]·140 δέομαι ὑμῶν, [ἔχω ἐμαυτῷ υἱὸν ἕνα μικρόν, λάβετε αὐτὸν καὶ σφάξατε ἀντὶ ἐμοῦ, καὶ ἐμὲ καταλίπατε.141

Καὶ] ἀποκριθέντες [οἱ ὑπηρέται] εἶπαν [αὐτῷ]· οὐ δυνησόμεθα [λαβεῖν τὸν υἱόν σου] ἐὰν μὴ [πρῶτον] ἀνενέγκωμεν τοῖς μείζοσιν [ἡμῶν].

----

133. *Lat*: in hac civitate.

134. *Lat*: et custodes occisi, et nunc manus carnificum sideraverunt.

135. *Lat* adds: quoniam nullum nobis deest victum.

136. *Lat*: ducentos septem.

137. *Lat*: in concilio.

138. *Lat* adds: esset eorum in cibum et sanguis ipsius in potum.

139. *Lat*: cum . . . duceretur unus ex senioribus illis, super quem sors ceciderat ad interficiendum.

140. *Lat*: ad carnifices.

141. *Lat*: ne me interficiatis, dabo inquid vobis pro me filium meum ad occidendum.

Immediately the swords fell *from the executioners'*
hands, and their hands became stone. When the rulers saw
what had happened, they cried, "Woe to us, for there are
magicians *here*[125] who even went into the prison and led
the people out! *For look, they have put these men too*
under a magic spell.[126] What should we do? *Go now, and*
gather up the elderly of the city; we are hungry."[127]

23. They *went* and gathered up **all the old people of**
the city, and found two hundred *seventeen*.[128] They
brought them to *the rulers*,[129] made them cast lots,[130]
and the lot fell on seven old people. One of those
selected[131] said to the *attendants*,[132] "I beg you! I
have a small son. Take him, slaughter him in my place,
and let me go."[133]

The *attendants* answered *him*, "We cannot *take your*
son unless we *first* take the matter up with *our*
superiors."

----

125. *Lat*: "in this city."

126. *Lat*: "And the guards are slain, and now they have
     petrified the hands of the executioners."

127. *Lat* adds: "because our food is gone."

128. One month's supply: 7 x 31 = 217. *Lat*: 207. *Syr*:
     216.

129. *Lat*: "to the council."

130. *Lat* adds: to see "who would be their food and whose
     blood their drink."

131. *Lat*: "When he was led away, one of those old people
     on whom the lot fell to be killed."

132. *Lat* always reads "executioners" for "attendants."

133. *Lat*: "Do not kill me. I will give you my son to
     kill in my place."

Καὶ ἀπελθόντες [οἱ ὑπηρέται] εἶπαν τοῖς ἄρχουσιν·
[καὶ ἀποκριθέντες οἱ ἄρχοντες εἶπαν τοῖς ὑπηρέταις ὅτι·
ἐὰν δώῃ ὑμῖν τὸν υἱὸν αὐτοῦ ἀντ᾽ αὐτοῦ, ἐάσατε αὐτὸν
ὑπάγειν.[142]

Καὶ ἐλθόντες οἱ ὑπηρέται εἶπαν τῷ γεραιῷ.] καὶ
[ἀποκριθεὶς] ὁ γεραιὸς εἶπεν [αὐτοῖς]· ἔχω [κὰι]
θυγατέρα [σὺν τῷ υἱῷ] μου· [λαβόντες αὐτοὺς][143] σφάξατε,
μόνον ἐμὲ ἐάσατε. καὶ παρέδωκεν αὐτοῦ τὰ παιδία τοῖς
[ὑπηρέταις] ἵνα σφάξωσιν αὐτὰ, ipsum vero dimiserunt
inlesum.

'Ελθόντων δὲ αὐτῶν ἐπὶ τὴν ληνόν,[144] ἔκλαιον δὲ τὰ
παιδία [πρὸς ἄλληλα],[145] καὶ ἐδέοντο [τῶν ὑπηρετῶν]
λέγοντα· δεόμεθα ὑμῶν,[146] μὴ ἡμᾶς ἀποκτείνητε [τῆς
μικρᾶς ἡλικίας ταύτης].[147] ἀλλ᾽ ἐάσατε πληρῶσαι τὰς
ἡλικίας ἡμῶν, καὶ οὕτως σφαγιάσατε [ἡμᾶς].[148] οἱ δὲ
[ὑπηρέται] οὐχ ὑπήκουσαν τοῖς παιδίοις [οὐδὲ

----

142. *C*: ite et accipite filium eius, et suspendite in
     statera, si est major patre, tollite et occidite
     eum nobis, si autem minor est pondere, ne eum
     accipiatis, que et factum est et inventum est
     iunior minor pondere.

143. *Lat*: et ipsam si vultis dabo vobis.

144. This phrase appears in only one Greek ms., though a
     phrase similar to it appears in *C*.

145. *Lat* adds: supplex volutabantur pedibus carnificum.

146. *Lat* adds: miseremini adolescentie nostre. *P*: ἀλλὰ
     σπλαχνίσθητι ἐπὶ τὰς ἡμῶν ἡλικίας.

147. *Lat*: nos modo quia infantulos sumus.

148. *Grp*, including *P*, *Syr*, and *Eth*, add: ἔθος γὰρ ἦν ἐν
     τῇ πόλει ἐκείνῃ, τοὺς τελευτῶντας οὐκ ἐνεταφίαζον,
     ἀλλὰ κατήσθιον αὐτούς.

The attendants went and informed the rulers, *and the rulers answered the attendants:* "If he gives you his son in his place, let him go."[134]

When the attendants came to the old man, they told him, and the old man said *to them,* "In addition to my son I also have a daughter. Take[135] and slaughter *them,* only let me go." He delivered up his children to the *attendants* for them to slaughter, **and they dismissed him unharmed.**

As they went to the trough, the children wept *together,*[136] and begged *the attendants,* "We beg you:[137] do not kill us *when we are so small,*[138] but let us reach full stature and then slaughter *us.*"[139] But the *attendants* did not listen to the children *nor have compassion on them, but brought them weeping and begging to the trough.*[140]

----

134. *C:* "Go and take his son and hang him on a scale. If he weighs more than the father, remove him and kill him for us. But if he weighs less, do not accept him. By doing this you will see if the younger weighs less."

135. *Lat:* "I will also give her to you if you wish."

136. *Lat* adds: "threw themselves at the feet of the executioners."

137. *Lat* and *P* add: "have mercy on our youth."

138. *Lat:* "for we are but children."

139. *Grp,* including *P* (similarly *Syr* and *Eth*), add: "It was customary in that city not to prepare the dead for burial, but to eat them."

140. *Lat:* "with hands outstretched he (sic) seized a sword in order that they might kill them."

ἐσπλαγχνίσθησαν ἐπ' αὐτοῖς, ἀλλὰ ἐπέφερον αὐτὰ ἐπὶ τὴν ληνὸν κλαίοντα καὶ δεόμενα].[149]

Καὶ ἐγένετο [ὡς ἤγαγον αὐτὰ τοῦ σφάξαι], θεασάμενος 'Ανδρέας [τὸ γεγονὸς[150] ἐδάκρυσεν, καὶ κλαίων] ἀνέβλεψεν εἰς τὸν οὐρανὸν καὶ εἶπεν· κύριε 'Ιησοῦ [Χριστέ], καθὼς ἐπήκουσάς μου εἰς τοὺς νεκροὺς καὶ οὐκ εἴασας καταβρωθῆναι αὐτούς, οὕτως καὶ νῦν ἐπάκουσόν μου[151] [τοῦ μὴ ὑπενεγκεῖν τοὺς δημίους τὸν θάνατον ἐπὶ τὰ παιδία ταῦτα,[152] ἀλλὰ ἀναλυθῆναι τὰς μαχαίρας ἐκ τῶν χειρῶν τῶν δημίων.[153]

Καὶ εὐθέως ἐλύθησαν αἱ μάχαιραι καὶ ἔπεσον][154] ἐκ τῶν χειρῶν [τῶν δημίων] ὥσπερ κηρὸς ἐν πυρί. καὶ τούτου γενομένου θεασάμενοι οἱ δήμιοι [τὸ γεγονὸς] ἐφοβήθησαν σφόδρα. καὶ [ἰδὼν] 'Ανδρέας [τὸ γινόμενον][155] ἐδόξασεν τὸν κύριον [ὅτι ὑπήκουσιν αὐτοῦ ἐν παντὶ ἔργῳ].

24. Καὶ θεασάμενοι οἱ ἄρχοντες [τὸ γεγονὸς][156] ἔκλαυσαν κλαυθμὸν μέγαν λέγοντες· [οὐαὶ ἡμῖν,] ὅτι τελευτ<ῶ>μεν νῦν.[157] τί μέλλομεν ποιεῖν;

----

149. *Lat*: extensas manus arripuit <g>ladiu<m> qualiter illos interficerent.

150. *Lat*: omnia que fiebant.

151. *Lat* adds: celeriter.

152. *Lat*: et nec permittas infantulos istos occidi.

153. This sentence is also missing in one important Greek ms. *Grp*, including *P* and *Syr*, add: ὥσπερ κηρὸν ἐν πυρί. *B*: sed deliquescant gladii eorum et arescant manus eorum.

154. *Lat*: sed gladi<o>s eorum tenentes, liquefiant.

155. *Lat* adds: repletus gaudio.

156. *Lat* adds: et gladii liquefacti.

157. The last three words are represented in *Lat* and in only one Greek ms.

As they brought them for slaughter, Andrew saw *what was happening*[141] *and cried.* He looked into heaven *weeping* and said, "Lord Jesus *Christ,* just as you listened to me in the case of the dead guards and did not let them be devoured, so now too, listen to me,[142] *so that the executioners may not bring death on these children.*[143] *Loosen the swords from the hands of the executioners."*[144]

Immediately the swords were loosened[145] and fell from the hands *of the executioners* like wax in fire. At that, when the executioners saw *what had happened,* they were terrified. When Andrew *saw what had happened,* he[146] glorified the Lord, *because he had responded to him in every instance.*

24. When the rulers saw *what had happened,*[147] they wept terribly saying, *"Woe to us,* for now we perish. What shall we do?"

----

141. *Lat:* "everything they were doing."

142. *Lat* adds: "quickly."

143. *Lat:* "Do not permit those children to be killed."

144. *Grp,* including *P,* and *Syr,* add: "like wax in fire." *B:* "their swords melted and their hands withered."

145. *Lat:* "when they grabbed their swords they melted."

146. *Lat* adds: "was full of joy."

147. *Lat* adds: "and the swords melting."

Καὶ ἰδοὺ ὁ διάβολος παρεγένετο ὁμοιωθεὶς γέροντι, καὶ [ἤρξατο] λέγειν [ἐν μέσῳ πάντων].[158] οὐαὶ ὑμῖν, ὅτι τελευτᾶτε νῦν μὴ ἔχοντες][159] διατροφάς. τί [ποιήσουσιν[160] ὑμᾶς πρόβατα καὶ βόες];[161] οὐ μὴ ἀρκέσουσιν ὑμῖν. ἀλλὰ si me vultis audire, [ἀναστάντες] ἐπιζητήσατε ὧδέ τινα [ἐν τῇ πόλει ἐπιδημήσαντα] ξένον ὀνόματι Ἀνδρέαν καὶ ἀποκτείνατε αὐτόν· εἰ δὲ μή γε, οὐκ ἐᾷ ὑμᾶς ταύτην ποιῆσαι τὴν πρᾶξιν ἔτι· αὐτὸς γὰρ ἀπέλυσεν τοὺς ἀνθρώπους ἐκ τῆς φυλακῆς. καὶ γὰρ ἔστιν ὁ ἄνθρωπος ἐν τῇ πόλει ταύτῃ, καὶ ὑμεῖς [οὐκ] οἴδατε αὐτόν. [νῦν οὖν] ἀναστάντες [ἐπιζητήσατε] αὐτόν, [ἵνα τοῦ λοιποῦ δυνηθῆτε τὰς τροφὰς ὑμῶν ἐπισυνάξαι.[162]

Ἦν δὲ ὁ Ἀνδρέας θεωρῶν τὸν διάβολον πῶς ὡμίλει τοῖς ὄχλοις]· ὁ δὲ διάβολος οὐκ ἐθεώρει τὸν μακάριον Ἀνδρέαν. τότε [ἀποκριθεὶς] Ἀνδρέας πρὸς διάβολον εἶπεν· [ὦ Βελία ἐχθρότατε, πάσης κτίσεως πολεμιστὴς ὑπάρχων].[163] ἀλλ' ὁ κύριός μου Ἰησοῦς Χριστὸς ταπεινώσει σε εἰς τὴν ἄβυσσον.

---

158. *B*: in presentia senioribus civitatis Marmedone.

159. *Lat*: non invenientes.

160. *Grm*: ποιήσωσιν.

161. *Lat*: Quid facimus? Nec oves neque boves habemus.

162. From this point until the end of chapter 26 *C* has only: Persuadente diabol<o>, insurrexerunt omnes adversus beatum Andream ut interficerent illum, querentes autem et invenerunt eum.

163. *AS*: Ana þu heardeste stræl to æghwilcre unrihtnesse; þu þe simle fihtest wið manna cyn. *B*: o sagitta durissima que super omne pestiferum gladium inferre dolorem non adquiescis, cuius ignominiosa deceptionis crudelitas a Christi discipulis in omnibus separatur.

Then the devil came looking like an old man and *began to* speak *in the midst of them all,*[148] "Woe to you, for now you are dying *for lack of*[149] food. What *good will sheep or cattle do you?*[150] They will never satisfy you. **If you want my opinion,** *get up and* search for a certain stranger here *residing in the city* named Andrew and kill him. If you do not, he will not allow you to carry out this practice ever again, for it is he who released the people from prison. Indeed, the man is in this city, and you do *not* recognize him. *So now,* arise, *seek* him *out, so that at last you can gather your food."*[151]

Andrew saw how the devil was speaking to the crowds, but the devil did not see the blessed Andrew. Then Andrew told the devil, *"O most cruel Belial, opponent of every creature,*[152] my Lord Jesus Christ will lower you into the abyss."

----

148. *B:* "before the elders of the city Marmedona."

149. *Lat:* "because you cannot find."

150. *Lat:* "What shall we do? We have no sheep or cattle."

151. *C:* "At the devil's persuasion they all rose up against the blessed Andrew in order to kill him. After searching they found him."

152. *AS:* "You hardened shaft to all wickedness, do you forever fight with humankind?" *B:* "O hardened arrow that never stops producing more sorrow than any ravaging sword, you whose shameful cruelty of deception Christ's disciples always detect!" *A* also calls the devil a "shaft."

Καὶ ἀκούσας ταῦτα ὁ διάβολος εἶπεν· τῆς μὲν φωνῆς σου ἀκούω [καὶ ἐπίσταμαι τῆς φωνῆς σου]· ποῦ δὲ ἕστηκας οὐ γινώσκω.

Καὶ [ἀποκριθεὶς] Ἀνδρέας εἶπεν [τῷ διαβόλῳ· [πρὸς τί οὖν] ἐπικέκλησαι [Ἀμαήλ];[164] οὐχ ὅτι τυφλὸς εἶ, μὴ βλέπων πάντας τοὺς ἁγίους;

Καὶ [ἀκούσας ταῦτα] ὁ διάβολος εἶπεν τοῖς πολίταις· περιβλέψασθε νῦν τὸν λαλοῦντα πρός με, ὅτι αὐτός ἐστιν.

Καὶ διαδραμόντες οἱ πολῖται ἔκλεισαν τὰς θύρας τῆς πόλεως καὶ ἐζήτουν τὸν μακάριον,[165] καὶ οὐκ ἐθεώρουν αὐτόν.[166] τότε ὁ κύριος ἐφανέρωσεν ἑαυτὸν τῷ Ἀνδρέᾳ καὶ εἶπεν αὐτῷ· Ἀνδρέα, ἀνάστηθι καὶ φανέρωσον σεαυτὸν εἰς αὐτούς, ἵνα μάθωσιν τὴν δύναμιν [τοῦ ἐνεργοῦντος αὐτοῖς διαβόλου].[167]

25. Τότε ἀναστὰς Ἀνδρέας ἐνώπιον πάντων εἶπεν· [ἰδοὺ] ἐγώ εἰμι Ἀνδρέας ὃν ζητεῖτε.

Ἐπέδραμαν δὲ [ἐπ᾽ αὐτὸν] οἱ ὄχλοι καὶ ἐκράτησαν αὐτὸν[168] λέγοντες· ἃ σὺ ἐποίησας ἡμῖν καὶ ἡμεῖς ποιήσομεν σοί. καὶ διελογίζοντο ἐν ἑαυτοῖς [λέγοντες]· ποίῳ θανάτῳ αὐτὸν ἀποκτείνωμεν;[169] [καὶ ἔλεγον πρὸς ἑαυτοὺς ὅτι ἐὰν ἄρωμεν αὐτοῦ τὴν κεφαλήν, ὁ θάνατος αὐτοῦ οὐκ ἔστιν βάσανος αὐτῷ. ἕτεροι πάλιν ἔλεγον ὅτι ἐὰν αὐτὸν κατακαύσωμεν ἐν πυρὶ καὶ δῶμεν αὐτοῦ τὸ σῶμα

----

164. *Grp*: Σαμαήλ, or Σαταναήλ. *P*: Σατάν.

165. *Grm* and *AS* add: Ἀνδρέαν.

166. *AS*: Þaet hie hine genamon. Cf. *ATh* 16.

167. *AS*: min mægen on þe wesan.

168. *GE*: adpraehensum Andream. *N*: καὶ συλλαβόμενοι τὸν ἀπόστολον.

169. Cf. *ATh* 21.

When the devil heard these things he said, "I hear
your voice, *and I recognize it,* but I do not know where
you are standing."

"Why were you nicknamed *Amael?"*[153] Andrew asked *the
devil.* "Was it not because you are blind, unable to see
all the saints?"

Hearing this, the devil said to the citizens, "Look
around now for the one who is speaking with me, for he
is the one."

The citizens ran about, shut the city gates, and
searched for the blessed one[154] but did not see him.[155]
Then the Lord revealed himself to Andrew and said to
him, "Andrew, arise and reveal yourself to them, so that
they might learn the power *of the devil who sways
them."*[156]

25. Then Andrew arose before them all and said,
"Look, I am Andrew whom you seek."

The crowds ran *to him,* seized him,[157] and said,
"What you have done to us we shall do to you." They
deliberated among themselves *saying,* "How shall we kill
him?" *They said to each other, "If we behead him, his
death will not be agonizing for him." Still others said,
"If we burn him with fire and give his body to feed our
superiors, this death is not torturous for him."*

----

153. *Grp,* perhaps rightly: "Samael," or "Satanael." *P:*
     "Satan."

154. *Grm* and *AS:* "Andrew."

155. *AS:* "that they might take him."

156. *AS:* "my power in you."

157. *GE:* "Andrew was seized." *N:* "seizing the apostle."

τοῖς μείζοσιν ἡμῶν εἰς βρῶσιν, οὗτος ὁ θάνατος οὐκ ἔστιν
βάσανος αὐτῷ].

Τότε [ἀποκριθεὶς εἷς ἐξ αὐτῶν εἰσελθόντος εἰς
αὐτὸν] τοῦ διαβόλου [καὶ πληρώσαντος αὐτοῦ τὴν καρδίαν]
ἔλεγεν τοῖς ὄχλοις ὅτι [καθὼς ἐνεδείξατο ἡμῖν, καὶ ἡμεῖς
ἐνδειξώμεθα αὐτῷ καὶ ἐξεύρωμεν αὐτῷ βασάνους δεινοτάτας.
ἀναστάντες οὖν] περιάψωμεν σχοινίον περὶ τὸν τράχηλον
αὐτοῦ καὶ διασύρωμεν αὐτὸν ἐν [πάσαις] ταῖς πλατείαις
[καὶ ῥύμαις] τῆς πόλεως [καθ᾽ ἑκάστην ἡμέραν] ἕως τῆς
τελευτῆς αὐτοῦ.[170] καὶ ὅταν τελευτήσῃ, διαμερίσωμεν
αὐτοῦ τὸ σῶμα τοῖς πολίταις [πᾶσιν καὶ διαδῶμεν αὐτὸ εἰς
βρῶσιν αὐτοῖς.][171]

Καὶ ἀκούσαντες οἱ ὄχλοι [ἐποίησαν καθὼς εἶπεν
αὐτοῖς].[172] καὶ περιάψαντες σχοινίον περὶ τὸν τράχηλον
αὐτοῦ διέσυρον αὐτὸν ἐν [πάσαις] ταῖς πλατείαις [καὶ
ῥύμαις] τῆς πόλεως,[173] καὶ συρομένου τοῦ μακαρίου
Ἀνδρέου αἱ σάρκες αὐτοῦ ἐκολλῶντο ἐν τῇ γῇ, καὶ τὸ αἷμα
αὐτοῦ ἦν ῥέον ὥσπερ ὕδωρ ἐπὶ τὴν γῆν. ὀψίας δὲ γενομένης
ἔβαλον αὐτὸν εἰς τὴν φυλακήν,[174] δήσαντες αὐτοῦ τὰς
χεῖρας εἰς τὰ ὀπίσθια· καὶ ἦν [παραλελυμένος σφόδρα.[175]

26. Πρωΐας δὲ γενομένης πάλιν ἐξήνεγκαν αὐτὸν καὶ
περιάψαντες σχοινίον περὶ τὸν τράχηλον αὐτοῦ διέσυρον
αὐτόν, καὶ πάλιν αἱ σάρκες αὐτοῦ ἐκολλῶντο ἐν τῇ γῇ καὶ

----

170. *N*: ἔσυρον ἐπὶ πᾶσαν τὴν πόλιν, δημοσίᾳ τοῦτον
βασανίζοντες. Cf. APh Act 15.15.

171. *Grm* om.

172. *AS*: hit him licode.

173. *GE*: ligatis   pedibus,   trahebant   per   plateas
civitatis.

174. *N*: καὶ ἐνέβαλον εἰς τὴν φυλακήν.

175. *AS*: and eall his lichama <wæs> gelysed.

Then *one of them whom* the devil *had entered and possessed,* said to the crowd, *"As he has done to us, let us do to him. Let us invent the most heinous tortures for him. Let us go,* tie a rope around his neck, and drag him through *all* the boulevards *and streets* of the city *each day* until he dies.[158] When he is dead, let us divide his body for *all* of the citizens *and pass it out for their food."*

Hearing this, the crowds *did as he had said to them.*[159] They tied a rope around his neck and dragged him through *all* the boulevards *and streets* of the city.[160] As the blessed Andrew was dragged, his flesh stuck to the ground, and his blood flowed on the ground like water. When evening came, they threw him into the prison[161] and tied his hands behind him. He was *utterly exhausted.*[162]

26. *Early the next morning, they brought him out again, tied a rope around his neck, and dragged him about. Again his flesh stuck to the ground and his blood flowed.*[163] The blessed Andrew wept *and prayed,* "My Lord

----

158. *N*: "they dragged him throughout the city, torturing him in public."

159. *AS*: "it pleased them."

160. *GE*: "they tied up his feet and dragged him through the boulevards of the city."

161. *N*: "and they threw him into the prison."

162. *AS*: "and all his body was crushed."

163. *AS*: "So also on the next day they did the same to him."

τὸ αἷμα αὐτοῦ ἦν ῥέον.]176 καὶ ἔκλαιεν ὁ μακάριος
Ἀνδρέας [καὶ ηὔχετο] λέγων· κύριέ μου Ἰησοῦ Χριστέ,
ἐλθὲ καὶ θέασαι ἃ ἐποίησαν me τῷ δούλῳ σου. ἀλλὰ ὑπομένω
διὰ τὴν ἐντολήν σου ἣν ἐνετείλω μοι λέγων· μὴ ποιήσῃς
κατὰ τὴν ἀπιστίαν αὐτῶν. 177 θέασαι οὖν κύριε ὅσας μοι
[βασάνους] παρέχουσιν· [σὺ γὰρ γινώσκεις κύριε τὴν
ἀνθρωπίνην σάρκα. 178 ἐγὼ γὰρ γινώσκω κύριε ὅτι οὐκ εἶ
μακρὰν ἀπὸ τῶν σῶν δούλων· ἀλλ' οὐδὲ ἐγὼ ἀντιλέγω διὰ
τὴν ἐντολήν σου ἣν ἐνετείλω μοι. εἰ δὲ μή γε, ἐποίουν
αὐτοὺς εἰς τὴν ἄβυσσον κατελθεῖν μετὰ τῆς πόλεως
αὐτῶν. 179 ἀλλ' οὐ μὴ ἐγκαταλείψω τὴν ἐντολήν σου ἣν
ἐνετείλω μοι ἕως θανάτου, ὅτι σὺ εἶ βοηθός μου κύριε·
μόνον μὴ ἐάσῃς τὸν ἐχθρὸν ἐπιγελάσαι μου.]180

Καὶ ταῦτα [τοῦ μακαρίου Ἀνδρέου] λέγοντος ὁ
διάβολος [ὄπισθεν περιεπάτει]181 καὶ ἔλεγεν τοῖς ὄχλοις·
τύπτετε αὐτοῦ τὸ στόμα ἵνα μὴ λαλῇ.

Ὀψίας δὲ γενομένης ἦραν τὸν Ἀνδρέαν καὶ ἔβαλον
αὐτὸν πάλιν εἰς τὴν φυλακήν, [δήσαντες αὐτοῦ τὰς χεῖρας
ὄπισθεν, καὶ εἴασαν αὐτὸν εἰς τὴν αὔριον πάλιν].

Καὶ παραλαβὼν ὁ διάβολος μεθ' ἑαυτοῦ ἑπτὰ δαίμονας,
οὓς ὁ μακάριος Ἀνδρέας ἐξέβαλεν ἐκ τῶν περιχώρων, καὶ
εἰσελθόντες ἐν τῇ φυλακῇ ἔστησαν ἐνώπιον τοῦ μακαρίου

----

176. *AS*: Swilce oþre dæge þæt ilce hie dydon.

177. Cf. *APh* Acts 8 and 15.25, 15.29, 15.31, 15.33,
    15.34, and 15.37.

178. Cf. *APh* Act 4.

179. Cf. *APh* Act 15.26.

180. Even though this section of the prayer is missing
    in *C* and in *AS*, *A* resonates with it, suggesting
    that some Latin version contained it or something
    similar.

181. *Lat* and *Grp* om.

Jesus Christ, come and see what they have done to **me** your servant. But I endure because of your command which you commanded me when you said, 'Do not respond in kind to their unbelief.' Now Lord, observe how many *tortures* they bring upon me, *for you, Lord, know human flesh. I know, Lord, that you are not far from your servants, and I do not dispute the command which you gave me. Otherwise, I would have made them and their city plunge into the abyss. But I shall never forsake your command which you commanded me, even to the point of death, because you, Lord, are my help. Only do not let the enemy mock me.* "

As *the blessed Andrew* said these things, the devil *was walking behind him* saying to the crowds, "Slap his mouth to shut him up!"

At nightfall they took Andrew, threw him again into the prison, *tied his hands behind him, and left him again until the next day.*

Taking with him seven demons whom the blessed Andrew had cast out of the vicinity, the devil entered the prison, stood before the blessed Andrew, and jeered at him cruelly. *The seven demons and the devil* taunted

'Ανδρέου καὶ ἐχλεύαζον αὐτὸν χλευασμὸν μέγα<ν>· [καὶ
ἀποκριθέντες οἱ ἑπτὰ δαίμονες σὺν τῷ διαβόλῳ] εἶπον [τῷ
μακαρίῳ 'Ανδρέᾳ· νῦν ἐνέπεσας εἰς τὰς χεῖρας ἡμῶν. 182
ποῦ ἐστιν ἡ δύναμίς σου καὶ ὁ φόβος σου καὶ ἡ δόξα σου
καὶ ἡ ὕψωσίς σου, 183 ὁ ἐπαίρων σεαυτὸν ἐφ' ἡμᾶς καὶ
ἀτιμάζων ἡμᾶς καὶ διηγούμενος τὰ ἔργα ἡμῶν τοῖς κατὰ
τόπον καὶ χώραν, καὶ ἐποίησας τὰ ἱερὰ ἡμῶν οἰκίας
ἐρήμους γενέσθαι ἵνα μὴ ἀνενεχθῶσιν θυσίαι ἐν αὐτοῖς,
ὅπως καὶ ἡμεῖς τερφθῶμεν; διὰ τοῦτο οὖν καὶ ἡμεῖς
ποιοῦμεν τὰ ἀντάξια καὶ ἀποκτενοῦμέν σε ὡς καὶ τὸν
διδάσκαλόν σου τὸν λεγόμενον 'Ιησοῦν ὃν ἀπέκτεινεν
Ἡρῴδης.]184

27. Καὶ [ἀποκριθεὶς] ὁ διάβολος ἔλεγεν τοῖς ἑπτὰ
δαίμοσιν [τοῖς πονηροῖς]·185 τεκνία μου, ἀποκτείνατε
τοῦτον τὸν ἀτιμάζοντα ἡμᾶς, 186 [ἵνα λοιπὸν πᾶσαι αἱ
χῶραι ἡμῶν γένωνται]. τότε ἐλθόντες οἱ ἑπτὰ δαίμονες
ἔστησαν ἐνώπιον [τοῦ 'Ανδρέου θελόντες αὐτὸν
ἀποκτεῖναι]· καὶ θεασάμενοι τὴν [σφραγῖδα]187 ἐπὶ τοῦ
μετώπου αὐτοῦ, [ἣν ἔδωκεν αὐτῷ ὁ κύριος], ἐφοβήθησαν,
καὶ οὐκ ἠδυνήθησαν προσεγγίσαι αὐτῷ, ἀλλ' ἔφυγον. 188 καὶ

----

182. Missing in *Lat* and in an important Greek ms. *AS*:
     Hwæt is þæt þu her gemetest? See however *A* which,
     like the Greek, contains a reference to Andrew's
     falling into the devil's power, suggesting that its
     antecendent Latin translation also contained a
     similar reading.

183. *AS*: hwilc gefreolseð þe nu of urum gewealde? Hwær
     is þin gilp and þin hiht?

184. *B*: quoniam actus nostros confundere non cessabat.

185. Also absent in one Greek ms.

186. *AS* adds: and ure weorc.

187. *Lat* (similarly *Eth*): signum . . . crucis.

188. In *C* those who were afraid to seize Andrew because
     of the sign of the cross were the residents of the
     city, not demons.

the blessed Andrew, "Now you have fallen into our hands.[164] Where are your power, your awesomeness, your glory, and your grandeur,[165] you who raise yourself up against us, dishonor us, narrate our deeds to the people in every place and region, you who make our temples deserted houses with the result that no sacrifices for our delight are offered up in them? For this reason we will retaliate. We will kill you as Herod killed your teacher called Jesus."[166]

27. The devil said to his seven *wicked* demons, "My children, kill him who dishonors us,[167] *so that at last all the regions will be ours.*" Then the seven demons came and stood before *Andrew wanting to kill him.* But when they saw the *seal*[168] on his forehead *which the Lord had given him,* they were afraid and were not able to approach him but fled. The devil said to them, "My children, why do you *flee from him and* not kill him?"

----

164. *AS*: "What is it you have found here?"

165. *AS*: "Who will deliver you now from our power? Where is your boasting and your hope?"

166. *B*: "because he has not ceased confounding our deeds."

167. *AS* adds: "and our works."

168. *Lat* (similarly *Eth*): "the sign of the cross."

εἶπεν αὐτοῖς ὁ διάβολος· τεκνία μου, διὰ τί [ἐφύγετε ἀπ'
αὐτοῦ καὶ] οὐκ ἀπεκτείνατε αὐτόν;

Καὶ ἀποκριθέντες οἱ δαίμονες εἶπον [τῷ διαβόλῳ]
ὅτι· ἡμεῖς οὐ δυνάμεθα [αὐτὸν ἀποκτεῖναι], εἴδομεν γὰρ
τὴν [σφραγῖδα]189 ἐπὶ τοῦ μετώπου αὐτοῦ καὶ ἐφοβήθημεν
[αὐτόν].190 ἐπιστάμεθα γὰρ αὐτὸν πρὶν ἢ αὐτὸν ἐλθεῖν ἐν
τῇ θλίψει ταύτῃ [τῆς ταπεινώσεως αὐτοῦ·191 ἀλλὰ] σὺ
[ἀπελθὼν] ἀπόκτεινον αὐτὸν εἰ δυνατὸς εἶ· ἡμεῖς [γὰρ]
οὐχ ὑπακούομέν σου, μή ποτε ὁ θεὸς ἰάσεται αὐτὸν καὶ
παραδώσει ἡμᾶς εἰς βασάνους [πικράς].192

Καὶ ἀποκριθεὶς [εἶς ἐκ τῶν διαμόνων εἶπεν]· οὐ
δυνάμεθα ἡμεῖς [αὐτὸν] ἀποκτεῖναι· ἀλλὰ [δεῦτε]193
ἐπιγελάσωμεν αὐτῷ ἐν τῇ θλίψει ταύτῃ.194

[Καὶ ἐλθόντες οἱ δαίμονες σὺν τῷ διαβόλῳ πρὸς τὸν
μακάριον Ἀνδρέαν ἔστησαν ἐνώπιον αὐτοῦ καὶ] ἐχλεύαζον
αὐτὸν καὶ ἔλεγον [αὐτῷ· ἰδοὺ καὶ σὺ] Ἀνδρέα [ἦλθες εἰς
αἰσχύνην ἀτιμίας καὶ εἰς βασάνους]·195 καὶ τίς ἐστιν ὁ
δυνάμενός σε ῥύσασθαι;

----

189. *Lat*: crucem.

190. Also absent in *Grp* and *P*.

191. *AS*: he ure wæs wealdend.

192. Also missing in *P*. *AS*: wyrsan.

193. *Lat*: conprehendite illum et claudite.

194. *Grp* add: τῆς ταπεινώσεως αὐτοῦ. *Lat* adds: et
     tribulatione maxima.

195. *Lat*: quid est hoc quod venisti hic in derisum
     nostrum? Si adicimus tibi universa et orribilia
     tormenta.

The demons answered *the devil,* "We cannot *kill him,* for we saw the *seal*[169] on his forehead and were afraid *of him,* for we knew him before he came into this torment *of his humiliation.*[170] You *go* and kill him if you can, *for* we do not obey you, lest God heal him and deliver us up to *bitter*[171] tortures."

"We cannot kill *him,*" said *one of the demons,* "but *come,*[172] let us mock him in this torment."[173]

The demons and the devil came to the blessed Andrew, stood before him, and mocked him saying, "*Look* Andrew, *you too have come to dishonorable shame and tortures.*[174] Who can rescue you?"

---

169. *Lat:* "cross."

170. *AS:* "he was our master."

171. *AS:* "worse."

172. *Lat:* "seize him and shut him up."

173. *Grp* add: "of his humiliation." *Lat* adds: "and extreme tribulation."

174. *Lat:* "Why did you come here to mock us? If we afflict you with every type of terrible torture."

Καὶ ταῦτα ἀκούσας ὁ μακάριος ᾿Ανδρέας [ἔκλαιεν μεγάλως·[196] καὶ ἦλθεν αὐτῷ φωνὴ λέγουσα]· ᾿Ανδρέα, διὰ τί κλαίεις; [ἦν δὲ ἡ φωνὴ ἐκείνη τοῦ διαβόλου]· μετήλλαξεν γὰρ [τὴν φωνὴν αὐτοῦ] ὁ διάβολος.

[Τότε] ἀποκριθεὶς ὁ ᾿Ανδρέας [εἶπεν· κλαίω ὅτι ἐνετείλατό μοι] ὁ κύριός μου λέγων· [μακροθύμησον ἐπ᾿ αὐτοῖς·[197] εἰ δὲ μή γε, ἔδειξα ὑμῖν <μου δύναμιν>].[198]

Καὶ [ἀποκριθεὶς] ὁ διάβολος εἶπεν τῷ ᾿Ανδρέᾳ·[199] εἴ τί ἐστίν σοι δυνατόν, ποίησον.[200]

Καὶ ἀποκριθεὶς ὁ ᾿Ανδρέας [εἶπεν]· ἐὰν ἀποκτείνητέ με ἐνταῦθα, οὐ μὴ ποιήσω κατὰ τὸ θέλημα τὸ ὑμῶν, ἀλλὰ κατὰ τὸ θέλημα [τοῦ πέμψαντός με][201] ᾿Ιησοῦ Χριστοῦ. [διὰ τοῦτο οὖν ταῦτά μοι ἐνδείκνυσθε, ἵνα ἐγκαταλείψω τὴν ἐντολὴν τοῦ κυρίου μου· ἐὰν γάρ μοι ὁ κύριος] ἐπισκοπὴν ποιήσῃ ἐν τῇ πόλει ταύτῃ, παιδεύσω ὑμᾶς [καθὼς ἄξιοί ἐστε]. καὶ ταῦτα ἀκούσαντες οἱ ἑπτὰ δαίμονες ἔφυγον [σὺν τῷ διαβόλῳ].[202]

28. Πρωΐας δὲ γενομένης[203] [ἐξήνεγκαν τὸν ᾿Ανδρέαν πάλιν καὶ περιάψαντες σχοινίον περὶ τὸν τράχηλον αὐτοῦ

----

196. Lat: nullum ei dedit responsum, sed tantum convertit faciem suam ad celum, flens intra semedipsum, oravit ad dominum.

197. Lat: omnia sufferre mala que nobis inferuntur.

198. This sentence requires an object which I have supplied to make sense in context.

199. Lat: audi me Andrea.

200. Lat: ne invanum recipias maiora tormenta.

201. Lat, P, and Grp om.

202. This last phrase is also missing in one important Greek ms.

203. C adds: miserunt ad carcerem, et.

After the blessed Andrew heard these things *he wept greatly,*[175] *and a voice came to him saying,* "Andrew, why do you weep?" *(The voice was the devil's,* for the devil altered *his voice.)*

"*I weep,*" answered Andrew, "*because* my Lord *commanded me,* 'Be patient with them.'[176] *Had he not, I would have shown you <my power>.*"

The devil *answered Andrew,*[177] "*If you have some such power, use it.*"[178]

"Even if you kill me here," answered Andrew, "I will never do your will but the will of Jesus Christ *who* sent me.[179] *For this reason then you do these things to me, so that I might neglect the command of my Lord, for if the Lord* visits this city *for my sake,* I will punish you *as you deserve.*" When the seven demons heard these things, they fled *with the devil.*

28. The next morning they[180] again fetched Andrew, tied a rope around his neck, and dragged him.[181] Again his flesh stuck *to the earth,* and his blood *flowed on*

----

175. *Lat:* "He gave no response, but turned his face toward heaven, wept silently, and prayed to the Lord."

176. *Lat:* "suffer every evil they inflict upon us."

177. *Lat:* "Listen to me, Andrew."

178. *Lat:* "lest you receive worse torments needlessly."

179. Cf. John 4:34 and 5:30.

180. *C* adds: "sent to the prison and."

181. *C* adds: "through the streets and boulevards of the city."

ἔσυρον αὐτόν,[204] καὶ πάλιν αἱ σάρκες αὐτοῦ ἐκολλῶντο [ἐν τῇ γῇ], καὶ τὸ αἷμα αὐτοῦ [ἔρρεν ὥσπερ ὕδωρ ἐπὶ τὴν γῆν].[205] καὶ συρόμενος ὁ μακάριος ἔκλαιεν[206] λέγων· κύριέ μου Ἰησοῦ Χριστέ, ἀρκεταί εἰσιν αἱ βάσανοι αὗται· ἐξητόνησα γάρ. ὁρᾷς ὅσα ὁ ἐχθρὸς ἐνεδείξατό μοι μετὰ τῶν ἑαυτοῦ δαιμόνων· σὺ [γὰρ] κύριε μνήσθητι ὅτι [ἐποίησας τρεῖς ὥρας] ἐπὶ τοῦ σταυροῦ καὶ [ὠλιγοψύχησας] λέγων·[207] πάτερ [μου],[208] ἵνα τί με ἐγκατέλιπας; [ἰδοὺ κύριε][209] ἐν τρισὶν ἡμέραις διασύρομαι ἐν ταῖς πλατείαις καὶ ῥύμαις τῆς πόλεως ταύτης· καὶ [μάλιστα] γινώσκων κύριε [τὴν ἀνθρωπίνην σάρκα] ὅτι ἀσθενής ἐστιν· ἐπίταξον οὖν κύριέ [μου] ἀναλαβεῖν τὸ πνεῦμά μου ἀπ᾽ ἐμοῦ, [ἵνα λοιπὸν ἀναπαύσεως τύχω]. ποῦ εἰσιν οἱ λόγοι σου κύριε οὓς ἐλάλησας πρὸς ἡμᾶς ἐπιστηρίζων ἡμᾶς, ὅτι[210] ἐὰν περιπατήσητε μετ᾽ ἐμοῦ,[211] οὐ μὴ ἀπολέσητε μίαν τρίχα ἐκ τῆς κεφαλῆς ὑμῶν; πρόσσεχες [οὖν] κύριε καὶ θέασαι ὅτι αἱ σάρκες μου καὶ αἱ τρίχες τῆς κεφαλῆς μου ἐκολλήθησαν τῇ γῇ·[212] [ἰδοὺ γάρ] εἰμι διασυρόμενος ἡμέρας τρεῖς ἐν

---

204. C adds: per omnes vicos et plateas civitatis.

205. N: ἔσυρον ἐπὶ πᾶσαν τὴν πόλιν, δημοσίᾳ τοῦτον βασανίζοντες. GE: ligatis pedibus, trahebant per plateas civitatis.

206. Lat adds: voce magna.

207. Lat adds: ad patrem.

208. One important Greek ms. om.

209. Grp om.

210. Lat adds: si me audieritis, et.

211. Grm: ὅτε περιεπατήσαμεν μετὰ σοῦ, λέγων ἡμῖν.

212. GE: Iam enim capilli capitis eius evellebantur, et sanguis defluebat a capite, et oravit ad Dominum, dicens: Aperi, quaeso, Domine, oculos cordis eorum, ut cognoscant te Deum verum et desistant ab hac iniquitate; et ne statuas illis hoc in peccatum, quia nesciunt quid faciunt.

the ground like water.[182] As he was dragged, the blessed Andrew wept, saying,[183] "Lord Jesus Christ, these tortures are enough; I am exhausted. Look at what the enemy and his demons have done to me. Remember, O Lord, that you *spent three hours* on the cross and *you weakened,* for you said,[184] 'My Father, why have you forsaken me?'[185] *Look, Lord,* for three days I am dragged around in the boulevards and streets of this city. Lord, *especially* because you know that *human flesh* is weak, command my spirit to leave me, *my* Lord, *so that at last I may attain rest.* Lord, where are your words which you spoke to us to strengthen us, telling us, 'If you[186] walk with me,[187] you will not lose one hair from your head?'[188] *Therefore,* Lord, look and see that my flesh and the hairs of my head stick to the ground,[189] *for* I have been dragged around in heinous tortures for three days, and you, my Lord, have not revealed yourself to me

---

182. *N*: "they dragged him throughout the city, torturing him in public." *GE*: "they tied up his feet and dragged him through the boulevards of the city."

183. *Lat* adds: "with a loud voice."

184. *Lat* adds: "to the Father."

185. Cf. Mark 15:34 and Matt 27:46.

186. *Lat* adds: "obey me and."

187. Instead of the preceding phrase *Grm* read: "When we walked with you."

188. Cf. Luke 21:18 and Acts 27:34.

189. *GE*: "For already the hairs of his head were plucked out, and blood flowed from his head. He prayed to the Lord, saying, 'O Lord, I pray, open the eyes of their hearts, that they might recognize you, the true God and end this iniquity. Do not hold this against them as sin, for they know not what they do.'"

βασάνοις δειναῖς, καὶ οὐκ ἐφανέρωσάς μοι σεαυτὸν κύριέ
μου ἵνα ἐπισχυρίσῃς μου τὴν καρδίαν· [καὶ ὠλιγοψύχησα
σφόδρα].²¹³ ταῦτα [λέγων] ὁ μακάριος Ἀνδρέας
[διεσύρετο].²¹⁴

Τότε ἦλθεν αὐτῷ φωνή²¹⁵ ἑβραϊστὶ λέγουσα· ἡμέτερε
Ἀνδρέα, ὁ οὐρανὸς καὶ ἡ γῆ παρελεύσεται, οἱ δὲ λόγοι
μου οὐ μὴ παρέλθωσιν. πρόσσχες οὖν καὶ θέασαι ὄπισθέν
σου [τὰς πεσούσας] σου σάρκας καὶ τρίχας τί
γεγόνασιν.²¹⁶

[Καὶ στραφεὶς] ὁ Ἀνδρέας εἶδεν μεγάλα δένδρα
[φυέντα]²¹⁷ καρποφόρα·²¹⁸ καὶ [ἀποκριθεὶς] εἶπεν· ἔγνων
γὰρ κύριε ὅτι οὐκ ἐγκατέλιπάς με.

Ὀψίας δὲ γεναμένης²¹⁹ ἐνέβαλον αὐτὸν εἰς τὴν
φυλακήν,²²⁰ ἤδη ἀτονήσαντα ἐπὶ πολύ·²²¹ καὶ ἔλεγον ἐν
ἑαυτοῖς [οἱ ἄνδρες τῆς πόλεως· τάχα] τελευτᾷ ἐν τῇ νυκτὶ
ταύτῃ·²²² [ἠτόνησεν] γάρ, [καὶ] αἱ σάρκες αὐτοῦ
ἐδαπανήθησαν.

----

213. *Lat*: ut non deficerem.

214. *Lat*: cum intra se orasset.

215. *Lat* adds: domini.

216. Cf. *APh* Act 15.37.

217. Also missing in *P*.

218. Cf. *APh* Act 15.37 and 42.

219. *Grm* add: ἦραν αὐτὸν πάλιν καί.

220. *Grm* add: δήσαντες αὐτοῦ τὰς χεῖρας ὄπισθεν. *N*: καὶ
ἐνέβαλον εἰς τὴν φυλακήν.

221. *Grm* add: καὶ ἦν παραλελυμένος σφόδρα.

222. *Grm* add: καὶ οὐχ εὑρίσκομεν αὐτὸν ζῶντα ἐν τῇ ἑξῆς
ἡμέρᾳ.

to fortify my heart. *I am utterly exhausted.*"[190] The blessed Andrew said these things *as he was dragged about.*[191]

Then a voice[192] came to him in Hebrew, "Our Andrew, heaven and earth will pass away, but my words will never pass away.[193] Therefore, look and see behind you at what has happened to your *fallen* flesh and hair."

Andrew *turned and* saw large fruit-bearing trees *sprouting*, and he *responded*, "I know, Lord, that you have not forsaken me."

When evening came,[194] they threw him into the prison.[195] Already he was exceedingly weak.[196] *The men of the city* said to each other, "He will *probably* die during the night,[197] for he is *weak and* his flesh spent."

---

190. *Lat*: "so that I not weaken."

191. *Lat*: "as he prayed within himself."

192. *Lat* adds: "of the Lord."

193. Cf. Mark 13:21, Matt 24:35, and Luke 21:33.

194. *Grm* add: "they again lifted him up and."

195. *Grm* add: "and tied his hands behind him." *N*: "and they threw him into the prison."

196. *Grm* add: "and utterly disabled."

197. *Grm* add: "We will not find him alive tomorrow."

29. Ὁ δὲ κύριος παρεγένετο ἐν τῇ φυλακῇ, καὶ
ἐκτείνας τὴν χεῖρα αὐτοῦ εἶπεν [τῷ ᾿Ανδρέᾳ· ἐπίδος μοι
τὴν χεῖρά σου καὶ] ἀνάστηθι [ὑγιής].

Καὶ θεασάμενος [ὁ ᾿Ανδρέας τὸν κύριον ἐπέδωκεν αὐτῷ
τὴν χεῖρα αὐτοῦ] καὶ ἀνέστη ὑγιής, καὶ πεσὼν
προσεκύνησεν αὐτῷ καὶ εἶπεν· εὐχαριστῶ σοι κύριέ μου
᾿Ιησοῦ Χριστέ.

Καὶ θεασάμενος ὁ ᾿Ανδρέας εἰς μέσον τῆς φυλακῆς
εἶδεν στῦλον ἑστῶτα, καὶ ἐπὶ τὸν στῦλον ἀνδριὰς
ἐπικείμενος ἀλαβαστρινός·[223] καὶ[224] ἥπλωσεν τὰς χεῖρας
αὐτοῦ,[225] καὶ εἶπεν [τῷ στύλῳ καὶ τῷ ἐπ᾿ αὐτῷ
ἀνδριάντι]·[226] φοβήθητι τὸν τύπον τοῦ σταυροῦ,[227] ὃν
φρίσσει ὁ οὐρανὸς καὶ ἡ γῆ, [καὶ][228] ἀποβαλέτω ὁ ἀνδριὰς
[ὁ ἐπικείμενος ἐπὶ τὸν στῦλον] ὕδωρ πολὺ διὰ τοῦ
στόματος αὐτοῦ ὡς καταλυσμοῦ,[229] ἵνα παιδευθῶσιν οἱ ἐν
τῇ πόλει ταύτῃ.[230] [μὴ φοβηθῇς ὦ λίθε καὶ εἴπῃς ὅτι ἐγὼ
λίθος εἰμὶ καὶ οὐκ εἰμὶ ἄξιος αἰνέσαι τὸν κύριον· καὶ
γὰρ καὶ ὑμεῖς τετιμημένοι ἐστέ. ἡμᾶς γὰρ ἔπλασεν ὁ
κύριος ἀπὸ γῆς, ὑμεῖς δὲ καθαροί ἐστε· διὰ τοῦτο ἔδωκεν
ὁ θεὸς ἐξ ὑμῶν τῷ λαῷ αὐτοῦ τὰς πλάκας τοῦ νόμου· οὐ γὰρ
ἔγραψεν ἐν πλαξὶν χρυσαῖς ἢ ἀργυραῖς ἀλλ᾿ ἐν πλαξὶν

----

223. *N*: καὶ προσσχὼν ἀνδριάντι τινὶ λιθίνῳ ἑστῶτι
ἄντικρυς τῆς φυλακῆς.

224. *Grm* add: ἀνελθὼν ὁ ᾿Ανδρέας ἐπὶ τὸν ἀνδριάντα.

225. *Grm* add: ἑπτάκις.

226. *N*: ἐκτείνας τὴν χεῖρα καὶ σφραγίσας εἶπεν· σοι λέγω
τῷ ἀνδριάντι.

227. *N*: φοβήθητι τὸ σημεῖον τοῦ σταυροῦ.

228. *Lat* adds: precipio tibi ut.

229. *N*: καὶ ἐξάγαγε ὕδωρ.

230. *N*: ὅπως ἰδόντες οἱ ταύτην τὴν πόλιν κατοικοῦντες
ἀπηνέστατοι ἄνθρωποι παιδευθῶσιν.

29. The Lord appeared in the prison, and extending his hand he said *to Andrew, "Give me your hand and* stand up *whole."*

When *Andrew* saw *the Lord Jesus, he gave him his hand* and stood up whole. He fell, worshiped him, and said, "I thank you, my Lord Jesus Christ."

When Andrew looked into the middle of the prison, he saw a standing pillar and on the pillar rested an alabaster statue.[198] He[199] stretched out his hands,[200] and said *to the pillar and the statue on it,*[201] "Fear the sign of the cross, at which heaven and earth tremble,[202] and[203] let the statue *sitting on the pillar* spew from its mouth water as abundant as a flood,[204] so that the residents of this city may be punished.[205] *Do not fear, O stone, and say 'I am just a stone and unworthy to praise the Lord,' for in fact you too have been honored. The Lord molded us from the earth, but you are pure. Therefore, God gave to his people the tablets of the law made from you. He did not write on gold or silver tablets but on tablets of stone. So now, O statue, carry out this plan."*

----

198. *N:* "and he noticed a stone statue standing adjacent to the prison."

199. *Grm* add: "Andrew scaled the statue."

200. *Grm* add: "seven times."

201. *N:* "extended his hand, made the sign of the cross, and said: 'I tell you, O statue.'"

202. *N:* "fear the sign of the cross."

203. *Lat* adds: "I command you to."

204. *N:* "and send forth water."

205. *N:* "so that the cruel people living in this city who see this may be punished."

λιθίναις. νῦν οὖν ποίησον ὦ ἀνδρία τὴν οἰκονομίαν
ταύτην].231

Ταῦτα εἰπόντος τοῦ μακαρίου Ἀνδρέου εὐθὺς ἀπέβαλεν
ὁ λίθινος ἀνδριὰς ἐκ τοῦ στόματος αὐτοῦ ὕδωρ πολὺ ὥσπερ
[ἐκ διώρυγός τινος],232 καὶ ὑψώθη τὸ ὕδωρ [ἐπὶ τὴν
γῆν],233 καὶ ἦν ἁλμυρὸν σφόδρα κατεσθίον σάρκας
ἀνθρώπων.234

30. Πρωΐας δὲ γεναμένης [θεασάμενοι οἱ ἄνδρες τῆς
πόλεως235 ἤρξαντο φεύγειν λέγοντες ἐν ἑαυτοῖς· οὐαὶ
ἡμῖν, ὅτι τελευτῶμεν νῦν.236 καὶ ἀπέκτεινεν τὸ ὕδωρ τὰ
κτήνη αὐτῶν καὶ τὰ τέκνα αὐτῶν].237 καὶ ἤρξαντο φεύγειν
ἐκ τῆς πόλεως.

----

231. Even though C, B, and AS omit the section in
brackets, A lines 1508-21 leave little doubt that
the Latin version behind it, like the Greek,
extolled the virtues of the statue. However, the
passage also is missing in O, Syr, Eth, and Arm, as
well as in GE, N, and E.

232. C: tanquam fluvius torrens. N: ἐξῆλθεν εὐθέως ὕδωρ
ἐκ τοῦ στόματος τοῦ ἀνδράντος εἰς πλῆθος ὡσεὶ
κατακλυσμοῦ.

233. C: usque ad summum.

234. C adds: plurimos populos, et iumentas. B: ab homine
usque ad pecus vel omnem creaturam viventem. AS
(similarly Syr): heora bearn and hyra nytenu.

235. N: ὅπερ θεασάμενοι οἱ τῆς πόλεως κάτοικοι ἐπὶ πολὺ
ὑψούμενον.

236. GE: Et statim timor magna factus est super
habitatores civitatis illius.

237. Even though this section is missing in Lat, the
reference here to the destruction of cattle and
children appears at the end of the preceding
chapter in both C and AS. Cf. Photius Bibliotheca
114: νεκρῶν δὲ ἀνθρώπων καὶ βοῶν καὶ κτηνῶν ἄλλων
. . . ἀναστάσεις.

As soon as the blessed Andrew had said these things, the stone statue spewed from its mouth a great quantity of water as *from a trench,*[206] and the water rose *on the earth.*[207] It was exceedingly brackish and consumed human flesh.[208]

30. When morning came, *the men of the city saw what had happened*[209] *and began to flee, saying to themselves, "Woe to us, for now we die!"*[210] *The water killed their cattle and their children,*[211] and they began to flee the city.

----

206. *C:* "like a rushing river." *N:* "immediately the water came out of the mouth of the statue in quantity as from a flood."

207. *C:* "to the summit."

208. *C* adds: "most of the people and domestic animals." *B:* "from human to cattle and every living creature." *AS* (similarly *Syr*): "their children and their cattle."

209. *N:* "when the inhabitants of the city saw the water mounting up."

210. *GE:* "And immediately great fear came over the inhabitants of that city."

211. Photius, *Bibliotheca* 114 says that one of the apocryphal Acts he read mentioned the reviving "of dead people and cattle and other domestic animals."

Τότε ὁ ᾿Ανδρέας εἶπεν [πρὸς τὸν κύριον λέγων]·[238] κύριε ᾿Ιησοῦ Χριστέ, ἔφθην[239] ἐπιχειρῆσαι καὶ ἐποιῆσαι τὸ σημεῖον τοῦτο ἐν τῇ πόλει ταύτῃ. μή με ἐγκαταλίπῃς, ἀλλ᾿ ἀπόστειλον [Μιχαὴλ τὸν ἀρχ]άγγελόν σου ἐν νεφέλῃ πυρός, καὶ περιτείχισον τὴν πόλιν ταύτην, ἵνα ἐάν τις θελήσῃ ἐκφυγεῖν ἐξ αὐτῆς μὴ δυνηθῇ ἐξελθεῖν τοῦ πυρός.

Καὶ εὐθέως κατῆλθεν νεφέλη πυρὸς καὶ ἐκύκλωσεν πᾶσαν τὴν πόλιν [ὡς τεῖχος]. καὶ [μαθὼν][240] ὁ ᾿Ανδρέας [τὴν γενομένην οἰκονομίαν] εὐλόγει τὸν κύριον. τὸ δὲ ὕδωρ ὑψώθη ἕως τραχήλου τῶν ἀνδρῶν[241] καὶ ἦν κατεσθίον αὐτοὺς σφόδρα.

Καὶ ἔκλαιον [καὶ ἐβόων][242] πάντες λέγοντες· οὐαὶ ἡμῖν· ταῦτα γὰρ πάντα ἐπῆλθεν ἐφ᾿ ἡμᾶς διὰ τὸν ξένον τὸν ὄντα ἐν τῇ φυλακῇ, ὃν βασάνοις παρεδώκαμεν.[243] τί οὖν μέλλομεν ποιεῖν; πορευθῶμεν εἰς τὴν φυλακὴν καὶ ἀπολύσωμεν αὐτόν, μή ποτε ἀποθάνωμεν ἐν τῷ ὕδατι τούτῳ τοῦ κατακλυσμοῦ· ἀλλὰ βοήσωμεν ἅπαντες ὅτι πιστεύομέν σοι [ὁ θεὸς][244] τοῦ ξένου ἀνθρώπου· καὶ ἆρον ἀφ᾿ ἡμῶν [τὸ ὕδωρ τοῦτο].[245] καὶ ἐξῆλθον ἅπαντες βοῶντες [φωνῇ

----

238. One important Greek ms. om.

239. Following *P*. This rare use of φθάνω apparently confounded the scribes transcribing the text, who variously wrote ἔφην, ὤφθην, ὀφθείς, ἐφ᾿ ὅν, and ἐφ᾿ ᾧ. *C* reads "per virtutem tuam." Bonnet, who apparently had not consulted *P* here, gave up in confusion: "ego frustra quaesivi."

240. *Lat*: cum vidisset.

241. *Grm*: ἐκείνων.

242. *Lat* and one Greek ms. om.

243. *N*: καὶ ἐννοήσαντες διὰ τὴν εἰς τὸν ἀπόστολον παροινίαν τοῦτο γενέσθαι.

244. *AS*: Drihten.

245. *AS*: þas earfoðnesse.

Then Andrew said *to the Lord,* "Lord Jesus Christ, I already have undertaken and performed this sign in this city. Do not forsake me but send your *arch*angel *Michael* in a fiery cloud and wall up this city so that if any should want to flee it they will not be able to pass through the fire."

Immediately a cloud of fire descended and encircled the entire city *like a wall.* When Andrew *learned*[212] that *the plan had been achieved,* he blessed the Lord. The water rose to the necks of the[213] men and was devouring them viciously.

"Woe to us," they all cried *and shouted,* "for all these things came upon us because of the stranger in prison whom we delivered over to tortures.[214] What will we do? Let us go to the prison and free him, lest we die in this deluge of water. Let us all cry out, 'We believe in you, O *God*[215] of this stranger! Take *this water*[216] from us.'" All went out crying *in a loud voice,* "O God *of this stranger, remove this water from us.*"[217]

----

212. *Lat:* "saw."

213. *Grm:* "those."

214. *N:* "and when they considered that this came about because of their drunken violence against the apostle."

215. *AS:* "Lord."

216. *AS:* "these afflictions."

217. *N:* "running into the prison, they fell before the apostle weeping and quivering, seeking to stanch this death-dealing threat."

μεγάλη· ὁ θεὸς τοῦ ξένου ἀνθρώπου τούτου, ἆρον ἀφ' ἡμῶν
τὸ ὕδωρ τοῦτο].²⁴⁶

Καὶ ἔγνω ὁ Ἀνδρέας ὅτι [ἡ ψυχὴ αὐτῶν ὑπετάγη πρὸς
αὐτόν],²⁴⁷ τότε [ὁ μακάριος Ἀνδρέας] εἶπεν πρὸς τὸν
ἀλαβαστρινὸν ἀνδριάντα·²⁴⁸ παῦσαι λοιπὸν ἀποβάλλων τὸ
ὕδωρ ἐκ τοῦ στόματός σου,²⁴⁹ [διότι ὁ καιρὸς τῆς
ἀναπαύσεως παρῆλθεν· ἰδοὺ γὰρ ἐξέρχομαι καὶ κηρύσσω τὸν
λόγον τοῦ κυρίου.²⁵⁰ λέγω δέ σοι τῷ στύλῳ τῷ λιθίνῳ ὅτι
ἐὰν πιστεύσωσιν οἱ τῆς πόλεως ταύτης, οἰκοδομήσω
ἐκκλησίαν καὶ στήσω σε ἐν αὐτῇ, ὅτι ἐποίησάς μοι τὴν
διακονίαν ταύτην.]²⁵¹

Καὶ ἐπαύσατο [ὁ ἀνδριὰς τοῦ ῥέειν καὶ] οὐκέτι
ἐξήνεγκεν ὕδωρ.²⁵² καὶ ἐξῆλθεν Ἀνδρέας ἐκ τῆς
φυλακῆς,²⁵³ καὶ τὸ ὕδωρ διέτρεχεν ἀπὸ τῶν ποδῶν [τοῦ

----

246. Both C and A have short speeches at this point, but
they share little in common or with Gr or P. N:
δρομαῖοι ἐλθόντες εἰς τὴν φυλακὴν μετὰ κλαυθμοῦ
μεγάλου ἐν τρόμῳ προέπεσαν τῷ ἀποστόλῳ, αἰτούμενοι
στῆσαι τὴν τοιαύτην φθοροποιὸν ἀπειλήν.

247. C: ut omnes credentes in domino Iesu. AS: hie to
Drihtene wæron gehwerfede.

248. N: θεασάμενος δὲ ὁ πρωτόκλητος τὴν αὐτῶν εἰλικρινῆ
ἐπιστροφὴν καὶ μετάνοιαν καὶ σπλαγχνισθεὶς εἶπεν τῷ
ἀνδριάντι.

249. Lat adds: per nomen domini precipio tibi. N: μηκέτι
ἐξέλθῃ ὕδωρ ἐκ τοῦ στόματός σου.

250. N: ἰδοὺ γὰρ ἐξέρχομαι κηρύξαι τῷ λαῷ τούτῳ.

251. This section is missing in C and AS, presumably
because of its reference to Andrew's placing the
statue in the church. Cf. APh Act 15.36.

252. AS adds: heora muþe. N: καὶ τούτου ῥηθέντος
παραχρῆμα ἐπαύσατο ἡ τοῦ ὕδατος ῥύσις.

253. N: τότε ἐξελθὼν ἀπὸ τῆς εἱρκτῆς ὁ ἀπόστολος.

Andrew knew that *their souls were submissive to him.*[218] Then *the blessed Andrew* said to the alabaster statue,[219] "Now at last stop spewing water from your mouth,[220] *for the time of rest has come. For behold, I am leaving to preach the word of the Lord.*[221] *I say to you, stone pillar, that if the inhabitants of this city believe, I will build a church and place you in it, because you did this service for me.*"

The statue ceased *flowing and* no longer emitted water.[222] Andrew left the prison,[223] and the water ran from the feet *of the blessed Andrew.*[224] When the *citi-*

----

218. *C*: "that all believe in the Lord Jesus." *AS*: "they turned to the Lord."

219. *N*: "When the First-Called saw their sincere turnabout and repentance, he was moved to compassion and said to the statue."

220. *Lat* adds: "I command you in the Lord's name." *N*: "no longer issue water from your mouth."

221. *N*: "for I am leaving to preach to this people."

222. *AS* adds: "from its mouth." *N*: "as soon as he had said this, the flow of water ceased."

223. *N*: "then the apostle left the jail."

224. *Gr* adds: "Then the entire crowd saw him and all cried out."

μακαρίου ᾿Ανδρέου]. ²⁵⁴ καὶ ἐξελθόντες οἱ [τῆς πόλεως] ἐπὶ τὰς θύρας τῆς φυλακῆς ἐβόησαν λέγοντες· ²⁵⁵ ἐλέησον ἡμᾶς ὁ θεὸς τοῦ ξένου ἀνδρός, καὶ μὴ ποιήσῃς μεθ᾽ ἡμῶν²⁵⁶ καθ᾽ ἃ ἐποιήσαμεν τῷ ἀνδρὶ τούτῳ. ²⁵⁷

31. Καὶ ἐλθὼν ὁ γέρων ὁ παραδοὺς τὰ παιδία αὐτοῦ ἵνα σφάξωσιν αὐτὰ ἀντ᾽ αὐτοῦ, [ἐδέετο τῶν ποδῶν τοῦ μακαρίου ᾿Ανδρέου]²⁵⁸ λέγων· ἐλέησόν με.

Καὶ [ἀποκριθεὶς] ὁ [ἅγιος] ᾿Ανδρέας εἶπεν [τῷ γεραιῷ· θαυμάζω] πῶς σὺ λέγεις· ἐλέησόν με· [σὺ οὖν] οὐκ ἠλέησας τὰ τέκνα σου, ἀλλὰ παρέδωκας αὐτὰ ἀντὶ σοῦ· ²⁵⁹ λέγω οὖν σοι οἵαν ὥραν ἀπέρχεται τὸ ὕδωρ τοῦτο, εἰς τὴν ἄβυσσον πορευθῇς καὶ σὺ μετὰ τῶν δεκατεσσάρων δημίων τῶν φονε<υ>όντων τοὺς ἀνθρώπους καθ᾽ ἑκάστην ἡμέραν, [καὶ] μείνητε ἐν τῷ ᾅδῃ ἕως ἂν [ἐπιστρέψω ἄλλο ἅπαξ καὶ ἀνενέγκω ὑμᾶς]. ²⁶⁰ νῦν οὖν πορεύεσθε εἰς τὴν ἄβυσσον, [ἵνα ὑποδείξω τούτοις τοῖς δημίοις] τὸν τόπον τῆς

----

254. *Gr* adds: τότε πᾶς ὁ ὄχλος ἰδὼν αὐτὸν ἐβόουν ἅπαντες. These last two sentences appear in *Gr* at the end of the chapter and not here, as in *Lat*. Presumably they were relocated because of the choreographic awkwardness produced by Andrew's leaving the prison and then the Myrmidons finding him still there. By rearranging these sentences, *Gr* has the Myrmidons arriving at the prison first and then Andrew leaving.

255. *GE*: et dimissum apostolum, dicebant.

256. *Grm* add: κατὰ τὴν ἀπιστίαν ἡμῶν.

257. *Grm* add: ἀλλ᾽ ἔξελε ἀφ᾽ ἡμῶν τὸ ὕδωρ τοῦτο. *GE*: peccavimus in te, nescientes quid faceremus. Rogamus ergo, Domine, ut remittas nobis delictum et demonstres nobis viam salutis, ne descendat ira Dei super civitatem hanc.

258. *GE*: Haec enim dicentes, prostrati erant solo ante pedes Andreae.

259. *Grm* add: τοῦ σφαγῆναι.

260. *Lat*: ad diem iusti iudicii. Cf. *APh* Act 15.31.

zenry went to the doors of the prison, they cried out,[225] "Have mercy on us, God of this stranger. Do not treat us[226] as we treated this man."[227]

31. The old man who had delivered up his children for slaughter in his place came *and entreated at the feet of the blessed Andrew,*[228] "Have mercy on me."

"*I am amazed,*" said the *holy* Andrew *to the old man,* "that you can say, 'Have mercy on me,' when you did not have mercy on your own children but delivered them up in your place.[229] Therefore I tell you, at that hour when the water recedes, you will go into the abyss, you and the fourteen executioners who killed people daily, *and* the lot of you will stay in Hades until *I turn once again and raise you.*[230] So now, go into the abyss *so that I may show these executioners* the place of your[231]

----

225. *GE:* "when the apostle was released, they said."

226. *Grm:* "according to our unbelief."

227. *Grm* add: "but remove this water from us." *GE:* "We have sinned against you, not knowing what we were doing; therefore, we ask you, sir, pardon our transgression and show us the way of salvation, lest the wrath of God descend on this city."

228. *GE:* "Having said this, they lay on the ground at Andrew's feet."

229. *Grm* add: "for slaughter."

230. *Lat:* "until the day of judgment."

231. *Grm:* "their."

φονεύσεως ὑμῶν[261] [καὶ τὸν τόπον τῆς εἰρήνης, καὶ τῷ γ<ε>ραιῷ τούτῳ τὸν τόπον τῆς ἀγαπήσεως καὶ τῆς παραδόσεως] τῶν τέκνων αὐτοῦ.[262] νῦν οὖν ἀκολουθήσατέ μοι [πάντες].

Ἀκολουθούντων δὲ [τῶν ἀνδρῶν τῆς πόλεως] ἦν τὸ ὕδωρ διαχωριζόμενον [ἐκ τῶν ποδῶν τοῦ μακαρίου] Ἀνδρέου[263] ἕως ὅτε ἦλθεν εἰς τὸν τόπον [τῆς ληνοῦ][264] ἔνθα τοὺς ἀνθρώπους ἐσφαγίαζον.[265] καὶ ἀναβλέψας εἰς τὸν οὐρανὸν ὁ μακάριος Ἀνδρέας ηὔξατο ἀπέναντι παντὸς τοῦ ὄχλου, καὶ ἀνεῴχθη ἡ γῆ καὶ κατέπιε τὸ ὕδωρ σὺν τῷ γεραιῷ,[266] εἰς τὴν ἄβυσσον κατηνέχθη σὺν τοῖς δημίοις.[267]

Καὶ θεασάμενοι [οἱ ἄνδρες][268] τὸ γεγονὸς ἐφοβήθησαν σφόδρα καὶ [ἤρξαντο] λέγειν· οὐαὶ ἡμῖν, ὅτι ὁ ἄνθρωπος οὗτος ἐκ θεοῦ ἐστιν, καὶ νῦν ἀποκτείνει ἡμᾶς διὰ τὰς θλίψεις ἃς πεποιήκαμεν αὐτῷ. ἰδοὺ γὰρ τί εἶπεν τοῖς δημίοις καὶ τῷ γεραιῷ συνέβη [αὐτοῖς]. νῦν οὖν κελεύσει τῷ πυρὶ[269] καὶ καύσει ἡμᾶς.

----

261. *Grm*: αὐτῶν.

262. *C* adds: conversus vero sanctus Andreas ad populum dixit.

263. *Lat* adds: dextra levaque.

264. *Lat* perhaps rightly: toro.

265. *Lat* adds: et ubi sanguis decurrebat.

266. *Lat* adds: qui filios suos tradiderat.

267. Cf. *APh* Act 15.27.

268. *C*: omnes qui cum eo ibi adherant.

269. *Lat* adds: de celo.

murders *and the place of peace,* and to this old man the *place of love and the surrender* of his children.[232] Now *everyone* follow me."

As *the men of the city* followed him, the water divided[233] before *the feet of the blessed* Andrew until he came to the place of *the trough*[234] where they used to slaughter people.[235] Looking up into heaven, the blessed Andrew prayed before the entire crowd, and the earth opened and devoured the water along with the old man,[236] and he and the executioners were carried down into the abyss.

When *the men*[237] saw what happened, they were terrified and *began to* say, "Woe to us, for this person is from God, and now he kills us for the torments which we inflicted on him. For look, what he said to the executioners and the old man has happened *to them.* Now he will command the fire[238] and it will burn us."

----

232. *C* adds: "The holy Andrew turned to the people and said."

233. *Lat* adds: "right and left."

234. L, perhaps rightly: "mound."

235. *Lat* adds: "and where the blood ran off."

236. *Lat* adds: "who had betrayed his children."

237. *C*: "all who clung to him there."

238. *Lat* adds: "from heaven."

Καὶ ἀκούσας Ἀνδρέας εἶπεν πρὸς αὐτούς· μὴ φοβεῖσθε τεκνία μου· [κἀκείνους γὰρ οὐ μὴ ἐάσω εἰς τὸν ᾅδην,[270] ἀλλ' ἐπορεύθησαν ἐκεῖνοι] ἵνα ὑμεῖς πιστεύσητε εἰς τὸν κύριον [ἡμῶν] Ἰησοῦν Χριστόν.[271]

32. Τότε ἐκέλευσεν ὁ μακάριος Ἀνδρέας ἐνεχθῆναι πάντας τοὺς τελευτήσαντας ἐν τῷ ὕδατι, καὶ οὐκ ἴσχυσαν ἐνέγκαι αὐτούς· πολὺς γὰρ ἦν τελευτήσας ὄχλος [ἀνδρῶν τε] καὶ γυναικῶν καὶ παιδίων καὶ κτηνῶν. τότε ηὔξατο Ἀνδρέας,[272] καὶ πάντες ἀνέζησαν.[273]

Καὶ μετὰ ταῦτα ἐχάραξε τύπον ἐκκλησίας καὶ ἐποίησεν οἰκοδομηθῆναι τὴν ἐκκλησίαν εἰς τὸν τόπον ὅπου ὁ στῦλος ἐν τῇ φυλακῇ <ἵ>στατο.[274] καὶ βαπτίσας παρέδωκεν αὐτοῖς τὰς ἐντολὰς τοῦ κυρίου ἡμῶν Ἰησοῦ Χριστοῦ[275] λέγων

---

270. AS: forþon þe þas þe on þis wætere syndon eft hie libbað.

271. C adds: qui habet potestatem in celo et in terra, in mare, et in abyssum. Cf. APh Act 15.31.

272. C: domine Iesu Christe, mitte spiritum sanctum tuum de celis, et allevas omnes animas que in hanc aquam mortui sunt, ab homine usque ad pecus, ut omnes credant in nomine sancto tuo. AS contains an equivalent to the same prayer except for the words from "mortui" to "pecus."

273. Cf. Photius Bibliotheca 114: νεκρῶν δὲ ἀνθρώπων καὶ βοῶν καὶ κτηνῶν ἄλλων παραλογωτάτας καὶ μειρακιώδεις τερατεύεται ἀναστάσεις. At this point P adds a sentence to explain what happened to the wall of fire and to those Andrew had rescued from prison who were to eat figs until he arrived.

274. So P. B: in loco ubi statua fuerat. C: in eodem loco. AS: on þær stowe þær se swer stod. A: þær sio geogoð aras, þurh fæder fulwiht ond se flod onsprang. V: quod est in medio urbis ipsius nam Myrmidonie.

275. Lat adds: ordinavit eis episcopum unum de principibus.

After hearing this, Andrew said to them, "My little
children, do not be afraid; *for I will not let even them
stay in Hades.*[239] *They went there* so that you should
believe in *our* Lord Jesus Christ."[240]

32. Then the blessed Andrew commanded all those who
had died in the water to be brought to him, but they
were unable to bring them because a great multitude had
died, of *men*, women, children, and beasts. Then Andrew
prayed,[241] and all revived.[242]

Later, he drew up plans for a church and had the
church built on the spot where the pillar in the prison
had stood.[243] After baptizing them, he handed on to them

----

239. *AS*: "for those who are now in this water will live
     again."

240. *C* adds: "who has power in heaven, on earth, in the
     sea, and in the abyss."

241. Neither *Gr* nor *A* provide content to this prayer,
     but from *C* and *AS* one can reconstruct the following
     (the words in square brackets do not appear in *AS*):
     "Lord Jesus Christ, send your holy spirit from
     heaven and raise up all the souls [who died] in
     this water, [from humans to sheep], so that all may
     believe in your holy name."

242. Photius *Bibliotheca* 114: "He tells fabulous tales
     about irrational and childish resurrections from
     the dead of people and cattle and other domestic
     animals."

243. So *P*. *B*: "in the place where the statue had been."
     C: "on that spot." *AS*: "on the spot where the
     column stood." And *A*: "upon the spot where those
     young men arose by baptism, even where the flood
     sprang forth." *V* says the church was "in the middle
     of that city" where pagan worship had taken place.
     No Greek, Latin, or Anglo-Saxon version says Andrew
     made good on his earlier promise to place the
     water-spewing statue in the church, but the Syriac
     does: "And they brought the pillar which had made
     the water flow and set it up in the church."

[πρὸς αὐτούς]·276 στήκετε πρὸς ταῦτα, ἵνα γνῶτε τὰ μυστήρια τοῦ κυρίου ἡμῶν Ἰησοῦ Χριστοῦ quoniam magna est virtus eius. [οὐ παραδώσω ὑμῖν νῦν] ἀλλὰ πορεύομαι πρὸς τοὺς μαθητάς μου.

Καὶ ἐδέοντο αὐτοῦ πάντες· [δεόμεθά σου], ποίησον πρὸς ἡμᾶς ὀλίγας ἡμέρας, [ὅπως κορεσθῶμεν τῆς σῆς πηγῆς],277 ὅτι ἡμεῖς νεόφυτοί ἐσμεν.

Καὶ δεομένων αὐτῶν οὐκ ἐπείθετο, ἀλλ' εἶπεν αὐτοῖς· πορεύσομαι [πρῶτον πρὸς τοὺς μαθητάς μου]. καὶ ἠκολούθουν ὄπισθεν [τὰ παιδία] κλαίοντα καὶ δεόμενα [σὺν τοῖς ἀνδράσιν, καὶ ἔβαλαν σποδὸν ἐπὶ τὰς κεφαλὰς αὐτῶν· καὶ οὐκ ἐπείθετο αὐτοῖς] ἀλλ' εἶπεν· πορεύσομαι πρὸς τοὺς μαθητάς μου, καὶ μετὰ ταῦτα ἐπανέλθω πρὸς ὑμᾶς. καὶ ἐπορεύετο τὴν ὁδὸν αὐτοῦ.278

33. Καὶ κατῆλθεν ὁ κύριος Ἰησοῦς γενόμενος ὅμοιος μικρῷ παιδίῳ εὐπρεπεῖ, [καὶ συναντήσας τὸν Ἀνδρέαν] εἶπεν· Ἀνδρέα, διὰ τί ἐξελθὼν ἔασας αὐτοὺς ἀκάρπους, καὶ οὐκ ἐσπλαγχνίσθης ἐπὶ τοῖς παιδίοις τοῖς ἀκολου-

---

276. *GE*: Quibus ille erectis praedicabat Dominum Iesum Christum et miracula quae fecit in hoc mundo, et qualiter ipsum mundum iam pereuntem proprio cruore redemit. At ill<i> credentes baptizati sunt in nomine Patris et Filii et Spiritus sancti, accepta peccatorum remissione. *N*: βαπτίσας τε καὶ ἐκκλησίαν οἰκοδομήσας. Cf. APh Act 15.36 and 41.

277. *Lat*: et ne nos modo deseras, quousque nos firme<m>ur in dominicam integram fidem. *AS*: þæt þu us gedafra gedo.

278. *Lat* adds: et illi ceperunt gravissime flere.

the commands of our Lord Jesus Christ[244] telling *them*, "Stand by these, so that you might know the mysteries of our Lord Jesus Christ **for his power is great.** *I will not hand them on to you now;* instead, I am going to my disciples."

"We beg you," they all implored, "stay with us a few days, *so that we might be sated from your fountain,*[245] because we are neophytes."

Even though they begged him, he was not persuaded but said to them, "I will go *first to my disciples."* And *the children with the men* followed behind weeping and begging, *and threw ashes on their heads.*[246] *He was still not persuaded by them* but said, "I will go to my disciples, and later I will return to you." He went on his way.[247]

33. The Lord Jesus, having become like a beautiful small child, descended *and greeted Andrew* saying,

----

244. *Lat* adds: "ordained one of their rulers as their bishop." *V* names the bishop Plato; *A* names him Platan. In *P*, Plato plays an important role almost from the beginning of Andrew's ministry in Myrmidonia. See also *The Martyrdom of Matthew.*

   GE: "when they had been raised, he preached the Lord Jesus Christ and the miracles he had performed in this world, and how he redeemed this perishing world by shedding his own blood. Those who believed were baptized in the name of the Father, and of the Son, and of the Holy Spirit, receiving the remission of sins." *N:* "he baptized (them) and built a church."

245. *Lat:* "and do not desert us until we are confirmed in sound dominical faith." *AS:* "that you may establish tranquillity among us."

246. Cf. Jonah 3:5 (LXX).

247. *Lat* adds: "and they began to weep bitterly."

θοῦσιν ὄπισθέν σου [καὶ τῶν] δεομένων [ἀνδρῶν ὅτι·
ποίησον μεθ᾽ ἡμῶν ἡμέρας ὀλίγας]; ἡ γὰρ βοὴ αὐτῶν καὶ ὁ
κλαυθμὸς ἀνέβη²⁷⁹ εἰς οὐρανούς. νῦν οὖν ἐπιστρέψας
εἴσελθε εἰς τὴν πόλιν καὶ παράμεινον ἐκεῖ ἡμέρας ἑπτά,
ἕως οὗ ἐπιστηρίζω τὰς ψυχὰς αὐτῶν ἐν τῇ πίστει·²⁸⁰ καὶ
τότε [ἐξέλθῃς ἐκ τῆς πόλεως ταύτης, καὶ] ἀπελεύσῃ εἰς
τὴν πόλιν [τῶν βαρβάρων²⁸¹ σὺ] καὶ οἱ μαθηταί σου. [καὶ
μετὰ τὸ εἰσελθεῖν σε ἐν τῇ πόλει ἐκείνῃ, καὶ κηρύξαι τὸ
εὐαγγέλιόν μου ἐν αὐτῇ,²⁸² καὶ ἐξέλθῃς ἀπ᾽ αὐτῶν καὶ
πάλιν εἰσέλθῃς εἰς τὴν πόλιν ταύτην], καὶ ἀνενέγκῃς
cunctos τοὺς ἄνδρας τοὺς ἐν τῇ ἀβύσσῳ.

Τότε ᾽Ανδρέας ἐπιστρέψας εἰσῆλθεν ἐν τῇ πόλει
<Μυρμιδονίᾳ>²⁸³ λέγων· εὐλογήσω σε κύριέ μου ᾽Ιησοῦ
Χριστέ, ὁ σῶσαι θέλων πᾶσαν ψυχήν, ὅτι οὐκ ἔασάς με
ἐξελθεῖν ἐκ τῆς πόλεως ταύτης σὺν τῷ θυμῷ μου. [καὶ
εἰσελθόντες αὐτοῦ εἰς τὴν πόλιν] ἰδόντες αὐτὸν ἐχάρησαν
χαρὰν μεγάλην σφόδρα.²⁸⁴

Καὶ ἐποίησεν [ἐκεῖ]²⁸⁵ ἡμέρας ἑπτὰ διδάσκων καὶ
ἐπιστηρίζων αὐτοὺς ἐπὶ τὸν κύριον ᾽Ιησοῦν Χριστόν.²⁸⁶
καὶ πληρωθέντων τῶν ἑπτὰ ἡμέρων ἐγένετο ἐν τῷ

----

279. *Lat* adds: ad me.

280. Cf. *AXP* 38.

281. *P*. καὶ πορεύσει ἐξαφιλιώτου, ἔνθα ἐστὶν ὁ
συναπόστολος Ματθαῖος.

282. This last clause is missing in *Grm* as well as in
Lat.

283. *Lat*: Mermedonia. *Gr* om.

284. Cf. *AXP* 38.

285. *Lat*: cum illis.

286. *N*: καὶ ἑπτὰ ἡμέρας προσμείνας κατεφώτισεν αὐτοὺς
καὶ ἐστήριξεν ἐν τῇ πίστει τοῦ Χριστοῦ. Cf. *APh* Act
15.16: καὶ ἐστηρίζοντο ἐν τῇ πίστει. *AXP* 38.

"Andrew, why do you depart leaving them fruitless, and why do you have no compassion on the children following after you *and on the men* who implore, 'Stay with us a few days'? Their cry and weeping rose[248] to heaven. So now, turn back, go into the city, and stay there seven days until I strengthen their souls in the faith. Then *you may leave this city and* you will go into the city *of the barbarians,*[249] *you* and your disciples. *After you enter that city and preach my gospel there, you may leave them and again come into this city* and bring up **all** the men in the abyss."

Then Andrew turned and entered the city **Myrmidonia** saying, "I bless you, my Lord Jesus Christ who wants to save every soul, that you did not permit me to leave this city in my rage." *When he entered the city* they saw him and were jubilant.

He spent seven days *there*[250] teaching and confirming them in the Lord Jesus Christ.[251] At the completion of seven days, the time came for *the blessed Andrew* to leave. All **the people of Myrmidonia** were

---

248. *Lat* adds: "to me."

249. *P*: "and you will go to the east, where your fellow apostle Matthew is."

250. *Lat*: "with them."

251. *N*: "He remained seven days and enlightened and confirmed them in the faith of Christ."

ἐκπορεύεσθαι [τὸν μακάριον ᾿Ανδρέαν], συνήχθησαν πάντες
populus <Μυρμιδονίας>[287] [ἐπ᾽ αὐτὸν] ἀπὸ παιδίου ἕως
πρεσβυτέρου, καὶ προέπεμψαν[288] αὐτὸν[289] λέγοντες· εἷς
θεὸς ᾿Ανδρέου,[290] κύριος ᾿Ιησοῦς Χριστός, ᾧ ἡ δόξα καὶ
τὸ κράτος εἰς τοὺς αἰῶνας, ἀμήν.

----

287. *Lat*: Mermedonie. *Gr* om.

288. *Grm*: προέπεμπαν. One Greek ms. adds here: ἐν
Πάτραις τῆς ᾿Αχαΐας, and then presents a version of
Andrew's passion (viz. *M*). Cf. *ATh* 68.

289. *GE*: Andreas autem recedens ab eo loco, venit in
regionem suam. Cf. *AXP* 39.

290. *Grm*: εἷς.

gathered *to him,* young and old, and sent him off[252]
saying, "One is the God of Andrew: the[253] Lord Jesus
Christ, to whom be glory and power forever. Amen."

----

252. *GE:* "Andrew left that place and went to his own
     region."

253. *Grm:* "there is one."

EXCURSUS A

Andrew's Return to Myrmidonia

The *AAMt* stops here quite unexpectedly. Andrew was
to have left the city to rejoin his disciples in the
east (chapters 32 and 33, cf. 21), evangelized "the city
of the barbarians," and returned to Myrmidonia to raise
up the old man and the fourteen executioners who by then
would have visited places of eternal bliss and torment
(33). He never does any of this. Although the author or
authors may have intended this tantalizing incompletion,
it would seem more likely that the narrative originally
continued in the *AA*.[1] Two influential sources behind the
AAMt recounted experiences of the netherworld. The book
of Jonah sent the prophet into the earth (2:7 [LXX]: εἰς
γῆν), into the watery bowels of Hades (2:3: ἐκ κοιλίας
ᾅδου), where the abyss engulfed him (2:6: ἄβυσσος
ἐκύκλωσέν με) until he repented of his disobedience.
According to the *APe*, a youth raised back to life
revealed a conversation he heard on the other side of
the grave and thus produced faith in those who listen.[2]

P (*Paris gr. 1313*), an unpublished Greek recension
of the *AAMt*, may retain traces of this lost episode.
Andrew leaves Myrmidonia for the east where he finds his
disciples and Matthew (sic). He reports what happened to
him in Myrmidonia and says, "it is time for us to leave
for Myrmeke (ἐπὶ τὴν Μυρμήκην), inasmuch as our Lord
Jesus Christ commanded that those swallowed up in the
abyss be retrieved alive." When they arrive in the city,
they pray, and the old man and the executioners boil up

----

1. See the Introduction.

2. *APe* (*AV*) 28.

out of the earth and lie dead on the ground. Andrew then
tells Matthew and bishop Plato to grab each by the hand
and raise them up. They do so, everyone is confirmed in
the faith, and Andrew leaves with his disciples for
Amasia, precisely where the apostle next appears in
Gregory's epitome.

Although some information given here corresponds
with the ancient Acts--such as Myrmidonia, the raising
of those in the abyss, and Andrew's journey to Amasia--P
undoubtedly has taken great liberties with its source.
Before returning to exhume those swallowed by the abyss,
Andrew was to have gone to "the city of the barbarians."
Those exhumed presumably were to recount their
adventures in the netherworld in order to strengthen the
faith of others. These events do not occur in P. Thus,
even if the author of the recension now represented by P
had access to a version of the Acts narrating the
raising of the Myrmidons, one no longer can recover with
confidence the content of this episode.

Fortunately, traces also may appear in the Acts
which imitated the AA. The APh says that Philip ordered
an abyss to swallow hostile Snake-People ('Οφιανοί), a
crowd of "about seven thousand men not to mention women
and children" (Act 15.27). During their descent into
Hades they witnessed "the judgments of those who did not
confess the Crucified." Rebuked by Jesus for his lack of
compassion, Philip raised them up again, and they
believed because of what they had seen (Act 15.32). In
the AJPr, the Ephesians tried in vain to stone the
apostle, who caused the earth to swallow eight hundred
until they repented. He raised them up again and they
believed (34-35 [Zahn]). There is no visit to the
netherworld in the AXP, but chapters 38-39 do suggest
its author had read of Andrew's departure from
Myrmidonia for "the city of the barbarians." Polyxena's

departure from Greece closely followed *AAMt* 33, and soon
after she set sail, she too found herself on an island
of bellicose savages.[3] The most elaborate parallel to
this lost passage in the *AA* appears in the *ATh*. A woman
who had been murdered returned from the dead to retell
in graphic and gripping detail what she had seen in
hell. Thomas preached and "all the people believed"
(55-59).

Something similar probably took place in the *AA*
when Andrew and his disciples returned to Myrmidonia.
The executioners whom Andrew promised to raise from the
abyss would have told of their visit to "the place of
murder and the place of peace," and the old man who had
betrayed his children would have told of "the place of
love and of the betrayal of his children" (chapter 31).

If the *AA* once continued the narrative and indeed
recounted the raising of the Myrmidons, one must
explain, if possible, why this section has vanished, not
only from our texts of the *AAMt*, but also from Gregory's
epitome, Epiphanius, *Laudatio*, and *Narratio*. Codex 179
of Photius's *Bibliotheca* may supply a clue.

Photius mentions a fourth century Manichaean,
Agapius, who marshalled his theological proofs "from the
so-called Acts of the twelve apostles, especially those
of Andrew." The sentence immediately following reads:

> He [Agapius] also holds to metempsychosis. He
> sends off to God those who have achieved the
> zenith of virtue, consigns to fire and
> darkness those who achieved the nadir of
> wickedness, and brings down into bodies once
> more those who conducted their lives somewhere
> between these two extremes.

----

3. See Introduction, 44-45.

The flow of this passage suggests that Agapius found this doctrine expressed in the *AA*, but it is not immediately apparent how he would have found this in the undisputed fragments of the Acts that have come down to us. Perhaps Agapius' prooftext is lost without a trace, but it is also possible that the prooftext was the anticipated completion of the *AAMt*. That is, he might have related the Myrmidons' visit to "the place of peace" to "those who have achieved the zenith of virtue," applied the visit to "the place of murders" to "those who have achieved the nadir if wickedness," and argued that Andrew's rescue of the Myrmidons proves that individuals return from the dead.

The narration of tours of the netherworld was a common way to articulate reincarnation. According to Homer, during Odysseus's visit with the shades he saw Lede, the mother of the Dioscuri, Castor and Pollux, semi-divine heroes who each day alternated coming back to life.[4] Pythagoras, a dogmatic proponent of metempsychosis, was said to have visited the netherworld where he saw *inter alia* Hesiod and Homer punished for their theologies.[5] Aristotle complained about reincarnation as presented "in the Pythagorean stories" (κατὰ τοὺς Πυθαγορικοὺς μύθους).[6] Book Six of Virgil's *Aeneid*, modeled after the Odysseus's *nekyia*, told of certain souls allowed to reenter their bodies.[7] Plutarch narrated in detail two μύθοι of descents into Hades that

----

4. *Odyssey* 11.298-304.

5. According to a fragment of Hieronymus Rhodius in Diogenes Laertius 8.21.

6. *On the Soul* 1.3.407b.20-25.

7. *Aeneid* 6.703-51.

taught metempsychosis.[8] Lucian never tired of ridiculing such *nekyiai* and their attending doctrines of reincarnation. For example, in *Menippus* 20 (almost certainly following Menippus's own now-lost *Nekyia*) the souls of the rich

> will be sent back up into life and enter into donkeys until they shall have passed two hundred and fifty thousand years in the said condition, transmigrating from donkey to donkey, bearing burdens, and being driven by the poor. (Loeb)

See also Lucian's *Lover of Lies* 24-27 and *True Story I.*

Perhaps the most famous and certainly the most elaborate tour of the netherworld is the myth of Er in Book Ten of Plato's *Republic*.[9] Er, a soldier slain on the battlefield, is permitted to return to earth in order to disclose to mortals how the gods reward the righteous and punish the wicked with higher or lower reincarnations. Photius says that Agapius used not only the *AA* but also Plato to support metempyschosis.[10] No other passage in Plato is more likely to have inspired Photius's remarks than the myth of Er. The point to be made here is not that the *AA* actually advocated metempsychosis, but that tours of hell were vulnerable to metempsychotic interpretations.

If Manichaeans like Agapius did indeed use Andrew's raising of the Myrmidons in such a manner, it might explain why this passage disappeared except as a

----

8. The descent of Thespesius in *Divine Vengeance* 563B-568 and the descent of Timarchus in *The Sign of Socrates* 589F-592E.

9. See also *Phaedo* 111-14.

10. "Without shame he makes use of the martyrs and of those who loved Greek religion, especially Plato, to support his own fight with God" (codex 114).

promise. Ancient ecclesiastics frequently complained that the AA had been interpolated by heretics. For example, Philaster of Brescia (late fourth century) insisted that Manichaeans "added to" (*addiderunt*) and "abridged" (*tulerunt*) Andrew's Acts.[11] Priscillian of Avila, Philasters' Spanish contemporary, recommended that scribes purge from apocrypha whatever seemed to have been inserted by "miserable heretics."[12] An unknown author who wrote sometime between 400 and 600 and whose *Passion of John* was transmitted among the works of Melito of Sardis, states that the AJ, the ATh, and the AA contained true statements concerning the miracles performed through the apostles, but on the subject of doctrine were full of lies.[13] This same sentiment characterized Gregory's epitomizing of the AA, abbreviating the miracles but often excising entire discourses. Turibius of Astorga (mid-fifth century) complained that Mani and his disciples "composed or interpolated" apocryphal books, especially the AA.[14] John of Thessalonica (late seventh century) speaks approvingly of authors long before him who redacted the apocryphal Acts in order to repair the damage done them by heretical additions. He explicitly mentions the AA along with those of Peter, Paul, and John.[15]

----

11. *Diversarum hereseon liber* 88 (CSEL 9.255-56).

12. Tractate 3 (CSEL 18.46): *In quibus tamen omnibus libris non est metus, si qua ab infelicibus hereticis sunt inserta, delere et <quae> profetis vel evangeliis non inveniuntur consentire respuere.*

13. *Passio Ioannis* (*PL* 5.1239), see Prieur, *Acta Andreae*, 118.

14. *PL* 54:694: *libros omnes apocryphos vel compositos, vel infectos esse, manifestum est: specialiter autem Actus illos qui vocantur S. Andreae.*

15. See Dvornik, *Apostolicity*, 190, and Prieur, *Acta Andreae*, 113-18.

This widespread assumption that the original *AA* had been embellished by heretics could explain why certain passages failed to be transcribed. Anti-Manichaeanism has cheated us of much of the apocryphal Acts.[16] Therefore, it is reasonable to suggest that Gregory, the authors of the Byzantine Βίοι, and the author responsible for detaching the *AAMt* from the rest of the *AA* refused to narrate Andrew's return to raise the Myrmidons because of a desire to sanitize the Acts of Manichaean metempsychotic viruses.

----

16. See Junod and Kaestli, *Histoire*, 50-86.

Part Two:

GREGORY'S EPITOME AND PARALLELS

INTRODUCTION TO PART II

Josef Flamion has established once and for all that Gregory of Tours held in his hands a Latin translation of the *AA* and that his epitome (=*GE* [*BHL 430*]) is the most comprehensive witness to its content.[1] Although Gregory's account retains the geographical sequence of his *Vorlage*, he everywhere rationalizes the narrative, removing fabulous or romantic elements in favor of historical verisimilitude.[2] To be sure, by modern standards he was naively credulous about miracles, but he nevertheless flattened the high adventure and romance of the Acts into palatable hagiographic *legenda* which few pious readers of his day would have thought unhistorical. Because he found the prolixity of the Acts tedious and its discourses offensive, he repeatedly omitted speeches and prayers, replacing them with discourses of his own.[3] A comparison with parallel versions shows that he took particular exception to two commitments of the ancient Acts. First, the Acts required celibacy, but Gregory either completely ignored such obligations or softened them into denunciations of prostitution, adultery, or incest.[4] Second, the Acts

----

1. *Actes d'André*, 213-63.

2. Ibid., 221, and Prieur, *Acta Andreae*, 10-12.

3. Prieur, *Acta Andreae*, 8-12.

4. Flamion, *Actes d'André*, 247 and 254-58.

berated military service and contained at least two
stories of soldiers abandoning arms. Gregory passed over
both in silence.[5] His radical epitomizing also muddled
geographical and time references, creating impossible
scenarios. Characters appear unannounced and then
quietly evaporate.[6] One cannot read Gregory's rough
cuttings without astonishment at the apparent
massiveness of the original work.

Fortunately, the modern reader is not wholly at the
mercy of Gregory's stuffy tastes and clumsy pen. *The
Epistle of Titus* (fifth century) alludes to the double
wedding in *GE* 11,[7] *The Manichaean Psalm-Book* (fourth
century?) alludes to the extinguished fire in *GE* 12,[8]
and *Oxyrhynchus Papyrus 851* (fifth or sixth centuries),
almost certainly a Greek fragment from the Acts,

----

5. Cf. *GE* 18 and *Papyrus Coptic Utrecht 1*.

6. Such clumsiness is common in Gregory. Although Erich
   Auerbach praises the bishop's literary energy,
   concreteness, and color, he also recognizes his
   penchant to narrate "in a confused and imprecise
   manner" (*Mimesis: The Representation of Reality in
   Western Literature*, trans. Willard R. Trask
   [Princeton: Princeton University Press, 1968], 82).
   "Gregory's language . . . is but imperfectly equipped
   to organize facts; as soon as a complex of events
   ceases to be very simple, he is no longer able to
   present it as a coherent whole. His language
   organizes badly or not at all. . . . Gregory has
   nothing to hand except his grammatically confused,
   syntactically impoverished, and almost sophomoric
   Latin" (ibid., 89-90).

7. D. de Bryne, "Epistula Titi, discipuli Pauli, de
   dispositione sanctimonii," *Revue Bénédictine* 37
   (1925): 47-72.

8. C. R. C. Allberry, *A Manichaean Psalm-Book*, Manichaean Manuscripts in the Chester Beatty Collections
   2 (Stuttgart: W. Kohlhammer, 1938).

corresponds with a few lines in *GE* 18.[9] More instructive
is a Sahidic Coptic excerpt calling itself "The Act of
Andrew" (ⲧⲡⲣⲁϫⲉⲓⲥ ⲛⲁⲛⲁⲣⲉⲁⲥ), conventionally known as
Papyrus Coptic Utrecht 1. The first eight pages are
lost, but the singular "Act" in the title suggests it
narrated only the content of the Acts parallel to the
first few lines of *GE* 18. This fragment surely retains
information suppressed by Gregory, especially the
denunciation of military service; nevertheless, there
remain lacunae at several important places and the
content of the rest is not easily harmonized with
undisputed passages of the Acts. In other words, *Papyrus
Coptic Utrecht 1* may not be a faithful translation but a
tendentious recension.

The single most important parallel to Gregory for
appreciating the general content of the Acts is a Βίος
written by Epiphanius, "monk and priest," from the
monastery of Callistratus in Constantinople.[10] Early in
the ninth century, he and a colleague left
Constantinople for a tour of various cites purportedly
evangelized by Andrew. Among his sources he lists
Clement of Rome, Evagrius of Sicily, and a catalogue of
the apostles and the seventy disciples falsely
attributed to Epiphanius of Cyprus.[11] The reference to
Clement presumably refers to the Ps.-Clementines.[12]
Although the monk of Callistratus does not list the *AA*
among his sources, he obviously knew a version of

----

9. Bernard Pyne Grenfell and Arthur S. Hunt, *The
   Oxyrhynchus Papyri* (London: Egypt Exploration Fund,
   1908), 6:18.

10. *PG* 120:216-60 (*BHG* 102).

11. Flamion, *Actes d'André*, 70-74, and Prieur, *Acta
    Andreae*, 18-19.

12. Ibid., 74-75.

Andrew's passion and other sources whose content ultimately derived from the Acts.

The determination of how much of this material once appeared in the Acts is impeded by three major obstacles. First, Epiphanius gathered some of his information from local legends which may well have issued from the *AA*, but whose paternity can no longer be proved. Second, Epiphanius was not an historian but a panegyrist quite capable of fetching content from his private stock. Third, Albert Dressel based his edition on a manuscript of questionable fidelity.[13] Prieur consulted other manuscripts of Epiphanius whose readings appear to be more primitive and that beg for a new edition.[14] In spite of these obstacles, one cannot afford to ignore Epiphanius's *Life* (=*E*) altogether.

Later in the ninth century, Nicetas the Paphlagonian wrote his own panegyric of Andrew conventionally referred to as *Laudatio* (=*L* [*BHG* 100]), the bulk of which merely recasts Epiphanius's *Life*.[15] Even so, readings from *Laudatio* are recorded here insofar as they frequently preserve readings from Epiphanius more faithfully than Dressel's edition of Epiphanius.

Once Andrew arrives in Patras, Nicetas switches to a second source, a recension of Andrew's passion known also to the author of *Martyrium prius* (=*M* [*BHG* 96], late

----

13. *Epiphanii monachi et presbyteri edita et inedita* (Paris and Leipzig: Brockhaus and Avenarius, 1843).

14. *Acta Andreae*, 19-20.

15. Bonnet, *Acta Andreae*, 3-44. Flamion provides a brilliant assessment of Nicetas' recasting of Epiphanius (*Actes d'André*, 206-12; see also 57-62).

eighth century).[16] *Martyrium prius* alludes to the story of Matthew (sic) in Myrmenis (sic) and then states that the apostle traveled to Bithynia, Macedonia, and Achaea prior to arriving at Patras. It begins narrating Andrew's ministry in detail, however, only after he arrives in Patras (para. *GE* 22). In spite of its derivation from an intermediate recension, *Martyrium prius*, especially when compared with *Laudatio*, is now the most valuable witness to the episodes following Andrew's first arrival in Patras.[17]

Narratio (=*N* [*BHG* 99], late eighth century) also parallels Gregory's epitome.[18] Its author knew some version of Andrew's passion as well as Andrean traditions from other sources, some of which themselves may have used the ancient Acts. The text of the passion is suspiciously identical with that in Epiphanius, suggesting Epiphanius and the redactor of *Narratio* both carefully recopied a common source or, more likely, that someone later touched up the passion in Epiphanius to conform with *Narratio*.[19] Insofar as the life of Andrew attributed to Symeon Metaphrastes derives from Epiphanius,[20] and that of Ps.-Abdias from Gregory of Tours, they are not incorporated into this edition.

----

16. Prieur's edition of the Acts contains a new edition also of *Martyrium prius* (*Acta Andreae*, 684-703). See also his discussion of the relationship between *M* and *L* (14-17).

17. Flamion, *Acts d'André*, 62-69.

18. Bonnet, *Acta Andreae*, 46-64, and Prieur, *Acta Andreae* 17-18.

19. Prieur, *Acta Andreae*, 18-20.

20. Flamion, *Actes d'André*, 85-87.

ABBREVIATIONS TO THE APPARATUS FOR PART II

AAMt   *The Acts of Andrew and Matthias.*

AJPr   *The Acts of John by Prochorus.* Zahn, *Acta Joannis*, 1-252.

APe   *The Acts of Peter. AAA* 1:45-117.

APh   *The Acts of Philip. AAA* 2.2:1-98.

APl   *The Acts of Paul.*

ATh   *The Acts of Thomas. AAA* 2.2:99-291.

E   *The Life of Andrew* (*BHG* 102), Epiphanius the monk. *PG* 120:216-60.

GE   Gregory's epitome (*BHL* 430). Bonnet, "Liber de miraculis," 821-46, reproduced in Prieur, *Acta Andreae*, 555-631.

L   *Laudatio* (*BHG* 100). Bonnet, *Acta Andreae*, 3-44.

M   *Martyrium prius* (*BHG* 96). Prieur, *Acta Andreae*, 675-703.

N   *Narratio* (*BHG* 99). Bonnet, *Acta Andreae*, 46-64.

P   *Paris gr. 1313.* Unpublished.

PCU   *Papyrus Coptic Utrecht 1.*

2. Cumque deambularet cum discipulis suis, accessit ad eum caecus quidam et ait: Andreas apostole Christi, scio, quia potes mihi reddere visum, sed nolo eum recipere, nisi depraecor, ut iubeas his qui tecum sunt conferre mihi pecuniam, de qua vestitum habeam sufficientem et victum.

Cui beatus Andreas: Vere, inquid, cognosco, quia non est haec vox hominis, sed diaboli, qui non sinit homini isti recipere visum. Et conversus tetigit oculos eius, et confestim recepit lumen et glorificabat Deum.

Cumque indumentum haberet vile et hispidum, ait apostolus: Auferte ab eo vestimenta sordida et date ei indumentum novum. Expoliantibus se paene omnibus, ait apostolus: Quod sufficit, haec accipiat. Et sic, accepto vestimento, gratias agens, rediit ad domum suam.

3. Demetrii autem primi civitatis Amaseorum erat puer Aegyptius, quem amore unico diligebat. Orta autem in eum febre, spiritum ex<h>alavit. Denique, audita

2.[1] While he was walking with his disciples,[2] a blind man approached him and said, "Andrew, apostle of Christ, I know that you are able to restore my sight, but I do not want to receive it. Rather, I ask that you order those with you to give me money for adequate clothing and food."

The blessed Andrew said to him, "I know truly that this is not the voice of a human but of the devil, who does not allow that man to regain his sight." Turning around, Andrew touched his eyes, and immediately he received light and glorified God.

Because the man's clothing was cheap and coarse, the apostle said, "Remove his filthy rags and give him new clothing." Nearly everyone was primping him, so the apostle said, "Let him have only the essentials." So the man took the clothing, gave thanks, and returned to his home.

3. Demetrius, the leader of the community of Amasians,[3] had an Egyptian boy whom he cherished with unparalleled love. A fever overtook the boy, and he

----

1. Chapter one tells the story of the Myrmidons.

2. The setting for this story is Amasia, even though the city is not mentioned until chapter 3.

3. *P* also sends Andrew off to Amasia after Myrmidonia. According to *E*, after Andrew left the cannibals--in Sinope!--he went to Amisus, where he was entertained by a Jew named Domitian. Andrew delivered a long speech in the synagogue, and the residents brought their sick and demoniacs to be healed. Many believed (224B-228D; cf. 242B). So too in *GE*, Andrew preached "at great length," performed a miracle, and converted the residents. Although these similarities might suggest that *E* and *GE* recorded the same story but confused like-sounding names (Amasia/Amisus; Demetrius/Domitian), it is safest to assume these accounts are unrelated.

Demetrius signa quae faciebat beatus apostolus, venit ad eum, et procidens cum lacrimis ante pedes eius, ait: Nihil tibi difficile confido, minister Dei. Ecce enim puer meus, quem unice diligebam, mortuus est, et rogo, ut adeas domum meam et reddas eum mihi.

Haec audiens beatus apostolus, condolens lacrimis eius, venit ad domum in qua puer iacebat, et praedicans diutissime ea quae ad salutem populi pertinebant, conversus ad feretrum, ait: Tibi dico, puer, in nomine Iesu Christi, fili Dei, surge et sta sanus. Et confestim surrexit puer Aegyptius, et reddidit illum domino suo. Tunc omnes qui erant increduli crediderunt Deo et baptizati sunt ab apostolo sancto.

4. Puer quidam Sostratus nomine christianus venit secretius ad beatum Andream, dicens: Mater mea concupivit formam speciei meae et iugiter me insectatur, ut commisceam ei. Quod ego infandum execrans refugi. At illa, felle commota, adiit proconsulem, ut crimen suum proiciat in me. Et scio, cum accusatus fuero, quia nihil ad haec respondebo; satius enim duco vitam amittere quam matris detegere crimen. Nunc autem tibi haec confiteor, ut digneris pro me Dominum exorare, ne innocens caream praesenti vita.

Haec eo dicente, venerunt ministri proconsulis arcersientes eum. Beatus vero apostolus, facta oratione, surrexit et abiit cum puero.

expired. Later, when Demetrius heard of the signs the blessed apostle was performing, he came to him, fell at his feet with tears, and said, "I am sure that nothing is difficult for you, O servant of God. Behold my boy, whom I love to an extraordinary degree, is dead. I ask that you come to my house and restore him to me."

When the blessed apostle heard this, he was moved by his tears and went to the house where the boy lay. After preaching at great length matters pertaining to the salvation of the people,[4] he turned to the bier and said, "Lad, I tell you in the name of Jesus Christ, the Son of God, arise and stand up, healed." Immediately the Egyptian boy arose, and Andrew returned him to his master. Then all the unbelievers believed in God and were baptized by the holy apostle.

4.[5] A Christian youth named Sostratus came secretly to the blessed Andrew and said, "My mother craved my beautiful looks and keeps pestering me to sleep with her. Because I curse this unspeakable act, I ran away. But she, crazed with venom, went to the proconsul in order to cast on me her own wrongdoing. I know that when accused I will make no defense, for I would rather relinquish my life than expose my mother's guilt. Now I admit this to you so that you might concede to pray to the Lord for me, lest I be deprived of this present life even though I am innocent."

While he was saying this, the proconsul's assistants came to arrest him. Then after a speech,[6] the

----

4. Gregory here has reduced an originally long speech into a single dependent clause.

5. Presumably this episode too takes place in Amasia.

6. The source behind *GE* seems to have contained here an extended discourse, perhaps denouncing incest.

Mater autem instanter accusabat eum, dicens: Hic, domine proconsul, oblitus maternae pietatis affectum, stuprose in me conversus, vix potui eripi, ne ab eo violarer.

Cui ait proconsul: Dic, puer, si vera sunt ista quae mater tua prosequitur. At ille tacebat. Iterum atque iterum proconsul interrogabat, et nihil respondit. Durante autem eo in silentio, proconsul habebat cum suis consilium, quid ageret; mater autem pueri coepit flere.

Ad quam beatus Andreas apostolus ait: O infelix, quae fletus emittis amaritudinis ob stuprum, quod in filium agere voluisti, quam in tantum concupiscentia praecipitavit, ut unicum amittere filium, libidine inflammante, non metuas.

Haec eo dicente, ait mulier: Audi, proconsul; postquam filius meus haec agere voluit, homini huic adhaesit et non discessit ab eo.

Proconsul autem de his ira commotus, iussit puerum in culeum parricidae recludi et in flumine proici, Andream autem in carcere retrudi, donec, excogitata supplicia, et ipsum perderet.

blessed apostle arose and went with the lad.

His mother urgently denounced him saying, "Lord proconsul, I was barely able to escape being violated by this lad who disregarded the feelings of respect due to a mother and who turned on me out of debauchery."

"Speak, boy, whether those things your mother has charged are true," the proconsul told him. He was silent. Again and again the proconsul interrogated him, but he made no response. Because he maintained his silence, the proconsul took counsel with his confidants about what to do. The boy's mother began to weep.

"Wretch!" the blessed apostle then told her. "You shed bitter tears for the disgrace you wished to inflict on your son, you whom desire so incited that in your blazing lust you did not fear to lose your only son."

When he had said this, the mother said, "Listen, proconsul. Ever since my son decided to commit this outrage, he has clung to this man and has not separated from him."

Infuriated by these charges, the proconsul gave orders for the boy to be sewn into the leather bag for parricides and thrown in the river,[7] and for Andrew to

----

Similarly, later in the story references appear to two prayers, but nothing is said about their content.

7. The custom of sewing parricides into a *culleum*, or leather bag, and throwing them into the river is distinctively Roman (Cicero *Pro Sexto Roscio Amerino* 25, Quintillian 7.8.6, Juvenal *Satire* 8.214, and Seneca *De clementia* 1.15), and one which Roman administrators did not hesitate to use in the eastern provinces. Cicero's brother, Quintus Cicero, executed two Mysian parricides in Smyrna by this means (Cicero *Ep. ad Q. Fratrem* 1.2.2). Inasmuch as Sostratus had not killed a parent, this punishment seems parti-cularly inappropriate. Furthermore, Suetonius insists

Orante autem beato apostolo, terrae motus magnus cum tonitruo gravi factus est, et proconsul de sede cecidit, et omnes terrae decubuerunt; mater vero pueri percussa aruit et mortua est. Tunc proconsul prostratus pedibus sancti apostoli, ait: Miserere pereuntibus, famule Dei, ne nos terra deglutiat.

Orante autem beato apostolo, cessavit terrae motus, fulgora quoque ac tonitrua quieverunt. Ipse autem circumiens eos qui turbati iacebant, cunctos reddidit sanos. Proconsul vero suscipiens verbum Dei, credidit in Domino cum omni domo sua, et baptizati sunt ab apostolo Dei.

5. Gratini[1] quoque Senopinsis[2] filus, dum in balneum mulierum lavaretur, a daemone, perdito sensu, graviter cruciabatur. Gratinus autem misit epistolam ad proconsulem, in qua rogabat, ut Andream exoraret ad se venire. Sed et ipse adpraehensus febre, graviter aegrotabat, uxor vero eius ab etrope[3] intumuerat. Deprecante igitur proconsule, Andreas, ascenso vehiculo, venit ad civitatem.

---

1. Greek: Γρατῖνος, a name is not otherwise attested.

2. I.e., *Sinopensis*.

3. I.e., *hydrope*.

be incarcerated. Once the mode of his execution had been determined, the proconsul would destroy him as well.

But as the blessed apostle prayed, there was a great earthquake and frightful thunder. The proconsul fell from his seat, everyone sprawled on the ground. Lightning struck the boy's mother; she withered up and died. Then the proconsul fell at the feet of the holy apostle and said, "O servant of God, have mercy on those who are perishing, lest the earth swallow us."

When the blessed apostle prayed, the earthquake stopped; the lightning and the thunder were quiet. Then he went around to those lying about terrified and raised them all up healthy.[8] The proconsul received the word of God, believed in the Lord with his whole house, and they were baptized by the apostle of God.[9]

5. While being washed in a women's bath, the son of Gratinus of Sinope was tortured senseless by a demon.[10] Gratinus sent a letter to the proconsul asking that he prevail on Andrew to come to him. Gratinus himself was gravely ill with fever, and his wife swollen with

----

that the culleum "was inflicted only on those who pleaded guilty" (*Augustus* 33), which Sostratus obviously had not done.

8. Apparently Andrew never revived the boy's mother.

9. This story undoubtedly inspired a strikingly similar episode in the *AJPr* (Zahn, 135-50), where a boy named Sosipater escapes his mother's lustful designs, a proconsul, and a culleum full of serpents. Prieur suggests that the name Sosipater may have appeared also in the ancient *AA* and that Gregory may have corrupted it into Sostratus (*Acta Andreae*, 41-42).

10. Apparently Andrew is still in Amasia at this time. *GE* fails to account for the lad's presence in a woman's bath, but surely he was doing something indecorous, say peeping or making love. For lovers in baths see also *GE* 23 and 27.

Cumque introisset in domum Gratini, conturbavit spiritus malus puerum, et venit et procidit ante pedes apostoli. Quem ille increpans: Discede, inquit, humanae generis inimice, a famulo Dei; et statim multo clamitans discessit ab eo.

Et veniens ad stratum viri, ait: Recte aegrotas incommode, qui, relicto proprio toro, misceris scorto. Surge in nomine domini Iesu Christi et sta sanus et noli ultra peccare, ne maiorem aegrotationem incurras; et sanatus est.

Mulieri quoque dixit: Decepit te, o mulier, concupiscentia oculorum, ut, relicto coniuge, aliis miscearis. Et ait: Domine Iesu Christe, deprecor piam misericordiam tuam, ut exaudias servum tuum et praestes, ut, si haec mulier ad caenum libidinis quod prius gessit fuerit revoluta, non sanetur omnino. Certe, si scis, Domine, cuius potentia etiam futura praenoscuntur, quod se abstinere possit ab hoc flagitio, te iubente sanetur. Haec eo dicente, disrupto per inferiorem partem humore,[4] sanata est cum viro suo.

---

4. Bonnet: *humorem*.

dropsy. At the proconsul's request, Andrew mounted a
carriage and went to the city.[11]

When he entered the home of Gratinus, the evil
spirit threw the boy into convulsions, and the boy fell
at the apostle's feet. Andrew rebuked him: "Depart from
God's servant, O enemy of the human race!" Immediately
he cried aloud and came out of him.

Andrew went to Gratinus's bed and said, "Your grave
illness is quite appropriate: you left your own marriage
bed and slept with a prostitute. Arise in the name of
the Lord Jesus Christ, stand up whole, and sin no more,
lest you incur a worse ailment."[12] He was healed.

To the woman he said, "O woman, the lust of the
eyes has deceived you, so that you too leave your
husband and sleep with others."[13] And he said, "Lord
Jesus Christ, I entreat your kind mercy that you might
listen to your servant and be ready, so that if this
woman returns to the lewd filth which she formerly
practiced, she may by no means be healed. O Lord, by
whose power future events are known, if you know that
she is able to abstain from this disgrace, let her be

----

11. Presumably this is the same proconsul who had become
    a believer in the previous story.

12. Cf. John 5:14.

13. Gregory's account in no way prepares the reader for
    Andrew's acerbic denunciations of Gratinus and his
    wife, who are sick as punishments for *affaires de
    coeur*. One might suspect that Gregory has deleted
    earlier episodes of their infidelities, but it is
    also possible that the original Acts debunked sex
    between Gratinus and his wife. The radical
    asceticism of the Acts disallowed sex even in
    marriage, and it is clear elsewhere that Gregory
    transformed obligatory, absolute celibacy in his
    source into a rejection of incest (e.g. *GE* 11).

Beatus autem apostolus fregit panem et dedit ei.
Quae gratias agens, accepit et credidit in Domino cum
omni domo sua; nec deinceps illa aut vir eius scelus
quod prius admiserant perpetrarunt.

Misit quoque postea Gratinus magna munera sancto
apostolo per famulos suos. Ipse postmodum secutus est
cum uxore, prostratique coram eo, rogabant, ut acciperet
munera eorum. Quibus ille ait: Non est meum haec
accipere, dilectissimi, sed potius vestrum est ea
indigentibus erogare. Et nihil accipit ex his quae
offerebantur.

healed at your command." When he had said this, she
passed liquids and was healed, along with her husband.

Then the blessed apostle broke bread and gave it to
her. When she had given thanks, she took it and believed
in the Lord with all her house. Thereafter neither she
nor her husband perpetrated the abomination they had
committed before.

Later, Gratinus sent lavish gifts to the holy
apostle at the hands of his servants. Afterwards he
followed along with his wife; they fell before him and
asked him to receive their gifts. "My dear friends," he
told them, "I cannot accept these things; rather, they
are yours to expend for the poor." He accepted nothing
they offered.

EXCURSUS B
Andrew in Sinope

The preceding story is the only narrative *GE* places in Sinope, but the city figures prominently in Byzantine witnesses to the *AA*. *N* places Andrew's conversion of Myrmidons in Sinope, although they no longer are ant-people or even cannibals. When Epiphanius the monk visited Sinope in the ninth century, the local residents claimed their city had been home to savage Jews who had attacked Andrew and Matthias; however, we also find evidence in *E* that the savages were Scythians: "they went to Sinope, a city of Pontus, among those called Scythians" (220A; cf. 221A). Andrew and Matthias exorcise demons from the vicinity and heal many demoniacs and infirm. From Sinope Andrew goes to Scythia (following *Ps.-Epiphanius*), and later Andrew returns to Sinope, ordains bishop Philologos, and goes on to Byzantium.

Sinope is not the only place in *E* where Andrew encounters cannibals. The apostle leaves Nicea for a mountain to the east during a local Greek festival. Demons possess the celebrants, and all begin eating their own flesh until Andrew intervenes (232D--233A). In Amastra too we find cannibals.

> When Andrew entered the city, he found many disciples and stayed with them. The city was populated entirely by Jews. When they heard that Andrew had arrived--that is, he who had opened the prison and let out the prisoners-- they convened and attempted to burn down the house. They grabbed Andrew, pummeled him with rocks, dragged him about, and bit his flesh like dogs. One of them bit and chopped a finger off his right hand. This is why they are called ἀνθρωποφάγοι to this day. They dragged him through the city, beat him, stoned him, bit him, and finally threw him half dead out of town.

Immediately the Lord appeared to him and said,
"Arise, my disciple, and go into the city. Do
not fear them, for I am with you." He restored
his finger.

Andrew arose and went into the city. When they
saw his tenacity, his gentleness, and how he
exhorted them, they were stunned and began to
listen to him. They were amazed when they
heard his teachings. He interpreted the
scriptures, and they received the word of
Christ. They came together bringing the ill
whom Andrew healed by calling on Christ.
(240C--241A)

This passage apparently relies on popular local
tradition probably influenced by the *AA*, but too
indirectly to help in reconstructing the content of the
Acts itself.

L has Andrew travel to Sinope three times. For the
first and last visits *L* simply follows *E* (7 and 31).
Andrew's second visit, however, is *L*'s version of
Andrew's confrontation with the cannibals at Amastra,
only *L* does not call them ἀνθρωποφάγοι but, more
moderately, δακτυλοφάγοι, "finger-biters" (25). None of
these passages about Sinope in *N*, *E*, or *L* should be
considered primary witnesses to Andrew's adventures in
Sinope as told by the ancient Acts.

6. Post haec ad Niceam proficiscitur, ubi erant septem daemones inter monumenta commorantes, sita secus viam. Homines quoque praetereuntes meridie lapidabant et multos iam neci mortis adfecerant.[5] Veniente autem beato apostolo, exiit ei obviam tota civitas cum ramis olivarum, proclamantes laudes atque dicentes: Salus nostra in manu tua, homo Dei, et exponentes omnem rei ordinem.

Ait beatus apostolus: Si creditis in dominum Iesum Christum, filium omnipotentis Dei, cum Spiritu sancto unum Deum, liberabimini eius auxilio ab hac infestatione daemoniorum.

At illi clamabant, dicentes: Quaecumque praedicaveris credimus et obaud<i>emus iussioni tuae, tantum ut liberemur ab ista temptatione.

At ille gratias agens Deo pro eorum fide, iussit ipsos daemonas in conspectu omnis populi eius adsistere; qui venerunt in similitudinem canum. Conversus autem beatus apostolus ad populum, ait: Ecce daemonas, qui adversati sunt vobis; si autem creditis, quod in nomine Iesu Christi possim eis imperare, ut desistant a vobis, confitemini coram me.

At illi clamaverunt dicentes: Credimus, Iesum Christum filium Dei esse, quem praedicas.

Tunc beatus Andreas imperavit daemonibus, dicens: Ite in loca arida et infructuosa, nullum paenitus hominum nocentes neque accessum habentes, ubicumque

----

5. The phrase *multos iam neci mortis adfecerent*, translated here "and killed many," is quite awkward and the manuscripts attempt--unsuccessfully--to correct the problem by various philological sleights-of-hand.

6. After this, he departed for Nicea, where there were seven demons lingering among the roadside tombs, who stoned passersby in broad daylight and already had killed many.[14] As the blessed apostle approached, all the residents came to meet him on the way carrying olive branches and praised him: "Our salvation is in your hands, O man of God." They described the entire situation.

The blessed apostle said, "If you believe in the Lord Jesus Christ, the Son of God Almighty, with the Holy Spirit--one God--you will be freed by his help from this infestation of demons."

"We believe in the one you have preached," they cried, "and we will obey your command, providing we are freed of this scourge."

He thanked God for their faith and ordered the demons to present themselves before all the people, but they came in the form of dogs. The blessed apostle turned to the people and said, "Behold the demons who afflicted you. If you believe that in the name of Jesus Christ I can command them to leave you, declare it before me."

"We believe that Jesus Christ whom you preach is the Son of God," they cried.

Then the blessed Andrew commanded the demons: "Go to arid and barren places,[15] harm absolutely no one, and enter no place where the name of the Lord is invoked until you receive your due punishment of eternal fire."

----

14. The influence of the Garasene demoniac is clear (Mark 5:1-20; Matt 8:28-34; Luke 8:26-39).

15. Cf. Matt 12:43-45 and *AJPr* 124.13-15.

nomen Domini fuerit invocatum, donec accipiatis debitum
vobis supplicium ignis aeterni.

Haec   eo   dicente,   daemon<e>s,   dato   rugitu,
evanuerunt ex oculis adstantium, et sic civitas liberata
est.   Baptizavit   autem   illos   beatus   apostolus   et
instituit eis episcopum Calestum, virum sapientem et
inrepraehensibiliter custodientem quae a doctore
susceperat.

When he said these things, the demons growled and
vanished from the eyes of those present. The population
was   freed.   The   blessed   apostle   baptized   them   and
installed Callistus as their bishop, a wise man who
guarded blamelessly what he had received from the
teacher.[16]

---

16. The ending of the story seems particularly truncated
    and implies Callistus earlier had been instructed by
    Andrew in the faith. This is the only place in GE or
    in undisputed sections of the AA where Andrew
    installs a bishop. E and L also mention a bishop in
    Nicea named Dracontius (E 240B and L 21). E and L do
    mention a Callistus, not in Nicea but in Chalcedon:
    "A man there named Callistus was smitten by a demon
    and   died.   Andrew   raised   him   up   by   prayer   and
    publicly exposed the artifices of the ruler of
    demons" (E 240C [L 22]).

EXCURSUS C

Andrew in Nicea

Another version of the previous story appears in *N* as the very first of Andrew's adventures. The author claims the story had "been recorded by some of the historians of that city," but the similarities with *GE* suggest that the ultimate source may have been none other than the *AA*.[1] It would seem most likely that the story was lifted from the ancient Acts by "historians" of Nicea and later incorporated into *N*.

> When crossing the province of Bithynia he entered one of its cities called Nicea, and after teaching the saving word there, he performed a marvel, as has been recorded by some of the historians of that city. In a plot of the archevil one, evil spirits sat at the east gate making the place impassable to people. When the First-called learned this, he went to the place, and by calling on Christ our God he banished the spirits, purged the place of their ambush, and rendered it unhindered to all wanting to walk by. (4)

In the second of Andrew's three missionary journeys narrated by *E* (and also by *L*) one finds the following stories, probably received from Nicean folk tradition ("they say . . ."), but whose relationship to the ancient Acts cannot be ruled out altogether.

> When Andrew arrived, he preached Christ to them, and encouraged them to receive the word of the Lord . . . . Greeks had a statue of Apollo, which produced oracles and visions. Those who received an oracle from it would repeat the oracle but they were not able to speak again, for a demon stopped up their ears and mouths and they remained deaf and dumb. Among them were many Athenians and demoniacs.

----

1. Prieur, *Acta Andreae*, 17-18, 83, and 582 n.2.

Andrew said to them, "You cannot be delivered
from demons or diseases unless you come to
sound teaching." Some of them consented but
lied.

There was a high rocky peak about nine miles
away. They say that in it lived an immense
dragon that used to harm many. Andrew went to
it with two disciples, and grabbed an iron rod
which he always used to steady himself. When
they drew near, the dragon came out to them.
Andrew shoved the iron rod into one of the
dragon's eyes and it came out the other. The
dragon expired immediately. When this had
happened, many believed in the Lord.

Then Andrew returned to Nicea and began to
teach. After the killing of the dragon by the
ambush at the rocky peak, eight bandits lived
there, for it was like a grove. They committed
many murders. Two of them were demoniacs.

Andrew, summoned by the local residents, went
to them. The demoniacs advanced to meet him
with shouts. Andrew rebuked them and by the
time they arrived the demons had departed. The
erstwhile demoniacs tied up their hands, were
purified of the demons, and came to Andrew in
their right minds. When the others saw what
had happened they were stupefied, threw away
their weapons, came to the apostle, and threw
themselves at his feet.

But he said with a voice gentle and calming,
"My children, why do you do this? Why do you
do to others what you yourselves hate? Do you
not know that he is the maker of the small and
the great and will reward each according to
one's works? You do not want to be blinded, so
why are you malicious? You do not want to
perish, so why do you steal? God has given you
health and strength, so that you might work
and prosper from your work and need nothing,
and that you might provide for those who have
nothing. From now on, cease doing these wicked
acts which you do. Go to your homes. God will
have mercy on you, the rulers will praise you,
and you will find reward." He was speaking to
them the word of God. Amazed, they stayed with
him that day, and he baptized them.

And when they returned, they found a large
rock along the road [L calls this place
Katzapos], where there was a statue of Artemis

in which lived many spirits granting visions
and seeking sacrifices. From the ninth hour to
the third they permitted no one to come along
that road. Andrew came with his disciples and
stayed there. The demons fled like crows
crying, "O power from Jesus the Galilean! His
disciples pursue us everywhere!" Andrew ripped
down the statue and set up a cross. The rock
and the area were purified of demons. The
region was quite appropriately named Nicea
[i.e. "Victory"].

Nearby was a thicket where a dragon and a
hoard of demons lived, to whom the Greeks
would offer sacrifices [*L* names the place
Daukomeos]. A statue of Aphrodite was there.
When Andrew and his disciples went to the
place, he knelt, prayed, arose, lifted his
hand, and sealed the place [with the sign of
the cross]. The dragon and the demons fled and
from then on the place was inhabited. (*E*
229B--232C [=*L* 15-19])

In the section immediately following, Andrew and
his disciples go to a nearby mountain (*L*: Mount Klidos)
during a Greek festival. The demons enter the
participants and cause them to eat their own flesh.
Andrew descends the mountain, seals them with the sign
of the cross, and cures their cannibalism.

7. Denique adpropinquans portam Nicomediae, ecce efferebatur mortuus in grabatto, cuius pater senex servorum sustentatus manibus vix obsequium funeris valebat inpendere. Mater quoque hac aetate gravata, sparsis crinibus, sequebatur heiulando cadaver, dicens: Vae mihi, cuius usque ad hoc tempus aetas producta est, ut funeris mei apparatum in filii funus expendam.

Cumque haec et his similia deplorantes cadaver vociferando prosequerentur, affuit apostolus Dei, condolensque lacrimis eorum, ait: Dicite mihi, quaeso, quid huic puero contigit, ut ab hac luce migravit?

At illi prae timore nihil respondentes, a famulis apostolus haec audivit: Dum esset, inquiunt, iuvenis iste in cubiculo solus, advenerunt subito septem canes et inruerunt in eum. Ab his igitur miserrime discerptus, cecedit et mortuus est.

Tunc beatus Andreas suspirans et in caelum oculos erigens, cum lacrimis ait: Scio, Domine, quia daemonum eorum fuit insidia, quos expuli a Nicea urbe. Et nunc rogo, Iesu benigne, ut resuscites eum, ne congaudeat adversarius humani generis de eius interitu.

Et haec dicens, ait ad patrem: Quid dabis mihi, si restituero tibi filium tuum salvum?

Et ille: Nihil eo habeo praetiosius, ipsum enim dabo, si ad vitam surrexerit te iubente.

7. Later, when he approached the gate of Nicomedia, a dead man was being carried out of the city on a bier.[17] His old father, supported by the hands of slaves, scarcely was able to pay for the funeral. His mother, bent over with age, hair unkempt, followed the corpse wailing: "Woe is me, for I have lived so long that I am spending for my son's funeral what I had saved for my own."

As they followed the corpse, screaming and mourning these and related misfortunes, the apostle of God arrived, and moved by their tears he said, "Please tell me what happened to this boy for him to have departed from this light."

They were afraid to answer, but from the servants the apostle heard this: "When this youth was alone in his bedroom, all of a sudden seven dogs rushed in and attacked him. He was savagely mangled by them, fell, and died."

Then the blessed apostle sighed, raised his eyes toward heaven, and spoke through his tears: "Lord, I know that the attack was the work of the demons that I expelled from Nicea.[18] I now ask you, O gracious Jesus, to revive him, lest the enemy of humankind rejoice at his destruction."

When he had said this, he asked the boy's father, "What will you give me if I restore your son to you healthy?"

"I have nothing more valuable than he. If he revives at your command, I will give him to you."

----

17. Cf. Luke 7:11-17, *AJPr* 1 and esp. 80-85.

18. *GE* 6.

Beatus vero apostolus iterum, expansis ad caelum manibus, oravit, dicens: Redeat, quaeso, Domine, anima pueri, ut, isto resuscitato, relictis cuncti idolis ad te convertantur, fiatque eius vivificatio salus omnium pereuntium, ut iam non subdantur morti, sed tui effecti, vitam mereantur aeternam. Respondentibus fidelibus: Amen.

Conversus ad feretrum ait: In nomine Iesu Christi, surge et sta super pedes tuos.

Et statim, ammirante populo, surrexit, ita ut omnes qui aderant voce magna clamarent: Magnus est Deus Christus, quem praedicat servus eius Andreas.

Parentes enim pueri multa munera dederunt filio suo, quae beato apostolo obtulit; sed ille nihil ex his accepit. Puerum tantum secum usque ad Macedoniam abire praecipiens, salutaribus verbis instruxit.

8. Egressus inde apostolus Domini navem conscendit, ingressusque Helispontum fretum, navigabat, ut veniret Bizantium. Et ecce commotum est mare, et incubuit super eos ventus validus, et mergebatur navis. Denique, praestolantibus cunctis periculum mortis, oravit beatus Andreas ad Dominum, praecipiensque vento, siluit; fluctus autem maris quieverunt, et tranquillitas data est. Ereptique omnes a praesenti discrimine, Bizantium pervenerunt.

Again the blessed apostle raised his hands to heaven and prayed, "O Lord, I ask that the lad's breath return, so that by his resuscitation all may turn to you from forsaken idols. May his reviving cause the salvation of all the lost, so that they may no longer be subject to death but may win eternal life by having been made yours." The faithful responded, "Amen."

Turning to the bier he said, "In the name of Jesus Christ, rise and stand on your feet."

To the astonishment of the people he arose at once, and all present shouted with a loud voice, "Great is the God Christ, whom his servant Andrew preaches."

The boy's parents gave their son many gifts which he offered to the blessed apostle, but Andrew accepted none of them. He did take the boy to travel with him all the way to Macedonia, and taught him with saving words.[19]

8. Leaving there, the Lord's apostle boarded a ship and sailed the Hellespont to get to Byzantium. A storm arose on the sea, a strong wind pressed down on them, and the ship foundered. At last, just when everyone was expecting to perish, the blessed Andrew prayed to the Lord, commanded the wind, and was silent. The raging waves of the sea became placid, and there was calm. Having been saved from the immediate crisis, they reached Byzantium.

----

19. Though Andrew takes the boy to Macedonia we hear nothing more about him in *GE*. *E* says that when Andrew traveled from Nicea to Nicomedia he restored the life of a certain Callistus who, like the boy in this story, had been killed by a demon (240C). According to *E*, however, Andrew left Callistus in Chalcedon, not Macedonia.

EXCURSUS D
Andrew in Byzantium

N says that Andrew,

after having sailed down through the same
Pontus Euxinus [Black Sea] which flows toward
Byzantium, landed on the right bank, and after
arriving at a place called Argyropolis, and
having constructed there a church, he ordained
one of the seventy disciples called Stachys
whom also Paul the Apostle, the mouthpiece of
Christ, the vessel of election, mentions in
the Epistle to the Romans [16:9] as beloved
[by him], Bishop of Byzantium, and left him to
preach the word of salvation. He, because of
the pagan godlessness that prevailed in that
region, and the cruelty of the tyrant Zeuxippus, a worshiper of idols who held sway there,
turned toward western parts, illuminating with
his divine teaching the darkness of the West.[2]

According to Francis Dvornik, the author of *N*
inherited this tradition from *Ps.-Epiphanius*: "Stachys,
whom Paul also mentions in the same Epistle, was
instituted first Bishop of Byzantium by Andrew the
Apostle, in Argyropolis of Thrace."[3] Dvornik also argues
that *E* knew of the Stachys legend from *Ps.-Epiphanius*,
and that *Ps.-Dorotheus* knew of it from *N*.[4]

Furthermore, Dvornik shows that this installation
of Stachys cannot have originated prior to the fifth
century, inasmuch as the suburb of Constantinople called
Argyropolis received this name from Patriarch Atticus

----

2. *N* 8; cf. *E* 244C. The translation is that of Dvornik,
   Apostolicity, 172.

3. Ibid., 175. The text appears in Schermann, *Prophetarum vitae fabulosae*.

4. *Apostolicity*, 179-80. *L* 32 contains the same episode,
   derived directly from *E*.

(406-25).[5] The reference to Zeuxippus reflects a local
Byzantine legend that claimed a Zeuxippus as one of its
former kings.[6] His very name (Ζευξίππος = Zeus Hippios)
suggests he would have been "a worshiper of idols"; a
statue of Zeuxippus once commemorated the legendary spot
in Byzantium where Heracles, with the Zeus's help, tamed
Diomedes' steeds (ἵπποι). Later, Severus relocated the
statue to the new temple of Apollo. Thus Dvornik
concludes:

> Such a legendary name naturally stimulated the
> imagination of the people of Byzantium, and it
> is not surprising that Zeuxippus was given a
> place in their folklore. Because the name was
> connected with the history of Byzantium from
> pagan times, it was easy to make of him a
> persecutor of Christians, and the creators of
> the Andrew Legend could have had, therefore,
> little difficulty in finding a suitable name
> for a fictitious ruler of Byzantium in
> apostolic times, and, at the same time, in
> endowing their Legend with a semblance of
> verisimilitude.[7]

The origin of the Stachys legend, therefore, should
be attributed to the desire of Byzantines to provide
their city with apostolic pedigree. Rome long had
claimed Peter as the founder of the papacy, but
Byzantium could claim no founding apostle on the basis
of widely recognized textual and ancient authority. This
was no problem when Rome and Byzantium were on good
terms, but later tensions put pressures on the eastern
see to secure apostolic rootage. Andrew was perfectly
suited for the purpose. According to John 1:35-42, he
was the first apostle to come to Jesus and later

----

5. Socrates *Historia ecclesiastica* 7.25; see Dvornik,
   Apostolicity, 219.

6. Ibid., 218-19.

7. Ibid.

introduced Jesus to his brother Peter. Furthermore,
tradition and the AA had placed Andrew in the region of
the Black Sea, including Byzantium. The relics of the
apostle had been transferred to Constantinople in the
mid-fourth century by Constantius II to be deposited in
the Church of the Holy Apostles. Unfortunately, neither
the tradition nor the AA said Andrew had installed a
bishop there. What tradition lacked, pious imagination
provided--probably late in the seventh century. Dvornik
dates the earliest written reference to this
installation of Stachys (Ps.-Epiphanius) to the early
eighth century.[8] Even today, Eastern Orthodoxy appeals
to apostolic succession from Andrew and calls him
affectionately ὁ Πρωτοκλητός, "the First-Called." To be
sure, GE's absolute silence concerning Andrew's
activities in Byzantium is suspicious, but if the
ancient Acts recorded any mission here, it is now
completely veiled to us.

----

8. Ibid., 175-79.

9. Inde progressi, ut venirent Thracias, apparuit eis multitudo hominum a longe cum evaginatis gladiis, lanceas manu gestantes, quasi volentes in illis irruere. Quod cum vidisset Andreas apostolus, faciens crucis signum contra eos, ait: Oro, Domine, ut decidat pater eorum, qui haec eos agere instigavit. Conturbentur virtute divina, ne noceant sperantes in te.

Haec eo dicente, angelus Domini cum magno splendore praeteriens, tetigit gladios eorum, et corruerunt proni in terra. Transiensque beatus apostolus cum suis, nihil est nocitus; omnes enim, proiectis gladiis, adorabant eum. Angelus quoque Domini discessit ab eis cum magno lumine claritatis.

10. Sanctus vero apostolus pervenit ad Perintum civitatem Traciae maritimam et invenit ibi navem, quae in Machedoniam properaret. Apparuit enim ei iterum angelus Domini et iussit eum ingredi navem. Tunc praedicans in navi verbum Dei, credidit nauta in Dominum Iesum Christum et omnes qui cum eo erant, et glorific-

9. Proceeding from there in order to go to Thrace,[20] they came upon a multitude of men a long way off with swords drawn and brandishing spears as if they intended to attack. When the apostle Andrew saw them, he made the sign of the cross against them and said, "I pray, O Lord, that their father who incited them to do this would fall. May they be thrown into disorder by divine power, so that they cannot harm those who hope in you."

As he said this, an angel of the Lord passed by with great splendor, touched their swords, and they fell sprawling on the ground. The blessed apostle passed by with his entourage unscathed, for the entire throng threw away their swords and adored him. Then the angel of the Lord departed from them in a great bright light.

10. The holy apostle arrived at Perinthus,[21] a Thracian coastal city, and there found a boat about to leave for Macedonia. Again an angel of the Lord appeared to him and commanded him to board the boat. As he preached the word of God on board, a sailor and all who were with him believed in the Lord Jesus Christ, and the

----

20. Although several witnesses to the *AA* mention Thrace, only *GE* is blessed with narrative. *N* claims the apostle went from Nicea directly to Thrace and from there on to Scythia (4). It is quite possible that *N* here depends not on the *AA* but on *Ps.-Epiphanius* (see also *Ps.-Dorotheus* on Andrew's itinerary).

21. Perinthus was a port city about fifty miles due west of Byzantium. *E* calls the city Heraclea: "having left there [Byzantium] he went to Heraclea in Thrace. After a few days he left [for Macedonia]" (244C). If the ancient Acts narrated Andrew's ministry in Perinthus, all that is left to us is the reference in *E* to "a few days" there. *N* claims that after visiting Thrace, Andrew set out for Scythia and Sebastopolis Magna (4), but this seems to have been based on *Ps.-Epiphanius* and not on the *AA*.

abat apostolus sanctus Deum, quod nec in mari defuit qui
audiret praedicationem eius aut qui crederet filium Dei
omnipotentis.

11. Fuerunt autem duo viri in Philippis fratres, et
uni quidem erant duo filii, alteri filiae duae, quibus
erat facultas magna, eo quod essent valde nobiles.
Dixitque unus ad alterum: Ecce sunt nobis opes eximiae,
et non est de civibus qui dignae copuletur generationi
nostrae; sed veni, et fiat nobis una domus ex omnibus.
Filii mei accipiant filias tuas, ut opes nostrae
facilius coniungantur. Placuit hic sermo fratri, et
inito foedere, obligaverunt hanc conven<i>entiam per
arrabone<m> quod pater puerorum misit.

Dato igitur die nuptiarum, factum est verbum Domini
ad eos, dicens: Nolite coniungere filios vestros, donec
veniat famulus meus Andreas. Ipse enim vobis quae agere
debeatis ostendet. Iam enim thalamum praeparatum erat et
convivae vocati, et omne apparatum nuptiale in promptu
tenebatur.

Tertia vero die advenit apostolus, et videntes eum,
gavisi sunt magno gaudio, et occurrentes ei cum coronis,

holy apostle glorified God that even on the sea there was someone to hear his preaching and to believe in the son of God Almighty.[22]

11. There were two brothers at Philippi,[23] one of whom had two sons, the other two daughters; both were rich, for they were great nobles. One said to the other, "Look, we both have vast wealth, and there is no one in the city worthy of breeding with our clan. Come, let us merge our families into one. Let my sons marry your daughters, so that we might more easily consolidate our wealth." This speech pleased his brother, and once the pact was made they secured the deal with an earnest sent by the boys' father.

When the date for the wedding had been set, the word of the Lord came to them saying, "Do not marry your children until my servant Andrew comes, for he will show you what you should do." The nuptial chamber already had been prepared, the guests called, and all the wedding provisions were at the ready.

Three days later, the apostle arrived. When they saw him they were jubilant, ran to him with wreaths,

----

22. Once again *GE* surely has greatly abbreviated the original, which presumably included an angelic speech telling Andrew to go to Macedonia, a sermon to the crew, Andrew's prayer of thanksgiving, and some indication of the Macedonian city where he disembarked (Neapolis? Thessalonica?). A similar tale appears in the *APe* where Jesus commands Peter to go to Rome. Peter boards a boat at Caesarea, captain Theon converts, is baptized, and partakes of the eucharist before they arrive at Puteoli (*APe* [*AV*] 5; see also Acts 27 and *APl* 10).

23. *E* also mentions Andrew's visit to Macedonia but narrates no events (244C). *N* says that after visiting Byzantium the apostle went "through Thessaly" not Macedonia, although "Thessaly" may be a corruption of Thessalonica (9).

processerunt[6] ante pedes eius et dixerunt: Te a<d>moniti praestolamur, famulae Dei, ut venias et adnunties nobis quid faciamus. Accepimus enim verbum o<p>perir<i>[7] te, et, ne ante coniungerentur filii nostri, quam tu venires, indicatum est nobis.

Erat tunc vultus beati apostoli tamquam sol relucens, ita ut omnes admirarentur, et honorarent eum.[8] Quibus ait apostolus: Nolite, filioli, nolite seduci, nolite decipere hos iuvenes, quibus potest fructus apparere iustitiae; sed magis paenitentiam agite, quia deliquistis in Dominum, ut proximos sanguine velletis coniugio copulare. Non nos nuptias aut avertimus aut vitamus, cum ab initio Deus masculum iungi praecipisset et feminam, sed potius incesta damnamus.

Haec eo loquente, commoti parentes eorum, dixerunt: Oramus, domine, ut depraeceris pro nobis Deum tuum, quia nescientes fecimus hoc delictum.

Adolescentes autem videntes vultum apostoli splendere tamquam[9] angeli Dei, dicebant: Magna et inmaculata est doctrina tua, vir beatae, et nesciebamus; verum enim cognovimus, quia Deus loquitur in te.

Quibus sanctus apostolus ait: Custodite sine pollutione quae audistis, ut sit Deus vobiscum, et accipiatis mercedem operis vestri, id est sempiternam

----

6. Some mss.: *prociderunt.*

7. The text reads: *operire.*

8. Bonnet's text follows mss. reading *Deum* instead of *eum*, but it is more likely that some scribe thought it more appropriate for the Philippians to honor God than to honor Andrew and made the text say so by adding *d.*

9. Some mss. add: *vultum.*

fell at his feet, and said, "O servant of God, having been warned about you, we have been waiting for you to come and tell us what we should do. We got word to stall for you,[24] and were told that our children should not be married before you arrived."

Then the face of the blessed apostle shone like the sun to such a degree that all were amazed and honored him. The apostle told them, "No, my little ones! Do not be led astray! Do not deceive these young people in whom the fruit of justice might appear! Rather, repent, for you have sinned against the Lord by wanting to unite blood relatives in marriage. It is not that we forbid or shun weddings--from the beginning God commanded the male and the female to be joined together[25]--but we do condemn incest."

When he said this, their parents were disturbed and said, "Sir, we beg you to entreat your God for us, for we did this crime unwittingly."

When the young people saw that the face of the apostle shone like the face of an angel of God, they said, "Your teaching is great and untainted, O blessed man, but we did not know it. Truly, we now recognize that God speaks through you."

The holy apostle said to them, "Keep uncontaminated what you hear, so that God may be with you, and so that you may receive interest from your wealth--that is, everlasting life which never ends." When the apostle had said this and blessed them, he was silent.[26]

----

24. Unemended, Bonnet's text reads: "to hide you."

25. Gen 2:24.

26. *The Epistle of Titus* also refers to this story: "At last, when Andrew arrived at a wedding, he too, to

vitam, quae nullo clauditur fine. Haec dicens apostolus et benedicens eos, siluit.[10]

12. Erat quidam iuvenis in Tesalonica nobilis valde ac dives opibus Exuos nomine. Hic venit ad apostolum, nescientibus parentibus suis, et procidens ad pedes eius, rogabat eum, dicens: Ostende mihi, quaeso, famule Dei, viam veritatis. Cognovi enim, quod verus minister sis eius qui te misit.

Sanctus vero apostolus praedicavit ei Dominum Iesum Christum, et credidit adolescens, adherens sancto apostolo nihilque de parentibus meminens neque de facultatibus aliquam inpendens sollicitudinem.

Parentes autem requirentes eum, audierunt, quod in Philippis cum apostolo moraretur, et venientes cum muneribus, rogabant, ut separaretur ab eo; sed nolebat, dicens: Utinam nec vos has opes haberetis, ut mundi cognoscentes auctorem, qui est verus Deus, erueretis animas vestras ab ira futura.

Sanctus quoque apostolus descendit de tristico[11] et praedicabat eis verbum Dei; sed non audientibus, rediit ad puerum et clausit ostia domus. At illi, convocata cohorte, venerunt, ut incenderent domum illam in qua erat iuvenis, dicentes: Intereat puer, qui reliqui<t>

----

10. *The Epistle of Titus*: *Ut venisset denique et Andreas ad nupcias, et ipse, ad demonstrandam gloriam Dei, destinatos sibi coniuges deiunxit masculos et foeminas ab invicem et docuit eos singulari statu permanere sanctos*. Cf. ATh 4-16.

11. For the Greek word τριστέγῳ; cf. Acts 20:9.

12. At Thessalonica there was a young man,
exceedingly noble and rich, named Exochus. Without his
parents' knowledge, he came to the apostle, fell at his
feet, and asked, "O servant of God, please show me the
way of truth, for I recognize that you are a true
servant of him who sent you."

The holy apostle indeed preached to him the Lord
Jesus Christ. The youth believed and attached himself to
the holy apostle, forgetting about his parents and
altogether disregarding his financial affairs.[27]

When his parents inquired about him, they learned
that he was staying with the apostle in Philippi. They
brought gifts with them and begged the lad to abandon
him, but he refused saying, "If only you did not own
these riches, so that by knowing the creator of the
world, the true God, you might rescue your souls from
the wrath to come."

The holy apostle descended from the third story and
preached to them the word of God. When they did not
listen, he went back to the boy and shut the doors of
the house. They assembled an armed band and came to set
fire to the house where the youth was, saying, "Let the
lad perish who forsook his parents and native land."

----

demonstrate God's glory, disjoined men and women
whose marriages had been arranged and taught them to
continue being holy as singles." The foiled wedding
in ATh 4-16, which may have been inspired by this
story in the AA, likewise opposes marriage
absolutely. It would therefore appear that the story
in the AA also prohibited marriage itself, not
merely incest. See Prieur, Acta Andreae, 20-21 and
42-43.

27. Judging from the youth's response to Andrew's
preaching, it would appear that the content of the
omitted speech denounced wealth.

parentes et patriam. Et adhibentes fasces caractae[12] scyrpique[13] et facularum, coeperunt succendere domum.

Et cum iam flamma fereretur in altum, arreptam adolescens ampullam aquae, ait: Domine Iesu Christe, in cuius manu omnium elementorum natura consistit, qui arentia inficis et infecta facis arescere, qui ignita refrigeras et extincta succendens,[14] tu extingue hos ignes, ut tui non tepescant, sed magis accendantur ad fidem. Et haec dicens, ex<s>parsit desuper aquam ex ampulla, et statim omne incendium ita supitum[15] est, acsi non fuisset accensum.

Quod videntes parentes pueri, dicebant: Ecce iam filius noster magus effectus est. Et adhibentes scalas, volebant ascendere in tristico, ut eos interficerent gladio. Dominus autem excaecavit eos, ne viderent ascensum scalarum.

Cumque in hac perversitate durarent, quidam Lesemachus[16] e civibus ait: Ut quid, o viri, casso vos labore consumitis? Deus enim pugnat pro viris istis, et vos non cognoscitis? Sinite ab hac stultitia, ne vos caelestis ira consumat.

Haec eo dicente, conpuncti omnes corde, dicebant: Verus est Deus, quem isti colunt, quem et nos persequi temptavimus.

----

12. An awkward transliteration of χάρακος.

13. I.e.: *scirpique*.

14. Some mss.: *succendis*.

15. I.e.: *subitum*.

16. I.e.: *Lysimachus*.

They brought out bundles of stakes, reeds, and torches and began to ignite the house.

As the fire rose, the youth grabbed a small flask of water and said, "Lord Jesus Christ, by whose hand the nature of all the elements holds together, who moistens the parched and parches the moist, who cools what burns and ignites what has been snuffed out, extinguish these flames, so that these people may not be lukewarm toward you but may be set on fire for the faith." When he had said this, he sprinkled the water from the small flask, and immediately the entire fire was controlled so that it was as if it had never burned.

When the boy's parents saw this, they said, "Look, our son already has been turned into a sorcerer." They brought out a ladder and intended to scale up to the third story to slay them by sword, but the Lord blinded them so they could not see the ladder's ascent.

Because they persisted in this perversity, a citizen named Lysimachus said, "Men, why do you expend yourselves on this futile task? Do you not recognize that God fights for these men? Stop this foolishness lest the wrath of heaven consume you."

At these words, everyone was cut to the heart and said, "The god those men worship and whom we tried to oppose is the true God."

Haec eis dicentibus, cum iam tenebrae noctis advenissent, subito lumen effulsit, et omnium oculi inluminati sunt. Ascendentesque ubi erat apostolus Christi, invenerunt eum orantem; prostrati quoque in pavimento, clamabant dicentes: Quaesumus, domine, ut ores pro servis tuis, qui errore seducti sunt. Tanta enim omnes conpunctio cordis attigerat, ut diceret Lysemachus: Vere Christus est filius Dei, quem praedicat servus eius Andreas. Tunc erecti ab apostolo, conroborati sunt in fide, tantum parentes pueri non crediderunt.

Qui exsecrantes adolescentem, regressi sunt in patriam, subdentes omnia quae habebant publicis ditionibus. Post dies autem 50 unius horae momento expiraverunt; et post haec, pro eo quod diligerent omnes viri civitatis adolescentem propter bonitatem et mansuetudinem eius, omne patrimonium ei concessum est a publico, et erat possidens cuncta quae habuerant parentes eius. Non tamen ab apostolo discedebat, sed fructus praediorum in pauperum necessitatibus et curis indigentium expendebat.[17]

13. Rogavit autem adolescens beatum apostolum, ut proficiscerentur simul in Thesalonica, et cum venissent ibi, congregati sunt omnes ad eum; gaudebant enim videntes puerum. Tunc, congregatis omnibus in theatrum, praedicabat eis puer verbum Dei, ita ut sileret apostolus, et admirarentur[18] prudentiam eius. At illi clamaverunt, dicentes: Salva filium Carpiani civis nostri, quia valde aegrotat, et credimus in Iesum quem praedicas.

---

17. *The Manichaean Psalm-Book*: ⲚⲦⲀ ⲩⲦ ⲦⲤⲈⲦⲈ ⲀⲠ Ⲏ Ⲓ ⲆⲀⲢⲀ ⳑ (142.20).

18. Some mss.: *admiraretur*.

By the time they had said this, nightfall had come. Suddenly a light shone so that everyone could see. They ascended to the place where the apostle of Christ was and found him praying. Prostrate on the floor they cried out, "We ask you, sir, to pray for your servants who have been deceived by error." Everyone was so repentant that Lysimachus said, "Truly Christ whom his servant Andrew preaches is the son of God." Then the apostle raised them up and strengthened them in the faith; only the lad's parents did not believe.

They returned to their homeland cursing the youth and handed over all their belongings to the public authorities. Fifty days later, in the space of an hour, they both died. Then, because all the men of the city loved the youth for his goodness and gentleness, they turned over to him from the public treasury his entire patrimony. Now he possessed all that his parents had owned. Not even then did he separate from the apostle, but spent the income from the estate on the needs of the poor and the care of the indigent.[28]

13. The youth asked the blessed apostle to set out with him for Thessalonica. When they arrived there everyone swarmed to him, for they were glad to see the boy. Then, when everyone was gathered at the theater, the boy preached to them the word of God,[29] so that the apostle did not need to speak. The crowd was amazed at the boy's insight and cried out: "Save the son of

----

28. *The Manichaean Psalm-Book* also refers to this story. In a list of apostolic sufferings one learns of Andrew that "they set fire to the house beneath him" (142.20).

29. This is the only witness to the *AA* in which someone other than Andrew gives the major sermon.

Quibus ait beatus apostolus: Nihil est inpossibile apud Deum; sed tamen, ut credatis, adducite eum in conspectu nostro, et sanabit illum Dominus Iesus Christus.

Tunc pater eius abiit ad domum suam et dixit ad puerum: Hodie sanus eris, fili dilectissime Adimante; hoc enim erat nomen pueri.

Qui ait ad patrem: Vere enim effectum est somnium meum; nam ego vidi per visum virum hunc, qui me sanum redderet.

Et haec dicens, induit vestimenta sua, surrexitque a grabatto et pergebat ad theatrum cursu veloci, ita ut non possit a parentibus adsequi. Et procidens ad pedes beati apostoli, gratias agebat pro sanitate recepta. Populi autem stupebant, videntes eum post viginti tres annos ambulantem, et glorificabant Deum, dicentes, quia: Non est similis deo Andreae.

14. Unus autem e civibus, cuius filius habebat spiritum inmundum, rogabat beatum apostolum, dicens: Sana, quaeso, vir Dei, filium meum, quia male a daemonio vexatur. Daemon vero, sciens futurum se eici, seduxit puerum in secretum cubiculum et suffocavit eum, laqueo extorquens animam eius.

Denique pater pueri, cum invenisset illum mortuum, flevit multum et ait amicis suis: Ferte cadaver ad theatrum; confido enim, quod poterit resuscitare ab hospite qui praedicat Deum verum.

Carpianus, our fellow citizen, for he is gravely ill, and we will believe in the Jesus you preach."

The blessed apostle said to them, "Nothing is impossible for God.[30] Bring him before us, and the Lord Jesus Christ will heal him so that you may believe."

His father then went to his house and said to the boy, "Today you will be healed, my beloved Adimantus" (this was the boy's name).

"My dream has indeed come true," he told his father, "for in a vision I saw this man restoring me to health."

When he had said this, he clothed himself, rose from his cot, and proceeded to the theater, running so quickly that his parents could not follow. Falling at the blessed apostle's feet, he gave thanks for the health he had received. The crowd was stupefied at seeing him walk after twenty-three years, and they glorified God saying, "No one equals Andrew's God!"

14. One of the citizens whose son had an impure spirit asked the blessed apostle: "Please heal my son, man of God, for he is deeply disturbed by a demon."[31] Foreseeing his impending expulsion, the demon led the boy to a secluded room and strangled him, wringing out his life with a noose.

When the boy's father found him dead he wept profusely and said to his friends, "Take the carcass to

----

30. Cf. Luke 1:37.

31. It would appear that the father had been in the Thessalonian theater, had seen Andrew heal Adimantus, and desired Andrew to heal his son as well. Cf. *APe* (*AV*) 23-29.

Quo delato et posito coram apostolo, narravit ei, qualiter interfectus esset a daemone, dicens: Credo, homo Dei, quod etiam a morte per te possit resurgere.

Conversus autem apostolus ad populum, ait: Quid vobis proderit, viri Thesalonicenses, cum haec fieri videtis,[19] si non creditis?[20]

At illi dixerunt: Ne dubites, vir Dei, quia, isto resuscitato, omnes credimus.[21]

Haec illis dicentibus, ait apostolus: In nomine Iesu Christi, surge, puer; et statim surrexit. Et stupefactus omnis populus, clamabat dicens: Sufficit; nunc credimus cuncti Deo illi quem praedicas, famule Dei. Et deducentes eum ad domum cum facibus et lucernis, eo quod iam nox advenisset, introduxerunt eum in domum suam, ubi per triduum instruxit illos de his quae Dei erant.

15. Venit ad eum quidam vir de Philippis Medias nomine, cuius filius in debilitate nimia aegrotabat, et ait ad apostolum: Depraecor, o homo Dei, ut restituas mihi filium meum, quia debilitatus est corpore. Et haec dicens, flebat valde.

Beatus vero apostolus abstergens genas eius et caput manu dimulcens, dicebat: Confortare, fili; tantum crede, et inplentur voluntates tuae. Tunc adpraehendens manum eius, ibat in Philippis.

Cumque ingrederetur portam civitatis, occurrit ei senex, rogans pro filiis, quos pro culpa ineffabili

----

19. Some mss.: *videritis*.

20. Some mss.: *credideritis*.

21. Some mss.: *credemus*.

the theater, for I am sure that the stranger who proclaims the true God can revive him."

When the lad had been carried out and placed before the apostle, the father related how the boy had been killed by the demon and said, "Man of God, I believe that through you he can arise even from death."

The apostle turned to the crowd and said, "What will it profit you, men of Thessalonica, if you see this done and still do not believe?"

"Man of God," they said, "be assured that if he is raised we will all believe."

When they had said this the apostle said, "Lad, in the name of Jesus Christ arise." He arose at once. The entire crowd was amazed and cried out: "Servant of God, that is sufficient. All of us now believe in the God you preach." They led him out to the house with torches and lamps--it was already past nightfall--and brought him inside his house where Andrew taught them the things of God for three days.

15. A man from Philippi named Medias,[32] whose son was seriously crippled, came to the apostle and said, "I entreat you, man of God, to restore my son to me, for his body is crippled." He wept profusely as he spoke.

The blessed apostle wiped his cheeks, stroked his head, and said, "Be comforted, son. Only believe and your desires will come to pass." Then seizing his hand, he went to Philippi.

When he entered the city gate, an old man ran to him pleading for his children, whom Medias had forced

----

32. Greek: Μειδίας.

Medias carcerali supplicio detruserat, et erant
ulceribus putrefacti.

Conversus autem sanctus apostolus ad Median, dixit:
Audi, homo; tu deprecaris, ut sanetur filius tuus, cum
apud te vincti retineantur, quorum iam sunt carnes
exaese.[22] Et ideo, si praeces tuas ad Deum vis
proficisci, absolve prius miserorum catenam, ut et
filius tuus a debilitate laxetur; nam video inpedimentum
ferre precibus meis malitiam quam exerces.

Tunc Medias procidit ad pedes eius, et deosculans,
ait: Absolvantur hii duo et alii septem, de quibus nihil
audisti, tantum ut sanetur filius meus. Et iussit eos in
conspectu beati apostoli exhiberi. At illi, inpositis
eis manus, et per triduum abluens vulnera eorum,
sanitati restituit libertatique donavit.

Postea vero die ait ad puerum: Surge in nomine
Domini Iesu Christi, qui me misit, ut medear infirmitati
tuae. Et adpraehensa manu eius, levavit eum; qui statim
surrexit et ambulabat, magnificans Deum. Vocabatur enim
puer Philomedes, qui viginti duobus annis fuerat
debilis.

Clamantibus autem populis et dicentibus: Et nostris
medere infirmis, famule Dei Andreas.

Ait vero apostolus ad puerum: Vade per domos
aegrotantium et in nomine Iesu Christi, in quo sanatus
es, tu iube eos ex<s>urgere.

At ille, admirantibus populis, abiit per domos
infirmorum, invocatoque Christi nomine, restituebat eos

----

22. I.e.: *exesae.*

into confinement for unspeakable immorality and who festered with sores.

The holy apostle turned to Medias and said, "Listen mister, you beg for your son to be healed, yet at your own home you detain in shackles people with rotting flesh. If you want your prayers to come before God, first release the chains of those who suffer, so that your son too may be freed of his disability. I see that your cruelty impedes my prayers."

Medias then fell at his feet, kissed him, and said, "I will free these two and seven others unknown to you, so that my son may be healed." He ordered them arrayed before the blessed apostle, who laid hands on them, washed their wounds for three days, restored their health, and gave them freedom.

The next day Andrew said to the boy, "Rise up in the name of the Lord Jesus Christ who sent me to cure your infirmity." He took his hand, lifted him, and immediately the lad straightened up and walked, magnifying God. The name of the lad who had been crippled for twenty-two years was Philomedes.

"Andrew, servant of God," shouted the crowd, "heal our sick."

The apostle told the lad, "Go to the houses of the sick and command them to rise up in the name of Jesus Christ who healed you."

To the crowd's astonishment, he went off to the houses of the sick and restored them to health by in-

sanitati. Credidit autem omnis populus, offerensque[23] ei
munera, rogabant, ut audirent verbum Dei. Beatus vero
apostolus praedicans Deum verum, nihil de muneribus
accipiebat.

16. Denique Nicolaus quidam e civibus exhibens
carrucam deauratam cum quattuor mulis candidis equisque
eiusdem numeri et coloris, obtulit beato apostolo,
dicens: Haec accipe, famulae Dei, quia nihil repperi
inter res meas his amabilius, tantum ut sanetur filia
mea, quae nimio cruciatu vexatur.

Cui subridens beatus apostolus ait: Accipio quidem
munera tua, Nicolae, sed non haec visibilia. Nam, si pro
filia quae praetiosum[24] in domo tua habebas offeres,
quanto magis pro anima debes? Ego enim hoc a te accipere
cupio, ut homo ille interior agnoscat verum Deum
factorem suum creatoremque omnium, qui terrena respuat
et aeterna desideret, qui caduca neglegat, diligat
sempiterna, qui illa quae videntur abnuat et ea quae non
videntur contemplatione spirital<e>s intentiones
advertat, ut, cum his exercitatu sensu vigueris, vitam
aeternam consequi merearis, filiamque hic sanitati
redditam, etiam in illa aeternitatis gaudia perfruaris.

Haec eo dicente, persuasit omnibus, ut, relictis
idolis, Deum verum crederent. Filiam quoque ipsius
Nicolai sanavit ab infirmitate qua tenebatur, et omnes
magnificabant eum,[25] percurrente per totam Machedoniam
fama de virtutibus quae faciebat super infirmos.

----

23. Some mss.: *offerentesque*.

24. Some mss.: *praeciosa*.

25. Bonnet conjectures *Deum*.

voking the name of Christ. Then all the people believed, offered him gifts, and asked to hear the word of God. The blessed apostle preached the true God but accepted no gifts.

16.[33] Later, a citizen named Nicolaus displayed a gilded carriage with four white mules and four white horses and offered them to the blessed apostle saying, "Take these, servant of God, for I found none of my possessions dearer than these, only let my daughter, plagued by extreme torment, be healed."

The blessed apostle smiled and said to him, "I do indeed receive your gifts, Nicolaus, but not these visible ones. For if you offer the most precious things in your home for your daughter, how much more would you owe for your soul? Here is what I long to receive from you: that your inner self recognize the true God, its maker and the creator of all; that it reject the earthly and crave the eternal; that it neglect the fleeting and love the everlasting; that it deny what is seen and, by contemplation, cast spiritual glances at what is not seen. When you have become alert to these things by means of trained perception, you will merit attaining eternal life and your daughter's restored health, and still more that you may enjoy in her the delights of eternity."

By saying this, he persuaded everyone to forsake idols and to believe in the true God. He healed Nicolaus's daughter from her illness, and all praised him, while reports of his miracles on behalf of the sick spread throughout Macedonia.

----

33. This story, like the previous one, takes place in Philippi.

17. Sequenti vero die docente eo, ecce quidam adolescens exclamavit voce magna, dicens: Quid tibi et nobis, Andreas famule Dei? Venisti, ut nos a propriis sedibus exturbaris?

Tunc beatus apostolus, vocatum ad se iuvenem, ait: Enarra, auctor criminis, quod sit opus tuum.

Et ille: Ego, inquid, in hoc puero ab adolescentia eius inhabitavi, suspicans, quod numquam ab eo recederem. Die autem tertio audivi patrem illius dicentem amico suo: Vadam ad hominem famulum Dei Andream, et sanabit filium meum. Nunc autem timens cruciatos quos nobis inferis, veni, ut egrediar ab eo coram te. Et haec dicens, prostratus solo ante pedes apostoli, exiit a puero, et sanatus est et surgens glorificabat Deum.

Tantam enim gratiam Deus praestitit sancto apostolo, ut sponte omnes venirent ad audiendum verbum salutis et dicerent: Enarra nobis, homo Dei, quis est verus Deus, in cuius nomine nostros curas infirmos. Sed et philosophi veniebant et conquirebant cum eo, et nemo poterat resistere doctrinae eius.

18a. Dum autem haec agerentur, surrexit quidam inimicus praedicationis apostolicae et venit ad procon-

17. On the following day, while Andrew was teaching, a young man cried out in a loud voice: "What do you have to do with us, Andrew, God's servant?[34] Have you come here to chase us from our haunts?"

Then the blessed apostle called the youth to himself and said, "Tell me, contriver of crime, what is your work?"

"I have inhabited this boy from his youth," he said, "thinking I would never leave him. But three days ago I heard his father telling a friend, 'I will go to Andrew, God's servant, and he will heal my son.' Now I have come in order to desert him in your presence, for I fear the tortures you inflict on us." This said, he lay on the ground at the apostle's feet and left the boy. He was healed, rose up, and glorified God.

God displayed his grace through the holy apostle such that everyone voluntarily came to hear the word of salvation and said, "Tell us, man of God, who is the true God in whose name you cure our sick?" Even philosophers would come and debate with him, and no one could oppose his teaching.[35]

18a.[36] When these things had been done, an opponent of apostolic preaching arose and went to the proconsul

----

34. Cf. Mark 1:24 and Luke 4:34.

35. Cf. Acts 6:10.

36. What *GE* briefly narrates here probably occupied eight pages at the beginning of *Papyrus Coptic Utrecht* 1 (*PCU*). The singular "act" in the title of the document, *The Act of Andrew* (ⲧⲉⲡⲣⲁϫⲓⲥ ⲛ̅ⲁⲛⲁⲣⲉⲁⲥ), suggests it told but one story: Andrew's confrontation with Varianus and the demoniac (cf. The Coptic *Act of Peter* [BG 8502.4], which likewise contains only one episode).

sulem Virinum, dicens: Surrexit homo iniquus in Thesalonica, qui templa deorum praedicat destrui, caerimonias respui et omnia priscae legis decreta convelli. Unum deum tantum praedicat coli, cuius se etiam famulum protestatur.

Haec audiens proconsul, misit milites cum equitibus, qui eum exhiberent in conspectu eius. Qui venientes ad portam, didicerunt, in quam domum commoraretur apostolus. Ingredientes autem, cum vidissent vultum eius fulgore nimio resplendere, timore perterriti, ceciderunt ante pedes eius. Beatus vero apostolus narrabat audientibus, quae de eo proconsuli nuntiata fuissent. Et venientes populi cum gladiis et fustibus, volebant milites interficere; sed prohibuit eos sanctus apostolus.

Proconsul enim veniens, cum non invenisset apostolum in civitate qua praeceperat, fremuit ut leo et misit alios viginti.

Varianus[37] saying, "A troublemaker has arisen in Thessalonica,[38] preaching that the temples of the gods must be destroyed, the rites rejected, and all decrees of ancient law struck down. He also preaches that only one God should be worshiped, whose servant he declares himself to be."[39]

When the proconsul heard this, he sent infantry and cavalry to make Andrew appear before him. When they came to the gate, they determined in which house the apostle resided. But on entering and seeing his face shining brilliantly, they fell at his feet terrified. Then the blessed apostle told his audience what had been told to the proconsul concerning him. The crowd came with swords and clubs wanting to kill the soldiers, but the holy apostle restrained them.

When the proconsul came and did not find the apostle in the city where he had expected to find him, he roared like a lion and sent twenty additional soldiers.[40]

----

37. *PCU* seems to preserve the more original spelling of the name. *GE*: Virinus.

38. For discussions of the geographical problems with this episode see Gilles Quispel, "An Unknown Fragment of the Acts of Andrew [Pap. Copt. Utrecht 1]," *VC* 10 [1956]: 139), and Prieur, *Acta Andreae*, 1.44.

39. Originally, Varianus directed his venom at Andrew not for his berating pagan religion, as here in *GE*, but for his converting the proconsul's wife and repelling her from his bed. See Excursus F.

40. *PCU* speaks of four soldiers.

18b. (=*PCU*)

(page 9)

ⲡⲁⲡⲟⲥⲧⲟⲗⲟⲥ ⲛ̄ⲧⲉⲣⲉ̣ ⲁⲛⲇⲣⲉⲁⲥ ⲇⲉ
ⲡⲁⲡⲟⲥⲧⲟⲗⲟⲥ ⲙ̄ⲡⲉⲭ̄ⲥ̄ ⲥⲱⲧⲙ̄
ϫⲉ ⲥⲉⲁⲙⲁϩⲧⲉ ⲛ̄ⲛⲁⲧⲡⲟⲗⲓⲥ ⲉⲧⲃ[ⲏ]ⲏ̣
ⲧ̄ϥ̄. ⲁϥⲧⲱⲟⲩⲛ ⲁϥⲉⲓ ⲉⲃⲟⲗ ⲉⲧⲙ[ⲏ]ⲧ̣ⲉ
ⲛ̄ⲧⲉⲡⲗⲁⲧⲉⲓⲁ ⲡⲉⲭⲁϥ ⲛ̄ⲛⲉⲥⲛⲏ[ⲩ]
ϫⲉ ⲛ̄ⲟⲩϩⲱⲃ ⲁⲛ ⲡⲉ ⲉϩⲩⲡⲟⲕⲣⲓⲛⲓ̣.

ⲉⲧⲓ ⲇⲉ ⲉⲣⲉ ⲡⲁⲡⲟⲥⲧⲟⲗⲟⲥ ϫⲱ ⲛ̣̄[ⲛⲉ]ⲓ
ϣⲁϫⲉ ⲛⲉⲟⲩⲛ ⲟⲩϣⲏⲣⲉ ϣⲏⲙ [ⲉⲃⲟⲗ]
ϩ̄ⲙ ⲡⲉϥⲧⲟⲟⲩ ⲙ̄ⲙⲁ̣ⲧⲟ̈ⲓ ⲉ̣ⲣⲉ ⲟⲩⲇⲁ̣[ⲓ]ⲙ[ⲱⲛ]
ϩⲏⲡ ϩ̄ⲙ ⲡⲉϥⲥⲱⲙ[ⲁ] ⲛ̄ⲧⲉⲣⲉϥⲉ̣[ⲓ] ⲇⲉ̣
ⲛ̄ϭⲓ ⲡϣⲏⲣⲉ ϣⲏⲙ ⲉⲧⲙ̄ⲙⲁⲩ ⲙ̄[ⲡⲙ̄]
ⲧⲟ ⲉⲃⲟⲗ ⲙ̄ⲡⲁⲡⲟⲥⲧⲟⲗⲟⲥ ⲁ̣[ⲛ]ⲇⲣ[ⲉⲁⲥ ⲁϥ]
ⲱϣ ⲉⲃⲟⲗ ⲉϥϫⲱ ⲙ̄ⲙⲟⲥ ϫⲉ ⲱ ⲟⲩ[ⲁ]ⲣⲓ[ⲁ]ⲛ̣ⲉ̣
[ⲟ]ⲩ ⲡⲉ ⲛ̄ⲧⲁⲓ̈ⲁⲁϥ ⲛⲁⲕ ϫⲉ ⲉⲕⲉϫⲟ[ⲟ]ⲩ̣ⲧ̣
[ⲛ̄]ⲥⲁ ⲡⲉⲓ̈ⲑⲉⲟⲥⲉⲃⲏⲥ ⲛ̄ⲣⲱⲙⲉ. ⲛⲁⲓ
[ⲛ̄]ⲧⲉⲣ̣ⲉϥϫⲟⲟⲩ ⲛ̄ϭⲓ ⲡϣⲏⲣⲉ ϣⲏⲙ
[ⲁⲡⲇⲁⲓ]ⲙⲱ̣ⲛ ⲧⲁⲩⲟϥ ⲉⲡⲉⲥⲛⲧ ⲁϥⲧⲣⲉϥ
[ⲧⲁⲩⲉ] ⲥ̣ϩⲃⲏⲛⲧⲉ ⲉⲃⲟⲗ ⲛⲉϥϣⲃⲉⲣⲙⲁ
[ⲧⲟ̈ⲓ] ⲇⲉ ⲁⲩⲁⲙⲁϩⲧⲉ ⲙ̄ⲙⲟϥ ⲁⲩϭⲱ ⲉⲩ
[· · · ·]ⲉ ⲙ̄ⲙⲟϥ:

⠀⠀⠀⠀⠀⠀⠀ⲁⲛⲇⲣⲉⲁⲥ ⲇⲉ ⲁϥ
ϣⲛ̄ϩⲧⲏϥ ϩⲁ ⲡϣⲏⲣⲉ ϣⲏⲙ ⲡⲉϫⲁϥ
ⲛ̄ⲛⲉϥϣⲃⲣ̄ⲙⲁⲧⲟ̈ⲓ ϫⲉ ⲛ̄ⲧⲁⲧⲉⲧⲛ̄
ϣⲓⲡⲉ ϩⲏ<ⲧ> ⲉⲧⲉⲧⲛ̄ⲛⲁⲩ ⲉⲧⲉⲧⲛ̄ϥⲩ
ⲥⲓⲥ ⲉⲥⲥⲟⲟϩⲉ ⲙ̄ⲙⲱⲧⲛ̄ ⲉⲧⲃⲉ ⲟⲩ
ⲧⲉⲧⲛ̄ϥⲓ ⲙ̄ⲙⲁⲩ ⲙ̄ⲡⲁ̣ⲑⲗⲟⲛ ϫⲉ ⲛ̄
ⲛⲉϥⲥⲙ̄ⲙⲉ ⲙ̄ⲡⲉϥⲣ̄ⲣⲟ ϫⲉ ⲉϥⲉϫⲓ
ⲛ̄ⲟⲩⲃⲟⲏⲑⲓⲁ ⲛ̄ϥ̄ϭⲙ̄ϭⲟⲙ ⲙ̄ⲙⲓϣⲉ
ⲟⲩⲃⲉ ⲡⲇⲁⲓⲙⲱⲛ ⲉⲧϩⲏⲡ ϩⲛ̄ ⲛⲉϥ
ⲙⲉⲗⲟⲥ. ⲟⲩ ⲙⲟⲛⲟⲛ ϭⲉ ϫⲉ ⲉϥⲥⲙ̄
ⲙⲉ ⲉⲧⲃⲉ ⲡⲁⲓ̈ ⲁⲗⲗⲁ ⲉϥϣⲁϫⲉ ϩⲛ̄

18b. *Papyrus Coptic Utrecht 1* contains fragments of a translation calling itself "The Act of Andrew," which provides a fuller treatment of this narrative than *GE* 18b. The text printed below, apart from occasional conjectures concerning lacunae, is the reconstruction of Roelof Van den Broek.[41] The first eight pages of this papyrus no longer exist, but the singular "Act" in the title indicates that it told one story only, apparently the conversion of Varianus's wife (see *GE* 19 and Excursus F) and the proconsul's violent response. The context immediately preceding page 9 obviously told of four soldiers from Varianus arresting some of Andrew's adherents.

...) the apostle. When Andrew, the apostle of Christ, heard that they had arrested those who were in the city because of him, he rose up, went out into the middle of the street, and said to the brethren that there was no cause for concealing who they were.

While the apostle spoke these words, there was a young man among the four soldiers in whose body a demon was hidden. When that young man came before the apostle Andrew he cried out, "O Varianus, what have I done to you that you should send me against this religious man?" When the youth had said this, the demon threw him down and caused him to froth at the mouth. His fellow soldiers seized him and continued to (...) him.

But Andrew took pity on the youth and said to his fellow soldiers, "Are you not ashamed in my presence by seeing your nature rebuking you? Why do you remove the prize-money,[42] so that he cannot appeal to his king in order to receive help for finding the strength to fight

----

41. Published in Prieur, *Acta Andreae*, 656-71.

42. The ἄθλον was the prize awarded the winner in athletic contests.

ⲧⲁⲥⲡⲉ ⲙ̄ⲡⲡⲁⲗⲁⲧⲓⲟⲛ ϫⲉ ⲉⲣⲉ ⲡⲉϥ
ⲣ̄ⲣⲟ ⲥⲱⲧⲙ̄ ⲉⲣⲟϥ ϩⲛ̄ [ⲟ]ⲩϭⲉⲡⲏ ϯⲥ[ⲱ]
ⲧⲙ̄ ⲅⲁⲣ ⲉⲣⲟϥ ⲉϥϫⲱ ⲙ̄ⲙⲟⲥ ϫⲉ [ⲱ]
ⲟⲩⲁⲣⲓⲁⲛⲉ ⲟⲩ ⲡⲉ ⲛ̄ⲧⲁⲓ̈[ⲁⲁϥ ⲛⲁⲕ]
ϫⲉⲕⲁⲥ ⲉⲕⲉϫⲟ[ⲩⲧ ⲛ̄ⲥⲁ ⲡⲉⲓ̈]ⲑⲉⲟ
ⲥⲉⲃⲏ[ⲥ ⲛ̄ⲣⲱⲙⲉ ⲡⲁⲡⲟⲥⲧⲟⲗⲟⲥ ⲁⲛ]
ⲁⲣ[ⲉⲁⲥ

(lacuna of 6-8 lines of about 22 letters)

(page 10)

ⲉϩⲣⲁⲓ ⲉϫⲱⲓ̈ ⲡⲉⲓ̈ϩⲱⲃ ⲅⲁⲣ ⲛ̄ⲧⲁⲓ̈ⲁⲁϥ
ⲛ̄ⲧⲁⲓ̈ⲁⲁϥ ⲁⲛ ⲉⲃⲟⲗ ϩⲓⲧⲟⲟⲧ ⲁⲗⲗⲁ ⲛ̄
ⲧⲁⲩϯ ⲁⲛⲁⲅⲕⲏ ⲉⲣⲟⲓ̈ ϯⲛⲁϫⲱ ϭⲉ
ⲉⲣⲟⲕ ⲛ̄ⲧϭⲟⲙ ⲧⲏⲣⲥ̄ ⲙ̄ⲫⲱⲃ ⲡⲉⲓ̈
ϣⲏⲣⲉ ϣⲏⲙ ⲉⲧϩⲓⲧⲉ ϩⲙ̄ ⲡⲉϥⲥⲱⲙⲁ
ⲟⲩⲛⲧⲁϥ ⲙ̄ⲙⲁⲩ ⲛ̄ⲟⲩⲥⲱⲛⲉ ⲙ̄ⲡⲁⲣ
ⲑⲉ[ⲛ]ⲟⲥ ⲉⲩⲛⲟϭ ⲙ̄ⲡⲟⲗⲓⲧⲉⲩⲧⲏⲥ ⲧⲉ
ⲛ̄ⲁⲑⲗⲏⲧⲏⲥ ⲁⲗⲏⲑⲱⲥ ϯϫⲱ ⲙ̄ⲙⲟⲥ
ϫⲉ ⲥϩⲏⲛ ⲉϩⲟⲩⲛ ⲉⲡⲛⲟⲩⲧⲉ ⲉⲧⲃⲉ
ⲡⲉⲥⲧⲃ̄ⲃⲟ ⲙ̄ⲛ̄ ⲛⲉⲥⲡⲣⲟⲥⲉⲩⲭⲏ ⲙ̄ⲛ̄
ⲧⲉⲥⲁⲅⲁⲡⲏ. ϫⲉⲕⲁⲥ ϭⲉ ⲛ̄ⲛⲁϫⲱ ⲉⲣⲟⲕ
ⲛ̄ⲟⲩⲙⲏⲏϣⲉ ⲛ̄ϣⲁϫⲉ ⲛⲉⲟⲩⲛ
ⲟⲩⲁ ϣⲟⲟⲡ ϩⲁⲧⲙ̄ ⲡⲉⲥⲛⲓ̈ ⲉⲩⲛⲟϭ
ⲙ̄ⲙⲁⲅⲟⲥ ⲡⲉ ⲁⲥϣⲱⲡⲉ ϩⲣⲁⲓ̈ ϩⲛ̄
ⲟⲩϩⲟⲟⲩ ⲛ̄ⲧⲉⲓ̈ϩⲉ ⲙ̄ⲡⲛⲁⲩ ⲛ̄ⲣⲟⲩ[ϩⲉ]
ⲁⲧⲡⲁⲣⲑⲉⲛⲟⲥ ⲃⲱⲕ ⲉϩⲣⲁⲓ̈ ⲉϫⲛ̄ ⲧⲉ[ⲥ]
ϫⲉⲛⲉⲡⲱⲣ ⲉϥϣⲗⲏⲗ ⲁⲡϣⲏⲣⲉ̣ ϣⲏ[ⲙ]
ⲙ̄ⲙⲁⲅⲟⲥ ⲛⲁⲩ ⲉⲣⲟⲥ ⲉⲥϣⲗⲏ[ⲗ ⲁⲡ]
ⲥⲉⲙⲙⲁϥ ⲃⲱⲕ ⲉϩⲟⲩⲛ ⲉⲣⲟϥ [ⲉⲡⲟ]
ⲗⲉⲙⲓ ⲙ̄ⲛ̄ ϯⲛⲟϭ ⲛ̄ⲁⲑⲗⲏⲧⲏⲥ [ⲡⲉ]
ϫⲉ ⲡϣⲏⲣⲉ ϣⲏⲙ ⲙ̄ⲙⲁⲅⲟⲥ [ϩⲣⲁⲓ̈ ⲛ̄]
ϩⲏⲧϥ̄ ϫⲉ ⲉϣϫⲉ ⲁⲓ̈ⲣ̄ ϫⲟⲩⲧⲏ̣ [ⲛ̄]ⲣⲟ[ⲙ]
ⲡⲉ ϩⲁⲣⲁⲧϥ̄ ⲙ̄ⲡⲁⲥⲁϩ ϣⲁⲛϯⲧⲥⲁ̣
ⲃⲟ ⲉⲧⲉⲓ̈ⲧⲉⲭⲛⲏ ⲉⲓⲥϩⲏⲏⲧⲉ ⲧⲉⲛⲟⲩ
ⲧⲁⲓ̈ ⲧⲉ ⲧⲁⲣⲭⲏ ⲛ̄ⲧⲁⲧⲉⲭⲛⲏ. ⲉⲓ̈ⲧⲙ̄

against the demon hidden in his limbs? Not only is he making an appeal for this,[43] but he is speaking the language of the palace, so that his king might hear him at once. For I hear him saying, 'O Varianus, what have I done that you would send me out against this religious man?'" The apostle Andrew (....

> In the missing six to eight lines Andrew apparently turned to the demoniac and addressed the demon. The demon seems to have begged Andrew to do nothing rash.

"...) against me, for this act I have committed I did not commit on my own, but I was forced to do it. I will tell you the whole cause of the situation. This young man whose body is convulsed has a virgin sister who is a great devotee of asceticism.[44] I tell you truly that she is near to God because of her purity, her prayers, and her love. Now, to tell it without elaboration, there was someone living next door to her house who was a great magician. Here is what happened: One evening the virgin went up on her roof to pray, the young magician saw her at prayer, and Semmath entered into him to fight with this great ascetic.[45] The young magician said to himself, 'Even though I have spent twenty years under my teacher before acquiring this ability, this now is the

---

43. The antecedent of "this" seems to be the ἄθλον.

44. Lit. "athlete."

45. Lit. "athlete."

ϭⲙ̅ϭⲟⲙ ⲉⲧⲉⲓ̈ⲡⲁⲣⲑⲉⲛⲟⲥ. ⲛ̅ⲧⲛⲁ
ϣϭⲙ̅ϭⲟⲙ ⲛ̅ⲣ ⲗⲁⲁⲩ ⲛ̅ϩⲱⲃ ⲁⲛ: ⲡϩⲣ̅
ϣⲓⲣⲉ ⲇⲉ ⲙ̅ⲙⲁⲅⲟⲥ ⲁϥⲧⲁⲣⲕⲟ ⲛ̅ϩⲉⲛ
ⲛⲟϭ ⲛ̅ⲇⲩⲛⲁⲙⲓⲥ ⲉϩⲣⲁⲓ̈ ⲉⲝⲛ̅ ⲧⲡⲁⲣ
ⲑⲉⲛⲟⲥ ⲁϥⲭⲟⲟⲩⲥⲟⲩ ⲛ̅ⲥⲱⲥ. ⲛ̅ⲧⲉⲣⲉ
ⲛ̅ⲇⲁⲓⲙⲱⲛ ⲇⲉ ⲃⲱⲕ ⲉⲩⲛⲁⲡⲓⲣⲁⲍⲉ
ⲙ̅ⲙⲟⲥ ⲏ ⲉⲧⲣⲉⲩⲡⲓⲑⲉ ⲙ̅ⲙⲟⲥ
ⲁⲩⲣ̅ ⲧⲙⲓⲛⲉ ⲙ̅ⲡⲉⲥⲥⲟⲛ ⲁⲩⲧⲱϩⲙ̅
ⲉⲡⲣⲟ. ⲛ̅ⲧⲟⲥ ⲇⲉ ⲁⲥⲧⲱⲟⲩⲛ ⲁⲥⲉⲓ
[ⲉ]ϩⲣⲁⲓ̈ ⲉⲧⲣⲉⲥⲁⲟⲩⲱⲛ ⲉⲥⲙⲉⲉⲩⲉ ⲭⲉ
ⲡⲉⲥⲥⲟⲛ ⲡⲉ. ⲁⲥϣⲗⲏⲗ ⲇⲉ ⲛ̅ϣⲟⲣⲡ̅
[ⲉⲙⲁ]ⲧⲉ ⲉⲧⲣⲉⲛ̅ⲇⲁⲓⲙⲱⲛ ⲣ̅ ⲑⲉ ⲛ̅ⲛⲓ
[·····ⲛ̅ⲥⲉⲡ]ⲱϩⲧ ⲛ̅ⲥⲉϩⲱⲗ ⲉⲃⲟⲗ
[··············ϣⲏⲣⲉ] ϣⲏⲙ [

(lacuna of 4-6 lines of about 22 letters.
At this point, two pages are missing.)

(page 13)

ⲁⲥⲣⲓⲙⲉ [ⲛ̅]ϭ[ⲓ] ⲧⲡⲁⲣ[ⲑⲉ]ⲛⲟⲥ ⲛ̅
ⲛⲁϩⲣⲛ̅ ⲧ[ⲉ]ⲓ̈[ⲣⲟⲩ]ⲥⲓⲁ ⲧⲉⲓⲣⲟⲩⲥⲓⲁ ⲇⲉ
ⲡⲉⲭⲁⲥ ⲉⲧⲡ[ⲁⲣ]ⲑⲉⲛⲟⲥ ⲭⲉ ⲁϩⲣⲟ
ⲧⲉⲣⲓⲙⲉ ⲛ̅ⲧ[ⲉⲥ]ⲟⲟⲩⲛ ⲁⲛ ⲭⲉ ⲛⲉⲧ
ⲛⲁⲉⲓ ⲉⲡⲉⲓⲙⲁ [ⲟ]ⲩⲕ ⲉ[ⲝ]ⲉⲥⲧⲓ ⲛ̅ⲥⲉⲣⲓⲙⲉ
ⲡⲁⲓ̈ ⲅⲁⲣ ⲡⲉ ⲡ[ⲙⲁ······]ⲉ ⲛ̅ⲧⲉ
ⲛⲟⲩ ⲛⲉ[ⲓ̈]ⲇⲩⲛⲁⲙ[ⲓ]ⲥ [···] ⲉⲓ ⲛ̅ⲥⲱ [ⲧ]
ⲉⲓ̈ⲣⲟ[ⲩⲥⲓⲁ] ⲭ[ⲱ] ⲙ̅ⲙⲟ[ⲥ] ⲭⲉ [ⲁϩⲣⲟ] ⲧⲉⲣⲓⲙⲉ
ⲉⲡⲙⲟⲕϩ̅ ⲛϩⲏⲧ ⲇⲉ [·····]ⲟⲟⲩⲉ
ⲧⲉⲛⲟⲩ ϭⲉ ⲉⲣⲉⲣⲓ[ⲙ]ⲉ [ⲉⲧⲃⲉ] ⲡⲟⲩⲥⲟ̅
ⲉⲧⲃⲉ ⲭⲉ ⲟⲩⲛⲟⲩⲧ[ⲉ·····ⲛ]ⲙ̅ⲙⲁϥ
ⲛ̅ⲣⲁⲥⲧⲉ ϯⲛⲁⲭⲟⲟⲩϥ ⲛⲁ[ϩⲣ]ⲙ̅ ⲡⲁ
ⲡⲟⲥⲧⲟⲗⲟⲥ ⲁⲛⲇⲣⲉ[ⲁ]ⲥ ⲭ[ⲉ ⲉ]ϥⲛⲁ
ⲧⲁⲗϭⲟϥ ⲟⲩ ⲙⲟⲛⲟⲛ ⲇⲉ ⲭⲉ ϯⲛⲁ
ϯⲡ[ⲁ]ϩⲣⲉ ⲉⲣⲟϥ ⲁⲗⲗⲁ ϯⲛⲁⲧⲣⲉϥϩⲱⲕ
ⲉⲡⲡⲁⲗⲁⲧⲓⲟⲛ:

            ⲛⲁⲓ̈ ϭⲉ ⲛ̅ⲧⲉⲣⲉ
ⲡⲇⲁⲓⲙⲟⲛⲓⲟⲛ ⲭⲟⲟⲩ ⲡⲉⲭⲉ ⲡⲁⲡⲟ

beginning of my career. If I do not overpower this virgin, I will not be able to do anything.' So the young magician conjured up some great supernatural forces against the virgin and sent them after her. When the demons left to tempt her or to win her over, they acted like her brother and knocked at the door. She got up and went downstairs to open up, supposing it was her brother. But first she prayed fervently, with the result that the demons became like (...) <they> fell down and flew away (...) <the young> man (....."

> Two pages are missing, but it would appear that the magician, frustrated by his inability to overpower the virgin, used his powers against the soldier, this time with success. On learning of her brother's condition, the virgin went to her friend Eirusia for solace and guidance. The demon continues his story.

"...) The virgin wept before Eirusia, but Eirusia said to the virgin, 'Why are you crying? Do you not know that those who come to this place cannot cry? For this is the place (...) now these powers (...) come after you.' Eirusia told her, 'Why are you crying, while the grief (...). Now then, if you weep because of your brother because a god (...) with him, tomorrow I will send him to the apostle Andrew so that he may heal him, but not only so that I will bring him back to his senses, but I will cause him to arm himself for the palace.'"

ⲥⲧⲟⲗⲟⲥ ⲛⲁ ϫⲉ ⲛⲧⲁⲕⲉⲓⲙⲉ ⲛⲁϣ
ⲛⲍⲉ ⲉ[ⲙ]ⲙⲩⲥⲧⲏⲣ ⲓ ⲟⲛ ⲉⲧⲍⲏⲡ ⲛⲧⲉ
ⲡϫⲓⲥⲉ ϩⲟⲗⲱⲥ ⲟⲩⲙⲁⲧ̣[ⲟ]ⲓ̈ ⲉⲩϣⲁⲛ
ⲛⲟϫ̄ ⲉⲃⲟⲗ ϩⲙ̄ ⲡⲡⲁⲗⲁⲧⲓ[ⲟ]ⲛ ⲟⲩ
ⲕ ⲉ̣ⲝⲉⲥⲧⲓ ⲛⲁ ⲉⲧⲣⲉ̣ϥⲉⲓⲙⲉ ⲙ̄ⲙⲩ
ⲥⲧⲏⲣ ⲓ ⲟⲛ ⲙ̄ⲡⲡⲁⲗⲁ̣ⲧⲓ ⲟⲛ ⲁⲩⲱ ⲛⲁ̣ϣ
ⲛⲍⲉ [ⲉ]ϥⲛ̣ⲁⲉⲓⲙⲉ ⲉⲙⲙⲩⲥⲧⲏⲣ ⲓ ⲟⲛ
ⲉⲧⲍⲏ[ⲡ ⲛⲧⲉⲡ]ϫⲓⲥⲉ

       ⲡⲉϫ[ⲉ] ⲡⲁⲁⲓⲙⲟ
ⲛⲓ[ⲟⲛ ⲛ]ⲁ ϫⲉ [ⲁⲛ]ⲟ[ⲕ ⲁⲓⲉ]ⲓ ⲉϩⲣⲁⲓ
ϩⲛ̄ [ⲧ]ⲉ̣ⲓ̈ⲟⲩϣⲏ ⲉϩⲟⲩⲛ ⲙ̄ⲡⲉⲓ̈
ϣ[ⲏⲣ]ⲉ̣ ϣⲏⲙ ⲉⲟⲩ[ⲁ]ⲩ[ⲛ]ⲁⲙⲓⲥ ⲛⲧⲉ
ⲡ[ϫⲓⲥ]ⲉ [ⲁ]ⲥ̣ⲉⲓ ⲉϩⲟⲩ[ⲛ· · · ·]ⲣⲓⲱⲛ
ⲉⲧ[· · · · ·] ϣⲃⲉⲉ̣ⲣ̣ⲉ [ⲛ̄ⲧ]ⲡ̣ⲁ̣ⲣⲑⲉⲛⲟⲥ
ⲛ̄ϩⲏⲧ̄ ⲉⲃⲟⲗ ϩ[ⲙ̄· · · ·]ⲣ ⲉⲥⲉⲓ ⲉⲥ
ⲛⲁ̣ⲥⲱⲕ ⲉ̣ⲃⲟⲗ ⲛ̄[· · · · · ·] ⲉ̣[ⲧ]ⲙ̄ⲙⲁⲩ
ⲁⲧⲉⲥϣⲃⲉⲉⲣⲉ [ⲛⲧ]ⲡ[ⲁⲣⲑⲉⲛⲟ]ⲥ̣ ϫⲱ ⲙ̄
ⲙⲟⲥ ϫⲉ ⲙⲁ̣[· · · ·ⲙⲟⲕϩ̄] ⲛ̄ϩⲏⲧ
ⲧⲁϩⲟⲓ̈ ϫⲉ [· · · · · · · ·] ⲧⲱⲛ ⲁⲥⲉⲓ
ϭⲉ ⲉϩⲟⲩⲛ ⲛ̄ϭⲓ [ⲧⲛⲟϭ ⲛ̄ⲇⲩⲛ]ⲁ̣ⲙⲓⲥ ⲉⲃⲟⲗ
ϩⲙ̄ ⲡⲭ[ⲓ]ⲥ̣ⲉ̣ ⲉ̣ϩⲣⲁ̣[ⲓ̈ ϩⲛ̄ ⲧⲉⲓⲟ]ⲩϣⲏ ⲁⲥ
ⲧⲁ̣[· · · · · · · · · · ·] ⲉⲛⲧⲁⲓ̈
ϫ[ⲱ ⲙ̄ⲙⲟⲥ· · · · · · ·]ⲉ ⲇⲉ ⲛ̄ⲧⲉ
ⲣⲉ[· · · · · · · · · ·ⲉⲓ]ⲙⲉ ⲛⲉⲓ [

(lacuna of 3-5 lines of about 20 letters)

(page 14)

    ϫⲉ ⲉⲧⲃⲉ ⲟⲩ ϭⲉ ⲛ̄ⲅⲥⲧⲱⲧ ⲁⲛ ⲉⲕϫⲱ
ⲛ̄ⲙⲙⲩⲥⲧⲏⲣ ⲓ ⲟⲛ̣ ⲙ̄ⲡϫⲓⲥⲉ ϩⲟ
ⲗⲱⲥ ⲁⲛⲟⲕ ⲧ̇[ⲥⲧ]ⲱⲧ ϩⲛ̄ ⲛⲁⲙⲉⲗⲟⲥ
ⲧⲏⲣⲟⲩ ⲁⲩⲱ ⲧ̇[ϯ] ⲉⲟⲟⲩ ⲙ̄ⲡⲁⲣⲁ
ⲗⲏⲙⲡⲧⲱⲣ ⲉⲧ[ⲛ̄]ⲏⲩ ⲛ̄ⲥⲁ ⲛⲉ̣ⲯ̣ⲩ
ⲭⲟⲟⲩⲉ ⲛ̄ⲛⲉ̣ⲧ̣ⲟⲩⲁⲁⲃ: ⲱ̃ ⲛⲁ
ⲑⲗⲏⲧⲏⲥ ⲛ̄ⲧⲁⲣⲉⲧⲏ ⲛ̄ ⲉ ⲓ [ⲕ]ⲏ ⲁⲛ
ⲁⲧⲉⲧⲛ̄ⲁⲑⲗⲉⲓ ⲉⲓⲥ ⲡⲁⲅⲱⲛⲟⲑⲉ
ⲧⲏⲥ ⲥⲟⲃⲧⲉ ⲛⲏⲧⲛ̄ ⲙ̄ⲡⲉⲕⲗⲟⲙ

When the demon had finished saying these things, the apostle said to him, "How did you learn about the hidden mysteries of the height? Once they throw a soldier out of the palace, it is forbidden him to know the palatial mysteries, so how would he know the hidden mysteries of the height?"

The demon told him, "I descended into this night, into this young man, while a power of the height entered into (...) friend (fem.) of the virgin going from him in (...) while she moves from (...) there. The friend <of the virgin> said to her, '<Grief> touches me so that (...). Tonight <the great> power from the height came down, it did (...) which I said (...) but when (...) know these (....'"

> In the missing lines, the demon continues to explain how he learned about "the mystery of the height." It would appear that the legitimate heavenly power that had "entered" into Eirusia revealed these heavenly mysteries to the virgin, but the demon overheard them.

[Andrew speaks:] "Why then do you not tremble when you speak of the mysteries of the height? I tremble completely in all my limbs and I glorify the Receiver,[46] who comes after the souls of the saints. O athletes of virtue, you have not competed in vain. Behold, the judge prepares the imperishable crown for you. O warriors, you

---

46. Viz: παραλήμπτωρ. Cf. John 14:3.

ⲚⲀⲘⲀⲢⲀⲚⲦⲒⲚⲟⲚ: ⲱ̄ Ⲙ̄ⲠⲟⲖⲉ
ⲘⲒⲤⲦ[Ⲏ]Ⲥ Ⲛ̄ ⲉⲒⲔⲎ ⲀⲚ ⲀⲦⲉⲦⲚ̄Ⲕⲱ
ⲚⲎ[ⲦⲚ̄] Ⲛ̄ⲢⲈⲚⲢⲞⲠⲖⲞⲚ ⲘⲚ̄ ⲢⲈⲚ
ⲐⲨⲢⲰⲚ ⲀⲨⲱ Ⲛ̄ ⲉⲒⲔⲎ ⲀⲚ ⲀⲦⲉ
ⲦⲚ̄ⲢⲨⲠⲞⲘⲒⲚⲈ Ⲛ̄ⲢⲈⲚⲠⲞⲖⲈⲘⲞⲤ
ⲀⲠ̄Ⲣ̄ⲢⲞ ⲤⲞⲂⲦⲈ ⲚⲎⲦⲚ̄ Ⲙ̄ⲠⲠⲀ
ⲖⲀⲦⲒⲞⲚ: ⲱ̄ Ⲙ̄ⲠⲀⲢⲐⲈⲚⲞⲤ
Ⲛ̄ ⲉⲒⲔⲎ ⲀⲚ ⲀⲦⲉⲦⲚ̄ⲢⲀⲢⲈⲢ ⲉⲠⲦⲂ̄
ⲂⲞ ⲀⲨⲱ Ⲛ̄ ⲉⲒⲔⲎ ⲀⲚ ⲀⲦⲉⲦⲚ̄ⲢⲨ
ⲠⲞⲘⲒⲚⲈ ⲢⲚ̄ ⲢⲈⲚⲠⲢⲞⲤⲈⲨⲬⲎ
ⲉⲢⲈ ⲚⲈⲦⲚ̄ⲖⲀⲘⲠⲀⲤ ⲘⲞⲨⲢ ⲢⲚ̄
ⲦⲠⲀϢⲈ Ⲛ̄ⲦⲈⲨϢⲎ ϢⲀⲚⲦⲈ ⲦⲈⲒ
ⲤⲘⲎ ⲦⲀⲢⲈⲦⲎⲨⲦⲚ̄ ⲬⲈ ⲦⲞⲨⲚ
ⲦⲎⲨⲦⲚ̄ ⲀⲘⲎⲒ̈ⲦⲚ̄ ⲉⲂⲞⲖ ⲢⲀⲐⲎ
Ⲙ̄ⲠⲀⲦϢⲈⲖⲈⲈⲦ: ⲚⲀⲒ ⲆⲈ Ⲛ̄ⲦⲈ
ⲢⲈ ⲠⲀⲠⲞⲤⲦⲞⲖⲞⲤ ⲬⲞⲞⲨ [Ⲁ]ϤⲔⲞⲦϤ̄
ⲉⲠⲆⲀⲒⲘⲰⲚ ⲠⲈⲬⲀϤ Ⲛ̄[ⲀϤ] Ⲭⲉ
ⲎⲆⲎ ϬⲈ ⲠⲚⲀⲨ ⲠⲈ ⲉⲦⲢⲉ[ⲔⲈⲒ]
ⲉⲂⲞⲖ ⲢⲘ̄ ⲠⲈⲒϢⲎⲢⲈ ϢⲎⲘ
ⲬⲈⲔⲀⲤ ⲉϤ[ⲉ]ⲢⲰⲔ ⲉⲠⲠⲀⲖⲀⲦⲒ[Ⲟ]Ⲛ
Ⲛ̄ⲉⲠⲞⲨⲢⲀⲚⲒⲞⲚ

                  ⲠⲈⲬⲈ ⲠⲀⲆⲒ
ⲘⲰⲚ Ⲙ̄ⲠⲀⲠⲞⲤⲦⲞⲖⲞⲤ Ⲭⲉ
ⲀⲖⲎⲐⲰⲤ ⲱ̄ ⲠⲢⲰⲘⲈ Ⲙ̄ⲠⲚⲞⲨⲦⲈ
Ⲭⲉ Ⲙ̄ⲠⲒⲦⲀⲔⲈ ⲞⲨⲘⲈⲖⲞⲤ Ⲛ̄ⲦⲀϤ
Ⲛ̄ⲞⲨⲢⲞⲞⲨ ⲉⲦⲂⲈ Ⲛ̄ϬⲒⲬ ⲉⲦⲞⲨⲀ
ⲀⲂ Ⲛ̄ⲦⲉϤⲤⲰⲚⲈ ⲦⲈⲚⲞⲨ ϬⲈ
ϯⲚⲀⲂⲰⲔ [ⲉ]ⲂⲞⲖ ⲢⲘ̄ ⲠⲈⲒϢⲎ
ⲢⲈ ϢⲎⲘ ⲉⲘⲠⲒⲬⲒⲦϤ̄ Ⲛ̄ϬⲞⲚⲤ̄
ⲉⲠⲦⲎⲢϤ̄ [ⲢⲚ̄] ⲚⲈϤⲘⲈⲖⲞⲤ ⲚⲀⲒ
ⲆⲈ Ⲛ̄ⲦⲈⲢ[ⲉ Ⲡ]ⲆⲀⲒ[ⲘⲞⲚ]Ⲓ[Ⲟ]Ⲛ Ⲭ[ⲞⲞ]Ⲩ
ⲀϤⲉⲒ ⲉⲂⲞⲖ [ⲢⲘ̄ ⲠϢⲎⲢⲈ ϢⲎⲘ]
Ⲛ̄ⲦⲈⲢⲉϤ[· · · · · · · · ·ϢⲎⲢⲈ]
ϢⲎⲘ [

(lacuna of 1-3 lines of about 19 letters)

have not acquired weapons and shields or endured warfare in vain. The king has prepared the palace for you. O virgins, you have not guarded purity and endured in prayers in vain, your lamps glowing at midnight until this voice comes to you: 'Arise, go out to meet the bridegroom!'"[47]

When the apostle had said these things, he turned to the demon and said to him, "It is now time for you to come out of this young man, so that he may arm himself for the heavenly palace."

"Truly, O man of God," said the demon to the apostle, "I never harmed any of his limbs because of the holy hands of his sister, so now I will leave this young man to whose limbs I have done no violence whatsoever." After he had said these things, the demon <left the young man>.

When he had (...) the young man (...).

The lost line or lines surely narrated the young soldier's stripping off his uniform.

----

47. Cf. Matt 25:6.

(page 15)

ⲚⲦⲘⲚⲦⲘⲀⲦⲞⲒ ⲀϤ[ⲚⲞⲬϤ ⲈⲂⲞⲖ]
ⲘⲠⲈⲘⲦⲞ ⲈⲂⲞⲖ ⲘⲠⲀ̣[ⲠⲞⲤⲦ]Ⲟ
ⲖⲞⲤ ⲈϤⲬⲰ ⲘⲘⲞⲤ ⲬⲈ Ⲱ̃ [Ⲡ]ⲢⲰ
ⲘⲈ ⲘⲠⲚⲞⲨⲦⲈ ⲀⲒ̈ⲬⲞ ⲈⲂⲞⲖ Ⲛ̄
ⲬⲞⲨⲰⲦ Ⲛ̄ⲚⲞⲘⲒⲤⲘⲀⲦⲒⲞⲚ ϢⲀⲚ
ⲦⲔ̣Ⲱ ⲚⲀⲒ̈ ⲘⲠⲈⲒ̈ⲤⲬⲎⲘⲀ Ⲙ̄
ⲠⲢⲞⲤⲞⲨⲞⲈⲒϢ ⲦⲚⲞⲨ ϬⲈ ϨⲰⲰϤ
ⲦⲞ̣ⲨⲰϢ ⲈⲦ̣[Ⲙ̄]ⲠⲈⲦⲚ̄ⲦⲀⲒ̈ ⲦⲎⲢϤ̄
ϢⲀⲚⲦⲔⲰ ⲚⲀⲒ̈ ⲘⲠⲈⲒ̈ⲤⲬⲎⲘⲀ
Ⲛ̄ⲦⲈ ⲠⲈⲔⲚⲞⲨⲦⲈ:

              ⲠⲈⲬⲈ ⲚⲈϤ
ϢⲂⲢ̄ⲘⲀⲦⲞⲒ̈ ⲚⲀϤ ⲬⲈ Ⲱ̃ Ⲡ̄ϨⲢ̄ϢⲒ
ⲢⲈ Ⲛ̄ⲦⲀⲖⲀⲒⲠⲰⲢⲞⲤ ⲈⲔϢⲀⲚ
ⲀⲢⲚⲀ ⲘⲠⲈⲤⲬⲎⲘⲀ ⲘⲠⲢ̄ⲢⲞ ⲤⲈ
ⲚⲀⲔⲞⲖⲀⳘⲈ ⲘⲘⲞⲔ:

              ⲠⲈⲬⲈ ⲠϢⲎ
ⲢⲈ ϢⲎⲘ ⲚⲀⳘ ⲬⲈ ⲀⲚⲞⲔ ⲘⲈⲚ
ⲀⲚⲄ̄ ⲞⲨⲦⲀⲖⲀⲒⲠⲰⲢⲞⲤ ⲈⲦⲂⲈ ⲚⲀ
ⲚⲞⲂⲈ Ⲛ̄ϢⲞⲢⲠ̄ ⲈⲚⲈ ϨⲀⲘⲞⲒ ⲢⲰ
ⲈⲚⲈ ⲦⲀⲔⲞⲖⲀⲤⲒⲤ ⲘⲘⲀⲦⲈ ⲦⲈ ⲦⲀⲒ̈
ⲬⲈ̣ ⲀⲒ̈ⲀⲢⲚⲀ ⲘⲠⲈⲤⲬⲎⲘⲀ ⲘⲠⲈⲒⲢ̄
ⲢⲞ ⲀⲨⲰ Ⲛ̄ⲤⲈⲦⲘ̄ⲔⲞⲖⲀⳘⲈ ⲘⲘⲞⲒ̈
ⲬⲈ ⲀⲒ̈ⲔⲀⲦⲀⲫⲢⲞⲚⲒ ⲘⲠⲈⲤⲬⲎⲘⲀ
ⲘⲠⲢ̄ⲢⲞ ⲚⲚ[Ⲁ]ⲒⲰⲚ Ⲛ̄ⲀⲦⲘⲞⲨ
Ⲱ ⲚⲀⲦⲤⲞⲞⲨⲚ̣ Ⲛ̄ⲦⲈⲦⲚ̄ⲚⲀⲨ ⲀⲚ
ⲈⲠⲈⲒⲢⲰⲘⲈ ⲬⲈ ⲞⲨ ⲀϢ Ⲛ̄ϨⲈ ⲈⲠⲈ[Ⲓ]
ⲘⲘⲚ̄ ⲤⲚϤⲈ ⲄⲀ[Ⲣ] Ⲛ̄ⲦⲞⲞⲦϤ̄ ⲞⲨⲀⲈ
[Ⲥ]ⲔⲈⲨⲞⲤ Ⲙ̄ⲠⲞⲖⲈⲘ[Ⲓ]ⲔⲞⲚ ⲀⲨⲰ
ⲚⲈⲒⲚⲞϬ Ⲛ̄ϬⲞⲘ ⲈⲚⲈⲢⲄⲈⲒ ⲈⲂⲞⲖ ϨⲒ
ⲦⲞⲞⲦϤ̄.

ⲦⲈⲠⲢ̣Ⳓ︢Ⲓ[Ⲥ] Ⲛ̄ⲀⲚⲆⲢⲈⲀⲤ

...) of the military and <threw it> in front of the apostle, saying, "O man of God, I spent twenty coins to obtain these items of this temporary uniform, but now I want to give all that I own to obtain these items of the uniform of your God."

"O you unfortunate child!" his fellow-soldiers told him. "If you deny the uniform of the king, they will punish you."

The young man said to them, "I am indeed unfortunate because of my previous sins. Would that my punishment were only for denying the uniform of this king and not for despising the uniform of the king of the ages! You fools, do you not see what sort of man this is? There is no sword in his hand nor any instrument of war, and yet these great acts of power issue from his hand."

The Act of Andrew

EXCURSUS E
ANDREW AND THE DESERTER

"The Act of Andrew" in *PCU* intentionally ends here
with the words "There is no sword in his hand nor any
instrument of war, and yet these great acts of power issue
from his hand."[1] This final statement about Andrew's
weaponless might obviously occupies a commanding position
in the document, implying that whoever chose to copy this
particular episode did so in order to contrast thaumaturgy
and the military. In the Passion, Stratocles (i.e.,
"Battle-Praise") leaves the army to study philosophy and
then espouses non-violence, so it would appear that *PCU*
here reflects the anti-militarism of the original Acts.

This abrupt ending leaves the reader to assume that
Varianus would have punished the soldier for desertion,
just as the soldiers had warned: "If you deny the uniform
of the king, they will punish you." The predictable
punishment was death. In the *AP1*, Nero orders soldiers who
confessed to being "soldiers of the king of the ages"
tortured and slain (11 [=*Martyrdom* 2]). Tertullian knows
of a Christian soldier who sacrificed his life for
rejecting his uniform.[2] When a centurion named Marcellus
threw down his *cingulum*, or military belt, a prefect asked
him, "What was your intention in violating military

----

1. Following this line *PCU* continues with a narrative
   about the patriarch Joseph (Quispel, "Unknown
   Fragment," 129-30).

2. *De corona militis* 1. Here Tertullian says such uniforms
   included a *paenula*, or heavy cloak, military sandals, a
   sword, and a laurel wreath. Cf. Tertullian's famous
   squib in *De idololatria* 19.3: "The Lord, in disarming
   Peter, unbelted (*discinxit*) every soldier."

discipline by taking off your belt?" (*discingeres*).[3]
Marcellus intended, of course, to declare himself as a
servant of Christ; he was beheaded. Rejecting the *cingulum*
normally was a capital offense in fact, and always was
capital in Christian fiction.[4] One therefore should assume
that the soldier in the *AA* too was slain for his
divestiture.

Even though Gregory purged his account of all
political radicalism, including the soldier's desertion,
he does say that the soldier was slain--not by Varianus
but at the demon's departure. If one prefers the cause of
death anticipated in *PCU*, it would appear that the story
originally continued with Varianus's arrival and the
execution of the deserter. Andrew then raised him back to
life, just as he does in the next chapter.

----

3. *The Acts of Marcellus*, see Herbert Musurillo, *The Acts
   of the Christian Martyrs*, Oxford Early Christian Texts
   (Oxford: Oxford University Press, 1972), 250-59.

4. See also the Coptic *Martyrdom of Abadious* (Emile C.
   Amélineau, *Les Actes des martyrs de l'église copte*
   [Paris: E. Leroux, 1890], 75-77 and 112).

18c.[26] Interea venit proconsul cum magno furore, et
stans secus sanctum apostolum, eum videre non poterat.
Cui ille dixit: Ego sum quem quaeris, proconsul.

Et statim aperti sunt oculi eius, et vidit illum et
indignans ait: Quae est haec insania, ut contemnas
iussionem nostram et ministros nostros subicias dicioni
tuae? Vere enim te magum atque maleficum esse manifestum
est. Nunc autem feris te subiciam pro contemptu deorum
et nostro, et tunc videbis, si te possit eripere cruci-
fixus, quem praedicas.

Cui beatus apostolus ait: Oportet te credere,
proconsul, Deum verum et quem misit filium eius Iesum
Christum, praesertim cum videas unum de tuis militibus
interisse.

----

26. In place of *PCU*, *GE* reads: *Et ipsi ascendentes in
    domum, cum vidissent beatum apostolum, trubati,
    nihil dixerunt. Tunc proconsul haec audiens, iratus
    valde, misit multitudinem militum, qui eum cum vi
    adducerent. Quibus visis, apostolus dixit: Numquid
    propter me venistis?*

    *Et illi: Propter te, inquiunt, si tamen tu es magus,
    qui praedicas deos non coli.*

    *Quibus ille ait: Ego magus non sum, sed sum
    apostolus Dei mei Iesu Christi, quem praedico.*

    *Dum haec agerentur, unus militum arreptus a daemone,
    evaginato gladio, exclamans dixit: Quid mihi et
    tibi, Virine proconsul, ut mitteres me ad hominem,
    qui non solummodo extrudere ab hoc vase, verum etiam
    suis me virtutibus incendere potest? Utinam venires
    ad occursum eius et nihil mali ageres contra illum.
    Cum autem haec dixisset, daemonium egressum est a
    milite. Miles igitur cecidit et mortuus est.*

18c.[48] Meanwhile, the proconsul arrived in a fit of rage, and even though he stood next to the holy apostle, he was unable to see him. Andrew said, "I am the one you seek, proconsul."

Immediately his eyes were opened, he saw him and said indignantly, "What is this insanity such that you scorn our order and subject our subordinates to your authority? It is clear that you are a magician and a troublemaker. Now I will subject you to wild beasts for scorning us and our gods. Now you will see if the crucified one you proclaim can rescue you."

"Proconsul," said the blessed apostle, "you should believe in the true God and his son Jesus Christ whom he sent, especially when you see one of your soldiers killed."[49]

----

48. In place of *PCU*, *GE* reads: "They went into the house, and when they saw the blessed apostle, they were confounded and said nothing. The proconsul was incensed when he got word, and sent a large band of soldiers who were to bring him out by force. When they appeared, the apostle said to them, 'Have you come for me?'

    'For you,' they said, 'if you are the magician who preaches the gods should not be worshiped.'

    'I am not a magician,' he told them, 'but an apostle of my God, Jesus Christ, whom I preach.'

    Then one of the soldiers, seized by a demon, unsheathed his sword and cried, 'What do I have to do with you, proconsul Virinus, that you sent me to a man whose powers not only can drive me out of this vessel, but also can burn me? O that you would come to meet him and do him no harm.' When he had said this, the demon left the soldier; the soldier fell dead."

49. Of course, if Varianus himself had killed the boy, this last clause would be Gregory's own formulation.

Et prostratus ad orationem sanctus apostolus, cum
diutissime preces fundisset ad Dominum, tetigit militem,
dicens: Surge suscitat te Deus meus Iesus Christus, quem
praedico. Et statim surrexit miles et stetit sanus.

Cumque populus adclamaret: Gloria Deo nostro!

Proconsul ait: Nolite credere, o populi, nolite
credere magum.

At illi clamabant dicentes: Non est haec magica,[27]
sed est doctrina sana et vera.[28]

Proconsul dixit: Hominem istum ad bestias tradam et
de vobis scribam caesari, ut velociter pereatis, quia
contemnitis leges eius.

Illi autem volentes eum lapidibus obruere, dicebant: Scribe caesari, quia Machedonas[29] receperunt
verbum Dei et, contemptis idolis, Deum verum adorant.

Tunc iratus proconsul, recessit ad praetorium, et
facto mane intromisit feras in stadium et iussit trahi
et proici beatum apostolum in stadio. Quo adpraehenso,
trahebant per capillos, inpellentes fustibus, proiec-
tumque[30] in harena dimiserunt aprum ferocem et
orribilem; qui ter circuivit sanctum Dei et nihil

----

27. Some mss.: *magia*.

28. These last few paragraphs may also be preserved in
    Oxyrhynchus Papyrus 851: (recto) εἶπεν ὡς βούλῃ
    π[οί]ει. ὁ [δὲ ἡγε]μὼν εἶπεν πρὸς τοὺς ἀρχικυνηγούς·
    ἄγετε μοι ὧδε ζωνθαν (corrupt for ζῶντα ν[-] or even
    for ξένον ἄν[θρωπον]?) (verso) . . . ορ[..κύ]ριε
    [ἡγ]εμών, οὗτος ὁ ἄνθρωπος οὐκ ἐστιν μάγος, ἀλλὰ
    τάχα ὁ θεὸς αὐτοῦ μέγας ἐστιν.

29. Some mss.: *Machedones*.

30. Some mss.: *proiectoque*.

The holy apostle prostrated himself for prayer, and after he had poured forth an extremely long prayer to the Lord,[50] he touched the soldier and said, "Rise up! My God Jesus Christ whom I preach awakens you." Immediately the soldier rose and stood up, whole.

"Glory to our God!" shouted the people.

"O people, do not believe," said the proconsul, "do not believe the magician!"

"This is not magic," they cried, "but sound and true teaching."[51]

"I will hand this man over to the beasts and will write Caesar about you, so that you might die shortly for despising his laws," said the proconsul.

But they, fervid to stone him, said, "Write Caesar that the Macedonians received the word of God, detest idols, and worship the true God."

Then the enraged proconsul returned to the praetorium. The next morning he sent wild beasts into the stadium and ordered the blessed apostle dragged and flung into it. They seized him, dragged him by the hair, beat him with clubs, threw him into the arena, and dispatched a ferocious, horrible boar. The boar circled God's saint three times and did him no harm. When the crowd saw this, they gave glory to God.

----

50. Once again Gregory seems to have expunged a lengthy discourse.

51. *Oxyrynchus Papyrus 851*: (recto) "(...) he said: 'Do as you wish.' The governor said to the chief-hunters, 'Bring me here'" (the final word is corrupt, but might have read "living" or "the stranger"). (verso) (...) "'Lord governor, this person is not a magician, but perhaps his God is great.'"

nocuit. Videntes autem haec populi, dederunt gloriam
Deo.

Proconsul vero iussit iterum dimitti taurum; qui a
triginta militibus adductus et a duobus venatoribus
inpulsus, Andream non attigit, sed venatores discerpsit
in frusta.[31] et dans mugitum, cecidit et mortuus est. Et
statim adclamavit populus dicens: Verus Deus Christus.
Dum haec agerentur, angelus Domini visus est descendisse
de caelo et confortabat sanctum apostolum in stadio.

Denique proconsul fervens ira iussit leopardum
ferocissimum dimitti; qui dimissus reliquid populum,[32]
et ascendens ad sedem proconsulis, arripuit filium eius
et suffocavit eum. Tantaque insania proconsulem[33]
obtinu- erat, ut nihil de his aliquid aut doleret aut
diceret.

Tunc beatus apostolus conversus ad populum, dixit:
Cognoscite nunc, quia verum Deum colitis, cuius virtute
bestiae superatae sunt, quem nunc Virinus proconsul
ignorat. Sed ego, ut facilius credatis, etiam filium
illius in nomine Christi, quem praedico, suscitabo, ut
confundatur stultissimus pater eius. Et prostratus
terrae, diutissime oravit, adpraehensaque manu suffo-
cati, suscitavit eum. Haec videntes populi, magnificav-
erunt Deum et voluerunt Virinum interficere, sed
permissi non sunt ab apostolo. Virinus autem confusus
discessit in praetorium suum.

----

31. Following Prieur. Bonnet: *frustra*.

32. Or perhaps: *apostolum*.

33. Some mss.: *consulem*.

The proconsul again gave orders, this time that a bull be released, led in by thirty soldiers and provoked by two beast-fighting gladiators. It did not touch Andrew, but ripped the gladiators into pieces, gave a roar, and fell dead. Immediately the people shouted: "Christ is the true God!" When this happened, an angel of the Lord was seen descending from heaven who comforted the holy apostle in the stadium.

Seething with rage, the proconsul at last ordered a fierce leopard sent in. When dispatched, the leopard ignored the people,[52] leaped onto the proconsul's throne, seized his son, and strangled him. The proconsul was so overtaken by insanity that he felt no pain and said nothing whatever about these events.

The blessed apostle then turned to the people and said, "Realize now that you worship the true God, whose power overwhelmed the beasts and about whom the proconsul Varianus still knows nothing. I will revive his son in the name of Christ whom I preach, so that you might more easily believe and so that his thickheaded father may be confounded." For a long time he prayed, stretched out on the ground,[53] then, taking the corpse's hand, he awakened him. When the people saw this, they magnified God and would have killed Varianus, but the apostle would not allow it. Varianus left befuddled for his praetorium.[54]

----

52. Or perhaps: "the apostle."

53. It is likely the original contained the content of the prayer.

54. Andrew's fight with the beasts seems to have been modeled after similar contests in *APl* 3 (*Acts of Paul and Thecla* 33-36) and 7 (*Hamburg Papyrus* 5). See my discussion of this story in "From Audita to Legenda: Oral and Written Miracle Stories," *Forum* 2, 4 (1986): 15-26, esp. 20-21.

19. His ita gestis, adolescens quidam, qui erat iam cum apostolo, indicavit matri suae quae acta erant et arcessivit eam, ut veniret ad occursum sancti. Quae accedens, procidit ad pedes eius et quaerebat, ut audiret verbum Dei. Cui cum satisfactum fuisset depraecatione,[34] rogavit, ut accederet ad agrum eius, in quo serpens mirae magnitudinis erat, qui totam regionem illam devastabat.

Adpropinquante autem apostolo, sibila magna emittens, erecto capite, venit in obviam. Erat enim longitudo eius quinquaginta cubitorum, ut omnes qui aderant metu terrerentur et terrae decubarent.

Tunc sanctus Dei ait ad eum: Abde caput, funeste, quod erexisti in principio ad perniciem generis humani, et subde te famulis Dei ac morire.

Et statim serpens emittens gravem rugitum, circumdedit quercum magnam, quae propinqua erat, et obligans se circa eam, evomens rivum veneni cum sanguine, expiravit.

Sanctus vero apostolus pervenit ad praedium mulieris, in quo parvulus, quem serpens perculerat, mortuus decubabat. Et videns flere parentes eius, ait ad eos: Deus noster, qui vult vos salvos fieri, misit me huc, ut credatis in eum. Nunc autem abeuntes, videte mortuum interfectorem filii vestri.

At illi dixerunt, Nihil dolemus de morte fili, si ultionem ex inimico videmus.

----

34. The awkwardness of this phrase accounts for the variant *de praedicatione* and the omission of *depraecatione* altogether in some mss.

19. After this, a young man who already had been with the apostle told his mother what happened and summoned her to come to meet the saint. When she came, she fell at his feet and asked to hear the word of God. Her request granted, she asked him to come to her estate, where a snake of astonishing size was devastating the entire region.

As the apostle approached, the serpent hissed loudly, raised its head, and advanced to meet him. It was fifty cubits long,[55] and everyone there was gripped by terror and fell to the earth.

"Murderer!" said God's saint. "Hide the head you raised at the beginning for the destruction of humankind! Submit yourself to the servants of God and die!"

The snake immediately gave a deep roar, slithered around a mighty oak nearby, tied itself around it, vomited a stream of venom and blood, and perished.

The holy apostle traveled to the woman's estate, where a young boy smitten by the snake lay dead. When Andrew saw his parents weeping he said to them, "Our God, who wants you to be saved, sent me here so that you might believe in him. Go now and see that your son's murderer is dead."

"We will not grieve our son's death," they said, "if we see revenge on his enemy."

----

55. About eighty feet.

Illis vero abeuntibus, dixit apostolus ad uxorem proconsulis: Vade et suscita puerum.

Ad illa nihil dubitans, venit ad corpus et ait: In nomine Dei mei Iesu Christi, surge, puer, incolomis, et statim surrexit.

Parentes autem eius redeuntes cum gaudio, quod vidissent serpentem mortuum, invenerunt filium viventem, et prostrati coram pedibus apostoli, gratias agebant.

When they departed, the apostle said to the pronconsul's wife, "Go and revive the boy."

Without hesitation, she went to the corpse and said, "Lad, in the name of my God Jesus Christ rise up unscathed." He arose at once.

His parents returned jubilant at seeing the dead snake, and when they found their son alive, they fell at the apostle's feet and gave thanks.[56]

---

56. *E* tells of Andrew's two encounters with dragons near Nicea (229B-D and 232C-D [=*L* 16]). These stories probably are local legends unrelated to the ancient Acts.

EXCURSUS F
VARIANUS'S WIFE

In the preceding chapter, *GE* states that the wife of the proconsul Varianus raised the striken lad back to life. This is the first and last time that she appears in our texts of the *AA*, but surely her role in the original was more substantial. There can be little doubt that Gregory passed over events related to her conversion because he took issue with the radical celibacy of his source.[1] Varianus's irritation with Andrew in the *AA* had less to do with protecting pagan religion, as in *GE*, than with protecting his bed.

None of our texts of the *AA* names this woman. *PCU* mentions a believer names Eirusia, but one cannot identify her unambiguously with Varianus's wife. *The Manichaean Psalm-Book*, however, may supply important clues. Two different Manichaean poets extolled a woman named Aristobula in connection with other heroines of the *AA*. For example, in a hymn celebrating women of the apocryphal Acts who had fought for purity, one reads: "Maximilla and Aristobula--on them was great torture

----

1. Flamion, *Actes d'André*, 247-48; Quispel, "Unknown Fragment," 137-38; Prieur, *Acta Andreae*, 44-45. Two Latin passions, *Conversante et docente* (*Cd*) and *Épître grecque* (*Ep*), similarly change Aegeates' rage over Maximilla's continence to rage over the cessation of pagan rites. Flamion argues that the similarities between the charges against Andrew by Varianus and by Aegeates in *Cd* suggest "an analogous recasting of the texts" (*Actes d'André*, 247). In fact, it would appear that Gregory was inspired to replace Varianus's jealousy with a stock defense of Roman religion from having seen *Cd*. *Cd* 1: *tu es Andreas qui destruis templa deorum et persuades hominibus superstitiosam sectam quae nuper a vobis inventa est colere? GE: qui templa deorum praedicat destrui, caerimonias respui et omnia priscae legis decreta convelli. Unum deum tantum praedicat coli.*

inflicted" (143.13 [Allberry]). Maximilla is the heroine
of the conclusion the the *AA*; she too leaves her husband
in order to follow Christ. Similarly, one of the Hymns
of Heraclides lists holy women, including Mary
Magdalene, Martha, and Salome, Thecla and Eubula of the
APl, Drusiana of the *AJ*, and Mygdonia of the *ATh*. Nested
between Thecla and Eubula are the following lines:

> A shamer of the serpent is Maximilla the faithful,
> A receiver of good news is Iphidama her sister
>   also, imprisioned (?) in the prison.
> A champion of the fight [ἀγών] is Aristobula the
>   enduring one. (192.26-29 [Allberry])

In the *AA*, Iphidama is Maximilla's servant. In spite of
Aristobula's persistent identification with heroines of
the *AA*, scholars more commonly have identified her with
an obscure character also named Aristobula in *AJ* 59;
even though, nothing in her depiction in the *AJ*
corresponds with information about her in the Manichaean
hymns.

It is more reasonable to assume that she originally
appeared somewhere and prominently in the *AA*, and if so,
the most likely context is here, as the wife of
Varianus. By combining the information supplied by *GE*
and the Manichaean hymns, one might reconstruct the
following scenario. Aristobula converted to Andrew's
preaching and away from Varianus's embrace. Her husband
punished her "with great torture," but she was able to
attain her freedom and to travel with the apostle to the
woman's estate, where she raised the youth back to life.

20. Sequenti vero nocte visum vidit beatus apostolus, quem etiam fratribus enarravit, dicens: Audite, dilectissimi, somnium meum. Videbam, et ecce mons magnus erat in sublimi elevatus, qui nihil super se de terrenis rebus habebat, nisi tantum luce resplendens, ita ut mundum putaretur inluminare. Et ecce adstiterunt mihi dilectissimi fratres Petrus et Iohannes apostoli; et Iohannes quidem, extensa manu Petro apostolo, levabat eum in vertice[35] montis, et conversus ad me, rogabat ascendere post Petrum, dicens: Andreas, poculum Petri bibiturus es. Et extensis manibus, ait: Adpropinqua mihi et extende manus tuas, ut coniungantur manibus meis, et caput tuum capite meo societur. Quod cum fecissem, inventus sum brevior esse Iohanni; et post haec ait mihi: Vis cognoscere imaginem huius rei quam cernis, vel quis sit qui tibi loquitur?

Et ego aio: Desidero ista cognoscere.

Et ait mihi: Ego sum Verbum crucis, in qua pendebis in proximo propter nomen eius quem praedicas. Et multa alia mihi dixit, quae nunc silere oportet; prodebuntur tamen tunc cum ad hanc immolationem[36] accessero. Nunc autem conveniant omnes qui susceperunt verbum Dei, et commendem illos Domino Iesu Christo, ut eos in doctrina sua inmaculatos custodire dignetur. Ego vero iam resolvor a corpore et vado ad promissionem illam quam

----

35. Some mss.: *verticem*.

36. Some mss.: *aemulationem*.

20. The following night the blessed apostle saw a vision which he narrated to the other brethren: "My good friends, listen to my dream. I saw a great mountain raised on high with nothing earthly on it, and it so radiated with light that it seemed to illumine the world. And there standing with me, my beloved brothers, were the apostles Peter and John.[57] Extending his hand to the apostle Peter, John raised him to the mountain's summit, turned, and asked me to ascend after Peter saying, 'Andrew, you will drink Peter's cup.'[58] With his hands outstretched, he said, 'Come to me and stretch out your hands to join my hands, and let your head touch mine.' When I did so, I discovered myself to be shorter than John. 'Would you like to know,' he then asked, 'to what this symbol you see refers, or who it is who speaks with you?'

"'I long to know these things,' I said.

"'I am the word of the cross,' he said, 'on which you soon will hang for the name of the one you proclaim.' He also told me many other things about which I can say nothing now, but which will become apparent when I approach this sacrifice.[59] For now, let all who have received the word of God come together, and let me commend them to the Lord Jesus Christ, so that he may

----

57. The *AAMt* also places Peter on a mountain (*AAMt* 21).

58. I.e., he too will be crucified (cf. Mark 10:38-39, para. Matt 20:22-23, and John 21:18-19). Andrew's death and Peter's as recorded in the *APe* do indeed have much in common, apparently the result of imitation in the *AA*.

59. Andrew refuses to disclose the rest of this revelation concerning his death, choosing instead to do so as he approaches his cross. This anticipates his address to the cross: "I know you mystery, why you were planted" (Passion 54[4]).

mihi pollicere[37] dignatus est Regnator caelorum et terrae, qui est filius omnipotentis Dei, cum Spiritu sancto verus Deus, permanens in saecula sempiterna. Haec audientes fratres, flebant valde et cedebant palmis facies suas cum gemitu magno.

Denique convenientibus cunctis, ait iterum: Scitote, dilectissimi, me discessurum a vobis, sed credo in Iesum, cuius verbum praedico, quia custodiet vos a malo, ut non divellatur ab inimico haec messis, quam in vobis servi, id est cognitio et doctrina Iesu Christi Domini mei. Vos autem orate iugiter et state fortes in fide, ut, evulsam Dominus omnem zizaniam scandali, tamquam triticum mundum in horreo vos caelesti congregare dignetur. Et sic per dies quinque docebat eos et confirmabat in praeceptis Dei.

Post haec autem expansis manibus oravit ad Dominum, dicens: Custodi, quaeso, Domine, gregem hunc, qui iam tuam cognovit salutem, ut non praevaleat illi malignus, sed quae, te iubente, me dispensante, suscepit, inviolatum[38] custodire mereatur in saecula saeculorum.

Et haec dicens, omnes qui aderant responderunt: Amen.

Et accipiens panem, gratias agens fregit et dedit omnibus, dicens: Accipite gratiam quem[39] vobis tradit per me famulum suum Christus Dominus Deus noster. Et osculans singulos atque commendans Domino, in Thesalonica profectus est, ibique biduo docens, discessit ab eis.

----

37. Perhaps: *polliceri*.

38. Some mss.: *inviolata*.

39. Some mss.: *quam*.

keep them untarnished in his teaching. For I am already being untied from the body, and I go to that promise he saw fit to promise me--he who is Ruler of the heavens and earth, the son of God Almighty, with the Holy Spirit, the true God enduring for ages everlasting." When the brethren heard these things they wept effusively, slapped their faces, and groaned.

When all had come together, he said, "Dear friends, you should know that I will be leaving you, but I trust in Jesus, whose word I preach, that he will keep you from evil, so that the enemy may not shred this harvest which I tended among you, namely, the knowledge and teaching of Jesus Christ my Lord. Therefore, pray continually and stand strong in the faith, so that the Lord may uproot every offensive weed and may consider you worthy of gathering into the heavenly granary as pure wheat."[60] In this manner he taught them and strengthened them in the commandments of God for five days.

After this, with hands outstretched, he prayed to the Lord: "O Lord, please guard this flock which already knows your salvation, so that the wicked one will not prevail, and that it may be entitled to guard forever unharmed what it received at your command and by my guidance."

When he had said this, all present responded, "Amen!"

He took bread, gave thanks, broke it, and gave it to all saying, "Receive the grace which Christ the Lord our God gives you through me his servant." When he had kissed everyone and commended them to the Lord, he went

----

60. Cf. Matt 13:30.

21. Multi autem ex Machedonia fideles profecti sunt cum eo, quorum fuerunt duae naves. Quaerebant autem omnes, ut illam navem in qua apostolus vehebatur conscenderent, desiderantes eum audire loquentem, scilicet ut nec in mari eis deesset verbum Dei. Quibus ait apostolus: Novi desiderium vestrum, dilectissimi, sed navis haec parvula est. Ergo pueri cum inpedimentis in maiore conscendant nave, vos vero in ista quae minor est nobiscum properabitis. Et dato eis Anthimo, qui consolaret eos, iussit aliam conscendere navem, quam propre sibi semper iussit adesse, ut et ipsi viderent eum et audirent verbum Dei.

Dormiente autem eo parumper, quidam vento modico inpulsus, cecidit in mari. Anthimus autem excitavit eum, dicens: Succurre, doctor bonae; periit autem unus de famulis tuis.

Expergefactus autem apostolus, increpavit ventum, et siluit, et mare tranquillum est redditum. Homo vero qui ceciderat, unda famulante, ad navem devectus est. Cuius manum Anthimus adpraehensam, levavit eum in navi, et omnes admirati sunt virtutem apostoli, quod etiam et mare oboediebat ei. Duodecima igitur die Patras Achaiae civitatem adpulsi sunt, egressique navem, in quodam diversorio morabantur.[40]

---

40. N 9: Διελθών τε τὴν Θεσσαλίαν καὶ Ἑλλάδα καὶ το<ῖ>ς ἐν αὐταῖς ταῖς πόλεσιν τὸ τῆς οἰκονομίας Χριστοῦ τοῦ θεοῦ μυστήριον ἐκθέμενος αὐτόθεν μέτεισιν πρὸς τὴν Ἀχαΐαν.

on to Thessalonica. He taught there for two days and left them.

21. Many of the faithful from Macedonia went with him in two boats. All sought to board the boat carrying the apostle, longing to hear him talk, so that not even while sailing would they be without the word of God. The apostle said to them, "I know your desire, dear friends, but this boat is small. Therefore, let the young men and baggage board the larger ship, and you travel with us in this smaller one." He gave them Anthimus to comfort them,[61] and commanded them to board the other boat, which he ordered always to be nearby, so that they too might see him and hear the word of God.

While he napped, someone was jarred by a moderate wind and fell into the sea. Anthimus wakened him saying, "Good teacher, help! One of your servants perishes!"

The apostle awoke and rebuked the wind. It was silent and the sea once again became calm. The person who had fallen in was carried to the ship with the help of a wave. Anthimus took his hand, lifted him on board, and all were amazed at the power of the apostle, for even the sea obeyed him.[62] After twelve days, they landed at Patras, a city in Achaea, disembarked, and stayed at some residence.[63]

----

61. The Anthimus mentioned here appears nowhere else in our sources. Presumably he was one of Andrew's followers whose earlier roles, if any, Gregory passed over in silence.

62. Cf. Mark 4:41, para. Matt 8:27 and Luke 8:25.

63. *N* 9: "He passed through Thessaly and Greece, and after he had exposed the mystery of the dispensation of God's Christ to the residents of the cities in those regions, he left there for Achaea." This story almost certainly inspired a similar account of a lad tossed into the sea in *AJPr* 48,3-50,5.

EXCURSUS G
ANDREW'S ARRIVAL IN PATRAS

The last four words of the preceeding chapter suggest that the apostle stayed in an inn (*in quodam diversorio morabantur*). *E* and *L*, on the other hand, state that when Andrew arrived in Patras, a certain Sosius entertained him and was healed by the apostle of a serious illness.[1] *GE* too refers to this Sosius, though much later in the narrative (chapter 30). Prieur prefers the Greek witnesses here to *GE*,[2] but he does not explain why Gregory would have omitted Sosius's hospitality if he had found it in his source. Furthermore, *E* (followed by *L*) goes on immediately to narrate a healing that seems to parallel the healing in *GE* 30, suggesting that the monk from Callistratos, like Gregory, read of Sosius first in connection with that healing story, not here, when Andrew first arrives in Patras. The Greek lives moved Sosius to this early passage in order to provide the apostle with housing *tout de suite*. Certainty on this matter is impossible, except that Sosius probably played a more important role in the ancient *AA* than is now visible in our sources.

Equally uncertain is the reconstruction of the following chapter, where *GE* may be compared with the now-lost martyrdom source used by *M* (*Martyrium prius*) and *L*.

----

1. *L* 33: "He and the disciples with him disembarked and entered Patras, an Achaean city, and were entertained by a certain resident of the city named Sosius, who was healed quiet remarkably and thus was saved from deadly illness" (ἐν Πάτραις δὲ πόλει τῆς Ἀχαΐας εἰσελθὼν μετὰ τῶν σὺν αὐτῷ μαθητῶν κατήχθη ξενισθεὶς παρά τινι τῆς αὐτῆς πόλεως οἰκήτορι Σοσσίῳ τοὔνομα· ὃν παρ' ἐλπίδας ἰάσατο περισωσάμενο<ν> ἐκ νόσου θανατηφόρου (cf. *E* 244D).

2. *Acta Andreae*, 46-48.

Although these Greek recensions for the most part preserve the better readings, *GE* account cannot be ruled out altogether. Here Lesbius claims that he had sent troops to the proconsul of Macedonia, viz. Varianus, to bring Andrew to Patras for execution, but the ship was lost at sea. *M* and *L* say nothing concerning this failed expedition, but one would hardly expect them to, insofar as neither had mentioned Andrew's earlier problems with a proconsul in Macedonia. Therefore, it is quite possible that such a back-reference in the ancient Acts, now preserved only by *GE*, was deleted from the Greek recensions to avoid confusion.

The attempt in this edition to coordinate *GE* with *M* and *L* is only modestly successful, due to the unevenness of the sources. Even so, it seems better to present an eclectic reconstruction than to settle for choosing one version over the other. Purists will be able to distinguish between the two versions by comparing the text with the footnotes or by consulting Prieur.

22. (=M 3b-6 [L 34]) Καὶ εἰσελθόντος αὐτοῦ εἰς τὴν πόλιν φήμη διεδόθη ὅτι ἄνθρωπος ξένος ἦλθεν εἰς τὴν πόλιν γυμνός, φησίν, ἔρημος, μηδὲν ἐπιφερόμενος εἰς ἐφόδιον ἀλλ' ἢ μόνον ὄνομά τινος Ἰησοῦ, δι' οὗ σημεῖα καὶ τέρατα ποιεῖ μεγάλα καὶ νόσους παύει καὶ δαίμονας ἐκβάλλει καὶ νεκροὺς ἀναστᾷ καὶ λεπροὺς ἰᾶται καὶ πᾶν πάθος θεραπεύει.[41] ὁ δὲ ἀνθύπατος Λέσβιος ταῦτα ἀκούσας ἐταράχθη λέγων· μάγος ἐστὶν καὶ ἀπατεών· οὐ χρὴ ἡμᾶς προσέχειν αὐτόν, ζητεῖν δὲ μᾶλλον παρὰ τῶν θεῶν τὴν εὐεργεσίαν. καὶ ἠβουλήθη συλλαβόμενος αυτὸν ἀνελεῖν.

Νυκτὸς δὲ ἐπιστὰς ἄγγελος κυρίου τῷ ἀνθυπάτῳ Λεσβίῳ μετὰ ἐμφανείας μεγάλης καὶ ἀπειλῆς φοβερᾶς εἶπεν· τί παθὼν παρὰ τοῦ ξένου Ἀνδρεὰ κακῶς ἐλογίσω διαχειρίσασθαι αὐτὸν καὶ παρελογίσω τὸν θεὸν ὃν κηρύσσει; καὶ νῦν ἰδοὺ χεὶρ κυρίου αὐτοῦ ἐπὶ σὲ καὶ ἔσῃ παραπλὴξ ἕως οὗ ἐπιγνῷς δι' αὐτοῦ τὴν ἀλήθειαν. καὶ γενόμενος ἀπ' αὐτοῦ ὁ ἄγγελος ἀφανής, ἐκεῖνος ἐτέθη ἄφωνος.

Καὶ μετ' οὐ πολὺ ὀλίγον ἀνανήψας ἐκάλει τοὺς διακονοῦντας αὐτῷ στρατιώτας καὶ ἔλεγεν αὐτοῖς μετὰ δακρύων· ἐλεήσατέ με, σπεύσατε ἀναζητῆσαι ἐν τῇ πόλει ξένον τινὰ ἄνθρωπον λιτὸν Ἀνδρέαν λεγόμενον, ὃς κηρύσσει ξένον θεόν· δι' οὗ δυνήσομαι ἐπιγνῶναι τὴν ἀλήθειαν.[42] καὶ

----

41. *GE: Denique cum eum multi rogarent, ut in domibus eorum ingrederetur, dixit: Vivit Dominus, quia non vadam, nisi quo praeceperit Deus meus. Et nocte dormiens, nihil revelationis accepit. Altera vero nocte, cum esset ex hoc tristis, audivit vocem dicentem sibi: Andreas, ego semper tecum sum et non te derelinquo. Haec autem audiens, glorificabat Deum pro hac visione.*

42. *GE: Lisbius vero proconsul admonitus est per visum, ut susciperet hominem Dei. At ille misit ad hominem qui eos hospitio reciperat et rogavit, ut adduceret sibi beatum apostolum.*

22. When he entered the city, a rumor spread that a stranger had entered the city, reportedly naked, destitute, and bringing with him for his journey nothing but the name of a certain person named Jesus through whom he performs signs and great wonders, eradicates diseases, casts out demons, raises the dead, cures lepers, and heals every kind of suffering.[64] When the proconsul Lesbius heard this, he was disturbed and said, "He is a magician and charlatan. We must not give him attention, but rather seek help from the gods." He wanted to arrest and destroy him.

At night an angel of the Lord appeared to the proconsul Lesbius and with great fanfare and an awesome threat said, "What have you suffered from this stranger Andrew such that you wickedly contrived to lay hands on him and cheated the God he preaches? Now behold the hand of his Lord is on you, and you will be crazed until you know the truth through him." The angel vanished from him and he was struck dumb.

Not longer after, partially regaining his senses, he called his bodyguard and with tears said to them, "Take pity on me. Quickly search the city for a certain stranger, a tramp called Andrew who preaches a foreign god through whom I will be able to learn the truth."[65] They

----

64. Perhaps at this point Andrew healed and converted Sosius; see *GE* 30 (Prieur, *Acta Andreae*, 46-47 and 61). *GE*: "Later, when many people asked him to come to their homes, he said, 'As the Lord lives, I go nowhere unless my God commands it.' That night as he slept, he received no revelation. On the next night, as he was agonizing over this silence, he heard a voice saying to him, 'Andrew, I am with you always and will not leave you.' When he heard this, he glorified God for this vision.'"

65. Cf. *AAMt* 24. *GE*: "The proconsul Lesbius was warned in a vision to receive the man of God, and he sent for

μετὰ σπουδῆς ἀναζητήσαντες τὸν μακάριον Ἀνδρέαν καὶ
εὑρόντες αὐτὸν ἄγουσιν πρὸς τὸν ἀνθύπατον·43

Et ille: Ego, inquid, sum qui execrabam viam quam
doces et misi milites cum navibus ad proconsulem
Machedoniae, ut vinctum te transmittens mihi, morte
damnarem. Sed naufragia perferentes, numquam potuerunt
accedere quo iussi sunt. Cumque in hac intentione durarem,
ut distruerem viam tuam, apparuerunt mihi duo viri
Aethiopes, qui me flagris cedebant, dicentes: Non possumus
hic iam ullam potestatem habere, quia venit homo ille quem
persequi cogitabas. Et nunc in hac nocte, in qua adhuc
potestatem habemus, ulciscimur nos in te. Et sic graviter
caesum, recesserunt a me. Nunc autem tu, vir Dei,
deprecare Dominum, ut dimittens mihi hoc delictum, saner
ab infirmitate qua teneor.44

Καὶ ὁ μακάριος ἀπόστολος κατανυγεὶς καὶ ἐπιδακρύσας
τοῖς λόγοις τοῦ ἱκέτου, ὑψώσας τοὺς ὀφθαλμοὺς αὐτοῦ εἰς
τὸν οὐρανόν, ἐπιτιθεὶς τὴν χεῖρα αὐτοῦ τὴν δεξιὰν τῷ παντὶ
σώματι αὐτοῦ εἶπεν· ὁ ἐμὸς θεὸς Ἰησοῦς Χριστός, ὁ
ἀγνοούμενος ὑπὸ τοῦ κόσμου, νῦν δὲ δι' ἡμῶν φανερούμενος·
ὁ υἱὸς τοῦ θεοῦ τοῦ λόγου· ὁ πρὸ πάντων ὢν καὶ ἐν πᾶσιν

----

43. GE: Quod cum ille audisset, venit ad proconsulem, et
    ingressus cubiculum eius, vidit eum iacentem clausis
    oculis quasi mortuum. Pungensque latus illius, ait:
    Surge et enarra nobis quae tibi contigit.

44. M: ὁ δὲ ἀνθύπατος θεασάμενος αὐτὸν πίπτει πρὸς τοὺς
    πόδας αὐτοῦ καὶ δεόμενος αὐτοῦ ἔλεγεν· ἄνθρωπε τοῦ
    θεοῦ, ξένε καὶ γνῶστα ξένου θεοῦ, ἐλέησον ἄνθρωπον
    πεπλανημένον, ἄνθρωπον τῆς ἀληθείας ξένον, ἄνθρωπον
    κατεστιγμένον ταῖς κηλῖσι τῶν ἁμαρτημάτων, ἄνθρωπον
    θεοὺς εἰδότα πολλοὺς ψευδεῖς καὶ τὸν μόνον θεὸν τὸν
    ἀληθινὸν ἀγνοοῦντα· δέομαι τοῦ ἐν σοὶ θεοῦ, ὄρεξάι μοι
    χεῖρα σωτηρίας· ἄνοιξόν μοι θύραν γνώσεως· ἐπίλαμψόν
    μοι φῶς δικαιοσύνης.

ardently sought out the blessed Andrew, and when they found him they brought him to the proconsul.[66]

"I am the one who cursed the 'way' which you teach," he said, "and I sent soldiers and ships to the proconsul of Macedonia to send you to me bound, so that I might condemn you to death. But they suffered shipwreck and were unable to get where they had been commanded to go. Because I persisted in my intention to destroy your 'way,' two Ethiopians [i.e., demons] appeared to me, beat me with whips, and said, 'We are no longer able to exercise power here, because that man you planned to persecute is on his way. And now, this very night, while we still have power, we will avenge ourselves on you.' I was thus severely beaten and they left me. Now, O man of God, pray to the Lord, so that by his forgiving me this crime I may be cured of my infirmity."[67]

The blessed apostle, stunned and tearful at the words of the penitent, lifted up his eyes toward heaven, placed his right hand over his entire body, and said: "O my God Jesus Christ, unknown by the world but now revealed through us, you, Son of God, the Word, who was before all

----

the person who receives and invites guests to bring the blessed apostle to him."

66. *GE*: "When Andrew learned of the invitation, he went to the proconsul, entered his private chamber, and saw him lying prone, eyes closed, nearly dead. Poking his side, Andrew said, 'Get up and tell us what happened to you.'"

67. *M*: "Seeing him, the proconsul fell at his feet and begged him: 'Man of God, stranger and acquaintance of a strange god, take pity on one deceived, one estranged from the truth, one spotted with the stains of sins, one who knows many false gods but who is ignorant of the only true God. I beg the God in you, stretch out to me the hand of salvation, open to me the door of knowledge, shine on me the light of righteousness.'"

χωρῶν· ἅψαι τοῦ δούλου σου καὶ σκεῦος σὸν ἀπεργασάμενος
ἴασαι, ἵνα καὶ αὐτὸς ἔσται τῶν σῶν ἀνθρώπων, κηρύσσων τὴν
σὴν δραστήριον δύναμιν. καὶ παραχρῆμα πιάσας αὐτὸν τῆς
δεξιᾶς χειρὸς ἀνέστησεν.

'Αναστὰς δὲ ἀνθωμολογεῖτο τῷ κυρίῳ λέγων· ὄντως οὗτος
θεός, ἄνθρωπε ξένε, οὐ δεόμενος ὡρῶν οὔτε ἡμερῶν οὔτε
χρόνων· διὰ τοῦτο πρόσκειμαί σοι μετὰ παντὸς τοῦ οἴκου
μου· πιστεύω εἰς τὸν ἀποστείλαντά σε πρὸς ἡμᾶς.

Καὶ ὁ 'Ανδρέας πρὸς αὐτὸν ἔφη· ἐπειδὴ μεγάλως
πεπίστευκας εἰς τὸν ἀποστείλαντά με, περισσοτέρως καὶ τῆς
γνώσεως ἐμπλησθήσῃ. [45]

----

45. *GE*: *Haec eo coram omni populo narrante, beatus
apostolus praedicabat assidue verbum Dei, et credebant
omnes. Proconsul vero sanatus, credidit et
conroboratus est in fide.*

M 6 (=L 35) continues: 'Ως δὲ ἐν τούτοις ἦν καὶ πᾶσα ἡ
πόλις ἔχαιρεν ἐπὶ τῇ σωτηρίᾳ τοῦ ἀνθυπάτου, πανταχόθεν
συνήρχοντο ὄχλοι ἐπιφερόμενοι τοὺς ἀσθενοῦντας
ποικίλαις νόσοις· καὶ ἐπευξάμενος αὐτοῖς καὶ
ἐπικαλεσάμενος τὸν κύριον 'Ιησοῦν, ἐπιθεὶς τὰς χεῖρας
πάντας ἰάσατο· καὶ θάμβος κατέλαβεν πάντας τοὺς
κατοικοῦντας τὴν πόλιν, καὶ βοῶντες ἔκραζον· μεγάλη ἡ
δύναμις τοῦ ξένου θεοῦ· μέγας ὁ θεὸς ὁ κηρυσσόμενος
ὑπὸ τοῦ ξένου 'Ανδρέα· (*M only:* ἡμεῖς ἀπὸ τῆς σήμερον
τὰ ξόανα τῶν εἰδώλων ἡμῶν ἀπολλύωμεν, τὰ ἄλση αὐτῶν
ἐκκόπτωμεν, τὰς στήλας αὐτῶν συντρίβωμεν, τὴν πολύθεον
γνῶσιν τῶν ματαίων δαιμόνων ἐκτρεπώμεθα· τὸν μόνον
θεὸν τὸν δ' 'Ανδρέου κηρυσσόμενον ἐπιγινώσκωμεν· μέγας
ὁ θεὸς 'Ανδρέου.) καὶ πάντες ὁμοθυμαδὸν ὁρμήσαντες ἐπὶ
τοὺς ναοὺς τοὺς θεοὺς αὐτῶν ἐνέπρησαν, ἐλέπτυναν,
ἐξέκοψαν, ἐξουθένησαν, κατεπάτησαν, ἀπώλεσαν λέγοντες·
μόνος ὁ 'Ανδρέου θεὸς ὀνομαζέσθω. καὶ ὁ ἀνθύπατος
Λέσβιος συνέχαιρεν τῇ βοῇ τοῦ δήμου καὶ τῷ ἔργῳ τοῦ
ὄχλου.

things and who pervades all things, touch your servant and heal him, thereby perfecting your vessel, so that even he may be among your people, preaching your vigorous power." Immediately he grasped his right hand and raised him up.

After rising, he gave thanks to the Lord and said: "Stranger, surely he is God who needs neither hours nor days nor seasons. Therefore, I devote myself and all my house to you. I believe in the one who sent you to us."

"Since you have believed so greatly in the one who sent me," Andrew told him, "you will be abundantly filled with knowledge."[68]

----

68. *GE*: "When he had narrated this to all the people, the blessed apostle preached the word of God continually, and all believed. The proconsul was healed, believed, and was strengthened in the faith."

M (=*L*) continues: "While matters were in this state, and while the entire city was rejoicing at the proconsul's salvation, crowds gathered from everywhere bringing those who were sick with various diseases. He prayed for them, called on the Lord Jesus, laid his hands on them, and healed everyone. Astonishment overtook all those living in the city, who shouted out, 'Great is the power of the foreign God! Great is the God preached by the stranger Andrew. (*M* only: From today on let us destroy the statues of our idols, let us cut down their groves, let us crush their monuments, let us reject the polytheistic knowledge of vain demons. Let us recognize rather the only God, the one preached by Andrew. Great is the God of Andrew!') Together they all rushed to the temples and burned up, pulverized, cut down, scorned, trampled on, and destroyed their gods saying, 'Let Andrew's God alone be named.' The proconsul Lesbius likewise rejoiced at the cry of the citizenry and exulted at the action of the crowd."

GE says nothing concerning such renunciations of idolatry, probably because this passage never appeared in the ancient Acts. Pagan piety was not a major concern of the *AA*. Notice that in the passion section *M* (and probably its source) made the cause of Andrew's eventual martyrdom not his conversion of Maximilla to continence but his denunciations of pagan deities. On

23. Igitur Trofimae, quae quondam concubina proconsulis fuerat et alio iam viro sociata erat, reliquid virum suum et adherebat apostolicae doctrinae et ob hoc plerumque in domo proconsulis veniebat, in quam iugiter docebat apostolus. Iratus autem vir eius venit ad dominam suam, dicens: Trofima recolens scortum, quod cum domino meo proconsule agere consueverat, ei nunc iterato commiscetur.

At illa succensa felle, ait: Idcirco ergo me reliquid vir meus et iam sex mensibus non coniungitur mihi, eo quod diligat ancillam suam. Et vocato procuratore, iussit eam scorto damnari. Nec mora, deducitur ad lupanar ac lenoni donatur. Sed nihil horum Lisbius sciebat, requirens tamen eam, ab uxore deludebatur.

At illa ingressa lupanar, orabat assidue, cumque venissent qui eam contingerent, ponebat euangelium quod secum habebat ad pectus suum, et statim omnes vires perdebant accedentes ad eam. Quidam vero inpudicissimus veniens, ut inluderet ei, resistente autem ea, disrupit vestimenta eius, et cecidit euangelium ad terra. Trofimae vero lacrimans, extensis ad caelum manibus, dixit: Ne patiaris me, Domine, pollui, ob cuius nomine diligo castitatem.

23. Then Trophime, at one time the proconsul's mistress and currently the lover of yet another man, left her husband and devoted herself to apostolic teaching. For this purpose she often visited the house of the proconsul where the apostle constantly taught. Her enraged husband came to her lady[69] and said, "Trophime is resuming her former prostitution with my master the proconsul, and now once again sleeps with him."

Ablaze with bitterness, she said, "So that is why my husband deserted me and for the last six months has not made love with me: he prefers his maidservant!"[70] She summoned the steward and ordered Trophime condemned to prostitution. Without delay she was led away to a brothel and given to a pimp. Lesbius knew nothing of these developments, and when he inquired about Trophime, his wife lied to him.

Trophime entered the brothel and prayed incessantly. Whenever men came to touch her, she would place the Gospel which she had with her on her breast, and all the men would fail to approach her. A particularly shameless rogue came to violate her, and when she resisted, he tore off her clothes, and the Gospel fell to the ground. Trophime wept, stretched her hands toward heaven, and said, "Do not let me be defiled, O Lord, for whose name I value chastity!"

----

the other hand, Prieur argues that the episode concerning idols appeared in the original *AA* and supplied the emperor's motivation for replacing Lesbius with Aegeates (*Acta Andreae*, 48-49).

69. I.e. Lesbius's wife.

70. Surely Lesbius abandoned his wife's bed because he adhered to Andrew's ascetic message (Prieur, *Acta Andreae*, 49).

Et statim apparuit ei angelus Domini, et iuvenis cecidit ante pedes eius et mortuus est. At illa confortata, benedicebat et glorificabat Dominum, qui non permiserat eam deludi. Sed postmodum in nomine Iesu Christi resuscitavit puerum, et omnis civitas cucurrit ad hoc spectaculum.

Uxor vero proconsulis abiit ad balneum cum procuratore suo. Cumque lavarentur simul, apparuit eis daemon teterrimus, a quo percussi ambo ceciderunt et mortui sunt. Et ecce planctus magnus factus est, et nuntiatum est apostolo et proconsuli, quod uxor eius cum lenone mortua erat.

Tunc beatus Andreas haec audiens, ait populo: Videte, dilectissimi, quantum praevalet inimicus, nam Trofime propter pudicitiam damnaverunt scorto. Nunc autem iudicium Dei adfuit, et ecce materfamilias, quae eam in lupanar poni iussit, cum lenone suo percussa in balneum, cecidit et mortua est.

Haec eo dicente, ecce advenit nutrix eius, quae prae senectute manibus deportabatur aliorum, scissis vestibus, cum clamore magno, et deposita coram apostolo, rogare coepit, dicens: Scimus, quia dilectus Dei es, et quaecumque petieris Deum tuum praestat tibi. Nunc autem miserere mei et resuscita illam.

Immediately an angel of the Lord appeared to the
youth, and he fell at the angel's feet and died. When she
had been comforted, she blessed and glorified the Lord who
had not allowed her to be abused. Later she raised the lad
in the name of Jesus Christ, and all the city ran to the
sight.[71]

The wife of the proconsul went off to the bath with
her pimp. While they were washing together, a hideous
demon appeared to them and beat them both such that they
fell and died. There was great wailing, and it was told to
the apostle and the proconsul that Lesbius's wife and the
pimp were dead.

When the blessed Andrew heard the news, he said to
the people, "Dear friends, see how the enemy prevails, for
they condemned Trophime to prostitution on account of
chastity.[72] But now God's judgment has arrived. Behold,
the pimp and the lady of the house who ordered Trophime
put in a brothel have been battered to death in the bath."

When he had said this, the lady's nurse arrived, who
because of old age was carried about in the arms of
others, her clothing ripped, crying loudly. She was placed
before the apostle and began to beg him, "We know that you
are beloved of God, and that whatever you ask your God he
accomplishes for you.[73] Now have mercy on me and raise
her."

----

71. Cf. *AJ* 63-86, esp. 82-83, where Drusiana raises to
    life a man who had violated her.

72. Prieur suggests that the chastity at issue is not that
    of Trophime but that of Lesbius (*Acta Andreae*, 49-50).

73. Cf. Mark 11:24, para. Matt 21:22, and John 14:13-14.

Condolens beatus apostolus super lacrimas mulieris, conversus ad proconsulem, ait: Vis, ut resuscitetur?

Cui ille: Absit, inquid, ut vivat, quae tantum flagitii commisit in domo mea.

Et apostolus: Noli, ait, sic agere; miserere enim nos oportet petentibus, ut misericordiam consequamur a Deo.

Haec eo dicente, perrexit proconsul ad praetorium; sanctus vero apostolus iussit corpus exhiberi in medium, et accedens, ait: Rogo, benigne domine Iesu Christe, ut resuscitetur haec mulier, et cognoscant omnes, quia tu es dominus Deus solus misericors et iustus, qui non pateris innocentes perire. Et conversus, tetigit caput mulieris, dicens: Surge in nomine Iesu Christi Dei mei.

Et statim surrexit mulier. Quae, d<e>misso vultu, flens et gemens, respiciebat in terram. Cui apostolus: Ingredere in cubiculum tuum et esto secretius orans, donec conforteris a Domino.

Cui illa respondit: Facito me prius cum Trofime pacificam, in qua tantum mali congessi.

Sanctus apostolus dixit: Noli timere, non enim meminit Trofimae malorum neque ultionem expectat, sed gratias agit Deo in omnibus quae accesserit[46] ei. Et vocata Trofimae, pacificavit eam[47] cum Calisto, uxore proconsulis, quae resuscitata erat.

Lysbius vero in tantum proficit in fide, ut quadam die accedens ad apostolum, omnia ei confiteretur peccata sua. Cui sanctus apostolus dixit: Gratias ago Deo, fili,

----

46. Some mss.: *acciderint* or *occiderunt*.

47. Some mss.: *eas*.

The blessed apostle, moved by the woman's tears, turned to the proconsul and said, "Do you want her revived?"

"Let her not live," he said, "for having committed such a scandal in my house!"

"Don't act like that," said the apostle, "for we should show mercy to those seeking it, so that we may obtain mercy from God."

When Andrew had said this, the proconsul went to the praetorium, and the holy apostle ordered the body displayed before everyone. He approached the body and said, "Kind Lord Jesus Christ, I ask that this woman be revived, and that all may know that you are the Lord God, who alone is merciful and just, who does not allow the innocent to perish." He turned around, touched the head of the woman and said, "Rise up in the name of Jesus Christ, my God."

Immediately the woman rose up, wept, moaned, hung her head, and looked at the ground. "Go to your room," the apostle told her, "and pray in secret until you are comforted by the Lord."

"Let me first make peace with Trophime," she replied, "on whom I have brought so much harm."

"Have no fear," said the holy apostle, "for Trophime does not hold these wicked acts against you nor does she seek revenge, but gives thanks to God for whatever happens to her." When Trophime was summoned, he reconciled her with Callisto, the proconsul's wife, who had been raised.

Lesbius so progressed in the faith that one day he came to the apostle to confess all his sins. The holy apostle told him, "I thank God, my son, that you fear the

quod times futurum iudicium. Sed viriliter age et
confortare in Dominum quem credis. Et tenens manum eis,
deambulabat in litore.[48]

24. Post deambulationem vero cum sedisset, sedebant
et singuli qui cum eo erant super arenam, audientes verbum
Dei. Et ecce cadaver e<v>ectum[49] in mari proiectum est
ante pedes apostoli in litore. Tunc sanctus Andreas
apostolus exultans in Domino, ait: Oportet hunc
resuscitari, ut cognoscamus, quid in eum adversarius est
operatus. Et fusa oratione, tenens manum mortui, erexit
illum, et statim revixit et loquebatur. Cumque nudus
esset, dedit ei tunicam, dicens: Dic nobis ordinem, expone
omnia quae contigerunt tibi.

----

48. *M* 7 (=*L* 36): ῾Ως δὲ ὄχλος ἱκανὸς παρενόχλησεν, καὶ ὁ
λόγος τοῦ μακαρίου ᾿Ανδρέα καὶ τὸ κήρυγμα αὐτοῦ
ἀκωλύτως εἰς πάντας διέδραμεν, ὁ δὲ καῖσαρ διάδοχον τῷ
Λεσβίῳ πέμψας παύει αὐτὸν τῆς ἀρχῆς. καὶ ὁ Λέσβιος
δεξάμενος τὸ πρόσταγμα τοῦ βασιλέως μετὰ χαρᾶς ἦλθεν
πρὸς τὸν μακάριον ᾿Ανδρέαν λέγων· νῦν μᾶλλον πιστεύσω
τῷ κυρίῳ ἀποδυσάμενος τὴν κενὴν δόξαν καὶ τὸ ἄνθος τοῦ
κόσμου ἀποθέμενος καὶ τὸν περισπασμὸν τοῦ βίου
ἀπορρίψας. δέξαι με οὖν συνέκδημόν σου, ἄνθρωπε τοῦ
θεοῦ· δέξαι με πιστὸν πιστῶς λαλοῦντα καὶ
διαμαρτυράμενον πᾶσιν ἀνθρώποις τὰ περὶ τοῦ κοινοῦ
σωτῆρος Χριστοῦ. καὶ καταλιπὼν τὸ πραιτώριον σὺν τῷ
᾿Ανδρέᾳ διῆγεν (*L* adds: ἐν πάσῃ τῇ τῆς ᾿Αχαΐας
περιχώρῳ συνεφεπόμενος αὐτῷ τὸ θεῖον κήρυγμα
καταγγέλλοντι).

49. Bonnet: *enectum.*

coming judgment. Be of courage and strong in the Lord in whom you believe." He took his hand and walked with him on the seashore.[74]

24. After the walk, while he was sitting, other individuals too would sit with him on the sand hearing the word of God, when a corpse that had rotted in the sea was thrown onto shore at the apostle's feet. Then the holy apostle rejoiced in the Lord and said, "This corpse should be resuscitated, so that we might learn what the enemy has done to him." After he had uttered a prayer,[75] he grabbed the dead man's hand, lifted him up, and immediately he came to life and began to speak. Because the man was nude, Andrew gave him a tunic and said, "Explain to us in detail all that happened to you."

----

74. The Greek witnesses say nothing about this episode with Trophime, but in *M* 7 (=*L* 36) one finds a passage referring to Lesbius's leaving Patras to travel with the apostle. The proconsul's motivation for this departure from Patras, according to *M*, was the emperor's sending of Aegeates to replace him. It is perhaps more likely that Aegeates did not come on the scene in the ancient *AA* until later in the story, as in *GE* (but see Prieur, *Acta Andreae*, 48-49). Here is the passage in *M*: "Because a great crowd was causing a disturbance, and because the word of the blessed Andrew and his preaching spread everywhere unresisted, the emperor sent a successor for Lesbius and terminated his rule. On receiving the imperial decree, Lesbius went with joy to the blessed Andrew and said, 'Now I will believe in the Lord even more, because I have shed vain glory, put off the pride of the world, and thrown aside the distraction of life. Therefore, O man of God, take me as your fellow traveler. Receive me as a devotee who speaks faithfully and witnesses to all people concerning our common savior, Christ.' Leaving the praetorium, he traveled with Andrew" (*L* adds: "touring all the territory of Achaea with the announcer of the divine preaching").

75. Presumably the original gave the content of the prayer.

At ille respondit: Nihil tibi occultabo, quicumque sis homo. Ego sum Sostrati filius civis Machedonis, qui nuper ab Italia adveni. Sed cum redissem ad propria, audivi doctrinam surrexisse novam, quam nullus hominum prius audivit, sed et signa prodigiaque ac medelas magnas fieri a quodam doctore, qui se veri Dei adfirmat esse discipulum. Ego autem, cum haec audissem, properavi, ut eum videre possim; non enim aliud arbitrabam, nisi ipse esset Deus qui talia ageret. Cumque navigarem cum pueris et amicis meis, subito orta tempestas, commoto mari, obpraessi fluctibus sumus. Et utinam simul proiecti fuissemus, ut et illi resuscitati fuissent a te sicut et ego!

Et haec dicens, volvebat multum in corde suo et arbitrabatur, quod ipse esset apostolus quem quaerebat. Et procidens ad pedes eius, ait: Scio, quia tu es famulus Dei veri. Rogo pro his qui mecum fuerunt, ut et ipsi, te inpertiente, vitam mereantur, ut cognoscant Deum verum, quem praedicas.

Tunc sanctus apostolus repletus Spiritu sancto, praedicabat ei constanter verbum Dei, ita ut miraretur puer super doctrina eius. Et expansis manibus, ait: Ostende, quaeso, domine, et reliquorum cadavera mortuorum, ut et ipsi cognoscant te Deum verum et solum.

Haec eo dicente, statim apparuerunt 30 et 9 corpora ad litus, unda famulante, devecta. Tunc, flente iuvene, omnes simul flere coeperunt, prostratique ante pedes apostoli, rogabant, ut et isti resuscitarentur. Sed et Philopater--hoc enim erat nomen pueri--dicebat: Genitor

"I will hide nothing from you, whoever you are," he said. "I am the son of Sostratus, a citizen of Macedonia, recently arrived from Italy. When I returned home I heard that a new teaching had arisen which no one had ever heard before, and that a certain teacher who asserts that he is a disciple of the true God performs signs, portents, and wondrous cures. When I heard these things, I hurried to see him, for I decided only this: that it was God himself who was doing such things. While I was sailing with my slaves and friends, a storm suddenly broke out, the sea was wild, and we were overcome by the turbulence. If only we had been thrown up on shore together, so that the others too might have been revived by you as I was!"

When he had said these things, he turned many things over in his mind[76] and decided that this person was the apostle whom he had sought. He fell at his feet and said, "I know that you are a servant of the true God. I entreat you for those who were with me, that they too may regain life with your help, so that they may know the true God whom you preach."

Then the holy apostle, full of the Holy Spirit, continuously preached to him the word of God, to the extent that the boy marveled at his teaching.[77] Then he raised his hands and said, "O Lord, I ask that you bring forth the rest of the corpses, that they too may know that you are the true and only God."

After he had said this, immediately thirty-nine corpses appeared on the shore, washed up by a cooperative wave. At the youth's weeping, everyone else began to weep, and falling at the apostle's feet they asked that these

----

76. Literally: heart.

77. Presumably the original Acts provided the content of this discourse.

meus per bonam voluntatem, inpositis necessariis, cum
magna pecunia misit me huc. Nunc autem, si audierit quae
mihi contigerunt, blasphemat Deum tuum et doctrinam eius
refutat. Sed absit, ut ita fiat.

Flentibus autem omnibus, rogavit apostolus, ut
congregarentur corpora simul; sparsim enim proiecta
fuerant. Congregatis igitur omnibus in unum, ait
apostolus: Quem vis prius resuscitare?

At ille dixit: Warum[50] conlactaneum meum.

Tunc flexis in terram genibus palmisque extensis ad
caelum, diutissime oravit, cum lacrimis dicens: Iesu bone,
resuscita hunc mortuum, qui cum Philopatore nutritus est,
ut cognoscat gloriam tuam, et magnificetur nomen tuum in
populis. Et statim surrexit puer, et admirabantur omnes
qui aderant.

Apostolus autem iterum super singulos orationem
fundens, ait: Quaeso, Domine Iesu, ut et isti resurgant,
qui de profundo aequoris sunt delati. Tunc iussit
fratribus, ut unusquisque tenens mortuum diceret:
Resuscitat te Iesus Christus, filius Dei vivi. Quod cum
factum fuisset, suscitati sunt 30 et 8, et glorificaverunt
Deum qui aderant, dicentes: Non est similis tibi, Domine.

Lysbius vero multa munera obtulit Philopatori,
dicens: Non te contristet amissio facultatum, nec recedas
a famulo Dei. Et erat semper cum apostolo, intendens
omnibus quae dicebantur ab eo.

----

50. Other mss.: *Wicharum* or *Waharam*; Greek probably Βᾶρος,
    from the Latin *Varus*.

too be revived. For his part, Philopater (this was the lad's name) said, "With good intentions my father laded the ship with necessities[78] and sent me here with much money. But now if he hears what has happened to me, he might blaspheme your God and suppress his teaching. May it not be so!"

As everyone wept, the apostle asked that the bodies be collected, for they had been scattered about. When all had been brought together, the apostle said, "Whom do you wish raised first?"

"Varus," he said, "my foster brother."

Then Andrew knelt to the ground, raised the palms of his hands to heaven, and prayed for a long time weeping, "Good Jesus, raise this dead man who was reared with Philopater, that he may know your glory and that your name may be magnified among the people."[79] Immediately the boy rose up, and all present were astonished.

The apostle again poured out prayer for each one of the others saying, "Lord Jesus, I ask that these who have been swept here from the depths of the sea also may rise again." Then he ordered each of the brothers to take a corpse and say, "Jesus Christ, the son of the living God, revives you." When this was done, the thirty-eight were aroused, and the spectators glorified God: "None is like you, O Lord."

Lesbius gave Philopater many gifts, saying, "Do not let the economic loss sadden you, and do not depart from

----

78. Or: "staffed the ship with my comrades."

79. The phrase "prayed for a long time" suggests the prayer in the original was much longer than the single sentence we find here in GE.

25. Erat enim mulier Caliopa nomine, quae homicidae coniuncta, conceptum suscipit inlicitum. Ubi vero tempus pariendi venit, artabatur doloribus magnis et partum proferre non poterat. Quae ait sorori suae: Vade, quaeso, et invoca Dianam deam nostram, ut misereatur mei. Ipse enim habet studium obstetricandi.

Faciente autem sorore quae sibi imperata fuerant, venit ad eam nocte diabolus, dicens: Quid me casso invocas, cum tibi nihil prodesse possim? Sed magis vade ad apostolum Dei Andream in Achaia, et ipse miserebitur sorori tuae.

Surrexit igitur mulier et venit ad apostolum et narravit ei omnia haec. At ille nihil moratus venit in Chorinthum ad domum mulieris aegrotantis; erat enim Lysbius proconsul cum eo. Videns vero beatus apostolus mulierem gravium dolorum cruciatu torqueri, ait: Recte haec pateris, quae male nupsisti, quae doloso concipiens, dolores intolerabiles sustines. Insuper consuluisti daemonia, quae neque ulli neque sibi prodesse possunt. Crede nunc Iesum Christum, filium Dei, et proice puerperium. Verumtamen mortuum egredietur quod indigne concepisti.

Credidit mulier, et egredientibus cunctis de cubiculo, proiecit partum mortuum; et sic a doloribus liberata est.

the servant of God." So he was continuously with the apostle, attentive to everything he said.

25. There was a woman named Caliope who had slept with a murderer and conceived out of wedlock. When the time for her delivery came, she had hard labor and was not able to deliver. She said to her sister, "Please go and invoke our goddess Diana[80] to take pity on me, for she is the deity of childbirthing."

When the sister did as she had been ordered, the devil came to her at night and said, "Why do you uselessly invoke me, since I am unable to help you? Go instead to Andrew the apostle of God in Achaea, and he will take pity on your sister."

So the woman arose and went to the apostle and told him everything. Without delay, he went to Corinth to the house of the suffering woman. Now then, Lesbius the proconsul was with him. When the blessed apostle saw the woman writhing from the tortures of hard labor, he said, "It is quite fitting that you suffer these pains! You endure intolerable torments because you married badly and conceived with a trickster. Furthermore, you consulted demons who cannot help anyone, not even themselves. Now believe in Jesus Christ, the son of God, and bring forth your infant, but the baby will be stillborn because you conceived it unworthily."

The woman believed, and when everyone had left the room, she birthed a dead baby. Thus was she relieved of her suffering.[81]

----

80. Greek: Artemis.

81. *AJPr* 115-16 tells a similar tale, presumably because it had been inspired by this section of the *AA*.

26. Cum autem multa signa et prodigia faceret beatus apostolus in Chorintho, Sostratus, pater Philopatoris, admonitus per visum, ut apostolum visitaret, venit in Achaia, et cum non invenisset eum, pervenit in Chorintho. Cumque cum Lysbio et aliis deambularet, cognovit eum Sostratus, sicut ei iam per somnium erat ostensus, complexusque pedes eius, ait: Miserere mei, quaeso, famulae Dei, sicut et filio meo misertus es.

Philopater autem ait apostolo: Hic est pater meus quem cernis. Nunc autem interrogat, quid eum oporteat agere.

Et beatus apostolus ait: Scio, quia pro cognoscenda veritate ad nos venerit. Gratias agimus Domino nostro Iesu Christo, qui se credentibus revelare dignatur.

Leontius autem, servus Sostrati, ait ad eum: Vides, domine, qua luce refulgeat vultus hominis huius?

Cui ille: Video, inquid, dilectissime, et ideo non discedamus ab eo, sed simul cum illo vivamus et audiamus verba vitae aeternae.

Et sequenti die obtulit apostolo munera multa; sanctus vero Dei dixit ad eum: Non est meum accipere aliud ex vobis, nisi vos ipsos lucri faciam, cum credideritis in Iesum, qui me misit euangelizare in hunc locum. Si pecuniam desiderassem, Lysbium diciorem repperissem, qui me multo ditare potuerat; nam vos in his conferte mihi, in quibus vobis proficiat ad salutem.

27. Post dies autem paucos iussit sibi balneum praeparari, et cum venisset lavandi gratia, vidit senem daemonium habentem et trementem valde. Quem dum admiraretur, alius puer adolescens egressus de piscina, procidit ad pedes apostoli, dicens: Quid nobis et tibi, Andreas? Venisti huc, ut destruas nos a sedibus nostris?

26. When the blessed apostle had done many signs and portents in Corinth, Sostratus, Philopater's father, was warned in a vision to visit the apostle. He went to Achaea, but when he did not find him, he went on to Corinth. As Andrew was walking with Lesbius and others, Sostratus recognized him, for he looked just like he had in the dream. Embracing his feet he said, "Please take pity on me, servant of God, as you took pity on my son."

Philopater told the apostle: "This man you see is my father. He now asks what he should do."

"I know," said the blessed apostle, "that he comes to us in order to know the truth. We thank our Lord Jesus Christ who deigns to reveal himself to those who believe."

Sostratus's slave Leontius said to him: "Master, do you see how the man's face shines with light?"

"I see, dear friend," said Sostratus, "and for that reason we should not separate from him, but let us live together with him and hear the words of eternal life."

On the next day, he offered the apostle many gifts, but God's saint told him, "I cannot accept anything from you, but I would make you yourselves my prize by your believing in Jesus who sent me to evangelize in this place. Had I desired money, I would have prevailed on the more opulent Lesbius who could make me exceedingly wealthy. Offer me instead whatever promotes your salvation."

27. A few days later he ordered a bath prepared for him, and when he went there to bathe, he saw an old man possessed of a demon trembling terribly. As he wondered at him, a young boy came from the pool, fell at the apostle's feet, and said, "What do we have to do with you, Andrew? Have you come here to drive us from our dwellings?"

Erectus autem, adstante populo, dixit apostolus:
Nolite timere, sed credite in Iesum salvatorem nostrum.

Clamantibus autem omnibus: Credimus quae praedicas.

Increpavit utrumque daemonem, et egressi sunt a
corporibus obsessis, dimissique vel senex vel adolescens,
redierunt ad propria sua.

Beatus vero apostolus lavans, disserebat, quia:
Inimicus generis humani ubique insidiatur, sive in
lavacris sive in fluminibus. Et idcirco nomen Domini
assidue invocandum erit, ut is qui vult insidiari non
habeat potestatem. Quod videntes viri civitatis, veniebant
et adferebant aegrotos, ponentes ante eum, et curabantur.
Sed et de aliis civitatibus veniebant cum infirmis, et
ipsi sanabantur et libenter audiebant verbum Dei.

28. Dum haec agerentur, ecce quidam senex Nicolaus
nomine, scissis vestibus, venit ad apostolum, dicens:
Famule Dei, ecce 74 anni sunt vitae meae, in quibus non
discessi ab inmunditiis et scorto ac fornicatione,
plerumque praeceps deductus ad lupanar, et exercebam
inlicita. Et nunc tertia dies est, in qua audivi miracula
quae agis et praedicationes tuas, quae sunt plenae verbis
vitalibus. Cogitabam enim mecum, ut, relicto hoc opere,
venirem ad te, ut mihi ostenderes meliora. Sed dum haec
cogitarem, veniebat mihi alius sensus, ut haec relinquerem
et non facerem bonum quod cogitabam. Luctante igitur
conscientia mea, accepi euangelium et oravi Dominum, ut
haec aliquando me faceret oblivisci. Post dies vero paucos

The apostle rose up and said to the bystanders, "Do not be afraid, but believe in Jesus our Savior."

"We believe what you preach," they all cried.

He rebuked each demon, and they deserted the haunted bodies. The old man and the youth were given leave and returned to their own homes.

As the blessed apostle bathed, he discoursed as follows: "The enemy of humankind lies in ambush everywhere, whether in baths or in rivers. For that reason one must continually invoke the name of the Lord, so that he who wants to ambush you will have no power." When the men of the city saw this, they left, brought back the sick and placed them before him. They were healed. People also came from other cities bringing the sick, and these too were healed and gladly heard the word of God.

28.[82] While this was going on, an old man named Nicolaus came to the apostle wearing torn clothing and saying, "Servant of God, I have lived for seventy-four years, and during this time I persisted in debauchery, prostitution, and fornication. Often I ran impulsively to the brothel and engaged in illicit sex. But two days ago I heard of the miracles you do and your speeches which are full of lifegiving words. I thought to myself that I would abandon my debauchery and come to you, in order that you show me a better course. But while I considered this, another feeling came over me, namely, that I should abandon and not do the good I had intended. Then, in a struggle of conscience, I took a Gospel and prayed to the Lord to make me forget these things once and for all. A few days later, when my perverse thoughts were inflamed, I

----

82. This episode apparently takes place in Sparta; see *GE* 29.

oblitus euangelii, quod super me erat, inflammante
cogitatione perversa, abii iterum ad lupanar. Et ecce
mulier meretrix videns me, ait: Egredere, senex, egredere;
angelus enim Dei es tu. Ne contingas me neque adpropinques
in hoc loco; video enim in te misterium magnum. Cumque ego
obstupefactus cogitarem quid hoc esset, recolui, quod
euangelium mecum habebam. Et conversus, veni ad te famulum
Dei, ut miserearis erroribus meis; spes enim mihi est
maxima, quod non peream, si oraveris pro humilitate mea.

Haec audiens beatus Andreas, cum multa contra
fornicatione deseruisset, prostratus genibus, expansis
manibus, tacitus orabat, emittens gemitus cum lacrimis ab
ora diei sexta usque in horam nonam. Surgens autem, abluta
facie, nihil accipere voluit, dicens: Non gustabo, donec
cognoscam, si miserebitur Deus huic homini, et si sit
reputandus inter salvatos. Et ieiunans altera die, nihil
ei revelatum est de homine usque ad quintum diem, in quo
flens vehementer, dicebat: Domine, pro mortuis obtinemus
pietatem tuam, et nunc iste, qui tua cognoscere desiderat
magnalia, cur non revertatur, ut sanes illum?

Haec eo dicente, vox de caelis delata est, dicens:
Obtines, Andreas, pro sene; sed sicut tu ieiuniis
fatigatus es, ita et ipse studeat ieiunium, ut salvetur.
Et vocans eum, praedicavit ei abstinentiam.

Die vero sexta vocavit suos et rogavit, ut orarent
universi pro eo. Qui prostrati solo, orabant dicentes:
Domine pie, misericors, remitte homini delictum suum. Quo
facto, et ipse gustavit et ceteros manducare permisit.

went again to a brothel unaware of the Gospel I had with me. A whore saw me and said, 'Get away, get away, old man, for you are an angel of God! Do not touch me or approach this place, for I see in you a great mystery.' Stupefied, I considered what this mystery might be, and I remembered that I had a Gospel with me. I spun around and came to you, servant of God, so that you may have pity on my vices. I have the greatest hope that I will not perish if you pray for my wretchedness."

When the blessed Andrew heard this, he spoke much against fornication,[83] knelt, stretched out his hands, prayed silently, uttered groans, and wept from the sixth hour to the ninth. Then he arose, washed his face, and desired to eat nothing: "I will not eat until I know if God will take pity on this man, and if he should be counted among the saved." He fasted the next day as well, and nothing was revealed to him about this man until the fifth day, on which he wept violently and said, "Lord, we obtain your mercy for the dead, so why is this man who desires to know your marvelous deeds not able to reform that you may heal him?"

When he had said this, a voice descended from heaven saying, "Andrew, you have obtained your request for the old man. But for him to be saved, he must fast until he is exhausted, just as you have." Andrew called the old man and preached abstinence.[84]

On the sixth day, he summoned his followers and asked them all to pray for Nicolaus. They prostrated themselves on the ground and prayed, "Kind, compassionate Lord,

----

83. The ancient *AA* here may have contained a speech on celibacy.

84. Here again *GE* seems to have deleted a discourse.

Nicolaus autem rediens ad domum suam, omnia quae habebat distribuit indigentibus; ipse quoque multum se excruciavit, ita ut per sex menses nihil aliud quam aquam acciperet et pane arido vesceretur. Exacta enim digna paenitentia, excessit a saeculo. Beatus autem apostolus non erat praesens, sed in loco quo erat vox ad eum facta est, dicens: Andreas, meus effectus est Nicolaus, pro quo depraecatus es. At ille gratias agens, narravit fratribus, Nicolaum excessisse de corpore, orans, ut in pace quiesceret.

29. (=*M* 8a [*L* 37]) In quo loco dum commoraretur, venit ad eum Antiphanes civis Megarinsis et ait ad eum: Si qua est in te bonitas iuxta praeceptum Salvatoris, quem praedicas, beate Andreas, nunc ostende et libera domum meam de insidia qua temptatur. Ecce enim valde turbata est.

Cui sanctus apostolus: Enarra, ait, nobis, homo, quae contigerit[51] tibi.

Et ille: Dum de itinere, inquid, reversus domui fuissem et ingrederem ianuam atrii mei, ecce audivi vocem ianitoris miserrime declamantem. Cumque interrogassem, quae essent haec voces, narraverunt mihi qui aderant, ipsum cum uxore et filio male a daemonio torqueri. Ascendens vero ad superiora domus, vidi alios pueros stridentes dentibus et in me impetum facientes et adridentes risos insanos. Quos cum praeterirem, ascendi iterum ad alia superiora, in qua coniux iacebat ab his verberata gravissime. Quae ita erat amentiae fatigatione turbata, ut, caesariem super oculos dimissam, neque aspicere neque me cognoscere possit. Hanc ergo, rogo, ut restituas mihi tantum, de ceteris vero curam non habeo.

----

51. Some mss.: *contigerint* or *contingerunt*.

forgive this man's offense." Once this was done, Andrew nibbled a bit and allowed the others to eat.

Nicolaus returned home and gave all his possessions to the poor. He so tortured himself that for six months he drank only water and ate only dry bread. Having performed the proper penance, he passed from this world. The blessed apostle was not present, but a voice came to him where he was, saying, "Andrew, Nicolaus, for whom you interceded, has become mine." He gave thanks, told the brethren that Nicolaus had departed from the body, and prayed that he might rest in peace.

29. When he was staying at that place,[85] Antiphanes, a citizen of Megara, came to him and said, "Blessed Andrew, if you have any of the kindness commanded by the Savior whom you preach, show it now and free my house from the calamity threatening it, for it is exceedingly troubled."

"Tell us, sir, what happened to you," said the apostle.

"When I returned home from a journey," said he, "I passed through the entrance to my atrium and heard the voice of my porter crying miserably. When I asked why, those present told me that he was severely tortured by a demon, along with his wife and son. When I went upstairs, I saw other servants grinding their teeth, attacking me, and laughing hysterically. I went past them up to the top floor where my wife was lying, having been badly battered by them. She was so disturbed, so weary with madness, hair falling in front of her eyes, that she could not see or recognize me. Her alone I ask you to restore to me; I'm not concerned about the others."

----

85. Sparta. See below.

Tunc sanctus apostolus misericordia motus, ait: Non
est enim acceptio personarum apud Deum, qui propterea
venit, ut cunctos salvos faceret pereuntes. Et ait: Eamus
ad domum eius.

Cumque procedens a Lachedaemone venisset in Megara,
ingressi sunt ianuam domus, et statim omnes daemones unius
vocis impetu clamaverunt, dicentes: Ut quid nos hic,
Andreas sanctae, persequeris? Ut quid domum non tibi
concessam adis? Quae tua sunt posside, quae nobis concessa
sunt ne adicias penetrare.

Sed sanctus apostolus nimis de his admirans, ascendit
in cubiculum quo mulier decubabat, et facta oratione,
adpraehensam manum eius, ait: Sanat te Dominus Iesus
Christus. Et statim surrexit mulier a lectulo et
benedicebat Deum. Similiter et singulis quibusque qui a
daemonio vexabantur inponens manum, sanitati restituit
habuitque deinceps Anthiphanem et uxorem eius firmissimos
adiutores ad praedicandum verbum Dei.

Καὶ ὅραμα ἐν τούτοις βλέπει ὁ μακάριος ᾿Ανδρέας·
ἔδοξεν τὸν σωτῆρα Χριστὸν ἑστάναι ἄντικρυς αὐτοῦ καὶ
λέγοντα αὐτῷ· ᾿Ανδρέα ἐπίθες τὸ πνεῦμα ἐπὶ τὸν Λέσβιον καὶ

Then, moved with compassion, the holy apostle said, "There is no respect of persons with God,[86] who came in order to save all the lost." He said, "Let us go to his house."

He left Lacedaemon, came to Megara, and passed through the entrance to the house. Immediately all the demons cried out with the fury of a single voice, "Holy Andrew, why do you persecute us here? Why are you in a house not given to you? Occupy those houses which are yours, but do not in addition infiltrate those given to us."

The holy apostle was astonished at them, and went upstairs to the bedroom where the woman lay. After he prayed, he took her hand and said, "May the Lord Jesus Christ heal you."[87] Immediately the woman got up from the cot and blessed God. In the same manner, he laid hands on each one who had been harassed by a demon, restored them to health, and accepted Antiphanes and his wife as exceptionally strong associates for preaching the word of God.[88]

The blessed Andrew then saw a vision. It seemed that the savior Christ stood before him telling him, "Andrew, place the Spirit on Lesbius and give him your grace. Take

----

86. Cf. Acts 10:34, Rom 2:11, Gal 2:6, Eph 6:9, and Col 3:25.

87. Cf. Acts 9:34.

88. An Antiphanes also appears in Passion 15, whom Prieur suggests is one and the same as the Antiphanes here in *GE* 29 (*Acta Andreae*, 638, n. 29.1). Inasmuch as *GE* does not contain the following passage, one cannot be certain that this section actually appeared in the ancient *AA*.

δὸς αὐτῷ τῆς χάριτός σου· καὶ ἄρας τὸν σταυρόν σου ἀκολούθει μοι· αὔριον[52] γὰρ ἐκβαλῶ σε ἐκ τοῦ κόσμου· σπεῦδε ἐν Πάτραις. διυπνισθεὶς δὲ ὁ ἀπόστολος τὴν ὄψιν τοῦ ὁράματος τοῖς παροῦσιν ἐγνώρισεν· καὶ τὸ τέλος ἐξεδέχετο τοῦ λόγου.[53]

30. (=E 244D-245B, L 33 and 38)[54] [Εἰσῆλθε δὲ ὁ Ἀνδρέας μετὰ τῶν μαθητῶν αὐτοῦ, καὶ προσελάβετο αὐτοὺς ἀνὴρ ὀνόματι Σώσιος, ὃν ἰάσατο Ἀνδρέας ἀπὸ ἀσθενείας θανατικῆς.[55] διερχόμενος δὲ τὴν πόλιν εἶδεν ἄνθρωπον ἐρριμένον ἐπὶ τῆς κοπρίας παραλελυμένον· καὶ προσελθὼν αὐτῷ ὁ Ἀνδρέας, δούς τε αὐτῷ χεῖρα ἀνέστησε τῇ ἐπικλήσει τοῦ Χριστοῦ.[56]

Καὶ τούτου διαφημισθέντος Μαξιμίλλα, ἡ γυνὴ ἀνθυπάτου, ἔπεμψε τὴν πιστὴν αὐτῆς Ἐφιδαμίαν, ἱκανὴν

---

52. Perhaps: τάχιον, cf. L.

53. *M* continues: Καὶ ἰδού τις εἰσπηδήσας τῷ ἀποστόλῳ λέγει· ὁ Αἰγεάτης ὁ τὴν ἀνθυπατείαν ἐγκεχειρισμένος, ὁ ἀποσταλεὶς παρὰ τοῦ Καίσαρος, ἐνετεύχθη εἰς τὰ μέρη τῆς Ἀχαΐας παρά τινων δούλων τοῦ διαβόλου κακῶν καὶ ἐχθρῶν ἀνθρώπων. *L:* καὶ καθὼς προσετέτακτο ποιήσας αὐθημερὸν ταῖς Πάτραις παρουσιάζει.

54. The reconstruction of the following four stories is eclectic due to the wide divergences in the extant versions. Square brackets in the text and *italics* in the translation indicate passages found only in the Greek versions (*E* and *L*). Passages only in *GE* appear in **bold** in the translation. When possible, the text printed represents agreements between *GE* and one of the Greek witnesses. When *GE* is absent and *E* and *L* disagree, *E* usually gets the nod.

55. *L* 33: ἐν Πάτραις δὲ πόλει τῆς Ἀχαΐας εἰσελθὼν μετὰ τῶν σὺν αὐτῷ μαθητῶν κατήχθη ξενισθεὶς παρά τινι τῆς αὐτῆς πόλεως οἰκήτορι Σοσσίῳ τοὔνομα· ὃν παρ' ἐλπίδας ἰάσατο περισωσάμενο<ν> ἐκ νόσου θανατηφόρου. Cf. *E* 244D.

56. *GE: Veniens vero beatus apostolus Patras civitate, in qua proconsul Egeas erat, qui nuper Lysbio successerat.*

up your cross and follow me,[89] for tomorrow[90] I will cast
you from the world. Hasten to Patras." On awaking, the
apostle disclosed to those with him the seeing of the
vision, and he awaited the completion of the word.[91]

30. *Andrew and his disciples entered (Patras), and a
man named Sosius, whom Andrew healed of a terminal
illness, received them.*[92] *As he walked about the city, he
saw a paralytic thrown on a dungheap. Andrew approached
him, gave him his hand, and raised him up by calling on
Christ.*[93]

*As reports of the healing circulated, Maximilla, the
proconsul's wife, sent her faithful servant Iphidama, who*

----

89. Cf. Mark 8:34, para. Matt 16:24, Luke 9:23, and Matt
    10:38, para. Luke 14:27.

90. Or: "soon."

91. *M* continues: "Then someone burst in upon the apostle
    and said, 'The Emperor sent Aegeates to administer the
    proconsulship, and wicked slaves of the devil, enemies
    of humankind, have introduced him into the regions of
    Achaea.'" *L*: "Doing as he had been ordered, he arrives
    in Patras that very day." Prieur suggests that a
    Coptic fragment in the Bodleian Library might provide
    clues concerning the content of this vision (*Acta
    Andreae*, 50; in this volume see 444-49.)

92. This unexpected appearance of Sosius requires some
    explaining. According to *E* and *L*, Sosius hosted Andrew
    when the apostle first returned to Patras; *L* 33: "He
    and the disciples with him disembarked and entered
    Patras, an Achaean city, and were entertained by a
    certain resident of the city named Sosius, whom Andrew
    healed quite remarkably and who thus escaped a deadly
    illness" (cf. *E* 244D; see Excursus G). The references
    to Sosius in *GE*, *E*, and *L* suggest that he played a
    larger role in the original, which probably narrated
    his healing more expansively than in a relative
    clause.

93. *GE*: "Then the blessed apostle came to the city of
    Patras, where Aegeates was proconsul, having recently
    succeeded Lesbius."

οὖσαν ἰδεῖν καὶ λαλῆσαι καὶ ἀκοῦσαι τοῦ ᾿Ανδρέου. ἐλθοῦσα δὲ ἡ ᾿Εφιδαμία κατήντησε τὸν Σώσιον, μαθητὴν τοῦ ᾿Ανδρέου, πρὸς ὃν ἐξενίζετο. ὁ δὲ κατήχησεν αὐτὴν τὸν λόγον τοῦ θεοῦ καὶ τὴν ἰδίαν ἴασιν.]⁵⁷ καὶ εἰσήγαγεν αὐτὴν πρὸς τὸν ᾿Ανδρέαν καὶ πεσοῦσα εἰς τοὺς πόδας αὐτοῦ [ἤκουσε τῶν λόγων αὐτοῦ· καὶ ἀπήγγειλε πρὸς τὴν κυρίαν αὐτῆς.

Μεθ᾿ ἡμέρας δέ τινας ἠσθένησε Μαξιμίλλα, ἡ γυνὴ τοῦ ἀνθυπάτου. καὶ τῶν ἰατρῶν ἀποκαμόντων ἀπογνωσθεῖσα ἀπέστειλε τὴν ᾿Εφιδαμίαν καὶ προσκαλεῖται τὸν ᾿Ανδρέαν.] Ait: Andreas sanctae, rogat te domina mea Maximilla, quae magnis febribus retenetur, ut accedas ad eam, libenter enim vult audire doctrinam tuam. Nam et proconsul, coniux eius, stat ante lectulum, flens gladiumque in manu tenens, ut, cum illa spiritum ex<h>alaverit, iste se mucrone perfodeat.

῾Ο δὲ συνῆλθεν αὐτῇ μετὰ τῶν μαθητῶν αὐτοῦ. καὶ εἰσελθὼν ad cubiculum in quo mulier iacebat incommoda,⁵⁸ εὗρε τὸν ἀνθύπατον κρατοῦντα μάχαιραν [καὶ ἐκδεχόμενον τὸν θάνατον τῆς ἑαυτοῦ γυναικός, βουλόμενον ἑαυτὸν ἀνελεῖν,⁵⁹ συνθνηξόμενον αὐτῇ. ὁ δὲ ᾿Ανδρέας πραείᾳ τῇ φωνῇ εἶπε πρὸς αὐτόν·] Nihil tibi nunc mali feceris. ἀπόστρεψον τὴν μάχαιραν, τέκνον, εἰς τὸν τόπον αὐτῆς. Erit enim tempus, quando ad nos exerendus erit.⁶⁰ Sed nihil intellegens praesis, dedit accendi locum.

----

57. *GE: et accessit ad eum quaedam mulier Efidama nomine, quae ex doctrina Sosiae cuiusdam apostolici discipuli iam conversa fuerat.*

58. *E*: εἰς τὴν οἰκίαν.

59. *L* adds: ἐκείνης θνησκούσης.

60. *E*: καὶ ἐπικάλεσαι κύριον τὸν θεὸν τοῦ οὐρανοῦ καὶ τῆς γῆς πιστεύσας αὐτῷ. Similarly *L*, which adds: κἀκεῖνος εἰστήκει σιωπῶν καὶ μηδὲν ἀποκρινόμενος.

was worthy to see, speak with, and hear Andrew. When Iphidama left, she met Sosius, Andrew's disciple, from whom he received hospitality. He instructed her in the word of God and in divine healing.[94] When he brought her to Andrew she fell at his feet *and listened to his words. Then she told her mistress.*

A few days later, Maximilla, the proconsul's wife took sick. Despairing of the physicians who proved useless, she sent Iphidama and summoned Andrew. **"Holy Andrew," Iphidama said, "my mistress Maximilla, who is suffering from a high fever, asks you to come to her, for she eagerly desires to hear your teaching. Her husband the proconsul stands at the cot weeping and wielding a sword in his hand, so that when she expires he can stab himself with the blade."**

He and his disciples went with her and entered **the bedroom where the unfortunate woman lay.**[95] He found the proconsul clasping a sword *and awaiting his wife's demise, wishing to do away with himself so as to die with her.*[96] *Andrew spoke to him softly,* **"Do yourself no harm.**[97] Put your sword back in its scabbard, child,[98] **for a time will come when it will be drawn against us."**[99] **The ruler understood nothing, but allowed him to pass.**

----

94. *GE*: "A certain woman named Iphidama came to him, who already had been converted through the teaching of Sosius, an apostolic disciple."

95. *E*: "the house."

96. *L* adds: "if she should die."

97. Cf. Acts 16:28.

98. Cf. Matt 26:52.

99. *E*: "and call on the Lord, the God of heaven and earth believing in him." *L* adds: "And he stood there dumbfounded, making no reply."

Tunc apostolus veniens ante lectum infirmae,
[ἐπετίμησε δὲ τῷ πυρετῷ λέγων· ἀπόστηθι ἀπ' αὐτῆς, ὁ
πυρετός.] καὶ ἐπέθηκεν ἐπ' αὐτῇ τὰς χεῖρας, καὶ εὐθέως
ἵδρωσεν, et discessit ab ea febris. καὶ μετ' ὀλίγον
ἐζήτησε φαγεῖν.[61] ἐδίδου δὲ αὐτῷ ὡς centum argenteos[62]
εἰπών· λάβε τὸν μισθόν σου.

'Ο δὲ οὐκ ἀπεδέξατο εἰπῶν, [ἡμεῖς δωρέαν ἐλάβομεν,
δωρέαν δίδομεν. προσένεγκε δὲ μᾶλλον, εἰ δύνασαι, σεαυτὸν
τῷ θεῷ.[63]

31. (=E 245C, L 39) Ἐκεῖθέν τε ἐξελθόντες [ὁ
μακάριος ὑπεστηρίζετο παρὰ τῶν οἰκείων μαθητῶν κεκμηκὼς
ὑπὸ τοῦ γήρως.][64] καὶ ὁρᾷ τινα [εἰς τὸν ἔμβολον][65]
κατακείμενον [καὶ προσαιτοῦντα, ὅστις εἶχε χρόνους πολλοὺς
παραλυτικῶς]. Cui multi e civibus stipem porrigebant, unde
alimentum haberet. καὶ λέγει αὐτῷ ὁ Ἀνδρέας· ἰαταί σε
Ἰησοῦς ὁ Χριστός. [καὶ ἔδωκεν αὐτῷ χεῖρα· εὐθέως δὲ
ἐγένετο ὑγιὴς ὁ ἄνθρωπος, καὶ ἔτρεχε διὰ μέσης τῆς πόλεως,
δεικνύων ἑαυτὸν καὶ] δοξάζων τὸν θεόν.

32. (=E 245C, L 40) Καὶ προβὰς ἐκεῖθεν εἶδεν ἄνδρα
μετὰ γυναικὸς καὶ παιδίου τυφλούς, et ait: Vere diaboli

----

61. *E* continues: καὶ παραχρῆμα ἠγέρθη. τοῦτο θεωρήσαντες
    πολλοὶ ἐπίστευσαν. ὁ δὲ Αἰγεάτης ὡς ἰατρῷ προσεῖχε τῷ
    Ἀνδρέᾳ· ἦν γὰρ Ἕλλην, καὶ οὐκ ἤθελε τὸν λόγον τοῦ
    θεοῦ ἀκούειν. *L*: καὶ ῥωσθεῖσα παρ' ἐλπίδας ἀνέστη
    δοξάζουσα τὸν θεόν. πολλοί τε τῶν τεθεωμένων τὸ
    παράδοξον τῆς ἰάσεως ἐπίστευσαν ἐπὶ τὸν κύριον· ὁ δὲ
    ἀνθύπατος ἑλληνικαῖς πλάναις ἐξαπατώμενος οὐκ ἠνείχετο
    τῶν θείων λογίων ἀκούειν.

62. *E*: χιλίους χρυσοῦς. *L*: χιλίους χρυσίνους.

63. So *E*. *L*: οὗτος ὁ μισθὸς παρὰ σοὶ μενέτω· σοῦ γάρ ἐστιν
    ἄξιος· ὁ δὲ ἐμὸς μισθὸς ἐν τάχει πρὸς ἐμὲ ἐπελεύσεται,
    λέγων τοῦτο περὶ τῆς Μαξιμίλλης.

64. *E*: ὑπεβάσταζον τὸν Ἀνδρέαν· ἦν γὰρ πρεσβύτης.

65. *GE*: stercore.

The apostle then went to the sick woman's cot *and rebuked the fever saying, "Fever, leave her alone!"* He placed his hands on her, and immediately she broke into a sweat, **and the fever left her.** A little later she wanted to eat.[100] Aegeates offered him **one hundred silver coins**[101] *and said, "Take your pay."*

Andrew refused to take anything, *saying, "We received a gift, we give a gift. Rather, offer yourself to God, if you can."*[102]

31. Leaving there, *the blessed one, weary with old age, was propped up by his own disciples,*[103] and he saw someone who had been paralyzed for a long time lying *inside the portico*[104] begging. **Many of the citizens used to give him a pitance for his food.** Andrew says to him, "Jesus the Christ heals you!" *He gave him his hand, and at once the man became well. He ran through the middle of the city showing himself off* and glorifying God.

32. As he went on from there, he saw a man with his wife and son, all blind, **and he said, "Truly this is the**

----

100. *E* continues: "and immediately she arose. Many who saw this believed. But Aegeates, being Greek, mistook Andrew for a doctor, and was unwilling to hear the word of God." *L*: "Having been strengthened beyond expectation, she rose up and glorified God. Many of those who saw the incredible healing believed on the Lord, but the proconsul, beguiled by Greek errors, would not allow himself to hear the divine oracles."

101. *E* and *L* inflate Aegeates' generosity to "one thousand gold coins."

102. So *E*. *L*: "'Retain this reward, for it is worthy of you. My reward will come to me quickly,' by which he meant Maximilla." This story in *GE* is similar to *ATh* 82–89.

103. *E*: "they propped Andrew up, for he was old."

104. *GE*: "in feces."

hoc est opus. Ecce enim quos et mente caecavit et corpore.
Et ait: Ecce ego vobis in nomine Dei mei Iesu Christi
corporalium oculorum restituo lumen; ipse quoque mentium
vestrarum tenebras reserare dignetur, ut, cognita luce,
quae inluminat omnem hominem venientem in hunc mundum,
salve esse possitis. καὶ ἥψατο τῶν ὀφθαλμῶν αὐτῶν, καὶ
εὐθέως ἀνέβλεψαν, καὶ κατεφίλουν τοὺς πόδας αὐτοῦ,
[δοξάζοντες καὶ εὐχαριστοῦντες τὸν θεόν. θεωροῦντες δὲ
ὄχλοι ἐξεπλήσσοντο θαυμάζοντες, καὶ πολλοὶ ἐπίστευον.]66

33. (=E 245C-D, L 41)67 Καί τινες προσελθόντες
παρεκάλουν αὐτῷ μὴ ὀκνῆσαι καὶ μέχρι τοῦ λιμένος
παραγενέσθαι· ἄνδρα γάρ τινα [τῶν ἀρχαίων εὐγενῆ τε καὶ
περιφανῆ ὁλόξηρον καὶ εἰδεχθῆ ὑπὸ λέπρας γεγονότα καὶ
δυσωδίας πλείστης ἀπόζοντα ἔλεγον ἐπὶ κοπρίας ἐρρῖφθαι·
ᾧπερ οἱ παριόντες ψωμοὺς ὡς κυνὶ προσρίπτουσιν, οὐ
τολμῶντες αὐτῷ προσεγγίσαι ὅλως ἡλκωμένῳ·68 καὶ γὰρ ὅλαι
αἱ Πάτραι] πολλάκις ἰατροῖς πολλὰ ὑπέσχοντο δώσειν ὅπως
ἰαθῇ, διὰ τὸ ναυάρχου τινὸς υἱὸν ἐνδόξου παρ' αὐτοῖς
γεγενῆσθαι· ἀλλ' οὐκ ἴσχυσεν ὑπ' οὐδενὸς παραμυθίας τινὸς
κἂν γοῦν μικρᾶς ἐπιτυχεῖν.

----

66. *GE*: *et dicebant, quia: Non est alius Deus nisi quem
praedicat famulus eius Andreas.*

67. The text printed here comes basically from *L*, which
shares many readings with *E* and *GE* that they do not
share with each other. Of the three versions of this
story, *L* appears to be closest to the original, either
because the author had independent access to the
ancient Acts, or because he knew a more expansive
version of *E* than those now extant, or because the
source he shared with *M* contained this passage. See
Prieur, *Acta Andreae*, 50-51.

68. *E* adds: ἀλλ' ὅταν προσφέρωσιν αὐτῷ τὴν τροφήν, τὰς
ῥῖνας αὐτῶν κρατοῦντες, ταχέως ἀναχωροῦσιν.

work of the devil, for he has blinded them in mind and body." To them he said, "In the name of my God, Jesus Christ, I restore to you the light of your physical eyes. He also deigns to unlock the darkness of your minds, so that you may be saved by recognizing the light which illumines everyone who comes into this world."[105] He touched their eyes, and immediately they received their sight and kissed his feet, *glorifying and thanking God. When the crowd saw this, they were struck with astonishment, and many believed.*[106]

33. Some people came to him and asked him not to recoil from going also to the harbor, for they said that there, thrown on a dungheap, was a certain man, *one of the ancients, of noble pedigree and renown, who had become shriveled and hideous with leprosy and who reeked with stench. "Passers-by throw scraps to him as to a dog, not daring to approach anyone so utterly ulcerated.*[107] Time *and again all of Patras* has offered to give handsome sums to physicians to heal him, because he was the son of one of their celebrated fleet commanders, but he was unable to get even the slightest relief from any of them."

----

105. Cf. John 1:9.

106. *GE*: "and they said, 'There is no other God but the one whom his servant Andrew preaches.'"

107. *E* adds: "When they bring him food they hold their noses and leave quickly."

Ταῦτα ἀκούσας ὁ 'Ανδρέας,[69] σπλαγχνισθεὶς πρὸς αὐτὸν
παραγίνεται· [πολλοί τε τῶν τοῦ ὄχλου συνῆλθον αὐτῷ, τὸ
μέλλον συμβαίνειν ἱστορήσοντες. καὶ προσελθὼν αὐτῷ μόνος,
μηδενὸς ὑπομένοντος τῆς δυσώδους ἀποφορᾶς ἀνασχέσθαι,
εἶπεν αὐτῷ· ἧκον πρός σε ἵνα σε ἰάσωμαι διὰ τοῦ ἐμοῦ
ἰατροῦ.

Κἀκεῖνος ἀπεκρίνατο· μή τι φίλε ὁ σὸς ἰατρὸς θεός
ἐστιν, οὐ γὰρ ἄνθρωπος; ἀνθρώπων γάρ με οὐδείς ἐστιν ὁ
ἰώμενος.

Καὶ ὁ 'Ανδρέας εἶπεν αὐτῷ· ὄντως σῳζόμενόν σε
καταμανθάνω· ἄρτι γάρ σοι ὁ θεὸς παρέσται ἀνιστῶν σε
ἐντεῦθεν, φωναῖς ὑπ' ἐμοῦ καλούμενος ὁραταῖς. τῶν δὲ φωνῶν
τὴν δύναμιν ἐν ἑαυτῷ ὄψει ὑγιὴς βαδίζων ἅμα ἐμοί.

Καὶ εἰπὼν ταῦτα πρὸς τὸν νοσοῦντα, ἔκπληκτον
γενόμενον ἐπὶ τῇ ὑποσχέσει αὐτοῦ, προσηύξατο·] καὶ μετὰ
τὴν εὐχὴν ἀποδύει τὸν ἀσθενῆ πάντα ὅσα ἠμφίεστο ῥακία,
σεσηπότα καὶ αὐτὰ ἀπὸ τῶν πολλῶν ἑλκῶν καὶ ἀποτροπαίων τοῦ
πρεσβύτου ἀποστάζοντα ὑγρῶν· ὧν πεσόντων εἰς γῆν σκώληκες
πολλοὶ τὸν τόπον ἐπλήρωσαν. [ἦν οὖν πάνυ ὀλιγοστὸν τὸ ἀπὸ
γῆς ἔνθα κατέκειτο οὗτος ἐπὶ θάλασσαν διάστημα·] ἐκέλευσεν
οὖν αὐτῷ ἀναστάντα βαδίσαι ἅμα αὐτῷ. [κἀκεῖνος δυνάμει τῇ
τοῦ κυρίου ἀναστὰς μηδὲ ὑπό τινος κρατούμενος συνάψει τῷ
ἀποστόλῳ, πολλῶν ὑγρῶν ἀπορεόντων αὐτοῦ καὶ τοῦ παντὸς
σώματος μυδῶντος, ὡς καὶ τὸν τόπον καθ' ὃν ἐβάδιζε
διάβροχον γίνεσθαι καὶ ὁρᾶσθαι τοῦτον προδήλως ὑπὸ πάντων·
τοσαύτη γὰρ ἦν ἡ τῶν ὑγρῶν ἀπορροή.]

'Ως δὲ ἐγένοντο ἀμφότεροι εἰς τὴν θάλασσαν, εἶπεν
πάλιν πρὸς αὐτὸν ὁ ἀπόστολος· ἄρτι σου τὸ σῶμα ἀπολούω,
ὅπως τοῦτο ὑγιὲς καταστῇ· τὴν γὰρ ψυχήν σου δι' ἑαυτοῦ
λούσεις. καὶ ἄρας αὐτὸν καθῆκεν εἰς τὴν θάλασσαν καὶ
ἀνήγαγεν αὐτὸν εὐθέως ὅλον ὑγιῆ τῇ χάριτι τοῦ κυρίου, μήτε

----

69. L: ὁ συμπαθέστατος μύστης Χριστοῦ.

When Andrew[108] heard this, he was moved to compassion and went to him. *Many of those in the crowd went with him, inquisitive about what would happen, but because no one else could tolerate the efflux of stench, only Andrew approached the man.* "I have come to you," Andrew told him, "so that I might heal you through my physician."

"Friend," he said, "is your physician divine or human? No human can heal me."

"I detect that you are truly being saved," Andrew told him, "for even now God is present with you to raise you up from here, for I have called to him with visible sounds. You will see in yourself the power of the sounds, for you will walk with me healed."

When he had said this to the sick man, who was shocked by Andrew's promise, the apostle prayed, and after prayer he stripped the invalid of all the rags he was wearing, which were putrid and dripping with pus from the old man's many revolting sores. As the rags dropped to the earth, many maggots filled the spot. *There was a short distance between the ground where he was lying and the sea,* and Andrew commanded him to get up and walk with him. *By the Lord's power, he stood up without any assistance and went off with the apostle, as large quantitites of pus dribbled from him and as his entire body oozed. So abundant was the flow of pus that wherever he walked there was a trail of moisture clearly visible to everyone.*

When they both got to the sea, the apostle again spoke to him: "Now I wash your body so that it might be made well. You yourself will wash your soul." He lifted him up, brought him into the sea, and brought him out. By the Lord's grace, the man immediately became whole,

----

108. *L:* "Christ's most compassionate initiate."

σπιλάδα ἔχοντα ἐν τῷ σώματι [μήτε ἕλκος μήτε τραῦμα μήτε
οὐλήν, ἀλλά τινα ἐρρωμένον, καὶ εἰλικρινὲς σῶμα ἔχοντα· ὃν
ἰδόντες πάντες ἔκθαμβοι ἐγένοντο καὶ φωναῖς μεγίσταις παρὰ
τὸν αἰγιαλὸν ἐδόξαζον τὸν θεόν, ὡς εὐθέως ἀκουσθῆναι τὸ
γενόμενον τῷ ἀνθυπάτῳ.

Τοῦ δὲ ἀποστόλου κελεύσαντος ἱμάτιον αὐτῷ δοθῆναι, τῇ
χαρᾷ ἐπαρθεὶς ὁ πρὶν παρειμένος καὶ ἀσθενὴς οὐκ ἠνέσχετο,]
ἀλλὰ γυμνὸς βοῶν ἔτρεχε διὰ μέσης τῆς πόλεως, [ὅπως αὐτὸν
ἴδωσιν οἱ πρὶν ἐπιστάμενοι, ὁποῖον ἠπίσταντο καὶ ὁποῖος
ἐγεγόνει· καὶ ἀνελθὼν εἰς τὴν ἀγορὰν αὐτῶν ἐκραύγαζεν·
εὐχαριστῶ σοι θεὲ τῷ πέμψαντί μοι τὸν σὸν ἄνθρωπον·
εὐχαριστῶ σοι τῷ ἐλεήσαντί με, ὃν πᾶς ἄνθρωπος ἀπήλπισε,
σὺ δὲ μόνος ἐπεσπλαγχνίσθης· ᾧ οὐδεὶς ἐτόλμα προσελθεῖν,
νῦν δὲ πάντες προσέρχονται εἰς δόξαν τὴν σήν. καὶ πολλὰ
λέγων τοιαῦτα γυμνὸς ὢν μόλις ἠνέσχετο ἐλθόντος τοῦ
ἀποστόλου καὶ ἐπιτιμήσαντος αὐτῷ ἐνδύσασθαι. δεξάμενος οὖν
τὰ ἱμάτια καὶ ἐνδυσάμενος ἠκολούθει τῷ ἀποστόλῳ· ὃν πάντες
ἑώρων ὑγιῆ γεγενημένον καὶ κατεπλήττοντο.]

without a blemish on his body--*no ulcer, no wound, no scar*--but was vibrant and had a pure body. *Everyone who saw him was amazed and glorified God with loud voices at the beach, with the result that the proconsul heard right away what had happened.*

Just when the apostle commanded him to be given clothes, the one who earlier had been neglected and weak was now so transported by joy that he did not want to take them, but ran through the city naked and screaming, so that his prior acquaintances could contrast what they had known him to be with what he had become. He went to their agora and shouted: "I thank you, O God who sent your man to me! I thank you, you who had mercy on me! Everyone had given up hope for me, but you alone showed compassion. No one dared to draw near to me, but now all draw near to your glory." As he was speaking many such things, stark naked, he still hesitated taking the clothing until the apostle arrived and scolded him to get dressed. When he had taken the garments and dressed himself, he followed the apostle. Everyone saw that he had become well and they were astounded.

Part Three:

THE PASSION OF ANDREW

INTRODUCTION TO PART III

Prior to Prieur's edition, all publications of the passion of Andrew relied on Flamion's reconstruction, which he pieced together from *N*, *E*, *M*, *L* (all of which are treated in the Introduction to Part II) a Greek martyrdom conventionally known as *Martyrium alterum* (*Ma* [*BHG* 97-98]),[1] *Vaticanus gr. 808* (*V* [*BHG* 95], an extensive Greek fragment),[2] and two Latin passions, *l'Épître* (*Ep* [*BHG* 94 and *BHL* 428], sixth century)[3] and *Conversante et docente* (*Cd* [*BHL* 429], sixth century).[4] Flamion also drew

----

1. *AAA* 2.1:58-64. Bonnet used two manuscripts (eleventh and fourteenth centuries) that represent two divergent recensions.

2. *AAA* 2.1:38-45, tenth or eleventh centuries.

3. *AAA* 2.1:1-37. Although *Ep* also exists in two independent Greek versions (*Ep*gr.1 and *Ep*gr.2), Bonnet has shown that this passion was composed in Latin ("La passion d'André en quelle langue a-t-elle été écrit?" *ByZ* 3 [1894]: 458-69). One of the Greek translations, however, incorporates readings from a Greek passion that seems to have been very close to the original (*Ep*gr.2). Bonnet's Latin text derives from twelve manuscripts from the eighth to the twelfth centuries; *Ep*gr.1 derives from four manuscripts from the eleventh to sixteenth; *Ep*gr.2 from nine manuscripts from the tenth to the sixteenth.

4. Maximillian Bonnet, *Acta Andreae*, 66-70. This edition, based on five manuscripts from the ninth to the twelfth centuries, first appeared in *AnBoll* 13 (1894): 374-78.

on two notices from Evodius of Uzala that allude to content not expressed in the witnesses listed above.[5]

New manuscript discoveries and renewed attention to the Armenian passion render Flamion's reconstruction entirely obsolete. The single most important witness to the passion, and our only witness to long sections of it, is a Greek recension surviving in two manuscripts originally discovered by Prieur and published in an inferior edition by Theodore Détorakis (=HS [BHG 94h]).[6] An unpublished Greek recension, Ann Arbor gr. 36 (C [BHG 99c]), though more truncated and not beginning until chapter 51, shares many readings with HS and almost certainly likewise derived from an early transmissional stratum. The Armenian passion (Arm [BHO 52], sixth or seventh centuries) does not begin until chapter 47, but by comparing it with HS and C there can be no doubt that it too was based on a reliable Greek version, perhaps on the Acts itself.[7] At several points the Armenian alone preserves original readings.

Both Prieur and I base our editions primarily on HS, C, Arm, and V, occasionally incorporating readings from L, M and Ep. Prieur uses the apparatus to identify parallels in the Armenian but does not incorporate these readings into the textual reconstruction itself. This edition, on

----

5. *De fide contra Manichaeos*, ed. Joseph Zycha, CSEL 25 (1891).

6. *The Acts of the Second International Congress of Peloponnesian Studies* (Athens, 1981-1982), 1.333-52.

7. Chérubin Tchérakian, *Ankanon Girkʻ Arakʻelakankʻ*, Tʻangaran Haykakan Hin eue nor Dproutʻeanc G [*Non-Canonical Apostolic Writings*, Armenian Treasury of Ancient and Recent Writings 3] (Venice, 1904), 146-67. Tchérakian based his edition on three manuscripts. This text has been translated into French by Louis Leloir in *Écrits apocryphes*, 228-57.

the other hand, integrates many Armenian readings into the text when they seem to reflect the original, or reproduces them in the notes when of particular interest. I am indebted to Thomas J. Samuelian for translating the Armenian. Readings from other recensions are recorded here only when potentially primitive. Prieur frequently divides the chapters awkwardly. Rather than repeating the awkwardness here, I have indicated with asterisks (*) where Prieur makes a break between chapters different from that chosen in this edition. Excursus H discusses the bedeviling confusion in our sources concerning the content of Andrew's speech to the cross.

ABBREVIATIONS TO THE APPARATUS FOR PART III

Arm   Armenian passion. Tchérakian, *Ankanon Girk'*
        Arak'elankank', 146-67. Trans. Leloir, *Écrits*
        apocryphes, 228-57.

C   *Ann Arbor gr. 36* (*BHG* 99c). Unpublished.

Cd   *Conversante et docente* (*BHL* 429). Bonnet, *Acta*
        Andreae, 66-70.

E   *The Life of Andrew* (*BHG* 102), Epiphanius the
        monk. *PG* 120: 216-60.

Ep   *l'Épître* (*BHG* 94 and *BHL* 428). *AAA* 2.1:1-37.

GE   Gregory's epitome (*BHL* 430).Bonnet, "Liber de
        miraclus," 821-46, reproduced in Prieur, *Acta*
        Andreae, 555-631.

HS   *Jerusalem, St. Sabas, 103* and *Sinai gr. 526*
        (*BHG* 94h). Détorakis, *The Acts of the Second*
        International Congress of Peloponnesian Studies,
        1.333-52.

L   *Laudatio* (*BHG* 100). Bonnet, *Acta Andreae*
        3-44.

M   *Martyrium prius* (*BHG* 96). Prieur, *Acta*
        Andreae, 675-703.

Ma   *Martyrium alterum* (*BHG* 97-98). *AAA* 2.1:58-64.

N   *Narratio* (*BHG* 99). Bonnet, *Acta Andreae*, 46-64.

V   *Vaticanus gr. 808* (*BHG* 95). *AAA* 2.1:38-45.

1. Ὁ δὲ ἀνθύπατος Αἰγεάτης ἅμα τῷ ἰαθῆναι τὴν γυναικὰ αὐτοῦ ἐξεδήμησεν εἰς τὴν Ῥώμην πρὸς τὸν καίσαρα Νέρωνα. * Στρατοκλῆς ὁ τοῦ Αἰγεάτου ἀδελφὸς αἰτησάμενος Καίσαρα τὸ μὴ στρατεύεσθαι, ἐπὶ φιλοσοφίαν δὲ τραπῆναι, παρεγένετο ἀπὸ τῆς Ἰταλίας εἰς Πάτρας ἐκείνης ὥρας· καὶ θορύβου καταλαβόντος τὸ πᾶν πραιτώριον τοῦ Ἀριστοκλέους,[1] ἕνεκεν τοῦ διὰ ἱκανοῦ χρόνου ἐληλυθότος πρὸς Αἰγεάτην, καὶ ἡ Μαξιμίλλα ἐξῆλθεν ἐκ τοῦ κοιτῶνος εἰς ἀπάντησιν αὐτοῦ ἡδομένη, καὶ ἀσπαζομένη τὸν Στρατοκλέα εἴσεισιν ἅμα αὐτῷ. καὶ αἰθρίας λαμπρᾶς γενομένης αὐτὴ μὲν παρ' αὐτῇ γεγόνει, ὁ δὲ Στρατοκλῆς τὸ καθῆκον τὸ πρὸς τοὺς φίλους ἀπεπλήρου προσηνῶς πᾶσι προσφερόμενος καὶ ἀσπαζόμενος πάντας ἐπιεικῶς καὶ μετρίως.

2. Καὶ ἐν τούτῳ ὄντος αὐτοῦ παῖς τις τῶν πρὸς χεῖρα τοῦ Ἀριστοκλέους[2] ὑπὸ δαίμονος πληγεὶς[3] ἐν κοπρῶνι ἔκειτο παραπλήξ, ὃν ἔστεργε πάνυ, ὃν θεασάμενος[4] εἶπεν· εἴθε μηδέποτε ἀφίγμην, ἀλλ' ἐν θαλάσσῃ ἂν ἀπωλόμην, ὅπως μοι τοῦτο μὴ συμβεβήκῃ· οὐ γὰρ ἂν δυναίμην, φίλοι--ἀπιδὼν εἰς τοὺς σὺν αὐτῷ--δίχα τούτου ζῆν. καὶ ταῦτα λέγων τὰς ὄψεις ἐπάτασσεν, ἐντάραχος γενόμενος καὶ ἀπρεπὴς τοῦ ἰδέσθαι καὶ διηπόρει τι πράξει.

Καὶ ἡ Μαξιμίλλα ἀκούσασα ἔξεισι τοῦ κοιτῶνος καὶ αὐτὴ τεθορυβημένη καί φησι τῷ Στρατοκλεῖ· ἄφροντις ἴσθι, ἀδελφέ, τοῦ παιδὸς ἕνεκα· ἄρτι σωθήσεται. ἔστι γάρ τις ἐπιδημήσας τῇ πόλει ταύτῃ ἀνὴρ θεοσεβέστατος, ὃς δύναται

----

1. Prieur: Στρατοκλέους ἕνεκεν.

2. Prieur: Στρατοκλέους. *L* adds: εἰς ὑπηρεσίαν παρείπετο τῶν πάνυ πιστοτάτων, λίαν αὐτῷ στεργόμενος, Ἀλκμανᾶς τε προσαγορευόμενος.

3. *L*: τούτου δὴ πονηρῷ δαιμονίῳ ληφθέντος ἀθρόον, καὶ χαλεπῶς ὑπ' αὐτοῦ ἐνοχλουμένου. *E*: ἐκυλίετο ἀφρίζων.

4. *L*: οὐ μετρίᾳ συνείχετο λύπῃ Στρατοκλῆς. Similarly *E*.

1. At the same time that his wife was healed, the proconsul Aegeates took leave for Rome, to the emperor Nero. * Stratocles, Aegeates' brother, who had petitioned Caesar not to serve in the army but to pursue philosophy, arrived in Patras from Italy at that very moment. Excitement overtook the entire praetorium of Aristocles,[1] because Stratocles had not come to visit Aegeates for a long time. Maximilla too left the bedroom delighted to greet him, and when she had welcomed Stratocles, she entered with him. At daybreak, she was alone while Stratocles fulfilled his duty to his friends, comporting himself gently to everyone and greeting them all graciously and with decorum.

2. As he was thus engaged, one of the boys under the supervision of Aristocles,[2] one whom Stratocles loved dearly, was stricken by a demon[3] and lay in feces out of his mind. When Stratocles saw him[4] he said, "If only I had never come here but perished at sea this would not have happened to me! Friends," glancing at those with him, "I cannot live without him." As he said this, he hit himself about the eyes and became disturbed and unfit to be seen. He was at a loss about what to do.

When Maximilla heard about this, she too emerged upset from her bedroom and said to Stratocles, "Don't worry about your servant, brother. Soon he will be healed,

----

1. Prieur: "on account of Stratocles."

2. Prieur: "Stratocles." *L* adds: "who had been talked into serving with the most trustworthy, whom Stratocles loved dearly, Alcman by name."

3. *L*: "all of a sudden was taken over by a wicked demon and was miserably troubled by it." *E*: "rolled about in a froth."

4. *L*: "Stratocles was overcome with excessive sorrow."

οὐ μόνον δαίμονας φυγαδεῦσαι, ἀλλ' εἰ καί τι τῶν
ἀποτροπαίων καὶ δεινῶν καταλάβοι πάθος, ἐκεῖνος ἰάσεται.
οὕτως πεποίθαμεν αὐτῷ, ἀλλ' ὡς καὶ πεῖραν αὐτοῦ ἔχοντες
λέγομεν ταῦτα. καὶ ἡ 'Ιφιδάμα τὰ αὐτὰ ἔλεγεν πρὸς τὸν
Στρατοκλέα, κατέχουσα αὐτὸν μή τι τῶν δεινῶν τολμήσειεν
ἀνιώμενος ἄγαν.

3. Καὶ ὡς παραμυθοῦνται αὐτὸν αἱ ἀμφότεραι,
παραγίνεται ὁ 'Ανδρέας εἰς τὸ πραιτώριον συνθέμενος τῇ
Μαξιμίλλῃ ἐλθεῖν πρὸς αὐτόν. καὶ εἰσβὰς τοῦ πυλῶνος
ἔλεγεν· ἐνέργειά τις ἔνδον ἀγωνίζεται.⁵ σπεύσωμεν,
ἀδελφοί. καὶ μηδὲ πυθόμενός τινος εἴσεισιν εὐθέως δρομαίως
ἔνθα ὁ παῖς τοῦ Στρατοκέους ἤφριζεν διάστροφος ὅλος
γενόμενος.

"Ον ἰδόντες πάντες ἄφνω οἱ διὰ τὰς βοὰς τοῦ Στρατοκλέους δραμόντες⁶ μειδιῶντα καὶ διιστῶντα τοὺς παρόντας
καὶ αὐτῷ τόπον ποιοῦντα μέχρις ἂν ἔλθῃ πρὸς τὸν κείμενον
ἐπὶ γῆς παῖδα, διηπόρουν ὅστις εἴη. καὶ οἱ μὲν πάλαι αὐτὸν
ἐπιστάμενοι καὶ πεπειραμένοι, ὥς τινι θεῷ φοβούμενοι τόπον
ἐδίδουν. οἱ δὲ τοῦ Στρατοκλέους δοῦλοι ἰδόντες αὐτὸν
εὐτελῆ καὶ λιτὸν ἄνδρα καὶ τύπτειν ἐπειρῶντο· οὓς οἱ
λοιποὶ θεασάμενοι ἐνυβρίζοντας αὐτῷ ἐπετίμησαν αὐτοῖς
ἀγνοοῦσιν ὃ ἐτόλμων. κἀκεῖνοι ἠρεμήσαντες τὸ τέλος ἰδεῖν
ἔμενον.

4. Καὶ εὐθέως τῇ Μαξιμίλλῃ καὶ τῇ 'Ιφιδάμα ἀνήγγειλέ
τις τὸν μακάριον ἀφιγμένον. κἀκεῖναι χαρᾶς πλησθεῖσαι καὶ
ἀναπηδήσασαι τῶν τόπων ἔφθασαν πρὸς τὸν Στρατοκλέα· ἐλθὲ
τοιγαροῦν ὀψόμενος πῶς σου ὁ παῖς ῥώννυται.

'Αναστὰς οὖν καὶ αὐτὸς ἅμα αὐταῖς ἐβάδιζεν. ἰδὼν δὲ ὁ
Στρατοκλῆς ὄχλον πάμπολυν περιεστῶτα τῷ παιδὶ αὐτοῦ ἠρέμα

----

5. L adds: σκάνδαλον ποιῆσαι· τοιγαροῦν.

6. L: συνδραμόντες τὸν 'Ανδρεαν.

for there is a most God-fearing man sojourning in this city who not only can dispell demons, but if some menacing and serious sickness overcomes someone, he cures it. We have thus come to trust in him, but we say this as those who have put him to the test." Iphidama likewise said such things to Stratocles to restrain him from venturing some rash act, inasmuch as he was altogether distraught.

3. While both women were consoling Stratocles, Andrew, having agreed with Maximilla that he would go to the boy, arrived at the praetorium. On entering the gate he said, "Some force is fighting inside;[5] hurry brothers!" He asked questions of no one but burst inside to the place where Stratocles' lad was foaming at the mouth, entirely contorted.

Those who came dashing because of Stratocles' ruckus had no idea who Andrew was when they saw him smiling and shoving aside those who were present, making a path in order to get to the lad lying on the ground. Those who already had met Andrew and had seen him at work gave ground, fearing him like some god. Stratocles' servants, on the other hand, viewed him as a shabby tramp and tried to beat him up. When the rest saw them maltreating him, they rebuked them for not knowing what they were doing. When they settled down, they waited to see the outcome.

4. Just then someone told Maximilla and Iphidama that the blessed one had arrived. They were elated, sped from their rooms, and hurried to Stratocles: "Come and you will see how your servant is healed."

Stratocles too got up and walked with them, and when he saw the enormous crowd standing around his servant, he

----

5. *L*: "to create an attack; therefore."

εἶπεν· θέαμα γέγονας ἐλθὼν εἰς τὴν Ἀχαΐαν, Ἀλκμάνα--τοῦτο γὰρ ἦν τῷ παιδὶ ὄνομα.

Καὶ ὁ Ἀνδρέας ἀπεῖδεν εἰς τὴν Μαξιμίλλαν καὶ ἀφορῶν εἰς αὐτὴν[7] ἔλεγεν ταῦτα· τὸ μάλιστα δυσωποῦν, τέκνον μου, τοὺς ἐκ πολλῆς ζάλης καὶ[8] πλάνης ἐπὶ τὴν τοῦ θεοῦ πίστιν ἐπιστρέφοντας[9] τοῦτό ἐστιν τὰ ἀπεγνωσμένα τοῖς πολλοῖς πάθη ταῦτα ὁρᾶν θεραπευόμενα. ἰδοὺ γὰρ ὃ λέγω καὶ νῦν ὁρῶ ἐνταῦθα γινόμενον. μάγοι ἑστήκασι[10] μηδὲν δυνάμενοι ποιῆσαι, οἳ καὶ ἀπεγνώκασι τὸν παῖδα, καὶ ἄλλοι οὓς κοινῇ πάντες ὁρῶμεν περιέργους· διὰ τί μὴ δεδύνηνται τὸν δεινὸν τοῦτον δαίμονα ἀπελάσαι τοῦ ταλαιπώρου παιδός; ἐπειδὴ συγγενεῖς αὐτοῦ ὑπάρχουσιν. τοῦτο γὰρ ἐπὶ τοῦ παρόντος ὄχλου χρήσιμον λέγειν.

5. Καὶ μηδὲν μελλήσας ἀναστὰς ἔφη·[11] ὁ μάγοις μὴ ἐπακούων θεός, ὁ περιέργοις μὴ παρέχων ἑαυτὸν θεός, ὁ τῶν ἀλλοτρίων ἀφιστάμενος θεός, ὁ τὰ σὰ παρέχων ἀεὶ τοῖς ἰδίοις θεός,[12] καὶ νῦν παράσχου τὴν δέησίν μου ταχινὴν γενέσθαι ἀπέναντι τούτων ἁπάντων ἐν τῷ παιδὶ τοῦ Στρατοκλέους, φυγαδεύων τὸν δαίμονα, ὃν οἱ συγγενεῖς αὐτοῦ μὴ δεδύνηνται φυγαδεῦσαι.

----

7. *L* om: καὶ . . . αὐτήν.

8. *L* om: ζάλης καί.

9. *L*: ἐπιστρέφειν.

10. *L* adds: καὶ φαρμακοὶ καὶ περίεργοι.

11. *L*: προσηύξατο.

12. *L* om: ὁ μάγοις . . . ἰδίοις θεός. It reads instead: ὁ τοῖς σοῖς ἀεὶ ὑπακούων θεός, ὁ τὰ σὰ τοῖς ἰδίοις ἀεὶ παρέχων.

said quietly, "Alcman," (this was the boy's name) "you have become a spectacle by coming to Achaea!"

Andrew stared at Maximilla, and while looking at her he said the following: "My child, this is what is most distressing to those who are turning to a faith in God away from a great tempest and wandering: to see these ailments cured which many considered beyond help. Look, even now I see what I am saying coming to pass. Magicians[6] are standing here helpless to do anything, both those who had given up on the lad and others whom we all see huckstering in public. Why have they been unable to expel this fearsome demon from the pitiful lad? Because they are kindred to it.[7] It is useful to say this before the present crowd."

5. Without delay he got up and said,[8] "O God who does not give heed to magicians, O God who does not offer yourself to the quacks, O God who withdraws from things foreign (to yourself), O God who always offers your possessions to your own,[9] even now, in the presence of all these people, grant my request quickly with respect to Stratocles' servant by banishing the demon whom those who are its kindred could not."

----

6. *L* adds: "along with sorcerers and quacks."

7. This is the first occurrence in the Passion of the notion of συγγενεία so common and important at the end of the book. In order to alert the English reader to these occurrences, συγγενεία and its cognates will be translated with cognates of "kindred."

8. *L*: "prayed."

9. The beginning of the prayer in *L* reads: "O God who always gives heed to your own, who always offers your possessions to your own."

Καὶ εὐθέως ὁ δαίμων ἔπανδρον[13] φωνὴν ἀφεὶς ἔλεγεν·
φεύγω, δοῦλε τοῦ θεοῦ ἄνθρωπε, φεύγω οὐ μόνον τοῦ παιδὸς
τούτου, ἀλλὰ καὶ τῆς πόλεως ὅλης ταύτης.

Καὶ ὁ Ἀνδρέας αὐτῷ εἶπεν· οὐ μόνον σε τῆς πόλεως
ταύτης κελεύω φυγαδευθῆναι, ἀλλ᾽ εἰ καί που ἴχνος
ἀδελφικόν μου ὑπάρχει, εἴργω σε τῶν χώρων ἐκείνων μὴ
ἐπιβῆναι.

Καὶ ἀποστάντος τοῦ δαίμονος ὁ Ἀλκμάνης ἀνέστη ἀπὸ
τῆς γῆς, χεῖρα αὐτῷ ὀρέξαντος τοῦ Ἀνδρέου, καὶ
συνεβάδιζεν αὐτῷ σωφρονῶν καὶ εὐσταθῶν καὶ εὐτάκτως ὁμιλῶν
καὶ ἥδιστα ὁρῶν τὸν Ἀνδρέαν[14] καὶ τὸν αὐτοῦ δεσπότην,
ἐξετάζων τὴν αἰτίαν τοῦ ἔνδον ὄχλου. ὁ δὲ αὐτῷ ἀπεκρίνατο·
οὐδένα χρή σε τῶν ἀλλοτρίων σου μανθάνειν. ἀρκεῖ ἡμῖν
ἰδοῦσιν ἐν σοὶ ὃ εἴδομεν.

6. Καὶ ἐν τούτῳ ὄντων αὐτῶν ἡ Μαξιμίλλα ἀποκρατοῦσα
τὴν χεῖρα τοῦ Ἀνδρέου καὶ τοῦ Στρατοκλέους εἴσεισιν εἰς
τὸν κοιτῶνα, συνεισῆλθον δὲ αὐτοῖς καὶ ὁπόσοι ἦσαν ἐκεῖ
ἀδελφοί. καὶ καθεσθέντες ἀφεώρων εἰς τὸν μακάριον
Ἀνδρέαν, ὅπως τι φθέγξηται. καὶ ἡ Μαξιμίλλα ἐσπουδάκει
τοῦ Στρατοκλέους ἕνεκεν τὸν ἀπόστολον ὁμιλῆσαι, ὅπως
πιστεύσῃ εἰς τὸν κύριον. ὁ γὰρ ἀδελφὸς αὐτοῦ Αἰγεάτης
βλασφημότατος ὑπῆρχε καὶ ταλαιπωρότατος περὶ τὰ κρείσσονα.

7. Ὁ οὖν Ἀνδρέας ἤρξατο λέγειν πρὸς τὸν Στρατοκλέα·
* ὅτι μέν, ὦ Στρατοκλῆ, κεκίνησαι ὑπὸ τοῦ γεγονότος εὖ
οἶδα. ὅτι δὲ καὶ τὸν ἐν σοὶ νῦν ἡσυχάζοντα ἐχρῆν ἄνθρωπόν
με εὐθῦναι εἰς τοὐμφανὲς καὶ τοῦτο ἐπίσταμαι. τὸ γὰρ ὅλως
διαπορεῖν σε καὶ ἐννοεῖν τὸ γεγονὸς ὁπόθεν ἢ πῶς γέγονεν
δεῖγμα μέγιστον ὑπάρχει τῆς ἐν σοὶ ψυχῆς τεταραγμένης·
κἀμὲ εὖ διατίθησιν ἡ ἐν σοὶ ἀπορία καὶ ἐποχὴ καὶ θάμβωσις.
ἀποκύησον δὲ τέκνον ὃ ἔχεις, καὶ μὴ μόνον ὠδῖσιν σεαυτὸν

---

13. *L*: ἀνθρωπίνην.

14. *L* ends the story here, leaving only *HS*.

Immediately the demon relented and said in a masculine[10] voice, "I flee, servant of God! I flee not only from this lad but also from this entire city."

"I command you to flee not only from this city," Andrew told him, "but I bar you from setting foot in any of those regions where there is so much as a trace of my brethren."

When the demon had left, Alcman got up from the ground, Andrew extended his hand to him, and the lad walked with him, self-composed, steady on his feet, conducting coherent conversation, affectionately looking at Andrew and his master, and inquiring about the cause for the crowd inside. Andrew told him, "There is no need for you to learn about anything alien to you. It is enough for us to see in you what we have seen."

6. While they were thus occupied, Maximilla took Andrew and Stratocles by the hand and entered her bedroom along with any of the brethren who were there. Once seated, they fixed their eyes on the blessed Andrew so that he might speak. For the sake of Stratocles, Maximilla had been eager for the apostle to talk so that he might believe in the Lord. His brother Aegeates was altogether blasphemous and despicable with respect to what is superior.

7. "O Stratocles," Andrew began, * "I know well that you are moved by what has happened, but I also am certain that I must bring out into the open the person now latent within you. Your total bewilderment and pondering of the source and cause of what has happened are the greatest proofs that the soul within you is troubled, and the perplexity, hesitation, and astonishment in you please me.

----

10. *L*: "human."

παραδίδου. οὐκ εἰμι ἀμύητος μαιευτικῆς, ἀλλ' οὐδὲ
μαντικῆς. ἔστι <τι> ὃ ἀποτίκτεις, <ὃ> ἐγὼ φιλῶ. ἔστι τι ὃ
σιγᾷς, ὃ ἐγὼ ἐρῶ, ὃ καὶ εἰς ἔνδον ἐγὼ ἀναθρέψω. οἶδα τὸν
σιγῶντα· οἶδα τὸν ποθοῦντα. ἤδη μοι λαλεῖ ὁ καινός σου
ἄνθρωπος· ἤδη μοι ἐντυγχάνει ἃ πέπονθε πολλοῖς χρόνοις
ἀεί. αἰσχύνεται τὴν πρὶν αὐτοῦ θεοσέβειαν· λυπεῖται ἐπὶ τῇ
πρώτῃ αὐτοῦ πολιτείᾳ· μάταια τὰ πρὶν αὐτοῦ θρησκεύματα
ἅπαντα τίθεται· διαπορεῖ τίς ἡ ὄντως θεοσέβεια·
ἀπονειδίζει σιγῶν τοῖς αὐτοῦ πρὶν θεοῖς ματαίοις· πάσχει
ἀλήτης γεγονὼς παιδείας ἕνεκεν. τίς ἡ πρὶν αὐτοῦ
φιλοσοφία; νῦν ἔγνω ὅτι ματαία. ὁρᾷ ὅτι κενὴ καὶ
χαμαιριφής· νῦν μανθάνει ὅτι οὐδὲν τῶν δεόντων ὑπισχνεῖται
νῦν ὁμολογεῖ ὅτι οὐδὲν τῶν χρησίμων ἐπαγγέλεται. τί γάρ;
οὐ ταῦτα λέγει, Στρατοκλῆ, ὁ ἐν σοὶ ἄνθρωπος;

8. Καὶ ὁ Στρατοκλῆς μετὰ τὸ στενάξαι μέγα ἀπεκρίνατο
ταῦτα· μαντικώτατε ἄνθρωπε καὶ ἀληθῶς ἄγγελε θεοῦ ζῶντος,
καὶ οὐκ ἀποστήσομαί σου μέχρις ἐμαυτὸν γνωρίζω κατεγνωκὼς
ἐκείνων ἁπάντων καὶ ὧν με σὺ ἤλεγξας ματαί<ω>ς[15] ἐν αὐτοῖς
κατατριβέντα.

Καὶ ἦν σὺν τῷ ἀποστόλῳ Στρατοκλῆς νυκτὸς καὶ ἡμέρας
μὴ ἀπολειπόμενος αὐτοῦ, τὰ μὲν ἐξετάζων καὶ μανθάνων καὶ
διαναπαυόμενος, τὰ δὲ σιωπῶν καὶ ἡδόμενος. ἀληθῶς φίλος
σωτηρίας ἀκροάσεως γεγονώς· ὅστις τοῖς ἑαυτοῦ πᾶσι χαίρειν
φράσας μόνος μετὰ μόνου τοῦ ἀποστόλου διάγειν ἐβούλετο.
οὐκέτι γὰρ ἐπί τινος ὅλως ἐξήταζε τὸν μακάριον, ἀλλ' ἢ τῶν
λοιπῶν ἀδελφῶν ἄλλο τι πρασσόντων αὐτὸς ἰδιάζων ἐπυνθάνετο
αὐτοῦ, εἰς ὕπνον τρεπομένων αὐτὸς διαγρυπνῶν καὶ μηδὲ τὸν
Ἀνδρέαν ἐῶν καθεύδειν διανεπαύετο ἀγαλλιῶν.

---

15. *HS*: ματαίοις. So also Prieur.

Bring to birth the child you are carrying and do not give yourself over to labor pains alone. I am no novice at midwifery or divination. I desire what you are birthing. I love what you are stifling. I will suckle what is within you. I know the one who is silent. I know the one who aspires. Already your new self speaks to me. Already I encounter those things he has suffered for so long. He is ashamed of his former religion; he mourns his former public conduct; he considers all his former worship vacuous; he has no idea what true religion is; he tacitly reproaches the useless gods of his past; having become a vagabond, he suffers in order to become educated. Whatever his former philosophy, he now knows that it was hollow. He sees that it is destitute and worthless. Now he learns that it promises nothing essential. Now he admits that it pledges nothing useful. Right? Does the person inside you not say these things, Stratocles?"

8. After a loud groan, Stratocles answered as follows: "Most prophetic man, truly a messenger of the living God, I too will not separate from you until I recognize myself by having despised all those things about which you rebuked me for idly squandering my time in them."

Stratocles was with the apostle night and day and never left him, sometimes examining, learning from, and interrupting him, and other times remaining silent and enjoying himself, having truly become enamored of saving attentiveness. Declaring that he would bid adieu to all his possessions, he decided to live alone, with no one else but the apostle. He ceased altogether examining the blessed one when anyone else was present, but while the rest of the believers were doing something else, he questioned him in private. When the others fell asleep, he would lie awake and by his enthusiastic interruptions would not let Andrew sleep.

9. Οὐκ ἠρέμει δὲ ὁ Ἀνδρέας πρὸς τοὺς ἀδελφοὺς τὰς τοῦ Στρατοκλέους πεύσεις ἐκφαίνων εἰπὼν πρὸς αὐτόν· δισσῶς τὸ ὠφελεῖσθαι καρπίζου, ὦ Στρατοκλῆ, καὶ ἰδίᾳ μου ἀναπυνθανόμενος καὶ ἐπὶ τῶν ἀδελφῶν τὰ αὐτὰ ἀκούων. οὕτως γάρ σοι μᾶλλον ἐγκατατιθήσεται ἃ ποθεῖς καὶ ζητεῖς. οὐ γάρ ἐστι δίκαιον μὴ οὐχὶ καὶ τοῖς ὁμοίοις τὰς σὰς ὠδῖνας ἐκτίθεσθαι. ὡς γὰρ ἡ ὠδίνουσα γυνή· τῶν πόνων καταλαβόντων αὐτὴν καὶ τοῦ βρέφους βιαζομένου ὑπό τινος γενέσθαι δυνάμεως μὴ μένειν ἔνδον, ἀλλ' εἰς τὸ ἔξω ἐκθλίβεσθαι, καὶ τοῦτο ταῖς παρούσαις γυναιξὶ τῶν αὐτῶν μυστηρίων μετεχούσαις ἐστὶ γάρ τι πρόδηλον καὶ οὐκ ἀσυμφανές· κέκραγεν αὐτὸ τὸ τεχθὲν προκεκραγυίας τῆς μητρός. εἶτα τῷ βρέφει μετὰ τὸ τεχθῆναι λοιπὸν θεραπείαν προσάγουσί τινα ἣν αὐταὶ ἴσασιν αἱ μεμυημέναι, ὅπως τῶν ζωογονουμένων τι εἴη τὸ ὅσον ἐπ' αὐταῖς. οὕτως δὲ καὶ ἡμᾶς, τέκνον μου Στρατοκλῆ, τὰ σὰ κυήματα εἰς μέσον φέρειν δεῖ καὶ μὴ ἠρεμεῖν, ἵνα ὑπὸ πλειόνων τῶν συγγενῶν ἀναγράφηται καὶ προαγάγηται εἰς ἐπίδοσιν τῶν σωτηρίων λόγων, ὧν κοινωνόν σε εὗρον.

10. Μακαρίως οὖν διάγοντος τοῦ Στρατοκλέους καὶ στηριζομένου λοιπὸν ἐπὶ πάντων τῶν αὐτοῦ συγγενῶν λόγων καὶ ἑδραίαν ψυχὴν ἐσχηκότος καὶ πίστιν βεβαίαν καὶ ἀπαράλλακτον ἐπὶ τὸν κύριον, ἠγαλλία ἡ Μαξιμίλλα ἅμα τῇ Ἰφιδάμᾳ· καὶ ὁ Ἀλκμάνης δὲ θεραπευθεὶς οὐκέτι τῆς πίστεως ἀφίστατο. νυκτὸς οὖν καὶ ἡμέρας εὐφραινομένων αὐτῶν καὶ ἐπιστηριζομένων τῷ Χριστῷ, χάριν ἔχων ὅ τε Στρατοκλῆς καὶ ἡ Μαξιμίλλα καὶ ἡ Ἰφιδάμα καὶ ὁ Ἀλκμάνης ἅμα πολλοῖς ἑτέροις ἀδελφοῖς τῆς ἐν κυρίῳ σφραγῖδος κατηξιώθησαν.[16]

---

16. L: ἀξιωθῆναι.

9. Andrew would not keep quiet but exposed Stratocles' inquiries to the brethren by telling him, "Stratocles, double your harvest by asking me questions in private and by hearing the same in the presence of the brethren, for in this way what you desire and seek will all the more surely be stored up in you. It is not right for you to conceal your labor pains even from your peers. Take the example of a woman in labor: When the labor pains overcome her and the fetus is pressured by some power to come forth--not to stay within but to be squeezed outside--the fetus becomes obvious and noticeable to the attending women who take part in such mysteries (it was the fetus itself that cried out when the mother cried out earlier). Then, postpartum, these initiates at last provide for the newborn whatever care they know, so that, insofar as it is up to them, the fetus might be born alive. Likewise, Stratocles my child, we too must not be passive but bring your embryos into the open, so that they may be registered and be brought to the donative of saving words by many kindred, whose associate I found you to be."

10. Maximilla and Iphidama rejoiced that Stratocles was conducting himself in a pious manner, at last was firmly established upon all the words that were akin to him, and possessed a steady soul and a firm and unalterable faith in the Lord. Alcman, after his cure, no longer resisted the faith. Because they were rejoicing and being confirmed in Christ night and day, Stratocles, full of gratitude, Maximilla, Iphidama, Alcman, along with many of the other brethren, were deemed worthy of the Lord's seal.

11. Οἷς εἶπεν ὁ Ἀνδρέας· * ἐὰν τοῦτον τὸν τύπον φυλάξητε, τεκνία μου, ἀνεπίδεκτον ἄλλων σφραγίδων ἐντυπουσῶν τὰς ἐναντίας γλυφάς, θεὸς ὑμᾶς ἐπαινέσεται καὶ εἰς τὰ αὐτοῦ δέξεται. διαυγοῦς γὰρ φαινομένης τῆς τοιαύτης ὀπτασίας ἐν ταῖς ὑμετέραις ψυχαῖς μάλιστα ἀπαλλασσομέναις τῶν σωμάτων, αἱ κολαστήριοι δυνάμεις καὶ ἐξουσίαι κακαὶ καὶ ἄρχοντες δεινοὶ καὶ ἄγγελοι πύρινοι καὶ δαίμονες αἰσχροὶ καὶ ἐνέργειαι ῥυπαραὶ μὴ φέρουσαι τὸ καταλειφθῆναι ὑφ᾽ ὑμῶν, ἐπειδὴ οὔκ εἰσι τοῦ συμβόλου[17] τῆς σφραγῖδος φωτὸς ὄντος συγγενοῦς, κατατρέχουσι καὶ καταδύουσι φεύγουσαι εἰς τὸ συγγενὲς αὐτῶν σκότος καὶ πῦρ καὶ ὁμίχλας καὶ εἴ τί ἐστι ἐπινοούμενον κολαστήριον ἐπάγγελμα. εἰ δὲ ῥυπώσητε τὸ λαμπρὸν τῆς δεδομένης ὑμῖν χάριτος, κατορχήσονται ὑμῶν καὶ διαπαίξουσιν αἱ δειναὶ ἐκεῖναι δυνάμεις ἄλλη ἄλλως χορεύουσαι. ἀπαιτήσει γὰρ ἑκάστη τὸ ἴδιον καθάπερ τις ἀλαζὼν καὶ τύραννος· καὶ τότε ὑμῖν ὄφελος οὐδὲν ἔσται παρακαλοῦσι τὸν τῆς σφραγῖδος ὑμῶν θεόν, ἣν ὑμεῖς ἀποστάντες αὐτοῦ ἐμιάνατε. (**12.**) φυλάξωμεν οὖν, τεκνία μου, τὴν πιστευθεῖσαν ἡμῖν παρακαταθήκην.[18] ἀποδώσωμεν τῷ παρακαταθεμένῳ ἡμῖν αὐτὴν ἄσπιλον. εἴπωμεν ἐκεῖ γενόμενοι πρὸς αὐτόν· ἰδοὺ ἀνύβριστόν σου τὴν χάριν ἐκομίσαμέν σοι, τί ἡμῖν τῶν σῶν χαρίζῃ; ἀποκρίνεται οὖν ἡμῖν εὐθέως· χαριοῦμαι ὑμῖν ἐμαυτόν· πᾶν γὰρ ὃ ἐγώ εἰμι καὶ δίδωμι τοῖς ἐμοῖς. εἰ γὰρ φῶς θέλετε ἀκάμμυτον, ἐγώ εἰμι. εἰ ζωὴν γενέσει μὴ ὑποπίπτουσαν, ἐγώ εἰμι· εἰ ἀνάπαυσιν πόνων ματαίων, ἔχετέ με τὴν ἀνάπαυσιν· εἰ φίλον παρέχοντα μὴ ἐπίγεια, ἐγώ εἰμι ὁ φίλος ὑμῶν· εἰ πατέρα

----

17. *HS* actually reads: συμβούλου.

18. At this point *E* and *L* agree against *HS*. Readings in *L* but not in *E* appear in pointed brackets: ἐπιμελεῖσθαί <τε> ψυχῆς <ὡς ἀθανάτου>, σώματος δὲ καταφρονεῖν <ὡς φθείρεσθαι μέλλοντος>. ἀγνεύειν, ἐγκρατεύεσθαι, παρθενεύειν, σωφρονεῖν, ἀδικεῖσθαι καὶ μὴ ἀδικεῖν, μὴ φλυαρεῖν <L: βαττολογεῖν>, μηδὲ ψεύδεσθαι <εἰς ἀλλήλους>, ἀλλ᾽ ἀδιαλείπτως <τῷ θεῷ εὐχαριστοῦντας> προσεύχεσθαι.

11. "My children," Andrew told them, * "if you keep this seal's impression unconfused with other seals that imprint different designs, God will commend you and receive you to his domain. Because such a radiant image appears in your souls which are essentially set loose from your bodies, the punishing powers, evil authorities, fearsome rulers, fiery angels, hideous demons, and foul forces, who cannot endure being forsaken by you, since they have nothing to do with the symbol of the seal since it is kindred to light, run aground and sink during their flight to their kindred: darkness, fire, gloom, and whatever other impending punishment one might imagine. But if you pollute the brilliance of the grace given you, those awful powers will taunt you and toy with you by dancing here and there. Like an impostor or a tyrant, each will demand its own. Then it will do you no good to call on the God of your seal which you defiled by apostasizing from him. (**12.**) So, my children, let us guard the deposit entrusted to us.[11] Let us return the deposit spotless to the one who entrusted it to us. When we arrive there, let us say to him, 'Look, we brought you your gift unabused. Which of your possessions will you give us?' He will answer us at once, 'I will give you myself. All that I am I give to my own. If you desire unflickering light, I am it. If you desire a life not subject to coming-to-be, I am it. If you desire rest from futile labor, you have me as your rest. If you desire a friend who supplies goods not of this world, I am your friend. If you desire a father for those who are rejected on earth, I am your father. If

----

11. Here *E* and *L* agree against *HS*. Additions in *L* appear in bold: "Let us care for the soul **as though it were immortal**, disdain the body **as though it were about to perish**. Be pure, chaste, virgin, prudent. Suffer injustice, but do not be unjust. Do not joke around (*L*: **"speak of trifles"**) or lie **to each other** but constantly **give thanks to God** in prayer."

τοῖς ἐπὶ γῆς παραιτουμένοις, ἐγὼ ὑμῶν πατήρ· εἰ ἀδελφὸν
γνήσιον τῶν μὴ γνησίων ἀδελφῶν χωρίζοντα ὑμᾶς, ἐγώ εἰμι
ἀδελφὸς ὑμῶν· καὶ εἴ τι ὑμῖν φιλικώτερον ὃ ποθεῖτε καὶ
ζητεῖτε, ἐμὲ ἔχετε ἐν πᾶσι τοῖς ἐμοῖς καὶ τὰ ἐμὰ πάντα ἐν
ὑμῖν. ταῦτα ἡμῖν, ἀγαπητοί, ἀποκρίνεται ὁ κύριος ἡμῶν.

Καὶ λαλήσαντος ταῦτα τοῦ Ἀνδρέα, τῶν ἀδελφῶν οἱ μὲν
ἔκλαιον, οἱ δὲ ἠγαλλιῶντο. μάλιστα δὲ ὁ Στρατοκλῆς
νεόφυτος γεγενημένος εἰς ὕψος ἤλατο τῇ διανοίᾳ, ὡς πάντα
τὰ αὐτοῦ ἀπολείπειν, μόνῳ δὲ τῷ λόγῳ προσαρτῆσαι ἑαυτόν.

13. (=GE 35) Ἀγαλλιάσεως οὖν μεγάλης οὔσης ἐν τοῖς
ἀδελφοῖς, νυκτὸς καὶ ἡμέρας συνερχομένων αὐτῶν ἐν τῷ
πραιτωρίῳ πρὸς τὴν Μαξιμίλλαν, κυριακῆς οὔσης παραγίνεται
ὁ ἀνθύπατος,[19] τῶν ἀδελφῶν συνηγμένων ἐν τῷ κοιτῶνι[20]
αὐτοῦ καὶ ἀκρωμένων τοῦ Ἀνδρέα. ὡς δὲ ἠγγέλη τῇ
Μαξιμίλλῃ ὁ ἀνὴρ ἀφιγμένος, οὐ μικρῶς ἐθορυβεῖτο τὸ
ἀποβαῖνον προσδοκῶσα, ὀνομάτων πολλῶν κατειλημμένων ἔνδον
ὑπ᾽ αὐτοῦ.

Ὁ δὲ Ἀνδρέας ἰδὼν αὐτὴν ἠπορημένην εἶπεν πρὸς τὸν
κύριον· κύριε Ἰησοῦ, μὴ εἰσερχέσθω εἰς τοῦτον τὸν κοιτῶνα
ὁ Αἰγεάτης μέχρις οἱ σοὶ δοῦλοι ἀδεῶς ἐξέλθωσιν ἐντεῦθεν,
σοῦ ἕνεκεν συνεληλυθότες, καὶ τῆς Μαξιμίλλης ἀεὶ ἡμᾶς
λιπαρούσης, ἵνα ἐνταῦθα συνερχώμεθα καὶ ἀναπαυώμεθα. ἀλλ᾽
ὡς ἀξίαν αὐτὴν ἔκρινας καταξιῶσαι τῆς σῆς βασιλείας,
ἐπιστηριχθήτω μᾶλλον ἅμα τῷ Στρατοκλεῖ· καὶ λέοντος
ἠγριωμένου ὁρμὴν καθ᾽ ἡμῶν ὡπλισμένου κατάσβεσον περισώσας
ἡμᾶς ἅπαντας.

Καὶ ὁ ἀνθύπατος Αἰγεάτης εἰσελθὼν ὑπὸ τῆς γαστρὸς
ὠχλήθη καὶ ᾔτει σέλλαν καὶ πολλὴν ὥραν καθεζόμενος
ἐπεμελεῖτο ἑαυτοῦ. καὶ τῶν ἀδελφῶν πάντων ἐξιόντων

---

19. *E* adds: ἀπὸ τοῦ Καίσαρος. *L*: ἐκ Ῥώμης. *GE*: abierat in
Machedonia.

20. *GE*: in praetorio.

you desire a legitimate brother to set you apart from bastard brothers, I am your brother. If you desire and seek anything more valuable to you, you have me with all that is mine and all that is mine will be in you.' Beloved, our Lord gives us this reply."

After Andrew said these things, some of the brethren cried, others rejoiced, but because he had become a neophyte, Stratocles in particular was so elevated in his mind that he forsook all his possessions and devoted himself to the word alone.

13. There was great joy among the brethren as they gathered together night and day at the praetorium with Maximilla. On the Lord's day, when the brethren were assembled in Aegeates' bedroom[12] listening to Andrew, the proconsul arrived.[13] When her husband's arrival was announced to Maximilla she panicked, anticipating the outcome, that he would apprehend so many people inside.

When Andrew saw her perplexity, he said to the Lord, "Do not permit Aegeates to enter this bedroom, Lord Jesus, until your servants can leave here without fear, for they have come together for your sake, and Maximilla constantly pleads with us to meet and take our rest here. Inasmuch as you have judged her worthy to deserve your kingdom, may she be especially emboldened, and Stratocles too. Save us all by repelling that savage lion armed to attack us."

As the proconsul Aegeates came in, he got an urge for a bowel movement, asked for a chamber pot, and spent a long time sitting, attending to himself. He did not notice

----

12. *GE*: "in the praetorium."

13. *E* says Aegeates came "from the emperor." *L*: "from Rome." According to *GE*, Aegeates "was off in Macedonia." See Prieur, *Acta Andreae*, 52.

ἔμπροσθεν αὐτοῦ οὐχ ἑώρα. ὁ γὰρ ᾿Ανδρέας ἑκάστῳ τὴν χεῖρα
ἐπιτιθεὶς ἔλεγεν· ᾿Ιησοῦς περισκεπάσει ὑμῶν τὸ φαινόμενον
ἀπὸ τοῦ Αἰγεάτου, ἵνα τὸ μὴ ὁρώμενον ὑμῶν στηριχθείη ἐπ᾿
αὐτόν. ὕστερον δὲ πάντων ἔξεισιν αὐτὸς σφραγισάμενος
ἑαυτόν.

14. ῾Ως δὲ καὶ ἡ τοιαύτη χάρις τοῦ κυρίου ἐτελέσθη, ὁ
Στρατοκλῆς ἐξελθὼν περιπτύσσεται τὸν ἀδελφόν, οὐκ ἐκ ψυχῆς
ἀγαλλιῶν, ἀλλὰ τῇ ὄψει μειδιῶν, ὡς διὰ πολλοῦ χρόνου τὸν
ἀδελφὸν ἀπειληφώς. καὶ οἱ λοιποὶ δὲ αὐτοῦ δοῦλοι καὶ
ἀπελεύθεροι ὁμοίως αὐτὸν ἠσπάζοντο.

Αὐτὸς δὲ ἠπείγετο εἰς τὸν κοιτῶνα εἰσελθεῖν τοπάζων
τὴν Μαξιμίλλαν ἔτι καθεύδειν· ἤρα γὰρ αὐτῆς. ἐκείνη δὲ ἦν
εὐχομένη. ὡς δὲ εἶδεν αὐτὸν ἐπιστραφεῖσα εἰς γῆν ἀπεῖδεν.

Κἀκεῖνος αὐτῇ ἔφη· δός μοι πρῶτον τὴν δεξιάν σου·
φιλήσω ἣν λοιπὸν οὐκ ἂν γυναῖκα προσαγορεύσω, ἀλλὰ
δέσποιναν, οὕτως διαναπεπαυμένου μου ἐπὶ τῇ σωφροσύνῃ καὶ
φιλίᾳ τῇ πρός με.

῎Ωετο γὰρ ὁ τάλας κατειληφὼς αὐτὴν εὐχομένην ὅτι περὶ
αὐτοῦ ηὔχετο· εὐχομένης γὰρ αὐτῆς ἐκεῖνος τὸ ἴδιον ὄνομα
ἀκούσας ἠγάσθη· τοῦτο δὲ ἦν τὸ λεγόμενον ὑπὸ τῆς
Μαξιμίλλης· καὶ ῥῦσαί με λοιπὸν ἀπὸ τῆς μιαρᾶς μίξεως
Αἰγεάτου καὶ φύλαξόν με καθαρὰν καὶ σώφρονα, σοὶ τῷ θεῷ
μου ὑπηρετοῦσαν μόνῳ. ὡς δὲ καὶ τῷ στόματι ἤγγιζε φιλῆσαι
τοῦτο θέλων, ἐκείνη αὐτὸν διωθεῖτο λέγουσα· οὐ θέμις,
Αἰγεάτα, μετὰ τὴν εὐχὴν ἀνδρὸς στόμα γυναικείῳ στόματι
προσψαῦσαι.

all the brethren exit in front of him. For Andrew laid his hand on each one and said, "Jesus will screen your appearance from Aegeates, in order to secure your invisibility before him." Last of all, Andrew sealed himself and left.[14]

14. When this grace of the Lord was completed, Stratocles, because he had been away from his brother for a long time, went out and embraced Aegeates, with a smile on his face but with no joy in his soul. The rest of his servants and freedmen greeted him in the same manner.

But Aegeates, out of passion for Maximilla, rushed into the bedroom assuming she was still asleep. She was at prayer. When she saw him, she looked away toward the ground.

"First give me your right hand," he told her. "I will kiss the woman I will call no longer 'wife' but 'lady,' so that I may find relief in your chastity and love for me."

For when the wretch overtook her at prayer, he supposed she was praying for him and was delighted to hear his own name mentioned while she prayed. This is what Maximilla actually said: "Rescue me at last from Aegeates' filthy intercourse and keep me pure and chaste, giving service only to you, my God." When he approached her mouth intending to kiss it, she pushed him back and said, "Aegeates, after prayer a woman's mouth should never touch a man's."

----

14. At this point the reader is to assume that only Aegeates is left in the bedroom. The next chapter, however, places him somewhere outside, presumably outside of the praetorium, and places Maximilla in her own bedroom "still asleep" (ἔτι καθεύδειν). This non sequitur may simply indicate the author's lack of narrative control, but it may also suggest that HS has failed to report an episode that interrupted these two chapters.

Καὶ ὁ ἀνθύπατος ἐκπλαγεὶς αὐτῆς τὸ αὐστηρὸν τῆς ὄψεως ἀπέστη αὐτῆς. καὶ ἀποδυσάμενος τὴν ἐνόδιον ἐσθῆτα ἡσύχασεν, καὶ κατακλιθεὶς ἐκάθευδεν, πολλὴν διανύσας ὁδόν.

15. Ἡ δὲ Μαξιμίλλα τῇ Ἰφιδάμᾳ ἔφη· γενοῦ, ἀδελφή, πρὸς τὸν μακάριον, ὅπως ἐλθὼν ἐνθάδε τούτου κοιμωμένου ἐπιθείς μοι τὴν χεῖρα εὔξηται.

Ἡ δὲ μὴ μελλήσασα δρομαία παραγίνεται πρὸς τὸν Ἀνδρέαν καὶ ἀναγγείλασα τὴν ἀξίωσιν τῆς πιστοτάτης Μαξιμίλλης, παραγίνεται ὁ Ἀνδρέας καὶ εἴσεισιν εἰς ἕτερον κοιτῶνα ἔνθα ἦν ἡ Μαξιμίλλα. καὶ ὁ Στρατοκλῆς δὲ συνεισῆλθε τῷ ἀποστόλῳ, σὺν αὐτῷ ἐλθὼν ἀπὸ τῆς ξενίας τοῦ μακαρίου. ὅτε γὰρ τὸν ἀδελφὸν ἀπησπάσατο ἐπύθετο τὴν ξενίαν ἔνθα ὁ τοῦ κυρίου ἀπόστολος ᾤκει. καὶ ξεναγηθεὶς ὑπό τινος ἀδελφοῦ Ἀντιφάνους συνεισῆλθε τῷ μακαρίῳ.

16. Ὁ δὲ Ἀνδρέας ἐπιθεὶς τὴν χεῖρα τῇ Μαξιμίλλᾳ ηὔχετο οὕτως· * δέομαί σου, ὁ θεός μου κύριε Ἰησοῦ Χριστέ, ὁ ἐπιστάμενος τὸ μέλλον ἔσεσθαι, σοὶ τὴν χρηστήν μου παῖδα Μαξιμίλλαν παρατίθημι. ἐνισχυσάτω σου ὁ λόγος καὶ ἡ δύναμις ἐν αὐτῇ· καὶ καταγωνισάσθω τὸ ἐν αὐτῇ πνεῦμα καὶ τὸν Αἰγεάτην ὑβριστὴν καὶ ἀντίδικον ὄφιν· καὶ διαμεινάτω λοιπόν, κύριε, καθαρὰ ἡ ψυχὴ ἡ ἐν αὐτῇ ἀφαγνισθεῖσα τῷ σῷ ὀνόματι· μάλιστα τοῦ μιαροῦ τούτου

Taken back by the sternness of her face, the proconsul left her. Because he had just completed a long journey, he put off his traveling clothes, relaxed, and lay down to slept.

15. Maximilla then told Iphidama, "Sister, go to the blessed one so that he may come here to pray and lay his hand on me while Aegeates is sleeping."

Without hesitation she ran to Andrew, and after she reported the request of faithful Maximilla, Andrew went and entered another bedroom where Maximilla was. Stratocles also entered with the apostle, having come with the blessed one from his guest residence. For after Stratocles had greeted his brother, he asked about the accommodations where the Lord's apostle was staying. Guided about by a brother named Antiphanes, Stratocles entered with the blessed one.[15]

16. Andrew laid his hand on Maximilla and prayed as follows, * "I ask you, my God, Lord Jesus Christ, who knows the future, I entrust to you my child, the worthy Maximilla. May your word and power be mighty in her, and may the spirit that is in her struggle even against Aegeates, that insolent and hostile snake. O Lord, may her soul remain forever pure, sanctified by your name. In

----

15. The awkwardness of the preceding three sentences issues in part from the absence in *HS* of any earlier reference to Antiphanes or anyone else entertaining Andrew in Patras. *M* 9 also mentions an Antiphanes as Andrew's host in Patras, and *GE* 29 mentions a wealthy man named Antiphanes apparently in Megara. These traces suggest that Antiphanes was more important in the ancient *AA* than our sources allow us to see. Presumably, when Antiphanes and his wife converted in Megara (so *GE*), they became patrons to Andrew, traveled with him from Megara to Patras, and hosted him there (so *HS* and *M*). Prieur doubts that these two characters sharing the same name, Antiphanes, are the same person (*Acta Andreae*, 462, n. 2).

μιάσματος περιφύλαξον αὐτήν, δέσποτα· καὶ τὸν ἄγριον καὶ
ἀεὶ ἀπαίδευτον ἐχθρὸν ἡμῶν κατακοίμησον ἀπὸ τοῦ φαινομένου
αὐτῆς ἀνδρός, καὶ ἅρμοσον αὐτὴν τῷ ἔσω ἀνδρί, ὃν μάλιστα
σὺ γνωρίζεις, οὗ ἕνεκεν τὸ πᾶν σου μυστήριον τῆς
οἰκονομίας τετέλεσται, ὅπως οὕτως ἑδραίαν τὴν ἐν σοὶ
πίστιν ἔχουσα τὴν ἰδίαν συγγένειαν συλλάβῃ, τῶν
προσποιητῶν καὶ ὄντως ἐχθρῶν χωρισθεῖσα. καὶ εὐξάμενος
οὕτω καὶ παραθέμενος τῷ κυρίῳ τὴν Μαξιμίλλαν, πάλιν ἐξῄει
ἅμα τῷ Στρατοκλεῖ.

17. Ἡ οὖν Μαξιμίλλα σκέπτεταί τι τοιοῦτον. παιδίσκην
πάνυ εὔμορφον καὶ φύσει ἄτακτον ὑπερβολῇ, ὀνόματι Εὐκλίαν,
προσεκαλέσατο καί φησιν αὐτῇ ὃ καὶ αὐτὴ ἥδετο καὶ
ἐπεθύμει· εὐεργέτιν με ἕξεις ὧν δέῃ πάντων, εἴ μοι συνθοῖο
καὶ φυλάξειας ἅ σοι προσανατίθεμαι. καὶ εἰποῦσα πρὸς τὴν
Εὐκλίαν ἃ ἐβούλετο, καὶ πιστευθεῖσα ὑπ' αὐτῆς, τοῦ λοιποῦ
ἁγνῶς βουλομένη διάγειν ἔσχεν καὶ τὴν τοιαύτην παραμυθίαν
ἐπὶ χρόνον ἱκανόν. ὡς γὰρ ἔθος ἐστὶ γυναικὶ εὐτρεπίζεσθαι
τὰ τοῦ ἐναντίου εὐτρεπίσματα, τούτοις οἷσπερ ἂν κοσμοῦσα
τὴν Εὐκλίαν, ἐπέτρεψε κατακλίνεσθαι αὐτὴν ὡς αὐτὴ τῷ
Αἰγεάτῃ. ᾗ καὶ χρώμενος ὡς τῇ ἑαυτοῦ συμβίῳ ἀφίει
ἀνισταμένην αὐτὴν ἀπιέναι εἰς τὸν ἴδιον κοιτῶνα ἑαυτῆς·
τοῦτο γὰρ ἦν τῇ Μαξιμίλλῃ ἔθος. διαναπεπαυμένη οὖν καὶ
ἀγαλλιῶσα ἐν τῷ κυρίῳ μὴ ἀπολειπομένη τοῦ Ἀνδρέα,
ἐλάνθανεν ἐπὶ πλεῖον τοῦτο ποιοῦσα.[21]

---

21. Evodius of Uzala, *De fide contra Manichaeos* 38:
    *Maximilla . . . subposuerit marito suo ancillam suam,
    Eucliam nomine, exornans eam . . . adversariis
    lenociniis et fucationibus, et eam nocte pro se
    vicariam subponens, ut illo nesciens cum ea tamquam
    cum uxore concumberet* (CSEL 25.968). *E* and *L*: ἀλλὰ
    προσεποιήσατο νοσεῖν.

particular, protect her, O Master, from this disgusting pollution. With respect to our savage and ever boorish enemy, cause her to sleep apart from her visible husband and wed her to her inner husband, whom you above all recognize, and for whose sake the entire mystery of your plan of salvation has been accomplished. If she has such a firm faith in you, may she obtain her own proper kinship through separation from masquerading (friends) but actual enemies." When he had prayed thus and entrusted Maximilla to the Lord, he left with Stratocles once again.

17. Maximilla then planned the following. She summoned a shapely, exceedingly wanton servant-girl named Euclia and told her what she delighted in and desired. "You will have me as a benefactor of all your needs, providing you scheme with me and carry out what I advise." Because she wanted to live chastely from that time on, Maximilla told Euclia what she wanted and got her word agreeing to it, and so for some time she employed the following subterfuge. Just as a woman customarily adorns herself to look like her rival, Maximilla groomed Euclia in just such finery and put her forward to sleep with Aegeates in her stead. Having used her as his lover, he let her get up and go to her own bedroom, just as Maximilla used to. By so doing, Maximilla escaped detection for some time, and thereby got relief, rejoiced in the Lord, and never left Andrew.[16]

----

16. Evodius of Uzala paraphrases this section of the Acts as follows: "Maximilla . . . imposed on her husband her maid-servant Euclia by making her up . . . with devious finery and cosmetics and by substituting her in her place at night, so that without his knowing it, he would sleep with her as with a wife" (*De fide contra Manichaeos* 38). *E* and *L* offer another ruse for Maximilla not sleeping with Aegeates: "but she pretended to be sick."

18. Ἡ δὲ Εὐκλία μηνῶν ὀκτὼ διεληλυθότων ἠξίωσε τὴν δέσποιναν ἐλευθερίας τυχεῖν. κἀκείνη αὐτῆς ἡμέρας παρέσχεν αὐτῇ ὃ ᾐτήσατο. πάλιν μετ' ὀλίγας ἡμέρας ᾔτησε καὶ χρῆμα οὐκ ὀλίγον· κἀκείνη δέδωκεν αὐτῇ ἀμελλητί· εἶτα καὶ τῶν κοσμίων αὐτῆς τινα· ἡ δὲ οὐκ ἀντεῖπεν. καὶ ἁπαξαπλῶς ἱμάτια, ὀθόνας, περιθέματα ἑκάστοτε λαμβάνουσα παρὰ τῆς Μαξιμίλλης οὐκ ἠρκέσθη, ἀλλὰ τοῖς συνδούλοις τὸ πρᾶγμα περίφαντον ἐποίησεν, καυχωμένη ὥσπερ καὶ ἐπαιρομένη.

Κἀκεῖνοι ἐπὶ τῷ καυχᾶσθαι τὴν Εὐκλίαν ἀγανακτήσαν-τες, τὰ μὲν πρῶτα ἐπεστόμιζον αὐτὴν διαλοιδορούμενοι. ἡ δὲ γελῶσα πρὸς αὐτοὺς ἐδείκνυεν αὐτοῖς τὰ παρὰ τῆς δεσποίνης δεδομένα αὐτῇ δῶρα· ἃ γνωρίσαντες οἱ τῆς Εὐκλίας σύνδουλοι ἠπόρουν ὃ πράξωσιν. ἡ δὲ Εὐκλία αὐτοῖς πίστιν ὧν ἔλεγεν ἔτι μᾶλλον παρέχεσθαι βουληθεῖσα ἐπέστησεν οἰνωμένου τοῦ ἑαυτῆς δεσπότου πρὸς τῇ κεφαλῇ αὐτοῦ δύο τινάς, ὅπως πεισθεῖεν ὅτι ὄντως αὐτῷ παρακατακλίνεται ὡς αὐτὴ οὖσα ἡ Μαξίμιλλα. διυπνίσασα γὰρ αὐτόν, βαθεῖ ὕπνῳ κατανηνεγμένον, ἤκουσεν ἅμα τοῖς αὐτῇ συνδούλοις ἐπιτηρουμένοις τὸ πρᾶγμα· ἡ κυρία μου Μαξιμίλλα, τί βραδέως; ἡ δὲ ἐσίγα. κἀκεῖνοι ἐφεστῶτες ἠρέμα ἐξῄεσαν τοῦ κοιτῶνος.

19. Ἡ δὲ Μαξιμίλλα οἰομένη ἀφλύαρον καὶ πιστὴν ὑπάρχειν τὴν Εὐκλίαν διὰ τὰ αὐτῇ δῶρα δεδομένα, ταῖς νυξὶ παρὰ τῷ Ἀνδρέᾳ διανεπαύετο ἅμα τῷ Στρατοκλεῖ καὶ τοῖς λοιποῖς πᾶσιν ἀδελφοῖς. ὁ δὲ Ἀνδρέας θεασάμενος ὄναρ εἶπεν πρὸς τοὺς ἀδελφοὺς ἀκουούσης καὶ τῆς Μαξιμίλλης· καινίζεταί τι σήμερον ἐν τῇ τοῦ Αἰγεάτου οἰκίᾳ κατασκεύασμα, ταραχῆς καὶ ὀργῆς γέμον. ἡ δὲ Μαξιμίλλα ἐδέετο αὐτοῦ μαθεῖν ὅ τι εἴη τοῦτο. ὁ δέ φησιν· ὃ μετ' ὀλίγον γνωρίζεις μὴ σπεῦδε παρ' ἐμοῦ μαθεῖν.

18. When eight months had elapsed, Euclia demanded that her lady procure her freedom. That same day, Maximilla granted her whatever she asked. A few days later, she made more demands, this time a large sum of money, and Maximilla gave it to her without hesitation. When Euclia demanded some of her jewelry, Maximilla did not object. In a word, even though Euclia regularly took clothing, fine linen, and headbands from Maximilla, she was not content but flaunted the affair before the other servants, boasting like a show-off.

The slaves, though peeved at Euclia's bragging, at first curbed themselves from lashing out at her. But she would laugh at them when showing them the gifts her mistress had given her. Euclia's fellow servants recognized them but were at a loss about what to do. Wishing to provide even greater proof of what she was saying, Euclia stationed two of them at the head of her master's bed when he was drunk, in order to convince them that she was indeed sleeping with him as though she were Maximilla. When she woke him from a deep sleep, she and the fellow servants observing the situation heard: "Maximilla, my lady, why so late?" Euclia said nothing, and the attending servants left the bedroom without a peep.

19. But Maximilla, supposing that Euclia was true to her word and reliable because of the gifts given her, spent her nights resting with Andrew along with Stratocles and all the other brethren. Andrew saw a vision, and as Maximilla listened, he told the brethren, "Today at the home of Aegeates some new contrivance is brewing, brimming with trouble and wrath." Maximilla begged him to disclose what this might be, but he said, "Do not be eager to learn from me what you are to recognize soon enough."

20. Ἡ δὲ συνήθως μεταμφιασθεῖσα τὴν ἐσθῆτα ἁπάντων ὁρώντων εἴσεισιν εἰς τὸν τοῦ πραιτωρίου πυλῶνα. * οἱ δὲ ἀπὸ τῆς οἰκίας τὸ πρᾶγμα μεμαθηκότες καὶ πῶς καθ᾽ ἑκάστην ἡμέραν ἅμα τῷ Στρατοκλεῖ ἀπήρχετο πρὸς τὸν Ἀνδρέαν καὶ ποίᾳ ὥρᾳ εἰς τὸν κοιτῶνα τὸν ἴδιον εἰσῄει, ἐλάβοντο αὐτῆς ὥς τινος ἀλλοδαπῆς· κἀκείνης τῆς ὥρας εἰς τὸ πραιτώριον τοῦ ἀνθυπάτου εἰσερχομένης καὶ ἀντιτεινούσης ἵνα μὴ ὀφθῇ, βίᾳ ὥσπερ ἀποκαλύψαντες αὐτὴν ἑώρων τὴν αὐτῶν δέσποιναν. καὶ οἱ μὲν αὐτῶν τὸ πρᾶγμα περίφαντον ἐβούλοντο ποιῆσαι καὶ τῷ Αἰγεάτῃ ἀγγέλλειν, οἱ δὲ ἐπεῖχον στοργὴν ὑποκρίσει πρὸς τὴν δέσποιναν ἀγόμενοι, ἐπεστόμιζον τοὺς σὺν αὐτοῖς καὶ τύπτοντες ὡς μεμηνότας διώθουν αὐτοὺς ἐκεῖθεν. καὶ οὕτως ἐκείνων διαμαχομένων πρὸς ἀλλήλους ἡ Μαξιμίλλα εἰσεπήδησεν εἰς τὸν ἑαυτῆς κοιτῶνα εὐχομένη τῷ κυρίῳ ἀποστραφῆναι πᾶν πονηρὸν ἀπ᾽ αὐτῆς.

21. Καὶ μετὰ ὥραν μίαν εἰσέβαλον πρὸς αὐτὴν οἱ διαμαχόμενοι τοῖς ὁμοδούλοις ὑπὲρ αὐτῆς, θωπείας λόγους ἀγγέλλοντες αὐτῇ, λήψεσθαί τι προσδοκῶντες ὡσανεὶ δοῦλοι τοῦ Αἰγεάτου· οὓς οὐκ ἀπηξίωσεν ἡ μακαρῖτις ὧν ἠξίουν, ἀλλὰ προσκαλεσαμένη τὴν Ἰφιδάμαν ἔφη· δῶμεν τούτοις ὧν εἰσιν ἄξιοι. καὶ οὕτως κελεύσασα δοθῆναι αὐτοῖς δηνάρια χίλια, ὑποκρίσει προσποιησαμένοις αὐτὴν φιλεῖν, ἐνετείλατο μηδενὶ τὸ πρᾶγμα δῆλον ποιῆσαι.

Οἱ δὲ καὶ πολλὰ διομοσάμενοι σιγήσειν τὸ ὀφθὲν αὐτοῖς, ὑφοδηγούμενοι ὑπὸ τοῦ πατρὸς αὐτῶν τοῦ διαβόλου, εὐθέως πρὸς τὸν ἴδιον δεσπότην εἰσέβαλον, ἔχοντες μεθ᾽ ἑαυτῶν καὶ τὸ χρῆμα. καὶ τὸ ὅλον διήγημα ἤγγελλον αὐτῷ καὶ ὅπως αὐτοῖς ἡ ἰδία συνδούλη ὑπέβαλε τὸ τῆς Μαξιμίλλης τεχνασθὲν πρᾶγμα, μηκέτι βουλομένης κοινοῦσθαι τῷ Αἰγεάτῃ, ἀπεστραμμένη<ς>[22] τὴν πρὸς αὐτὸν μῖξιν ὥς τι δεινὸν καὶ αἰσχρὸν ἔργον.

---

22. *HS* actually reads: ἀπεστραμμένη.

20. She altered her customary attire and entered the praetorium gate in plain sight. * The household servants who had known about the affair--how it was that every day she and Stratocles sneaked off to Andrew, and at what hour she returned to her own bedroom--took her for some foreigner. She sneaked into the proconsul's praetorium at that hour trying to escape detection. When they had forcibly exposed her, they noticed she was their mistress. Some of them wanted to divulge the ruse and to tattle to Aegeates, while the others, motivated by hypocrisy toward their mistress, feigned fondness for her and silenced the others, assaulted them as though they were insane, and drove them out. While the slaves were fighting each other, Maximilla burst into her bedroom and prayed that the Lord would fend her from every evil.

21. One hour later, those who had fought on Maximilla's behalf against their fellow servants set upon her, fawning, expecting to receive some payoff, just as though they were servants of Aegeates. The blessed lady considered them deserving of their request and summoned Iphidama: "Let's give them their due." She ordered that those who had hypocritically simulated affection for her be given one thousand denarii and commanded them to disclose the matter to no one.

Even though they solemnly swore themselves to silence about what they had seen, at the instigation of their father the devil, they went to their master immediately, money in hand, and told him the whole story, including how their own fellow servant submitted to the plan Maximilla devised because she no longer wanted to sleep with Aegeates, repulsed by sex with him as a heinous and despicable act.

22. Καὶ ὁ ἀνθύπατος πάντα ἀκριβευσάμενος καὶ ὅπως ἡ Εὐκλία παρεκατεκλίνετο αὐτῷ ὡς αὐτὴ οὖσα ἡ σύμβιος, <καὶ> ὡμολόγησε τοῖς ἰδίοις συνδούλοις, ἣν καὶ αὐτὴν ἀνακρίνας ἔμαθεν τὴν ὅλην αἰτίαν· ἥτις βασανιζομένη πάντα ὡμολόγησεν ἃ παρὰ τῆς δεσποίνης ἔλαβεν τοῦ σιγῆσαι ἕνεκεν.

'Εφ' ᾗ πάνυ ἀγανακτήσας διότι ἐκαυχήσατο πρὸς τοὺς συνδούλους ἐκεῖνά τε εἶπεν ὑποδιαβάλλουσα τὴν δέσποιναν--ἐβούλετο γὰρ σεσιγῆσθαι τὸ πρᾶγμα, φιλοστόργως διακείμενος πρὸς τὴν σύμβιον--τὴν μὲν Εὐκλίαν ἐγλωσσοτόμησεν καὶ ἠκρωτηρίασεν, κελεύσας αὐτὴν ἔξω ῥιφῆναι· ἥτις μετὰ ἡμέρας ἄτροφος μείνασα, κυσὶν βορὰ ἐγένετο. τοὺς δὲ λοιποὺς αὐτοῦ δούλους τοὺς εἰρηκότας πρὸς αὐτὸν ἃ δὴ εἶπον, τρεῖς ὄντας, ἐσταύρωσεν.

23. Καὶ ἐφ' ἑαυτοῦ μεμενηκὼς καὶ μηδὲν ὅλως γευσάμενος ἐκείνης τῆς ἡμέρας διὰ τὴν ἀνίαν, διαπορῶν τὴν πολλὴν μεταβολὴν τῆς Μαξιμίλλης τῆς πρὶν πρὸς αὐτὸν διαθέσεως, καὶ πολλὰ ἀποδακρύσας καὶ ὀνειδίσας τοῖς θεοῖς αὐτοῦ, εἴσεισι πρὸς τὴν σύμβιον· καὶ προσπεσὼν τοῖς ποσὶν αὐτῆς μετὰ δακρύων ἔλεγεν· ἅπτομαί σου τῶν ποδῶν, ἀνὴρ συμβίου ἔτη ἤδη συγγεγονώς σοι δύο καὶ δέκα, ἣν ἀεὶ ὥσπερ τινὰ θεὰν ἐτιθέμην σὲ καὶ νῦν τίθημι σωφροσύνης ἕνεκεν καὶ τοῦ λοιποῦ σου ἤθους κοσμίου ὄντος· ὅπερ ἐνδέχεται, ἀνθρώπου καὶ σοῦ οὔσης, πρὸς ὀλίγον μεταβεβλῆσθαι. εἰ μὲν οὖν ἔστι τι τοιοῦτον ὅπερ οὐκ ἂν προσδοκήσαιμι τὸ ὑπεισιόν μοι περί τινος ἑτέρου ἀνδρός, συγγνωμονήσω καὶ αὐτὸς κρύψω καθὰ καὶ αὐτὴ πολλά μου ἠνέσχου ἀφραίνοντος. εἰ δὲ καὶ ἕτερόν τι χαλεπώτερον τούτου εἴη διαζευγνῦόν σε ἐμοῦ, ὁμολόγησον τοῦτο καὶ τάχα ἰάσομαι ἐγνωκὼς πρὸς τὸ μηδὲν ὅλως σοι ἀντιλέγειν.

'Η δὲ τοσοῦτον αὐτῷ ἐπεῖπεν πολλὰ λιπαροῦντι καὶ δεομένῳ· φιλῶ, Αἰγεάτα, φιλῶ. καὶ ὃ φιλῶ οὐδὲν τῶν ἐν τῷ κόσμῳ ἐστὶν τούτῳ ὥστε γενέσθαι σοι κατάδηλον, καί με νυκτὸς καὶ ἡμέρας ἐξάπτει καὶ φλέγει τῇ πρὸς αὐτὸ στοργῇ·

22. The proconsul learned everything in detail, how Euclia had shared his bed as though she were his spouse, and how she confessed to have done so to her fellow slaves. Through interrogation he also discovered her motivation, for under torture she confessed to all the payoffs she received from her lady for keeping quiet.

The proconsul, furious at her for boasting to her fellow servants and for saying these things in order to defame her mistress--he wanted the matter hushed up since he was still affectionate for his spouse--cut out Euclia's tongue, mutilated her, and ordered her thrown outside. She stayed there without food for several days before she became food for the dogs. The rest of the servants who had told their story to him--there were three of them--he crucified.

23. Stricken by grief, Aegeates stayed in seclusion that day and ate nothing at all, baffled by the great change in Maximilla's attitude toward him. After crying for some time and reproaching his gods, he went to his spouse, fell at her feet weeping, and said, "I cling to your feet, I who have been your husband now for twelve years, who always revered you as a goddess and still do because of your chastity and your generally refined character, even though it might have been tarnished somewhat, since even you are human. So if you are keeping some secret from me about another man--something I never would have suspected--I will make allowances and I myself will cover it up, just as you often put up with my foolishness. Or if there is something else even more serious than this that separates you from me, confess it and I will quickly remedy the situation, for I know it is entirely useless to contradict you."

While he persistently cajoled and begged, she told him, "I am in love, Aegeates. I am in love, and the object

ὃ οὐκ ἂν αὐτὸς ἴδοις δύσκολον ὄν, οὔτ' ἂν ἐμὲ τούτου
χωρίσαις, ἀδύνατον γάρ. ἔα οὖν με αὐτῷ προσομιλεῖν, μὲ καὶ
μόνῳ αὐτῷ προσαναπαύεσθαι.

24. Ὁ δὲ ἀνθύπατος ἐξελθὼν ἀπ' αὐτῆς καί τις ὥσπερ
ἐμμανὴς ἠπόρει ὃ πράξει· οὐ γὰρ ἐτόλμα τι τῶν μὴ
προσηκόντων πρὸς τὴν μακαρῖτιν διαπράξασθαι, πολλῷ αὐτοῦ
διασημοτάτην τοῦ γένους ἕνεκεν ὑπάρχουσαν. καὶ δὴ τῷ
Στρατοκλεῖ συμβαδίζοντι ἔλεγεν· ἀδελφέ, καὶ μόνε μοι τοῦ
παντὸς ἡμῶν γένους τεθνεῶτος συγγενῆ γνήσιε, τὴν σύμβιόν
μου γενομένην ἐν ἐκστάσει ἢ μανίᾳ οὐκ ἐπίσταμαι.

Καὶ ὡς ἤρξατό τι ἕτερον λέγειν πρὸς τὸν ἀδελφὸν
ἀθυμῶν, τῶν σὺν αὐτῷ τις δούλων εἷς πρὸς τὸ οὖς ἔφη·
δέσποτα, εἰ ἄρα βούλῃ τὸ πρᾶγμα ἐκμαθεῖν, τοῦ Στρατοκλέους
πύθου καί σε αὐτὸς διαναπαύσει, ἐπίσταται γὰρ ἅπαντα τὰ
κατὰ τὴν σύμβιόν σου. εἰ δὲ ἤδη τὸ πᾶν πρᾶγμα γνῶναι
βούλῃ, ἐγώ σοι ἐμφανίσω.

25. Καὶ ἑλκύσας αὐτὸν ἰδίᾳ εἶπεν· * ἔστι τις ξένος
ἐπιδημήσας οὐ μόνον τῇ πόλει ταύτῃ ἀλλὰ καὶ ὅλῃ τῇ Ἀχαΐᾳ
περίφαντος γενόμενος. οὗτος δυνάμεις μεγίστας καὶ
θεραπείας ὑπὲρ ἀνθρώπων ἰσχὺν διαπράττεται, ὡς καὶ αὐτὸς
ἐκ μέρους μαρτυρῶ παρατυχὼν καὶ θεασάμενος νεκροὺς ὑπ'
αὐτοῦ ἐγειρομένους. τὰ δὲ ὅλα ὅπως εἰδείης, θεοσέβειαν
ἐπαγγέλλεται καὶ ἀληθῶς ταύτην δείκνυσι καὶ εἰς τὸ φανερὸν
διαλάμπουσαν. τούτῳ οὖν τῷ ξένῳ καὶ ἡ δέσποινά μου
προηγησαμένης τῆς Ἰφιδάμας ἐγνωρίσθη. καὶ εἰς τοσοῦτον
ἐχώρησε τῷ αὐτοῦ πόθῳ ὡς μηδένα ἄλλον ὅλως αὐτοῦ στέργειν
πλέον, ἵνα μὴ καὶ σοῦ εἴπω. οὐ μόνον δὲ οὕτως τῷ ἀνδρὶ

of my love is not of this world and therefore is imperceptible to you. Night and day it kindles and enflames me with love for it. You cannot see it for it is difficult to see, and you cannot separate me from it, for that is impossible. Let me have intercourse and take my rest with it alone."

24. The proconsul left her like some maniac, not knowing what to do. He did not dare commit any impropriety against the blessed woman, for her pedigree far outstripped his. He said to Stratocles who was walking with him, "Brother and my only legitimate kin insofar as our entire family has died off, I do not know if my wife is in a state of ecstacy or lunacy."

And as he dispiritedly began to tell Stratocles something else, one of his attending servants whispered in his ear, "Master, if you would learn of this affair in detail, ask Stratocles; he will satisfy your curiosity, for he knows all about your wife. But if you would know of the entire matter right now, I will apprise you."

25. He drew Aegeates aside and told him privately, * "There is a certain stranger sojourning here who has become renowned not only in this city but throughout Achaea. He performs great miracles and cures exceeding human strength, as I in part can corroborate in that I was present and saw him revive corpses.[17] And so that you may know the whole story, he proclaims a reverence for the divine and truly shows it to be shining forth into public view. My mistress, following Iphidama's lead, became acquainted with this stranger. She has so given way to desire for him that she loves no one more than him, including you I would say. Not only has she become

----

17. Presumably these corpses are those cast up by the sea according to *GE* 24.

συνεκράθη, ἀλλὰ καὶ τὸν ἀδελφόν σου Στρατοκλέα τῷ αὐτῷ
πόθῳ περιέδησεν ᾧπερ καὶ αὐτὴ δέδεται, μόνον ἕνα θεὸν τὸν
δι᾽ ἐκείνου αὐτοῖς γνωρισθέντα ὁμολογοῦντες, ἄλλον μηδένα
ὅλως ἐπὶ τὴν γῆν ὑπάρχειν. ἀλλὰ καὶ τὸ πάντων
μανιωδέστατον πρασσόμενον ὑπὸ τοῦ ἀδελφοῦ σου ἄκουσον. ὁ
γένους τοιούτου ὤν, ὁ ἐνδοξότατος ἐν τῇ ᾽Αχαΐᾳ Αἰγεάτου
ἀδελφὸς χρηματίζων τοῦ ἀνθυπάτου, ἑαυτῷ ληκύθιον εἰς τὸ
γυμνάσιον εἰσκομίζει. ὁ δούλους πολλοὺς ἔχων αὐτοδιάκων
δείκνυται, λάχανα ὠνούμενος καὶ ἄρτους καὶ τὰ λοιπὰ
ἐπιτήδεια διὰ μέσης τῆς πόλεως βαδίζων φέρει, ἀναίσχυντός
τις ὁρώμενος πᾶσιν ἁπαξαπλῶς.

26. Καὶ ὡς ὡμίλει ταῦτα ὁ νέος τῷ ἰδίῳ δεσπότῃ
βαδίζοντι διὰ τὸ πολλὴν αὐτὸν ὥραν εἰς γῆν ὁρᾶν, ὁρᾷ
πόρρωθεν ᾽Ανδρέαν καὶ εἰς ἐξάκουστον κεκραγὼς εἶπεν·
δέσποτα, ἰδοὺ ὁ ἄνθρωπος δι᾽ ὃν ἡ οἰκία σου ἀκαταστατεῖ
νῦν. καὶ ὁ πᾶς ὄχλος ἐπεστράφη πρὸς τὴν ἐκείνου βοὴν
ὀψόμενος τὴν αἰτίαν. καὶ μηδὲν ἕτερον εἰρηκὼς ἀφίησι τὸν
ἀνθύπατον ὁ ὅμοιος αὐτῷ δεινός, ὥσπερ καὶ αὐτοῦ ἀδελφός,
οὐ γὰρ δὴ δοῦλος, καὶ δρομαίως πορευθεὶς λαμβάνεται τοῦ
᾽Ανδρέα καὶ βίᾳ αὐτὸν ἄγει πρὸς τὸν Αἰγεάτην, περιβαλὼν
αὐτοῦ τῷ αὐχένι ᾧ ἐχρῆτο ἐπὶ τοῦ ὤμου ὁ μακάριος σαβάνιον.

῞Ον ἰδὼν ὁ ἀνθύπατος ἐγνώρισε καὶ εἶπεν· σὺ εἶ ὁ ποτέ
μου τὴν σύμβιον ἰασάμενος, ᾧ ἠβουλήθην χρῆμα ἱκανὸν
χαρίσασθαι καὶ οὐκ ἠβουλήθης. τίς ἡ περὶ σὲ δόξα δίδαξον
κἀμέ, ἢ ἡ τοσαύτη σου δύναμις, ἵνα πένης οὕτως καὶ λιτὸς
ὁρώμενος καὶ ἤδη πρεσβύτης πλουσίους ἔχῃς ἐραστὰς καὶ
πένητας καὶ μέχρι καὶ βρεφῶν ὡς πυνθάνομαι.

intimately involved with the man, she has tied up your brother Stratocles with the same passion for him that has tied her up. They confess but one God, the one that man disclosed to them, denying the existence of every other on earth. But listen to what your brother did that was craziest of all. Even though he is of noble stock, the most honored man in Achaea, addressed as brother of the proconsul Aegeates, he carries his own little oil flask to the gymnasium. Even though he owns many slaves, he appears in public doing his own chores--buying his own vegetables, bread, and other necessities and carrying them on foot through the center of the city--making himself look simply repulsive to everyone."

26. He told this to his master who was taking a stroll, staring at the ground for a long time, and then the youth spotted Andrew from a distance and shouted out loud: "Look, master! There is the man responsible for the present disruption of your household." The entire crowd turned to see the cause of his outburst. Without another word, the youth--who was as fearsome as Aegeates, as though he were his brother and not really his slave--ran from the proconsul, seized Andrew, and forcibly brought him to Aegeates, wrapping around his neck the towel that the blessed one used to wear over his shoulder.[18]

When the proconsul saw him, he recognized him and said, "You are the one who once cured my wife and who refused a considerable sum of money I wanted to donate. Teach me too about your renown and what sort of power you have, such that you have lovers, so I hear, who are rich and poor, including infants, even though you appear in this manner like a simple old tramp."

----

18. Cf. *ATh* 106.

Ὁ δὲ πᾶς ὄχλος παρὼν φιλοστόργως διακείμενος πρὸς
τὸν ἀπόστολον μαθὼν τὸν ἀνθύπατον αὐτῷ προσομιλοῦντα
προσέτρεχεν τῷ τόπῳ ἔνθα αὐτῷ ὡμίλει, διαπορῶν τὴν
αἰτίαν.23 καὶ μὴ μελλήσας ὁ Αἰγεάτης ἐκέλευσεν αὐτὸν ἐγ-
κλεισθῆναι24 εἰπὼν τοῦτο· ὄψῃ, λυμεών, τὰς εἰς Μαξιμίλλαν
εὐεργεσίας σου ταύτας δι' ἐμοῦ εὐχαρίστους ἀποδιδομένας
σοι.

----

23. M 9b-10: Σὺν δὲ τῇ βίᾳ παραχρῆμα συνήχθη πᾶσα ἡ πόλις
    ἐπὶ τὰς θύρας τοῦ Ἀντιφάνους βοῶσα καὶ λέγουσα·
    Καῖσαρ ἀπέστειλεν τὸν ἀνθύπατον εἰς ἄμυναν μὲν τῶν
    κακῶν, ἔπαινον δὲ τῶν ἀγαθῶν. τί οὖν τὸν δοῦλον τοῦ
    θεοῦ ζητεῖ ὁ Αἰγεάτης; μαθεῖν βουλόμεθα. ἡμῶν γὰρ
    Ἀνδρέας ὁ ἀπόστολος τοῦ ξένου θεοῦ καὶ πατὴρ (two
    mss. add: καὶ μήτηρ) καὶ διδάσκαλος καὶ ἰατρὸς
    καθέστηκεν. μὴ βιάζεσθε ἡμῶν τὸν πατέρα· μὴ ἐμποδίζετε
    ἡμῶν τὸν διδάσκαλον· μὴ αἴρετε ἡμῶν τὸν ἰατρόν· μὴ
    σκοτίσητε ἡμῶν τὸν φωστῆρα· μὴ ἀποστερήσητε ἡμῶν τὴν
    ζωήν· μὴ ἀδικήσητε ἡμῶν τὸν ποιμένα· καὶ γὰρ ἡμεῖς
    πάντες ἕτοιμοι ἐσμὲν ὑπὲρ αὐτοῦ ἀποθανεῖν, ἐπειδὴ
    πάντας ἡμᾶς τῷ ζωοποιῷ Χριστῷ ὡς ἀρνία παρέστησεν.
    ταῦτα αὐτῶν βοώντων φοβηθεὶς ὁ μακάριος μήποτε τὸ
    πλῆθος διαχειρίσωνται τοὺς ἀποσταλέντας παρὰ τοῦ
    Αἰγεάτου, ἐξελθὼν τῆς οἰκίας καὶ μέσον σταθεὶς τῶν
    ὄχλων κατέσεισεν αὐτοὺς τῇ χειρὶ σιγᾶν· καὶ στὰς ἐπί
    τινος ὑψηλοῦ τόπου ἤμελλεν ἀνοίγειν τὸ στόμα, καὶ
    πάντες μιᾷ φωνῇ ἐβόησαν· μέγας ὁ θεὸς τοῦ ξένου
    Ἀνδρέα, ὃς διῆλθεν διὰ τοῦ δούλου αὐτοῦ εὐεργετῶν
    πάντας τοὺς καταδυναστευομένους ὑπὸ τοῦ διαβόλου. καὶ
    φησὶν ὁ Ἀνδρέας· ἀδελφοὶ οἱ κληθέντες ὑπὸ τοῦ Χριστοῦ
    καὶ οἱ ἐκλεχθέντες ὑπὸ τῆς χάριτος τοῦ λόγου· οὐ τοῦτο
    μόνον χάρις ἐστὶν ἵνα εἰς τὸν ἀποστείλαντά με
    πιστεύσητε, ἀλλ' ἵνα καὶ ὑπὲρ αὐτοῦ ἀποθάνητε.
    παύσασθε οὖν θορύβους ποιοῦντες, μήποτε ὡς αἴτιοι
    στάσεως καὶ ἀρχηγοὶ πολέμου εὐθύνας ἀποδῶμεν καὶ οὐχ
    ὡς πολῖται θεοσεβείας· ἄφετε πορευθῶ πρὸς τὸν
    Αἰγεάτην· συγχωρήσατε τοῖς κρατοῦσίν με· ἀποθανὼν γὰρ
    μᾶλλον ὀφθήσομαι ὑμῖν σήμερον τὴν ὁδὸν τῆς ἀναστάσεως
    ὑποδεικνύων. καὶ οὕτως μόλις καταπαύσας τοὺς ὄχλους
    παρέδωκεν ἑαυτὸν τοῖς δημίοις. οἱ δὲ δήμιοι ὡς θῆρες
    καὶ οὐκ ἄνθρωποι, ὡς λύκοι ἁπαλὸν καὶ καλὸν ἀρνίον
    ἁρπάσαντες τοῖς ὀδοῦσιν, ἐν πληγαῖς ἀνηκέστοις καὶ
    μάστιξιν φοβεροῖς ὥσπερ κύνα οὕτως συνέτριβον πάντα τὰ
    μέλη αὐτοῦ. μετὰ δὲ ταῦτα ἤγαγον αὐτὸν τῷ μιαρωτάτῳ
    Αἰγεάτῃ.

24. N adds: ἐν φρουρᾷ πλησίον τῆς αὐτόθι θαλάσσης.

The entire crowd on hand dearly loved the apostle,
and when they learned that the proconsul was speaking with
him but not knowing why, they ran to the place where he
was talking with Andrew.[19] Without hesitation, Aegeates

----

19. *M* 9b-10 gives a different account of the arrest of
Andrew in which the role of the crowd is much more
significant. Instead of the slaveboy bringing Andrew
to Aegeates, Aegeates sends his henchmen to arrest the
apostle at the house of Antiphanes, Andrew's host.
"Immediately the entire city violently assembled at
the door of Antiphanes shouting: 'Caesar sent the
proconsul to punish the wicked and praise the good.
Why then does Aegeates seek the servant of God? We
want to know! For Andrew the apostle of the foreign
god has become our father (two mss. add: and mother)
and teacher and healer. Do not commit violence against
our father! Do not manacle our teacher! Do not kill
our physician! Do not darken our illuminator! Do not
steal our life! Do no injustice to our shepherd, for
all of us are prepared to die for him, because he
presented us all like sacrificial lambs to the life-
giving Christ.' As they were shouting this, the
blessed one feared the throng would lay their hands on
those who had been sent by Aegeates, so he left the
house, stood in the middle of the crowd, and waved his
hands for them to be quiet. He stood on a high spot
and was about to open his mouth when everyone shouted
in unison: 'Great is the God of the stranger Andrew
who came among us through his servant and helped all
those who had been overcome by the devil.' Andrew
said, 'Brethren, called by Christ and chosen by the
grace of the Word, grace consists not only in your
believing in the one who sent me but also in your
dying for him. Stop causing a disturbance. Let us give
account of ourselves, not as originators of rebellion
or instigators of war but as citizens of piety. Let me
go to Aegeates. Give room to those who are arresting
me, for after I die, I will appear to you today,
demonstrating the way of resurrection.' So saying, he
barely quieted the crowd and handed himself over to
the executioners. The executioners, like beasts not
humans, grabbed him with their teeth--like wolves on a
tender and beautiful lamb. With barbarous blows and
ferocious floggings, like dogs they mangled all his
body parts. After this, they led him off to disgusting
Aegeates." According to Prieur, correspondences
between this passage and *Ep* 2-6 indicate that in the
original *AA* Andrew did indeed denounce pagan temples
(*Acta Andreae*, 53-59).

27. Καὶ βραχὺ διαλιπὼν εἴσεισι πρὸς τὴν Μαξιμίλλαν καὶ καταλαμβάνει αὐτὴν ἅμα τῇ Ἰφιδάμᾳ ἄρτον μετὰ ἐλαιῶν ἐσθίουσαν--ἦν γὰρ καὶ τὸ τῆς ὥρας οὕτως ἔχον--καί φησιν αὐτῇ· ἐγώ, Μαχιμίλλα, εὐπορήσας τοῦ διδασκάλου σου καὶ κατακλείσας αὐτὸν τὰς περὶ αὐτοῦ ἀγγελίας εἰσκομίζω, ὅτι με οὐκ ἐκφεύξεται, ἀλλὰ κακῶς ἀπολεῖται.

Καὶ ἡ μακαρῖτις αὐτῷ ἀπεκρίνατο· οὐκ ἔστι τῶν δυναμένων ἀποκλεισθῆναι ὁ ἐμὸς διδάσκαλος· οὐ γάρ ἐστι ληπτός, οὐδὲ ὄψει δεικτός. οὐδενὸς οὖν τῶν τοιούτων ἐπικρατὴς γεγονώς, Αἰγεᾶτα, μέθες τὸ τοιοῦτόν σου καύχημα. κἀκεῖνος μειδιῶν ἐξῆλθεν, καταλιπὼν αὐτὴν ἐσθίουσαν.

Καὶ ἡ Μαξιμίλλα τῇ Ἰφιδάμᾳ ἔφη· ἀδελφή, ἡμεῖς νῦν ἐσθίομεν καὶ ὁ μετὰ τὸν κύριον ἡμῶν εὐεργέτης κατακέκλεισται. ἄπελθε ἐν ὀνόματι κυρίου, Ἰφιδάμα, μέχρι τοῦ φρουρίου, μάθε ὅπου τυγχάνει τὸ δεσμωτήριον. πιστεύω δὲ ὅτι ἑσπέρας γενομένης δυνησόμεθα ἰδεῖν τὸν ἀπόστολον τοῦ κυρίου καὶ ὅτι οὐθείς με ὄψεται ἀπιοῦσαν, ἢ μόνος Ἰησοῦς καὶ σὺ ἡ ξεναγοῦσά με.

28. Καὶ ἡ Ἰφιδάμα μεταμφιασθεῖσα τὴν συνήθη ἐσθῆτα πιστῶς ὥρμα. πυθομένη οὖν τὸ δεσμωτήριον ποῦ εἴη καὶ ἐπιστᾶσα τῷ τόπῳ ὁρᾷ ὄχλον πολὺν πρὸ τοῦ πυλῶνος τοῦ δεσμωτηρίου ἑστῶτα. καὶ ἐξήτασε τὴν τοῦ ὄχλου συγκρότησιν, καί τις αὐτῇ ἀπεκρίνατο· Ἀνδρέα τοῦ εὐσεβεστάτου ἕνεκεν κατακλεισθέντος ὑπὸ τοῦ Αἰγεάτου.

Καὶ ὡς προσέστη ὥραν μίαν ἡ πιστοτάτη Ἰφιδάμα, εἶδεν τὸν πυλῶνα τοῦ δεσμωτηρίου ἀνοιχθέντα καὶ θαρσήσασα εἶπεν· Ἰησοῦ, συνείσελθέ μοι πρὸς τὸν σὸν δοῦλον, δέομαί σου. καὶ μηδενὶ κατάφορος γενομένη εἰσῆλθε καὶ κατέλαβε τὸν ἀπόστολον ὁμιλοῦντα τοῖς σὺν αὐτῷ κατακλείστοις, οὓς ἤδη εἰς τὴν πίστιν τοῦ κυρίου παρακαλῶν ἐστήριζεν.

ordered him locked up,[20] saying, "Corrupter! You will see
my rewards to you for your benefactions to Maximilla."

27. A short time later, Aegeates left and went to
Maximilla and discovered her eating bread and olives with
Iphidama—it was the right time for it—and said to her,
"Maximilla, now that I have captured your teacher and
locked him up, I bring you news about him: he will not
escape from me but will suffer a horrible death."

"My teacher is not someone who can be detained," the
blessed lady answered, "for he is not apprehensible or
perceptible. Inasmuch as you have never overpowered anyone
like this, Aegeates, stop this boasting." He left smiling,
leaving her to eat.

"Sister," Maximilla said to Iphidama, "here we are
eating while our benefactor (second to the Lord himself)
is imprisoned. Go to the garrison in the name of the Lord,
Iphidama, and find out where the prison is. I believe that
at nightfall we will be able to see the Lord's apostle and
that no one will see me leaving except Jesus and you, my
guide."

28. Iphidama changed out of her usual garb and
dutifully rushed off. Once she discovered where the prison
was, she went there and saw a large crowd standing at the
prison gate. She inquired why the crowd had formed, and
someone told her, "Because of the most pious Andrew,
locked up by Aegeates."

When the faithful Iphidama had stood there for an
hour, she saw the prison gate opened, and encouraged by
this, she said, "Jesus, I ask you to go in with me to your
servant." No one detected her as she entered and found the

----

20. *N* adds: "in a garrison next to the sea."

29. Καὶ ἐπιστραφεὶς εἶδεν τὴν Ἰφιδάμαν καὶ ἐπαρθεὶς τῇ ψυχῇ εἶπεν πρὸς τὸν κύριον· δόξα σοι, Ἰησοῦ Χριστέ, ἀληθῶν λόγων καὶ ὑποσχέσεων πρύτανις, ὃς εὐθαρσίαν τοῖς συνδούλοις δίδως, ὅπερ εἶ σὺ μόνος, ᾧ κεχρημένοι πάντες καταγωνίζονται τοὺς ἐναντίους. ἰδοὺ γὰρ ἡ Ἰφιδάμα ἡ σή, ἣν ἐπίσταμαι φρουρουμένην ἅμα τῇ δεσποίνῃ, ἧκεν ἐνθάδε πόθῳ τῷ πρὸς ἡμᾶς ἀγομένη, ἣν περισκέπασον αὐτὸς καὶ νῦν ἀπιοῦσαν τῇ σῇ περιβολῇ καὶ ἑσπέρας παραγινομένην ἅμα τῇ δεσποίνῃ, ὅπως μή τινι τῶν ἐχθρῶν κατάδηλοι γένωνται, ἐπεὶ καὶ μέχρις ὧδε γενομένου μου σπεύδουσιν τρόπον τινὰ συνδεδεμέναι μοι, ἃς φύλαξον αὐτὸς καὶ φιλοστόργους οὔσας, κύριε, καὶ φιλοθέους.

Καὶ εὐξάμενος ἐπὶ τῇ Ἰφιδάμᾳ ἀπέλυσεν αὐτὴν ὁ Ἀνδρέας εἰρηκώς· καὶ τοῦ δεσμωτηρίου φθάσει σε ὁ πυλὼν ἠνεῳγμένος καὶ ἐρχομένων ὑμῶν ἐνταῦθα ὀψίας ἀνεῳχθήσεται, καὶ ἀγαλλιάσεσθε ἐν τῷ κυρίῳ καὶ πάλιν ἀπελεύσεσθε, ὅπως καὶ διὰ τούτων εἴητε στηριζόμεναι ἐπὶ τὸν κύριον ἡμῶν.

30. Καὶ εὐθέως ἐξελθοῦσα ἡ Ἰφιδάμα εὗρεν οὕτως ἅπαντα καθὼς Ἀνδρέας αὐτῇ εἶπεν. καὶ γενομένη πρὸς τὴν Μαξιμίλλαν διηγεῖτο αὐτῇ τὴν τοῦ μακαρίου γενναίαν ψυχὴν καὶ προαίρεσιν, ὅτι μηδὲ ἐγκεκλεισμένος ἠρεμεῖ, ἀλλὰ καὶ τοὺς σὺν αὐτῷ κατακλείστους προέτρεπεν, καὶ ὅτι ἐμεγαλύνετο τῇ δυνάμει τοῦ κυρίου, καὶ ὁπόσα αὐτῇ ἄλλα ὡμίλησεν ἔνδον διηγεῖτο αὐτῇ ἀμφοτέρων ἕνεκεν.

Καὶ ἡ Μαξιμίλλα ἀκούσασα πάντα ἅπερ αὐτῇ ἡ Ἰφιδάμα διηγεῖτο ὡς παρὰ τοῦ ἀποστόλου ἠγαλλία τῷ πνεύματι εἰρηκυῖα· δόξα σοι, κύριε, ὅτι σου ἀδεῶς τὸν ἀπόστολον πάλιν ὁρᾶν μέλλω. οὐδὲ γὰρ εἰ λεγεὼν ὅλη φυλάττοι με κατα-

apostle speaking with his fellow inmates, whom he already had strengthened by encouraging them to believe in the Lord.

29. When he turned and saw Iphidama, his soul was elated and he said to the Lord, "Glory be to you, Jesus Christ, ruler of true words and promises, who instills courage in my fellow servants. All who make use of you conquer their enemies, for you alone exist. Behold your Iphidama, driven by desire for us, has come here. I know that she and her mistress are under surveillance. Shield her with your covering both now as she leaves and this evening when she returns with her mistress, so that they will be invisible to their enemies. For as long as I have been here, they have made every effort to be bound together with me. Guard them yourself, Lord, for they are affectionate and god-loving."

When he had prayed for Iphidama, Andrew dismissed her and said, "The prison gate will be opened before you get there, and when you and Maximilla return here this evening, it will have been opened, and you will rejoice in the Lord and leave again, so that by these events too you both might be confirmed in our Lord."

30. Iphidama left at once and found everything to be just as Andrew had predicted. When she came to Maximilla, she narrated to her the blessed one's noble soul and resolve; namely, that even though imprisoned he was not quiet, but in fact urged on his fellow inmates and extolled the Lord's power. She also recounted to her whatever else he said to her inside the prison that pertained to them both.

When Maximilla heard everything Iphidama told her about the apostle, she exulted in spirit and said, "Glory be to you, O Lord, for I am about to see your apostle

κλείσασα ὡς μὴ ἰδεῖν τὸν ἀπόστολόν σου ἰσχύσειεν ἄν·
πηρωθήσεται γὰρ τῇ τοῦ κυρίου φωτεινῇ ὄψει καὶ τῇ παρρησίᾳ
τοῦ δούλου αὐτοῦ τῇ πρὸς τὸν θεόν. καὶ εἰποῦσα ταῦτα
προσεδόκα λοιπὸν λύχνους ἀφθήσεσθαι ὅπως ἐξέλθοι.

31. Ὁ δὲ ἀνθύπατος εἶπέν τισι τῶν παρ᾽ αὐτοῦ· τὴν
τόλμαν τῆς Μαξιμίλλης ἐπίσταμαι διὰ τὸ μὴ φροντίζειν μου.
αἱ μὲν οὖν θύραι τοῦ πραιτωρίου μὴ οὕτως φρουρείσθωσαν,
ἀλλὰ τέσσαρες ἀπίτωσαν εἰς τὸ δεσμωτήριον καὶ τῷ
δεσμοφύλακι φήσουσιν· ἤδη ἡ θύρα ἣν πεπίστευσαι ἠσφαλίσθω.
καὶ ὅρα μή τινι τῶν πολὺ δυναμένων ὑπὸ δυσωπίας ἢ
θεραπείας πεισθεὶς ἀνεῴξῃς, μηδὲ εἰ καὶ αὐτὸς ἔλθοιμι,
ἐπεὶ κεφαλὴν οὐχ ἕξεις. καὶ ἑτέροις δὲ ἐκέλευσε τέσσαρσι
περὶ τὸν κοιτῶνα αὐτῆς γενέσθαι καὶ ἐπιτηρεῖν εἰ
ἐξέρχοιτο. οἱ μὲν οὖν πρότεροι τέσσαρες ἔσπευσαν εἰς τὸ
δεσμωτήριον, καὶ οἱ λοιποὶ δὲ καθὰ ἐκελεύσθησαν πρὸ τοῦ
κοιτῶνος τῆς μακαρίτιδος ἀνέστρεφον. ὁ δὲ κατηραμένος
Αἰγεάτης ἐπὶ τὸ δεῖπνον ἐτράπη.

32. Ἡ δὲ Μαξιμίλλα τῷ κυρίῳ περὶ πολλὴν ὥραν
εὐξαμένη ἅμα τῇ Ἰφιδάμᾳ καὶ εἰποῦσα πάλιν τῷ κυρίῳ· ὥρα
λοιπόν, κύριε, ἀπιέναι πρὸς τὸν δοῦλόν σου, ἔξεισι τοῦ
κοιτῶνος ἅμα τῇ Ἰφιδάμᾳ εἰποῦσα· καὶ μεθ᾽ ἡμῶν ἴσθι,
κύριε, καὶ τῶν ὧδε μὴ ἀπολειφθῇς.

Καὶ γενομένη εἰς τὸν τοῦ δεσμωτηρίου πυλῶνα εὑρίσκει
τινὰ παιδαρίσκον εὔμορφον ἑστῶτα ἠνεῳγμένων τῶν θυρῶν καὶ
λέγοντα αὐταῖς· εἴσβατε ἀμφότεραι πρὸς τὸν ἀπόστολον τοῦ
κυρίου ὑμῶν πάλαι προσδοκῶντα ὑμᾶς. καὶ προδραμὼν αὐτὸς
εἴσεισι πρὸς τὸν Ἀνδρέαν καί φησιν αὐτῷ· ἰδού, Ἀνδρέα,
ἔχεις ταύτας ἀγαλλιώσας ἐν τῷ κυρίῳ σου· στηριζέσθωσαν ἐν
αὐτῷ ὁμιλοῦντός σου.

again without fear. Even if an entire legion kept me locked up under key, it would not be strong enough to prevent me from seeing your apostle. It would be blinded by the radiant appearance of the Lord and by the boldness of his servant before God." Having said this, she waited for lamps to be lit so that she could leave.

31. The proconsul said to some of those who were with him, "I know Maximilla's audacity, because she never obeys me. Therefore, leave the praetorium doors unguarded but have four men go off to the prison and tell the jailer, 'Right now, secure the door for which you are responsible! See that you do not open it for any of the dignitaries, even if you are won over by intimidation or bribery--not even if I should come myself--or you will be missing your head!'" He commanded four others posted around her bedroom to detect if she should come out. The first four sped to the prison, while the others paced in front of the blessed woman's bedroom as ordered. The cursed Aegeates went to supper.

32. Maximilla prayed with Iphidama to the Lord for a long time, telling the Lord again, "Lord, at last it is time for me to go to your servant." She left the bedroom with Iphidama, saying, "Lord, be with us and do not forsake those who are here."[21]

When she arrived at the prison gate, she found a beautiful young boy standing before opened doors who told them, "Both of you go in to your Lord's apostle who has been expecting you for some time." Running ahead of them, he went to Andrew and told him, "Look, Andrew, these women

----

21. Presumably the women were able to slip by boudoir surveillance because of the covering they were given to make them invisible.

The following quotation from Evodius of Uzala
(*De fide contra Manichaeos* 38) seems to refer to
this episode: *cum eadem Maximilla et Iphidama
simul issent ad audiendum apostolum Andream,
puerulus quidam speciosus, quem vult Leucius vel
deum vel certe angelum intelligi, commendaverit
eas Andreae apostolo et perrexerit ad praetorium
Egetis et ingressus cubiculum eorum [earum?]
finxerit vocem muliebrem quasi Maximillae
murmurantis de doloribus sexus feminei et
Iphidamiae respondentis. Quae colloquia cum
audisset Egetes credens eas ibi esse,
discesserit.*

33 (1). (...) περὶ ὑμᾶς τὸ πᾶν τῆς ἀτονίας ἐστίν;
οὔπω ἐλέγχεσθε ὑφ' ἑαυτῶν, μηδέπω φέροντες τὴν ἐκείνου
χρηστότητα; αἰδεσθῶμεν, συνησθῶμεν ἑαυτοῖς ἐπὶ τῇ ἐκείνου
ἀφθόνῳ κοινωνίᾳ. εἴπωμεν ἑαυτοῖς· μακάριον ἡμῶν τὸ γένος,
ὑπὸ τίνος ἠγάπηται. μακαρία ἡμῶν ἡ ὕπαρξις, ὑπὸ τίνος
ἠλέηται. οὐκ ἐσμέν τινες χαμαιριφεῖς, ὑπὸ τοιούτου ὕψους
γνωρισθέντες· οὐκ ἐσμὲν χρόνου, εἶτα ὑπὸ χρόνου λυόμενοι·
οὐκ ἐσμὲν κινήσεως τέχνη, πάλιν ὑφ' ἑαυτῆς ἀφανιζομένη,
οὐδὲ γενέσεως αἰτία, εἰς <τὸ> αὐτὸ τελευτῶντες. ἐσμέν
τινες ἄρα μεγέθους ἐπίβουλοι· ἐσμὲν ἴδιοι καὶ τάχα τοῦ
ἐλεοῦντος· ἐσμὲν τοῦ κρείττονος· διὰ τοῦτο ἀπὸ τοῦ
χείρονος φεύγομεν· ἐσμὲν τοῦ καλοῦ, δι' ο<ὖ> τὸ αἰσχρὸν
ἀπωθούμεθα· τοῦ δικαίου, δι' οὗ τὸ ἄδικον ῥίπτομεν· τοῦ
ἐλεήμονος, δι' οὗ τὸν ἀνελεήμονα ἀφίεμεν· τοῦ σῴζοντος,
δι' οὗ τὸν ἀπολλύντα ἐγνωρίσαμεν· τοῦ φωτός, δι' οὗ τὸ
σκότος ἐρρίψαμεν· τοῦ ἑνός, δι' οὗ τὰ πολλὰ ἀπεστράμμεθα·

have come to you rejoicing in your Lord. May they be strengthened in him by your speech."

> Evodius of Uzala, *De fide contra Manichaeos* 38 seems to refer to this episode: "when this same Maximilla and Iphidama together went to hear the apostle Andrew, a beautiful child, whom Leucius wants to be taken as God or at least as an angel, brought them to the apostle Andrew, then went on to Aegeates' praetorium, entered their bedroom, and mimicked a woman's voice to sound like Maximilla grumbling over the sufferings of the female sex and Iphidama responding. When Aegeates heard this conversation, he thought they were there and went away."

> *HS* seems to have omitted not only this story of Jesus' ventriloquism but a substantial speech as well. The last section of this speech is preserved in *Vaticanus gr. 808* (*V*), a fragment of Andrew's passion that runs parallel to *HS* for the next several chapters.

33 (1). "(...) is everything about you lax? Have you still not convinced yourselves that you do not yet bear his goodness? Let us stand in awe and rejoice with each other over our abundant partnership with him. Let us say to each other: 'Blessed is our race, for someone has loved it. Blessed is our existence, for someone has shown it mercy. We are not cast to the ground, for we have been recognized by such a height. We do not belong to time, so as to be dissolved by time. We are not the product of motion, which disappears of its own accord, nor the cause of coming-to-be, so as to wind up in the same condition. Rather, we are those who aspire to greatness. We belong to the one who indeed shows mercy. We belong to the better, therefore we flee the worse. We belong to the good, through <whom> we shove aside the disgraceful; to the just, through whom we reject the unjust; to the merciful, through whom we abandon the unmerciful; to the savior, through whom we have recognized the destroyer; to the light, through whom we have cast off the darkness; to the one, through whom we have turned from the many; to the

τοῦ ὑπερουρανίου, δι' οὗ τὰ ἐπίγεια ἐμάθομεν· τοῦ
μένοντος, δι' οὗ τὰ <μὴ> μένοντα εἴδομεν· [...] ἄξιον
εὐχαριστίαν ἢ παρρησίαν ἢ ὕμνον ἢ καύχημα προελόμενοι
εἰπεῖν εἰς τὸν ἐλεήσαντα ἡμᾶς θεὸν ἀλλ' ἢ γνωρισθῆναι ὑπ'
αὐτοῦ.

34 (2). Καὶ δὴ προσομιλήσαντος αὐταῖς ἐπὶ πολλὰς
ὥρας, τέλος²⁵ ἀπεπέμψατο αὐτὰς²⁶ εἰρηκώς· πορεύεσθε ἐν
εἰρήνῃ. εὖ ἴστε γὰρ ὅτι οὔτε ὑμᾶς ἐμοῦ ἀπολείπεσθαι
πάντοτε²⁷ ὅλως, δοῦλαι²⁸ τοῦ Χριστοῦ,²⁹ διὰ τὴν ἐν αὐτῷ
ἀγάπην, οὐδ' αὖ πάλιν αὐτὸς ἀπολειφθήσομαι ὑμῶν διὰ τὴν
ἐκείνου μεσιτείαν. καὶ ἀπηλλάγη ἕκαστος εἰς τὰ αὐτοῦ.³⁰

Καὶ ἦν ἡ τοιαύτη ἀγαλλίασις αὐτῶν ἐπὶ ἡμέρας ἱκανὰς
γενομένη, ἐν αἷς οὐκ ἔσχεν ὁ Αἰγεάτης ἔννοιαν ἐπεξελθεῖν
τὴν κατὰ τὸν ἀπόστολον αἰτίαν. ἐστηρίζοντο οὖν ἑκάστοτε³¹
ἐπὶ τὴν τοῦ κυρίου ἐλπίδα, ἐπισυναγόμενοι ἀφόβως πάντες³²
εἰς τὸ δεσμωτήριον, ἅμα τῇ Μαξιμίλλῃ καὶ τῇ 'Ιφιδάμᾳ καὶ
τοῖς λοιποῖς ἀδιαλείπτως ἔχουσιν περισκεπόμενοι τῇ
περιβολῇ καὶ χάριτι τοῦ κυρίου.

----

25. *V*: καὶ ὁμιλήσας τοῖς ἀδελφοῖς τὰ τοιαῦτα.

26. For αὐτάς *N* and *V* read: ἕκαστον εἰς τὰ ἴδια εἰπὼν
    αὐτοῖς.

27. The speech to this point appears only in *HS*. *V* reads
    similarly: ὑμεῖς ἐμοῦ ἀπολείπεσθέ ποτε.

28. *V*: δοῦλοι.

29. *HS*: κυρίου.

30. *N*: καὶ οὕτως οἱ ἀδελφοὶ περιπτυξάμενοι αὐτὸν ἐξῆλθον
    ἀπὸ τοῦ δεσμωτηρίου.

31. *HS*: ἐστηρίζετο οὖν πᾶν τὸ πλῆθος τῶν πιστῶν. *N*:
    ἐστηρίζοντο τῇ αὐτοῦ διδαχῇ παιδευόμενοι.

32. *V*: καὶ συλλεγόμενοι πάντες ἀφόβως.

heavenly, through whom we have learned about the earthly;
to the enduring, through whom we see things that do <not>
endure.' (There is no more) worthy (reason for our)
resolving to give thanks, to speak boldly, to sing a hymn,
or to boast before the God who had mercy on us than that
we have been recognized by him."

34 (2). And after he had spoken with the women for
some time,[22] he at last sent them away saying,[23] "Go in
peace. For you well know, O maidservants[24] of Christ,[25]
that because of his love I will never entirely abandon
you, and that because of his mediation, you will never
again abandon me." Each one left for home.[26]

For several days, while Aegeates had no thought of
pressing charges against the apostle, there was great joy
among them.[27] Every day they were strengthened in the hope
of the Lord; they convened fearlessly at the prison and
were incessantly with Maximilla and Iphidama and the
others, because they were screened by the covering and
grace of the Lord.

35 (3). One day, while Aegeates sat as judge, he
remembered his business with Andrew. Like a maniac, he
left the case at hand, rose from the bench, and dashed to

----

22. *V*: "And after he had spoken such things to the
    brethren."

23. *N* and *V*: "everyone to their own homes and said to
    them."

24. *V*: "servants."

25. *HS*: "the Lord."

26. *N*: "And when the brethren embraced him, they left the
    prison."

27. *HS*: "The entire crowd of believers was confirmed." *N*:
    "They were confirmed by being instructed in his
    teaching."

35 (3). Καὶ ὁ Αἰγεάτης δικάζων ἡμέρας μιᾶς εἰς
ὑπόμνησιν ἔσχεν τὴν περὶ τὸν Ἀνδρέαν χρείαν. καὶ ὥσπερ
τις ἐμμανὴς γεγονὼς ἀφίησιν ἣν ἐν χερσὶν δίκην ἔσχεν, καὶ
ἀνίσταται τοῦ βήματος. καὶ δρομαίως παραγίνεται εἰς τὸ
πραιτώριον, ἐμβράσσων τῇ Μαξιμίλλῃ ἅμα καὶ κολακεύων.[33] ἡ
δὲ Μαξιμίλλα ἐφθάκει αὐτὸν ἀπὸ τοῦ δεσμωτηρίου εἰσβάλλουσα
τῇ οἰκίᾳ.

36 (4). Καὶ εἰσβαλὼν[34] πρὸς αὐτὴν ἔλεγεν· * ἄξιόν με
θέμενοι οἱ σοὶ γονεῖς, Μαξιμίλλα, τῆς συμβιώσεώς σου
κατηγγύησάν μοι τὸν σὸν γάμον,[35] μήτε πρὸς πλοῦτον
ἀπιδόντες, μήτε πρὸς γένος μήτε πρὸς δόξαν, ἀλλὰ τάχα πρὸς
τὸ τῆς ψυχῆς μου εὔγνωμον. καὶ ἵνα μὴ <εἴπω> πολλὰ ὧν
ἐβουλόμην εἰς ὄνειδός σου ἐκφέρειν, ὧν τε ἐγὼ ὑπὸ τῶν
γονέων σου ἔπαθον εὐεργεσιῶν, ὧν τε αὐτὴ ὑπ' ἐμοῦ τιμῶν
καὶ θεραπειῶν ἔτυχες, ὥσπερ δέσποινά μου διαγραφεῖσα, τῷ
παντὶ ἡμῶν βίῳ, ἓν τοῦτο μόνον ἥκω νῦν παρὰ σοῦ
μαθησόμενος ἀπολιπὼν τὸ δικαστήριον συνετῶς. εἰ μὲν εἴης
ἐκείνη ὁποία ἦσθα πάλαι, συμβιοῦσά μοι ὃν ἠπιστάμεθα
τρόπον,[36] συγκαθεύδουσά μοι, συγγινομένη, συντεκνοῦσα, καὶ
σὲ εὖ κατὰ πάντα ποιήσαιμι, ἐπεὶ μᾶλλον καὶ ὃν ἔχω ἐν τῷ
δεσμωτηρίῳ ξένον ἀπολύσω. εἰ δὲ μὴ βούλῃ, σοὶ μὲν χαλεπὸν
οὐδὲν προσάγοιμι,[37] οὐδὲ γὰρ δύναμαι, δι' ἐκείνου δὲ ὃν
μάλιστα ἐμοῦ στέργεις πλέον ἀνιάσω σε.[38] πρὸς ὁπότερον

---

33. N: ὡς κολακεύσων καὶ θωπεύσων τῇ Μαξιμίλλῃ πεισθῆναι
αὐτῷ καὶ πρὸς αὐτὸν αὖθις καθὰ τὸ πρότερον
ἀνθυποστρέψαι τῇ ἑνώσει.

34. V: εἰσελθών.

35. V: γαμβρόν.

36. N: καὶ ἵνα τί τοῦτο πεποίηκας, ἀποστᾶσα τῆς ἐμῆς
συμβιώσεως καὶ κολληθεῖσα τῷ ξένῳ καὶ ἀλήτῃ τούτῳ;
δεῦρο ἐπιστράφηθι πρός με.

37. V: ἀγάγοιμι.

38. V: ἐκεῖνον δὲ ὃν μάλιστα ἐμοῦ στέργεις πλεῖον ἀνιάσω.
N: εἰ δὲ μὴ βουληθῇς ταῖς ἐμαῖς πεισθῆναι παραινέσεσιν

the praetorium seething with turbulence at Maximilla but flattering her all the same.[28] Maximilla got home from the prison before he arrived.

36 (4). When he went in to her, he said, *
"Maximilla, because your parents thought me worthy to be your mate, they pledged you to me in marriage[29] without regard to wealth, heredity, or reputation, considering only the kindness of my soul. Just now I intentionally left the court and came here not to enumerate the many matters I had wanted to bring forth to your disgrace--such as the benefits I enjoyed from your parents, or the honors and favors you received from me during our entire lives, such as your designation as my lady--but simply to learn from you this one thing. If you would be the woman you once were, living together with me as we are accustomed to[30]--sleeping with me, having sex with me, conceiving children with me--I would treat you well in every way. What is more, I will release the stranger whom I have in prison. But if you should not choose this course, I will do you no harm--I am unable to--but I will torment you indirectly through the one you love more than me.[31] Answer me tomorrow, Maximilla, after you have considered which of

----

28. *N*: "in order to flatter and wheedle Maximilla to persuade her to take up at once her former sexual relations with him."

29. *V*: "pledged me to be your wooer."

30. *N*: "Why have you done this, forsaking your spouse and clinging to this stranger and vagabond? Return to me again."

31. *V*: "I will intensify torturing the one you love more than me." *N*: "If you are unwilling to be persuaded by my exhortations which I am now presenting in order to disgrace you, I will never do you any harm, for even if I were able to I would not want it, remembering your erstwhile love and cohabitation with me."

τοιγαροῦν ὃ βούλῃ, Μαξιμίλλα, σκεψαμένη αὔριον ἀπόκριναι·
ἐγὼ γὰρ πρὸς τοῦτο μόνον ὅλως ὥπλισμαι.[39] * καὶ εἰπὼν
ταῦτα ἔξεισιν.[40]

37 (5). Ἡ δὲ Μαξιμίλλα πάλιν κατὰ τὴν συνήθη ὥραν
ἅμα τῇ Ἰφιδάμᾳ παραγίνεται πρὸς τὸν Ἀνδρέαν· καὶ τὰς
χεῖρας αὐτοῦ εἰς τὰς ἰδίας ὄψεις θεῖσα καὶ τῷ στόματι
προσφέρουσα κατεφίλει· καὶ ἤρξατο τὸ πᾶν τῆς ἀξιώσεως
Αἰγεάτου προσαναφέρειν αὐτῷ.

Καὶ ὁ Ἀνδρέας αὐτῇ ἀπεκρίνατο· ἠπιστάμην[41] μέν, ὦ
παιδίον μου Μαξιμίλλα, καὶ αὐτὴν[42] κεκινημένην σε
ἀντιβαίνειν πρὸς τὸ πᾶν τῆς συνουσίας ἐπάγγελμα, μυσαροῦ
βίου καὶ ῥυπαροῦ βουλομένη<ν> χωρίζεσθαι· καὶ τοῦτό μοι ἐκ
πολλοῦ κεκράτητο[43] τῆς εὐνοίας, ἤδη δὲ καὶ τὴν ἐμὴν γνώμην
ἐπιμαρτυρῆσαι βούλει. ἐπιμαρτυρῶ,[44] Μαξιμίλλα,[45] μὴ πράξῃς
τοῦτο· μὴ ἡττηθῇς ὑπὸ τῆς Αἰγεάτου ἀπειλῆς·[46] μὴ κινηθῇς

αἷς νῦν πρὸς σὲ δυσωπῶν διεξέρχομαι, εἰς σὲ οὐδαμῶς
κακόν τι διαπράξομαι· δυνάμενος γὰρ οὐ βεβούλημαι,
μεμνημένος σου τῆς ἀρχαιοτάτης φιλίας καὶ
συναναστροφῆς.

39. N: οὐκοῦν ὦ γύναι τὸ συμφέρον σοι καὶ ἐμοὶ
διαμεριμνήσασα πειθηνιός μοι κατὰ πάντα γενοῦ, τῇ
αὔριον περὶ τούτου λόγον ὑφέξασα (ὑφέξουσα?).

40. N: καὶ ταῦτα διαλεχθεὶς τῇ ἑαυτοῦ γυναικὶ αὖθις ἐπὶ τὸ
δικαστήριον ἀνεχώρησεν.

41. V: ἐπίσταμαι.

42. HS: ἀφ᾽ ἑαυτῆς.

43. HS: κεκράτυντο.

44. HS: ἐπεὶ δὲ καὶ τὴν ἐμὴν γνώμην ἐπιμαρτυρῆσαι βούλῃ,
καὶ μαρτυρῶ.

45. N: ὦ τέκνον μου Μαξιμίλλα, εἰ τῆς ἐμῆς νουθεσίας καὶ
διδαχῆς τὴν ἄγκυραν βεβαίαν κατασχεῖν βούλῃ καὶ τῆς
εἰς Χριστὸν πίστεως οὐδαμῶς ἀποστῆναι.

46. N: μὴ πράξῃς τοῦτο ὅπερ ὁ Αἰγεάτης κολακεύων δολερῶς
ὑποκρίνεται.

the two options you want, for I am fully prepared to carry out this threat."[32] * Having said this, he left.[33]

37 (5). At the usual time, Maximilla again went with Iphidama to Andrew. Putting his hands on her eyes and then bringing them to her mouth, she kissed them and began to seek his advice about every aspect of Aegeates' ultimatum.

"O Maximilla my child," Andrew replied, "I know that you too have been moved to resist any proposition of sexual intercourse and wish to be disassociated from a foul and filthy way of life. For a long time this conviction has dominated my thinking, but still you want me to bear witness to my intent.[34] I bear you witness, Maximilla:[35] do not commit this act. Do not submit to Aegeates' threat.[36] Do not be moved by his speech.[37] Do not fear his disgusting schemes.[38] Do not be conquered by his artful flatteries. Do not consent to yield yourself to his filthy[39] wizardry. Endure each of his tortures by

----

32. *N*: "Therefore, woman, be obedient to me in every respect, consider its benefits to both of us, and go on record concerning this matter tomorrow."

33. *N*: "And having spoken these things to his wife, he retreated immediately for the court."

34. *HS*: "since you want me to affirm my intent, and I bear witness."

35. *N*: "O Maximilla, my child, if you wish to possess the solid anchor of my admonition and teaching and never to apostasize from faith in Christ."

36. *N*: "Do not commit this act which Aegeates feigns with treacherous flattery."

37. *N*: "Even if he promises to do nothing terrible to you, do not be shaken by his vapid speeches."

38. *HS*: "his hostilities and plots." *N*: "Do not become softened by his sordid schemes."

39. *HS* adds: "and wicked."

ὑπὸ τῆς ἐκείνου ὁμιλίας·[47] μὴ φοβηθῇς τὰς αἰσχρὰς αὐτοῦ
συμβουλίας·[48] μὴ νικηθῇς ταῖς ἐντέχνοις αὐτοῦ κολακείαις·
μὴ θελήσῃς ἐκδοῦναι σεαυτὴν[49] ταῖς ῥυπαραῖς αὐτοῦ[50]
γοητείαις. ἀλλ' ὑπόμεινον πᾶσαν αὐτοῦ τὴν βάσανον ὁρῶσα
εἰς ἡμᾶς πρὸς ὀλίγον, καὶ ὅλον αὐτὸν ὄψῃ ναρκῶντα καὶ
μαραινόμενον ἀπό τε σοῦ καὶ πάντων τῶν συγγενῶν σου.[51] ὃ
γὰρ μάλιστα ἐχρῆν με εἰπεῖν πρὸς σέ--οὐ γὰρ ἡσυχάζω καὶ
διὰ σοῦ ὁρώμενον καὶ γινόμενον πρᾶγμα ποιήσας--ὑπέδραμέν
με· καὶ εἰκότως ἐν σοὶ τὴν Εὔαν ὁρῶ μετανοοῦσαν καὶ ἐν
ἐμοὶ τὸν Ἀδὰμ ἐπιστρέφοντα. ὃ γὰρ ἐκείνη ἔπαθεν ἀγνοοῦσα,
σὺ νῦν, πρὸς ἧς ἀποτείνομαι ψυχήν, κατορθοῖς ἐπιστρέφουσα.
καὶ ὅπερ ὁ σὺν ἐκείνῃ καταχθεὶς καὶ ἀπολισθήσας ἑαυτοῦ
νοῦς ἔπαθεν, ἐγὼ σὺν σοί, τῇ γνωριζούσῃ ἑαυτὴν ἀναγομένην,
διορθοῦμαι. τὸ γὰρ ἐκείνης ἐνδεές, αὐτὴ ἰάσω μὴ τὰ ὅμοια
παθοῦσα. καὶ τὸ ἐκείνου ἀτελές, ἐγὼ τετέλεκα προσφυγὼν
θεῷ· καὶ ὃ ἐκείνη παρήκουσεν, σὺ ἤκουσας· καὶ ὃ ἐκεῖνος
συνέθετο, ἐγὼ φεύγω· καὶ ἃ ἐκεῖνοι ἐσφάλησαν, ἡμεῖς
ἐγνωρίσαμεν. τὸ γὰρ διορθῶσαι ἑκάστου τὸ ἴδιον πταῖσμα
ἐπανορθοῦν τέτακται.

38 (6). Ἐγὼ μὲν οὖν ταῦτα εἰπὼν ὡς εἶπον, εἴποιμι ἂν
δὲ καὶ τὰ ἑξῆς· εὖγε ὦ φύσις σῳζομένη μὴ ἰσχύσασα ἑαυτὴν
μηδὲ ἀποκρύψασα· εὖγε ψυχὴ βοῶσα ἃ ἔπαθες καὶ ἐπανιοῦσα
ἐφ' ἑαυτήν· εὖγε ἄνθρωπε καταμανθάνων τὰ μὴ σὰ καὶ ἐπὶ τὰ
σὰ ἐπειγόμενος· εὖγε ὁ ἀκούων τῶν λεγομένων· ὡς μείζονά σε

----

47. So V. N: εἰ καὶ κατὰ σοῦ μηδὲν δεινὸν πράξειν
    ἐπαγγέλλεται, μὴ σαλευθῇς ὑπὸ τῶν αὐτοῦ φαύλων
    ὁμιλιῶν.

48. HS: τὰς ἐκείνου ἔχθρας καὶ ἐπιβουλάς. N: καὶ μὴ
    χαυνωθῇς ταῖς αὐτοῦ ῥυπαραῖς συμβουλίαις.

49. V: ἑαυτήν σου. At this point N goes its own way, with
    only remote similarities to HS and V.

50. HS adds: καὶ κακαῖς.

51. HS's version of the speech ends here. The following
    comes exclusively from V.

looking to us for a while, and you will see him entirely numb and wasting away from you and from all of your kindred. Inasmuch as I do not keep silent in making the matter visible and actual through you, the most important thing I should say to you now comes to me: I rightly see in you Eve repenting and in me Adam converting. For what she suffered through ignorance, you--whose soul I seek-- must now redress through conversion. The very thing suffered by the mind which was brought down with her and slipped away from itself, I make right with you, through your recognition that you are being raised up. You healed her deficiency by not experiencing the same passions, and I have perfected Adam's imperfection by fleeing to God for refuge. What Eve disobeyed, you obeyed; what Adam agreed to, I flee; the things that tripped them up, we have recognized. For it is ordained that each person correct his or her own fall.

38 (6). Having said these things as I said them, I would also say this: Well done, O nature being saved, for you are neither overbearing nor in hiding. Well done, O soul crying out what you suffered and returning to yourself. Well done, O human who learns what is not yours and speeds on to what is yours. Well done, O hearer of what is being said, for I know that you are greater than

καταμανθάνω νοουμέν<ω>ν ἢ λεγομέν<ω>ν· ὡς δυνατώτερόν σε
γνωρίζω τῶν δοξάντων καταδυναστεύειν σου· ὡς ἐμπρεπέστερον
τῶν εἰς αἴσχη καταβαλλόντων σε, τῶν εἰς αἰχμαλωσίαν
ἀπαγαγόντων σε. ταῦτα οὖν ἅπαντα καταμαθών, ἄνθρωπε, ἐν
ἑαυτῷ, ὅτι ἄϋλος ὑπάρχεις, ὅτι ἅγιος, ὅτι φῶς, ὅτι
συγγενὴς τοῦ ἀγεννήτου, ὅτι νοερός, ὅτι οὐράνιος, ὅτι
διαυγής, ὅτι καθαρός, ὅτι ὑπὲρ σάρκα, ὅτι ὑπὲρ κόσμον, ὅτι
ὑπὲρ ἀρχάς, ὅτι ὑπὲρ ἐξουσίας, ἐφ᾽ ὧν ὄντως εἶ, συλλαβὼν
ἑαυτὸν ἐν καταστάσει σου, καὶ ἀπολαβὼν νόει ἐν ᾧ
ὑπερέχεις, καὶ ἰδὼν τὸ σὸν πρόσωπον ἐν τῇ οὐσίᾳ σου, τὰ
πάντα διαρρήξας δεσμά, οὐ λέγω τὰ περὶ γενέσεως ἀλλὰ καὶ
τὰ ὑπὲρ γένεσιν, ὧν σοι προσηγορίας <ἐ>θέμεθα ὑπερμεγέθεις
οὔσας, πόθησον ἐκεῖνον ἰδεῖν ὀφθέντα σοι, οὐ γενόμενον, ὃν
τάχα εἷς μόνος γνωρίσῃ θαρρῶν.

39 (7). Ταῦτα εἶπον ἐπὶ σοῦ, Μαξιμίλλα· τῇ γὰρ
δυνάμει καὶ εἰς σὲ τείνει τὰ εἰρημένα. ὅνπερ τρόπον[52] ὁ
᾽Αδὰμ ἐν τῇ Εὔᾳ ἀπέθανεν συνθέμενος τῇ ἐκείνης ὁμιλίᾳ,[53]
οὕτως καὶ ἐγὼ νῦν ἐν σοὶ ζῶ φυλασσούσῃ τὴν τοῦ κυρίου
ἐντολὴν καὶ διαβιβαζούσῃ ἑαυτὴν πρὸς τὸ τῆς οὐσίας ἀξίωμα.
τὰς δὲ Αἰγεάτου ἀπειλὰς ἐκπάτει, Μαξιμίλλα, εἰδυῖα ὅτι
θεὸν ἔχομεν τὸν ἐλεοῦντα ἡμᾶς· καὶ μή σε οἱ ἐκείνου ψόφοι
κινείτωσαν, ἀλλὰ μεῖνον ἁγνή· κἀμὲ μὴ μόνον τιμωρείσθω
βασάνοις ταῖς κατὰ τὰ δεσμά, ἀλλὰ καὶ θηρσὶ παραβαλλέτω
καὶ πυρὶ φλεξάτω καὶ κατὰ κρημνοῦ ριψάτω.[54] καὶ τί γάρ;
ἑνὸς ὄντος τούτου τοῦ σώματος, ὅπως θέλει τούτῳ
καταχρησάσθω, συγγενοῦς ὄντος αὐτοῦ.

---

52. *HS*: ὥσπερ γάρ.

53. *V*: ὁμολογίᾳ.

54. *N*: ἡμῖν δὲ ὅσα ἔξεστιν τῷ ἀνθυπάτῳ ἐπαπειλεῖν μὴ
    λόγοις μόνον ἀλλὰ καὶ ἔργοις ταῦτα διεξερχέσθω κατὰ τὸ
    αὐτῷ δοκοῦν· εἴτε θηρίοις ἐκδιδότω βορρᾷ, εἴτε πυρὶ
    κατακαυσάτω, εἴτε βύθῳ ἀκοντιζέτω, εἴτε ξίφει τεμνέτω,
    εἴτε σταυρῷ προσηλωσάτω.

what is thought or said; I recognize that you are more powerful than those who presume to dominate you; more distinguished than those who cast you down to shame, than those who lead you away to captivity. O human being, if you understand all these things in yourself--that you are immaterial, holy, light, akin to the unbegotten, intellectual, heavenly, transparent, pure, beyond the flesh, beyond the world, beyond the powers, beyond the authorities over whom you really are, if you comprehend yourself in your condition, if you perceive with the mind through which you excel, if you see your face in your essence, having broken every shackle--I mean not only those shackles acquired by coming-into-being but also those beyond the realm of coming-into-being, whose magnificent names we have presented to you--then desire to see him who was revealed to you without coming into being, whom you alone soon will recognize, if you take courage.

39 (7). "I said these things in your presence, Maximilla, because the force of what has been said extends also to you. Just as Adam died in Eve through his complicity[40] with her, so also I now live in you through your observing the commandment of the Lord and through your transporting yourself to a state worthy of your essence. Scorn Aegeates' threats, Maximilla, for you know that we have a God who has compassion on us. Do not let his blatherings move you but remain chaste. Let him not only avenge himself on me with the tortures of captivity, let him also throw me to the beasts, burn me with fire, and throw me off a cliff.[41] So what? Let him destroy this

----

40. *V:* "agreement."

41. *N:* "Whatever means are available to the proconsul for intimidating us, not only in speech but also in deeds, let him carry them out as he sees fit. Let him hand us over to the beasts as meat, or burn us with fire, or

40 (8). Πρὸς σὲ δέ μοι πάλιν ὁ λόγος, Μαξιμίλλα· λέγω σοι, μὴ ἐκδῷς ἑαυτὴν τῷ Αἰγεάτῃ· στῆθι πρὸς τὰς ἐκείνου ἐνέδρας, καὶ μάλιστα θεασαμένου μου Μαξιμίλλα τὸν κύριόν μοι λέγοντά μοι· ὁ τοῦ Αἰγεάτου πατήρ, ᾿Ανδρέα, διάβολος τούτου σε τοῦ δεσμωτηρίου δι᾿ αὐτοῦ ἐκλύσει. σὸν οὖν ἔστω λοιπὸν φυλάξαι σεαυτὴν ἁγνήν, καθαράν, ἁγίαν, ἄσπιλον, εἰλικρινῆ, ἀμοίχευτον, ἀσυνδιάθετον ταῖς ὁμιλίαις τοῦ ἀλλοτρίου ἡμῶν, ἄθρυπτον, ἄθραυστον, ἄκλαυστον, ἄτρωτον, ἀχείμαστον, ἀμέριστον, ἀσκανδάλιστον, ἀσυμπαθῆ πρὸς τὰ τοῦ Κάϊν ἔργα. ἐὰν γὰρ μὴ ἐκδῷς ἑαυτήν, Μαξιμίλλα, πρὸς τὰ τούτων ἐναντία, καὶ αὐτὸς ἀναπαύσομαι οὕτως βιασθεὶς ἀναλῦσαι τοῦ βίου τούτου ὑπὲρ σοῦ, τοῦτ᾿ ἔστιν ὑπὲρ ἐμαυτοῦ. εἰ δὲ ἐγὼ ἀπελαθείην ἐντεῦθεν, τάχα καὶ ἑτέρους συγγενεῖς μου ὠφελῆσαι δυνάμενος διὰ σέ, αὐτὴ δὲ πεισθῇς ταῖς Αἰγεάτου ὁμιλίαις καὶ τοῦ πατρὸς αὐτοῦ ὄφεως κολακείαις, ὥστ᾿ ἂν ἐπὶ τὰ πρῶτά σου ἔργα τραπῆναι, ἴσθι με ἕνεκέν σου κολασθησόμενον μέχρις ἂν αὐτὴ μεταγνῷς ὅτι μὴ ὑπὲρ ἀξίας ψυχῆς τὸ τοῦ βίου ζῆν ἀπέπτυσα. **(41 [9].)** δέομαί σου οὖν τοῦ φρονίμου ἀνδρὸς ὅπως διαμείνῃ εὔοψις νοῦς· δέομαί σου τοῦ μὴ φαινομένου νοῦ ὅπως αὐτὸς διαφυλαχθῇ· παρακαλῶ σ<ε>, τὸν ᾿Ιησοῦν φίλησον· μη ἡττηθῇς τῷ χείρονι· συλλαβοῦ κἀμοί, ὃν παρακαλῶ ἄνθρωπον, ἵνα τέλειος γένωμαι· βοήθησον καὶ ἐμοί, ἵνα γνωρίσῃς τὴν ἀληθῆ σου φύσιν· συμπάθησόν μου τῷ πάθει, ἵνα γνωρίσῃς ὃ πάσχω καὶ τοῦ παθεῖν φεύξῃ. ἴδε ἃ αὐτὸς ὁρῶ, καὶ ἃ ὁρᾷς πηρώσει

body as he will, for it is only one body and it is akin to him.

40 (8). "Once again my speech is for you, Maximilla. I say to you, do not yield yourself to Aegeates. Stand up against his ambushes, especially, Maximilla, since I saw the Lord saying to me, 'Andrew, Aegeates' father, the devil, will use him to release you from this prison.'[42] So from now on keep yourself chaste and pure, holy, unsullied, unalloyed, unadulterated, unassociated with anything foreign to us, unbroken, undamaged, unweeping, unwounded, unvexed by storms, undivided, unfalling, unsympathetic to the works of Cain. For if you do not give yourself up to their opposites, Maximilla, I will rest, even if I am forcibly unloosed from this life for your sake--that is, for my sake. If I am driven from here, perhaps I can help others of my kindred because of you, but if you become won over by the seductions of Aegeates and the flatteries of the serpent, his father, so that you return to your former sexual acts, know this: I will be punished there because of you, until you yourself realize that I despised living this life because of an unworthy soul. (**41 [9].**) Therefore, I beg you, wise man ($\dot{\alpha}\nu\dot{\eta}\rho$), that your clearsighted[43] mind stand firm. I beg you, mind unseen, that you may be protected. I entreat you, love Jesus. Do not be overcome by the inferior. You whom I entreat as a man ($\dot{\alpha}\nu\theta\rho\omega\pi\sigma\varsigma$), assist me in my becoming perfect. Help me too, so that you may recognize your true nature. Suffer with my suffering, so that you may recognize what I suffer and escape suffering. See what I see, and what you see will blind you. See what you

----

impale us in the depths of the sea, or slash us with a sword, or nail us to a cross."

42. Viz., the body.

43. Or: "beautiful."

σε· ἴδε ἃ δεῖ, καὶ ἃ μὴ δεῖ οὐκ ὄψῃ· ἄκουσον ὧν λέγω, καὶ
ἅπερ ἤκουσας ῥῖψον. * ταῦτα εἶπον πρὸς σὲ καὶ πάντα τὸν
ἀκούοντα, εἰ ἄρα ἀκούσῃ.

42 (10). Σὺ δὲ ὁ Στρατοκλῆς, ἀπιδὼν πρὸς αὐτὸν
ἔλεγεν, τί οὕτως συνέχῃ πολλοῖς δακρύοις, καὶ στένεις εἰς
ἐξάκουστον; τίς ἡ περὶ σὲ δυσθυμία; τί τὸ πολύ σου ἄλγος ἢ
ἡ πολλὴ ἀνία;[55] γνωρίζεις τὰ λεγόμενα, καὶ διὰ τί σε
εὔχομαι, τέκνον, ὅπως διατεθῇ<ς>; μανθάνεις πρὸς τίνας
εἴρηται τὰ εἰρημένα; ἥψατό σου ἕκαστον τῆς διανοίας;
ἔθιγέν σου τοῦ διανοητικοῦ μέρους; ἔχω μένοντα τὸν
ἀκούσαντά μου; εὑρίσκω ἐν σοὶ ἐμαυτόν; ἔστιν τις ἐν σοὶ
ὁμιλήσα<ς> ὃν ἐγὼ ὁρῶ ἴδιόν μου; ἀγαπ<ᾷ> τὸν ἐν ἐμοὶ
λαλήσαντα, καὶ βούλεται αὐτῷ κοινωνῆσαι; θέλει αὐτῷ
συνενωθῆναι; σπεύδει αὐτῷ φιλωθῆναι; ποθεῖ αὐτῷ συζυγῆναι;
εὑρίσκει τινὰ ἐν αὐτῷ ἀνάπαυσιν; ἔχει ποῦ κλῖναι τὴν
κεφαλήν; μὴ ἐναντιοῦταί τι αὐτῷ ἐκεῖ; μὴ τραχύνεται; μὴ
ἀντικρούει; μὴ ἀπεχθάνεται; μὴ φεύγει; μὴ ἀγριοῦται; μὴ
ἐκκλίνει; μὴ ἀπέστραπται; μὴ ἐξορμᾷ; μὴ βαρύνεται; μὴ
πολεμεῖ; μὴ πρὸς ἑτέρους ὁμιλεῖ; μὴ ὑφ' ἑτέρων
κολακεύεται; μὴ ἑτέροις συντίθεται; μὴ ἄλλα αὐτῷ διοχλεῖ;
μή τις ἀλλότριός μου ἔσω; μὴ ἀντίδικος; μὴ λυμεών; μὴ
ἐχθρός; μὴ γόης; μὴ περίεργος; μὴ στρεβλός; μὴ ὕπουλος; μὴ
δόλιος; μὴ μισάνθρωπος; μὴ μισολόγος; μὴ τυράννων ὅμοιος;
μὴ ἀλαζών; μὴ ἐπηρμένος; μὴ μανιώδης; μὴ ὄφεως συγγενής;
μὴ διαβόλου ὅπλον; μὴ πυρὸς συνήγορος; μὴ σκότους ἴδιος;
μή τις ἐν σοὶ ὃς οὐκ ἀνέξεταί μου, Στρατοκλῆ, λέγοντος
ταῦτα; τίς γάρ; ἀπόκριναι· μὴ μάτην λαλῶ; μὴ μάτην εἶπον;
οὔ φησιν ὁ ἐν σοί, Στρατοκλῆ, πάλιν δακρύσας ἄνθρωπος.[56]

---

55. V actually reads: ἄνοια.

56. At this point HS and N resume.

should, and you will not see what you should not. Hear
what I say and throw off whatever you heard (from
Aegeates). * I have said these things to you and to any
who hear, if perchance you might hear.

42 (10). "But to you, Stratocles," he said, looking
at him, "why are you afflicted with many tears and why do
you groan out loud? Why do you despair? Why your great
grief and great sorrow? You recognize what has been said,
so why do I beg you, child, that you live accordingly? Do
you know to whom I have said these things? Has each
engaged your mind? Has it reached your intellectual
faculty? Do I still have the one who listened to me? Do I
find myself in you? Is there someone in you speaking whom
I see as my own? Does he love the one who has spoken in me
and does he desire to have fellowship with him? Does he
wish to be united with him? Does he strive to become loved
by him? Does he long to be yoked with him? Does he find
any rest in him? Does he have anywhere to lay his head?[44]
Surely there is nothing in you to resist him--nothing to
be turbulent against him, nothing to counteract him,
nothing to hate him, nothing to flee from him, nothing to
be savage to him, nothing to shun him, nothing that has
turned away from him, nothing to rush from him, nothing to
be oppressed, nothing to fight him, nothing to associate
with others, nothing to be flattered by others, nothing to
conspire with others, no other things to disturb him,
nothing in you alien to me, no opponent, no corrupter, no
enemy, no magician, no charlatan, no pervert, no deceiver,
no traitor, no misanthrope, no hater of rational
discourse, no one similar to tryants, no boaster, no snob,
no maniac, no kindred of the snake, no weapon of the
devil, no advocate for fire, no property of darkness--is
there? Stratocles, surely there is no one in you to oppose

----

44. Cf. Matt 8:20 and Luke 9:58.

43 (11). Ἐν τούτοις ὁ Στρατοκλῆς εἴσεισι πρὸς τὸν Ἀνδρέαν κλαίων καὶ ὀδυρόμενος. ὁ οὖν Ἀνδρέας λαβόμενος τῆς χειρὸς τοῦ Στρατοκλέους εἶπεν· ἔχω ὃν ἐζήτουν·[57] εὖρον ὃν ἐπόθουν· κρατῶ ὃν ἠγάπων· ἀναπαύομαι ἐφ᾽ ὃν προσεδόκουν· τὸ γὰρ ἔτι μᾶλλον στένειν σε καὶ ἀκαθέκτως δακρύειν[58] σύμβολόν μοι γέγονεν πρὸς τὸ ἤδη ἀναπεπαῦσθαι, ὅτι οὐ μάτην πεποίημαι πρὸς σὲ τοὺς συγγενεῖς μου λόγους.

44 (12). Καὶ ὁ Στρατοκλῆς αὐτῷ ἀπεκρίνατο· μὴ νόμιζε, μακαριώτατε Ἀνδρέα, ὅτι ἕτερόν τί ἐστι τὸ ἀνιῶν με ἀλλ᾽ ἢ σύ. οἱ γὰρ διὰ σοῦ ἐξιόντες λόγοι πυρὶ ἀκοντιζόμενοι εἰς ἐμὲ ἐοίκασι, καὶ ἐμοῦ ἕκαστος αὐτῶν καθικνεῖται ὡς ἀληθῶς ἀνακαίων ἐκκαίων με. καὶ καταφλέγων[59] πρὸς τὴν σὴν στοργήν·[60] καὶ τὸ παθητικὸν μέρος τῆς ψυχῆς μου, τὸ πρὸς τοῖς ἠκουσμένοις ὄν, τὸ μετὰ τοῦ ἀνιᾶν μαντευόμενον[61] κολάζεται. ἀπαλλάσσῃ γὰρ αὐτός, καὶ εὖ οἶδα ὅτι καλῶς· τὴν δὲ μετὰ ταῦτά σου ἐπιμέλειαν καὶ στοργὴν ζητῶν ποῦ εὕρω ἢ ἐν τίνι; τὰ μὲν σπέρματα τῶν σωτηρίων λόγων δέδεγμαι, σοῦ ὄντος μοι τοῦ σπορέως. τὸ δὲ ἀναβλαστῆσαι ταῦτα καὶ ἐκφῦναι οὐχ ἑτέρου ἀλλ᾽ ἢ σοῦ δεῖται, Ἀνδρέα μακαριώτατε. καὶ τί γὰρ ἔχω σοι εἰπεῖν, δοῦλε τοῦ θεοῦ, ἀλλ᾽ ἢ τοῦτο; πολλοῦ ἐλέου δέομαι καὶ βοηθείας τῆς παρὰ σοῦ, ὅπως δυναίμην ἄξιος γενέσθαι ὧν ἔχω σου σπερμάτων· ἃ οὐκ ἄλλως

---

57. V: ἔχω ὃν ἠγάπων.

58. N: τί οὕτως δακρύων ἀκαθέκτως οὐ διαλιμπάνεις καὶ στένων οὐκ ἐφησυχάζεις; ὁρῶ γάρ σου τὸν ἀδιάπαυσον ὀδυρμὸν καὶ χαίρω.

59. N: κατέφλεξάν μου.

60. N: τὴν καρδίαν καὶ πρὸς πίστιν τοῦ ὑπὸ σοῦ εἵλκυσαν καταγγελλομένου Χριστοῦ καὶ στοργὴν τῆς σῆς μακαριότητος, καὶ τὴν ἐμὴν ἀκανθώδη καὶ κεχερσωμένην ὁμαλίσαντες ψυχήν.

61. V: τὴν μετὰ τούτων ἀνίαν μαντευόμενος.

my saying these things, is there? Who is it? Answer! I do
not speak in vain, do I? I have not spoken in vain, have
I? 'No!' says the person in you who weeps once again,
Stratocles."

43 (11). Then Stratocles approached Andrew weeping
and wailing. Andrew took Stratocles' hand and said, "I
have the one I sought.[45] I have found the one I desired. I
hold the one I loved. I rest because of the one I have
waited for. The very fact that you are still groaning
louder and are weeping uncontrollably[46] symbolizes for me
that I have already achieved rest, because not in vain
have I spoken to you the words which are akin to me."

44 (12). "Most blessed Andrew," Stratocles replied,
"do not think that there is anything that vexes me but
you, for the words which came from you are like flaming
javelins impaling me. Each of them strikes me and truly
blazes and burns with love for you.[47] The sensitive part
of my soul, which is disposed toward what I have heard, is
tormented in that it presages with anguish (what will take
place).[48] For you yourself may leave, and I know well that
it is good that you do so. But after this, where and in
whom will I seek and find your concern and love? I
received the seeds of the words of salvation while you
were my sower; for them to shoot up and reproduce requires
no one else but you, blessed Andrew. What do I have to say

----

45. *V*: "I have the one I loved."

46. *N*: "Why do you not stop weeping uncontrollably or
    silence your groaning? I see your incessant mourning
    and I rejoice."

47. *N*: "they enflame my heart and draw it toward faith in
    the Christ announced by you and to love of your
    blessedness, by leveling out my thorny and parched
    soul."

48. *V*: "in that it presages the grief that attends them."

ἀπίδω ἄπληκτα ὄντα⁶² καὶ εἰς τὸ φανερὸν ἀνίσχοντα, μὴ οὐχί σου βουληθέντος καὶ εὐξαμένου ὑπὲρ αὐτῶν καὶ ἐμοῦ ὅλου.

45 (13). Καὶ ὁ Ἀνδρέας αὐτῷ ἀπεκρίνατο· ταῦτα ἦν, τέκνον, ἃ καὶ αὐτὸς ἑώρων ἐν σοί. καὶ μου τὸν κύριον δοξάζω, ὅτι μου ἡ περὶ σὲ ἔννοια οὐκ ἐκενεμβάτησεν, ⁶³ ἀλλ' οἶδεν ὃ εἶπεν. ὅπως δὲ εἰδῆτε, αὔριόν με ὁ Αἰγεάτης εἰς τὸ ἀνασκολοπισθῆναι παραδίδωσιν. ἡ γὰρ τοῦ κυρίου δούλη⁶⁴ Μαξιμίλλα ταράξει τὸν ἐν αὐτῷ ἐχθρόν, ⁶⁵ οὗ ἐστιν ἐκεῖνος ἴδιος, μὴ συντιθεμένη αὐτῷ τὰ αὐτῇ ἀλλότρια ἔργα. ⁶⁶ καὶ εἰς ἐμὲ στραφεὶς δόξει ἑαυτὸν παρηγορεῖν.

46 (14). Ἡ δὲ Μαξιμίλλα ταῦτα τοῦ ἀποστόλου λέγοντος οὐ παρῆν· ἐκείνη γὰρ τοὺς λόγους κατακούσασα οὓς πρὸς αὐτὴν ἀπετείνατο, ⁶⁷ καὶ τρόπον τινὰ διατεθεῖσα ἀπ' αὐτῶν καὶ γενομένη τοῦτο ὅπερ οἱ λόγοι ἐδείκνυον, ἐξορμήσασα οὐκ ἀκρίτως οὐδὲ ἀστοχάστως παραγίνεται⁶⁸ εἰς τὸ πραιτώριον. καὶ τῷ παντὶ βίῳ ἅμα τῇ τῆς σαρκὸς μητρὶ κακίᾳ καὶ τοῖς⁶⁹ τῆς σαρκὸς χαίρειν φράσασα, ⁷⁰ καὶ τοῦ Αἰγεάτου προσανενέγκαντος⁷¹ αὐτῇ τὴν ὁμοίαν αὐτῷ ἀξίωσιν, περὶ ἧς ἔφησεν αὐτῇ διασκέψασθαι, εἰ ἄρα βούλοιτο αὐτῷ

---

62. V: ἐπιδώσει ἄληκτα. Prieur: ἐπιδώσει ἄπληκτα.

63. V: οὐ κενεμβάτησεν.

64. N: οἰκέτις.

65. N: διοχλήσει τὸν ἐνοικοῦντα αὐτὸν ἀνθρωποκτόνον ὄφιν.

66. V: αὐτῆς ἀλλότρια.

67. N: ὑπακούσασα τοῦ ἀποστόλου λόγων.

68. V: παρεγένετο. N: ἀνεχώρησεν.

69. V om.: τῇ τῆς σαρκὸς μητρὶ κακίᾳ καὶ τοῖς.

70. N adds: καὶ μόνῳ τῷ θεῷ συνεῖναι ᾧπερ καὶ νενύμφευται.

71. V: ἀνενεγκόντος. N: προσκαλεσάμενος.

to you but this, servant of God? I need the great compassion and help that comes from you in order to be worthy of these seeds I already have from you, which I might not otherwise see unmolested[49] and sprouting into the open without your willing it and praying for them and for my entire self."

45 (13). "Child," answered Andrew, "these things are what I myself also found in you. I glorify my Lord that my estimation of you was not groundless, but knew what it said. So that you (pl.) may know, tomorrow Aegeates will hand me over to be impaled on a stake.[50] Maximilla, the Lord's servant,[51] will trouble the enemy[52] in him to whom he belongs, and will not consent with him to do anything alien to her. By turning against me he will presume to console himself."

46 (14). Maximilla was not present when the apostle said this, for when she heard the words that applied to her[53] and in some way was changed by them, she became what the words themselves had signified. She rushed out deliberately and resolutely and went to the praetorium. Because she had bidden farewell to her whole life as well as to wickedness, the mother of the flesh, and to things pertaining to the flesh,[54] when Aegeates brought up his characteristically reprehensible ultimatum which he had

----

49. V: "will otherwise not produce without stopping." Prieur: "will otherwise not produce unmolested."

50. I.e., crucified.

51. N: "domestic servant."

52. N: "will disturb the murderous serpent resident in him."

53. N: "when she heeded the words of the apostle."

54. N adds: "and cohabited with God alone, whom she also had married."

συγκαθεύδειν,[72] ἀπειπαμένης δέ, περὶ τὴν τοῦ ᾿Ανδρέα ἀναίρεσιν λοιπὸν ἐτέτραπτο, καὶ ἐσκέπτετο ποίῳ θανάτῳ αὐτὸν περιβάλοι. καὶ ὡς ἐπεκράτησεν αὐτῷ τὸ πάντων μᾶλλον τὸ ἀνασκολοπισθῆναι, ἀπιὼν μὲν αὐτὸς[73] ἅμα τοῖς ὁμοίοις ὡς θὴρ ἐσιτίζετο.[74]

47 (15). ῾Η δὲ Μαξιμίλλα, προηγουμένου αὐτῆς τοῦ κυρίου ἰδέᾳ τοῦ ᾿Ανδρέα, ἅμα τῇ ᾿Ιφιδάμᾳ πάλιν παραγίνεται εἰς τὸ δεσμωτήριον· καὶ ὄχλου πλείονος ἔνδον ὄντος τῶν ἀδελφῶν καταλαμβάνει αὐτὸν λόγους ποιούμενον τοιούτους· * ἐγώ, ἀδελφοί, ἐξεπέμφθην ὑπὸ τοῦ κυρίου ἀπόστολος εἰς τὰ κλίματα ταῦτα ὧν με κατηξίωσεν ὁ κύριός μου, διδάξαι μὲν οὐδένα, ὑπομνῆσαι δὲ πάντα τὸν συγγενῆ τῶν λόγων ἄνθρωπον ὅτι ἐν κακοῖς τοῖς προσκαίροις διάγουσιν οἱ πάντες ἄνθρωποι[75] τερπόμενοι ταῖς ἐπιβλαβέσιν αὐτῶν φαντασίαις, ὧν ἀεὶ καὶ ὑμᾶς παρεκάλεσα ἐκστῆναι, καὶ ἐπὶ τὰ μόνιμα ἐπείγεσθαι προ<έ>τρεψα[76] καὶ πάντων <τῶν> ῥευστῶν τὴν φυγὴν ποιήσασθαι· ὁρᾶτε γὰρ μηδένα ὑμῶν ἱστάμενον, ἀλλὰ τὰ πάντα εὐμετάβολα μέχρι ἠθῶν ἀνθρωπίνων· τοῦτο δὲ συμβαίνει διὰ τὴν ἀπαίδευτον ψυχὴν τὴν εἰς φύσιν πλανηθεῖσαν καὶ τὰ τῆς πλάνης ἐνέχυρα κατέχουσαν. μακαρίους οὖν ἐκείνους τίθεμαι τοὺς κατηκόους τῶν κεκηρυγμένων λόγων γεγονότας καὶ δι᾿ αὐτῶν μυστήρια ὀπτριζομένους περὶ τὴν ἰδίαν φύσιν, ἧς ἕνεκεν τὰ πάντα ᾠκοδόμηται.[77] **(48 [16].)** ἐντέλλομαι

---

72. **N:** βούλοιτο πρὸς αὐτὸν ὡς πάλαι διατεθῆναι.

73. **N:** τῆς οὖν ὥρας προτρεπομένης ἐπὶ τὸ ἄριστον πρό-
εισιν.

74. **V om.:** ὡς θήρ. **N:** ἅμα τοῖς ὁμοίοις αὐτῷ γαστριδούλοις σιτίζεσθαι οἷά τις θὴρ αἱμοβόρος τῷ θυμῷ βρέμων πρὸς βορὰν σαρκῶν ἀθῴων.

75. **V om.** οἱ πάντες ἄνθρωποι.

76. Following Bonnet's hypothetical reconstruction. The text actually reads: προτρέψασθαι.

77. **Arm:** խնամարկեցաւ.

told her to ponder--namely, whether she would be willing
to sleep with him[55]--she rebuffed him. He turned attention
at last to the destruction of Andrew and considered what
kind of death he might impose on him. Of all the options
crucifixion[56] most preoccupied him. Then he went off[57]
with his cronies and ate like a wild animal.[58]

47 (15). Maximilla, led by the Lord disguised as
Andrew, went to the prison again with Iphidamia. A great
crowd of the brethren was inside when she found him
speaking the following: * "Brethren, the Lord sent me as
an apostle to these regions of which my Lord considered me
worthy, not to teach anyone, but to remind everyone akin
to these words that all people pass their time among
ephemeral evils reveling in their destructive fantasies,
which I have continually encouraged you to shun. I have
urged you to pursue things that are stable, and to flee
from all that undulates. Look, not one of you stands firm,
but everything--including human conventions--is in flux.
This happens because of the uneducated soul's wandering
into nature and retaining the pledges of its mistake.
Therefore, I consider blessed those who have obeyed the
words preached and who through them observe, as in a
mirror, the mysteries concerning their proper nature, for
the sake of which all things were constructed.[59] (48
[16].) Therefore, I command you, beloved children, to
build firmly on the foundation laid for you, which is

----

55. *N*: "whether she would be willing to respond to him as
    before."

56. More literally: "impaling on a stake."

57. *N*: "At the prescribed hour he went off to breakfast."

58. *N*: "to eat with gluttons like himself, roaring with
    rage for the meat of innocent flesh like a
    bloodthirsty wild animal."

59. *Arm*: "were provided for."

τοιγαροῦν, ἠγαπημένα τέκνα, ἐποικοδομεῖσθε[78] ἑδραίως ἐπὶ
τῷ θεμελίῳ τῷ καταβεβλημένῳ ὑμῖν, ὄντι ἀσαλεύτῳ καὶ
ἀνεπιβουλεύτῳ παντὶ τῷ πονηρευομένῳ. ἐπὶ τοῦτον τὸν
θεμέλιον ῥιζώθητε· στηρίχθητε μνημονεύοντες ὧν ὅσα τε
γεγόνασιν συναναστρέφοντός μου πᾶσιν ὑμῖν. εἴδετε δι' ἐμοῦ
ἔργα γεγονότα οἷς οὐκ ἔχετε ἀπιστῆσαι αὐτοί, γεγονότα
σημεῖα τοιαῦτα[79] ἃ καὶ τάχα ἡ ἄλαλος φύσις κεκράξεται·
λόγους ὑμῖν παρέδωκα οὓς εὔχομαι οὕτως καταδέχεσθαι ὑφ'
ὑμῶν ὡς αὐτοὶ οἱ λόγοι θέλουσιν. στηρίζεσθε οὖν, ἀγαπητοί,
ἐπὶ πᾶσιν οἷς εἴδετε, οἷς ἠκούσατε, οἷς ἐκοινωνήσατε· καὶ
ὑμᾶς ὁ θεὸς εἰς ὃν ἐπισπεύσατε ἐλεήσας εὐαρέστους
παραστήσει ἑαυτῷ ἀναπεπαυμένους εἰς ἅπαντας αἰῶνας. (49
[17].) τὸ δὲ περὶ ἐμὲ μέλλον συμβαίνειν μὴ οὕτως ταρασσέτω
ὑμᾶς ὥς τι ξένον θαῦμα, ὅτι ὁ τοῦ θεοῦ δοῦλος, ᾧ πολλὰ
παρέσχετο αὐτὸς ὁ θεὸς δι' ἔργων καὶ λόγων,[80] οὗτος βίᾳ
ὑπὸ ἀνθρώπου πονηροῦ ἀπελαύνεται τούτου τοῦ προσκαίρου
βίου· οὐ μόνον γὰρ περὶ ἐμὲ τὸ τοιοῦτον συμβήσεται, ἀλλὰ
καὶ εἰς πάντας τοὺς <'Ιησοῦν> ἠγαπηκότας καὶ εἰς αὐτὸν
πεπιστευκότας καὶ αὐτὸν ὁμολογοῦντας. ὁ πάντα ἀναιδὴς
διάβολος τὰ ἴδια τέκνα ὁπλίσει κατ' αὐτῶν, ὅπως αὐτῷ
συνθῶνται· καὶ οὐχ ἕξει ὃ βούλεται. καὶ διὰ τί ταῦτα
ἐπιχειρεῖ ἐγὼ φράσω· ἀπὸ μὲν τῆς πάντων ἀρχῆς, καὶ εἰ δεῖ
λέγειν, ἐξ οὗπερ ὁ ἄναρχος τῇ ὑπ' αὐτὸν ἀρχῇ κατῆλθεν
ἀπωθῆναι [...][81] ὁ πολέμιος εἰρήνης ἀλλότριος, τὸν μὴ
ἴδιον, ἀλλὰ μόνον τινὰ τῶν ἀσθενεστέρων καὶ <μὴ> περιφανῆ
καὶ μηδέπω δυνάμενον γνωρίζεσθαι. καὶ διὰ τὸ μηδὲ αὐτὸν
ἐπίστασθαι, τούτου ἕνεκεν ἐκεῖνον ὑπ' αὐτοῦ ἐχρῆν

----

78. Bonnet suggests: ἐποικοδομεῖσθαι. So Prieur.

79. Arm adds: զոր կարծեմ թէ .

80. Arm: վասն զի Աստուած ծառայիցն իւրոց սապղս է վարձս յաղագս
գործոց և բանից.

81. V, the only Greek witness to this passage, seems
defective here. Arm: եկն յերկիր, զի զնա մերժեցէ ի
մէնջ, և կորուսցէ.

unshakable and impregnable to the stratagems of the
wicked. Be planted on this foundation. Stand firm,
remembering everything that happened while I was living
with all of you. You saw acts performed through me which
you yourselves cannot disbelieve; such signs performed[60]
that perhaps even mute nature would have cried out in
acclaim. I have handed over to you words which I pray you
received in the way the words themselves would want. Dear
friends, stand firm in everything you have seen, heard,
and participated in, and God, in whom you have believed,
because he had mercy, will present you to himself as
acceptable, forever at rest. (**49 [17].**) Do not let what is
going to happen to me trouble you as though it were some
strange marvel, namely that God's servant, by whom God
himself provided many things through acts and words,[61]
will be violently driven from this passing life by a
wicked man. This violence will not come upon me only, but
also on all who have loved, believed, and confessed
<Jesus>. The devil, entirely void of shame, will arm his
own children against them, so that they may join forces
with him. But he will not obtain what he wants. I will
tell you why he undertakes these things.[62] From the
beginning of all things, in other words, from that time
when the one without beginning descended to that realm
under him to drive away (...).[63] The enemy, a stranger to
peace, (oppresses) the one not belonging to him, but is
merely one of the weaker, inconspicuous, and thus far
unable to be recognized. And because this person does not

----

60. *Arm* adds: "which I think."

61. *Arm*: "for God will give his servants reward for their
    deeds and words."

62. At this point the speech in *Arm* deviates greatly from
    the Greek.

63. *V* is defective. *Arm*: "came to earth that he might
    drive him from us and destroy him."

πολεμεῖσθαι.⁸² δόξας γὰρ αὐτὸν ἔχειν καὶ δεσπόζειν αὐτοῦ
εἰσαεί, τοσοῦτον αὐτῷ ἀντιφέρεται ὡς τὴν αὐτῶν ἔχθραν
φιλίας παραπλησίαν ἐργάζεσθαι. ὑποβάλλων γὰρ αὐτῷ τὰ ἴδια
πολλάκις διέγραψεν ἐνήδονα ὄντα καὶ ἀπατηλά, δι' ὧν αὐτοῦ
περικρατεῖν ἐδόκει· ἐχρθὸς μὲν οὐ<κ>⁸³ ἐδείκνυτο εἰς τὸ
φανερόν, προσποιούμενος φιλίαν τὴν αὐτοῦ ἀξίαν.⁸⁴ (50
[18].) καὶ τοῦτο ἦν αὐτῷ ἔργον ἐπὶ πολὺ γινόμενον, ὡς εἰς
λήθην γνωρίζεσθαι ἐκείνῳ, γνωρίσαι <δὲ> αὐτόν· τοῦτ' ἔστιν
οὗτος διὰ τὰ ἑαυτοῦ δῶρα [...].⁸⁵ ἀλλ' ὅτε τὸ τῆς χάριτος
μυστήριον ἐξήφθη, καὶ ἡ βουλὴ τῆς ἀναπαύσεως ἐφανερώθη,
καὶ τὸ τοῦ λόγου φῶς ἐδείχθη, καὶ τὸ σῳζόμενον γένος
ἠλέγχθη τὸ πρὶν ἡδοναῖς πολεμούμενον, ἰδὼν ὁ ἀλλότριος
καταφρονούμενον ἑαυτὸν καὶ τὰ ἑαυτοῦ δῶρα διαγελώμενα,⁸⁶
δι' ὧν αὐτοῦ ἐδόκει κατοφρυοῦσθαι, διὰ τὴν τοῦ ἐλεήσαντος
χρηστότητα, ἤρξατο πρὸς ἡμᾶς μίσει καὶ ἔχθρᾳ καὶ
ἐπεξαναστάσει ἀντιπλέκειν. καὶ τοῦτο ἐν ἔργῳ τέθεικεν⁸⁷ μὴ
παύσασθαι ἀφ' ἡμῶν μέχρις ἂν εἰς ἃ νομίζει χωρίσωμεν. τότε
μὲν γὰρ ἀμέριμνος ἦν ὁ ἡμῖν ἀλλότριος, καὶ φιλίαν
προσεποιεῖτο στέλλεσθαι πρὸς ἡμᾶς τὴν αὐτοῦ ἀξίαν· εἶχεν

----

82. **Arm:** զի ինքն տկար է և անզոր և անբրիյթ տեսլեամբ. պատրէ
զմիտս այնոցիկ որ ոչն ճանաչեն զնատուած: Եւ վասն այնորիկ
եկն Տէրն պատերազմեցաւ ընդ նմա, և ընկէց ի փառաց, և
յիշխանութենէն, զոր կարծեցուցանէր խորատոյ լեալ յայնուռնդու
դ֊ոիւնոց. և մեզ ծանոյց արարիչն Աստուած զիւր հայրն փառաց
մշտնջենաւոր, զի զնա սիրեսցուք և զպատոտիրանն նորա արասցուք.
և ես մեզ բաղում անգամ գրեցի զպատեր խորամանկութեան
բանսարկուին.

83. **The ms. reads:** οὖν.

84. **Arm:** զի ինքն Թշնամին ոչ երևեցուցանէր զիւր թոյնն նենգաւորս,
այլ ի մերս անապակս և ի չարիս պղծութեան գմարդիկ
արկանելով.

85. **Arm:** զի այն իսկ է նորա գործ, զի ի մուացութիւնս և ի
հեղգութիւնս ածցէ գմարդիկ առ ի խոտորեցուցանելոյ յարարչէն
մերմէ Աստուծոյ. և հանիցէ յաւիտենական կենացն.

86. **V:** τὸν ἀλλότριον αὐτὸν . . . διαγελώμενον.

87. **V:** τέθειται.

understand, he has to wage war with him.[64] Insofar as the
enemy also aspires to dominate him forever, he opposes him
in a manner that makes their hostility resemble a
friendship. In order to place him under his control, he
often flaunted his own pleasure-loving and deceitful
traits, supposing that through these he would subjugate
him. By faking a friendship befitting his victim, he did
not display himself openly as an enemy.[65] (50 [18].) This
activity took place for so long that the victim forgot to
recognize it. <But> the devil recognized it; that is,
because of his gifts he (was not seen to be an enemy).[66]
But when the mystery of grace was set aflame, and the plan
for rest was revealed, and the light of the word was set
forth, and the race being saved was proved to have been
previously at war with pleasures, and when the enemy saw
himself scorned and his gifts, through which he thought to
intimidate, ridiculed because of the goodness of the
merciful one, he began to entangle us in hate, hostility,
and insurrection. He has made it his business not to leave
us alone until we give way to the things that he values.
For when this was the case, our opponent had nothing to
worry about, and he pretended to depict his status as
friendly to us. He had no fear that we would revolt
inasmuch as we had been deceived by him. But let us not

----

64. *Arm*: "And since the Lord came to wage war against him
    who was thought to be submerged in the abyss of hell,
    having fallen from glory and power, our creator God
    acquainted us with his father of eternal glory, that
    we might love him and do his commandments. I have
    written you many times about the base deceit of the
    troublemaker."

65. *Arm*: "for the enemy himself did not reveal his
    deceitful poisons, but by throwing people into
    prodigal love and the evils of turpitude."

66. *Arm*: "for that is his work, that into forgetfulness
    and sloth he leads people, in order to lead us astray
    from God our creator and to remove us from eternal
    life."

δὲ καὶ τὸ μὴ φοβεῖσθαι μὴ ἀποστῶμεν, πεπλανημένοι ὑπ'
αὐτοῦ. Բայց մեք մի՞ ի րաց կացցուք ի Քրիստոսէ խարելութեամբ
Բշնամլոյն, որով՞ենակ յայտնեցաւ մեզ խնամակալութիւն նորա և
լուսաւորեաց զմեզ։ Իսկ զԲշնամլոյն զորութիւն և զյանդգնութիւն
սկսրացոյց.[88] τὸ γὰρ κρυπτόμενον αὐτοῦ τῆς φύσεως καὶ τὸ
δοκοῦν λανθάνειν, τοῦτο ἤλεγξεν καὶ ὁμολογεῖν ὅ ἐστιν
παρεσκεύασεν. ἐπιστάμενοι τοιγαροῦν τὸ μέλλον ἔσεσθαι,
ἀδελφοί, διυπνιζώμεθα καὶ πρὸς τὸ ἀπηλλάχθαι αὐτοῦ
γιγνώμεθα, μὴ δυσφοροῦντες μηδὲ χειμαζόμενοι,[89] μηδὲ
ἀποκομίζοντες αὐτοῦ ἴχνη ἐπὶ τῶν ψυχῶν τὰ μὴ ἴδια ἡμῶν.
ἀλλ' ὅλοι ἐν ὅλῳ τῷ λόγῳ ἐπ<αι>ωρούμενοι τὸ τέλος πάντες
ἀσμένως προσδεξώμεθα καὶ τὴν ἀπ' αὐτοῦ φυγὴν ποιήσωμεν,
ὅπως καὶ αὐτὸς λοιπὸν δειχθῇ ὅστις ἐστὶ τὴν φύσιν, ἡμῶν
ἐπὶ τὰ ἡμέτερα ἀνιπταμένων.[90]

51 (1).[91] Ὁμιλοῦντος δὲ ταῦτα τοῦ Ἀνδρέα τοῖς
ἀδελφοῖς δι' ὅλης τῆς νυκτὸς καὶ εὐχομένου, καὶ κοινῇ
πάντων ἀγαλλιώντων καὶ στηριζομένων ἐπὶ τὸν κύριον, τῇ
ἐξῆς ἐξ ἑωθινοῦ[92] μεταπεμψάμενος ὁ Αἰγεάτης τὸν Ἀνδρέαν
ἐκ τοῦ δεσμωτηρίου εἶπεν αὐτῷ· τὸ τέλος τῆς περὶ σὲ
κρίσεως ἤγγικεν, ξένε ἄνθρωπε καὶ ἀλλότριε τοῦ νῦν βίου[93]
καὶ ἐχθρὲ τῆς ἐμῆς οἰκίας[94] καὶ λυμεὼν τοῦ παντός μου
οἴκου. τί γὰρ τὸ δόξαν σοι εἰσπηδῆσαι ἀλλοτρίοις τόποις

----

88. V is corrupt here. Prieur reads: τὸ δὲ τῆς οἰκονομίας
χρῆμα ἐξαφθέν, οὐ λέγω ἰσχυροτέραν [...].

89. V: σχηματιζόμενοι.

90. V ends here. Arm: և մեք զփրկութիւն անձանց մերոց անմաալ
պաշհեսցուք.

91. Here begins the section of the AA traditionally
regarded as Andrew's martyrdom.

92. N: ἔωθεν. C: ὀρθρίσας πάνυ. Ma1: ὀρθρίσας. Ma2: ἐξεώθη.

93. Only Ma1, C, and Arm read: τοῦ νῦν βίου. N: τοῦ
ἡμετέρου ἔθνους.

94. N: τῆς τῶν θεῶν εὐμενείας.

stand aside from Christ by the deceit of the enemy,
because the providence of God has been revealed to us and
has enlightened us. He has weakened the enemy's power and
arrogance.[67] For the hidden aspect of the devil's nature
and what seemed to be unnoticed, this Christ exposed and
forced to confess what it was. Therefore, brethren, since
we understand what will happen, let us awaken and separate
ourselves from him. Let us not be vexed or agitated by the
storm,[68] and let us not transport on our souls traces of
the devil which are not ours. But since we have been
entirely buoyed up by the whole word, let us all eagerly
anticipate the goal and let us take flight from him, so
that at last he may be exposed for what he is by nature,
as we fly off to those things which are ours."[69]

51 (1). Throughout the night Andrew spoke these
things to the brethren, prayed, and all rejoiced together
and were confirmed in the Lord. Early in the morning,[70]
Aegeates summoned Andrew from prison and said to him, "The
time to complete my judgment against you has arrived, you
stranger, alien to this present life,[71] enemy of my
home,[72] and corrupter of my entire house. Why did you
decide to burst into places alien to you and corrupt a
wife who used to please me in every way[73] and never slept

----

67. These last two sentences appear only in *Arm*. *V* is
    corrupt at this point: "But when the matter of God's
    plan was kindled, I do not say stronger (...)."

68. *V*: "not demean ourselves."

69. *Arm*: "and let us keep without error the salvation of
    our souls."

70. *C* and *Ma*1: "Waking early in the morning."

71. *N*: "our race."

72. *N*: "of the favor of the gods."

73. *C* adds: "whom I knew (sexually)."

καὶ ὑποδιαφθεῖραι γυναῖκα πάλαι ἀρεσκομένην μοι ὅλην[95] καὶ
μηδενὶ ἑτέρῳ προσαναπαυομένην; ἐφ' ᾧ ἔμαθον πεισθεὶς παρ'
αὐτῆς νῦν σοὶ καὶ τῷ σῷ θεῷ χαίρειν. τοιγαροῦν ἀπόλαυε τῶν
ἐμῶν δωρεῶν.[96]

Καὶ ἑπτὰ μάστιξιν ἐκέλευσεν αὐτὸν μαστιχθῆναι·
ὕστερον δὲ[97] εἰς τὸ ἀνασκολοπισθῆναι αὐτὸν ἔπεμψεν,
κελεύσας τοῖς δημίοις μὴ ἥλοις αὐτὸν ἐμπαρῆναι ἀλλὰ
σχοινίοις δεθέντα τανύσαι, <καὶ> ἀδιατμήτους αὐτοῦ τὰς
ἀγκύλας καταλειφθῆναι[98] ἵνα, ὡς ἐνόμιζεν, ἔτι μᾶλλον αὐτὸν
κολάσῃ.

Καὶ ἦν τοῦτο πᾶσι πρόδηλον· διεδόθη γὰρ ἐν ὅλαις
Πάτραις φημισθὲν[99] ὅτι ὁ ξένος, ὁ δίκαιος,[100] ὁ τὸν θεὸν
ἔχων ὑπὸ τοῦ ἀνοσίου Αἰγεάτου ἀνασκολοπίζεται, μηδὲν
ἄτοπον ποιήσας. καὶ σὺν ἑνὶ πάντες ἠγανάκτουν.[101]

52 (2). Ὡς δὲ ἦγον[102] αὐτὸν εἰς τὸν τόπον οἱ δήμιοι
τὸ κελευσθὲν εἰς πέρας ἀγαγεῖν[103] βουλόμενοι, ὁ Στρατοκλῆς

----

95. C adds: ἣν ἔγνωκα.

96. N adds: τε καὶ ἀμοιβῶν ἀνθ' ὧν εἰς ἐμὲ διεπράξω.

97. N: παρέδωκεν (similarly E and L).

98. This reconstruction conflates the recensions. E, Cd, Ep, and Arm mention the ropes. N, HS, Ma, and C mention the unbroken knees. Both appear later in Aegeates' commands to the executioners. Prieur omits μὴ ἥλοις αὐτὸν ἐμπαρῆναι ἀλλὰ σχοινίοις δεθέντα τανύσαι, καί.

99. So C and Ma1. Ma2: φήμη. HS: ἐφημίσθη. N: διαβοωμένη.

100. N adds: καὶ Χριστοῦ δοῦλος. E: δοῦλος Χριστοῦ.

101. N and E add: διὰ τὸ ἀνόσιον τῆς κρίσεως. Ma2: κατὰ τοῦ Αἰγεάτου.

102. So HS and Ma2. C and Ma1: ἤγαγον. N and E: διῆγον.

103. HS and C: τῷ κελευσθέντι πέρας ἐπαγαγεῖν.

with another man? She has convinced me that she now rejoices in you and your God. So enjoy my gifts!"[74]

He commanded that Andrew be flogged with seven whips. Then he sent him off[75] to be crucified[76] and commanded the executioners not to impale him with nails but to stretch him out tied up with ropes, <and> to leave his knees uncut, supposing that by so doing he would punish Andrew even more cruelly.

This matter became known to everyone, for it was rumored throughout Patras that the stranger, the righteous one,[77] the man who possessed God, was being crucified by the impious Aegeates, even though he had done nothing improper. All alike were outraged.[78]

52 (2). As the executioners led him to the place intending to carry out their orders, Stratocles, who had

---

74. *N* adds: "and compensations for what you accomplished against me."

75. *N* (similarly *E* and *L*): "delivered him up."

76. Literally: "fixed to a pole," *passim*.

77. *N* and *E* add: "servant of Christ."

78. *N* and *E* add: "because of the profanity of the judgment." *Ma2*: "against Aegeates."

πυθόμενος τὸ συμβὰν δρομαίως παραγίνεται[104] καὶ ὁρᾷ τὸν
μακάριον ὑπὸ τῶν δημίων βίᾳ συρόμενον ὥς τι κακὸν
ποιήσαντα·[105] ὧν οὐκ ἐφείσατο, ἀλλὰ πληγὰς ἑκάστῳ αὐτῶν
ἐντριψάμενος[106] καὶ τοὺς χιτωνίσκους αὐτῶν διαρρήξας
ἄνωθεν ἕως κάτω ἀπέσπασε τὸν Ἀνδρέαν, εἰπὼν πρὸς αὐτούς·
καὶ ἐν τούτῳ τῷ μακαρίῳ χάριν δότε παιδεύσαντί με καὶ τὸ
πολὺ τῆς ὀργῆς ἐπέχειν[107] διδάξαντι· ἐπεὶ ἔδειξα ἂν ὑμῖν
τί Στρατοκλῆς δύναται καὶ τί ὁ μιαρὸς Αἰγεάτης·
μεμαθήκαμεν δὲ φέρειν[108] τὰ ἐπαγόμενα. καὶ κρατῶν[109] τῆς
χειρὸς τοῦ ἀποστόλου ἀπῄει σὺν αὐτῷ εἰς τὸν παραθαλάσσιον
τόπον, ἔνθα ἐχρῆν αὐτὸν ἀναρτηθῆναι.[110]

53 (3). Οἱ δὲ στρατιῶται πορευθέντες ἐπεδείκνυον
ἑαυτοὺς τῷ Αἰγεάτῃ δηλοῦντες αὐτῷ τὰ γεγονότα. κἀκεῖνος
αὐτοῖς ἀπεκρίνατο· ἑτέρας λαβόντες[111] ἐσθῆτας πορεύθητε[112]
ἔνθα τὸ κελευσθὲν ὑμῖν διατέτακται πρᾶξαι. καὶ ὁπότε τῷ
καταδικασθέντι φίλων τὴν ἀφ᾽ ὑμῶν ἀπαλλαγὴν ποιήσασθαι
τηνικαῦτα ὑπακούσατε. τῷ μέντοι Στρατοκλεῖ μηδὲ ὅλως
ὀφθῆτε τὸ ὅσον τὸ ἐφ᾽ ὑμῖν, ἀλλὰ μηδὲ ἀντείπητε εἴ τινος
ὅλως[113] χρῄζει ὑμῶν. οἶδα γὰρ τὸ τῆς ψυχῆς αὐτοῦ

----

104. N and E: καταλαμβάνει.

105. N and E: βίᾳ ἑλκόμενον ὑπὸ τῶν δημίων ὥσπερ τινὰ
κακοῦργον εἰς κρίσιν.

106. HS: ἐντρίψας. Ma1: ἐκτριψάμενος.

107. Ma1: ἐπέσχεν. C: ἐπίσχειν.

108. Ma1: γὰρ ὑποφέρειν.

109. So C and Ma1. HS: ἀποκρατῶν. N and E: περικρατῶν. Ma2:
κρατοῦντες.

110. Ma1: σταυρωθῆναι. N and E: ἔνθα καὶ ηὐτρέπιστο
τελειωθῆναι αὐτόν.

111. Ma1: βαλλόντας.

112. HS: πορευθέντες.

learned what was happening, arrived[79] at a run and saw the executioners violently dragging off the blessed one like a criminal.[80] Stratocles did not spare any of them but gave each a beating, ripped their clothing from top to bottom, tore Andrew away, and told them, "Thank the blessed one for educating me and teaching me to check my violent temper. Otherwise, I would have demonstrated for you what Stratocles and Aegeates the rogue are capable of. For we (believers) have learned to endure our afflictions." He grabbed the apostle's hand and went away with him to the seaside location where he was to be hung up.[81]

53 (3). The soldiers left and presented themselves to Aegeates explaining what had happened. "Change your clothes," the proconsul answered, "and go back there to perform your duties. When you rid yourselves of the convict's friends, then obey your orders. Avoid as best you can letting Stratocles see you, and do not argue if he should require from you anything at all. For I know the nobility[82] of his soul, such that if provoked he probably would spare not even me." They did exactly as Aegeates told them.

----

79. *N* and *E*: "caught up."

80. *N* and *E*: "violently hauled off by the executioners like some criminal to judgment."

81. *Ma*1: "to be crucified." *N* and *E*: "where it was arranged that he be terminated."

82. *Ma* and two mss. of *Arm* read instead: "rashness."

εὐγενὲς[114] οἷόν ἐστιν, ὡς τάχα κἀμοῦ ἀφειδήσει, εἰ ἄρα
παροξυνθείη. κἀκεῖνοι οὕτως ἐποίησαν[115] καθὼς ὁ Αἰγεάτης
εἶπεν αὐτοῖς.

Ὁ δὲ Στρατοκλῆς βαδίζων ἅμα τῷ ἀποστόλῳ ἐρχομένῳ ἐπὶ
τὸν προκείμενον τόπον ἐπηπόρει[116] διαγανακτῶν πρὸς τὸν
Αἰγεάτην ἔσθ’ ὅτε καὶ ἠρέμα διαλοιδορούμενος αὐτόν.

Καὶ ὁ ’Ανδρέας[117] αὐτῷ ἀπεκρίνατο· τέκνον μου
Στρατοκλῆ, ἀκίνητόν σε βούλομαι τοῦ λοιποῦ τὸν νοῦν
κτήσασθαι,[118] καὶ μὴ ἀναμένειν ὑπ’ ἄλλου νουθετεῖσθαι,
παρὰ δὲ σεαυτοῦ λαμβάνειν τὸ τοιοῦτον, καὶ μήτε ἔσωθέν σε
διατίθεσθαι πρὸς τὰ δοκοῦντα χαλεπά, μήτε εἰς τὸ φανερὸν
ἐξάπτεσθαι· πρέπει γὰρ τὸν ’Ιησοῦ δοῦλον ’Ιησοῦ ἄξιον
εἶναι. ἐρῶ δέ τι πρὸς σὲ ἕτερον καὶ τοὺς σὺν ἐμοὶ
βαδίζοντας ἀδελφοὺς περὶ τῶν ἀλλοτρίων ἡμῖν ἀνθρώπων. ἡ
δαιμονικὴ φύσις μέχρις μὴ ἔχῃ τὴν αἱματώδη τροφὴν μηδὲ τὸ
δι’ αὐτῆς νόστιμον ἀνασπᾷ μὴ ἀναιρουμένων ζῴων, ἐξασθενεῖ
καὶ εἰς οὐδὲν χωρεῖ νεκρουμένη ὅλη. εἰ δὲ ἔχει ὃ ποθεῖ καὶ
στερρύνεται καὶ εὐρύνεται καὶ ἐξανίσταται αὔξουσα οἷς
ἥδεται. τοιοῦτόν τι, τέκνον, συμβαίνει περὶ τοὺς ἐκτὸς
ἀνθρώπους οἳ νεκροῦνται μὴ ἐξαπτομένων ἡμῶν πρὸς ὃ
ἐξάπτουσιν. ἀλλὰ καὶ ἐν ἡμῖν αὐτοῖς ὁ ἀντιπρόσωπος
ἄνθρωπος, ὁπόταν τι τολμήσῃ καὶ μὴ τὸν συνθέμενον εὕρῃ,
τύπτεται καὶ ἐρείδεται ὅλος εἰς γῆν νεκρούμενος ὅτι μὴ[119]

---

113. C: ὁ λόγος. HS om.: ὅλως.

114. Ma and two mss. of Arm: προπετές.

115. Ma1: ποιήσαντες.

116. So HS. Ma1: ἐπείπερ. C: ἐπιπόρει.

117. N, E, and Ma1: ἀπόστολος.

118. HS: κεκτῆσθαι. Ma1: κέκτισται. C: κτεῖσθαι.

119. Ma1: οὐκ.

Stratocles walked with the apostle to the designated spot, but he was perturbed, furious with Aegeates, now and then railing against him under his breath.

"Stratocles my child," Andrew[83] responded, "from now on I want you to keep your mind unwavering, and do not wait for advice from someone else, but take such advice from yourself--that you not be inwardly oriented toward seeming hardships nor attached to mere appearances--for it is fitting for a servant of Jesus to be worthy of Jesus. I will tell you and the brethren walking with me something else about people alien to us. As long as the demonic nature lacks its bloody food and cannot suck up its nutrition in that animals are not slain, it weakens and recedes to nothingness, becoming entirely dead. But if it has what it longs for, it firms up, expands, and rises up, growing by means of those foods it enjoys. This situation, child, obtains to those outside who die when we do not attach ourselves to what they are attached to. But even that self within ourselves which is contrary (to our true nature), when it dares to do something and cannot find anyone to consent with it, it is beaten and totally crushed to the earth, dead, because it did not complete what it undertook. Let us keep this image always before our eyes, children, so that we not grow drowsy and the opponent intrude and slaughter us.

----

83. *N*, *E*, and *Ma*1: "the apostle."

ἐτέλεσεν ὃ ἐπελάβετο.[120] πρὸ ὀφθαλμῶν οὖν, τεκνία, ἀεὶ
τοῦτον ἔχωμεν μήπως ἀποκοιμηθέντων ἡμῶν ὡς ἀντίδικος
ἐπεμβὰς ἀποσφάξῃ ἡμᾶς.

 այլ յոր ինչ դև քն յորդորէն և վարեն զնոսա ի չար ախտան: Ասեմ
և այլ ազգ առ ձեզ. քանզի Հասևալ եմք ի կատարած առաջիկայ
ճանապարհիս մերոյ, քանզի մարտ եղեալ կռուին ընդ մեզ դև քն
յաղագս քաղցր և Հեշտ պատուիրանացն Աստուծոյ, քանզի նման է,
որպէս ինձ թուի, Թագաւորական ԹուՆոյ արծուոյ, որ Թուքի
յերկրէ ի բարձունս, արեգական ճառագայթիւքն պայծառացեալ,
վայելուչ գեղով երևեալ գարդարեալ յինքեան ընուԹենէն բարձրաԹուիչ
լինելով, իսկ երԷ առ երկրաս Թուիցէ այն որ ԹեԹև ԹւՆքն իւրովք
բարձրաԹուիչ լիներ Թողեալ գուղողորդ սովորական Թուիցն լուսաքնակս,
ապականի յերկրէ, ճանրանան նմին ԹԽքն. և այլախոս է իսկ արծուին.
զի ԹԽքտ և իւր քնուԹիւնն պաառճաճ է երկրի, սակայն ԹԽոցն
անվայելուչ է նիստն, զի ի քարշեալն ընդ երկիր, երևույԹ զնա տեսղացն
ցուցանէ:

---

120. Ma1: ἐνελάβετο.

At this point *Arm* continues with an extended simile of an eagle. *N* and *E* also may reflect this passage: "Let us strive to renew the inner human, to let it fly to God in whom is all our desire."[84] *N* and *E* also suggest that their versions of the speech are truncated: "After he had spoken these things *and many others* to Stratocles and those with him on the way."[85] The best evidence for the inclusion of this speech comes from a similar speech comparing the soul with an eagle in Act 3 of the *APh*, which almost certainly relies on a text of the *AA* that contained this discourse. It would therefore appear that *Arm* is our most reliable witness to this passage, though it would be unwise to put too much confidence in its precise fidelity.

"I will tell you other things, because you have arrived at the end of the road before you, and because the demons pitched battle against us on account of the sweet and pleasant commandments of God. For it seems to me that it is like the regal bird, the eagle, that flies from earth on high, and is adorned with the rays of sunlight, by nature high-flying, appearing adorned with resplendent beauty. If he, soaring with light wings, flies around the earth, having left the usual traveling orbit of those living in light, he is corrupted by the earth, and his wings grow heavy. And the eagle is indeed transfigured, for although his nature is appropriate to the earth, nesting is unbecoming to his wings. While being drawn to earth, he appears ridiculous to those who see him.

----

84. Σπευδάσωμέν τε ἀνανεῶσαι τὸν ἔσωθεν καὶ πρὸς θεὸν τοῦτον ἀναπτερῶσαι, ἐν ᾧ ἡ πᾶσα ἡμῶν ἔφεσις ὑπάρχει.

85. Ταῦτα καὶ ἕτερα πλείονα τῷ τε (*E*: τότε) Στρατοκλεῖ καὶ τοῖς συνοῦσιν (*E*: σὺν αὐτῷ) διαλεχθεὶς κατὰ τὴν ὁδόν. Cf. *C*: εἰπὼν δὲ πρὸς αὐτὸν πολλά, καὶ νουθετήσας πάντας τοῖς ἀδελφοῖς. *Cd*: *Andreas vero cum plurimis eos adloqueretur verbis.*

Այսպիսի ինչ երքարք և մեզ է գիտելի գմերմէ քնուրթենէս. մինչդեռ գործն արծուոյ Թուչիցիմք յերկնաւոր լոյսն մեր քնական, և զարդարիցեմք գմեզ լուսեղէն պատուիրանաւն և հոգեղինացն առաքինութեամբք, թեթևացեալ այսութիւք և պայծառացեալք լիցուք ի քնական լապտերացն և վայելչացեալք անձինք մեր օրինակաւս այսուիկ հրաուեալ լիցուք ի քնական լապտերացն և վայելչացեալք ի վերայ բուսոյ ասման գեղեցիկ և հոգևոր թևոց մերոց։ Չի գոր օրինակ արծուին զելս իւրոյ Թուճմանն յերկինս ի քարձունս առնիցէ, երևելի ամենցուն լինի, և յիւր իսկ Թեւս պանծանայ և հաճոյ աչաց հայելոյ, և գեղեցիկ մարդկան երեւեալ ի վերուստ ի խոնարհ, նոյնպէս և մեք ի վեր քարձրութիւնն վերասցուք և յընդդիմակցացն մերոց ոչ յումեք ծանրացեալք, և առաքինութեամբք մերովք քարի վարս ցուցեալ իւրաքանչիւր յարմարեալ գնացիւք. Համբստ խորհրդով ընտիրք երևեցուք, զանազան առաքինութիւնն ի կիր արկանելով. և այս քանք այսպէս չարագ ծեսցին, գի իւրովին գիւր օգուտն ծանիցէ մարդն, գի դժնեայ և անարգ է խորհուրդ չարին, և փուքայ գմեզ ծոյլս կազմել առ ի կամս ասաւծութեանն։ Քանգի երկնային օրինօքն եղեաք խրատեալք երկրաւորքս զանց արասցուք գչար գործովք, և նորոգեցուք ի քնութեան մեր գքարի գործն մեր, Թերևս առցուք գործէն արծուոյ քնութեան որ միսանգամ նորոգի։ Դարձեալ գնոյն առակ ես ճեզ ասացից, ապա յայնժամ երևեսցի որ ոք իցէ քարեզարդ և վայելուչ, յորժամ ի մեռելոց յարիցէ. յայնժամ երևի մարդն արժանի քոլոր տեսողացն պայծառ գեղով ընդ առաջ վերանալով Տեառն. իսկ եթէ մնասցէ յերկրի, ապա երևեսցի ի խոնարհագոյն ճալուցն ծաղր եղեալ, վասն գի նմանեցոյց գինքն յետին Թուչնոյն։

"Such things, brothers, are also known to us about our nature. When, like the eagle, we fly toward our natural heavenly light and adorn ourselves with the luminous commandments and the virtues of the spiritual, we will be levitated by these and made to glow from natural lanterns and to be resplendent upon the growth of the plant of our beautiful and spiritual wings. Like the eagle, as the soul makes its upward ascent to heaven on high, it becomes visible to everyone, proud of its own wings, a pleasure for the eyes to look upon, appearing beautiful on high to people below; so also shall we ascend to the heights and not be weighed down by any of our opponents, by dint of our virtue having shown good conduct, each with his appropriate course. With humble thoughts we will appear chosen, practicing various virtues, and these words will be written, that each one will know his good, since the thoughts of the evil one are atrocious and disrespectful, and he hastens to make us lax in our will toward godliness. For we mortals were admonished by heavenly laws that we should avoid evil deeds, and we should renew in our natures our good work. Perhaps we might take wing like the example of the eagle of nature,[86] which was renewed again. Again I will tell you the same parable: When it will appear that someone is well-endowed and resplendent, then he will rise from the dead. Then a person appears worthy to all who see him, with splendid beauty going up to the Lord. But if he remain on earth, he will appear the most humble--a joke to common fowl--for he will make himself resemble the lowliest bird.

----

86. The phoenix.

Զայս այժմիկ և յաղագս իմոյ արծուոյս ասացից, զի ես այսքան
առաքինութիւնս ընդ իս տպաւոր կարգեցի, զորէն կատարեալ
արդարոցն որ առաջի ամենայն աշխարհի են պսակելոց, յորժամ
զերկրային մարմինս ի բաց դիցէ, և միսանգամ յարուցեալ զերկնային
փառս զգեցցի. և յայնժամ ի փափագելի արքայութիւնն մտցեն ընծալով
ընդ Հրեշտակս յանանց ուրախութիւնն Աստուծոյ. * ἀλλ' οὖν
μέχρις ὧδε τὸ πέρας τοῦ λόγου· καὶ γὰρ τοῦτον ἡγοῦμαι τὸν
τόπον, ἐφ' ὃν ὁμιλοῦντες παρεγενόμεθα· σημεῖον γάρ μοι ὁ
πεπηγὼς σταυρὸς δηλοῖ τοῦ τόπου.[121]

54 (4). Καὶ ἀπολιπὼν πάντας πρόσεισι τῷ σταυρῷ καὶ
φησὶν αὐτῷ μετὰ φωνῆς· χαίροις, ὦ σταυρέ, καὶ γὰρ χαίροις
ὄντως. εὖ γε οἶδα καὶ ἀναπαυόμενόν σε λοιπὸν ἐκ πολλοῦ
κεκμηκότα, πεπηγμένον καὶ ἀναμένοντά με. ἥκω ἐπὶ σὲ ὃν
ἐπίσταμαι·[122] γνωρίζω σου τὸ μυστήριον δι' ὃ καὶ πέπηγας.
τοιγαροῦν καθαρὲ καὶ φωτεινὲ καὶ ὅλε ζωῆς καὶ φέγγους
σταυρέ, δέξαι με τὸν πολλὰ κεκμηκότα.

Καὶ εἰπὼν ταῦτα ὁ μακαριώτατος ἑστὼς ἐπὶ τῆς γῆς καὶ
ἀτενὲς ὁρῶν εἰς τὸν σταυρὸν ἀνῆλθεν ἐν αὐτῷ
παρακελευσάμενος τοῖς ἀδελφοῖς ἥκειν τοὺς δημίους καὶ

---

121. The text printed here follows *HS*; the other versions
differ greatly. *Arm*: մինչև ցայս տեղի է առակս. քանզի և
այս տեղի է ժողովեստ միաբանութեան, քանզի ցրջեալ նշան խաչիս
ազդէ որ ի տեղւոջս յայսմիկ ենե կանգնեալ առ ի փրկութիւն
անձին իմոյ. *N* and *E*: κατέλαβον τὸν τόπον ἔνθα ἤμελλεν
τελειοῦσθαι· καὶ θεασάμενος πεπηγότα τὸν σταυρὸν πρὸς
τὸ χεῖλος τῆς θαλαττίας ψάμμου. *M*: ὡς δὲ ἦλθεν ἐπὶ
τὸν τόπον βλέπει τὸ ξύλον πεπηγμένον. *L*: ὡς οὖν ἐπὶ
τὸν τόπον τῆς καταδίκης ὁ μακάριος ἀπήγετο, κατιδὼν
πόρρωθεν τὸ ξύλον πεπηγός. *Ma1*: ἔφθασαν τὸν τόπον
ἔνθα ἤμελλεν σταυρωθῆναι. *Cd*: pervenit ad locum
vidensque de longe crucem. *Ep*: cumque pervenisset ad
locum ubi crux parata erat, videns eam a longe.

122. *M* and *Arm* add: ἴδιόν μου. *L*: ἴδιον. One ms. of *M*
(similarly *N*, *Cd*, and *Ep*) and *Arm*: ἧκον πρὸς σὲ τὸν
ποθήσαντά με.

"And now I will tell you this about my eagle, for I
established as an ideal for myself this much virtue, after
the example of the perfectly just who are crowned before
all the world, when he will put off the earthly body and
the next time arise clothed in heavenly glory, and then
into coveted paradise will they enter rejoicing with the
angels in the infinite joy of God. * This is the end of my
speech, for I think that while we were speaking we arrived
at the designated place. The planted cross is a sign to me
indicating the spot."[87]

54 (4). He left everyone, approached the cross, and
spoke to it in a loud voice: "Greetings, O cross!
Greetings indeed! I know well that, though you have been
weary for a long time, planted and awaiting me, even you
now at last can rest. I come to you, whom I have known.[88]
I recognize your mystery, why you were planted. So then,
cross that is pure, radiant, full of life and light,
receive me, I who have been weary for so long."

The blessed one said these things standing on the
ground looking intently at the cross. When he came to it,

----

87. These last two sentences come from *HS*. *Arm*: "Up to
    this point the parable is apt, for it is appropriate
    for the collective unity, for the sign of the cross,
    which stands out, signifies that in this place it was
    erected for the salvation of my soul." *N* and *E*: "he
    arrived at the place where he was about to be killed.
    And when he saw the cross planted by the edge of the
    seashore." *M*: "When he came to the place, he saw the
    wood planted." *L*: "when the blessed one was brought to
    the place of execution, he saw from afar the wood
    planted. *Ma*1: "they proceeded to the place where he
    was about to be crucified." *Cd*: "he went to the place
    and saw the cross from a distance." *Ep*: "and when he
    arrived at the place where the cross was readied, he
    saw it at a distance."

88. M, *Arm*, and *L* add: "as my own." One ms. of *M* (echoed
    in *N*, *Cd*, and *Ep*) and *Arm* also add: "I come to you who
    long for me."

ποιεῖν ἃ ἐκελεύσθησαν·[123] εἰστήκεισαν γὰρ πόρρωθεν. κἀκεῖνοι ἐλθόντες μόνον ἀπέδησαν αὐτοῦ τοὺς πόδας καὶ τὰς μασχάλας,[124] μηδὲν προσπερονήσαντες αὐτοῦ, μήτε τὰς χεῖρας μήτε τοὺς πόδας μήτε μὴν τὰς ἀγκύλας ὑποτεμόντες, ταύτην τὴν ἐντολὴν ἐσχηκότες παρὰ τοῦ ἀνθυπάτου. ἀνιᾶσαι γὰρ αὐτὸν ἐβούλετο ἀνηρτημένον, καὶ νυκτὸς ζῶντα ὑπὸ κυνῶν βρωθῆναι.[125]

---

123. So *Ma*2 and *C*. *N*: τὰ αὐτοῖς κελευσθέντα. *E*: τὰ κελευσθέντα αὐτοῖς. *Ma*1: τὸ κελευσθέν. *HS*: ὃ ἐκελεύσθησαν. *Ep*gr.2: τὰ ἐγκελευσθέντα αὐτοῖς.

124. *Ma*1 and *M*: τὰς χεῖρας. *Cd*: manus. *E* and *Ep*gr.2 mention only the feet.

125. *N* and *E*: βρωθείη. *Ma*1: βρωθέντα.

he commanded the brethren to summon the executioners who were standing far away to carry out their orders. When they came, they tied up only his feet and armpits,[89] without nailing up his hands or feet nor severing his knees because of what the proconsul had commanded them, for Aegeates intended to torment him by his being hung and his being eaten by dogs if still alive at night.

----

89. *Ma₁*, *M*, and *Cd*: "hands."

EXCURSUS H
ANDREW'S SPEECH TO THE CROSS

The address to the cross as presented in the previous chapter conforms with what one can reconstruct with confidence from *HS*, *C*, *Ma*, *E*, *Cd*, and *Ep*. Other witnesses, however, greatly expand the speech, viz. *M* and *L* (derived from a common source), *Arm*, and *N*, which for the most part goes its own way. Similarities between the Armenian and the Greek recensions *M* and *L* surely derived from an even earlier stage of textual transmission, possibly from the ancient Acts itself. Furthermore, parallels between these more expansive versions and Peter's speech to his cross in the *APe*, which served as a model for the author of the *AA*, might indeed suggest that portions of this longer version may have once appeared in the Acts.

At the beginning of this expanded version, *Arm* seems to be the most reliable, in large part because it is more likely that its series of seven questions came to be answered in the versions now preserved in Greek than that the revelation of the mystery of the cross according to the Greek became obfuscated by the interrogatives in the Armenian. Unfortunately, *Arm* too is derivative. This excursus presents a hypothetical reconstruction of an archetype of the longer speech by comparing the Greek witnesses with *Arm*. The relationship of this reconstruction with the shorter version of the speech must remain moot. The following begins after the words "why you were planted" (δι' ὃ καὶ πέπηγας) in the discourse as it appears in Passion 54 (4).[1]

---

1. Prieur places the witnesses in parallel columns for comparison (*Acta Andreae*, 737-45).

ուսանիմ զքո տեսակդ վասն որոյ կացերդ.[1] տեսի իմն
ի քեզ որպէս և իս գծագրեմ զքող երէ գոր իմանամն գոս.
գոր և որպէս տեսանեմս սիրեմ, գոր իմանամս, և ըմրունիմ ի
քէն. գինչ ձև է քո, ոյ խաչ. գինչ խոտորնակն.[2]   գինչ
մէջն.[3]   գինչ է աներևոյթ իքեզ. գինչ է երևելիդ քո.
ո՞րշափ ճաճկեալդ, ո՞որքան երևիադ ալադագո ընկերին քո
ապապակի, ո որքան երկնեաղ, գտանիս որ լոեն քեզ.[4] ὦ
ὄνομα σταυροῦ, πραγμάτων ἀνάμεστον ὅλον·[5] εὖγε, ὦ σταυρέ,
τὴν περιφορὰν τοῦ κόσμου πεδήσας·[6]   վ́ա́չ տեսիլ րունութեան,

----

1. M (similarly L): πέπηξαι γὰρ ἐν τῷ κόσμῳ ἵνα τὰ ἄστατα
στηρίξῃς· καὶ τὸ μέν σου εἰς οὐρανοὺ ἀνατείνεται ἵνα
τὸν οὐράνιον λόγον σημαίνῃς.

2. M (similarly L): τὸ δέ σου ἥπλωται δεξιᾷ καὶ ἀριστερᾷ
ἵνα τὴν φθονερὰν καὶ ἀντικειμένην δύναμιν τροπώσῃ καὶ
τὸν κόσμον (L: τὰ διεσκορπισμένα) συναγάγῃ εἰς ἕν.

3. M (similarly L): τὸ δέ σου πέπηκται εἰς τὴν γῆν ἵνα τὰ
εἰς γῆν καὶ τὰ ἐν τοῖς καταχθονίοις συνάψῃς τοῖς
ἐπουρανίοις.

4. M (similarly L): ὦ σταυρέ, μηχάνημα σωτήριον τοῦ
ὑψίστου· ὦ σταυρέ, τρόπαιον νίκης Χριστοῦ κατ' ἐχθρῶν·
ὦ σταυρέ, ἐπὶ γῆς φυτευθείς, τὸν δὲ καρπὸν ἐν οὐρανοῖς
ἔχων.

5. Cf. APe 37 (Martyrdom 8): ὦ ὄνομα σταυροῦ, μυστήριον
ἀπόκρυφον. Aɣm: ո անունն խաչի, լի ամենա՞ն իրոք. գինչ
գարմանք, գինչ պարտ է ասել քեզ, ա լլ Անդրէաս. յորժամ
ամենա՞ն ընութեանս մերոյ Աստուած հա՞յր, Յիսուս յորժամ
գխորհուրդն իր տեղւն մարդկան հա՞ղորդեցոյց որ
անաստուածք էին յա՞նմ ժամանակի դատաւորք, ոչ
հուր ունէին, ոչ մուր, ոչ վիրապս և ոչ խեղդելիս, ոչ
կապանս, և ոչ սով, ոչ քանդ, և ոչ քարինս, և ոչ ալլ
ինչ մեքենայս. իմացան թէ կատարեցէ, յոր իշխեցին
ճեռնարկել, ալ գիւաչ: Վ́աչ ով խաչ, կոչեցեալ ամենին
զօրութիւն: Վ́ա́չ ձև ինաստուն ի քանչ իմաստնոյ ձևացեալ. Նոքա
անգիտանայ ին, բայց մեք ճանեաք, և նովաւ ողորմութիւն գտաք. որ
ցուցանես գքեզ ինձ. այդ յորդորէ ասել ինձ .

6. Arm: Վ́ա́չ ով խաչ. որ գրաւմամբք աշխարհիս վաղեցեր.

"I study your image for which you stood.[2] I saw mine in you as I etched yours upon me. If what I perceive is you existing, I like what I see, what I perceive, what I understand from you. What is your shape, O cross? What is your crossbeam?[3] Where is the center?[4] What is invisible in you? What is apparent? To what extent are you hidden? To what extent are you revealed through the cry of your companion (the gallows)? To what extent do you travail to find those who hear you?[5] O name of the cross, entirely filled with deeds![6] Well done, O cross, who restrained the

----

2. *M* (similarly *L*): "For you have been planted in the world to stabilize the unstable. One of your timbers extends into heaven so that you might symbolize the heavenly word."

3. *M* (similarly *L*): "Your crossbeam spreads to the right and left so that you might put to flight the jealous and opposing power and gather the world (*L*: things scattered abroad) into a unity."

4. *M* (similarly *L*): "Your base has been planted into the earth so that you might unite with things in heaven all that is upon the earth and beneath it."

5. *M* (similarly *L*): "O cross, implement of salvation of the Most High! O cross, trophy of Christ's victory over his enemies! O cross, planted on earth but bearing fruit in heaven!"

6. Cf. *APe* 37 (Martyrdom 8): "O name of the cross, hidden mystery!" *Arm*: O name of the cross, filled with all things! What a marvel! What should one say to you, alter Andrew? When God, father of our entire nature, Jesus, communicated his thought to ignorant men who were judges without God at that time, they had neither fire nor sword or dungeons nor strangling ropes nor chains nor starvation nor prison nor stoning nor other instruments (of torture). They learned that he, on whom they dared to lay a hand, would instead consume the cross. Well done, O cross, called 'perfect power!' Well done, intelligent form, born of an intelligent word! They did not know you, but we have recognized and because of this we have found mercy. You manifest yourself to me; it induces me to speak."

որ Հանապազ զրուն բռնաւորութիւն բռնաւորես. εὖγε, μορφὴ
συνέσεως τὴν ἄμορφον μορφώσασα· վա՛զ կապ անկապելի որ կապեցեր
զառաջին անկապան. վա՛զ աներևույթն տանջանաց, որ երն իսկ յառաջ
աներևոյթ և անզննելի. վա՛զ խրատտուիդ, որ խրատէ զանխրատու. [7]
εὖγε, ὦ σταυρέ, τὸν δεσπότην ἐνδυσάμενος [8] καὶ τὸν λῃστὴν
καρποφορήσας [9] καὶ τὸν ἀπόστολον εἰς μετάνοιαν καλέσας καὶ
ἡμᾶς εἰσδέξασθαι μὴ ἀπαξιώσας. [10] τοιγαροῦν καθαρὲ καὶ
φωτεινὲ καὶ ὅλε ζωῆς καὶ φέγγους σταυρέ, δέξαι με τὸν
πολλὰ κεκμηκότα. [11] ἀλλὰ μέχρι πόσου ταῦτα λέγω καὶ οὐ
περιπλέκομαι τῷ σταυρῷ, ἵνα ἐν τῷ σταυρῷ ζωοποιηθῶ, καὶ

----

7. **M:** εὖγε ἀφανὴς κόλασις φανερῶς δὲ κολάζουσα τὴν
ὑπόστασιν τῆς πολυθέου γνώσεως καὶ τὸν ἐφευρετὴν ταύτης
ἐκ τῆς ἀνθρωπότητος ἐκδιώκων.

8. **L:** ὁ τὸν δεσπότην ὡς βότρυν βαστάσας.

9. **N:** Χαίροις σταυρὲ δι' οὗ ὁ λῃστὴς παράδεισον ᾤκησεν.

10. **Arm continues:**   վա՛զ քեզ քրիստոս որ մնաս ինձ պարկիլ ի
խաչիս, վասն որոյ դու Համբերէիր որում չէիր արժանի. վա՛զ
նախատանացդ որ յազագս մարդկութեան Համբերեցեր ընդդէմ
անամօրին զի զնա ամաչեցուցես. վա՛զ որ ոչ փախար յայժմանէ,
որ ոչն կարէր ճանաչել զոր ինքն գործեաց. բարուք Համբերեցեր
տանջողացն զքեզ, քանզի ոչ գիտէին զինչ գործեցին.
փրիեցեր զՀշուառացեալսն, և ոչ ի բաց մերժեցեր զՊշնամանիչսն
անխնակալութեամբդ   քո ծանեաք   զշնորհս քո,   զի ոչ
Պշնամանեցեր, այլ յորժան դարձան առ քեզ ընկալար զնոսա,
և ուրախացեալք ի քեզ խոստովանեցին ի քո բարերարութիւնդ.

11. **So HS with echoes in other witnesses. Arm:** Այլ այժմ
ընկալ զմեզ որ յայժմանէ Հրաժարեցաք. ընկալ զմեզ զտառապեալս,
և ազատսա Տէր որ ի քեզ ապաւինեցաք.

error of the world!⁷ Well done, vision of violence, that
continually and violently treats violence with violence!
Well done, shape of understanding, who shaped the
shapeless! Well done, unbounded bond, that bound up the
first one to be unbounded! Well done, for the tortures of
the invisible, previously invisible and incomprehensible!
Well done, giver of correction, who corrects the one who
needs no correction![8] Well done, O cross, who put on the
Master,[9] produced the thief as your fruit,[10] called the
apostle to repentance, and did not disqualify us from
being received.[11] So then, cross, pure, radiant, and full
of life and light, receive me, the one who for so long has
been weary.[12] But how long shall I say these things
without being embraced by the cross, so that in the cross
I may be made to live, and through the cross I may exit

----

7. Or: "who held together the revolving vault of the
universe!" *Arm*: "Well done, O cross, who leaped over
the distractions of the world!"

8. *M*: "Well done, invisible punishment, who punished
visibly the essence of polytheistic knowledge and
expelled its inventor from humankind!"

9. *L*: "bore the Master like a bunch of grapes."

10. *N*: "Greetings, O cross, by means of whom the thief
inhabited paradise."

11. *Arm* continues: "Bravo to you, Christ, who remains for
me deliverance on the cross, who endured that which
you did not deserve. Bravo for the insults you endured
for humankind before the shameless one, for you shall
shame him. Bravo that you did not flee from the one
who could not know what he did. With goodness you
endured your torturers, since they did not know what
they had done. You saved the wretched and did not
reject your enemies. By your absence of malice we knew
your grace, for you did not become hostile, but when
they turned to you, you accepted them. And those who
rejoice in you bore witness to your beneficence."

12. *Arm*: "But now accept us who renounced this (life),
accept us who suffer, and deliver us, Lord, who have
taken refuge in you."

διὰ σταυροῦ τὸν κοινὸν θάνατον τοῦ βίου ἐξέλθω;[12]
προσέρχεσθε οἱ ὑπηρέται τῆς ἐμῆς χαρᾶς καὶ οἱ διάκονοι τοῦ
Αἰγεάτου καὶ πληρῶσατε τῶν ἀμφοτέρων τὸ βούλημα καὶ
προσδεσμεῖτε τὸν ἀμνὸν τῷ πάθει,[13] τὸν ἄνθρωπον τῷ
δημιουργῷ, τὴν ψυχὴν τῷ σωτῆρι.[14]

---

12. Arm: այլ մինչև յետք դայդ ապիցեմ, և ոչ դոր դու ցուցանես
ո՛ իսաչ, կացեալ առաջի քո յանձն առնեմ քեզ զլսոյս իմ. քանզի
ոչ է մեզ ժամանակ այլ մերձեցեալ յերկելիսս յայսմ ոչ իսաչ.

13. L: τῷ ξύλῳ.

14. Cf. APe 37 (Martyrdom 8): ἀξιῶ οὖν ὑμᾶς τοὺς δημίους,
οὕτως με σταυρώσατε, ἐπὶ τὴν κεφαλὴν καὶ μὴ ἄλλως.

life in a death like his?[13] Approach, you ministers of my
joy and servants of Aegeates; fulfill the intention of us
both and bind the lamb to the suffering,[14] the mortal to
its crafter, the soul to its savior."[15]

----

13. *Arm*: "But until when shall I say this and not that
    which you showed, O cross? Standing before you I
    commend to you those who are listening, for there is
    not for us any other time to approach this vision, O
    cross."

14. *L*: "to the wood."

15. Cf. *APe* 37 (Martyrdom 8): "Therefore, I ask you
    executioners, crucify me topsy-turvy and in no other
    way."

55 (5). Οἱ δὲ ἀδελφοὶ περιεστῶτες, ὧν τάχα οὐδὲ τὸν ἀριθμὸν δυνατὸν ἐξαριθμήσασθαι[126] τοσούτων ὄντων,[127] θεασάμενοι ἐκείνους ἀποστάντας καὶ μηδὲν πεποιηκότας περὶ τὸν μακάριον ὧν οἱ ἀνακρεμάμενοι πάσχουσιν,[128] προσεδόκουν τι πάλιν ἀκούσεσθαι[129] αὐτοῦ, καὶ γὰρ κρεμάμενος ἐκίνει αὐτοῦ τὴν κεφαλὴν μειδιῶν.[130]

Καὶ ὁ Στρατοκλῆς αὐτοῦ ἐπύθετο· τὶ μειδιᾷς, δοῦλε τοῦ θεοῦ Ἀνδρέα; ἢ μὴ ὁ γέλως σου ἡμᾶς πενθεῖν καὶ κλαίειν ποιεῖ ὅτι σοῦ στερισκόμεθα;

Καὶ ὁ Ἀνδρέας αὐτῷ ἀπεκρίνατο· οὐ μὴ γελάσω, τέκνον μου Στρατοκλῆ, τὴν κενὴν ἐνέδραν τοῦ Αἰγεάτου, δι' ἧς οἴεται ἡμᾶς τιμωρεῖσθαι; οὐδέπω πέπεισται ὅτι ἀλλότριοι αὐτοῦ ἐσμὲν καὶ τῶν ἐπιβουλῶν αὐτοῦ. οὐκ ἔχει τὸ ἀκούειν, ἐπεὶ εἰ εἶχεν, ἀκηκόη ἂν ὅτι ὁ Ἰησοῦ ἄνθρωπος ἀτιμώρητός ἐστιν λοιπὸν αὐτῷ γνωρισθείς.

56 (6). Καὶ εἰπὼν ταῦτα ἀπεκρίνατο πᾶσιν κοινὸν λόγον, καὶ γὰρ τὰ ἔθνη συνέτρεχον ἀγανακτοῦντα ἐπὶ τῇ ἀδίκῳ κρίσει τοῦ Αἰγεάτου· ἄνδρες, οἱ παρεστῶτές μοι καὶ γυναῖκες καὶ παῖδες καὶ πρεσβῦται καὶ δοῦλοι καὶ ἐλεύθεροι καὶ ὁπόσοι ἄλλοι μέλλετε ἀκούειν· εἰ τοῦτο ἡγεῖσθε τὸ τέλος τῆς ζωῆς τῆς προσκαίρου τὸ τεθνάναι, ἤδη ἀπαλλάσσεσθε τοῦ τόπου τούτου.[131] καὶ εἰ τὴν σύνοδον τῆς

----

126. *C*: ἐξαριθμῆσαι.

127. The Latin passions read: *viginti milia hominum.*

128. *N* and *E*, corroborated somewhat by **Arm**: οὐδὲν τῶν ἀνασκολοπιζομένων ἐποίησαν αὐτῷ.

129. *N* and *Ep*gr.2 add: παρ'. So Prieur.

130. *N* and *Ma*2 add: τῷ προσώπῳ.

131. **Arm**: աֆա ֆրագարիֆմ ի կենագս յայցզանէ. This would suggest that the Greek text it translated read: ἴδε ἀπαλλάσσω

55 (5). The brethren standing around, so many they were nearly innumerable,[90] when they saw that the executioners had withdrawn and had carried out against the blessed one none of the usual procedures suffered by those who are hung,[91] they expected to hear something more from him, for even while hanging he shook his head and smiled.[92]

"Why do you smile, Andrew, servant of God?" asked Stratocles. "Should your laughter not make us mourn and weep because we are being deprived of you?"

"Shall I not laugh, Stratocles my child," Andrew answered, "at Aegeates' futile trap by which he presumes to avenge himself on us? He has not yet been persuaded that we are alien to him and his designs. He is not able to hear, since if he were able, he would have heard that the person who belongs to Jesus and who has been recognized by him in the end cannot be punished.

56 (6). When Andrew had said these things, he addressed a general speech to everyone, for even the pagans had hurried to the site, infuriated at Aegeates' unjust decision. "Men who are present with me, women, children, old, slaves, free, and any others who would hear: if you suppose this act of dying is the end of ephemeral life, leave this place at once.[93] If you understand the conjunction of the soul with a body to be the soul itself, so that after the separation (of the two)

----

90. The Latin passions do number them: 20,000.

91. *N* and E, corroborated to some extent by *Arm*: "did to him nothing customary to those who are crucified."

92. *N* and *Ma2* add: "on his face."

93. *Arm*, perhaps correctly: "Behold I renounce this life." *Ep*gr.2: "abandon this entire life."

ψυχῆς τὴν εἰς σῶμα αὐτὴν τὴν ψυχὴν[132] τίθεσθε, ὡς μετὰ τὸν
χωρισμὸν μηκέτι ὑπάρχειν τι, θηρίων ὑπονοίας ἔχετε καὶ
θηρσὶν ὑμᾶς δεινοῖς ἐναριθμεῖν ἀναγκαῖον. καὶ εἰ τὰ
παρόντα ἡδέα ἀγαπᾶτε καὶ ἐκ παντὸς ταῦτα μεταδιώκετε,
τὸ[133] ἀπ' αὐτῶν μόνον καρπούμενοι, λησταῖς ἐστὲ ὅμοιοι.
καὶ εἰ τὸ φαινόμενον μόνον τοῦτο οἴεσθε ἑαυτοὺς εἶναι
μηδὲν δ' ἕτερον παρὰ τοῦτο, ἀγνοίας ἐστὲ καὶ ἀμαθείας
δοῦλοι. καὶ εἰ τοῦτο καταμανθάνετε τὸ νυκτερινὸν φῶς μόνον
ὑπάρχειν, πρὸς δὲ τούτῳ μηδέν, συγγενεῖς ἐστὲ τῆς νυκτὸς
ταύτης. καὶ εἰ τροφὴν ἑαυτῶν τὴν γεώδη νομίζετε τὴν
παρεκτικὴν ὄγκον τοῦ σώματος καὶ δύναμιν συστάσεως
αἵματος, γήϊνοί ἐστὲ καὶ αὐτοί. καὶ εἰ τὸ σῶμα ἄνισον
ἔχοντες[134] οἴεσθε εὐδαιμονεῖν, ὄντως ἐστὲ κακοδαίμονες.[135]
καὶ εἰ τὰ ἐκτὸς ὑμῶν εὐτυχήματα μακαρίζει ὑμ<ᾶ>ς, ὄντως
ἐστὲ ἀθλιώτατοι. և երէ ամուսնութեան հեշտութիւնք և
խառնակութիւնք ուրախացուցանէ զձեզ, և որ ի նոցանէ ապտեղութիւնն
է, լի ցաւովք տրտմեցուցանէ զձեզ. և երէ մննդեան բաղում որդեաց
ցանկանայցէք և որ ի նոցանէ ձանձրալի թշուառութիւնն ծնանիցի ձեզ,
 նեղեսցէ զձեզ. καὶ εἰ τὰ λοιπὰ ὑμῶν κτήματα ἰδίοις ἐπαίρει
ἑαυτοῖς, τὸ πρόσκαιρον αὐτῶν ὀνειδιζέτω ὑμᾶς.[136] (57 [6].)
τί γὰρ ὄφελος ὑμῖν ἐστιν τὰ ἐκτὸς κεκτημένοις, ἑαυτοὺς δὲ
μή; ἢ τίς ἐκ τοῦ ἐκτὸς γένους ἔπαρσις, τῆς ἐν ὑμῖν ψυχῆς
αἰχμαλώτου ταῖς ἐπιθυμίαις πεπραμένης; և զինչ հեշտութեան
և որդեծնութեան ցանկալ յորժամ յետոյ բաժանել ունիմք ես ի միմեանց.
քանզի և ոչ զինչ օք զինչ առնէ. կամ ով կինչ իրրում խնամ տանիցի

τοῦ βίου τούτου. *Epgr.*2: πάντα τὸν βίον τοῦτον
ἀπολείπεσθε.

132. *HS*: αὐτῇ τῇ ψυχῇ.

133. Perhaps: τά.

134. *Arm*: երէ զմարմինդ անաւտ կարծէք զոյ, և լինել բարերախտիկք.

135. *Arm*: ապա երկրայինք էք իրրև զնոսա.

136. *Arm*: և երէ զաւել ստացութեան մեծութիւնն հեշտութեամբ
սիրիցէք ապականութեամբն իւրով, նախատեսցէ զձեզ.

nothing at all exists, you possess the intelligence of animals and one would have to list you among ferocious beasts. And if you love immediate pleasures and pursue them above all, in order to enjoy their fruits exclusively, you are like thieves. And if you suppose that you are merely that which can be seen and nothing more, you are slaves of folly and ignorance. And if you perceive that only this nocturnal light exists and nothing in addition to it, you are kindred to this night. And if you think that your earthly food is capable of creating bodily mass and the blood's constitutive power, you yourselves are earthly. And if you suppose that you are happy even though you have an inequitable body,[94] you actually are miserable.[95] And if your external prosperity makes you happy, you truly are most wretched. And if the pleasure and intercourse of marriage please you, and if the corruption which is from them, full of pain, makes you sad, and if you are in need of sustenance for your many children, and if the annoying poverty they cause is known to you, it will upset you. And if the rest of your possessions draw you to themselves as though you belonged to them, may their impermanence reproach you.[96] (**57 [6].**) What benefit is there for you who gain for yourselves external goods but do not gain your very selves? What pride issues from external ancestry if the soul in you is held captive, sold to desires? And why do we desire pleasure and childbearing, for later we have to separate? No one knows what he does. Who will take care of his wife when he is preoccupied merely by the passions of desire? Or why all the rest of the concern for externals, while

----

94. *Arm*: "If you think the body to be free of disease and to be fortunate."

95. *Arm*: "then you are earthly like them."

96. *Arm*: "And if you are pleased with great wealth together with its corruption, it will insult you."

 զրաջեալ տոփանօք ցանկութեան. ἢ τίς ἡ λοιπὴ ἅπασα ἐπιμέλεια
ἡ περὶ τὰ ἐκτός, ὑμῶν αὐτῶν ὃ ἐστὲ ὅ<ν>τως[137]
ἀμελούντων;[138] ἀλλὰ μετάθετε,[139] παρακαλῶ πάντας ὑμᾶς, τὸν
ἐπίπονον βίον, τὸν μάταιον, τὸν μανιώδη, τὸν ἀλαζόνα,[140]
τὸν κενόν, τὸν φθαρτόν, τὸν πρόσκαιρον, τὸν ἡδονῶν
φίλον,[141] τὸν χρόνου δοῦλον, τὸν μέθης παῖδα, τὸν ἀσωτίας
πάροικον, τὸν φιλαργυρίας ἴδιον, τὸν ὀργῆς συγγενῆ, τὸν
δόλου βραβευτήν, τὸν φόνων σύμμαχον, τὸν ἔχθρας πρύτανιν,
τὸν ἐπιθυμίας χορηγόν, τὸν μοιχειῶν ἄρχοντα, τὸν ζήλων
μεσίτην, τὸν φόνων ἐκδείκτην. δέομαι ὑμῶν, πάντα τὸν βίον
τοῦτον ἀπολίπετε, οἱ ἐμοῦ ἕνεκεν συνεληλυθότες ἐνταῦθα,
καὶ σπεύσατε καταλαβεῖν τὴν ἐμὴν ψυχὴν ἐπειγομένην εἰς τὰ
ὑπὲρ χρόνον, εἰς τὰ ὑπὲρ νόμον, εἰς τὰ ὑπὲρ λόγον, εἰς τὰ
ὑπὲρ σῶμα, εἰς τὰ ὑπὲρ ἡδονὰς πικρὰς καὶ ἀθεμίτους καὶ
πόνου παντὸς ἀναμέστους. εἴθε δὲ ἑωρᾶτε νῦν καὶ αὐτοὶ περὶ
ὧν λέγω τοῖς τῆς ψυχῆς ὀφθαλμοῖς· καὶ ἔπεσθε τῇ ἐνδιαθέτῳ
μου φιλίᾳ· καὶ καταμάθετε τοὺς ἐμοὺς πόνους ὑπὲρ ὧν νῦν
διαλέγομαι πρὸς ὑμᾶς· καὶ ἀρραβωνίσασθέ μου τὸν νοῦν· καὶ
ἑτέραν ὑμῖν κοινωνίαν κοινωνήσατε. καὶ περιβάλλετε ἑαυτοὺς
ἐμαῖς ἡνίαις[142] καὶ διασμήξατε ὑμῶν τὰς ἀκοὰς ἀκοῦσαι ἃ
λέγω.[143] καὶ πάντων ἀπαξαπλῶς τῶν προσκαίρων πεφεύγετε,

----

137. *HS* actually reads: οὕτως. So Prieur.

138. *Arm*: կաս զինչ խնամ այն ինչ որ յարտաքին ստացուածոյն
Լինիցի յորմէ ակամայ իսկ ստոյգ Լինիցիմք զրկեալք.

139. *C*: μάθετε.

140. *C*: ἀλάστορα.

141. *Arm* adds: և տրոտութեան ընդունիչ, և անյագութեան
դրացիի, և չար ցանկութեանց ծնիչ.

142. This clause appears only in *C* and *Arm*, and neither
yields a satisfactory meaning. *C*: ὑπερβάλλετε ἑαυτοὺς
ἐμαῖς ἡνοίαις, but the last word is corrupt, perhaps
for ἡνίαις, ἀνοίαις, ἐννοίαις, or ἀνίαις, as printed
above. *Arm* reads: Արկէք զզեղ ընդ իմով վշտօքս, suggesting that the Greek it translated read περιβάλλετε
ἑαυτοὺς ἐμαῖς ἀνίαις. The confusion of περι- and
ὑπερ- is common. The reading preferred in the text

you yourselves neglect what you actually are?[97] I exhort
you all rather to rid yourselves[98] of this life which is
painful, vain, crazy, boastful,[99] empty, perishable,
transitory, the friend of pleasures,[100] the slave of time,
the servant of drunkenness, the sojourner of debauchery,
the possession of greed, the kindred of wrath, the umpire
of treachery, the ally of murders, the prince of hatred,
the patron of desire, the master of adulteries, the
mediator of jealousies, the instigator of murders. I
entreat you who have come here together for my sake,
abandon this entire life and hasten to overtake my soul
which speeds toward things beyond time, beyond law, beyond
speech, beyond body, beyond bitter and lawless pleasures
full of every pain. Observe now, even you, with the eyes
of your souls, those things about which I speak. Follow
after my deep-seated love. Learn of my sufferings about
which I am now speaking with you. Take my mind as a
downpayment. Participate in another fellowship for
yourselves. Wrap yourselves with my lashes,[101] and wipe
your ears to hear what I say.[102] Flee from everything

----

97. *Arm*: "And what value is the concern for external
   possessions, which surely will be forcibly stripped
   from us?"

98. *C*: "to learn."

99. *C*: "vengeful."

100. *Arm* adds: "and the bearer of grief, the neighbor of
    insatiety, the breeder of evil desires."

101. The text is uncertain. *Arm*: "Throw about you my
    afflictions." Prieur: "Submit yourselves to my
    reins."

102. *Arm* adds: "Cleanse your minds to understand what I
    want."

σὺν ἐμοὶ[144] δὲ καὶ νῦν ἐπείχθητε· (58 [6]) ἀλλὰ καὶ νῦν εὖ
οἶδα οὐκ ἀνηκόους ὑμᾶς τῶν ἐμῶν λόγων ὄντας· արդարեւ Հեզս
տեսանեմ զձեզ որպէս և կամիմ. ի բաց լինել ձեզ յարտաքին կերպարանաց
զի ներքինս մեր մարմն լիցի: Ողջունեմ զձեզ չնորհօքն Աստուծոյ
և սիրովն որ առ Նա, և առաւել ձերով մարմանութեամբդ
որ առ մշմանս, Հեռանալ ձեզ ի վնասակարացն և դիմել ի Նա և
ի բարին և ի մշամտութիւնն որ առ Նա է և ի մարմանութիւնն
որ ի սոյն. ἠρέμα τοιγαροῦν ἄνδρες θαρροῦσιν ἐπὶ τὴν τοῦ
θεοῦ ἡμῶν γνῶσιν.[145] ἄπειμι προετοιμάσα<ι> τὰς ἐκεῖ ὁδούς
τοῖς μὲν συνθεμένοις μοι καὶ καθαρᾷ πίστει[146] καὶ φιλίᾳ τῇ
πρὸς αὐτὸν ἀπηρτισμένοις, πῦρ κοιμίζων, σκότους φυγαδεύων,
κάμινον σβεννύων, σκώλ<η>κα θανατῶν, ἀπειλὴν ἐκκόπτων,
δαίμονας ἐπιστομίζων, ἀρχοντικὰς φιμῶν δυνάμεις καὶ
καταλύων, ἐξουσίας δυναστεύων, διάβολον ῥίπτων, Σατανᾶν
ἀποβάλλων, κακίαν κολάζων·[147] τοῖς δὲ μὴ φιλίᾳ τῇ πρὸς
θεὸν ἐληλυθ<ό>σιν ἀλλ᾽ ὑποκρίσει, καὶ ἡδονῶν τῶν ἀκάρπων
ἕνεκεν, καὶ περιεργίᾳ ἑαυτοὺς ὑποβεβληκόσιν καὶ ἀπιστίᾳ
καὶ τῇ λοιπῇ ἀγνωσίᾳ[148] καὶ μηδὲν εἶναι ἕτερον μετὰ τὴν
ἐνθάδε λύσιν ὑπ<ει>λ<η>φ<ό>σιν· πάντα ταῦτα ἐξίπταται καὶ
κινεῖται καὶ φέρεται καὶ ἀνίπταται καὶ κατατρέχει καὶ
πολεμεῖ καὶ κρατεῖ καὶ ἄρχει καὶ τιμωρεῖ καὶ φλέγει καὶ
μέμηνεν[149] καὶ συνέχει καὶ κολάζει καὶ ἐπεξέρχεται· ἀλλὰ

----

above prefers the Armenian witness to περιβάλλετε and
reads ἠνίαις instead of ἠνοίαις in C. Prieur:
ὑποβάλετε ἑαυτοὺς ἐμαῖς ἠνίαις.

143. Arm adds: սրբեցէք զմիտս ձեր իմանալ զոր կամիմ.

144. Ep[gr.2]: καὶ πάντων ἀπαξαπλῶς τῶν προσκαίρων
καταφρονήσατε.

145. Arm: ձեօք և փութասցին ձանաչել զգարարիչն Աստուած.

146. Arm adds: սուրբ Հաւատովք և գիտութեամբք, և սիրով
զինքեանս իջէն պարսպեալ.

147. Arm adds: և վերագոյն են քան զամենայն Հիւթս.

148. Arm: Հանդերձ այլանդակ և օտար վարիւք.

149. Arm adds: անչէջ Հրով.

merely temporal. Even now speed away with me. (**58 [6]**.)
Even now I know that you are not inattentive to my words.
Truly I see you mild as I want it, and to be far away from
external forms, for the internal is our unity. I greet you
with the grace of God and with love which is due him and
even more with your consent to each other, to keep us away
from those who do harm, and to apply to him, and to the
good, and to the innocence which is to him and to the
accord which is in them. For this reason men quietly take
courage in the knowledge of our God.[103] On the one hand, I
am leaving to prepare routes there for those who align
themselves with me and are equipped with a pure faith[104]
and with love for him; I am stifling the fire, banishing
the shadows, extinguishing the furnace, killing the worm,
eradicating the threat, gagging the demons, muzzling and
destroying the ruling powers, dominating the authorities,
throwing down the devil, casting out Satan, and punishing
wickedness.[105] On the other hand, with respect to those
who have come here not out of love for God but out of
hypocrisy and because of unfruitful pleasures, who have
submitted themselves to superstition, disbelief, and every
other ignorance,[106] and who suppose nothing else exists
after one's release from here, all these monsters fly out,
become agitated, rush forth, take wing, ravage, fight,
conquer, rule, wreak vengence, enflame, rage,[107] afflict,
punish, and attack. They blaze, exercize violence, and do
not withdraw or relent, but rejoice, exult, smile, mock,

----

103. *Arm*: "Through you, and they strive to know God the
     creator."

104. *Arm* adds: "are protected by holy faith, knowledge,
     and love."

105. *Arm* adds: "and are superior to all matter."

106. *Arm*: "with distorted and alien ways."

107. *Arm* adds: "with an inextinguishable fire."

καὶ ἐκκαίει καὶ βιάζεται καὶ οὐκ ἀφίσταται οὐδὲ ἐξίσταται·
ἀλλὰ καὶ χαίρει καὶ ἀγαλλιᾷ καὶ μειδιᾷ καὶ καταγελᾷ καὶ
ἀναπαύεται καὶ πᾶσι τοῖς ὁμοίοις τέρπεται, ἔχον<τα> τοὺς
εἰς αὐτὰ ἐμπίπτοντας ἀπιστήσαντας τῷ θεῷ μου.[150] καὶ
ἔλεσθε τοιγαροῦν, ἄνδρες, ὁπότερα βούλεσθε, ἐφ᾽ ὑμῖν γὰρ
τέθειται τὸ τοιοῦτον.

59 (6). Καὶ οἱ ὄχλοι ἀκούσαντες[151] τῶν εἰρημένων ὑπὸ
τοῦ Ἀνδρέα καὶ τρόπον τινὰ ᾑρημένοι ὑπ᾽ αὐτοῦ οὐκ
ἀφίσταντο τοῦ τόπου. καὶ ὁ μακαριώτατος μᾶλλον προήγετο[152]
λέγειν πρὸς αὐτοὺς πλείονα ὧν εἰρήκει, καὶ τοσαῦτα ἦν, ὡς
ἔστιν τεκμαίρεσθαι τοὺς ἀκούοντας. τριῶν νυχθημέρων αὐτοῖς
προσωμίλει, καὶ οὐδεὶς ὅλως καμὼν ἐχωρίζετο αὐτοῦ.

Ὡς δὲ καὶ τῇ τετάρτῃ[153] ἡμέρᾳ τὸ γενναῖον αὐτοῦ
ἐθεάσαντο[154] καὶ τὸ ἀκαμπὲς τῆς διανοίας καὶ τὸ πολὺ τῶν
λόγων[155] καὶ τὸ χρηστὸν τῆς προτροπῆς καὶ τὸ εὐσταθὲς τῆς
ψυχῆς καὶ τὸ σῶφρον[156] τοῦ πνεύματος καὶ τὸ ἑδραῖον τοῦ
νοῦ καὶ τὸ εἰλικρινὲς τοῦ λογισμοῦ ἀγανακτήσαντες πρὸς τὸν
Αἰγεάτην σὺν ἑνὶ πάντες ἔσπευδον ἐπὶ τὸ βῆμα. καὶ
καθεζομένου αὐτοῦ κατεβόων· τίς ἡ κρίσις σου, ἀνθύπατε;
κακῶς ἐδίκασας· ἀδίκως[157] ἔκρινας· ἀνοσιώτατα ʼτὰ
δικαστήριά σου· τί ἠδίκησεν ὁ ἀνήρ; τί κακὸν ἔπραξεν; ἡ

----

150. Arm reads quite differently from ἀλλὰ καὶ χαίρει to
θεῷ μου: ԱՄԲՆԵԲԵԱՆ Ա ՈՐ ՆՄԱՆ ՍՈՐԻՆ ԵՆ ԱՆՃԱԵԱՈՐ Ա
ՈՐԱՐԱԳԵԱԼ Բ ՀԵՍՈՒԵԸՆՅ, ՎՄԱՈՐԱՉ ԱՅՍ. Ա ԱՐԴԱՐԲ ՈՒՐԱՓ
ԼԻՆԻՆ Ա ԳՆՄԱՆ, Ա ԵՄԱՈՐ ԱՌԱՆԵՆ Ա ՀԱՆԴԵՐԻՆ.

151. C: κατακούσαντες.

152. Epgr.2: προσῆγε.

153. HS: ἐπιούσῃ.

154. C: ἀπεθεάσαντο.

155. N and Ma2: τοῦ λόγου.

156. HS and C: σοφόν. So Prieur.

157. Ma1 and C: κακῶς. N and E: ἀνοσίως.

and take their rest and delight in all who are similar to them, possessing those who succumbed to them by not believing in my God.[108] Choose then which of the two paths you prefer, for the choice is yours to decide.

59 (6). When the crowds heard Andrew's speech, they were won over by him, so to speak, and did not leave the spot. The blessed one proceeded to speak to them even longer than he had before, to such an extent that those who heard him took it as a sign. He spoke to them for three days and nights, and no one, no matter how weary, separated from him.

On the fourth[109] day, when they observed his nobility, the adamance of his thought, the sheer abundance of his words,[110] the value of his exhortation, the stability of his soul, the prudence[111] of his spirit, the firmness of his mind, and the precision of his reasoning, they were furious with Aegeates and together ran off to the tribunal. As he sat there they cried out, "What is this judgment of yours, O proconsul? You have judged wickedly! You have made an unjust[112] decision! Your courts are a sacrilege! What crime did the man commit? What evil has he done? The city is in uproar! You are wronging us all! You are grieving us all! Do not betray the city of the emperor! Grant the Achaeans the just man! Grant us this god-fearing man. Do not kill this man possessed of

----

108. *Arm*: "this will happen to all who resemble the faithless and alienated from God. And the just will be glad and joyful and make merry and rest."

109. *HS*: "next."

110. *N* and *Ma2*: "the greatness of the word."

111. *HS* and *C*: "wisdom."

112. *Ma1* and *C*: "wicked." *N* and *E*: "unholy."

πόλις τεθορύβηται· πάντας ἡμᾶς ἀδικεῖς· πάντας ἡμᾶς
λυπεῖς· μὴ προδῷς τὴν Καίσαρος πόλιν· χάρισαι Ἀχαιοῖς
ἄνδρα δίκαιον· χάρισαι ἡμῖν ἄνδρα θεοσεβῆ· μὴ ἀποκτείνῃς
ἄνδρα ἔνθεον· μὴ ἀνέλῃς ἄνδρα εὐσεβῆ· τέσσαρσιν ἡμέραις
κρεμάμενος ζῇ. μηδὲν φαγὼν ἡμᾶς τῶν λόγων αὐτοῦ ἐχόρτασεν·
κάθελε τὸν ἄνδρα καὶ πάντες φιλοσοφήσομεν· λῦσον τὸν
σώφρονα καὶ ὅλαι Πάτραι δίκαιαι· ἀπόλυσον τὸν ἔμφρονα καὶ
πᾶσα ἡ Ἀχαΐα ἐλεηθήσεται.

60 (7). Ὡς δὲ παρήκουσεν ὁ Αἰγεάτης τὰ πρῶτα, τῷ
ὄχλῳ διανεύων τῇ χειρὶ ἀναχωρεῖν αὐτοὺς τοῦ βήματος, θυμοῦ
πλησθέντες ἐτόλμων τι εἰς αὐτόν, ὄντες τὸν ἀριθμὸν ὡς
δισχίλιοι·[158] οὓς θεασάμενος ὁ ἀνθύπατος τρόπον τινὰ
ἐμμανὴς γενόμενος,[159] δεδοικὼς μή τι νεώτερον πάθοι,[160]
ἀναστὰς τοῦ βήματος συνάπτει αὐτοῖς ὑποσχόμενος ἀπολύειν
τὸν μακάριον Ἀνδρέαν.[161]

Ἔφθανον οὖν αὐτὸ τοῦτο τῷ ἀποστόλῳ δηλοῦντες καὶ τὴν
αἰτίαν δι᾿ ἣν παραγίνεται ἐπὶ τὸν τόπον. ἀγαλλιῶντος οὖν
τοῦ ὄχλου ὅτι ἔμελλεν ὁ μακάριος Ἀνδρέας λύεσθαι,[162]
παραγενομένου τοῦ ἀνθυπάτου καὶ τῶν ἀδελφῶν δὲ πάντων ἅμα
τῇ Μαξιμίλλῃ χαιρόντων,

61 (8). ἀκούσας δὲ ὁ Ἀνδρέας εἶπεν· * ὦ ἡ πολλὴ τῶν
ὑπ᾿ ἐμοῦ μαθητευθέντων νωθρία· ὦ ἡ ἐπικαλυφθεῖσα ἡμῖν μετὰ
πολλὰ μυστήρια ταχινὴ ὁμίχλη·[163] ὦ πόσα εἰρηκότες ἕως τοῦ

----

158. *C* and *Ep*gr.2: δισμύριοι. *Ma*1: δισμυρίους.

159. *HS*: ἐμμανεῖς γεγενημένους. So Prieur.

160. So *HS*, similarly *N*, *E*, and *L*. *Ma*1: τινα δεινὰ παθεῖν.
C: τι δεινότερον πάθοι. *Ep*gr.2: τι δεινὸν πάθῃ. *Cd*:
quid mali pateretur.

161. *N*, *E*, *HS*, and *Ma*2 om.: Ἀνδρέαν.

162. *C* and *Ep*gr.2: ἀπολύεσθαι.

163. *Arm*: ի՛լ յայտնեելոյ ձեզ բազում խորՀրդածութիւն.

God! Do not destroy this pious man. Even though he has been hanging for four days, he is still alive. Although he has eaten nothing, he has glutted us with his words. Bring the man down and we will all become philosophers. Untie the prudent one, and all Patras will be law-abiding. Release the sagacious one, and all Achaea will receive mercy."

60 (7). When Aegeates at first disregarded the crowd and gestured for them to leave the tribunal, they were enraged and were gaining courage to oppose him in some way; they numbered about two thousand.[113] When the proconsul saw them, he became rather crazed,[114] terrified that he might suffer a revolution.[115] He rose from the tribunal and went off with them, promising to release the blessed Andrew.

They ran ahead to disclose to the apostle this very fact as well as the reason for Aegeates' coming to the spot. The crowd was jubilant because the blessed Andrew was about to be untied, and when the proconsul arrived, all the brethren were rejoicing along with Maximilla.

61 (8). When Andrew heard this, he said, * "O the great lethargy of those I have taught! O the sudden fog engulfing us even after many mysteries![116] O, how much we have spoken up to the present, and we have not convinced our own! O, how much has happened so that we might flee

----

113. *C*, *Ep*gr.2, and *Ma*1: twenty thousand.

114. *HS*: "When the proconsul saw that they had become rather crazed."

115. *Ma*1, *C*, *Ep*gr.2, and *CD*: "might suffer some calamity."

116. *Arm*: "O, by revealing to you much thought."

νῦν οὐκ ἐπείσαμεν τοὺς ἰδίους· ὦ πόσα γέγονεν ἵνα τῶν
γηΐνων φύγωμεν·[164] ոչ քանի րնաստրութիւն յաղագս
մարմնականացս ասացան, և առաւել դղոյն կամիս. ոչ քանիցս
անգամ ապացեցի զի յաղտեղի սովորութեանցն հանիցդ զնոսա, այլ
առաւել յոչինչն յորդորեցան. τίς ἡ πολλὴ φιλία ἡ πρὸς τὴν
σάρκα;[165] ἢ τίς ἡ πολλὴ συμπλοκὴ πρὸς αὐτήν;[166] πάλιν με
παρακαλεῖτε ἐν τοῖς ῥευστοῖς ἀν<α>θῆναι;[167] εἰ δὲ
ἠπίστασθε ὅτι δεσμῶν μὲν ἐλύθην, ἑαυτῷ δὲ ἐδέθην,
ἐσπουδάκοιτε ἂν καὶ αὐτοὶ τῶν πολλῶν λυθῆναι, τῷ ἑνὶ δὲ
δεθῆναι.[168] καὶ τί εἴπω; ταῦτα ἃ γὰρ λέγω εὖ οἶδα ὅτι καὶ
γενήσεται· καὶ γὰρ ὑμᾶς αὐτοὺς δήσω σὺν ἐμαυτ<ῷ>,[169] καὶ

----

164. N: φυγεῖν τῆς προσπαθείας τῶν γηΐνων ἀλλ' ἔτι τούτοις
δέδενται καὶ ἐν αὐτοῖς ἐμμένουσιν καὶ οὐ βούλονται
τούτων ἀποστῆναι. Arm: ոչ որչափ սքանչելիք են զի
յերկրաւորացս փախիցեն, այլ առաւել յամօսիկ հարեալ կան.

165. So HS, similarly Arm. N and E: τίς ἡ τοσαύτη φιλία
καὶ ὁ ἔρως καὶ ἡ πρὸς τὴν σάρκα συνήθεια;

166. Arm adds: զի՞նչ է ցանկութիւնն որ ընդ նմին սերմանեցաւ.
զի՞նչ որ ի նմայն է. զի՞նչ է սովորութիւնն չար. զի՞նչ ապտեղի
կատակքն. դարձեալ զիս կամիցիք որ իմդ էք, քաղաքավարել
ընդ այլսդ.

167. The following appears only in N and E but quite
possibly belonged to the ancient Acts and dropped out
in our other witness by haplography caused by the
reptition of -θῆναι at the end of the preceding
sentence and at the end of this expansion. ἕως τίνος
τοῖς κοσμικοῖς καὶ προσκαίροις προσανέχετε; ἕως πότε
οὐ συνιεῖτε τὰ ὑπὲρ ἡμᾶς καὶ τὰ ἐκεῖ καταλαβεῖν
ἐπείγεσθε; ἄφετέ με λοιπὸν ἐν τῷ σχήματι ἐν ᾧ ὁρᾶτε
ἀναιρεθῆναι.

168. N and E add: οὕτως γάρ μοι κεκλήρωται τοῦ (E: ἐκ
τούτου) ἐκδημῆσαι τοῦ σώματος καὶ ἐνδημῆσαι πρὸς τὸν
κύριον, ᾧ καὶ συνεσταύρωμαι· ὅπερ δὴ καὶ γενήσεται.
Arm: երբ դիտացեալ էիք ի րաղումն զմի կապանս, և դուք
րաղումք զմի լուծանելով ապստանէիք. երբ լացեալ իցէ ձեր ի
վերայ կապանաց նորա, զգայիք վաղվաղակի զնա լուծանել. երբ
տեսեալ էր ձեր զայն որ ոչն է ր ինքեամր կապեալ, լուծանէիք
դուք զձեզ, զնա կապեցի. երբ դիտէիք դուք զնորա կապանն,
ձեզէն զինքեանս լուծանէիք, զի ընդ նմա կապիցէք.

169. C actually reads: ἐμαυτούς.

the earthly![117] O, what strong statements have been spoken against carnal things, and yet they want more of the same! O, how many times I have prayed that I might lift them from these filthy habits, but instead they were encouraged to nothingness! Why this excessive fondness for the flesh?[118] Why this great complicity with it?[119] Do you again encourage me to be put back[120] among things in flux?[121] If you understood that I have been loosened from ropes but tied up to myself, you yourselves would have been eager to be loosened from the many and to be tied to the one.[122] What should I say? I know well that what I am saying will happen, for you yourselves will I tie up with me, and after liberating myself, I will release myself from all things and become united with the one who came

----

117. *N* adds: "to flee the passionate attachment to earthly things; instead, they have been tied to them and remain in them and do not want to abandon them." *Arm*: "O, how wondrous they are who flee the earthly and moreover are driven toward earthly things."

118. *N* and *E*: "Why such a fondness and love and intimacy with the flesh?"

119. *Arm* adds: "What is your desire which has been fertilized by this? What is in it? What is your evil habit? What are the improper jokes? Again you who are mine will want to deal with others."

120. Or perhaps: "be put on ship."

121. *N* and *E*: "How long will you be devoted to the worldly and ephemeral? When will you comprehend things above us and hasten to lay hold of things there? Let me at last be destroyed in the manner you now see."

122. *N* and *E* add: "for it has been allotted to me to leave this body and to live with the Lord, with whom I too am being crucified. This indeed will happen." *Arm*: If you knew one rope among the many, you, the many, would be free by releasing the one. If you should cry about your bonds, you would feel immediately the release of them. If you saw the one, which was not himself tied, you would release yourself, for you are tied to him. If you know his bonds, you can untie yourself, that you might be tied to him."

ἐμαυτὸν ἐλευθερώσας ἀπολύσω πάντων συνενούμενος τῷ ὑπὲρ
πάντων γενομένῳ καὶ ὑπὲρ πάντας ὄντι.[170] (62 [8].) ἀλλ'
ἐπεὶ πρόσεισί μοι νῦν ὁ Αἰγεάτης σιγῶν τὰ ἐμὰ τέκνα
συνέχω.[171] ἃ δεῖ με πρὸς αὐτὸν εἰπόντα ἀναλῦσαι, ταῦτα
ἐρῶ.[172] τίνος χάριν πάλιν πρὸς ἡμᾶς,[173] Αἰγεᾶτα; τίνος
ἕνεκεν ὁ ἀλλότριος[174] ἡμῶν προσέρχῃ ἡμῖν; τί τολμῆσαι
πάλιν θέλων;[175] τί τεχνάσασθαι; τί μεταπέμψασθαι; εἰπεῖν
δὲ τί· λύσων ἡμᾶς πρόσει ὡς μετεγνωκώς; οὐδ' ἂν ἀληθῶς
μεταγνῷς, Αἰγεᾶτα, ἔτι[176] σοι συνθήσομαι· οὐδ' ἂν τὰ σὰ
ἅπαντα ὑπισχνῇ, ἀφίσταμαι ἐμαυτοῦ·[177] οὐδ' ἂν ἴδιόν μου
λέγῃς σαυτὸν[178] πεπίστευκά σοι. λύεις δέ, ἀνθύπατε, τὸν
δεθέντα; λύεις τὸν πεφευγότα;[179] λύεις τὸν ἐλευθερωθέντα;
λύεις τὸν γνωρισθέντα ὑπὸ τοῦ συγγενοῦς, τὸν ἐλεηθέντα,
τὸν φιληθέντα ὑπ' αὐτοῦ, τὸν ἀλλότριόν σου, τὸν ξένον[180]

----

170. Arm: Ա զիս ազատեալ արձակեցից յամենայն միաւանութենէ
     ձերմէ, զի երթայց առ այն որ ի վերն է քան զամենեսեան.

171. Arm: Արդ քանզի լռւթեամբ մօտ կայ առ իս եղիատէս և
     պաշարեալ կամի գողրեակս իմ.

172. So HS, C, Arm, and Ep$_{gr.2}$. N and E: καὶ στραφεὶς ἔφη
     (E: εἶπε) πρὸς Αἰγεάτην. M (similarly L): καὶ ὡς
     εἶδεν ὁ ἀπόστολος ἑστῶτα αὐτὸν ἄντικρυς αὐτοῦ, εἶπεν
     αὐτῷ μεγάλῃ τῇ φωνῇ. Cd: et cum vidisset Andreas
     Aegeatem dixit. Ep: quem videns sanctus Andreas
     dixit.

173. Ma1 and M add: ἐλήλυθας. Ep$_{gr.2}$: ἧκες. N and E:
     παραγέγονας. Ep: venisti.

174. N and E add: καὶ ἐχθρός.

175. N and E: τί τολμῆσαι βουλόμενος.

176. So C and L. Ep$_{gr.2}$: ἐπί. HS: οὔτι. Ma1: οἶτι.

177. Ma1: οὐκ ἀφίσταμαι τοῦ ἐμοῦ δεσπότου.

178. C: λέγεις σαυτόν. HS: βουλεύσῃς ἑαυτόν.

179. Arm: լուծանէս գփախուցեալս.

180. Arm: լուծանէս գծանօթացեալ ս ի յազգէն քումմէ որ
     ողորմութիւն եղիտ, որ ոչ քո են, այլ օտարացեալ են ի քէն որ
     նմայն երևեցաւ միայնոյ.

into being for all and who exists beyond all.[123] **(62 [8].)**
But now that Aegeates is coming to me, I will keep quiet
and embrace my children.[124] Whatever I must resolve by
speaking to him, these I will speak.[125] Aegeates, why have
you come to us again? Why should you who are foreign[126] to
us come to us? What do you want to attempt now? What do
you want to contrive? Whom do you wish to summon? Say
something! Have you come to untie us because you changed
your mind? Even if you really did change your mind,
Aegeates, I would never accede to you. Were you to promise
all your possessions, I would keep far from them.[127] Were
you to say you yourself were mine, I would not trust you.
Would you untie the one who is tied up, proconsul? Would
you untie the one who has fled?[128] Would you untie the one
who was liberated? Would you untie the one recognized by
his kindred, the one who received mercy, the one loved by

----

123. *Arm*: "and I will release myself free from your
     brotherhood, that I might go to him who is above
     all."

124. *Arm*: "But now that Aegeates has approached me in
     silence in order to surround, beseige my children."

125. *N* and *E*: "And turning, he said to Aegeates." *M*
     (similarly *L*): "And when the apostle saw him standing
     opposite him, he said in a loud voice." *CD*: "And when
     Andrew saw Aegeates, he said." *Ep*: "When the holy
     Andrew saw him, he said."

126. *N* and *E* add: "and hostile."

127. *Ma*1: "I would not abandon my master."

128. *Arm*: "Will you release those who have fled?"

τὸν ἐπιφανέντα σοι μόνον; ἔχω ᾧ συνέσομαι εἰσαεί· ἔχω ᾧ
συμπολιτεύσομαι εἰς ἀναριθμήτους αἰῶνας. πρὸς ἐκεῖνον
ἄπειμι· πρὸς ἐκεῖνον ἐπείγομαι, τὸν καὶ σὲ γνωρίσαντά μοι,
τὸν εἰρηκότα μοι· κατάμαθε τὸν Αἰγεάτην καὶ τὰ τούτου
δῶρα. μή σε φοβείτω ὁ δεινὸς ἐκεῖνος, μηδέ σε κρατεῖν
νομιζέτω ἐμὸν ὄντα. ἐχθρός σού ἐστιν· λυμεὼν ὑπάρχει,
ἀπατεών, διαφθορεύς, κατάλαλος, ἀγνώμων, μανιώδης,
περίεργος, φονεύς, ὑβριστής, κόλαξ, γόης, δεινός, ὀργίλος,
ἀσυμπαθής, καὶ πάσῃ τῇ περιβολῇ αὐτοῦ τῇ ὑλώδει
περινηθισμένος.[181] τοιγαροῦν ἐπιγνούς σε διὰ τοῦ
ἐπιστρέψαντός μοι ἀπαλλάσσομαί σου. εὖ οἶδα τυπτόμενόν σε
καὶ πενθήσαντα[182] ᾧ πρὸς ὃν λέγω, ἀνθύπατον, τὸν ὑπὲρ
αὐτὸν ἀναφυγόντος μου. ⸃καὶ γὰρ κλαύσῃ καὶ τύψῃ καὶ βρύξῃ
καὶ λυπηθήσῃ καὶ ἀθυμήσῃ καὶ κόψῃ καὶ ἀνιάσῃ[183] καὶ
παρασκευάσει ἅμα τῇ συγγενίδι σου θαλάσσῃ ἣν καὶ νῦν ὁρᾷς
κυμαινομένην ὀργίλως[184] ὅτι ὑμῶν ἀπήλλαγμαι[185] ἐγώ· ἡ
χάρις δι' ἐμοῦ τὸ τερπνόν, τὸ ὅσιον, τὸ δίκαιον, τὸ
ἀληθές, τὸ εὔχαρι, τὸ λάλον·[186] καὶ πᾶσιν οἷς ἐδόκεις δι'
ἐμοῦ κεκοσμῆσθαι.

----

181. This last clause appears only in C. N and E: καὶ ἡ
     περιβολὴ αὐτοῦ ὡς λύκου δορά. L: ἀπόστηθι τοίνυν ἀπ'
     ἐμοῦ, ἐργάτα πάσης ἀνομίας. Arm: աՆՖմարբր, ՖաՆղերἀ
     ամՆմաՆ ՆՆղասր և խխստ ֆար գոոբոՎ.բՆ.

182. Arm: ՍբՐֆ գխաֆֆֆ դու Բֆ Ւմ յոոդոոբֆոֆ գֆֆ Վⲁⲁⲣⲇ ҍ ֆֆ.
     Ա գխⲙⲝⲁ ֆֆ ‹ⲁⲣⲕⲁ‹Նⲝ ⲣⲅֆֆ Ա սգⲁⲁ.

183. Arm adds: Ա Բⲟ‹ⲝ գⲟⲟⲟⲣⲙⲝֆ ⲕⲝⲁ‹ ֆⲛ.

184. Arm adds: ⲣ ‹ⲙⲁ‹ֆ ⲇⲝⲝ Ա ⲁⲝⲝⲁⲣ‹ֆ.

185. C adds: ὁ ὑμῶν, which must be corrupt, perhaps a
     dittograph generated from ὅτι ὑμῶν, which stands
     immediately above it in the ms.

186. Perhaps: καλόν. Arm: ⲁⲟⲟⲣ ⲇ‹ⲙⲁⲣⲝⲁ ⲁⲟⲟⲟⲟⲁⲁⲟ‹ֆ ⲣⲁ‹ֆ
     ‹‹ⲝⲝ‹ⲁⲙⲝⲁⲁ‹ ⲣⲁⲣⲟ‹Բⲝⲁⲙⲣ ⟄ⲟⲝⲁⲟ.

him, the one alien to you,[129] the stranger who appeared so only to you? I possess the one with whom I will always be. I possess the one with whom I will be a compatriot for countless ages. It is to him that I go. It is to him that I speed on, to the one who made me recognize even you by saying to me: 'Mark Aegeates and his gifts. Do not let that rogue frighten you, and let him not suppose that he can seize you, for you are mine. He is your enemy. He is a corrupter, a cheat, a destroyer, a slanderer, a boor, a maniac, a busybody, a murderer, an insolent egotist, a flatterer, a magician, terrible, petulant, unmerciful, and decorated on all sides by his material[130] veneer.[131] Inasmuch as I recognized you through your turning to me, I am released from you. Proconsul, I know well that you bewail and mourn[132] because of what I am saying to you as I flee off to the one beyond you. You will weep, beat your breast, gnash your teeth, grieve, despair, lament, anguish,[133] and comport yourself like your relative the sea, which you now see furiously troubled by waves because I am leaving all of you.[134] The grace which came because of me is delightful, holy, just, true, charming, and

----

129. *Arm*: "Will you release those who are known to be from your nation who know mercy, who are not yours, but are alienated from you, who is revealed only to him?"

130. Or: "wooden."

131. *N* and *E*: "his covering is like wolf hide." *L*: "Keep from me the works of all lawlessness." *Arm*: "wicked in works."

132. *Arm*: "Do you not recognize that by my exhortation I redeem you from yourself and know that you strike yourself and mourn?"

133. *Arm* adds: "and abandon your miserable life."

134. *Arm* adds: "for it is like you, and like the world."

Καὶ ὁ ἀνθύπατος ἀκούσας ταῦτα ἔκθαμβος εἰστήκει,
τρόπον τινὰ ἐξεστηκώς.[187] ἀπιδὼν δὲ πάλιν πρὸς αὐτὸν ὁ
Ἀνδρέας εἶπεν·[188] ἀλλὰ νῦν ἐστάθης ἰδεῖν, ἐχθρὲ πᾶσιν
ἡμῖν Αἰγεᾶτα. ἤρεμος καὶ ἡσύχιος ἔστηκας καὶ μηδὲν
δυνάμενος ὧν τολμᾷς.[189] ἐγὼ δὲ καὶ οἱ ἐμοὶ συγγενεῖς ἐπὶ
τὰ ἡμῶν ἐπειγόμεθα, σὲ ἐῶντες εἶναι ὃ εἶ καὶ ὃ μὴ
ἐπίστασαι αὐτὸς περὶ σεαυτοῦ.

63 (9). Καὶ ὡς πάλιν ἐκεῖνος ἐτόλμα προσεγγίσαι τῷ
ξύλῳ ὥστε λῦσαι τὸν Ἀνδρέαν, τῆς πόλεως ὅλης θορυβούσης
αὐτόν, ὁ ἀπόστολος Ἀνδρέας μετὰ φωνῆς[190] εἶπεν· τὸν ἐπὶ
τοῦ σοῦ ξύλου δεθέντα Ἀνδρέαν μὴ ἐπιτρέψῃς πάλιν λυθῆναι,
δέσποτα· τὸν ἐπὶ τοῦ σοῦ μυστηρίου ὄντα, μὴ δῷς με ἀναιδεῖ
διαβόλῳ, Ἰησοῦ· τὸν ἐπὶ τῆς σῆς χάριτος κρεμασθέντα ὁ
ἀντίδικός σου μὴ λυέτω με, πάτερ.[191] τὸν ἐγνωκότα σου τὸ
μέγεθος ὁ μικρὸς μηκέτι ταπεινούτω.[192] ἀλλά με αὐτός,

----

187. *N* and *E* add: πάσης οὖν τῆς πόλεως θορυβούσης αὐτὸν
τοῦ ἀπολύειν (*E* adds: τὸν) Ἀνδρέαν. Similarly *Cd*.

188. *Arm* adds: Ո՞ որ ամենայն րնուրբանց գուցեր զբեզ. ո́ որ ոչ
իւէ րնդունանյ եղև բեզ, այլ Հանդերձաւ̇ս̇ ապապակէ. ո որ
ի սկզբանէ երեիր, և յանէրևույիս̇ լուծանի. որիՆակէն ա՛ե՛ր.որ
լիՆիբ դկնտաւ̇բ ի րնութիւն ազգակցին ձերոյ. ո որ̇չափ գուցա, զի
զոր ցանկայ̇ն տեսցունբ. ո որբան երևամ̇նաց րանւ, զի զազգակից̇ն
բշւամանեցէ. ո որ չարչարեցանւ, զի որ իչէն ցուցցի,բանիցս
անդա Հաւրերբա̇ց, զի մ̇ի ի Նմա̇Նէ յանդիմ̇ա̇Նեցցի. որ̇բան
աշխատեցա̇ւ, զի զա̇ա ի Նմա̇Նէ̇ իմա̇ցի. զ̇ո՞չ է իմա̇ցակա̇ն, ոչ
իւէ է րնդ վա̇յր, այլ ա̇մ̇են̇այ̇ն իւէ որ̇ի̇Նա̇կ̇ա̇ւ ե̇ղ̇ե̇ւ.

189. *Arm:* ա̇յլ ա̇յժմ̇ կ̇ա̇ց̇ե̇ր տ̇ե̇ս̇ա̇ն̇ե̇լ զ̇ո̇ւ̇ե̇զ̇ ե̇ղ̇ի̇ա̇ն̇ե̇ս̇ ի̇ր̇ր̇և զ̇ա̇ե̇ղ և զ̇զ̇ո̇ւ̇ա̇ծ̇.
և զ̇ի̇ զ̇ո̇ւ̇ս̇յ̇ո̇ւ̇ չ̇ո̇ւ̇Ն̇ի̇ս̇ ո̇ւ̇ ի̇չ̇ի̇ւ̇ա̇Ն̇. ի̇չ̇ե̇Ն̇ ի̇ր̇ր̇և զ̇ո̇ր̇ա̇ւ̇ո̇ր̇.

190. *N* and *E* add: ἀτενίσας εἰς τὸν οὐρανόν.

191. *N* and *E*: τὸν τανυσθέντα καθ' ὁμοιότητά σου μὴ ἐάσῃς
συσταλῆναι, πάτερ.

192. *N* and *E*: τοὺς ἐγνωκότας σου τὸ μέγεθος καὶ ποθήσαντας
(*E* adds: σε) καὶ ἀγαπήσαντας (*E* adds: σε) καὶ
πιστεύσαντας εἰς σὲ διὰ τοῦ ὑμῶν (*E*: δι' αὐτοῦ τοῦ)
κηρύγματος διαφύλαξον ἀπήμονας (*N* adds: ἀπὸ τοῦ
ἀντικειμένου δαίμονος) καὶ βεβαίωσον αὐτοὺς ἐν τῇ σῇ

articulate,[135] along with all the things by which you seemed to have been adorned through me."

When the proconsul heard these things he stood there flabbergasted and rather stunned.[136] Andrew looked at him again and said,[137] "Aegeates, enemy of us all, now you stand there watching. You stand there quiet and calm, unable to do anything you dare?[138] My kindred and I speed on to things our own, leaving you to be what you are and what you fail to understand about yourself."

63 (9). And when Aegeates again attempted to approach the wood to untie Andrew, the entire city was in an uproar at him. The apostle Andrew shouted:[139] "O Master, do not permit Andrew, the one tied to your wood, to be untied again. O Jesus, do not give me to the shameless devil, I who am attached to your mystery. O Father, do not let your

----

135. Perhaps: "good." *Arm*: "will with all the goodness of the holy and true divine word."

136. *N*, *E*, and *CD* add: "so the entire city was in an uproar for him to release Andrew."

137. *Arm*, which seems to be corrupt, adds: "O, you who have shown yourself to be outside of all nature. O, he who from the beginning appeared and is dissolved in the invisible; fearful examples, which are aimed at the nature of your like. O, how much was shown, that we might see what you desired. How he extended his words to vilify those like him. O, how he is tormented, for it will be shown how many times he has been patient, that he would not be scolded by him. How he worked, that from this he might know what is intelligible. Nothing is vain, but everything is by example."

138. *Arm*: "But now you stand and see us mild and lowly, Aegeates, and since you do not have these qualities, O prince, will you reign as a strongman?"

139. *N* and *E* add: "looking intently into heaven."

Χριστέ, ὃν ἐπόθησα, ὃν ἠγάπησα, ὃν οἶδα, ὃν ἔχω, ὃν φιλῶ,
οὗ εἰμί,[193] δέξαι με[194] ὅπως διὰ τῆς ἐμῆς ἐξόδου τῆς ἐπὶ
σὲ ἡ τῶν πολλῶν μου συγγενῶν σύνοδος[195] γένηται,
ἀναπαυομένων[196] ἐν τῇ σῇ μεγαλειότητι. καὶ εἰπὼν ταῦτα καὶ
δοξάσας ἐπὶ πλεῖον τὸν κύριον παρέδωκεν τὸ πνεῦμα,[197] ἐπὶ
τῇ εὐχαριστίᾳ αὐτοῦ, * κλαιόντων οὖν ἡμῶν[198] καὶ ἀνιωμένων
ἁπάντων ἐπὶ τῷ χωρισμῷ αὐτοῦ.

64 (10). Μετὰ δὲ τὴν ἔξοδον τοῦ μακαρίου ἀποστόλου, ἡ
Μαξιμίλλα ἅμα τῷ Στρατοκλεῖ μηδενὸς ὅλως φροντίσασα τῶν
παρεστώτων αὐτῇ προσελθοῦσα ἔλυσεν τὸ λείψανον τοῦ
μακαρίου, καὶ ὀψίας γενομένης, τὴν ἀναγκαίαν αὐτῷ
ἐπιμέλειαν προσαγαγοῦσα ἐκήδευσεν.[199]

πίστει καὶ χάρισαι αὐτοῖς τὴν πρὸς σὲ παρρησίαν τοῦ
δοξάζειν σὲ τὸν ἀληθινὸν θεόν.

193. *N* and *E*: ἐν ᾧ εἰμὶ καὶ ἔσομαι.

194. *N* and *E* add: ἐν εἰρήνῃ εἰς τὰς αἰωνίους (*N* adds: σου)
σκηνάς.

195. *N* and *HS*: εἴσοδος. *Ep*gr.2 adds: πρὸς σέ.

196. *N* and *Ep*gr.2 add: αὐτῶν.

197. *Ma*, *C*, and *Ep*gr.2 add: σὺν (*C*: ἐπὶ) τῇ εὐχαριστίᾳ (*C*
and *Ep*gr.2: αὐτοῦ).

198. *N*: ἁπάντων.

199. *HS* and *L*: κατέθαψεν. *N* and *E*: ἔθαψεν αὐτὸν πλησίον
τοῦ αἰγιαλοῦ, ἔνθα κατάκλειστος ὑπῆρχεν.

opponent untie me, I who am hanging upon your grace.[140]
May that runt no longer humiliate the one who has known
your greatness.[141] But you yourself, O Christ, you whom I
desired, whom I loved, whom I know, whom I possess, whom I
cherish, whose I am,[142] receive me,[143] so that by my
departure to you there may be a reunion[144] of my many
kindred, those who rest in your majesty." When he had said
these things and further glorified the Lord, he handed
over his spirit,[145] * so that we[146] wept and everyone
grieved his departure.

64 (10). After the departure of the blessed apostle,
Maximilla, accompanied by Stratocles, completely
disregarding those standing around her, came forward,
untied the corpse of the blessed one, and having provided
it with the necessary attention, buried it at
nightfall.[147]

----

140. *N* and *E*: "O Father, do not let the one stretched out
in your likeness be given slack."

141. *N* and *E*: "Those who have known your greatness, have
desired, loved, and believed in you through our (*E*:
his) preaching, keep these untroubled (*N* adds: from
the hostile demon), strengthen them in your faith,
and grant them boldness before you that they might
glorify you, the true God."

142. *N* and *E*: "in whom I am and will be."

143. *N* and *E* add: "in peace to (*N* adds: your) eternal
dwellings."

144. *N* and *HS*: "entrance."

145. *Ma*, *C*, and *Ep*gr.2 add: "with (*C* and *Ep*gr.2 add: his)
thanksgiving." So Prieur, *Acta Andreae*, 542 n. 64.1.

146. This unexpected first person plural appears in *HS*,
*Ma*2, and *CD*. *N*: "all."

147. *N* and *E* add: "beside the sea-shore where he had been
imprisoned."

Καὶ ἦν τοῦ Αἰγεάτου κεχωρισμένη διὰ τὴν θηριώδη αὐτοῦ ψυχὴν καὶ πολιτείαν ἄνομον· ὃν οὐδὲ προσήκατο τοῦ λοιποῦ ὅλως ὑποκρίσει αὐτοῦ προσφερομένου.²⁰⁰ ἀλλ᾽ ἑλομένη βίον σεμνὸν καὶ ἤρεμον τῇ ἀγάπῃ τοῦ Χριστοῦ κεχορηγημένη, μακαρίως ἅμα τοῖς ἀδελφοῖς διῆγεν· ἣν πολλὰ λιπαρήσας ὁ Αἰγεάτης καὶ ὑποσχόμενος πραγμάτων αὐτοῦ²⁰¹ δεσπόζειν αὐτὴν καὶ μὴ δυνηθεὶς πεῖσαι αὐτήν, νυκτὸς ἀναστὰς καὶ διαλαθὼν πάντας τοὺς αὐτοῦ ἀπὸ ὕψους μεγάλου²⁰² ῥίψας ἑαυτὸν ἐτελεύτησεν.

ʽΟ δὲ Στρατοκλῆς ὢν τοῦ Αἰγεάτου κατὰ τὸν σαρκικὸν ἀδελφὸς οὐκ ἠβουλήθη τῆς ὑπ᾽ αὐτοῦ καταληφθείσης οὐσίας θιγεῖν--καὶ γὰρ ἄτεκνος ὁ δεινὸς ἐτελεύτησεν--εἰπών· τὰ σά, Αἰγεᾶτα, ἅμα σοὶ πορευέσθω· ἐμοὶ δὲ ὁ ᾽Ιησοῦς²⁰³ εἴη φίλος κἀγὼ αὐτοῦ.²⁰⁴ τὸ δὲ πολὺ πλῆθος τῶν ἐκτὸς κακῶν καὶ τῶν ἔνδοθεν ἀπορρίπτων μου ἐκείνῳ τὰ ἐμαυτοῦ προσανατιθέμενος²⁰⁵ πᾶν τοὐναντίον διωθοῦμαι.

65 (11). ᾽Ενταῦθά που τὸ τέλος τῶν μακαρίων μου διηγημάτων ποιήσαιμι καὶ πράξεων καὶ μυστηρίων δυσφράστων ὄντων,²⁰⁶ ἵνα μὴ καὶ ἀφράστων²⁰⁷ εἴπω. ἡ κορωνὶς

----

200. Arm: Ա յայնմ հետէ ոչ կարէր աննալ ներգաւոր բանից նորա, զի մի ի կեղծաւորէն խարեսցի, այլ յանձն առեալ զպարկեշտ և զսէգ վարս սիրովն Աստուծոյ.

201. HS: τῶν αὐτοῦ ἁπάντων.

202. HS and Ma1: μεγίστου.

203. Ma2, N, and E: Χριστός. C and L: εἷς, which may derive from ὁ ἱς, a common abbreviation for ὁ ᾽Ιησοῦς.

204. Ma2, N, and E add: δοῦλος.

205. N and E: καὶ τὰ ἐμὰ πάντα αὐτῷ προσανατίθημι.

She separated from Aegeates because of his beastly soul and lawless public life. Thereafter, though he shammed good behavior, she had nothing whatever to do with him.[148] Choosing instead a life holy and quiet, provided for by the love of Christ, she spent her time happily with the brethren. Even though Aegeates often importuned her and offered her the opportunity to manage his affairs, he was not able to persuade her. One night, undetected by anyone in his household, he threw himself from a great height and died.

Stratocles, Aegeates' brother according to the flesh, did not want so much as to touch the property Aegeates left--the wretch died childless. He said, "May your possessions go with you, Aegeates! May Jesus[149] be my friend and I his![150] Casting from me the entire lot of external and internal evils and entrusting to that one everything I own, I thrust aside everything averse to him."

65 (11).[151] Hereabouts I should make an end of the blessed tales, acts, and mysteries difficult--or should I say impossible--to express. Let this stroke of the pen end

----

148. *Arm*: "from that time forward he could not obey his deceitful words, for he could not be fooled by the deceiver, but committed himself to honest and humble ways by the love of God."

149. *Ma2*, *N*, and *E*: "Christ." *C* and *L*: "one."

150. *Ma2*, *N*, and *E* add: "servant."

151. This postscript appears at the end of *HS* and *C*, with echoes in *Arm*, where the passage appears in direct discourse as a continuation of Stratocles' speech.

τελευτάτω.[208] καὶ ἐπεύξομαι πρῶτον μὲν ἐμαυτῷ ἀκοῦσαι τῶν εἰρημένων ὡς εἴρηται, καὶ τούτ<ω>ν εἰς τὸ συμφανές, εἶτα καὶ τῶν ἀφανῶν, διανοίᾳ δὲ ληπτῶν, ἐπείτα καὶ πᾶσι τοῖς διατιθεμένοις ὑπὸ τῶν εἰρημένων, κοινωνίαν ἔχειν ἐπίπαν θεοῦ δὲ ἀνοίγοντος τὰς ἀκόας τῶν ἐντυγχανόντων, ὅπως ᾖ ληπτὰ ἄπαντα αὐτοῦ τὰ χαρίσματα ἐν Χριστῷ Ἰησοῦ τῷ κυρίῳ ἡμῶν μεθ᾽ οὗ τῷ πατρὶ δόξα, τιμή, καὶ κράτος σὺν[209] τῷ παναγίῳ καὶ ἀγαθῷ καὶ ζωοποιῷ πνεύματι νῦν καὶ ἀεὶ καὶ εἰς τοὺς αἰῶνας τῶν αἰώνων, ἀμήν.

----

206. *C* om.: ὄντων.

207. *C*: ἀνέκφραστον.

208. *HS* omits that sentence. It appears in *C* and is echoed in *Arm*.

209. Instead of the section κοινωνίαν . . . σύν, *HS*: κοινὴν δοξολογίαν ἀναπέμψωμεν τῷ φιλανθρώπῳ θεῷ σὺν τῷ μονογενεῖ αὐτοῦ υἱῷ καί.

it. I will pray first for myself, that I heard what was
actually said, both the obvious and also the obscure,
comprehensible only to the intellect. Then I will pray for
all who are convinced by what was said, that they may have
fellowship with each other, as God opens the ears of the
listeners, in order to make comprehensible all his
gifts[152] in Christ Jesus our Lord, to whom, together with
the Father, be glory, honor, and power with[153] the all-
holy and good and life-giving Spirit, now and always,
forever and ever, amen.

---

152. Prieur suggests that the postscript originally ended
     here (*Acta Andreae*, 57 and 548 n. 65.2).

153. *HS*: "let us send up a common doxology to the
     philanthropic God with his unique son and."

Part Four:

RELATED MATERIALS

AUGUSTINE, *CONTRA FELICEM* 6 (*CSEL* 25.833)

Etenim speciosa figmenta, et ostentatio simulata, et coactio visibilium, nec quidem ex propria natura procedunt, sed ex eo homine, qui per se ipsum deterior factus est per seductionem.

BODLEIAN MS. COPT. F. 103 (P)

(I. Recto)

```
[·]·ρωмє·[··]єναγ єροῑ ϩм
'[·]·мєλοс єτ···[  ]'¹
τοτє πєχαϥ ν̄ϭι ῑⲥ̄ ν̄
αναρєαс χє ϩων єϩογν
єροῑ αναρєαс πєκρᾱ²
πє πκωϩτ ναῑατκ̄
ϩν̄ ν̄ρωмє· αϥογωϣⲃ̄
αϥογωϣⲃ̄ ν̄ϭι αναρє
αс πєχαϥ м̄πсωτ[ηρ]
χє † θє ναῑ єτραϣαχє ·α·³
τοτє π[є]χαϥ ναϥ χє
ϣαχє αναρєαс πєϲτγ
λος єτταχρηγ αϥογ
ωϣⲃ̄ ν̄ϭι αναρєαс πє
χαϥ χє ϥον'ϩ' ν̄ϭι πνογ
τє єτє πєκєιωτ πє
```

(I. Verso)

```
χє ν̄τ[αι]єι єβολ [ϩм]
πηєι м̄παєιωτ мν
ταмααγ αγω ϲονϩ
ν̄ϭι ταψγχη χє м̄πι
ογωϩ єτοοτ єβωκ
єϩογν єροϥ αγω м̄
πιναγ єπϩο м̄παιωτ
мν̄ ταмααγ ογαє м̄
πιναγ єπϩ[ο νν]αϣη
```

----

1. Probably: πιмєλοс єτ. The ϩм in line 1 and all of line 2 are in a second hand.

2. I.e.: πєκραν.

3. Probably: νακ, added by a second hand.

AUGUSTINE, *CONTRA FELICEM* 6

Augustine claimed that one of "Leucius's" Acta contained the following. It would appear likely that it belongs to the *AA*, but it cannot be placed with precision.

Pretentious imaginations, sham displays, and constrictions of things perceptible do not issue from one's true nature but from that human essence which demeans itself through seduction.

BODLEIAN MS. COPT. F. 103 (P)

John Barns suggests that this fragment might have belonged to the *AA*, but it could as easily have come from any number of apocrypha.[1] According to Prieur, if this passage derived from the *AA*, it might have appeared at the beginning or at *GE* 22 or at *GE* 29, for in each of these sections Christ appears to the apostle[2]

(I. Recto) (...) person (...) see me in the member which (....)

Then Jesus said to Andrew, "Come near me, Andrew. Your name is 'fire.' Blessed are you among all people."

Andrew answered and said to the Savior, "Let me speak to you."[3]

----

1. "A Coptic Apocryphal Fragment in the Bodleian Library," *JTS* n.s. 11 (1960): 74-75. Prieur reprints Barn's transcription, but botches up the columns at the bottom of page 22.

2. *Acta Andreae*, 24-25.

3. Or: "Give me the means so that I may speak to you."

ⲣⲉ ⲙⲛ̄ ⲧⲁⲥ[ϩⲓ]ⲙⲉ ⲁⲗⲗⲁ
ⲉⲛⲉⲓ̈ϥ[ⲓ ⲙⲡ]ⲁⲥⲧⲟ[ⲥ]ⲙ̄ⲡ[ⲁ]ⲁ[4]
   ʼⲡⲡⲁ̈ⲙⲁʼ[5]
ⲙⲏⲛⲉ ⲉⲓⲟⲩⲏϩ ⲛⲥ̱ⲱ̱ʼⲕʼ
ⲭⲓⲛ ⲉϩⲧⲟⲟⲩ ϣⲁ ⲣⲟⲩϩⲉ ʼⲉⲡʼ[6]
ⲉⲛⲉⲓ̱ⲕⲁⲁϥ ⲉ[ⲡ]ʼⲣʼⲉ̱ⲥ̱ⲏⲧ[7]
ⲁϥⲟⲩⲱϣⲃ ⲛ̄ϭⲓ ⲓ̄ⲥ ⲡⲉ
ⲭⲁϥ ⲭⲉ † ⲥⲟⲟⲩⲛ ⲁⲛ[ⲁⲣⲉⲁⲥ?

(II. Recto)

[
[· · · · ·] · · · [
[· · ·] · · ⲁⲩⲱ · · ⲉ[
· ·]ⲃⲉⲁⲩ· · ϩ · · ⲙⲙⲟⲟⲩ
ʼ[·] · · ⲟⲩ̱ⲉⲃⲟⲗ[·] · · · ⲣ̱ · · · · · · ʼ[8]
· ⲭ · · · · ⲣⲉ · · · · · ⲉ̱ⲃ̱ⲟⲗ
· ⲩ̱ⲁ̱ⲩ̱· · ϩⲙ· · · · · · ·
ⲧⲉⲉⲣⲉⲁ̱ⲣ̱· · · · · ⲉ̱ⲙ̱ⲡ̱ⲓ
ⲕⲁⲟⲩ̱ⲉⲃⲟⲗ · · · · ⲣ̱ⲟ̱ⲩ̱ · · · ʼ · · · · · · · ʼ[9]
· · · ⲉ[· · · · · ·] · · ⲧ̱ⲟⲩ·
ⲁⲥϣⲱⲡ[ⲉ · · · · · [· ⲉ · ·
ⲧⲁⲥ̱ϩ̱[· · · · · · ·] · · [
ⲣⲉⲕⲟ· [· · · · · · ·] · · · [[10]
ⲉⲕ· · [· · · · · · · ·] · ⲱ[
ⲛ̄ⲟ̱· [

(II. Verso)

[
ⲭ[· · · · · ·] · · · · [
[· · · ·] · ⲉ̱ⲣ̱ⲟ̱ⲟ̱ⲩ̱ ⲥⲁ· [

----

4. The ⲥ is illegible; above it appears the letter ⲩ.

5. ⲡ[ⲁ]ⲁ ʼⲡⲡⲁ̈ⲙⲁʼ are in a second hand.

6. A second hand added: ʼⲉⲡʼ.

7. The last four lines are corrupt. Barnes conjectures:
   <ⲉ>ⲛⲉⲓ̈ϥⲓ ⲙ̄ⲡⲁⲥⲧⲁⲩⲣⲟⲥ ⲙ̄ⲙⲏⲛⲉ ⲉⲓ̈ⲟⲩⲏϩ ⲛ̄ⲥⲱⲕ . . . ⲉⲙ̄ⲡⲓⲕⲁⲁϥ
   ⲉⲡⲉⲥⲏⲧ.

8. This line is in a second hand.

9. The last six indeciferable letters were written in the
   margin by a second hand.

10. Barnes restores: ⲧⲁⲥ̱ϩ̱[ⲓⲙⲉ ⲙⲛ̄ⲛⲁ]ϣⲏⲣⲉ ⲕⲟⲩ̱.[ⲓ.

Then he said to him, "Speak, Andrew, you strong pillar."

"As God who is your father lives," Andrew answered, (I. Verso) "(I swear) that I left the house of my father and my mother, and, as my soul lives, that I have not gone into it again. I have not looked on the face(s) of my father or my mother, nor have I looked on the face(s) of my children and my wife, but daily I was bearing my spiritual cross, following you and not laying it down from morning to night."[4]

Jesus answered and said, "I recognize this, Andrew (....)"

(II. Recto) "(...) my wife and my little children (....)"

---

4. This sentence is particularly corrupt, due in part to the work of a corrector. Even though Barns's reconstruction is plausible and meaningful, the exact sense of the sentence remains uncertain.

ⲞⲨⲔⲞⲨⲈⲒ ⲈⲞⲨⲀⲚ̄Ⲉ̣Ⲏ[ⲦⲚ]
ⲀⲚⲞ̣Ⲛ ⲈⲦ2Ⲁ [ⲡ]ⲈⲔⲣⲀⲚ
ⲰⲦⲎⲚ ⲤⲚⲦⲈ Ⲙ̄ⲡⲒⲈⲡⲒ
ⲐⲨⲘⲒ ⲈⲢ̣Ⲟ̣ⲞⲨ. ⲚⲀⲒ̈ ⲦⲈⲒ̈
ⲔⲈⲰⲦⲎⲚ ⲈⲦ2Ⲓ̈ⲰⲰⲦ
ⲈⲤ2ⲒⲰ[ⲰⲦ··]ⲈⲚ̄ⲞⲨⲀ
ⲈⲀ[······]·ⲰⲀⲡ¹¹
ⲬⲈ[······]ⲰⲈⲤⲈⲒ
Ⲭ·[······]·····
··[blank?]

---

11. Barnes restores: ⲚⲈ]ⲉ̣ Ⲛ̄ⲞⲨⲀ ⲈⲀ[ϥ.

(II. Verso) "(...) one smaller than one of us who bear your name. I have not desired two coats for myself, and even this coat which is on me is on me (....)"

BIBLIOGRAPHY

BIBLIOGRAPHY

Allberry, C. R. C. *A Manichaean Psalm-Book*. Manichaean Manuscripts in the Chester Beatty Collections 2. Stuttgart: W. Kohlhammer, 1938.

Amélineau, Emile C. *Les Actes des martyrs de l'église copte*. Paris: E. Leroux, 1890.

Auerbach, Erich. *Mimesis: The Representation of Reality in Western Literature*. Trans. Willard R. Trask. Princeton: Princeton University Press, 1968.

Baker, Alfred T. "The Passion of Saint Andrew." *Modern Language Review* 11 (1916): 420-49.

Bardenhewer, Otto. *Geschichte der altkirchlichen Literatur*. 3 vols. 2d ed. Freiburg: Herder, 1912-1914.

Barns, John. "A Coptic Apocryphal Fragment in the Bodleian Library." *Journal of Theological Studies* n.s. 11 (1960): 70-76.

Baumler, Ellen B. "Andrew in the City of the Cannibals: A Comparative Study of the Latin, Greek, and Old English Texts." Ph.D. diss., University of Kansas, 1985.

Bertin, Gerald A., and Alfred Foulet. "The Acts of Andrew in Old French Verse: The Gardner A. Sage Library Fragment." *Publications of the Modern Language Association of America* 81 (1966): 451-54.

Blatt, Franz. *Die lateinischen Bearbeitungen der Acta Andreae et Matthiae apud Anthropophagos*. Beihefte zur Zeitschrift für die neutestamentliche Wissenschaft 12. Giessen: Alfred Töpelmann, 1930.

Blumenthal, Martin. *Formen und Motive in den apokryphen Apostelgeschichten*. Texte und Untersuchungen zur Geschichte der altchristlichen Literatur 48.1. Leipzig: J. C. Hinrichs, 1933.

Bonnet, Maximilian, ed. *Acta Andreae cum laudatione contexta et Martyrium Andreae Graece: Passio Andreae Latine.* Supplementum codicis apocryphi 2. Paris: C. Klincksieck, 1895. Reprint of *Analecta Bollandiana* 13 [1894]: 309-78.

_____, ed. "Gregorii episcopi turonensis liber de miraculis beati Andreae apostoli." In *Monumenta Germaniae historica. Scriptores rerum Merovingicarum,* 821-46. Hannover: Impensis bibliopolii Aulici Hahniani, 1883.

_____, ed. "La passion d'André en quelle langue a-t-elle été écrit?" *Byzantinische Zeitschrift* 3 (1894): 458-69.

_____. See Lipsius, Richard Adelbert.

Bovon, François, ed. *Les Actes apocryphes des apôtres: Christianisme et monde païen.* Publications de la Faculté de Théologie de l'Université de Genève 4. Geneva: Labor et Fides, 1981.

_____. "Les Actes de Philippe." *Aufstieg und Niedergang der römischen Welt,* II.25.6:4432-4527. Berlin and New York: Walter de Gruyter, 1988.

Brooks, Kenneth R. *Andreas and the Fates of the Apostles.* Oxford: Clarendon Press, 1961.

Bryne, D. de. "Epistula Titi, discipuli Pauli, de dispositione sanctimonii." *Revue Bénédictine* 37 (1925): 47-72.

Budge, E. A. Wallis. *The Contendings of the Apostles.* London: Oxford University Press (Humphrey Milford), 1935.

Cureton, William. *Ancient Syriac Documents Relative to the Earliest Establishment of Christianity in Edessa and the Neigbouring Countries.* London: Williams and Norgate, 1864.

Delehaye, Hippolyte. *Synaxarium ecclesiae Constantinopolitanae. Acta Sanctorum, Propylaea, November.* Brussels: Société des Bollandistes, 1902.

Detorakis, Th. Τὸ ἀνέκδοτο μαρτύριο τοῦ ἀποστόλου Ἀνδρέα. In *Acts of the Second International Congress of Peleponesian Studies* 1.325-52. Athens, 1981-1982.

Diehl, Ernst, ed. *Inscriptiones latinae christianae veteres*. 4 vols. Rev. ed., ed. J. Moreau and H. I. Marrou. Dublin: Weidmanns, 1967-1970.

Dihle, Albrecht. "Neues zur Thomas-Tradition." *Jahrbuch für Antike und Christentum* 6 (1965): 54-70.

Dressel, Albert, ed. *Epiphanii monachi et presbyteri edita et inedita*. Paris and Leipzig: Brockhaus and Avenarius, 1843.

Dvornik, Francis. *The Idea of Apostolicity in Byzantium and the Legend of the Apostle Andrew*. Dumbarton Oaks Studies 4. Cambridge: Harvard University Press, 1958.

Ehrhard, Albert. *Die altchristliche Literatur und ihre Erforschung von 1884-1900*. Strassburger theologische Studien 1. Freiburg: Herder, 1900.

Flamion, Josef. *Les Actes apocryphes de l'apôtre André. Les Actes d'André et de Mathias, de Pierre et d'André et les textes apparentés*. Recueil de travaux d'histoire et de philologie 33. Louvain: Bureaux de Recueil, 1911.

Franko, Ivan. *Apocrypha and Legends (Codex apocryphus e manuscriptis ukraino-russicis collectus opera doctoris Joannis Franko)*. 5 vols. L'vov, 1896-1910. [in Russian]

_____. "Beiträge aus dem Kirchenslavischen zu den Apokryphen des Neuen Testaments." *Zeitschrift für die Neutestamentliche Wissenschaft* 3 (1902): 315-35.

Geyer, Paul, ed. *Itinera Hierosolymitana*. Corpus scriptorum ecclesiasticorum latinorum 39. Prague: F. Tempsky; and Leipzig: G. Freytag, 1898.

Gil, Juan. "Sobre el texto de los Acta Andreae et Matthiae apud anthropophagos." *Habis* 6 (1975): 177-94.

Goodwin, Charles Wycliffe. *The Anglo-Saxon Legends of St. Andrew and St. Veronica*. Cambridge: Macmillan, 1851.

Graesse, J. G. Th., ed. *Jacobus a Voragine, Legenda Aurea*. 2d ed. Leipzig: Impensis librariae Arnoldianae, 1850.

Grenfell, Bernard Pyne, and Arthur S. Hunt. *The Oxyrhynchus Papyri*. 6 vols. London: Egypt Exploration Fund, 1898-1919.

Gutschmid, Alfred von. "Die Königsnamen in den apokryphen Apostelgeschichten. Ein Beitrag zur Kenntnis des geschichtlichen Romans." *Rheinisches Museum für Philologie*, n.F. 19 (1864): 161-83 and 380-401. Reprinted in his *Kleine Schriften*, ed. Franz Rühl. Leipzig: B. G. Teubner, 1890.

Harnack, Adolf von. *Geschichte der altchristliche Literatur bis Eusebius*. Part 2, *Die Chronologie*. 2 vols. 2d ed., ed. K. Aland and F. Winkelmann. Leipzig: J. C. Hinrichs, 1893-1904. Reprint. Leipzig: J. C. Hinrichs, 1958.

Hefele, Karl J. von, *A History of the Councils of the Church*. Edinburgh: T. & T. Clark, 1871-1896.

Henry, R. *Photius: Bibliothèque*. 8 vols. Paris: Collection Byzantine, 1959-1977.

Hornschuh, M. "Acts of Andrew." In *New Testament Apocrypha*, ed. Edgar Hennecke and Wilhelm Schneemelcher, ET ed. Robert McL. Wilson, 2.390-403. Philadelphia: Westminster, 1967.

Istomin, K. "From the Slavo-Russian Manuscripts About the Apostle Andrew." *Vestnick archeologii i istorii* 16 (1904): 233-80. [in Russian]

Jacques, Xavier. "Les deux fragments conservés des Actes d'André et Paul. Cod. Borg Copt. 109, fasc. 132." *Orientalia* 38 (1969): 187-213.

James, Montague Rhodes. *Apocrypha anecdota*. Texts and Studies 2, 3 and 5,1. Cambridge: Cambridge University Press, 1893 and 1897. Reprint. Nendeln/Liechtenstein: Kraus, 1967.

_____. *The Apocryphal New Testament: Being the Apocryphal Gospels, Acts, Epistles, and Apocalypses with other Narratives and Fragments*. Oxford: Oxford University Press, 1924. Reprint. 1926-1975.

Javorskij, Julian Andreevich. *Novyia rukopisnyia nakhodki v oblasti starinnoi Karpatorusskoi pis'mennosti* (New Manuscript Findings in the Field of Ancient Carpatho-Russian Writings). Prague: Nákl, 1931. [in Russian]

Junod, Eric, "Origène, Eusèbe et la tradition sur la répartition des champs de mission des apôtres

(Eusèbe, *HE* III,1,1-3)." In *Les Actes apocryphes des apôtres. Christianisme et monde païen*, ed. François Bovon, 233-48. Publication de la Faculté de Théologie de l'Université de Genève 4. Geneva: Labor et Fides, 1981.

Junod, Eric, and Jean-Daniel Kaestli. *l'Histoire des Actes apocryphes des apôtres du IIIe au IXe siècle: le cas des Actes de Jean*. Cahiers de la Revue de Théologie et de Philosophie 7. Geneva, Lausanne, Neuchâtel, 1982.

_____. *Acta Iohannis*. Corpus Christianorum, Series Apocryphorum 1. Turnhout: Brepols, 1983.

Kaestli, Jean-Daniel. "Les scènes d'attribution des champs de mission et de départ de l'apôtre dans les Actes apocryphes." In *Les Actes apocryphes des apôtres. Christianisme et monde païen*, ed. François Bovon, 249-64. Publication de la Faculté de Théologie de l'Université de Genève 4. Geneva: Labor et Fides, 1981.

Konstantinidis, Chrysostom. "La fête de l'apôtre saint André dans l'église de Constantinople à l'époque byzantine et aux temps modernes." Mélanges en l'honneur de Mgr. M. Andrieu. *Revue des sciences religieuses* (1956): 243-61.

Kraft, B. "Andreas," s.v. *Lexicon für Theologie und Kirche*.

Krapp, George Philip. *Andreas and the Fates of the Apostles*. Boston: Ginn, 1906.

LaFargue, J. Michael. *Language and Gnosis: The Opening Scenes of the Acts of Thomas*. Harvard Dissertations in Religion 18. Philadelphia: Fortress, 1985.

Leloir, Louis. *Écrits apocryphes sur les apôtres. Traduction de l'édition arménienne de Venise. I. Pierre, Paul, André, Jacques, Jean*. Corpus Christianorum, Series Apocryphorum 3. Turnhout: Brepols, 1986.

_____. "La version arménienne des Actes apocryphes des apôtres et le Diatessaron." *New Testament Studies* 22 (1975-1976): 115-39.

Lemm, Oskar von. "Koptische apokryphe Apostelakten." *Mélanges asiatiques tirés du Bulletin Impériale des Sciences de Saint Pétersbourg* 10 (1890): 99-171.

Lipsius, Richard Adelbert. *Die apokryphen Apostel-geschichten und Apostellegenden. Ein Beitrag zur altchristlichen Literaturgeschichte*. 2 vols. in 3. Braunschweig: C. A. Schwetschke, 1883-1890.

Lipsius, Richard Adelbert, and Maximilian Bonnet. *Acta apostolorum apocrypha*. 3 vols. Leipzig: Hermann Mendelssohn, 1891-1903. Reprint. Darmstadt: Georg Olms Verlagsbuchhandlung, 1959.

Löfstedt, Bengt. "Zu de lateinischen Bearbeitungen der Acta Andreae et Matthiae apud Anthropophagos," *Habis* 6 (1975): 167-76.

MacDonald, Dennis Ronald. "*The Acts of Andrew and Matthias* and *The Acts of Andrew*," and "Response" to Jean-Marc Prieur. In *The Apocryphal Acts of Apostles, Semeia 38*, ed. Dennis R. MacDonald, 9-26 and 35-39. Decatur, GA: Scholars Press, 1986.

_____. "From Audita to Legenda: Oral and Written Miracle Stories." *Forum* 2,4 (1986): 15-26.

Martin, Henry Marie Radegonde. *Saint André*. Paris: H. Laurens, 1928.

Meineke, August, ed. *Stephan von Byzanz, Ethnika*. Graz: Akademische Druck-und Verlagsanstalt, 1958.

Morenz, S. "Der Apostel Andreas als Serapis." *Theologische Literaturzeitung* 72 (1947): 295-97.

Morris, R. *The Blickling Homilies of the Tenth Century*. Early English Text Society 63. London: N. Trübner, 1880.

Musurillo, Herbert. *The Acts of the Christian Martyrs*. Oxford Early Christian Texts. Oxford: Oxford University Press, 1972.

Mykytiuk, Bohdan Georg. *Die ukrainischen Andreas-bräuche und verwandtes Brauchtum*. Veröffent-lichungen des Osteuropa-Institutes München, Reihe Geschichte 47. Wiesbaden: Harrassowitz, 1979.

Nau, François N. "Actes coptes," s.v. *Dictionnaire d'histoire et de géographie ecclésiastiques*.

Novaković, S. "Apocrypha of One Serbian Cyrillic Collection of the Fourteenth Century." *Starine* 8 (1876): 55-69.

Peterson, Peter Megill. *Andrew, Brother of Simon Peter, His History and His Legends*. Supplements to Novum Testamentum 1. Leiden: E. J. Brill, 1958.

Preller, Ludwig, and Carl Robert. *Griechische Mythologie*. 2 vols. in 4. 4th ed. Berlin: Weidmann, 1964-1967.

Prieur, Jean-Marc. *Acta Andreae*. Corpus Christianorum, Series Apocryphorum 5 and 6. Turnhout: Brepols, 1989.

_____. "Les Actes apocryphes de l'apôtre André: Présentation des diverses tradition apocryphes et état de la question." *Aufstieg und Niedergang der römischen Welt* 2.25.6:4383-414.

_____. "La figure de l'apôtre dans les Actes apocryphes d'André." In *Les Actes apocryphes des apôtres. Christianisme et monde païen*, ed. François Bovon, 121-39. Publication de la Faculté de Théologie de l'Université de Genève 4. Geneva: Labor et Fides, 1981.

_____. "Response" to Dennis MacDonald. In *The Apocryphal Acts of Apostles, Semeia 38*, ed. Dennis R. MacDonald, 27-33. Decatur, GA: Scholars Press, 1986.

Quispel, Gilles. "An Unknown Fragment of the Acts of Andrew (Pap. Copt. Utrecht 1)." *Vigiliae Christianae* 10 (1956): 129-48.

Radermacher, L. "Zu den Acta Andreae et Matthiae." *Wiener Studien* 48 (1930): 108.

Reinach, Salomon. "Les apôtres chez les anthropophages." *Revue d'histoire et de littérature religieuse* 9 (1904): 305-20.

Santos Otero, Aurelio de. *Die handschriftliche Überlieferung der altslavischen Apokryphen*. 2 vols. Patristische Texte und Studien 20 and 23. Berlin and New York: Walter de Gruyter, 1978 and 1981.

Schermann, Theodor. *Prophetarum vitae fabulosae indices apostolorum discipulorumque Domini Dorotheo, Epiphanio, Hippolyto aliisque vindicata*. Leipzig: B. G. Teubner, 1907.

Schmidt, J. "Myrmidones," s.v. Pauly-Wissowa, *Real-Encyclopädie der klassichen Altertumswissenschaft*.

460   The Acts of Andrew

Tchérakian,   Chérubin.   *Ankanon   Girk'   Arak'elakank'*.
    T'angaran Haykakan Hin eue nor Dprout'eanc G [*Non-
    Canonical Apostolic Writings. Armenian Treasury of
    Ancient and Recent Writings* 3]. Venice, 1904.

Tissot, Yves. "Les Actes apocryphes de Thomas, exemple
    de recueil composite." In *Les Actes apocryphes des
    apôtres. Christianisme et monde païen*, ed. François
    Bovon,   223-32.   Publication   de   la   Faculté   de
    Théologie de l'Université de Genève 4. Geneva:
    Labor et Fides, 1981.

Vasil'evskij, Vasilij Grigor'evich. "Choždenei apostola
    Andreja v strane Mirmidonjan." *Žurnal ministerstva
    narodnago prosveščenija* (1877): 41-81 and 157-85.

Wright, William. *Apocryphal Acts of the Apostles. Edited
    from Syrian Manuscripts in the British Museum and
    Other Libraries*. London and Edinburgh: Williams and
    Norgate,   1871.   Reprint.   Amsterdam: Philo   Press,
    1968.

Wurm,   H.   ed.   "Decretales   selectae   ex   antiquissimis
    Romanorum   Pontificum   epistulis   decretalibus,"
    Apollinaris 12 (1939): 46-78.

Zahn, Theodor. *Acta Joannis*. Erlangen: Andreas Deichert,
    1880. Reprint. Hildesheim: H. A. Gerstenberg, 1975.

Zimmermann, B. "André (Saint), apôtre," s.v. *Diction-
    naire d'archéologie chrétienne et de liturgie*.

DATE DUE

HIGHSMITH   # 45220